GREAT
VACATIONS
WITH
YOUR KIDS

Revised Edition

About the Authors

DOROTHY JORDON is the founder and managing director of TWYCH, Travel With Your Children, a resource information center for parents planning successful and fun family vacations across the country or around the globe. This information is disseminated to thousands of families via a monthly newsletter, *Family Travel Times,* and two annually updated information guides: *Skiing with Children* and *Cruising with Children.* Ms. Jordon appears regularly on television and radio encouraging and supporting parents with advice on family travel, understanding that today's parents and their children are a unique breed who want to spend these very special times together. She lives in New York City with her husband and two sons, ages 9 and 12. She has been traveling with her children since her oldest was three weeks old.

MARJORIE A. COHEN is a freelance writer, author of six previous books: *Work, Study, and Travel Abroad: The Whole World Handbook; Where to Stay USA; The Teenagers Guide to Study, Travel and Adventure Abroad; Volunteer: The Comprehensive Guide to Voluntary Service in the U.S. and Abroad; The Budget Traveler's Latin America;* and the *Shoppers' Guide to New York.* She has also written travel articles for *Better Homes and Gardens, Child Magazine, Taxi,* and others and is a contributing editor to *Family Travel Times.* She lives with her husband and two daughters, ages 8 and 14, in New York City.

GREAT

VACATIONS

WITH

YOUR KIDS

REVISED EDITION

The Complete Guide to Family Vacations in the U.S. for Infants to Teenagers

DOROTHY JORDON

AND

MARJORIE ADOFF COHEN

A PLUME BOOK

PLUME
Published by the Penguin Group
Penguin Books USA Inc., 375 Hudson Street,
New York, New York 10014, U.S.A.
Penguin Books Ltd, 27 Wrights Lane,
London W8 5TZ, England
Penguin Books Australia Ltd, Ringwood,
Victoria, Australia
Penguin Books Canada Ltd, 10 Alcorn Avenue,
Toronto, Ontario, Canada, M4V 3B2
Penguin Books (N.Z.) Ltd, 182–190 Wairau Road,
Auckland 10, New Zealand

Penguin Books Ltd, Registered Offices:
Harmondsworth, Middlesex, England

Published by Plume, an imprint of New American Library, a division of
Penguin Books USA Inc. Previously published in a Dutton edition.

First Plume Printing, January, 1992

10 9 8 7 6 5 4 3 2

Copyright © 1987, 1990 by Dorothy Jordon and Marjorie Cohen

Cover photo: Bolton Valley Resort, Bolton Valley, Vermont, by Jerry LeBlond

Back cover photos: Keystone Resort, Keystone, Colorado; center photo of
picnic scene by Bob Winsett/Jeff Andrew

 REGISTERED TRADEMARK—MARCA REGISTRADA

Printed in the United States of America

Designed by Stanley S. Drate/Folio Graphics Co., Inc.

BOOKS ARE AVAILABLE AT QUANTITY DISCOUNTS WHEN USED TO
PROMOTE PRODUCTS OR SERVICES. FOR INFORMATION PLEASE
WRITE TO PREMIUM MARKETING DIVISION, PENGUIN BOOKS USA INC.,
375 HUDSON STREET, NEW YORK, NEW YORK 10014.

*This book is dedicated
to our own wonderful families—Elizabeth, Lucy,
Jordon, and Russell, our kids,
and Sy and David, our husbands*

CONTENTS

ACKNOWLEDGMENTS

This book would have been impossible to write without the help of many wonderful people. First, there are all those who took the time to answer our questions, the experts who were willing to share with us what they know, and all of the friends who couldn't wait to tell us about their own "great vacations" with their kids.

More specifically, we want to thank Sandra Soule, our editor for her patience and sound advice every step of the way and Carol Eannarino, the Managing Editor of *Family Travel Times,* who so willingly helped with research. We also want to thank Nancy Bolick, Cindy Lake Thomas, Jolene Davis, Jackie Fitzpatrick, and Margie Doherty for their help with the individual city sections and Debbie Joost for sharing her travel experiences with us. We'd also like to thank *Family Travel Times* contributors Louellen Berger, Sharla Feldscher, Claudia Lapin, Sally Lefèvre, Lori Martin, Gay Nagle Myers, Lisa Rosenthal, Candyce Stapen, Janet Tice, and Linda Wermuth.

To all of you who gave us your support and good will, our thanks.

INTRODUCTION

Trust us: you are going to have a wonderful vacation with your family this year. We've had a great time putting this book together, sorting through the possibilities. This second time around, we've had lots of fun uncovering new places for you to try—we've added at least 100 new listings since the first edition. New options seem to pop up daily. If we had all that fun just doing the paperwork, imagine how great it's going to be for you when you actually get to try it all out.

Some of you may have a little trepidation about traveling with your kids; others are seasoned family travelers. For the wary: you need, want, and deserve a family vacation. Think of how rare it is for all three, four, five, or six of you to be together at once. Think about those wild mornings when everyone's running off to school, to work, to the baby-sitter. Think of those nights—the rushed dinners, the meetings, the homework, the "stuff" of everyday life. Now think of how wonderful it would be to step out of the routine, to leave all of the hectic, tightly scheduled time behind and spend time together, not worrying about the clock, maybe even forgetting what day of the week it is. This really can happen.

Traveling with your kids has three advantages over other kinds of travel: with your kids along you get an entirely new perspective on what you're seeing, kids make friends for themselves and for you, and the adventurous spirit of your kids often leads you to experiences you may not have anticipated.

Although we think that family travel is great, we also know that it's different from other kinds of travel. Traveling with the kids requires a different approach to planning—it involves a different kind of travel than you did on your own, with your friends, or with your spouse before you had the kids. That's exactly why we have written this book: so that we can present first what's different and then, more importantly, show you how to cope with the differences. We cover the generalities of travel in the first part, the specifics in the second. What you'll read in the first section can be applied to any trip you take no matter how long, how far, or how elaborate. And each successive trip will become easier. We promise.

The second section gives you some specific suggestions of places to go and things to do. We admit it: we are trying to be all things to all people. We have included vacations that appeal to the rugged, outdoorsy types and vacations that appeal to the more sedentary among us. We talk about skiing down mountains, backpacking in wildernesses, and lying on beaches. There are vacations here that cost a lot, others that are quite inexpensive. Some of our suggestions take you thousands of miles from home, others only an hour or two away. Whatever you need or want in a family vacation, we think you'll find it here.

Fortunately, people in the travel industry are beginning to recognize and address the needs of families traveling together, but it's not always easy to find out just what they're up to. We have done all that for you. We have researched and uncovered information that's not easy to come by, so that you can spend your time on the parts that are fun—the choosing, the planning, and the doing.

Remember, too, that when we refer to a family vacation, we don't just mean mom, dad, and their 2.4 kids—we're talking about single parents plus their children; grandparents and their grandchildren; grandparents, parents, and kids together; and any other "family" configurations that are possible.

Time together as a family is precious time. Don't think we're naïve, though. We know that it's not going to be fun and games and laughter every minute (real life is not, after all, the "Cosby Show"), but the collective memories of a vacation together are very special for each member of a family and last a long, long time after the vacation is done.

All prices were correct at press time.
Changes may have occurred since.

1

GETTING READY

Ask 20 people what makes a great family vacation and you may very well get 20 different answers. But all great family vacations have some common denominators: they should be fun, they should be relatively carefree, they should include something of interest for every single member of the family, and they should provide lots of time together, away from the pressures of everyday life.

We've thought a lot about family vacations, and we've come up with what we call the six keys to great vacations. Everything in this book is related in one way or another to the six following principles:

1. Planning: Of all the six principles, this one is probably the most important. Planning your vacation with the individual needs of each member of your family in mind is the key to success. Begin with your youngest child and work your way up. Consider what each person's needs are and then how you can blend them all and make one smashing vacation out of it all. Work on all the details ahead of time. Be sure there are cribs, find out whether there's a children's program where you're going, ask whether you can warm the baby's bottle on the plane, and so on.

2. Participation: Be sure to include every member of your family in the planning process. The kids should be actively

involved from the very beginning. There are many reasons for this, but one of the most important and often overlooked is that kids have problems with "unknowns"—change and new places can be upsetting to them. By including your kids in the planning process from the beginning, many of the "unknowns" can be eliminated. We'll give examples of how to do this further on. And don't succumb to the fallacy that you should wait until the kids are old enough. One couple we know did that, and by the time they got to it, the kids were 15 and 16 and totally uninterested in a family vacation.

3. Alternating time together/time apart: You can't spend every minute of every day together on vacation any more than you can at home. Parents need time to be with each other without the kids, kids need to be off with other kids or adults, one parent may want to spend some time with just one kid—all kinds of configurations are possible and desirable. We've done lots of research on resorts and hotels with children's programs. We feel that it is through these programs that parents can best budget their time, but these programs aren't the only solution.

4. Go where you're wanted: You don't want to spend any time at a place where you're merely tolerated. You want to be welcomed. Some hotels just don't encourage families, and that's okay, too, but you want to avoid them. You want to be sure that the place you're going to stay will welcome you— that they're glad to have you with your children, that they like them and are able to handle their special needs.

5. Plan days that everyone is going to enjoy: Each day should be special and fun, and each day should have something for everyone. You don't have to spend day after day at a theme park; kids can enjoy all sorts of different things as long as their own needs relating to the activity are considered. Museum visits can be fun for kids as long as they don't involve endless hours of walking from painting to painting. And kids should have a chance to run around whenever possible. Stop at a playground on your way to a sightseeing attraction; let them scramble up and down a public statue and run in a park.

6. Attitude: Be realistic about what you can and can't expect on family vacations. Don't set yourself up for disappointment by having to cover every inch of a city. Choose carefully

what you plan to see and do, and remember that it's not how much you do but how good it feels doing it. Slow down. You rush around enough during your regular life. Adopt a vacation pace, and, even if it goes against your nature, force yourself to be flexible. Things are going to go wrong—everything will not be exactly as you planned. Anxiety is infectious; if you lose control, the kids probably will, too.

TRAVEL AGENTS

This leads us to our next topic—travel agents: Should you or shouldn't you use them?

As in most other areas, we have a definite opinion on the subject: we are very definitely pro–travel agent. The best thing about using a travel agent is that it gives you the luxury of "one-stop shopping": If the agent is a good one, you can have all your questions answered, fares and packages researched, reservations booked in just a few hours. Although much that you need to know as a parent traveling with children is not available to the travel agency network, with the information in this book you and your agent should be able to plan a great vacation.

Remember that even the best agents haven't been everywhere. But if they are good, they will have learned a lot from past clients and their colleagues. Although it might take you weeks to track down certain information, a good agent can accomplish miracles in five minutes to an hour with a computer and all the special resources available to the industry. A good example is airfares. Since deregulation of the airlines, the proliferation of airfares has been mindboggling. While this is often good for the consumer, it's enormously confusing. A good agent can sift through all of this with you and come up with the best deal. Sure, you can call airlines and get their lowest fare, but they're not going to tell you anything about what the competition has. Agents can also advise you on the reliability and general reputation of the travel wholesalers; they can decipher some of the fine print of packagers' brochures. The best part is that using travel agents won't cost you anything, and very often will save you money. They are paid their commissions by suppliers (airlines, hotels, car rental companies, tour operators). Don't be surprised, though, if a travel agent adds a service charge for booking some of the smaller hotels or resorts, which may not give commissions.

Good agents are able to work within your budget and even help you plan one. They know whom to go to for special fares, which tour operators have packages to your destination, plus unpublicized specials. Agents can be a great help with airfares. They can use their clout to get a "booked" seat and can have a wait list cleared much faster than you. Most agents' computers have something called *shopper's fares,* which provides a quick review of all the airlines that travel to any given destination. Think of all the time that one service can save. Another time saver: If you're stopping at more than one place, an agent can repeat the same information requests to the various hotels along your route.

You should pick your travel agent as carefully as you would your doctor or your car mechanic. How? One of the best ways is to ask for recommendations from friends whose opinions you trust and whose values you share. Consider factors such as destination or type (whether the agent specializes in the type of trip you're planning), accessibility and policies of the agency, and personality and qualifications of the individual agent.

Another factor to consider is whether the agency is a member of ASTA, the American Society of Travel Agents. Although there are good agencies who are not members, ASTA is a professional organization whose members have been in operation for at least three years. It has a tour payment protection plan (in case tour operators default) and is a ready resource for problems and complaints. More and more agents are now becoming certified travel consultants (CTCs), indicating at least five years' experience and completion of a two-year intensive study program. Although *CTC* after the agent's name is no guarantee, it does indicate that you're dealing with a professional—someone who is serious about what he is doing, serious enough to commit himself to a vigorous program of study. If the agent is a parent, better yet. He or she will be tuned in to the questions you need answered.

While you're considering the choice of an agent, take a look at the agency itself. Is it a pleasant place? What are their policies on service charges, refunds, payments? Are they an appointed agency of the airlines, Amtrak, and the cruise lines? Airline appointments indicate a certain basic financial investment and staff experience, plus the ability to write airline tickets.

You must like and respect the person you entrust your trip to and have confidence in his or her ability. You should feel able to ask questions, even the same ones repeatedly, no matter how silly they may seem. When working with an agent, be specific. "Sometime in

August" will not get the same response as "one week beginning between August 2 and 8." A prepared client simplifies the task for the agent. On the other hand, if you can be flexible about dates, a good agent may be able to arrange some savings.

A good agent will begin with a broad outline of your trip, respond and listen to your ideas and needs, and give specific suggestions. The agent should have an idea of your life-style, your "ideal vacation" and budget. He or she should ask, or you should volunteer the information, about what is an essential part of your vacation. Is a crib necessary? Do you want to be able to walk out your door onto the beach? Do you want daily maid service in an apartment? What do you like to do on vacation? Give an example of the places you've enjoyed in the past. A good agent can analyze these needs and pull them all together. A good agent can advise you on the amount of travel insurance you need, only enough to insure the part you may lose. For instance, if you're only liable for 50 percent of the ticket, only buy insurance for that amount.

All travel agents have a limited amount of time, so some of the detail work must be your responsibility. Check Appendix 3 for the tourist offices of each state you plan to visit and write to them. If you're an AAA member, use their guides and Triptik service. (See page 19.) Travel books and articles are fun for the family and often have good advice on "extras" or little-known area attractions. They can also help you to select your destination. Again, talk with friends who have been there.

We're delighted to report that more and more travel agents or consultants are tuning in to the special needs of families. One that we've discovered since our book first appeared is called Rascals in Paradise, and we're enthusiastic about the services they offer. Rascals is based in California and run by Deborah Baratta and Theresa Detchemendy, who are mothers of young kids. Their agency organizes group departures for three to six families at a time with all of the hassles taken care of in advance. "We block airline space; reserve space in small resorts, castles, barges, or boats; enlist teachers to organize activities for the young members of our groups, make babysitters available to be with each family every day as needed, and have separate children's menus and mealtimes." Rascals loves exotic destinations—they offer trips to Tahiti, the Cook Islands, and Thailand, along with tours to Europe, Hawaii, and the Caribbean. Rascals will also plan custom vacations for individual families with many of the same features as their escorted tours. Contact them at

650 Fifth Street, Suite 505, San Francisco, California 94107, 415-978-9800 or 800-U-RASCAL, or have your travel agent do it for you.

Another California-based business we discovered is Traveling with Children, 2313 Valley Street, Berkeley, California 94702, 415-848-0929. Here's how Daniel Hallinan, the owner, explains what his company does: "We do all of the standard travel agent work, such as booking airline flights and hotels, but we also do different things. Often it seems that many of our clients are coming simply for the reassurance that traveling with one's kids is both do-able and enjoyable. Much of our work consists of sending clients to the right sources. We rent houses and apartments for clients. Much of this work is noncommissionable so we charge our clients a $25 per hour consultation fee." Hallinan has been traveling with his own kids for 16 years, and the areas he knows best are Mexico, Hawaii, Europe, and the western U.S.

Janet Tice, co-author of *What to Do with the Kids This Year* (see page 259), operates a travel service called Families Welcome! that arranges vacations especially for individual families. Janet, mother of 9-year-old Fabiana, specializes in visiting cities with kids and offers special packages to London, Paris, and New York. Each package, designed for individual families traveling whenever they please, comes complete with a "Welcome Kit" filled with up-to-date resources and suggestions. Call 800-326-0724 or 919-968-6744 for information.

Another special travel service is one called Grandtravel, which is designed to cater to grandparents and grandchildren traveling together. Itineraries are planned to appeal to both generations and to include time together and time with peers. All tours include predeparture counseling—on what to do if the child gets homesick or the grandparents get tired—and tour escorts. Longer trips are scheduled for the summer; shorter trips coincide with school vacations. Some of Grandtravel's choices for trips in the United States include a week-long stay in Southern California, including San Diego, Hollywood, and Disneyland; a week in Washington, D.C.; a nine-day trip to the Southwest, called "American Indian Country"; "Our Western National Parks" with trips to Mt. Rushmore, Yellowstone, Grand Teton, and Grand Canyon National Parks; ten days in "Magnificent Colorado" and a 13-day "Alaskan Wilderness Adventure," which combines sightseeing with hiking and salmon fishing. For details, contact Grandtravel, The Ticket Counter, 6900 Wisconsin Avenue,

Suite 706, Chevy Chase, Maryland 20815, 800-247-7651 or 301-986-0790.

Another possibility for grandparents who want to take their grandchildren along but want some structure to their trip comes from the AARP's Travel Service, 4801 West 110th Street, Overland Park, Kansas 66211, 800-365-5358. In the U.S., AARP has special summer departures for its ten-day "American Heritage Tour," which begins in Philadelphia and travels south to Gettysburg, Washington, D.C., Shenandoah National Park, Richmond, and Williamsburg. Kids age 10 to 12 will get the most out of this tour, according to AARP. For grandparents who want to show their grandchildren Europe, AARP arranges special departures on their "Capitals and Countryside Tour of Western Europe," which includes jaunts in and out of England, Holland, Germany, France, and Switzerland.

Two other family-oriented travel services are International Family Adventures and Schilling Travel Service. International Family Adventures, pioneers in the field of exotic family vacations, takes groups of families as far afield as Africa, Asia, Australia, and Europe. For details, contact the owners, Anne and Hank Kahn, at P.O. Box 172, New Canaan, Connecticut 06840, or call during the day, 203-863-2106, evenings to 10:00 P.M., 203-972-3842.

Schilling Travel Service specializes in educational travel for families. For example, they recently arranged a trip to the U.S.S.R. for a group of grandparents and their grandchildren and intergenerational trips to Ireland and Africa. For information, contact Schilling Travel Service, 722 Second Avenue South, Minneapolis, Minnesota 55402, 612-332-1100 or 800-992-1903.

For families with handicapped children or parents, the not-for-profit ACCESS Foundation helps get your family on the road or in the air. According to director Danyaon Coston-Clark, they can plan your entire trip, accommodating every special need. They know which support services are available at the destination of your choice and how to get them. One of their most interesting programs is a home exchange service. Contact them at P.O. Box 356, Malverne, New York 11565, 516-887-5798.

A Word About Problems

Even the best agent can made mistakes. Check your documents carefully for dates, arrival and departure times, correct airports, guaranteed reservations at hotels and car rental agencies. Because the agent often acts as the middle person, it may not be his fault if you get a window instead of an aisle seat, a small hotel room, or water in the trunk of your rental car. If you feel you have a legitimate complaint, first go to the supplier, and then to the agency owner or manager to see what his response is. If you are still not satisfied, write to ASTA, the Better Business Bureau, or a local newspaper. As a last resort, you can go to your local small claims court.

PLANNING

Just as soon as you know where you're going, get the whole family involved in the planning. Not only is this fun, but it eliminates the children's wariness about the unknowns of travel. Think about it for a moment from your children's point of view. They are about to set out for a place they've never seen; to be surrounded by people they've never met; to sleep in a new room, in a new bed; and to eat foods cooked differently from what they're used to. Planning together, discussing what can be expected, will accomplish a great deal in allaying the fears of children. Preparation is the key. Take out a map and show the kids where you're going and the route you're going to take. Talk about distances in terms they can understand: "We'll be driving for four hours—that's like going to Grandma's house and back home again." Help them compose and address letters to tourist offices asking for information on the places you'll be visiting. (See Appendix for list of addresses.) Have them put their own names on the return address so that the responses can come to them. Kids love getting their own mail. Even if your children aren't old enough to read, they can enjoy the colorful pictures from a very early age. Let them point to or circle what they'd like to do. We give our kids different colored markers and let them go at it. From what's been circled, make up a list of what you're going to do, and don't forget your own desires.

Take a trip to the library with the kids and get some books that have some connection to an aspect of your trip. *Family Travel Times,* published monthly by Travel with Your Children (TWYCH), 80 Eighth Avenue, New York, New York 10011, runs a column called "The Bookshelf" with lots of suggestions for suitable books on whatever topics are discussed in that particular month's issue for parents and kids.

When we were getting ready to go to a dude ranch out west, we all headed for the card catalog and looked up Wyoming, dude ranches, and Custer. Each of the kids took out four books; the favorite turned out to be a textbook about Wyoming. We read a piece every night at bedtime: we read about the mountains, the towns we'd pass through en route to the ranch from the airport, rodeos, Indians, reservations, and horses. Ask your child's teacher whether there's anything that the class is studying that can be related to your travels. Whether or not the answer is yes, you can be sure that the trip will have invaluable educational value. Kids absorb so much. Even the youngest will learn.

Another great benefit of advance planning is that it's the best way we know to combat the "When are we going on vacation?" syndrome that can drive parents crazy. From the minute your kids find out about an upcoming vacation, they start asking, "Is today vacation?" or, if they're a bit older, "How many more days until we go?" One of the best ways, not to avoid the question, but to channel all that anticipation and excitement, is to involve the kids in the planning. One friend came to us and said that she was going to Walt Disney World with the family but that the kids were driving her wild asking about when they'd get going. We gave her a handful of brochures for her nonreader and a guidebook for her older child. When we saw her two days later, she was overflowing with gratitude. Between the two of them, the kids had planned exactly what they wanted to see and do. A pretrip calendar is good, too. Little ones can cross off the days; the older ones can plan final chores and packing.

Remember, as you plan a trip, that kids love to repeat the things they like; they like to go back to the places they enjoy. Be flexible enough in your planning so that repeats will be possible.

And one more thing while we're on the subject of planning. A funny thing happened on the way to this edition—one of us became the parent of a teenager. When our 12-year-old crossed over into the teens, we were presented with a whole new set of considerations for family trips. We found out that when you travel with a teenager, there must be other kids the same age around. If you're going to a resort, be sure that there's some central place for teenagers to go to "hang out." If activity programs begin too early in the day, you can be sure your teenager is going to miss them. Adolescents like to sleep late. Consider the all-important bathroom time that teenagers need, and if it's at all possible, try to get accommodations with two bathrooms, or at least with an extra sink and mirror. When you're on vacation, remember that it's not fair to make your teenager babysit too often for your younger kids—once in a while is fine, but after all, it's everybody's vacation. Try not to restrict your teenager's freedom too much when you're in a new place; give him or her the same kind of independence he or she would have at home. If you're going to travel to a city, why not call ahead to friends who may be able to put you in touch with other friends in that city who have teenage kids? Your kid and the new friend could meet for a movie or do some sightseeing together. And be absolutely sure that your teenager is in on the planning of the trip from the beginning.

DECIDING WHERE AND FOR HOW LONG

If we can believe the statistics we've been hearing, families are now taking shorter but more frequent vacations. People no longer pin all of their vacation hopes on one vacation per year. How long and how frequent your vacations are really depend on your own circumstances. No matter what the situation, the length of your vacation depends a great deal on how much money you can afford to spend. If you can afford two weeks at a certain ski resort as long as you don't opt for the children's program or ten days if you do, you probably should choose the shorter vacation with the children's program and enjoy the luxury of having a place where they can go to have fun and meet people their own age. It's value, not just bargains, that you have to consider.

Determining where you should go is more complicated than deciding how long. We advise parents to start out by asking themselves where they'd like to go if they didn't have kids. You can go practically any place you've ever wanted to go as long as you make the right arrangements and can be sure that your kids' needs can be met as well as your own. Let's take, as an example, a friend we know who always wanted to take a trip along the California coast. "If I were alone," she told us, "I'd be happy to ride in the car for four hours, but how can I do that with a 15-month-old?" Obviously, she can't. But she can cover the same territory by finding a good base for her travels and taking short day trips from that place. If she's determined to go someplace four hours from her "base," she can make sure that there is someone who can take care of her toddler for the day.

In spite of the extraordinary variety of vacation choices, when you think about it there are only three basic vacation types: (1) on the move, (2) staying in one place, and (3) a little of each. Which would you like?

One of the first things all of your family have to ask themselves is what they want from a vacation. If you have four people involved, there may be four answers. One person may love the beach; one may hate it; one may love to sightsee and be on the go; another may want to relax by the side of a pool. It's really not that difficult to accommodate everybody's tastes. Let's give some examples: A friend of ours is an avid sailor, but his kids and his wife despise boating. They like to be near water but not on it. They chose a week at a resort where the mother could relax on the beach while the father enjoyed unlimited sailing and the kids went to morning sports activities. Every day when the father came back from the sail, the whole family took a hike or a bike ride or went shelling. Everyone got to do what he or she liked separately, and they all did something they enjoyed together. A cardinal rule of successful vacations—no martyrs, *please.*

Another family we know is made up of ski-crazy kids, a mother who can take it or leave it, and a father who never liked skiing but has developed back problems that would prevent him from going even if he wanted to. The solution: a resort where the mother can ski, play tennis, and go to the spa while the kids are at ski school, and where the father can swim in the indoor pool and catch up on his reading.

Another success story is the family of a mother, a father, and a teenage son who didn't want to do anything with his parents. The solution: two weeks at a spot where the father could play tennis, the mother could horseback ride, and the teenager could go off on a five-day wilderness trek with expert guides and other kids his own age.

And finally we cite the family who had always dreamed of going to Alaska. When they checked on the airfare for six to and from their home city, their dream ended abruptly. But they were clever: They asked themselves what it was that so appealed to them about Alaska, and when they determined that it was the quiet, the wilderness, and the closeness to nature, they went camping in the Grand Tetons, only a four-hour car ride from their home.

The moral of all this is simple: All travel problems have solutions. All it takes is determination, some creative thinking, and research.

BOOKS THAT HELP

Throughout *Great Vacations* we refer to books that can help you with your planning—from choosing a place to go, to organizing your trip, to knowing what you want to do along the way or upon arrival.

To begin with, we recommend the following books, which do not fit neatly under any specific chapter. Some are guidebooks; others are how-to books. We've looked through them all and think that they're worth your consideration. Most are available at bookstores, but some from smaller publishers may have to be ordered directly by mail. See the list of publishers in Appendix 2 for addresses and the name of a catalog that specializes in books for traveling families. Let us know about any good books you find so that we can include them the next time around.

Trips with Children in New England by Harriet Webster, published by Yankee Books, publishers of *Yankee* magazine ($9.95). Webster's attitude is reflected in the dedication of her book: "For Ma who gave me the joy of travel, and for Jonathan who helps me pass it on to our kids." Her book is thorough and thoughtfully written and includes nature centers, hiking trails, science museums, animal farms, train and plane rides, and more. She's aimed her book at the 5-to-14 set, but families with younger kids can benefit from it just as much.

Favorite Weekends in New England, also by Harriet Webster and published by Yankee Books ($8.95). Although not specifically for kids, this book has a lot to interest them.

Favorite Daytrips in New England by Michael Schuman, published by Yankee Books ($8.95). A good book to use if you decide to base your vacation somewhere in New England. You can easily stretch most of the trips into a full vacation.

The Great Weekend Escape Book by Michael Spring, published by E. P. Dutton ($10.95). We can't keep this one on the shelf. In it, Spring gives you 26 choices from Virginia to Vermont. His taste is excellent; as he explains: "I wrote this as though you were a close friend who sat me down and said, 'Tell me about 26 glorious weekends.'" Every chapter includes a section called "For Kids" that gives some ideas on topics of special interest to families traveling together. It has our highest recommendation.

Daytrips, Getaway Weekends and Budget Vacations in the Mid-Atlantic States by Patricia and Robert Foulke, published by the Globe Pequot Press ($12.95). There are eight itineraries to choose from, ranging from the Adirondacks to Washington, D.C. The book is well organized, and the itineraries are appealing, with lots that are suitable for kids. The same authors have written *Daytrips and Budget Vacations in New England,* also published by Globe Pequot Press ($10.95), with six itineraries from the coast to mountains, from cities to villages.

America's Greatest Walks by Gary Yanker and Carol Tarlow, published by Addison-Wesley Publishing Company, Inc. ($10.95). No matter how old your kids are, walks are wonderful family activities. The authors have picked their favorite 100 walks—long walks and short walks, walks in cities, walks in woods, mountain hikes and strolls along beaches. A nice little book.

Super Family Vacations by Martha Shirk and Nancy Klepper, published by Harper and Row ($12.95). This is a great new addition to the books on the subject of traveling with kids. The authors, both mothers, profile 115 vacations for families in the U.S., including resorts, ranches, adventure trips, and nature places. They've done an admirable job.

Directory of Free Vacation and Travel Information edited by Raymond Carlson, Pilot Books ($3.95). An often overlooked source of good, free travel information are the local, state, and federal government tourism agencies in this country. This directory has them all and is available from the publisher, 103 Cooper Street, Babylon, New York 11702, for $3.95 plus $1 for postage and handling.

Traveling with Your Baby by Vicki Lansky, published by Bantam ($2.95). This is a compendium of practical and ingenious suggestions together with helpful checklists. Filled with hints, both from the author and other parents, this book gives you the tools to plan a happier trip the first time out. Lansky is a true student of family life, an observant parent, and, as such, provides information unavailable elsewhere.

Going Places: The Guide to Travel Guides by Greg Hayes and Joan Wright, published by Harvard Common Press ($17.95 paperback; $26.95 hard cover.) Take a look at this excellent source book either at your travel agent's office or at the library. In almost 800 pages the authors review and evaluate the guidebooks that they think are the most helpful to travelers. Besides reviews, *Going Places* includes helpful appendices with the names of travel bookstores, travel publishers, travel newsletters and magazines, and foreign language phrase books. This ambitious work is a most valuable tool.

Birnbaum's United States edited by Steve Birnbaum, published by Houghton Mifflin ($12.95). This overall guide to the U.S. is good, and we've used it often to give us a perspective on the place we're about to visit. Birnbaum's style is crisp and his information is useful.

Away for the Weekend: New England by Eleanor Berman, published by Clarkson N. Potter, Inc. ($11.95). When you've got a weekend to spare and you want to make the most of it, this book will help. The author organizes her choices by season and covers all six New England states.

Day Trips from Phoenix, Tucson, and Flagstaff by Pam Hait, published by Globe Pequot Press ($9.95). This is one of a series that includes titles on Baltimore, Cincinnati, and Houston. They're handy little books to have when you are going to be based in a city and want to venture beyond its boundaries.

Underground Guide to Kauai by Lenore W. Horowitz, Papoloa Press, 362 Selby Lane, Atherton, California 94025 ($5.95 plus $1.50 postage and handling). This popular guide has lots of detailed advice on Kauai's beaches for families. Horowitz's restaurant reviews are first-rate. There are sections on museums, special tours, hiking, camping, riding, running, shopping, and things to do with kids. Another nice section is called "Special Mornings with Daddy."

Off the Beaten Path, a series published by Globe Pequot Press ($8.95 each), each covering Pennsylvania, Northern California, Southern California, Georgia, Wisconsin, and Minnesota. The authors of this series uncover some of the lesser-known attractions of their states. There's lots here that would interest kids; many things that you may not know about even if you live in the state covered.

Celebrations: America's Best Festivals, Jamborees, Carnivals and Parades by Judith Young, published by Capra Press, P.O. Box 2068, Santa Barbara, California 93120 ($10.95). Here's a guide to some of the well-known and less well known celebrations—from Mardi Gras to the International Strange Music Weekend. The book is organized into regions and seasons so that you can find something to do near wherever you go whenever you go.

Guide Book to Free Industry Tours, published by Kaywaden Associates, P.O. Box 371, Hinsdale, Illinois, 60521. Sometimes it's lots of fun to visit a factory—how about a look at the Harley-Davidson plant or the factory where they make Peter Paul candy bars? This book lists loads of possibilities by state.

A Shunpikers Guide to the Northeast: Washington to Boston without Turnpikes or Interstates by Peter Exton, published by EPM, 1003 Turkey Run Road, McLean, Virginia 22101 ($9.95). The author quotes Cato the Elder who said, back in 200 B.C., that "wise men shun the mistakes of fools." That's why he's written this book with detailed instructions on how to avoid the main roads and enjoy the sidetrips.

Gulliver Travels: A Kid's Guide to Florida, published by Harcourt Brace Jovanovich ($6.95). One of a terrific series written just for kids and loaded with facts about the place they're going and what's the most fun to do once they're there. Further on in our book we mention the other books in the series—on New York, Washington, D.C., and Southern California—and look forward to two more that are scheduled to appear in 1991, on the national parks and Texas.

City Safaris: A Sierra Club Explorer's Guide to Urban Adventures for Grownups and Kids by Carolyn Shaffer and Erica Felder, published by Sierra Club ($9.95). In the words of the authors, this is "an explorer's kit." Much more than a guide, "it's a toolbox of games, hints and how-to's. With its contents you can design any number of city explorations to suit your needs and interests—everything from half-hour walks around the block for a four-year-old taking nothing but crayons and paper to designing a month-long environmental study project for a fourteen-year-old with camera, tape recorders, interviews, opinion polls and library research."

Discover Seattle with Kids: Where to Go and What to See in the Puget Sound Area by Rosanne Cohen, published by JASI/ Discover Books, P.O. Box 19786, Seattle, Washington 98109 ($8.95). In its fifth edition, this is a well-trusted guide to what's happening where for kids.

Going Places: Family Getaways in the Pacific Northwest by John Bigelow and Breck Longstreth, published by Northwest Parent Publishing, P.O. Box 22578, Seattle, Washington 98122 ($7.95), takes you beyond Seattle to adventures in British Columbia, western Washington, Idaho, and Oregon. It includes brief introductions to each area suggested as a side trip and recommendations for accommodations once you've arrived.

Exploring the Twin Cities with Children by Elizabeth French, published by Nodin Press, 525 North Third Street, Minneapolis 55401 ($4.95) is a small (69 pages) but comprehensive directory of activities in the Minneapolis–St. Paul area. We wish the sights were clustered, but since they're listed alphabetically, you'll need a map along with the book to do any planning.

Places to Go with Children in the Delaware Valley by Alice Rowan O'Brien, published by Chronicle Books ($9.95) was conceived out of the author's attempt to pry her 3-year-old couch potato away from weekend cartoons. Whether you like museums or would rather be out picking local fruit, this book will steer you in the right direction. Highlighted are the many family attractions in the valley's most populated areas—mid to northern Delaware, south to central New Jersey, and the five Pennsylvania counties that surround and include Philadelphia.

On the Road USA, published by Reader's Digest ($24.95), is a hardcover, oversized book with 1,000 attractions located anywhere from three to 30 minutes from interstate highway exit ramps. Perfect to relieve the boredom of superhighway driving. You'll find historic sites, theme and amusement parks, state parks, picnic spots, and ghost towns.

Books for the Kids to Read (or for you to read to them)

We've found three books that are just right to read to kids before the family goes off on vacation.

On Our Vacation by Anne Rockwell, published by E. P. Dutton ($12.95), is an adorable book for your youngest traveler— probably best for kids from 2 to 4. Bearchild and his family go off to their vacation island; lots of cute pictures of their trip.

Dinosaurs Travel: A Guide for Families on the Go by Laurie Krasny Brown and Marc Brown, published by Little Brown ($13.95), is a wonderful book that talks about all aspects of travel in kids' term, like riding the subway or bus, sleeping and eating away from home, taking the train, and getting ready for a trip.

My Family Vacation by Dayal Kaur Khalsa, Crown Publishers ($12.95). This book chronicles May's trip to Florida with her parents and her older brother, Richie. The brilliantly colored illustrations are lovely.

ABOUT OUR LISTINGS:

The properties we list in this book all welcome kids and all willingly responded to our many, many questions. We're relying on you, our readers, to let us know about your own experiences with our choices—good and bad—and to tell us about any new places we can list in the next edition.

ONE MORE REMINDER:

If you're looking for a place to play tennis, check the tennis and golf chapter but don't overlook Chapter 8 on resorts, Chapter 10 on skiing (many ski resorts turn into tennis and golf spots once the snow melts), and Chapter 11 on farms and dude ranches.

And don't forget the None of the Above listings beginning on page 469.

NOTE: Rates quoted here were accurate at press time but are subject to change.

NOTE: Be sure to check pages 481–82 for a list of publishers' addresses. Some books published by smaller publishers may not be readily available in bookstores but can be ordered directly from the publisher.

Send us your cards and letters. We want to hear from you about your own great vacation choices so that we can include them in the next edition. Write to Great Vacations with Your Kids, TWYCH, 80 Eighth Avenue, New York, New York 10011.

2

GETTING THERE

Whether you decide to travel by car, plane, train, or bus, preparation is the key. You can start, with younger children, by getting library books about the kind of transporation you'll be using. If this is your child's first airplane ride, try Pat and Joel Ross's *Your First Airplane Trip* or Dinah L. Moché's *We're Taking an Airplane Trip.* For car trips, scout out *The Car Trip* by Helen Oxenburg, Anne Alexander's *ABC of Cars and Trucks,* or Richard Scarry's *On Vacation.* In preparation for the first plane trip you can play a game of setting up rows of chairs in the configuration of a plane and taking turns being the pilot, the passenger, and the flight attendant. Be especially sure not to put any of your own fear of flying into your child's mind; most children are excited, not frightened by the idea of flying. Don't ruin it.

Talk to the kids about the distance you're traveling and the time it will take to get there. Use terms they can understand, like, "The flight will take five hours; that's as long as you are in school." If you're going to visit relatives or friends, get out photos and talk about them. However you decide to travel, don't start packing the night before you leave. Even if you're not the organized type, force yourself this once. Start making lists of everything you need to take a week ahead of time. Remember, too, that you don't have to keep your kids entertained every single minute of their trip, but that you do have to provide them with things that will keep them busy, involved, and comfortable. They need toys and games to play with alone and some they can play with you or their brothers and sisters.

Fatigue and hunger are the two things you want to avoid on any trip. It's always best to start a long trip with a nap. We like late flights so that the kids are nice and tired when they board the plane. We like to start car trips early, early in the morning: get up at 5:00, bundle the kids into a prepacked car, get going, and hope they'll go back to sleep.

Hunger is easy enough to avoid. Just be sure to pack a variety of snacks and let the kids carry their own food. Since it is vacation time we let them eat their snacks whenever they want. They like that! Even if there's going to be a meal on board your flight, even if there's a dining car on the train, you can be sure that your kids are going to get hungry long before anything is officially served. There are lots of possibilities for snacks—dry cereal, oranges (great for thirst, hunger, and even deodorizing a stuffy car), bananas, apples, cheese, crackers, unsalted popcorn and pretzels, and individual packages of apple sauce. As a parent you've probably realized that one of the greatest inventions of the 20th century is juice-in-a-box. What genius came up with it? If we knew, we'd dedicate this book to him or her. Just freeze the box the night before the trip, and it will stay cold for a long time. It will even serve as a refrigerator pack for the other food. (We used it once to keep our kids' antibiotics cold during a flight.)

BY CAR

We don't have to tell you about having your car tuned up before you go. And if you're not a member of the American Automobile Association, this is the time to sign up. For the chapter nearest you, check your phone book or call 800-336-HELP. Not only will you be able to call someone if you're stuck on the road but you'll also be able to take advantage of their trip planning service called "the Triptik," which highlights the easiest, quickest, or most scenic routes individualized for you. When the inevitable "Are we there yet?" comes, the Triptik gives a good graphic answer. (Other automobile clubs that offer trip planning services are the ALA Auto & Travel Club, 888 Worcester Street, Wellesley, Massachusetts 02181; All-state Motor Club, 34 Allstate Plaza, Northbrook, Illinois 60062; Amoco Motor Club, P.O. Box 9049, Des Moines, Iowa 50369-0010; and Chevron Travel Club, P.O. Box P, Concord, California 94524.)

Let each of your kids take a turn being the "navigator." Give the navigator a special hat or badge to make the assignment even more impressive. As we've said before, it's best to start you car trip early in the morning. Not only will you get a few hours of sleep from the kids, but you will also be able to avoid rush hour traffic and arrive wherever you're going well before bedtime. This last part is important: Kids who have some time to look around the new place a bit before dark will be less apprehensive when bedtime comes. If you can end your driving day early enough to do something active before bed—a swim or a romp in a playground—all the better. When you're planning your travel in the car, make a driving pit stop schedule and stick to it. Don't make the kids wait 25 extra minutes for a stop; that breaks your part of the bargain. You can expect a car trip with kids to take one-third longer than without; for example, a four and one-half trip becomes a six-hour drive. When you take your breaks, have them accomplish as much as possible—picnic; sightsee; get some exercise. Give the kids a signal ten minutes before you're going to stop so that they can put away their toys and find their shoes. When you stop, look for a shady spot and cover the seats so they won't overheat. When it's time to get back into the car, announce the change of navigator, rotate the seating positions, and so on.

Car seats are, of course, a given. You must use your seat belts, and your younger children need car seats. If you haven't bought your car seat, you can get a reprint of *Consumer Reports* magazine's article "Child Safety Seat" for $3 from Consumer Reports Reprints, 256 Washington Street, Mt. Vernon, New York 10553. If you buy a new car seat for the trip, give it a trial run before takeoff. In cold weather, tuck blankets around your baby *after* the belt is buckled. In hot weather, cover the seat with a towel to avoid having it heat up when the car is parked.

In Chapter 3 we talk about what to take along with you in a car or on any kind of transportation. That's where we suggest toys, games, first aid kit, clothing, and so on.

Arrange the car so that your kids can get at the toys or games they want without having to undo their seat belts. See the write-up on "Cargo Cat" on page 42. Take pillows and blankets, and don't forget premoistened paper towels and dry paper towels.

Before you leave, talk to your children a bit about exercising caution with strangers. The easiest rule to follow is probably "talk to anyone you'd like to when you're with me, but avoid strangers when you're alone."

Two mothers, Ellyce Field and Susan Shlom, have collaborated on a book that we think you'll find enormously useful if you plan to travel by car. It's called *Kids and Cars: A Parent's Survival Guide for Family Travel* and is full of solid, no-nonsense advice written in an entertaining, down-to-earth way. The authors pooled their own first-hand experience with surveys they took of 200 traveling families and advice from child psychologists and pediatricians. The book is really three books in one—a guide to car travel, a family keepsake, and an activity book. Copies are available from the publisher, Melius and Peterson, 526 Citizens Building, P.O. Box 925, Aberdeen, South Dakota 57402, for $8.95 each.

When Things Go Wrong

We've been told that a high-carbohydrate, low-fat diet a few days before a trip diminishes the incidence of car sickness. Sometimes car sickness can be caused by drinking too much milk or soft drink, reading in the car, being overdressed, having no air in the car, or just plain being overexcited. Ask your pediatrician for advice. If you're traveling during the summer in a hot climate (such as New York City!) prevent sun sickness by keeping your children's arms and heads lightly covered.

Meal Stops

When it's time to eat a real meal, our first choice is a picnic. Picnics avoid waiting to be served, and the chance to go shopping gets rid of some pent-up energy. If you're not going to picnic, choose a restaurant with an outdoor café or terrace on the beach or lakeside so that the kids can play while you wait for your food. Places that offer a serve-yourself buffet or a salad bar are good for immediate gratification, which in turn avoids premeal crankiness. Lots of times we let our kids sit in a booth right behind ours so that they can eat by themselves. They really do rise to the occasion. This really works best when you're traveling with another family, because the kids from both families can sit together.

While you're at the restaurant, you can refill your thermos and make bathroom stops.

Some Gadgets You May Want

A company called Children on the Go manufactures fine products that we think are quite clever. They include the Secure View Mirror ($7.95), which attaches to the windshield and gives you a view of your child in the back seat as you drive; a Totty Seat ($8.95), which is a portable potty seat that folds to five and a half square inches, comes in a vinyl travel pouch, and fits any regular toilet seat; a Beam Screen ($9.95), which attaches to the window next to your child to block out heat and glare from the sun; Splat Mat ($9.95), a three-foot by four-foot vinyl mat that can go under high chairs to catch the splats; and Travel Beams ($4.95), a battery-operated light that attaches to the car window for night reading or game playing. To order any of these products, you can write directly to the company: P.O. Box 396, Arlington Heights, Illinois 60005.

Car Rentals

There are a few basic points to consider when you're choosing a car rental company:

- How easy is it to get 24-hour service when you break down? What *exactly* is the cost of liability insurance? (Don't pay for more than you need; check your own coverage with your insurance company.)
- In plain English, what are the mileage charges? What does "unlimited" mileage really mean? What are the drop-off fees?
- If you're going to ski country, will the car have snow tires and a ski rack? If you're going to be in Florida, will it be air-conditioned?
- Ask ahead of time what will happen if the budget car you reserve is not available and a sleek, luxury model has to be substituted. Make *sure* you're not liable for the difference.
- And, finally, check on the availability and cost of car seats.

On this last point: although many people will use their own car seats (if you take them on a plane to your car rental destination, you can just check them through as baggage or use them on the plane), many people will prefer not to carry them along. We surveyed the major car rental companies to ask about car seat availability and came up with the following:

Alamo

Car seats are available for $3.50 per day and should be reserved when you reserve your car. Call 800-462-5266 for reservations.

Avis

Many of Avis's locations have car seats to rent. For a confirmed car seat rental you need to allow 48 hours' advance notice; for two car seats you need 72 hours. The charge is either $3 per day or $15 per week per car seat; if the rental is only one-way, there's an additional $15 charge. Call 800-331-1212 for reservations.

Budget Rent a Car Corporation

Since Budget is primarily a franchise operation, the availability of car seats varies. But according to a printout sent by one of the public relations people at Budget, many franchises do make them available. (Some that have children's seats do not have what they call "baby seats.") Seats are free at some locations, $2 to $5 per day at others. Some locations require deposits; others do not. Call 800-527-0700 for information on individual locations.

Hertz

Hertz guarantees child safety seats—the Century 2000 model—at all of their U.S. corporate locations and at most licensee locations with an advance reservation. The seats are $3 per day, $15 per week, and $40 for 18 to 30 days and may be used for infants and children up to 5. Call 800-654-3131.

National

Most National locations have AstroSeats, good for kids up to 42 inches and 42 pounds. Two days' advance booking is necessary to confirm, and the cost is $2 per day, $10 per week for local returns. Call 800-328-4567.

BY PLANE

When you're traveling by air, you'll have to be a bit more strict about what to bring along. You won't have as much room as you would in the car, and you won't be able to spread out as much. Air travel is exciting for kids and has its own set of pleasures and pains. We've already outlined the importance of preparing kids for flying with storybooks and games. You'll also have to prepare them for the possibility their ears will hurt when they take off and land. If you explain why this happens, it won't be so frightening. Explain, too, that you will be carrying some gum or their bottle to keep at takeoff and landing. If your child tends to have ear problems, try to arrange nonstop flights to avoid compounding his or her discomfort. And be sure that your child has plenty to drink on the flight to avoid dehydration. Whenever you fly, get to the airport early so that the preflight process can be orderly and unhurried.

The people at Logan International Airport have put together a consumer guide to flying with kids from toddler to teenager called *When Kids Fly*. It's an informative booklet and is available free from the Public Affairs Department, Massport, 10 Park Plaza, Boston, Massachusetts 02116-3971. Logan is one of the few airports in the U.S. that has a special play area for kids who are waiting for flights. It was developed in cooperation with the Boston Children's Museum and features two model aircraft, a baggage cart and fuel tanker. Kids can climb and play while parents read. Pittsburgh airport has a two-tiered play area with a slide, a clubhouse, kid-size chairs and tables, toys, books, a changing table, and even a place where mothers can nurse in privacy. Rudimentary children's nurseries can be found at airports in Los Angeles, Miami, Minneapolis, New York's LaGuardia, Orlando, and Seattle but they're nowhere near the quality of the Boston and Pittsburgh facilities. No U.S. airport has a lounge where parents can leave their kids under supervision—wouldn't that be a nice idea?

Airfares: What's Best

A travel agent can be an enormous help with airfares, and with all of the restrictions on special fares, an agent is more important now than ever before. He or she knows what the deals are and can help you sort out whether certain restrictions are really worth the money you save. Just about every airline has a special fare for kids 2 to 11 years (those 2 years and under fly free on their parents' laps, one lap child allowed per adult). Occasionally, a Kids Fly Free program will pop up. Again, your travel agent should know about it.

Where to Sit

Try to reserve your seat as early as you can. Sometimes it is possible to reserve when you book; other times you must wait until just before flight time. Everyone has a theory about what are the best seats, it seems. The one we hear so often is to reserve the bulkhead seat, the one up in front of the cabin with all the leg room. We don't agree because in the bulkhead seats the armrests don't move up, so the youngest children can't comfortably lie on your lap to rest. We always prefer aisle seats for kids. If you ask, your child will probably request a window seat, but the fascination of the window seat is limited to takeoff and landing—the four hours of clouds and blue sky in between is not very entertaining. The aisle seat lets them get in and out at will. We have a friend who reserves one aisle seat and one window seat when traveling with her 2-year-old. The premise is simple: she figures no regular travelers want to reserve the middle seat, and she ends up with an empty seat for her baby. We like to book two seats for us and two seats right behind us for our kids. That way the kids can sit together, we can sit together, or one of us can alternate sitting with each of the kids. The flexibility is nice.

For some suggestions on what to take so that the kids can amuse themselves on the plane, see Chapter 3.

Car Seats on the Plane

Practically all airlines we surveyed allowed passengers to use their approved car seat on flights, although some have an upper age limit and some require that you pay for the seat, even for under 2's. All seats manufactured after January 1, 1981 (the date that federal safety standards took effect), and bearing the proper label can be used on an airplane. Seats manufactured between January 1981 and February 26, 1985, should have a label that reads "This child restraint system conforms to all applicable Federal motor vehicle safety standards." A seat manufactured after February 26, 1985, should have a second label that reads "This restraint is certified for use in motor vehicles and aircraft." Put transparent tape over the label to be sure it doesn't come off. There is no question that having your child in a car seat is the safest way to fly. We also understand that it is not very convenient or economical since, unless there is an unused seat on the plane, you're going to have to pay for the seat for your child—even a lap-sized child. We repeat our advice: When you book your seats, book a window seat and an aisle seat where there are three across. Unless the flight is packed, that middle seat will remain empty. For children over 2 years who require a paid seat, just take your car seat on board. If you have any problem, just ask to see a supervisor. All of these car-seat-on-airplane regulations are relatively recent, so be patient with anyone who is confused. For a free copy of *Child/Infant Safety Seats Acceptable for Use in Aircraft* you can write to Community and Consumer Liaison Division, APA-200, Federal Aviation Administration, Washington, D.C. 20591, or you can call the Federal Aviation Administration's toll-free number, 800-FAA-SURE.

Unaccompanied Minors

We won't spend a lot of time on this subject since this book is primarily for families who travel together, but there are a few basics that you should know. Most airlines accept UMs (that's what unaccompanied minors are called in the trade) as young as five and even younger if you are willing to pay for an airline representative to travel with them. Kids between 12 and 15 can be considered UMs but only if you make a formal request and do some accompanying paperwork. We encourage you to do this so that if there are problems or delays, the airline will assume responsibility for them. UMs under 8 years of age will usually be limited to direct flights; kids 8 and over may go on connecting flights, even if they're on different airlines. Some airlines charge $20 or $25 for escorting the child from one flight to another, so check ahead. If your child is going to fly as a UM, be sure that you get to the gate early so that you can introduce him or her to the cabin crew. Make a travel card for your child that includes name, address, flight numbers, name of person who is meeting the child and contact numbers for you, a relative or a friend. Be sure they know how to make a collect call. The Department of Transportation and National Child Safety Council's brochure *Kids and Teens in Flight* includes general tips and a travel card similar to the one we describe. Call 202-366-2220 to order a copy. If, in spite of your careful planning, something happens and your child is marooned in a city far from home and destination, airlines may or may not take the responsibility for finding him or her a place to stay. Check policy with the airline before you book your ticket. A few last tips: Don't book the last flight of the day; don't book a flight too close to your own if you're heading off someplace else; order a special meal for your child and tell personnel and your child about the special meal.

What the Airlines Have for You

We took a survey of the various domestic airlines and compiled the following rundown on each airline. We asked the public relations/marketing department of the airlines to tell us about their children's fares (be aware that they are always subject to change), any special food and beverage service they have for kids, in-flight services, and so on. Our questionnaire asked about the availability of disposable diapers and bibs, bottles, bassinets, bottle warming, special seating, advance boarding, toy or game packets, cockpit visits, changing table in the bathroom, special arrangements for nursing mothers, and airport facilities for kids. If we don't mention any of these in the airline's listing, they aren't available. Armed with the information that follows, you may well know more than your travel agent or the reservationist you speak to. If the airline you're going to fly has kids' or infants' meals, you'll of course have to order them in advance. Go one step further, too. A few days before your flight, call and make sure your special order made it into the computer. No matter whether there'll be a meal or not, take your own snacks and drinks. The kids will be hungry before anything is served—we guarantee it.

Some airlines make special arrangements for nursing mothers; flight attendants help you find a comfortable spot. Baby bassinets can be reserved on some flights for infants up to about 20 pounds.

Aloha Airlines

Since this airline's average flight is only 20 minutes, there are no meals served. However, Aloha does offer a special children's rate for kids 2 to 11 and a student rate for older kids, all the way up to 25.

American Airlines

Certain markets have children's fares that are 20 percent lower than adult fares. There's a children's menu—hamburgers, hot dogs, fried chicken, and spaghetti. Give them six hours advance notice to arrange it. Car seats must fit under the seat or in an overhead bin. Expect special seating with advance notice, bottle warming, and advance boarding. If you ask ahead, a cockpit visit is possible.

Braniff

Kids 2 to 11 pay three-fourths the published fare. There are no kids' or infant meals available, but there is milk. Sometimes families can get special seating; they can always board early. A cockpit visit is sometimes possible, but don't plan on any sky cots (infants beds) when you fly Braniff.

Continental Airlines

There are no kids' or infants' meals available. Advance boarding is okay, and sometimes there's a game packet and a sky cot. Cockpit visits may be possible. Continental has a "Young Travelers Club" for children 12 and under with "clubrooms" in Houston and Denver airports. The clubrooms, for unaccompanied minors, are stocked with television, books, and games and provide "constant adult supervision."

Delta

Delta offers baby, toddler, and child meals. They are as follows: for baby, three jars of baby food (vegetable with meat, vegetable and fruit, oatmeal and milk); for toddlers, corn flakes with banana and milk, orange juice, and toast for breakfast, and peanut butter and grape jelly sandwich with a banana, animal crackers, and milk for lunch. For older children, breakfast is corn flakes, orange juice, melon, and a Danish. Lunch and dinner is either a hot dog or cheeseburger, potatoes, cole slaw, banana, milk, and a candy bar. A snack is also available for between meals: a peanut butter and jelly sandwich, apple, potato chips, milk, and a fudge brownie. Order the special meals when you make your reservation, but if you forget, you can ask for them up to three hours before flight time. Parents may use any FAA-approved car seat. Advance boarding is available, and children traveling with an adult (anyone 12 years or over) pay a 75 percent fare unless there's a special kids' fare at the time.

Delta has a program just for kids called "Fantastic Flyer." On every flight kids receive a Mickey Mouse visor and a copy of *Fantastic Flyer* magazine, filled with games, puzzles, and stories. Once kids have enrolled in the Fantastic Flyer program on board, they receive a membership pack in the mail—a poster, certificates, an ID card, and then every three months they receive the latest copy of *Fantastic Flyer*. Delta also offers packages and special rates for trips to Disney World and Disneyland.

United

Kids 2 to 11 years are entitled to discounts. For example, on a standard coach ticket, the child's fare is 75 percent of the adult fare. Bassinets are available at bulkhead seats only. Children's meals—hot dog, hamburger, chips, peanut butter and jelly, or spaghetti and meat balls—can be arranged with at least 24 hours' notice. Bottles may be warmed and a "Fun in Flight" kit is available. Cockpit visits are possible before takeoff.

USAir

In selected markets, a special family fare is available: One adult pays full fare, other adults get a discount, and the children's fare is extended to any child 17 and under. An example at press time: Pittsburgh to Orlando: first adult pays $514 round-trip, and each additional adult and each child pays $120. Family fare is not an advanced purchase plan, so it can be used at the last minute and for one-way or round-trip travel. Children's meals are available with 24 hours' advance notice. Car seats in vacant seats are fine. Bottle warming, advance boarding, a game packet, and a cockpit visit are all possible.

BY TRAIN

We go to Washington, D.C., every year to visit relatives, and the kids *love* the train trip. Train travel—as long as it is not for too long a distance—is great for kids. It's more of an adventure than the family car, there's enough room to move around during the trip, there are usually snacks to be had, there's a bathroom on board, and there's a lot to see out the window. The kids always seem to meet other kids on the train, too, and have fun going from seat to seat, playing with their new companions. Unfortunately, Amtrak has discontinued their family-plan fares. Now children 2 to 11 pay 50 percent of the full fare; children under 2 years may travel free. Amtrak dining cars have children's portions and an excellent game book called *Amtrak's Train Tricks* that's good for kids 3 years and older. On long-distance western trains, passengers get route guides with a map and description of what they're going to pass. These trains also have movies and games in the lounge car. The Chicago–San Francisco–Oakland *California Zephyr*, the Chicago–Los Angeles *Southwest Chief*, the Chicago–Seattle–Portland *Empire Builder*, and the Seattle–Los Angeles *Coast Starlight* also feature Sightseer Lounge cars with picture windows from floor to ceiling. For information on any of Amtrak's trains or services, call 800-USA-RAIL; ask them to send you a National Train Timetable. If Amtrak's listening, we'd like to go on record saying that we're disappointed in them for discontinuing their family-plan fares and we also wish that American train travel would catch up with its European counterpart kid-wise. Some European trains actually have "play cars" for kids and places to warm bottles and change diapers. Why are we so far behind?

BY BUS

We don't think buses are a great way to travel with kids. They are cramped, and kids can't really walk up and down the aisle for exercise. For short trips, when there's no other alternative, the bus experience will be improved if you're sure to pack food and take games, toys, and a tape recorder/radio for the kids. They'll have to sit near the window for good radio reception. Bus fares are generally inexpensive: children 5 to 11 pay half fare, and one child under 5 years can travel free for each fare-paying adult.

Once more, we refer you to Chapter 3 for details on what to take with you on your trip, whether you go by car, plane, train, or bus.

ABOUT OUR LISTINGS:

The properties we list in this book all welcome kids and all willingly responded to our many, many questions. We're relying on you, our readers, to let us know about your own experience with our choices—good and bad—and to tell us about any new places we can list in the next edition.

ONE MORE REMINDER:

If you're looking for a place to play tennis, check the tennis and golf chapter but don't overlook Chapter 8 on resorts, Chapter 10 on skiing (many ski resorts turn into tennis and golf spots once the snow melts), and Chapter 11 on farms and dude ranches.

And don't forget the None of the Above listings beginning on page 469.

NOTE: Rates quoted here were accurate at press time but are subject to change.

NOTE: Be sure to check pages 481–82 for a list of publishers' addresses. Some books published by smaller publishers may not be readily available in bookstores but can be ordered directly from the publisher.

Send us your cards and letters. We want to hear from you about your own great vacation choices so that we can include them in the next edition. Write to Great Vacations with Your Kids, TWYCH, 80 Eighth Avenue, New York, New York 10011.

3

WHAT TO TAKE

Although the particulars of what to take with you vary with the age of your children, the place you're going, and the way you plan to get there, the basics remain the same. Try not to overload yourself with unnecessary equipment, but don't forget the essentials: a portable crib may not be absolutely necessary, but a stroller will be. Think about the pieces of equipment you use each day—baby food grinder, for example—and take whatever will make your travels easier. And, unless you're heading into the wilderness, you will probably be able to rent, buy, or borrow whatever you need wherever you are going.

The basic rules for choosing clothes to take along is simple enough: take clothes that are comfortable, sturdy, and dark-colored with tops and bottoms that can easily be mixed and matched. Keep in mind that polyester and cotton shirts dry a lot faster than pure cotton, and forget about taking anything along that you love and your child doesn't. You don't want arguments about clothes while you're on vacation. When kids are old enough, let them help select what they'll bring such as five T-shirts and three pairs of shorts. You can fill in the rest.

One suggestion from a friend seems particularly clever: Pack a "nighttime bag" with pajamas, toothbrushes, toothpaste, favorite toys, and favorite blanket and put it all on top of the suitcase so that when you arrive at a place, you don't have to go through the entire bag looking for the night things. Always take rain gear, too, unless

31

you're desert-bound. We spent three very soggy days in Vermont in June with no boots, no raincoats, and no umbrellas. It was *miserable.*

A Word About Health

We advise taking along a basic first-aid kit. Unless you have some valid reason to worry about your child's health, don't. Again, unless you're going deep into the wilderness, there will always be medical help nearby. If it will make you feel more relaxed, call ahead to wherever you are going and check out medical facilities or ask your pediatrician to recommend someone who practices in the place you're going.

Our multipurpose first-aid kit contains the following:

- Band-Aids
- gauze pads and tape
- cotton balls
- antiseptic cream (something like Neosporin or Bacitracin)
- thermometer and Vaseline
- vitamins
- children's acetaminophen
- insect repellent
- needle and tweezers for splinter or tick removal and matches for sterilizing
- sunscreen
- first aid book

Be sure to have your medical/hospital insurance card with you, and if it will make you feel more secure, a copy of your favorite baby care book.

For Infants

If your child is 2 or under, here's a checklist of things to bring along:

- disposable diapers
- some kind of baby wipes
- diaper rash ointment or cream
- pacifier (and plenty of spares if your child is addicted)
- food

- formula or juice and lots of extra bottles and nipples
- bibs
- blanket
- waterproof sheet (we've always preferred a small plastic table-cloth to double as a changing "table" and at night, as a mattress protector)
- some plastic bags for dirty laundry

If you'd like a pre-packaged mini-pack for your baby that has all you need for a diaper change and cleanup, you can order one for $12.50 from a company called Travel Mini Pack, P.O. Box 571, Stony Point, New York 10980; it's available in a gingham quilted case or in one with a small flower print.

Some Things You May Not Have Considered

Through the years, we've found that there are a few things that we wished we had had, but didn't, so we pass the list on to you:

- a can opener
- a jackknife (one of our kids wears braces and needs apples, bagels, and other snacks cut up)
- flashlight with batteries
- sewing kit (all this has to be is one spool of black thread, one of white, a few needles, and a few safety pins)
- plastic bags in various sizes that close tight for toothbrushes, bits of wet soap, wet bathing suits and towels, sandy beach shoes

TOYS AND GAMES: WHAT TO TAKE AND WHERE TO PUT IT

Probably the most important point to remember about getting together toys, games, and assorted travel equipment is that your kids should be the ones who ultimately decide what goes. When you travel, your children have very little control over what they're going to see, what they'll do, where they'll sleep, and where they'll eat. This uncertainty can unnerve them. Children like structure, and when they travel, structure all but disappears. Giving them control over what toys and games they'll take with them will be a great comfort to them.

Several days before you leave (*please* don't wait for the last minute), have the kids choose a container for their goodies; a backpack is one of the best choices. Follow one simple rule—if you can carry it, you can take it. One friend has her kids carry their packed bags around their backyard for ten minutes, just long enough for them to see whether they can manage them. When they go back into the house they invariably eliminate a few things. If your child, like one of ours, *must* travel with his collection of *Mad* magazines, let him take one or two and pack the rest in his suitcase. Books and magazines are heavy and will be good to have at the destination as well.

Although the kids should choose their own toys and games, you are still in a good position to lobby for some of the things that you know will keep them busy and happy. You want them to take toys that will serve more than one purpose, toys and games that they can play with by themselves, as well as some that require your participation. Encourage your kids to avoid games with small bits and pieces; they'll only get lost or roll under the seat. Have them take some new toys and some old favorites, too. Younger children should have a stuffed animal and a blanket, for sure. Even if your child doesn't seem particularly attached to any one blanket or teddy, the time will come when he or she will need the comfort of a familiar object. Trust us on this one.

With our own experience in mind and after talking to friends who travel a great deal with their families, we've come up with the following "recommended" list. Pick what seems best from it, taking into account, of course, your children's individual interests:

Felt-tip Markers

Make sure markers are washable; if they come in a box, transfer them immediately into a plastic bag with a zipper or a box with a tight-fitting lid. The original containers are guaranteed to disintegrate in the course of the trip. When our youngest was still in a car seat, we put the markers in a drawstring bag and tied the bag to the car seat so that she'd be able to get them easiy.

Spiral Notebook

A spiral notebook will serve many purposes. It can be a travel diary for an older child, a drawing pad for any age, a scrapbook for the collecting types, and a workbook for others. One friend buys her kids hardcover artists' sketch books, different sizes for different ages. The hard cover serves as a good lap tray and prevents it from being mashed on the floor of the car. A clipboard is another good choice. A travel editor friend of ours makes a few match-up games for her 3-year-old in a notebook. Even very young children can draw a line between two apples or two chairs, and doing it makes them feel very grown up.

Glue Stick or Tube

What a wonderful invention the glue stick is—perfect for collages and scrapbooks as you go. And no mess!

Geometric Plastic "Snake"

Some kids love geometric snakes—there are no pieces to lose, and they can play for a long, long time creating new shapes.

Cards

Take a regular deck of cards and/or any of the special card games such as Fish or Crazy Eights.

Books

Books are a must (paperbacks preferred), no matter what the age of your child. Take some new ones and some old favorites. Take some that the kids can read themselves and some that you can read to them. (A collection of fairy tales is a good idea.)

One of the nicest catalogs of books for kids (tapes, too) that we've ever seen is the one compiled by Chinaberry Book Service. The books are all listed by level—from books for the very young to books that can be read by an advanced reader. Each book listed is lovingly reviewed; the choices are exceptional. We spent one entire night reading through the catalog, trying to narrow down our choices. For a catalog of your own, write to 2830 Via Orange Way, Suite B, Spring Valley, California 92078-1521, or call 800-777-5205.

Tape Recorder

A tape recorder runs a close tie with books as the greatest boon to travel with children. Think of the possibilities: you can take tapes with the kids' favorite stories on them or with stories they've never heard before. Song tapes (Wee Sing is the brand name of a series of 60-minute tapes that include "Nursery Rhymes and Lullabies," "Children's Songs and Finger Plays," "Silly Songs," and "Around the

Campfire"; lyrics are included and each costs $7.95) and tapes of Broadway shows ("My Fair Lady" and "Annie" took one family we know from Alsace–Lorraine all the way to Paris) are great entertainment during trips.

Two excellent tapes meant especially for use with kids while traveling are "Traffic Jams" and "Imagination." The first is a collection of songs for the car written and performed by Joe Scruggs. We all loved listening to the tape; the musical arrangements are terrific, real toe-tapping stuff. Copies are available from Educational Graphics, P.O. Box 180476, Austin, Texas 78718, 512-345-4664. Three other tapes by the same people, although not specifically for travel, "Late Last Night," "Abracadabra," and "Even Trolls Have Moms" also deserve our highest recommendation. All three tapes cost $9.95 each plus $1.50 for postage and handling. "Imagination" is the creation of Lulu and Shelly Richardson; it is a 40-minute tape with background music and sound effects—of what the creators call "interactions and travel games." "Imagination" is meant to be used by kids and adults together. The Richardsons think that 5- and 6-year-olds can enjoy the tape as long as there are older brothers and sisters participating. Otherwise, kids should be about 7 years old. The Richardsons have also put together a travel tape called "Christmas" that is especially designed to use en route at holiday time. Both tapes are available for $7.95 each from Family Travel Tapes, 9220 A-1 Parkway East, Suite 125, Birmingham, Alabama 35206, 205-836-0638; add $1.50 for one tape, $2.00 for two for postage and handling.

Yet another tape developed especially for car trips is "Games for the Road," the creation of Deborah Valentine, an educator. The tape is narrated by the "Fairy Gamemother," who explains how to play 23 different noncompetitive games, designed so that children and adults can play together no matter what their abilities are. A 15-page booklet explaining the games comes along with each tape. Valentine recommends her tape for kids aged 5 to 15. For copies, write to Valentine Productions, 3856 Grand Forest Drive, Norcross, Georgia 30092; send $8.95 plus $1.50 for shipping and handling.

Another independent producer, Golden Glow Recordings, offers two tapes that are nice for travel, although not specifically for trips. The two tapes are "Nitey-Nite," which helps put kids to sleep with lullabies accompanied by harp, guitar, recorder, flute, and keyboard, and "Good Morning Sunshine," with a side that helps wake kids up gently and another that is more up-tempo for the "wide-awake and raring-to-go." These tapes are $9.70 each and are available from Golden Glow Recordings at 800 Livermore, Yellow Springs, Ohio 45387.

For tapes of children's stories, usually two to two and one-half hours long, we recommend the catalog of Listen for Pleasure, One Columba Drive, Niagara Falls, New York 14305. Tapes cost $14.95 each plus postage, and the selection includes lots of favorites such as *Grimm's Fairy Tales, Little Women, Black Beauty,* and *The Secret Garden.* Another nice catalog of tapes for kids is put together by Music for Little People and is available by writing to Box 1460, Redway, California 95560.

Take blank tapes too, so that the kids can be creative. Have them interview each other, the flight attendants, the people sitting next to them on the plane. One friend turned what might have been a boring visit to a sculpture show into a real adventure for her two boys by letting them tape a running commentary on what they saw as they went around the exhibit. Or try a sightseeing tape; it will bring back the whole trip when you play it a few months later.

It's best to let each kid have his or her own tape recorder, ear plugs, and microphone to avoid conflicts. Take extra batteries, too.

Hand-held Video Games
Video games are great for passing time. Our kids like to trade with other kids on the plane.

Workbooks
There are lots of good activity books on the market. A few are reviewed here. If the place you're going to has a related coloring book or workbook (for instance, a coloring book of Colonial Williamsburg), it would be great to get it ahead of time. Local tourist offices should be able to tell you what's available.

Action Figures
The category of action figures includes a variety of creatures— GI Joe, He-Man, Barbie dolls, and My Little Pony, to name a few. Kids can stay happy and busy for hours making up adventures for their plastic friends.

Puppets
Even the youngest child can have fun with puppets, and they can substitute for stuffed animals when space is at a premium.

Magnetic Letters and Numbers

Taking magnetic alphabet and numbers breaks the rule about small pieces, but some kids may really enjoy taking these along. A cookie sheet makes a good stick-on surface.

Press-on Games

Colorforms makes kits that are widely available, but we much prefer the kind made in Denmark by UniSet and distributed in the United States by International Playthings, Inc., Riverdale, New Jersey 07457. Colorforms are more like commercials than toys, but UniSet makes an airport stick-on set, a doll's house, dinosaurs, a zoo, a circus, a supermarket, a map of the United States (unfortunately, the map is a little too big for lap play), and more.

Lego or Bristle Blocks

These are another exception to the bits and pieces rule, but these toys are excellent for even the youngest children. If you're going to be traveling in Europe, buy your Lego as you travel. By the end of your trip you'll have a wonderful collection for much less than it would ever cost at home.

Active Toys

If you're traveling by car, don't forget to pack a few things for the rest stops to get the kids moving. Consider an inflatable beach ball, bat and mitt, a jump rope, or, for the littlest ones, a bottle of bubbles to blow and to chase.

Surprise Package

Hide a "surprise" or "crisis" bag somewhere in your hand luggage, something to pull out when the going gets rough. It should be wrapped—comic papers make a good wrapping—and should have some minitreats in it: maybe some candy, a hand-held game, a new book, stickers, or a story tape. Consider picking up something at a tag sale to put into the surprise bag; all that matters is that it's new to your kids.

It's a good idea, too, to tell the kids that you'll buy them something new at the airport or bus or train station. We like those booklets with the invisible ink pens. Or have the children buy some postcards to write en route. They can even cut them up to make puzzles for their friends that can be mailed in an envelope.

Here let's take a very subjective look at some specific take-along toys, games, and books.

One company that puts out an excellent catalog of toys and games, *Toys to Grow On,* reserves a page for toys especially suited for travel. Send for a Toys to Grow On catalog from 2695 East Dominguez Street, P.O. Box 6261, Carson, California 90749, 213-537-8600 or 800-542-8338.

Mad Libs

Our whole family loves Mad Libs. It's a fill-in-the-blank game published by Price/Stern/Sloan and costs about $2 per pad. The pad is filled with stories with missing words; players supply the words, and the result is a convoluted, usually very amusing tale. Our youngest has been able to play since she was 3 years old, although it's most fun for older kids.

Travel Yahtzee, Travel Connect Four, Travel Battleship, Travel Mastermind, Travel Shut-the-Box

All of the games listed are good for kids; most of the ones we talked to, though, thought Travel Scrabble was a drag.

Tangoes

Tangoes is a clever puzzle game that can keep one or two players aged 5 on up busy for quite a while. The compact game, just right for travel, contains two sets of seven playing pieces in various shapes. The challenge is to fit the pieces together into any of 54 different patterns printed on accompanying cards. Answers are on the back of the card to help younger kids and, in our case, adults. It's not easy but it is stimulating and fun. The game can be ordered directly from Rex Games, Inc., 2001 California Street, Suite 204, San Francisco, California 94109, for $10.

Are We There Yet?

The *Are We There Yet?* activity book put together by Rand McNally ($3.95) claims to be for all ages, but we'd recommend it for ages 6 and up.

The Kids Book of Games for Cars, Trains and Planes

The *Kids Book,* by Rudi McToots, published by Bantam Books

($4.95), has 160 suggestions for keeping children amused. It's a clever book with lots of workable ideas clearly explained.

My Holiday Away Scrapbook: A Souvenir for Me to Keep

My Holiday Away Scrapbook, a booklet published in Great Britain by Longman, is written by two good friends of ours, Herb Mack and Ann Cook. It is not widely available here but should be. It's a kind of personal diary that helps kids keep track of their trip, think about what they're seeing and what they've done, and, when completed, serves as a very personalized record of their adventure. It includes graphs to make, a travel games, a record of how money was spent, a food log, a place to record the best and worst things about the trip, and more. The illustrations are delightful, and the idea is a terrific one. Copies are available for $2.50 in the United States through Eeyore's Books for Children, 2212 Broadway, New York, New York 10024. Add $1.50 for shipping.

Best Travel Activity Book Ever

Despite a bit of hyperbole by the publishers, Rand McNally's *Best Travel Activity Book Ever* is thick—320 pages—and would be best for kids 4 to 6 to use with the help of an older brother or sister or parent ($6.95).

Games to Play in the Car

Written by Michael Harwood and distributed in the United States by St. Martin's Press ($6.95), *Games to Play* is a little book that has some old and some new, all quite playable games for car rides. The suggestions for games for little ones are especially useful.

Questron Books

Random House publishes 24 *Questron* workbooks that are sold with an electronic wand. The books teach reading and number skills; the wand signals right and wrong loudly enough for the kids to hear but not loudly enough to bother anyone around them.

Things to Do in the Car

We like this book because it includes activities for kids as young as 2. Author Linda Hogdon begins with "Get to Know My Community," which is smart since most trips are right around the neighborhood. Next is "Math Skills to Think About," which encourages computing without paper and pencil. "Thinking Games," "Remembering Games," and "Expanding Conversation" all help kids notice more of what's going on outside the window and help develop language skills at the same time. The ideas here are inventive; we think you'll like it. Copies cost $4 plus $1 for postage and handling from Young Ideas Enterprises, 2928 Hill Drive, Troy, Michigan 48098.

Have a Good Trip

This is a workbook for kids 3 to 12. If your child can't read, you'll have to explain directions; if he or she can read, the book is good for independent play. For a copy send $1.95 plus 50 cents postage to Virginia and Sam Murray, 5065 Dover Street, Northeast, St. Petersburg, Florida 33703.

My Travel Book

Written by Andrew Vowles and Lynn Illingworth, this activity book includes games, songs, and trivia questions. It should keep older kids busy—you really have to be able to read quite well to use it. Copies are available from Hayes Publishing, 2045 Niagara Falls Boulevard, Unit 14, Niagara Falls, New York 14304, for $2.95.

The (World's First Ever) Pop-Up Games Book

By pop-up book superstar Ron van der Meer, it's great for train and plane trips. It's not a book, or a game, but both. Almost any age can play, but some simple math and reading skills make it even more fun to play without the help of parents. Published by Delacorte Press, the book is $9.95.

Puzzles

Although you wouldn't want to take them with you (just what you need is to have puzzle pieces all over the car), you might want to get a puzzle map of the U.S. or of the state or states that you'll be visiting for the kids to play with before you go. This is a good way to get the kids ready for the trip. The puzzles we recommend, part of the Austin-Pierce "Puzzlin' State" series, include interesting facts about the state so that kids get a painless social studies lesson while they put the puzzle together. Puzzles are available in many children's stores or from the Globe Pequot Press.

Between You and Me

A company called Between You and Me concentrates its energies on developing toys and products for travel with kids that are kid-tested, practical, and beautiful, too. We had the chance to use two of their pre-packed travel kits with our kids—the Primary Pak (for kids 5 to 7) and Elementary Pak (for kids 8 to 10)—and they were big hits. The materials are carefully chosen—there were Mad Libs, colored markers, activity books, lace-ups—all in a good-looking back pack with adjustable straps. The contents of the travel packs change all the time, so if you buy one now, you can get another for your next trip. The price is $24.95 each, and a Family Deluxe Pak, which is meant for families with kids of all different ages is $29.95. The Travel Paks are only some of the goodies that Between You and Me has to offer: A little bright blue plastic case ($7.95) that can have your child's name on it is adorable. One of our kids takes hers along to school every day with crayons, stickers, and other treasures in it. And what a clever idea they have in Cargo Cat—a stuffed animal that attaches to the back seat of a car and has vinyl pouches big enough to hold all books and activities for the trip ($15). To order any of their products or for a catalog, write to Between You and Me, 3419 Tony Drive, San Diego, California 92122-2305.

Sealed with a Kiss

Julie Winston handpicks the items she puts in her travel-toy collection, called "Sealed with a Kiss." Packages are available for kids ages 4–18. We ordered one with ten items, all individually wrapped, and our kids were kept busy for hours. The charge is $30, which includes shipping. Write to her at 6709 Tildenwood Lane, Rockville, Maryland 20852 or call 800-888-SWAK.

Games People Play

There are many games to play as you go that require no equipment whatsoever. Some are classics—20 Questions, G-H-O-S-T, Geography. Your kids will like playing them as much as you did when you were their age. Here are a few that may be new to you:

Alphabet Sentences

Make up sentences with at least five words that begin with the same letter, more words per sentence for older kids.

How Many Bridges?

Kids guess how many bridges you'll cross between two points, how many hills you'll climb, how many haystacks or horses or billboards you'll see. A certain number of points is given for the best guess, and points can add up to an ice cream cone or sticker reward.

Memory Game
The first person says, "I'm going on a trip and packing a toothbrush." The second repeats the sentence and adds an item, and on and on, until someone forgets.

Alphabet Game
We compete with each other to find each letter in the alphabet, in sequence, on road signs, license plates, and billboards: only one letter per sign per person. The first to finish the alphabet is the winner.

Similes
You can slip a little poetry by the kids without their knowing it. Have them finish sentences like "rain sounds like . . ." "tears taste like. . . ." For older kids, get more abstract with "anger feels like . . ." "joy feels like. . . ."

Navigator
The kids take turns being the navigator. One friend gives the navigator a special hat, a map, and special privileges. It's the navigator's job to follow the route on the map, estimate when the next exit will occur, figure a good spot for lunch, and answer the question "When are we going to be there?"

String-along Story
One person starts the story, then stops after about ten sentences, and the next person adds a piece. You may want to tape record the tale to play later.

Just Plain Singing
It's fun to just sing together. Let everyone have a chance to choose a song! Try a round or some harmony.

Toy Libraries
Years ago we walked into the children's room of a library along the Connecticut shore and saw a bookcase filled with fabulous toys, puzzles, and games that were there to be borrowed like books. We couldn't believe our good luck, and the kids were thrilled. We've

since discovered that there is an association of toy libraries called, appropriately enough, the U.S. Toy Library Association. They publish a directory of toy libraries in the United States; it costs $23 and is available from the association's headquarters, 2719 Broadway Avenue, Evanston, Illinois 60201.

4

WHERE TO STAY

When it comes to choosing a place to stay with your kids, there are lots of variables to consider, variables that you may never have thought about when you were traveling alone. For example, when you're traveling by yourself, it rarely matters whether the room you stay in has a bathtub or just a shower. But if you're traveling with a 3-year-old who is used to a bath and who has never taken a shower, the absence of a bathtub can be a real issue.

Because kids feel most secure when they can sleep in the same bed every night, if at all possible, try to arrange to stay in one place and travel from there. If that's not possible, do what you can to make them secure in their new surroundings by taking their own portable crib or at least by setting up a corner of the room just for them. Whenever possible, try to make one hotel your base of operations; it's hard on kids to have to move around a lot.

Some questions you should ask when choosing a place to stay are the following:

- How much space do you need? If you're accustomed to having a lot of space, don't cram yourself into a tiny room for your vacation. One room for a family of four is okay for a night or two, but for anything longer, consider two rooms or find a hotel with suites or rent a condo or an apartment. If budget is a problem, think about cutting a day or two off your vacation for the sake of more space; it really may be worth it. If you want two rooms in a hotel where kids stay free, try to book two singles. You may well save 25 to 40 percent over the cost of two doubles.

- What amenities do you want? If you're staying in a hotel, look for one that has a swimming pool, a nearby playground, a game room—a place where your kids can get rid of some of their excess energy. Indoor pools are wonderful in winter. Ask whether the hotel or motel will help find a baby-sitter. Most do. And if it will make you feel more comfortable, arrange to interview the sitter before you need him or her. You can ask for references, too. Find out whether room service is possible. We love to order breakfast from room service—two large breakfasts are usually plenty for a family with two small children—and then take our time to eat and plan our day. Find out whether there's a refrigerator in the room. Being able to store juice and milk and to make your own breakfast will save you quite a bit of money.

- What's the best location for your room? If you're in a motel, ask for the first floor. Ideally, the kids should be able to step outside to play where you can see them. Avoid rooms with balconies. We try to limit the number of required no's and don't's on a vacation; to that end we avoid stairs and try to get rooms at the ends of halls or near the soda or ice machine, where the kids don't have to be quite so restricted about making noise.

- Are there bathtubs or only showers? This is worth repeating. Vacation is no time to introduce little ones to a shower. If a room without a bath is unavoidable, try to make your child comfortable with showers before you leave for vacation.

- Are there restaurant facilities for kids? Determine whether there are high chairs or booster seats available in the restaurant of the hotel or motel. Even if you carry your own booster seat or one of those great collapsible infants chairs that attach to any table, ask about the availability of high chairs. Whether or not the restaurant supplies high chairs will give you a good idea of just how eager they really are to have kids there.

- Are there laundry facilities? It's great to have access to a washing machine and dryer, not just for getting clothes clean, but also for drying them after getting caught in the rain.

- Is the place you are considering near where you're going to sightsee? If you're going to be in a city and plan to do a lot of sightseeing, it's nice to stay at a well-located hotel. The extra money you may pay for a room may be what you save in transportation to and from another hotel.
- Are there special rates for kids? Most accommodations have special rates for children; most often kids can stay in a parent's room at no extra cost. Always ask about family plans or, in cities, about special weekend rates.
- Is there a children's program? More and more resort hotels are offering children's programming to their guests. We're delighted by this. We feel that even if you have no intention of taking advantage of the program—if your child is too young or you insist on complete family togetherness every minute of the day—you should still seek out accommodations with chidren's programs. The reason: If there's a children's program there are bound to be other kids, and one of the nicest parts of a vacation for kids is meeting new friends.

CHILDPROOFING A HOTEL ROOM

Your home is childproofed so your toddler won't get hurt, but what happens when you get to a hotel or motel for a short stay? Children's curiosity is something to encourage. We don't want to have to be saying "no" every few minutes to keep the kids out of trouble. It's simple enough to make your room safe. Just do these few things:

- Put away any of those matches that the hotel provides.
- Identify the danger spots—lamp cords, exposed outlets, curtain pulls that kids might get twisted in, open windows without screens. Tape down the cords, plug up the outlets, and open the window only from the top.
- Move the bed against a wall so that your child will have less chance of falling out. Extra pillows can keep the open side safe.
- If the hotel's crib has no bumpers, roll up an extra blanket or two and make your own.
- Put all glasses up out of the reach of your toddler.
- Check out all fire exits.

A Very Special Word About Children's Programs

We have a very definite philosophy about children's programs. It can best be introduced by quoting from a letter we received in response to a questionnaire we sent to a couple who run a dude ranch in the Ozarks:

Your questionnaire asks for activities for the children. It concerned me that if you are writing a book about "Great Vacations with Your Kids," why in the world would you be so concerned about activities where the child would be supervised by someone other than the parent? We try to set up an atmosphere where parent and child can relate to each other. Granted our parents love the idea that the kids can go on a supervised trail ride and they don't have to go every time, but that is not the intent and purpose of the vacation. Yes, they love to be able to have a person to watch their toddler for a few hours while they canoe, go shopping or just lie in the sun, but that isn't the main point of the trip! Families that come here, especially if they are from metropolitan areas, usually take three days to just unwind! If the kids are teenagers, in those three days they go from nagging, complaining "nothing to do" syndrome creeps, to real people! It is truly astounding! The parents who have spent more money than time with their children find out who their kids really are.

As soon as we read the letter, we wrote back explaining that we agree completely. Children's programs are not meant to be places where parents "dump" their kids. They should be places where kids can go to have fun with other kids, where they can do things they enjoy alongside their peers. That doesn't mean a full day away from their parents—maybe just an hour or two at a time is all you want. The author of the letter says herself that parents like the idea of having the kids go off on a supervised trail ride. That's the kind of thing we like, too. It's great to have a choice, to have the option of a supervised children's activity.

Besides being fun for the kids, a good children's program, we feel, is safer than a private baby-sitter, especially on a beach holiday since, in the case of an emergency, there is additional staff to turn to. Other advantages of places with children's programs is that these places are most likely to have ideas about family activities in the area and have heard your questions before.

Even if you have no intention at all of enrolling your kid in a supervised program, just the fact that it's there means that there will be other kids for him or her to play with. We believe, and we learned this from our own kids, that as much as we feel the need for time away from them once in a while, they need to play with kids their same age and not have to be forced into situations where they are expected to behave like miniature adults. Hotels that offer children's programs are also likely to have family activities for everyone to do together. A nice alternative to a children's program when one is not operating when you visit (most hotels offer children's programs only at holiday time and during the summer) is children's sports instruction. Sign your kids up for a golf lesson while you play a set of tennis.

Even if your kids aren't old enough to join a program, there are still benefits to staying at hotels that offer them. Since so many of the program participants have younger brothers and sisters, the hotel will be used to having little ones and will have high chairs and cribs available as well as baby-sitting. Some hotels will even let kids younger than the official minimum age participate in programs if a baby-sitter or parent is along. And, if the hotels with children's programs are too expensive for you, you should still ask whether it's possible for non-guests to participate. You can stay in a less expensive place and still have your kids in a quality program.

Hotels

In our city section (Chapter 7) we have some specific hotel suggestions and then, further on, in the very end of the book, Appendix 1 suggests some hotels. We've listed the hotels we do because they welcome children and, in some cases, because they have children's programs. If you are looking for a hotel on your own, you can certainly contact the tourist office of the place you're going, you can leave it to your travel agent, or you can consult a good guidebook that features accommodations. We list some of the best at the end of this chapter. When choosing the hotel, keep in mind the criteria we have already noted. And try to get to wherever you're going to stay by 5:00 P.M. so there'll be a chance to acclimate the kids long enough before bedtime.

Once you've arrived at the hotel of your choice, here are some simple things to do to prevent your kids from going crazy with boredom while they wait for you to check in. Have something in your bag that they haven't seen yet for them to do. Or let them sit down with some hotel brochures and circle what they want to see. If your kids are old enough, let them explore the lobby, but tell them to be sure that wherever they go, they can still see you.

As soon as you've checked in, take a walk around the hotel with the kids, teach them how to call the operator themselves, and choose a meeting place to use in case you get separated. If it's a large hotel, go to the room then back to the lobby, and then ask the kids whether they can lead the way back to the room. Remember too, the more comfortable the kids feel with their surroundings, the easier bedtime will be.

We have some wonderful news on the subject of hotels. For years we've been trying to convince a major U.S. hotel chain to make a real commitment to families. Other countries have chains that have done it—Crest in England, Sofitel in France, Happy Family Swiss Hotels in Switzerland, and Delta Hotels in Canada. Now it's finally happened in the U.S. Hyatt has decided to take the step, and we're delighted. The new family-oriented program is called Camp Hyatt and here's what it means:

- Eleven of the 13 Hyatt resorts offer a full day-camp program that operates holiday weeks, summers, and weekends year-round for kids 3 to 15 from 9:00 A.M. to 11:00 P.M. The cost is $25 per day or $5 per hour; meals are usually additional. Here's where you'll find the program: Scottsdale, Arizona (we tried this one out; it's fabulous); Monterey, California; Grand Champions, Palm Springs, California; Grand Cypress, Florida; Maui, Hawaii; Waikiloa, Hawaii; Lake Tahoe, Nevada; Hilton Head, South Carolina; Grand Cayman in the Caribbean; and the Cerromar Beach and Dorado Beach in Puerto Rico.
- Hyatt's nonresort hotels offer Friday and Saturday night activities for kids 3 to 15, from 6:00 to 10:00 P.M. year-round. The charge is $4 per hour with a snack included.
- A Kids' Frequent Stay program lets kids have their Hyatt "passport" validated after each stay; four stays and the kids get a Camp Hyatt carrypack.
- All Hyatt restaurants and room services offer children's menus with breakfast for $3 or under, lunch and dinner for $5 and less. Small portions of other menu items are half-price for kids 3 to 15.
- At check-in, kids get their passport, registration card, Camp Hyatt cap, and room service menu.
- Families can book a second room for kids at half-price (this is

subject to availability at time of booking, so it's best to reserve early).

- You can also always count on baby-sitting, having your kids under 18 stay in your room for free (under 12 in Hawaii), and being able to borrow from a supply of games that is kept at the concierge's desk.

For more information, call Hyatt at 800-233-1234.

Hyatt, like most of the other large hotel chains in the U.S., offers attractive weekend rates that are often 30 to 50 percent less than the regular midweek rates. This is great for families. To find out about the weekend packages, just call the following numbers: Hilton, 800-445-8667; Marriott, 800-228-9290; Omni, 800-843-6664; Ramada, 800-228-2828; Sheraton, 800-325-3535; and Westin, 800-228-3000.

ALL-SUITE HOTELS

There's something new happening in the hotel industry—the all-suite hotels—and they're great for traveling families. Although they were originally designed to attract business travelers, they've got what families need: extra space. Most of these all-suite hotels feature a separate bedroom or even two bedrooms, a living room, a dining area, and, almost always, a completely equipped kitchen, all for the cost of a standard hotel room. (Some are actually converted apartment buildings.) The price is usually calculated per suite, and weekend specials are common. Also, because these new accommodations have been well received, new ones are appearing all the time and competition is keen. That is all the better for us since the competition forces the hotels to offer more and more amenities: free breakfasts and local newspapers, pre-stocked refrigerators, and help in finding baby-sitters. Here we list some of the larger all-suite chains, with a short profile of each one. For more information on each—directories, rates, reservations, and so on—just call the toll-free number listed. You might also want to consult *The All Suite Hotel Guide* by Pamela Lanier ($13.95, John Muir Publications), which lists over 800 of this kind of hotel in the U.S. and abroad. Each listing describes the facilities, the amenities, and gives information on what attractions are nearby.

Aston Hotels and Resorts
2255 Kuhio Avenue
Honolulu, Hawaii 96815-2658
Telephone: 800-367-5124

Formerly the Hotel Corporation of the Pacific, this group of 37 hotels in California, Hawaii, and Mexico offers a choice from studios to three-bedroom villas. Children under 18 are free, the charge for a crib is $6. Each suite has a full kitchen, and high chairs and booster seats can be arranged through the concierge. Some properties have market facilities, and many have children's camps that run through the summer for children aged 5 to 12. Activities include sand sculpture, making shell jewelry, scuba lessons, Hawaiiana classes, and snorkeling. A sample rate: an oceanfront two-bedroom, two-bath suite at the Aston Kaanapali Shores costs $239 per day for up to four guests.

Embassy Suites
Xerox Centre
Suite 1700
222 Las Colinas Boulevard
Irving, Texas 75039
Telephone: 800-EMBASSY

This is the largest all-suite system in the United States. There are 87 hotels now, with 100 planned by 1990. This company is ambitious. Suites have two rooms, including a living room with a sofa bed, a dining/work area, a color television, refrigerator, wet bar, and in some places, microwave ovens or ranges. Included in the nightly rate, which averages about $79, is a complimentary full breakfast with eggs, pancakes, sausages, hash browns, cereals, juices, pastries, tea, or coffee. Guests are treated to complimentary cocktails each evening, too, if local laws allow. Breakfasts and drinks are served in the central atrium, a courtyard with ponds, pools, and tropical plants. All Embassy Suites have maid service and the choice of laundry service or self-service laundry. Baby-sitting can be arranged; sometimes advance notice is required. We thought you'd like to know, too, that Embassy received a very high rating from *Consumer Reports* and was rated number one in the hotel industry for customer service by *Fortune* magazine. Special weekend rates are available at most locations.

Guest Quarters Suite Hotels
30 Rowes Wharf
Boston, Massachusetts 02110
Telephone: 800-424-2900

Guest Quarters has 14 properties on the East Coast, two in Texas, one in Michigan, one in Santa Monica, California, and another in Chicago. All offer spacious one- or two-bedroom suites with a separate living/dining area with a sofa bed, kitchen or wet bar with refrigerator and, on request, a microwave oven. You can expect room service with children's menu; complimentary breakfast, an afternoon reception, and both self-service and valet laundry facilities. Baby-sitting may be arranged with 24 hours' advance notice. Most Guest Quarters properties also feature indoor or outdoor pools, whirlpools, saunas, and exercise rooms.

Paradise Management
Kukui Plaza C-207
50 South Beretania Street
Honolulu, Hawaii 96813
Telephone: 800-367-5205

Another Hawaiian-based company, Paradise Management, has 168 properties available ranging from condos to hotel suites to apartments to homes. Accommodations range from studio-size to three-bedroom, and often there's no charge for children staying with parents; cribs are available at some properties. Some have outside pools, children's pools, and jungle gyms and/or playgrounds.

Pickett Hotel Company
655 Metro Place South
Dublin, Ohio 43017
Telephone: 800-PICKETT

At present there are Pickett properties in Ohio, Georgia, Florida (one in Walt Disney World), North Carolina, Tennessee, and Indiana. Suites have one or two bedrooms, and rates are reasonable—children 17 and younger stay free with their parents (except at Walt Disney World). Cribs cost $15 extra per stay. Each suite has a refrigerator stocked with juices, soft drinks, mixes, and snacks; a wet bar and dining table, and a microwave oven on request. Built-in hair dryers, a coffee maker, garment steamers, bathrobes, and three televisions (one in the bathroom!) are also included. There's a complimentary full breakfast served every day. Baby-sitting can be arranged, and you can either do your own laundry or have it done for you. Properties have outdoor pools and whirlpools, and there's a children's playground at the Walt Disney World Resort.

The Residence Inn Company
One Marriott Drive
Washington, D.C. 20058
Telephone: 800-331-3131

By the time this book appears, Residence Inn plans to have 115 properties; some are in cities; most are in suburban areas; and they cover 30 states in all. The Residence Inns are very deliberately designed to remind you of a quiet, residential neighborhood. One- and two-bedroom suites are available, and all have a separate living room area. Suites have kitchens, and a shopping service to stock the refrigerator is available. All include a complimentary "hospitality hour" and a free breakfast of rolls and pastries, cereal, juice, milk, tea, and coffee and a free local newspaper. Practically all of the properties have an outdoor pool, a whirlpool, and a "Sport-Court." Other nice features are wood-burning fireplaces in most suites and reduced rates for extended stays (anything over a week is reduced about 20 percent); baby-sitting can be arranged, and there's free popcorn for everyone who checks in.

BUDGET MOTELS

On the basis of the logical premise that travelers were getting tired of paying high prices for motel rooms, a few entrepreneurs dreamed up the idea of the no-frills motel over 20 years ago. All the basic amenities—air-conditioning, television, even swimming pools—still remain, but often the coffee shop is across the street or there's no wall-to-wall carpeting on the floor. The budget motel phenomenon has spread, and now there are lots of low-cost facilities all across the United States in cities, suburbs, small towns, near theme parks, national parks, and all along interstates.

At any of the chains listed here, you should be able to count on a spacious room, comfortable beds, and basic hotel amenities—sometimes even wall-mounted hairdryers, in-room coffee makers, and remote-control color cable television. Competition is fierce out there, which is great for you and your family, especially when you're going to popular areas like Orlando, Williamsburg, and San Diego. Not only will you find the right room at the right price, but you'll have a choice. Many of the chains accept credit cards and don't charge for kids under 18 who share a room with their parents. You'll also find family rates, connecting rooms, weekend and vacation packages at many properties.

The hotel–motel industry generally classifies a budget motel chain as one that charges an average of $50 or less per night in most locations for a room with two double beds.

For a listing of what's available, state by state, you may want to send for a copy of Pilot Books' *National Directory of Budget Motels,* which lists over 2,200 such facilities. The book costs $4.95 and may be ordered from the publisher at 103 Cooper Street, Babylon, New York 11702.

Following is a list of some of this country's budget motel chains. You can call any of the 800 numbers listed and ask for a free directory of the chain's properties. Rates of the various low-cost motels vary from chain to chain, often even from motel to motel within a chain, but, in general, the more people you fit into one room, the more money you'll save. Whenever there's a special children's discount, we note it here.

Allstar Inns
2020 De La Vina Street
P.O. Box 3070
Santa Barbara, California 93130-3070
Telephone: 805-687-3383
Locations: Arizona, California, Nevada, New Mexico, Oregon, Texas, and Washington.

Budget Host Inns
2601 Jacksboro Highway
Caravan Suite 202
P.O. Box 10656
Fort Worth, Texas 76114
Telephone: 817-626-7064
Locations: In 38 states
For kids: All motels have cribs, charges range from $2 to $5 per night. Note: This is a network of 208 independent inns with different names, so be sure to get the right name at booking time.

Chalet Susse International, Inc.
Chalet Drive
Wilton, New Hampshire 03086-0657
Telephone: 800-258-1980 (in New Hampshire, 800-572-1880)
Locations: In nine states, primarily eastern

Courtyard by Marriott
Marriott Drive
Washington, D.C. 20058
Telephone: 800-321-2211
Locations: East Coast, Midwest, and South; 100 locations
For kids: Room with fold-out beds and suites available; pools and
   courtyards; restaurant with kids' menu.

Days Inns of America, Inc.
2751 Buford Highway, N.E.
Atlanta, Georgia 30324
Telephone: 800-325-2525
Locations: In 44 states and the District of Columbia
For kids: Sometimes children are free with an adult, other times, $1
   or $2 for kids 18 and under; some motels have "Stay and Kids
   Eat Free" plan (a free meal for every child under 12 accompanied
   by an adult, for instance).

Drury Inns
10801 Pear Tree Lane
St. Louis, Missouri 63074
Telephone: 800-325-8300
Locations: Midwest and South
For kids: Cribs, outdoor swimming pools, free breakfast

Econo Lodges of America, Inc.
6135 Park Road, Suite 200
Charlotte, North Carolina 28210
Telephone: 800-446-6900
Locations: In 43 states and Canada
For kids: Kids under 18 are free; cribs are free with Family Plan.

Excel Inns of America

4706 East Washington Avenue
Madison, Wisconsin 53704
Telephone: 800-356-8013
Locations: In Texas, Iowa, Minnesota, Michigan, Illinois, South
Dakota, and Wisconsin.
For kids: Free under 18 years and no charge for cribs; pools in Texas
locations.

E-Z 8 Motels

2484 Hotel Circle Place
San Diego, California 92108
Telephone: 619-291-4824 (Reservations must be made with
individual motels, no central number.)
Locations: In California, Nevada, and Arizona
For kids: Cribs are available, pools, laundry facilities.

Friendship Inns International, Inc.

2627 Paterson Plank Road
North Bergen, New Jersey 07047
Telephone: 800-453-4511
Locations: In 35 states and Canada
For kids: The policy for children's rates varies from place to place
because each inn is individually owned; free breakfast at some
locations.

Hampton Inns

6799 Great Oaks Road, Suite 100
Memphis, Tennessee 38138
Telephone: 800-HAMPTON
Locations: In most states
For kids: Under 18, stay free; free continental breakfast and in-room
movies.

Hospitality International (Scottish, Red Carpet, and Master Hosts Inns)

1152 Spring Street, Suite A
Atlanta, Georgia 30309
Telephone: 800-251-1962
Locations: 30 states plus Canada; over 250 inns in all.

Imperial 400 National, Inc.
1000 Wilson Boulevard, Suite 820
Arlington, Virginia 22209
Telephone: 800-368-4400 (in Virginia, 800-572-2200)
Locations: In 40 states
For kids: Children under 16 free; some properties have pools.

Knights Inns/Arborgate Inns
2255 Kimberly Parkway
Columbus, Ohio 43232
Telephone: 614-755-6230
Locations: 214 inns in 19 states
For kids: Most have pools; some have rooms with kitchenettes for
    extended stays.
Note: Once you have a directory, you can call each inn using an 800
    number and a special code.

La Quinta Inns
La Quinta Plaza
P.O. Box 790064
San Antonio, Texas 78279
Telephone: 800-531-5900
Locations: 200 locations in 29 states; 75 in Texas
For kids: Free for kids 18 and under in parents' room.
Note: This chain received the highest budget rating in *Consumer
    Reports* study of hotel chains under $40.

Motel 6, Inc.
51 Hitchcock Way
Santa Barbara, California 93105
Telephone: 805-682-6666
Locations: In 42 states, most in California, 450 in all.
For kids: Pools, free for kids 18 and under.

Quality International
10750 Columbia Pike
Silver Spring, Maryland 20901
This is the umbrella company for Quality Inns 800-228-5151,
    Comfort Inns 800-228-5150, and Clarion Hotels 800-CLARION.
Locations: All over the United States
For kids: Children 16 and under free in parents' room.

Red Roof Inns, Inc.
4355 Davidson Road
Hilliard, Ohio 43026-9699
Telephone: 800-843-7663
Locations: In 30 states
For kids: Free cribs and free in-room movie service.
Note: This chain recently received a very favorable rating from
   Consumer Reports.

Regal 8 Inns
P.O. Box 1268
Mount Vernon, Illinois 62864
Telephone: 800-851-8888
Locations: In 22 states
For kids: All have indoor or outdoor pools.

TraveLodge/Viscount Hotels/Thriftlodge
Corporate Headquarters, Trusthouse Forte Hotels, Inc.
1973 Friendship Drive
El Cajon, California 92090
Telephone: 800-255-3050

Vagabond Inns
Box 85011
San Diego, California 92138
Telephone: 800-522-1555
Locations: In California, Nevada, and Arizona
For kids: Kids 18 or younger stay free in their parents' room. A
   rollaway bed or crib is provided, when available, at no extra
   charge; pools.

HOME EXCHANGES

Exchanges and rentals are a possibility to consider well in advance of your trip because arranging a house, apartment, or condo swap or a rental is more complex than just reserving a hotel room. But think of the advantages: You'll have your own base of operations with all the comforts of home, or even more comforts in some cases. Exchanging homes means you'll certainly save money; all you pay for is transportation. If you rent, you may also save, compared to the cost of a hotel room.

How to Find an Exchange

Home exchanging means trading your home, your vacation home, boat, or recreational vehicle with another family. It requires research and energy, but it can be a wonderful option. An excellent booklet on the subject is *Your Place and Mine: A Guide to Vacation Home Exchange* written by Cindy Gum, a Californian who has exchanged her homes with families in Brussels, Miami, Copenhagen, and Alexandria, Virginia. Gum writes this book with enthusiasm, including what to consider before embarking on an exchange search, ways to go about it, and lots of practical advice for the actual exchange. Copies of Gum's 50-page booklet cost $4.95 plus $1 postage and handling and are available from the author, 18510 Hillview Drive, Monte Sereno, California 95030.

Using the services of an exchange club is the easiest and most efficient way to go about swapping or renting. (Many clubs arrange either trades or rentals.) Most of the clubs publish periodically updated directories listing subscriber properties with or without photographs and information on location, the family that lives there, and details of a variety of options such as a car or boat that may come with the house. Once you've found something that interests you in a directory; it's time for a letter of inquiry. Your letter should include a detailed description of your family, home, and community; nearby activities; climate; and your preferred dates of exchange. Ask questions about the things that are important to you. Is there a washing machine, a cozy place to read, a backyard for the kids to play in safely? Enclose a stamped, self-addressed envelope to make it easier for the people on the other end.

Once you've decided on the exchange, write everything down— the dates, number of participants, car insurance information, details of pet care, cleaning procedures, the way the telephone bill will be handled, and any instructions for care of any special equipment you may have. When you leave, Cindy Gum suggests leaving a personalized household information booklet as a guide to the newcomers; include auto repair numbers, emergency numbers, your pediatrician's number, names of friends and neighbors who can answer questions, some suggested restaurants, nearby sightseeing attractions, baby-sitters, and so on. Suggest that the exchange family do the same for you.

If you don't want to work through an exchange club, you can go the word-of-mouth route: tell all the people you know about what you're looking for and ask whether they have any connections. Or you can advertise in a professional journal, a college alumni magazine, or a newspaper in the location where you're headed. If you're planning a summer exchange, start the fall before.

Here we list some of the organizations that can facilitate exchanges. To find the best for you, contact several and compare. What would be ideal, of course, would be to find someone with kids the same age as your kids so that there'll be some toys and games for them and maybe even a jungle gym out in the backyard.

International Home Exchange Services (IHES) / Intervac U.S.
P.O. Box 3975
San Francisco, California 94119
Telephone: 415-435-3497

This organization arranged what was probably the most publicized home exchange in history: A San Francisco couple and their two children traded homes with the governor of Colorado for a week at Christmastime. Use of the Denver mansion included a holiday dinner cooked by the governor's personal chef; the governor got a three-story contemporary home five blocks from the marina. IHES publishes three directories each year—January, March, and May—containing 7,000 listings in over 25 countries. The listings are in a coded format, and the directory we looked through had some fabulous possibilities. Subscriptions cost $35. Hospitality exchanges are also offered; for example, extra rooms in a home are listed. For families who want to "swap" children on a cultural, student, or vacation exchange basis there's even a Youth Exchange option.

Interservice Home Exchange, Inc.
Box 387
Glen Echo, Maryland 20812
Telephone: 301-229-7567

Interservice publishes three catalogs per year. Deadline for the first catalog of the year is November 22. Once the third catalog is printed, in April, it's too late to be listed, but you can still join and receive the catalogs. Annual membership is $35, which includes a listing and three catalogs; unlisted membership costs the same. Photos cost $10 more, and a second home can be listed for an additional $8. If you don't find a swap you like, you can return the catalogs and get your money back. Besides home swapping, you can rent through Interservice, be a guest in someone's home in a "hospitality exchange," or even arrange to house-sit.

Global Home Exchange and Travel Services (GHETS)
P.O. Box 2015
South Burlington, Vermont 05403-2015
Telephone: 802-895-3825.

This organization, run by teachers, is a matchmaking service. There's no directory; rather, prospective exchangees contact GHETS, and they search for the right match. GHETS interviews all applicants, inspects prospective homes, and requires personal references. To arrange an exchange within the United States costs $250, $25 of which is a nonrefundable lifetime application fee. European-American exchanges cost $300. Applicants fill out a form providing details of their home and ten to 12 interior and exterior color photos, and the GHETS area coordinator gets to work finding a match. If a proposed exchange is rejected, GHETS tries a second time. GHETS also offers travel services and an optional vacation insurance plan.

Home Exchange International
185 Park Row
P.O. Box 878
New York, New York 10038-0272
Telephone: 212-349-5340

This is another matching organization; there's no directory. Applicants fill out a form and supply a set of photographs of both the inside and the outside of the house. Fees are based on the category of home you choose. Homes are rated by the staff in the United States; the ratings are, in ascending order, "quality," "superior," and "luxurious." The ratings are based on three factors—location (from easy access to a major resort or urban area to a central location in a highly desirable area); furnishings (from comfortable with some modern conveniences to elegant with most modern conveniences); and availability of a car. Fees for exchanges within the United States are for stays of 14 days or less, $150 to $250; 15 days to three months, $200 to $300; and over three months, $275 to $375. International exchanges are slightly higher. Home Exchange International has offices in New York, London, Paris, Milan, and Los Angeles.

Loan-a-Home
2 Park Lane, 6E
Mount Vernon, New York 10552
Telephone: 914-664-7640

Designed primarily to serve the academic and business communities, this organization helps people find homes to exchange or rent. Many teachers anticipating a sabbatical contact Loan-a-Home as soon as they know when their leave will begin. A check for $30 will get you a current directory and a supplement; there's one in December and another in June, with supplements in March and September. For $40 you'll get four issues: two directories and two supplements. There's no charge to have your own home listed. Subscribers handle all the details of the exchange themselves. For an additional $5 you can list a "housing wanted" notice in the directory.

Vacation Exchange Club
12006 111 Avenue, Unit 12
Youngtown, Arizona 85363
Telephone: 602-972-2186

VEC publishes two issues per year of what they call *The Exchange Book,* one in February and another in April. Approximately half the listings are in the United States, and half abroad. Even if you don't want to be listed, you can just order copies of the books. If you're listed, your cost if $24.70; if you're unlisted, it is $16. Each additional home listed costs $6, and photos are $9 extra. (For first-class mail, add $3.50; otherwise the books will be sent third class and can take three to six weeks to get to you.) Deadlines are December 15 for the February issue and February 15 for the April version. All follow-up home exchange details have to be arranged by the exchangees.

Some other possibilities with the VEC directory include renting from a subscriber (although the VEC people warn that their experience shows that subscribers take better care of exchanged homes than rented ones); a "double exchange"—two families from one area exchange with two from another; "hospitality"—staying as paying guests in a home; "exchange hospitality"—a stay in your home is swapped for a stay somewhere else at another time; "youth hospitality"—you and your teenagers offer hospitality to a young person from another country; bed and breakfast; and a request for a travel companion.

CONDOMINIUMS AND VILLA RENTALS

One of the best choices for families are *condos;* the name we've given to what the travel industry may call villas, leisure homes, vacation rentals, or apartments. With a condo you have space, kitchen facilities, often laundry facilities, and privacy. For skiing families with young kids, slope-side condos are great: at naptime you can just pick up your kids at the nursery, take them "home," and tuck them in for their naps. If you have older kids, you may prefer the "sociability" of a hotel or lodge to the privacy of a condo, and the option of having the kids go down to the lobby or to the restaurant by themselves.

In many of our chapters—Chapters 9 and 10, in particular—we list condo possibilities. And Vintage Books has published four regional guides to condos, all under the name *The Condo Lux Vacationer's Guide to Condominium Rentals* ($9.95 each). The guides, one each for *The Southeast, The Bahamas and Caribbean Islands, The Mountain States,* and *The Southwest and Hawaii,* are written by Jill A. Little. Each volume contains information on rentals, including policy toward children, details of the accommodations, a description of activities on site, and special facilities and services, plus accompanying photo.

Vacation Condominiums for Rent is a state-by-state guide to more than 500 vacation condos in the U.S. The book is written by Frank, Christine, Brian, and Bret Walsh, condo owners themselves, and is published by MarLor Press, 4304 Brigadoon Drive, St. Paul, Minnesota, 55126 ($12.50 includes postage). Each brief listing describes the condo's features, tells about any special attractions the property may offer (e.g., swimming pools and tennis courts) and lists seasonal discounts.

Hideaways International (listed below) publishes a "how-to" report that answers the most frequently asked questions about condo rentals. Copies are $7.50 and can be ordered from 15 Goldsmith Street, Box 1464, Littleton, Massachusetts 01460.

Other sources for condo rental information are local tourist offices, classified newspaper and magazine ads, airlines (for air and condo packages), travel agents, and vacation clubs that publish property directories listing exchanges and/or rentals.

A few words of advice on the subject of condo rentals:

• Property owners who rent directly may offer the lowest accommodation rates and the most personal service, comparable to a home exchange.

- Check with off-site management firms or with the owner if you're "dealing direct" on how frequently they visit their properties and whether they have on-site managers to help out once you're there.
- Begin planning at least two months in advance, four or more if you're going at a peak time to a prime location.
- As with a vacation home exchange, be sure you get, in writing, your dates and an exact description of what is included in your rental in terms of facilities, service, insurance, and so on.
- Especially if you have teenagers along, but good for all ages, are condo setups that include some kind of central meeting spot, like a pool or a game room.

Here are a few of the agencies in the U.S. that are ready and willing to arrange your vacation rental for you:

Hideaways International
15 Goldsmith Street
P.O. Box 1270
Littleton, Massachusetts 01460
Telephone: 617-486-8955 or 800-843-4433

Hideaways publishes a guide twice a year for its members—the cost is $75 annually—which lists condos, cottages, chalets, and chateaux for rent, exchange, and/or sale. Rental prices start at $350 and average about $900 per week. Listings include photos of the property, usually inside and out; detailed descriptions of features such as landscaping and nearby sports; and price. Members receive the name and telephone number of the contact person by calling Hideaways. The catalog also includes some travel articles and details on "Villa Values"—a plan whereby Hideaway members save 10 percent on bookings at condos in Florida, the Caribbean, Hawaii, New England, and Europe. Hideaways offers an elaborate array of travel services as well. Friends who have used Hideaways found that the prices of some of their rentals were *much* less than the same properties through other agents. This is because Hideaways put renter and owner together without a fee for an intermediary. They earn their fees on membership, not on each transaction. Our friends also liked the fact that Hideaways membership brings special fares on airlines and car rentals.

Vacation Home Rentals, Worldwide
235 Kensington Avenue
Norwood, New Jersey 07648
Telephone: 201-767-9393

VHR has a seductive brochure with photographs of what they call "the best in homes away from home." They specialize in renting homes in resort areas and "secret hideaways" all over the world. Included in VHR's repertoire are villas, condominiums, townhouse apartments, houses, chateaux, and estates. Rates range from $400 to $20,000 (yes, that's the right number of zeroes) per week, depending on quality, size, staff, location, season, and amenities. When the services of household personnel are not included in the rental, help can usually be arranged at extra cost with enough advance notice. VHR can also make related travel plans—airline reservations, car rentals, and so forth. The people at VHR sent us a batch of description sheets for some of their properties, and here's a sampling: a cathedral-ceilinged apartment on a working horse farm across from Lake Pontchartrain in New Orleans, complete with a swimming pool, gazebo, and tennis court. Kids must be 10 or over, rents are $1,400–$1,750 per week, depending on the season. Another choice in the U.S. is a villa for eight with three large bedrooms on Plantation Key in Florida. All bedrooms have both ocean and park views and the weekly rent year-round is $1,250.

Villa Holidays
One Southwest Crossing, Suite 255
Minneapolis, Minnesota 55344
Telephone: 612-942-1150 or 800-328-6262

Although most of this company's properties are in the Caribbean, they do have some rentals available in Hawaii. "All of the properties we represent are personally inspected . . . and feature the reliability of on-site property management."

Four Star Living
964 Third Avenue
39th Floor
New York, New York 10155
Telephone: 212-355-2755

This rental outfit was begun by Heidi Otto. She started renting her own villa in Mexico, and was so overwhelmed by the response that she decided to turn villa rental and sales into a business. "Whether it is an apartment for two or a chateau for 20, or any other type of listing including yachts, Four Star Living can help you." Although most of Four Star's properties are in the Caribbean, Mexico, and Europe, they list some in the U.S. A $45 registration fee is deductible from the cost of bookings.

Condominiums Unlimited
567 West A Street
P.O. Box 6085
Hayward, California 94540
Telephone: 415-785-5880

The folks at Condominiums Unlimited specialize in properties in Hawaii. They offer one-, two-, and three-bedroom condos with kitchens and many with large gardens just perfect for kids to run and play. Some of the outer island condos have special activities for young kids, and a few of the places on Maui have summer camps for kids 4 to 11.

Four Seasons Villas
P.O. Box 848
18 Jane Road
Marblehead, Massachusetts 01945
Telephone: 617-639-1055 or 800-338-0474

One of the reasons that Linda Freedman started Four Seasons was the need to find accommodations suitable for families. "Have you ever spent two weeks in a hotel room with an infant and a toddler? We did!" Four Seasons has properties in the Caribbean, Mexico, Bahamas, Florida, Cape Cod, the Berkshires in Massachusetts, California, and at a number of ski resorts. Rates begin at $500 per week for a one-bedroom condo off-season.

Condo Club, Inc.
18 Thomas Avenue
P.O. Box 8280
Red Bank, New Jersey 07701-8280
Telephone: 800-272-6636

Condo Club will book condo vacations for you in resort areas of the U.S.; they specialize in Florida, Hawaii, and the Carolinas. One recent example is a seven-night Hawaii package including four nights in Maui and three nights in Kauai for $270 per person with a rental car.

Club Costa Travel Club
7701 College Boulevard
Overland Park, Kansas 66210
Telephone: 800-225-0381

Membership in Club Costa costs $49 per year and with it you and your family get, among other things, discounts at vacation retreats all over the world. We looked through their catalog and found offerings in Arizona, California, Colorado, Florida, South Carolina, Virginia, and Hawaii. An example of what the club offers is a town home in the Rocky Mountains—three bedrooms, 3½ baths, 2,200 square feet of space with a kitchen, microwave, washer and dryer; free bus service to four major ski areas; and a clubhouse with indoor pool for $175 per night in ski season, $65 during the summer.

BED AND BREAKFASTS

In 1975 Betty Rundback wrote the first edition of *Bed and Breakfast U.S.A.* We remember it well: 16 pages, 40 listings. Rundback's current edition is over 650 pages long and lists almost 1,000 bed and breakfast spots and 145 reservation agencies. Bed and breakfast places—private homes or small family-operated inns—have certainly caught on in the past few years. We're delighted, because a bed and breakfast place can be a wonderful alternative to a hotel or motel for a family on vacation. We like bed and breakfasts because of their homey feeling and because, in our experience, the hosts have been very welcoming and unusually helpful in orienting us to the surrounding area. There is one thing you must be sure of, though, when choosing a bed and breakfast: You must make certain that the hosts welcome—and we mean welcome, not tolerate—kids. Some bed and breakfasts like to be thought of as adult hideaways, and the idea of an early-rising, talkative 2-year-old would send chills up the spines of some proprietors. To find out whether children are welcome, don't just rely on what the listing in a guidebook says. Check on your own.

Here are a few questions you should ask about any bed and breakfast you are considering:

- Are there kids of similar age in the host family? This is the ideal situation because there will be instant friends for your kids as well as some play equipment to share. There'll also be a lot more understanding if you have to keep some milk in the family refrigerator or warm up a bottle.
- What are the rooms like? Are there cribs or cots for the kids? Are adjoining rooms for parents and children possible? Ask about the bathroom; will you have to share it with other guests?
- Is breakfast included? Is it a continental or full breakfast? Are there booster seats and high chairs?
- Is there a play area inside or outside? Are there board games or some children's books? Is there a playground nearby?
- Is baby-sitting possible?
- Are there any "in-law apartments"—apartments with separate entrances that are part of a larger house (these are perfect for families).

Reservations Services

With the increased popularity of the bed and breakfast, reservation networks have sprung up all over the country. These networks match hosts and guests. Many of these services have brochures describing the homes that have registered. Reservations are made through the services, and most charge no fee because they work on a commission for the bed and breakfasts. Some agencies are *membership-based:* they charge a basic fee and then send descriptive directories "free" to members. In larger cities, many reservation services include apartments, condominiums, and even houses without any hosts in them. In our city sections (Chapter 7) we include some bed and breakfast networks. Most of the bed and breakfast guidebooks include listings of these reservation services along with individual listings.

As you'd expect, the proliferation of bed and breakfasts has been accompanied by the proliferation of books about bed and breakfasts. See the listings at the end of the chapter for some suggestions.

HOSTELS

According to the executive director of the New York Council of the American Youth Hostels (AYH), the trend at AYH is toward more and more family accommodations as the 250 hostels that cover the United States Hostels now set aside family rooms where families can be together and enjoy some privacy. No two hostels look alike—in the United States a hostel may be a lighthouse on the California coast, a dude ranch in the Rockies, or a converted lifeguard station in Cape Cod. Simplicity is the rule at hostels; everything is "do-it-yourself." Guests help with chores, and beds come with the basics: mattresses, pillows, and blankets. Sheet sleeping sacks are often available for rent or can be purchased from AYH at $12 for nylon or $13 for cotton blend; add $2.50 if ordering by mail.

It's the cost of a stay at a hostel that is most surprising. A hostel in a converted ski lodge in the Catskills costs $9.00 for adults and $4.50 for kids per night in high season. Some of the family rooms even have private baths.

In order to stay at any hostel in the United States or abroad (there are 5,000 in 61 other countries), you and your family will have to be members of AYH. Family membership for parents and children 17 and under costs $30. Members receive a directory listing all hostels in the United States, a monthly newsletter from their local council, and updates throughout the year on AYH activities. For details, contact your local council or the national headquarters, P.O. Box 37613, Washington, D.C. 20013.

BOOKS TO READ

On the subject of where to stay there are lots and lots of books that list recommendations. Here we list some we've seen and liked:

The Entire United States

Bed and Breakfast U.S.A. by Betty Rundback and Nancy
Kramer, published by E. P. Dutton ($10.95). This is the one
we mentioned before, our favorite. It's well organized,
covers the entire United States, and includes information for
each place listed and whether or not children are welcome.
We've used the book ourselves and have never been disappointed. There's a new edition each year.

America's Wonderful Little Hotels and Inns by Sandra Soule,
published by St. Martin's Press (East edition, $15.95; West
edition, $14.95). This is a comprehensive book full of great
reader-recommended inns, hotels, resorts, and lodges. Each
listing indicates whether children are welcome. We recommend this one highly, too.

*Bed and Breakfast America: The Great American Guest House
Book* by John Thaxton, published by Burt Franklin and
Company ($8.95). A no-nonsense guide to the species. Each
listing includes a notation about children.

*The Complete Guide to Bed and Breakfasts, Inns and
Guesthouses* by Pamela Lanier, published by John Muir
Publications, Inc. ($14.95). The write-ups are in a shorthand
style (we like a bit more detail), but there's a useful appendix
that includes a section called "Family Fun" with a list of
accommodations that are particularly recommended for
kids.

Recommended Family Inns of America by the authors of the
"Recommended Country Inns" series published by Globe
Pequot, $10.95. Here are country inns that truly welcome
families. Each of seven authors has contributed about 20
properties and the result is over 125 destinations coast to
coast that are happy to give lodging to you and yours. The
choices include some with farm animals, horseback riding,
nearby streams for swimming and fishing and/or hills for
skiing—not to mention those hearty, home-cooked meals
that country kitchens are famous for!

Guide to the Recommended Country Inns. This is a series of
regional guides—one to the West Coast ($11.95); one to the
Mid-Atlantic states ($10.95); one to New England ($11.95);
one to the Rocky Mountain region ($11.95); the South
($10.95); and the Midwest ($10.95). They're all published

by Globe Pequot Press, and although some of the inns welcome kids, others are very definitely meant to be romantic getaways for adults.

Bed and Breakfast American Style by Norman T. Simpson, published by Harper and Row ($10.95). Norman Simpson was one of the first to write about America's country inns. In this, his last book before he died, he lists private homes, guest houses, mansions, farmhouses, country and village inns, small hotels, and seaside and mountain lodges. The prose is good, the information is useful. Simpson includes a line in his listings that indicates whether the property welcomes kids or not and what age the hosts have set as a minimum.

The East

New England Bed and Breakfast by Corinne Madden Ross, East Woods Press/Globe Pequot Press ($8.95). Most of the bed and breakfasts listed here welcome families, and the listings include the availability of cribs. We like this one and the same publisher's *California Bed and Breakfast Book,* by Kathy Strong ($8.95).

Best Places to Stay in New England by Christina Tree and Bruce Shaw, published by Harvard Common Press ($14.95). The authors have two chapters of special interest to traveling families, "Family Finds" and "Family Resorts." All listings throughout the book indicate the hosts' attitude toward children.

Budget Dining and Lodging in New England by Frank and Franklin Sullivan, published by Globe Pequot Press ($9.95). There's no consistent indication of whether children are or are not welcome at the various listings, but it's a well-constructed book nevertheless.

Bed and Breakfast in the Mid-Atlantic States and *Bed and Breakfast in New England* by Bernice Chesler, published by Globe Pequot Press ($13.95 each). Chesler used to write a book on the whole Northeast but when her listings grew too big for one book, she divided them into two volumes. These are nice guides with useful sections in each listing called "In Residence," which give you the names and ages of any kids who live there (and names, too, of resident dogs and cats).

The West

Bed and Breakfast Colorado and Rocky Mountains West by Buddy Mays, published by Chronicle Press ($7.95). Here you'll find 50 places to stay, including lodges, ranches, and historic hotels. Loving descriptions give the mood of each place, and most of the places described welcome children.

Northwest Best Places by David Brewster and Kathryn Robinson, published by Sasquatch Books ($14.95). First written in 1975, this series was designed to be a "discriminating, thinking-person's alternative to guidebooks of the gushing-prose variety." *Best Places* rates restaurants and hotels on a one- to four-star basis and includes Washington, Oregon, and British Columbia. Lots of people have grown to depend on this one; we recommend it.

The Bed and Breakfast Traveler by Lewis Green, published by Globe Pequot Press ($10.95). One man's version of what's worth seeing on the West Coast with b and b's along the way.

Best Places to Stay in Hawaii by Bill Jamison and Cheryl Alters Jamison ($10.95); *Best Places to Stay in the Southwest* by Gail Rickey ($10.95); and *Best Places to Stay in the Northwest* by Marilyn McFarlane ($14.95) are all published by Harvard Common Press and all share just about the same format. It's a format we like; places are divided by category, e.g., City Stops, Coastal Cottages, Island Getaways, Ski Lodges, and indexes in the Southwest and Northwest versions help you find what you want if you have a special interest such as biking, rafting, or tennis. Whether or not children are welcome is indicated in each listing. Besides lodging, the Southwest and Northwest editions include suggested itineraries. Nice work.

For more books on places to stay, check individual city sections as well.

5

PLANNING YOUR DAYS AND NONE OF THE ABOVE

In this chapter we talk about how best to plan a day on vacation and then some of what we call "none of the above"—topics that are important but don't fit neatly into any other category: finding baby-sitters while you're away, some special advice for single parents traveling with their kids, a few words about theme parks and family reunions.

PLANNING A DAY

Here the password is "underplan." When the kids are with you, don't expect to cover as much territory as you would without them. Allow plenty of time for eating, bathroom visits, and dawdling. Plan something especially for the kids each day, and let them in on the planning sessions. We've found that it's best to save the kids' favorites for afternoon, so that they have something to look forward to when energy may be waning.

You can make lists with your sightseeing "goals." Recently we did this at Disney World and it worked very well. We really got to see everything we wanted even though we had only two days to do it. Clustered sightseeing is best: pick one area and explore it instead of dashing all over town. Find out where the nearest park is, and if the weather is nice enough, include a visit. Very young children find a full day of sightseeing boring and exhausting. How about half a day with you and then the rest of the day with other children? Go to informal restaurants as you sightsee, or, better still, have a picnic. Pick out a likely restaurant *before* you go into a museum or park— don't wait until you're starving and the kids are cranky to go on a restaurant search. (We learned that one the hard way.) Take along a stroller. Even if your kids seem too old for a stroller at home, it can be a lifesaver while you're sightseeing.

Part of the reason you should underplan when you've got your kids along is so that you don't ever have to feel rushed. When you're feeling pressured you get impatient, and when you get impatient you lose your temper. A leisurely pace will loosen things up enormously.

If there are some places you feel you must see and they are places that your kids really aren't going to like, arrange some baby-sitting. We'll give some advice on the subject later in this chapter.

Once your plans have been made, feel free to rearrange them. If the kids are really restless at a particular place, leave. That's one of the great benefits of cluster sightseeing—there's always an alternative nearby. There are some stalling tactics you can try in order to give a place a second chance, though: a lunch break (a picnic in the park would be nice), going out to the gift shop, or trying to find something else at the same place they might like. To be prepared for this, you should read the brochure beforehand and know some alternatives. If your kids are 6 years old or older, consider a guided tour or one of the taped guides.

When you are planning your day, don't dismiss the possibility of going to a movie or bowling or indoor mini-golf. These can be fun, particularly on a rainy or snowy day.

Whenever you go to a place that's large or likely to be crowded, be sure to choose a central meeting spot just in case you get separated. We teach our kids to call our first names if they can't see us. If they call "Mommy" or "Daddy," it's less noticeable. Be sure the children know where they're staying; rehearse them on the name of the hotel or motel. Make a name tag for your youngest kids. A cute, ready-made ID bracelet with decorations is marketed by Kid I.D.,

909 Marina Village Parkway, No. 232, Alameda, California 94501, 415-523-4309. Send $4.95 plus 50 cents for handling for your own version of this elastic and Velcro band with room for name and address inside.

And don't forget to ask, just as soon as you arrive at a sightseeing attraction, where the bathrooms are located. Don't wait until you have a bathroom emergency to try wending your way through the halls of some enormous museum trying to find the restrooms.

MUSEUM VISITS—MAKING THEM WORK

Museums really can be fun for kids just as long as you choose the right ones and prepare the kids for the visit. Here are some ideas that have worked for us: We start out early, before the crowds; we avoid mealtimes; and we plan to stay no more than two hours.

We visit the gift shop first. This may seem a bit peculiar, but we do it so that the kids can choose five or ten postcards they like best and then hunt for the originals as they walk through the museum. We return to the gift shop at the end of the visit, too; give the kids a limit as to how much they can spend; and let them get some kind of souvenir of the visit.

Since we want to avoid the "don't's" and "no's" as much as possible, we have the kids ask the guards whether something can be touched. This is the passing-the-buck theory, and it works.

Naturally, we want our kids to learn something from their visit, but we try not to overdo the pedantry. After one museum visit our daughter said, "That was great, but next time don't read to me so much. Let me just look at things."

We never take the kids to a museum we don't like. Martyrdom is unnecessary.

One of the things our kids like to do at a museum—or any sightseeing spot, in fact—is to take along their tape recorders, making narrative tapes of what they're looking at. The prerecorded tapes sold at museums are good, too, so long as your child is old enough to concentrate on them.

You shouldn't think of museums as merely places to view art; there are many other kinds as well. There are crafts museums, science museums, historical museums, ethnic museums, and a growing number of "hands-on" children's museums throughout the country.

The best thing about these children's museums is that they involve kids in the museum experience and provide settings where a child's natural curiosity, senses, imagination, and exuberance are used to their fullest. Your kids will love the hands-on exhibits, such as the bubble-blowing machine at the Philadelphia Children's Museum and the railroad station at the Children's Museum in St. Paul, where they can pitch right in and help load a flatbed car.

Children needn't be 4, 5, or 6 to enjoy a children's museum. Even an infant can begin to touch, feel, and smell, and a 2- or 3-year-old will have a great time getting involved in the "touch me" exhibits. In our city sections (Chapter 7), we list some specific children's museums. Our kids have spent some wonderful hours in some of these, and we've enjoyed them as much as they have. Honestly.

For those of you who like the unusual, the out-of-the-ordinary when it comes to museum going, a book called *Special Museums of the Northeast* by Nancy Frazier lists museums from Maine to Washington, D.C., that include whaling museums, a motorcycle museum, doll museums, one museum dedicated to the cranberry and another to the nut. The book costs $9.95 and is published by the Globe Pequot Press.

Our family also loves "living history" museums—re-creations of America's past, such as Mystic Seaport in Connecticut and Sturbridge Village in Massachusetts. For a guide to these special places, we recommend a book called *Experiencing America's Past* by Gerald and Patricia Gutek ($12.95) which took 15 years to research and includes 40 historic museums and villages all over the U.S. Besides descriptions of the museums themselves, the Guteks include information on where to stay and interesting side trips. The publisher of this guide is John Wiley and Sons, Inc., 605 Third Avenue, New York, New York 10158-0012.

If you're planning to visit a large museum, such as the American Museum of Natural History or the Metropolitan Museum of Art in New York, choose one or two areas of concentration—the rocks or the dinosaurs in the former, the costumes or the mummies in the latter.

We recently discovered an excellent little book called *Where's the Me in Museum?* that explores with sensitivity and wisdom the whole question of visiting museums with children. Milde Waterfall and Sarah Grusin quote Bruno Bettleheim: "Maybe children—maybe all of us, need museums most in order to learn to marvel or not to forget to marvel. Because we marvel at these wondrous objects . . . we eventually marvel at man, at what we are." That wonderful quote sets the tone for the rest of this thoughtful book, published by Vandamere Press, P.O. Box 5243, Arlington, Virginia 22205 ($7.95).

Doing Children's Museums, A Guide to 225 Hands-on Museums, by Joanne Cleaver, published by Williamson Publishing, $12.95. Don't let the name fool you. This book is much more than museums just for kids. Organized state by state, the listings include historical centers, science museums, and even such esoteric museums like The Health Adventure (in Ashville, North Carolina) and The Imaginarium (in Anchorage, Alaska). At these museums the usual dictum of "Hands-Off" changes to "Please-Touch!" If you like museums, here's a wonderful source for finding those that are certain to turn on every member of the family.

If there's something you desperately want to see in a museum and you know your kids aren't going to like it at all, or if you don't want any distractions, call the museum ahead of time and see whether you can coordinate your visit with a family or children's workshop. You'd be surprised at how often this is possible: Even some of the most "serious" museums offer collage making, building with clay, origami, and so on. Prepare your children first, though. Don't just spring the idea of a drop-off on them. Stay with them for a few minutes at the beginning of the session, explain that you'll be in the museum the whole time, and be sure to find out exactly when the program is over so that you can be sure to be on time to pick them up and admire their work.

If you're traveling with a very young child, and you need to be able to use a stroller, be sure to check in advance whether strollers are allowed. Some places even rent or lend strollers and back carriers, another detail to check.

Two books written especially to prepare kids to visit an art museum are *Let's Go to the Museum* by Virginia K. Levy and *Mommy, It's a Renoir,* by Aline D. Wolf.

Let's Go is written by an art teacher, Virginia K. Levy, who designed her book for 6-to-12-year-olds to use as a workbook with questions, spaces for answers, and room to compose some original works of art. The book is published by Harry Abrams, Inc., 100 Fifth Avenue, New York, New York 10011, and costs $8.95.

Mommy, It's a Renoir is meant for parents and teachers and presents the author's sytem of teaching art appreciation through the use of art postcards. The process becomes a game. Copies of the manual and volumes of the postcards (Easy, Intermediate, Advanced, or Famous Paintings) are available for $10.95 plus $1.50 for shipping from the publisher, Parent Child Press, P.O. Box 767, Altoona, Pennsylvania 16603. All five books are $49.50 plus $3.

Our favorite, though, for reading to the kids before any trip to a museum is *Visiting the Art Museum,* published by E. P. Dutton and written by Laurie Krasny Brown and Marc Brown ($11.95). Animated characters and full-color reproductions of art selected from museums all over the world combine to present an amusing and instructional-without-being-pedantic look at a museum. We recommend it highly.

FINDING BABY-SITTERS

Up to now we've talked about the time you're going to spend with your kids, but now it's time to discuss the time you're going to spend alone or with another adult. Be sure that you allow yourself some of this "grown-up" time; you really do deserve it. If you're staying at a place where there's a children's program, you'll have no problem arranging time for yourself to take a tennis clinic or visit a nearby museum or just go on a shopping spree. But particularly if you are in a city, you'll need to be more resourceful.

The first thing to do, before you leave, is ask people you know at home whether they have friends or relatives with children in the place where you're going. If so, you can call and ask about baby-sitting. Or maybe a business associate knows someone. Once you've arrived, you can try contacting the local college or university; often they have baby-sitting services as part of their student employment program. Nursing schools are good sources, as are senior citizen groups or churches or synagogues. Most hotels have access to sitters—either staff people who want extra work or an agency contact. Bonded baby-sitting agencies are also listed in the Yellow Pages. Of course, a baby-sitter must have references.

Always prepare your kids in advance for the arrival of a baby-sitter. That's important at home and even more important when you're on vacation. Plan a special evening for them to make it easier for them while you're gone. Vicky Lansky, a writer whose books on practical parenting are an excellent resource for families, has a book called *KoKo Bear's New Babysitter* ($3.95 from 18326 Minnetonka Boulevard, Deephaven, Minnesota 55391) designed for parents and kids to read together. In her story, KoKo meets a new babysitter and experiences all of the fears and worries that are usual for kids in that same situation. By reading the book, your kids will understand that what they are feeling is felt by others too. One of the practical suggestions that Lansky makes is to have the baby-sitter help your child make a drawing or something similar to give to you when you return—this will help to reassure him or her that you really are coming back. (See Lansky's *Dear Babysitter's Handbook*, $3.95, for more tips.)

Two experts, Linda and Bruce Wermuth—he's a child psychiatrist and she's a family therapist—told us that there are three key concepts in planning baby-sitting for kids: familiarity, clear expectations, and accountability. They had some practical suggestions for arranging all three:

- Bring familiar toys with you, especially for a younger child.
- Have the sitter arrive early so that he or she can see how you interact with your kids and so that your child can get acquainted gradually.
- Set clear expectations; this gives both the children and the sitter a healthy sense of what they have to look forward to.
- Don't be too specific or overpromise, but do give the kids a sense of some of the things they'll be doing (e.g., the sitter will take you to the beach to play and hunt for shells and then later, for lunch, you can go to the snack bar).
- Write down any special needs—naptimes, bedtime, eating requirements—so that everything is clear.
- Be accountable to your children. If you tell them you'll be back by 3:00 P.M., be sure to be back by then. This gives the kids a healthy sense of control and trust, and helps with any fears of abandonment.
- Don't overpromise and underdeliver. It's better to say you'll be back at 4:00 and appear at 3:30 than to say you'll be back at 3:00 and show up half an hour late.

As you can see, most of the above advice is really no different from what you would expect to do at home. But, when you're away and in a new place, it just all becomes more important, and what might be overlooked at home just can't be overlooked on vacation.

A SPECIAL WORD FOR SINGLE PARENTS

More and more single parents are traveling with their kids, and without a doubt, they face many problems that a two-parent family doesn't. Being the only adult can be lonely, and it can be exhausting; with no one to share the responsibility, a vacation can become a disappointment. To find out what advice to pass on to single parents, to find out how they can make their vacations fun and rewarding, we spoke to Phyllis Diamond, the founder and former president of a New York–based group called Kindred Spirits, an organization dedicated to arranging entertainment, travel, and education programs for single parents.

According to Diamond, you're not likely to meet a lot of other single parents while you travel, so it's best to arrange to team up with a friend and his or her kids and go as a group. Not only will you have more fun, but you will also be able to have the kids in one room and the adults in another so that there can be some private time. If your budget is really tight—and for many single parents this is the case— you can all share a room and save money. Diamond suggests that you set out on your vacation with the clear understanding that you will probably not meet other singles. If you have realistic expectations— if you aim to have a good time with your kids and forget about meeting Prince or Princess Charming—everything will work out fine.

Where should you go? Probably the best places are the ones where you'll find children's programs, and this book is crammed with suggestions. Diamond told us that many single parents think that Disney World is the greatest place to take their kids, but she says they're wrong: It is too lonely and too exhausting for one adult. One of the best things she thinks that single parents can do when vacation time comes around is rent a share in a beach house with other single parents and their kids. It's fun, it provides other kids and other adults, it needn't be too expensive, and it is usually not hard to arrange. Kindred Spirits sponsors some short trips during the year— a three-night cruise on the Long Island Sound on the QE 2 was one recent offering. For information on Kindred Spirits, write to them in care of Group Services, the 92nd Street Y, 1395 Lexington Avenue, New York, New York 10128, 212-427-6000.

An official of the American Youth Hostels (P.O. Box 37613, Washington, D.C. 20013) told us that his organization's ski trips are enormously popular with single parents and their kids. In fact, any "adventure"-type vacation is a good bet. See Chapter 6 for suggestions.

THEME PARKS

Once upon a time, there were amusement parks—familiar places with roller coasters, Ferris wheels, and endless arcade games. They were all pretty much the same. We used to lump this memory of an amusement park together with the idea of a theme park and tried to avoid the latter whenever possible. When avoidance was no longer possible, we were pleasantly surprised at what we found. What makes theme parks different from the amusement parks of our past is that theme parks focus on a particular area of interest and envelop you in it. The best of these parks leave you with a satisfied feeling that you just don't get from the traditional amusement park.

You'll find a theme park to suit just about every interest. Want to spend a day on safari? How about pretending you're living in colonial America or enjoying a day with the folks from "Sesame Street"? We asked Hermine and Barry Block, contributors to the trade publication *Tourist Attractions and Parks,* about their favorites. Most are open Memorial Day to Labor Day but always check to be sure.

But before the specifics, let's go over a few basic ground rules for getting the most out of your theme park experience:

- Plan ahead. Send for brochures and find out as much as you can about the park to be sure that it is appropriate to the ages and interests of your kids.
- Allot the right amount of time to the park you're going to visit. Don't ever consider "doing" Disney World in less than two days; you should really allow at least three to five.
- Arrive at the park early. The lines will be shorter, and you won't be in danger of being closed out when the park reaches maximum capacity. Have a map with your route outlined in order to save unnecessary walking.
- Decide which rides or activities are most important to you and head for them first.
- Eat properly. You can't survive happily on junk food for eight hours. Consider packing a lunch if the food available isn't the kind you or your kids like.
- Eat early. Attractions are less crowded at lunchtime, so while

everyone else is eating, go to it. You can always snack later on.

- Or, you can try breaking your day into two parts. Start out with a morning visit; go back to your hotel for lunch, a swim, a rest; and then return for the evening.

- Have one parent wait in line while others look around. Usually the theme parks have the wait time posted, and they're fairly accurate.

- If you're like us and can't get anywhere really early, wait until later and hit the popular rides when other people are eating.

- When you enter the park, go left. Most people go to the right, so there will be fewer crowds to the left.

- Don't forget to bring towels to water parks (we did once).

- Teach your kids to call you by your first names if they need you. So many kids will be calling "Mommy" and "Daddy" you may not be able to tell it's yours.

- Theme park vacations are costly. To go to a park and have to say "no" to the kids all the time is not fun. So, try to budget generously.

Some books on the subject of theme parks, one general and four specifically about the Disney offerings, may interest you. First is the *Directory of Theme and Amusement Parks* edited by Raymond Carlson and Elenor Popelka ($3.95, Pilot Books, 103 Cooper Street, Babylon, New York 11702), which is a state-by-state listing of over 450 parks throughout the U.S. Unfortunately, not much information is given beyond the bare-bones listings; it would have been helpful to include what the parks cost and more descriptive material.

There's no lack of description or information in the other four books: *The Best of Walt Disney World* and *The Best of Disneyland* by Steve Birnbaum (Houghton Mifflin, $6.95 for Disneyland and $9.95 for Disney World), are official guides, updated annually, and considered generally to be the definitive guides to both attractions. They cover just about every question you could possibly have. There are good hints on traveling with kids, all new attractions are included, and every ride is described in detail, including information on whether or not it might be too scary for some youngsters.

The other two books on the subject were researched by people not affiliated with Disney and therefore may be a bit more objective. They're called *The Unofficial Guide to Walt DisneyWorld and EP-COT* by Bob Schlinger and *The Unofficial Guide to Disneyland* by Schlinger and John Finley. A nice feature of these guides is the rating of each ride's overall appeal by age group. There are also one-day touring plans for families with small children. Prentice-Hall is the publisher and they cost $7.95 each. If you're determined to do Disney right, get both the official and unofficial guides and use the best parts of each.

And, if you're in Florida to visit Disney World but have time to see more of Central Florida than just the park, take a look at Frederick Pratson's *Guide to the Great Attractions of Orlando and Beyond*. It includes a chapter on Disney World but also goes on to cover other favorites such as Sea World, Boardwalk and Baseball, Busch Gardens, NASA Space Center, and other less well known spots. Published by Globe Pequot, this is a helpful guide to one of the most popular vacation spots in the country.

And now, on with the Blocks's choices:

Water Parks

On a hot day, what could be better than a park devoted to water. Water parks divide into two types: "participatory" such as Wet 'N' Wild, where you can splash in swimming holes and slide down water slides, and "viewing," like Sea World, where you're meant to watch, not play. If you choose a participatory park, be sure that there are activities for your younger kids. Sea World is a great example of the viewing kind of water park and it is much more than just Shamu. There are birds, botanical gardens, pearl diving exhibitions, and a playground for when the kids just need to run and play. Lots of fun for kids, too, is "Places of Learning," a combination playground and educational resource that includes a one-acre multicolor map of the U.S. with giant replicas of children's books. Call the individual Sea World locations for details: San Diego: 619-222-6363; Orlando: 407-351-3600; San Antonio: 512-523-3600 or 800-527-4757; Aurora, Ohio: 216-562-8101 or 800-637-4268.

Safari Parks

Experience the thrill of being in deepest darkest Africa without leaving the U.S. Here, again, there are many possibilities. In some you drive through in your car while the animals wander in the fields. Many come close to or even climb on your car. At others you see the animals while riding on transportation organized by the park (like monorails). The Blocks feel that the best overall safari theme park is Busch Gardens' Dark Continent in Tampa, Florida. (813-988-5171 or 813-971-8282 for recorded information). This 300-acre African themed family entertainment center has seven sections and is also considered one of the top zoos in the country. Lots of animal breeding is done here, and the nursery is sure to delight and thrill children, as will the 12 major rides, eight kiddie rides, three water-oriented rides, and a variety of entertaining animal shows. Rides are integrated with the themes. For example, you'll find the Congo River Rapids in the Congo area (where else!) and a large log flume ride at the Stanleyville Village area. The original lagooned Busch Gardens is now Bird Gardens with its own children's play area, Dwarf Village.

We spent a full day at Lion Country Safari in Wellington, Florida (20 minutes from West Palm Beach), where, after a drive through the animal park, we played miniature golf, went to the petting zoo, watched the monkeys frolic on their own island, and more.

Historic Parks

These transport you into another time or place. A prime example is Busch Gardens–The Old Country, three miles from historic Williamsburg, which features eight authentically detailed reproductions of 17th-century European hamlets of Great Britain, France, Germany, and Italy, sprinkled with an assortment of rides and entertainment. A visit here before or after Williamsburg is a nice contrast of life in colonial times compared to life in 17th-century Europe. The Kingsmill Resort, owned and operated by Anheuser-Busch, is ideal for families. Shuttle buses take you to The Old Country (3 minutes away) and Colonial Williamsburg (10 minutes). For information call 804-253-1703 or 1-800-832-5665.

Another historical park, quite different from The Old Country is Conner Prairie in Noblesville, Indiana (317-776-6000). Depicting the lives, times, values, and attitudes of the area's first settlers, this 1836 historic village includes a pioneer adventure area to give you a hands-on experience. Weave on an old loom, split wood, or make candles or soap. Costumed guides describe the daily life, culture, and politics of the time. While there are no rides here, there's plenty to see and do year-round.

We can't leave out Colonial Williamsburg, the first restoration village in the U.S. They have recreated the town of Williamsburg as it was in the late 18th century. It is truly fascinating walking through the streets watching craftsmen ply their trades (barrel making, gunsmithing, harness making among them). Ongoing events such as parades, horse-drawn carriage rides, militia drills and the like, transport you to another era. We highly recommend staying directly in the old town (try either the Williamsburg Inn or the Lodge, both of which welcome families, and ask about the renovated homes in town). There are special children's tours for kids as young as 4 and also family workshops. This is a "do not miss" that will instill a true sense of American history in your children. For information call 1-800-HISTORY.

Country and Western Music Parks

If you like country music, head to Tennessee, where it all started. The Blocks say that the best country music theme park, Opryland (615-428-9400), is right on the site of the Grand Ole Opry. Here you'll find a mixture of country-oriented amusement rides and entertainment. If you want tickets to the Opry itself, write ahead far in advance. And, if you're a Dolly Parton fan, you can visit Dollywood, Pigeon Forge, Tennessee (615-428-9400), now in its fourth year of operation. We haven't heard of any rock and roll theme parks yet, but please let us know if you come across one!

Educational Parks

If your kids love "Sesame Street," take them to Sesame Place in Langhorne, Pennsylvania (215-752-7070). Ninety minutes from New York City and 30 from Philadelphia, this enchanting place always leaves us wanting to return. Our kids are past viewing the TV show, but Sesame Place still appeals to them. Here they can plunge into thousands of the Count's Balls or ride the Sesame Streak Water Slide. Littler ones love the Rubber Duckie Rapids and are not left out at all in this park, basically dedicated to ages 3–14. Indoor fun is provided at an educational computer/video arcade (the only extra charge) and the television Dream Theatre. There is entertainment and a "natural food" factory with relatively healthful food to eat. There are no mechanical rides, everything encourages the child's own action, and action is everywhere. We've gone late in the season when none of the water rides are open and enjoyed it just as much as on a warm summer day when one can spend hours trying out all of the water activities. We always avoid busy, crowded summer weekends.

More educational fantasy can be found at EPCOT, part of Disney World in Orlando (407-824-8000). Here you travel through various World's Fair–type pavilions. You can visit the world of dinosaurs, where you experience what primeval forests were like, or take a trip to the future. EPCOT also features an interesting "tour" of foreign countries, but the most fun of all for our kids was the Journey into Imagination led by a cuddly little purple creature name Figment and his friend, Dreamfinder. While many say EPCOT is primarily for adults, that isn't what our kids think. They had substantially less interest in the World Showcase pavilions, but everything else seemed to captivate them, from lunch at the Living Seas to the Captain Eo movie featuring Michael Jackson. (For places to stay near Disney World, see Appendix 1.)

Recreational Parks

If you're into physical fitness and adventure, visit Action Park (201-827-2000), actually built on a ski slope in Vernon Valley, New Jersey. Here you can ride a giant waterslide or high-speed toboggan, pilot a speedboat, or drive a tank that shoots tennis balls. There's a special area devoted to younger children. If you crave action, this is the place to go! We consider this more of an amusement park, but the Blocks insist it is a theme park—and the theme is action.

Commercial Products Parks

These are theme parks built around a product. One of the best of these is Disney World in Orlando, Florida. Although Disney based his first park (Disneyland, Anaheim, California) primarily on Mickey Mouse and other animated characters, the emphasis at EPCOT has expanded to include science and technology. The Magic Kingdom combines the elements of both a water park (River Country) and nature area (Discovery Island). Disney World is so expansive that you'll need to devote at least three to five full days there. If you're not tied into a school vacation, avoid peak times and remember that Friday is traditionally the slowest day at the park. The weeks between Thanksgiving and Christmas are also considered slow times.

Our kids prefer to seek out the characters, which they find more interesting than anything else. We were surprised how the information shows, such as the Hall of Presidents, interested them more than some of the pure entertainment shows. Don't be afraid to try an exhibit you think might be over their heads. After all, Disney people are expert at knowing how to keep kids of all ages interested. Again, when kids get cranky and tired and you don't want to leave the park, head off and relax at River Country (we hope you remembered your bathing suits) for a few hours and try the park again later.

One of the newest attractions at Disney World is the Disney MGM Studios, a 135-acre attraction that is the only movie theme park in the world where visitors can actually watch movie and television production in action. The Great Movie Ride takes visitors through scenes from film classics such as "The Wizard of Oz" and "Mary Poppins." At the television theater, audience volunteers actually appear with TV superstars in scenes from famous shows, and visitors also get the chance to see Disney animation artists at work. Typhoon Lagoon is a new water theme park, four times the size of River Country, with a 95-foot mountain peak topped by a wrecked fishing boat. Mickey's BirthdayLand, another relatively new addition, is great for little kids. They board the Mickey Mouse Express at the Main Street Station for a ride to Duckburg and a tour of Mickey's house, where there's a surprise party for Mickey in progress. And try not to miss EPCOT's nighttime extravaganza—the 15-minute illuminations, fireworks, dancing lasers, and sensational lighting effects across the World Showcase courtyards. (Have the kids nap during the day so that they can stay awake for the show.)

At Disneyland in Anaheim, California (714-999-4565), the news is Splash Mountain, a thrill ride that debuted not long ago and features the world's longest flume drop with a top speed of 40 mph. Bear Country, in the northwestern part of the Magic Kingdom, has been renamed Critter Country and has a new woodsy theme, including miniature houses, nests, and lairs of a variety of "critters."

Another park based on a commercial product is Hersheypark (717-534-3900) in Pennsylvania. Here you'll learn how chocolate is made and experience all the thrills of a traditional amusement park besides. This park is a chocoholic's dream and can be done easily in 1½–3 days. We prefer the latter, since the lodging facilities themselves have so much to offer. (See page 477–478.)

We spent one full day at Hersheypark, where amusement rides and entertainment delighted all of us. We especially liked their solution to the height requirements on certain rides. When the kids were devastated by not being allowed to ride the bumper cars, they were immediately elated to learn that the same ride, child-sized, was just a few steps away.

PLANNING A FAMILY REUNION

A family reunion is perhaps the most memorable family vacation of all. Children meet relatives they've only heard about, take a real life lesson in family history and genealogy and participate in a mixture of generations, customs, ideas, and activities. A rewarding experience for the whole family, it can also be an awesome project for the organizers. We talked to some people who have had experience organizing reunions for their families, and we've put together some guidelines based on what they told us.

Types of reunions vary. Yours might revolve around a Sunday afternoon meal at a nearby country inn, a week-long Caribbean cruise, or a visit to a family-oriented resort. Before deciding what kind of reunion best fits your family, *decide who will plan the reunion.* In familes where reunions take place regularly, organizers are often rotated by some sort of system and determined at the end of each clan gathering. "I asked my brothers what they thought of the idea of a family reunion, and they thought it was great. But nobody wanted to do anything about it. Someone had to do it, so I did," says Carl Conley of Cape Coral, Florida, who arranged a successful reunion for 57 family members at the Canaan Valley Resort Park near Davis, West Virginia. Pam and Rikk Larsen of Cambridge, Massachusetts, have family reunions every five years. Their group includes 18 children. Traditionally the grandparents arranged it, but after one fiasco, Pam took things into her own hands and insisted they try a Club Med. She couldn't believe seeing her 74-year-old mother happy in a pareto!

Any organizer should start planning well in advance, preferably at least a year ahead. To get a more enthusiastic response, involve as many other family members as possible rather than announcing your plans as a fait accompli. Poll key family members and mesh their suggestions with your own. If there's time, send a questionnaire to each potential participant. That way, everyone feels part of the planning and is more likely to make that extra effort to attend. Here's a checklist to help you plan:

- *What kind of family are you?*
  What's the age range? If a number of teenagers are involved, make certain there will be something fun for them to do by themselves—maybe disco dancing or an active sports program. When grandparents and great-grandparents are involved, look for places for them to relax, perhaps a resort that attracts other senior citizens. Unlike our normal planning advice (start with your youngest and work your way up), here we say work from both the top and bottom age groups simultaneously.

• Do most of you like outdoor sports, indoor sports, sedentary activities, or a mixture of the above? The Larsens always try to select a resort with a children's program. The hotel they visited on their "fiasco" boasted a program in their brochure but nothing materialized until they insisted the hotel do "something, anything, to keep the kids happy." "Club Med was just perfect for our family," said Pam. "My folks could take rolls and rolls of film of all the grandchildren engaged in a wide variety of activities, and at dinnertime the adult contingent could catch up without the kids interrupting all the time. We are a multiracial, multinational family," she explained, "with six of ours and four of my brother's children being adopted. We seem to cause a commotion wherever we go. At Club Med you know that kids are welcome and, well, if someone cries or acts like a child, there's no guilt. It's okay, it's no big deal. What a difference it was for us. I just came back from the new Sandpiper Club in Florida. It will be perfect for our next reunion. We may not even wait five years! Here all the luxury my parents need and like is combined with the wonderful services and feelings Club Med brings." Many resorts who offer kids programs during summers and holidays will tailor a program to meet the needs of your group, whatever time of year. Lots of places listed in *Great Vacations* are perfect.

• *What special needs are involved?* If you need wheelchairs, high chairs, strollers, cribs, and the like, arrange for them in advance and get a confirmation in writing. Check on ramps and other accessibility if you have a disabled member joining you. Be sensitive to any special dietary requirements. You certainly don't want a main dinner to offer steak if there are members of the family who don't eat meat. Low-cholesterol and low-salt meals may be a necessity for other family members.

• *What's the budget?* Perhaps this item should come first. Find out the maximum amount that people can afford, whether there's any leeway, and what that amount has to include. Take advantage of your status by getting group rates, which can save money on meals, rooms, and transportation. Some hotels provide discounts for booking as few as five rooms! Consider the cost of the planning as well. Divide it by the number of people you feel will realistically attend and add it to the cost.

If you end up with a profit, buy a souvenir for the group or arrange to have photos sent to everyone.

- *Where will the reunion take place?* Many reunions, such as Carl Conley's, take place near the original family homestead. In contrast, Lindsley and David Homrighausen, whose family reunions take place every five years, are bicoastal affairs. "We switch East Coast and West Coast, which is fun. This year it's San Francisco." Other reunions occur in a convenient middle meeting ground. This determination may make a vast difference in who comes. A resort, a campground, a trailer park, a boat, a luxury liner, or a college campus, all of these are possibilities. "We had one reunion at Bucknell University in Lewisburg, Pennsylvania," says Homrighausen. "We kind of took over the campus. They had wonderful dorm apartments complete with kitchenettes, and we had full use of all of the facilities: pools, squash courts, etc." Check this out. Many campuses are actively looking for business and may present a fun and economical spot.

- *When should the reunion take place?* Summer is the most popular time since most people vacation then, but a New Year's Eve or Easter week gathering is always an alternative. Ideally, schedule it when the most family members can come.

- *Will there be a main event?* The focus of many reunions is a meal or banquet. David Hopkinson's reunion took place on the grounds of Yarmouth (Maine) Community Center and was attended by 77 family members aged 3 through 90. "Box lunches were provided, although people could bring their own. There were toys galore, frisbees and balls being thrown back and forth. Everybody had a grand time."

- *How long should the reunion last?* Although the Hopkinson reunion was a one-day affair, the Florida contingent of his family stayed in Maine an entire month. Carl Conley's lasted a weekend, and the Homrighausens' and Larsens' traditionally last a week. Offer the potential for flexible stays. Notify everybody of the options you offer. "We sent a flyer with a tear-off bottom sheet well ahead of time," explains Hopkinson. "This was the key to its success. We asked how many were coming, whether or not they wanted the box lunch, etc." This system makes it easier for both organizers and respondents. Ask for all the information you need on this flyer and include your phone number for any questions.

- *How do people pay?* Let everyone know when deposits are due and whether they should be sent to you or directly to the property. Don't forget to give a specific deadline, allowing for some last minute stragglers.

Most important, don't get so caught up with the planning that you lose sight of the fact that a reunion is fun. Leave time for exploration and spontaneity. Give everyone (and yourself) a chance to relax and to become acquainted and reacquainted. "Ours just rolled the way it was supposed to. Everybody was relaxed and had a grand time," says Conley.

6

ADVENTURE

If you just want to lie on a beach and soak up the rays, skip this chapter. But if you're in the mood for adventure, for getting out into the middle of the great outdoors with your family, consider some of the offerings here. Read on and you'll find out about rafting trips, llama treks, backpacking, nature study and mountaineering, and more.

Adventure vacations are "in" right now, so there are bound to be lots to choose from. Fortunately, more and more adventure tour operators are thinking "family." One woman who probably knows the most about adventure-type vacations is Pat Dickerman, author of *Adventure Travel North America,* who started writing on the subject long before it became trendy. The book is available for $14 book rate or $16 first-class from Adventure Guides, 36 East 57th Street, New York, New York 10022. For credit card orders, call 212-355-6334.

Bill and Pam Bryan of *Off the Beaten Path* say that they "plan personal itineraries in the northern Rockies," but somehow that doesn't convey all that these two do for vacationers. The Bryans design day-by-day personalized itineraries with advice on which ranch to choose, what fishing lodge would suit your family, even which restaurant would be best for you to stop at along your way from one spot to another. They know everything there is to know about Montana, Idaho, and Wyoming, and they can arrange the kind of experiences that no one else can, from a night on an Indian reservation to a chance to meet local "characters" that you might otherwise only hear about. The Bryans charge $200 to $350 for their services. Contact them at 109 East Main Street, Bozeman, Montana 59715, 406-586-1311.

A well-known organization that you may want to contact about adventure travel is Outward Bound. With schools located throughout the United States, Outward Bound is dedicated to wilderness education; with Outward Bound, "you'll learn to trust your own abilities and instincts while you learn to live comfortably in the wilderness." Outward Bound is "serious" adventure—it doesn't ask for lots of experience, but it does demand commitment and willingness to try new experiences. Outward Bound's minimum age for participation is never less than 14, so this would be a possibility only for a family with teenage kids. For information and a brochure, contact the national offices, 384 Field Point Road, Greenwich, Connecticut 06830, 800-243-8520.

Before we go into descriptions of specific programs, here's a rundown of some of the questions to ask when you're researching adventure vacations for your family:

- Exactly what is included?
- Where will you spend the nights?
- How well established is the tour operator?
- Will the tour operator give you the names of some people who have gone before you?
- What are the qualifications and experience of the staff that's going along with you?
- What is the size of the group?
- Do they often have families?
- What special services are available for kids?
- What's the minimum age? (We've found that most outfitters are flexible on this issue: If you want to do it, they'll do all they can to make it possible.)
- Do the operators have kids themselves?

It's possible that you may be a bit uneasy about spending your entire vacation on an adventure-type experience if the idea is new to you. What if you don't like it? What if the kids are unhappy? How about trying what we call a "taste of adventure"—sign up for just a day or two of adventure. Among the listings that follow there are half-day, one-day, or two-day experiences—just enough to give you an idea of whether this is the kind of thing you like. Or, long before it's time to sign up, try a similar kind of activity close to home—a day hike on nearby trails or a canoe trip on a river that's within driving distance.

We've divided this chapter into seven sections according to the type of adventure. Our categories are exploring nature, canoeing, rafting, pack trips, sailing, biking, and wagon train trips. We've included a variety of operators, all of whom expressed a willingness to welcome kids. The listings are alphabetical according to the state where the outfitter is located.

NATURE EXPLORATION/WILDERNESS TRIPS

America Wilderness Alliance/American Wilderness Adventures
7600 East Arapahoe Road, Suite 114
Englewood, Colorado 80112
Telephone: 303-771-0380, 800-322-9453
Trip Coordinators: Diane Eakle and Lisa Naplacic
Operating season: Year-round
Trips in: Montana, Idaho, Colorado, Alaska, California, Utah,
    Minnesota, Maine, Wyoming, Hawaii, Alaska, Oregon, Arizona

IN THEIR OWN WORDS: "Wilderness adventures are unmatched in memories and friendships. They are full of discovery, excitement, and surprises. You can enjoy a highly participatory trip, or one less challenging, whichever suits your inclination and mood."

THE TRIPS: The Alliance coordinates a number of trips, all involving adventure and all taking advantage of the great outdoors. They offer backpacking, kayaking, sailing, horseback riding, canoeing, pack tripping, fishing, rafting, and combination trips of two or more adventures at a time. One nice possibility: a three-day Family Escape trip that has participants either take horses or a train from Durango, Colorado, to the base camp. From the base camp, families take day rides and kids play rodeo-type games. Minimum age for this trip is 6.

EQUIPMENT: Everything is provided: "All you bring is a sense of adventure and your toothbrush."

RATES: Costs vary from trip to trip. The parent-child horseback trip costs $345 per person.

Wilderness Threshold Trips
Sierra Club
730 Polk Street
San Francisco, California 94109
Telephone: 415-776-2211
Owners: Nonprofit organization, founded in 1892, to help care for the country's wilderness areas and to fight to preserve them.
Operating season: June–August
Trips in: California, Arizona, New York

IN THEIR OWN WORDS: "Wilderness Threshold trips have one specific goal in mind—to make it easy for families to enjoy the outdoors together. . . . We welcome single parents, grandparents, or aunts and uncles."

THE TRIP: There are five trips offered, all designed to help families learn outdoor skills together, while increasing their awareness of an area's plant and animal life. Camps vary according to location: On wilderness trips, pack stock is used to carry food and equipment; on some trips, motor vehicles are used for equipment, while participants hike; and on lodge-based trips the "camp" may be just a few yards from the road. Groups meet and have breakfast and supper together. Families are free during the day for nature study, hiking, fishing, or swimming. Evenings often involve group activities. Some of the recent choices have been a week in Canyon de Chelly, Arizona, for families with kids 6 and over; a Toddler Tramp in New York's Finger Lake region; and a week at Tuolumne Meadows in Yosemite National Park for families with toddlers.

RATES: The pack trips range from $255 to $395 per adult; $170 to $285 per child.

Wilderness Southeast
711 Sandtown Road
Savannah, Georgia 31410
Telephone: 912-897-5108
Owner: Not-for-profit educational corporation
Operating season: Year-round
Trips in: Georgia, Florida

IN THEIR OWN WORDS: "We make adventuring easy. Adventurous vacations open you up to Nature's beauty, inspire you with new insights, and get you actively involved. . . . Wilderness Southeast is a school of the outdoors."

THE TRIPS: Wilderness Southeast recommends three of their trips for families with children 8 and over. One is their Okefenokee Cabin/Canoe trip: three or four days spent paddling through the swamp, observing and learning about alligators, the cypress forest, wading birds, and life under the lily pads. Accommodations are in cabins with showers at Stephen Foster State Park. Another trip suitable for families is the Smokies Basecamp/Hike: four days hiking the trails, stopping frequently to examine animal tracks, wildflowers, and changes in the forest type caused by elevation. This trip is held in October so that hikers have the added pleasure of being in the midst of the season's spectacular colors. Accommodations are in cabins. A third recommended trip is to Cumberland Island, the southernmost of Georgia's barrier islands, complete with remains from ancient Indian culture and the Revolutionary War era. Participants must be able to hike from three to six miles per day; accommodations are in tents at Sea Camp campground.

EQUIPMENT: Participants must bring their own sleeping bags, sleeping pads, daypacks, and waterproof duffel bags (all are available for rent). "The most important thing to bring on any program is your cheerful acceptance of whatever surprises the wilderness may hold for us."

RATES: The above trips range from $225 to $315 per person.

Chewonki Foundation
RR 2, Box 1200
Wiscasset, Maine 04578
Telephone: 207-882-7323
Owner: Nonprofit educational institution
Operating season: Year-round, most family activities between mid-August and Labor Day
Trips in: Maine

IN THEIR OWN WORDS: "Chewonki Foundation programs encourage participants to develop their personal potential, gain a sense of community, and heighten their interest in and sensitivity to the natural world."

THE TRIPS: Family wilderness trips last from six to fourteen days; there's no official minimum age, but 7 is probably the best cutoff. All participants must know how to swim. Trips are based on canoeing, hiking, kayaking, or sailing, for example, ten days canoeing down the Allagash Wilderness Waterway, seven days sailing along the coast of Maine, and six days of backpacking in Baxter State Park with camping in the Chimney and Russell Pond areas. Each trip has a maximum of ten participants, and two Chewonki leaders accompany each group. Responsibility for chores is shared so that everyone has a chance to learn camping skills.

For families interested in the natural history of the Maine coast, there's a seven-day workshop that includes daily fieldwork and evening discussions. There's no age minimum for workshops; participants live in simple screened cabins and eat in a central dining room. Wilderness trip participants sleep in tents and help with the preparation of all meals.

Custom-designed trips can also be arranged for groups of ten or more.

EQUIPMENT: Chewonki provides all general equipment. Participants bring their own sleeping bags and packs.

RATES: Wilderness trips range from $485 to $800 per person.

Canyonlands Field Institute/ED Ventures
Box 68
Moab, Utah 84532
Telephone: 801-259-7750
Owner: Nonprofit organization
Operating season: February–November
Trips in: Utah

IN THEIR OWN WORDS: "From river canyon to alpine meadow, you explore the ecology, geology, and archaeology of this amazing country through the naturalists' and the artists' perspectives."

THE TRIPS: ED Ventures is a long-time favorite of ours. It sponsors field seminars, backcountry trips, and natural history outings. The age minimum is 5 or 10, depending on the activity. The seminars use indoor and outdoor classrooms and are one to three days long. Participants arrange their own accommodations. The territory to be explored is Arches and Canyonlands National Parks, the canyons of the Green and Colorado Rivers, and the wilderness of the Colorado plateau—"wind and water have transformed this pastel landscape into a maze of silent passageways and majestic arches sheltering abundant signs of the Anasazi cliffdweller culture." Custom-designed trips are also possible for groups of two or more, and if you're just passing through, you can call ahead to arrange for the services for a day of a private naturalist who knows "how to turn kids and adults on to the natural world."

EQUIPMENT: Meals and outfitter services are provided for back-country trips. No minimum age has been set; call for advice on whether your kids are the right age.

RATES: Costs vary. A sample: "Sharing Nature with Children" is $18 for adults, $2 for kids.

National Wildlife Federation
1412 16th Street NW
Washington, D.C. 20036
Telephone: 703-790-4363
Owner: Nonprofit group
Operating season: June–August
Trips in: Colorado, Vermont, South Carolina

IN THEIR OWN WORDS: "Nature investigations are our primary focus as well as environmental education and conservation. . . . The entire family has a chance to participate in a wide variety of outdoor discovery activities—it's a 'camp' experience for the whole family."

THE TRIPS: The Federation operates four "Conservation Summits" each summer. Locations vary somewhat from year to year, but most recently these summits were held on Kiawah Island in South Carolina; in the Green Mountains at the University of Vermont; in the Pacific Northwest at Western Washington University in Bellingham; and, for teachers, in Colorado at the YMCA of the Rockies. Summits last from Sunday to Sunday in July and August (one week per location). Accommodations vary by location, from dormitories to condos.

At the summits, adults may make their own schedule, choosing from about 20 classes and field trips at each location. All are led by highly qualified naturalists. "You decide how much time you want to spend in active outings, discussions, and lectures or just relaxing amidst beautiful surroundings." Choices include wildlife photography, bird identification, hikes, folk music, field ecology, and outdoor skills. All summits, except the one for teachers, have specially organized kids' programs for youngsters from 3 to 17. (At the Teachers' Summit family activities are scheduled and kids may participate in the programs of the YMCA of the Rockies, which are quite extensive).

Teens aged 13 to 17 join the Teen Adventure Program, which involves outdoor skill sessions, rope course work, canoeing, orienteering, and hiking trips. Kids 5 to 12 are called Junior Naturalists and they spend their days involved in stream studies, wildlife investigation, bird walks, nature hikes, learning folk tales, games, and arts and crafts. Both the Teen Adventure and the Junior Naturalist programs meet from 8:30 A.M. to 3:00 P.M.

For even younger kids, the 3- and 4-year-olds, there's "Your Big Backyard," which operates from 8:00 A.M. to noon and includes micro-hikes, touch-and-feel expeditions, fun-with-nature crafts, and more.

Baby-sitting is available for kids under 3 and even for older kids during nonprogram hours in case you're tied up with one of your own activities.

RATES: Fees are separated into program fees and accommodation and meal fees and differ from one summit location to another. An example: The program fee for adults at the Washington Summit is $200, for teens and Junior Naturalists it's $130 and for the preschoolers it's $70. Room and board ranges from $238 to $261 for adults and is $150 for kids 2 to 8.

CANOEING

Adventures Unlimited
Route 6, Box 283
Milton, Florida 32570
Telephone: 904-623-6197 or 626-1669
Owners: The Sanborns
Operating season: Year-round
Trips in: Florida

IN THEIR OWN WORDS: "Our entire facility is set up for families. The campground has a playground and the streams are perfect for children because they're shallow and have a clear, sandy bottom."

THE TRIPS: The Sanborns operate a campground with a choice of tent camping or cabins. Four cabins come fully equipped and are ideal for families; two of the four have fireplaces. With the campground as a base, families can sign up for canoeing or tubing on some of the rivers of Northwest Florida. Or, if you'd prefer, Adventures Unlimited will customize a two- or three-day river canoe camping trip especially for your family. The Sanborns don't set a minimum age for their trips; they welcome young kids.

EQUIPMENT: For overnight canoe trips, fully outfitted canoes can be rented.

RATES: A family of four can spend the day canoeing or tubing for $18; overnight in a rustic cabin costs $20; in a deluxe version, $50.

Bear Track Outfitting Company
Box 51
Grand Marais, Minnesota 55604
Telephone: 218-387-1162
Owners: David and Cathi Williams
Operating season: Year-round
Trips in: Minnesota

IN THEIR OWN WORDS: "We are very receptive to families, having five children ourselves, from toddler to teenager. We believe our customers become part of our family."

THE TRIPS: The Williamses outfit canoeists, plan trips, and run a canoe camp for kids 11 to 17. Their territory is the Boundary Waters Canoe Area, one million acres of land and water in the northern third of the Superior National Forest, completely forested with hundreds of lakes, wildflowers, birds, wildlife, and game fish.

There's no age limit for the Bear Track trips, and life vests are provided for everyone. A typical canoe trip organized by the Williamses starts with an orientation—an introduction to the North Country, the equipment, and the route. After orientation, the group (usually ten people) packs its gear; early the next morning they set out from the canoe base at Seagull Lake. "We usually route families on a trip that has no real hard portages, has smaller lakes and sometimes base camping on a lake with day trips that include fishing, photography, swimming, exploring, bird and moose watching." Evenings are spent around the campfire, roasting marshmallows and watching the Northern Lights.

In the winter, Bear Track offers cross-country skiing tours and winter camping. "We don't recommend these for kids under 10—they can't keep warm." The trip lasts three days. The night before the tour begins, there's an orientation at Bully Creek Camp. On the first day, the group travels to the base camp and sets up; winter skills such as firewood cutting are taught. The days are short and the nights are long, so there's a lot of conversation and storytelling inside the wood-heated tents. During the day, group members ski, ice fish, or take photographs. On the third day, camp is broken and the group heads back to the starting point.

EQUIPMENT: Bear Track can outfit a canoeing family completely, with canoes, food, camping equipment, and lodging in their cabins.

RATES: The rates per person per day for canoe trips are $38 for two to three days, $32 for seven days or more. The more people in the group, the lower the cost. The winter camping expeditions cost from $360 to $500 (three to five days) for four people. Cabin rates are $35 to $45 per night for two.

Gunflint Northwoods Outfitters
Box 100 GT
Grand Marais, Minnesota 55604
Telephone: 800-328-3325
Owners: Bruce and Susan Kerfoot
Operating season: May 1–October 20 and December 15–April 1
Trips in: Minnesota

IN THEIR OWN WORDS: "With over 50 years outfitting by our family, we have the background and experience to expertly plan your trip with you. The Boundary Waters Canoe Area Wilderness is an ideal setting for a family canoe trip."

THE TRIPS: The Kerfoots custom plan trips for families, choosing from over 50 possible routes. Trips are all in the Boundary Waters Canoe Area and last from two to 14 days. For the younger or less experienced families, they can arrange trips on small lakes with easy portages; for the more experienced, there are more challenging routes. The package includes dinner, lodging, and breakfast before and after the trip; a route briefing; and complete outfitting for six days. The Kerfoots also offer canoeing lessons for anyone 6 years and older at no extra charge.

EQUIPMENT: The Kerfoots supply the canoe, life vests, sleeping bags and pads, cooking kits, duffels, a tent, food, and even the dish towels.

RATES: The "Family Package" costs $258 per adult, $110 for each child for five nights and six days.

North Star Canoe and Bike Rentals
Route 12-A
Ballock's Crossing
Cornish, New Hampshire 03745
Telephone: 603-542-5802
Owners: John and Linda Hammond
Operating season: May–October
Trips in: New Hampshire

IN THEIR OWN WORDS: "Leave your tensions and pressures of daily life at home and become absorbed in the serenity and magnificence of this historic river."

THE TRIP: The Hammonds, who live on a working farm located on the river, will help you plan any length canoe trip along the cool, clear waters of the Connecticut River, which forms the border of Vermont and New Hampshire. For beginners and families, North Star recommends that you start with their day trip. Then, when you're ready for overnight canoe camping, they'll route it for you and outfit you. They'll also help arrange a canoeing/bicycling combination trip—they call it "pedal-and-paddle." If you want a guide, that too is possible.

EQUIPMENT: North Star will rent canoes, paddles, life jackets, bicycles, and helmets.

RATES: The daily rate for canoe rental is $15 per person; overnights are $10 per person per canoe for each additional day. Groups of eight or more get a 10 percent discount; ages 12 and under get 20 percent off. A two-night pedal-and-paddle trip costs $200, with overnight accommodation in a country inn.

RAFTING

Outdoor Adventure River Specialists (OARS)
P. O. Box 67
Angels Camp, California 95222
Telephone: 209-736-4677, 800-346-6277
Owner/operator: George Wendt
Operating season: April–October
Trips in: California, Oregon, Arizona, Utah, Wyoming, Idaho

IN THEIR OWN WORDS: "River rafting is the ideal family activity because it appeals to all ages. It's challenging, fun, and healthy."

THE TRIPS: OARS is licensed to operate in California, Arizona, Utah, and Oregon. They recommend three of their trips for families: a five-day trip on the mostly smooth San Juan River in Utah, the one- or two-day trips on the South Fork of the American River in California from May through September, and the five-day trip on the Rogue River in Oregon. Kids 7 years and over are welcome on these trips.

EQUIPMENT: Food, waterproof duffels, guides, camping gear, and child-size life jackets are provided. You have to take your own tent, sleeping bags, and eating utensils.

RATES: Prices vary from $60 for the one-day trips to $545 for the five-day trip. Costs vary with the date. There are special rates for children; for instance, the $545 San Juan River trip is $495 for kids.

Sobek Expeditions
P. O. Box 1089
Angels Camp, California 95222
Telephone: 209-736-4524
Owner: John Yost
Operating season: Summer
Trips in: The Tetons, Rocky Mountains

THE TRIPS: Two trips that the Sobek people recommend for families are Riding and Rafting in the Tetons and Rocky Mountain High. The first is a combination of three days of horseback riding in the Teton Wilderness bordering Yellowstone National Park, followed by four days of rafting on Jackson Lake in the heart of Grand Teton National Park and the Snake River.

The second trip is actually to one of the ranches we list in Chapter 11—the Vista Verde Ranch in Colorado. With Sobek planning the one-week trip, you can have a whitewater rapid ride down the upper Colorado River, and a ride in a hot air balloon over the Elk River Valley, the river itself, and the surrounding mountains.

EQUIPMENT: For riding and Rafting in the Tetons, all meals are included, and all outdoor equipment except sleeping gear (which can be rented) is provided.

RATES: Riding and Rafting costs $895 for adults, $795 for children 11 and under. Minimum age is determined by parents and Sobek. Sleeping gear rents for $35. The Rocky Mountain vacation costs $1,050 for adults, $850 for children under 12, $750 for children under 6. The hot air balloon ride is extra—quite a bit extra in fact—at $125 for adults, $110 for children under 12.

Turtle River Rafting Company
507 McLoud Avenue
Mt. Shasta, California 96067
Telephone: 916-926-3223
Owner: David Wikander
Operating season: May–September
Trips in: California

IN THEIR OWN WORDS: "We are well known as a hands-on company. You can expect to paddle, get wet, laugh, play in kayaks, relax by the river, share in the preparation of meals, and become more knowledgeable about the river and its ways."

THE TRIPS: The Turtle River folks are enormously enthusiastic about kids and parents rafting together. They've put a lot of thought into their family programs and have come up with two types designed especially for families—or, in fact, for any adults and kids together. First, what they call Kids' Klamath is designed for kids ages 4 and over "with their favorite adults." These two-day trips take place along the gentle section of the Klamath River and they're a perfect introduction to rafting for the kids and the adults as well. Storytellers go along on some of the trips, kayaks are available on all. The second type, called Family Trips, last two or three days and are perfect for single parents as well as mothers and fathers, kids and grandparents all together. They're meant to promote "good fun, unity, learning and confidence." The minimum age is 8 on these Family Trips, although on one, the Gentle Klamath, kids 6 and over are welcome to join, gliding silently down the quiet river past sunbathing turtles and otters at play.

Besides the floating, participants get to enjoy swimming holes and broad sandy beaches, and plenty of fresh, healthful meals and snacks. Everyone prepares the evening meal together—togetherness is important but "we also have time on our trips to spend alone; walking, reading or relaxing near the river." Children do not need to know how to swim in order to participate, but they should feel comfortable floating in the water with a life jacket.

EQUIPMENT: Meals are usually provided, but lower-priced co-op meals plans are available (you bring your own food and you save money). You'll have to bring your own sleeping bag and tent, but other gear, including child-size life jackets, is provided.

RATES: The Kids Klamath and the Family Trips range in price from $120 for adults and $75 for kids 16 and under for a two-day trip, to $250 and $200 for a three-day trip.

Mariah Wilderness Expeditions
P. O. Box 248
Point Richmond, California 94807
Telephone: 415-233-2303
Owners: Donna Hunter and Nancy Byrnes
Operating season: Year-round
Trips in: California, Oregon, Grand Canyon

IN THEIR OWN WORDS: "We provide wilderness tours within a safe and supportive environment which encourages the family to play together and experience new adventures together."

The trips Mariah runs are one and two days long on the South Fork, the Middle Fork, and the North Fork of the American River and on the Merced River. A minimum age of 8 has been set. Of special interest are a set of two-day trips for fathers and sons, mothers and daughters, fathers and daughters, mothers and sons, and single parents and their children. A storyteller goes along to add to the fun.

EQUIPMENT: Participants take their own sleeping bags and tents.

RATES: The special-interest trips are $150 per person, with a 50 percent discount for kids 15 or under.

W. E. T. (Whitewater Expeditions and Tours)
P. O. Box 160024
Sacramento, California 95816
Telephone: 916-451-3241
Owner: Stephen P. Liles
Operating season: March–October
Trips in: California

IN THEIR OWN WORDS: "W. E. T. began in 1970 as a partnership between friends who wanted to share the joys of floating down a whitewater river. We're still friends and we still float the rivers ourselves. . . . Our trips are informal with flexible timetables and requirements."

THE TRIPS: We have a friend who took two teenagers, a grand-parent, and her 2½ year-old on one of W. E. T.'s trips, even though the minimum age is officially 6. She had a wonderful time and recommends W. E. T. highly—she was impressed with the staff and with the food—but she is not sure that she would recommend taking such a little one along. "It's important to carefully evaluate your child and your willingness to take on added responsibility in an unfamiliar situation, factoring in uncertainties like weather conditions." In her case, the latter came in the form of an unexpected hailstorm that hit just as the group was setting up tents at a campsite. From her description, though, of W. E. T.'s trip, there's no doubt that older children, their parents, and even their grandparents could have a fabulous few days on the river. Liles recommends three of his group's trips for families: the South Fork of the American River, the Lower Klamath and the East Carson (the latter is only available from April to June because it's a free-flowing snow-melt river, subject to the whims of nature). You may stay in a wilderness camp area— "We are proud to remain one of a dwindling few outfitters to provide wilderness camping"—or if you prefer, in off-river lodging or at a more developed campground. "More developed" means with a flush toilet and accessible by car. At mealtime your on-river guide turns chef. On our friend's trip, one dinner menu featured filet mignon "as tender as butter" along with pasta and pesto, fresh salads, and a pineapple upside-down cake that had been baked from scratch in the fire.

Liles advises that beginners start with a two-day trip, although he adds that a quick one-day trip "can thrill and rejuvenate anyone in need of the outdoors." For anyone who really wants to pull an escape and live with the river for a while, he recommends a six- to 12-day trip.

EQUIPMENT: Guide services, all food, life jackets, and waterproof bags are provided. Tents, sleeping bags, ground cloths and pads may be rented.

RATES: A sample: The two-day South Fork of the American River trip costs $180 on a weekend and $150 on weekdays for adults and $155 and $125 respectively for kids.

All-Outdoors Adventure Trips
2151 San Miguel Drive
Walnut Creek, California 94956
Telephone: 415-932-8993
Owner: George Armstrong
Operating season: April–September
Trips in: California

IN THEIR OWN WORDS: "If you enjoy nature's beauty, the exhilaration of a challenge, and the feeling of accomplishment when new knowledge and skills are gained, then All-Outdoors trips are for you."

THE TRIPS: Armstrong recommends two of his trips for families—one is on the American River South Fork, the other the Lower Klamath River. The South Fork trip may run for one or two days, and, when an overnight is involved, participants get to choose between camping at a commercial campsite or at a more remote wilderness camp. Accommodations in a country inn built during the Gold Rush years may also be arranged. The Lower Klamath trip lasts from one to three days and according to Armstrong, is an ideal choice for families since the river has challenging rapids alternating with relaxing floating through sleepy countryside. Kids must be at least 6 years old and must know how to swim in order to participate. Custom-designed trips may be arranged for you, your family and friends; organizers go along for free when there are 12 paying participants.

EQUIPMENT: Tents, waterproof duffels, and child-size life jackets (for kids 45 pounds and over) are provided. You'll need to bring your own sleeping bag.

RATES: The American River trip costs $169 for two days, including camping; $229 for bed and breakfast accommodations; the Lower Klamath trip costs $279 for three days during a weekend, $30 less during the week. Kids 17 and under are entitled to a 10 percent discount and, parents accompanying their kids on the Lower Klamath River trip get a 10 percent reduction as well.

Bill Dvorak's Kayak and Rafting Expeditions
17921 U. S. Highway 285
Nathrop, Colorado 81236
Telephone: 719-539-6851 or 800-824-3795
Owner: Bill and Jaci Dvorak

Operating season: March–September
Trips in: Utah, Colorado, New Mexico

IN THEIR OWN WORDS: "We've had 19 years' experience outfitting river trips that focus on child/adult relationship building. Our staff is attracted for that reason and therefore motivated as well as specifically trained to enhance and facilitate that kind of relationship."

THE TRIPS: Dvorak's groups have eight to 25 people, and his trips last from one to 12 days. He's set 5 years old as his minimum age for the following trips, which can be recommended for families: the Upper Colorado–Lower Gore Canyon trip, one to four days, suitable for beginners and old hands as well; the Green River Wilderness trip, five to six days, through one of the wildest desert wilderness places on the map; Slickrock Canyon trip, two to three days, on the Dolores River, where moderate rapids are good for beginning kayakers; the seven-day Lower Canyons-Ragan Canyon trip on the Rio Grande, warm water and warm weather along the border of Texas and Mexico; the one-half day Salida-to-Cotopaxi trip on the Arkansas River; and the one- to two-day Gunnison Gorge trip on the Gunnison River, designated a gold medal trout fishery by the Division of Wildlife.

The Dvoraks are flexible about their minimum age requirement: We know a family who took their 3-year-old who was joined by Bill and Jaci's then-3-year-old, too.

Rafting, kayaking, and canoeing lessons are available as well.

EQUIPMENT: Food, waterproof duffels, and life jackets are all provided. Take you own tent and sleeping bags and pad or rent them for $25 and $15, respectively.

RATES: Special trips planned with kids in mind lasting from two to six days are free for kids 16 and under. A sample: A trip for a family of four for three days on the Upper Colorado is $710.

River Runners Ltd.
11150 Highway 50
Salida, Colorado 81201
Telephone: 719-539-2144, 800-332-9100 (in Colorado) and
   800-525-2081
Owner: David H. Smith
Operating season: May 1–September 15
Trips in: Colorado

IN THEIR OWN WORDS: "Over 17 years of experience has allowed us to chart more river miles and take more guests down the Arkansas than anyone. . . . The Arkansas River, from Salida to Parkdale (often referred to as the Grand Canyon of the Arkansas) offers excellent rafting for those who wish to learn to paddle and also for the less adventuresome. The rapids here range from easy to moderate."

THE TRIPS: River Runners offers a range of trips that last from a few hours to three days. Some of the shorter trips are fine for kids as young as 4, but their two- and three-day trips are recommended for kids 10 and over. The three-day trip includes shooting the rapids, hiking, swimming, fishing, and relaxing around a campfire. Participants sleep in tents along the banks of the Arkansas.

EQUIPMENT: If you don't have your own tent or sleeping bag, you can rent with advance notice. Guides cook the food—"a feast of high country cookin'."

RATES: The three-day trip, which covers 75 miles and includes seven meals, costs $170 for adults and $130 for kids under 12.

Rocky Mountain River Tours
P. O. Box 2552
Boise, Idaho 83701
Telephone: 208-344-6668
Owners: David and Sheila Mills
Operating season: June–September, but the water is best for kids in July and August.
Trips in: Idaho

IN THEIR OWN WORDS: "Our crew of river guides is the backbone of our vacation business. . . . They love working as guides and meeting people. Eighty-two percent of our guests are referred by past guests and that says it all. . . ."

THE TRIPS: The Mills have been rafting and running paddle boats on the river for 18 years, "and we still look forward to our next trip!" The owners recommend rafting on the middle fork of the Salmon River for families: "It is a wonderful place for a family to share laughter, adventure, and to meet new friends." And we agree. The wide sandy beaches of the river are inviting and remarkably comfortable for sleeping under the stars on nice nights. The trips last six days, and July and August are the best times for kids. Children must be at least 6 years old to participate; they don't need to know how to swim because life jackets are always worn on the water. The trip allows for hiking, fishing, bird watching, sunbathing, and swimming. You may spot deer, elk, mountain sheep, or an occasional river otter family. Each night a different campsite is set up along the river; the menu is based on fresh fruit and vegetables, and there are no meals repeated in the six days. Sheila Mills has written Dutch oven cookbook and teaches the guides new recipes every summer. There's an orientation night before the trip begins on the lawn of a lodge in Stanley, Idaho.

EQUIPMENT: Rocky Mountain provides life jackets, tents, eating utensils, two waterproof bags per person for sleeping bags and clothing, and a camera container. Participants should take their own sleeping bags, or, if they prefer, they can rent a bag for $10.

RATES: The six-day trip costs $970, with a 10 percent discount for children 12 and under. The same discount applies for groups of ten or more friends or relatives.

River Odysseys West (R. O. W.)
P. O. Box 579
Coeur d'Alene, Idaho 83814
Telephone: 208-765-0841 or 800-451-6034
Owners: Peter Grubb and Betsy Bowen
Operating season: May 1–October 30
Trips in: Idaho, Oregon

IN THEIR OWN WORDS: "Families have always been an important part of our business and we love to have kids along. It's a fantastic experience for them. . . . Together we foster a spirit of sharing and support, allowing you to take part in as much or as little as you wish."

THE TRIPS: Grubb tells us that his first choice for a family trip is the five-day Lower Salmon Gorge adventure that begins every Monday through July and August. (Usually one week a summer is set aside exclusively for families, so check on the exact date). The minimum age is 6 on this trip, with equal portions of hot sun, warm water, crashing waves, white beaches, and steep canyons. The choice is yours—paddle rafts or oar-powered rafts or inflatable kayaks called "duckies."

We took this trip last summer and loved every moment. Our group consisted of eight kids and 12 adults with more women than men. It's hard to describe the sense of relaxation that pervades the entire group in just the first hour on the river. The sun-filled days gave way to crisp, cool evenings, where a special cameraderie developed among kids, adults, and guides.

Grubb's second choice for families is the Snake River through Hells Canyon trip, for three to six days from June to September. The Snake River has carved the deepest canyon in North America and is the home of the most powerful whitewater in the Pacific Northwest. Camping here is a bit more difficult than on the Salmon because there are no sandy beaches. A family on our trip had taken this trip the previous summer and loved it.

For both trips, participants camp out in tents provided by R. O. W. and spend evenings around the campfire. The food is quite impressive: fresh fruit with each meal, banana-walnut pancakes for breakfast (plain ones for fussy kids) and from-scratch German chocolate cake for dessert. All of this was prepared by the guides while the kids played and the adults enjoyed wine and snacks.

EQUIPMENT: Tents are provided, but you should have your own sleeping bag and pad. If you prefer, the sleeping outfit can be rented for $30 per trip. Child-size life jackets are available—minimum weight is normally 50 pounds. (They did find one for our then-33-pounder, so let them know in advance if like us you have a light-weight kid.)

RATES: The five-day Lower Salmon Gorge trip is $595 for adults, $535 for kids under 17; the Snake River through Hells Canyon is $395 and $345 for three days to $725 and $645 for six days.

Hughes River Expeditions, Inc.
P. O. Box 217
Cambridge, Idaho 83610
Telephone: 208-257-3477
Owners: Jerry Hughes and Carole Finley
Operating season: Late May–September
Trips in: Idaho, Oregon

IN THEIR OWN WORDS: "A river trip in the wilderness and a white-water river is an ideal and unique vacation opportunity for families. During the summer over half our clients are families with children 5 years and over. Hughes is a small, owner-operator style of business. . . . We have two small children—two girls 3 and 5—and we truly value family trips as an important segment of our business. . . . We can fit a particular family into a style of trip that fits its own interests and needs. . . ."

THE TRIPS: Jerry Hughes has been a professional guide on the rivers of the region for 24 years; he's had his own company for 13. He's outfitted some famous outdoor types, including Peter Ueberroth, Sir Edmund Hillary, and crews from the National Geographic Society.

Hughes's trips last from three to seven days. "We've taken children as young as 3 years but 5 years is a better age." It's best if the kids can swim, but because life jackets are worn at all times, it's not absolutely necessary.

Hughes's trips take place in the backcountry and whitewater rivers of Idaho and Eastern Oregon. According to Hughes, the ideal rivers for family vacations are the Middle Fork (five- and six-day trips from June to September), Snake River–Hells Canyon (three- to five-day trips June through September), Salmon Canyon (four-day trips in July and September) and Bruneau Canyon lands (four days in late May and June, for kids over 12).

The trip Hughes thinks is best for the youngest kids is the Salmon River Canyon one. "We have taken kids of 3 to 5 years on this one many times and they always have a ball. Highlights are the largest sand bar camps in the West for kids to play on, warm swimming temperatures, good bass fishing, sturgeon fishing from camp and beautiful country all around."

EQUIPMENT: Hughes will provide you with just about everything—a roomy four-person tent for every two guests, waterproof gear packs, foam-lined camera boxes (you have to supply your own camera), tarps, and comfortable camp chairs. Sleeping bags and pads are available at no extra charge. Each expedition carries a "river library" of books and articles about the area. The accompanying staff does all the camp work and cooking, and the menu includes fresh meats and fish, fresh fruits and vegetables, and Dutch oven-baked biscuits, muffins, and cakes. Take your own fishing tackle and clothes for layering.

RATES: Trips cost from $480 to $960 per person, and there's a 10 percent discount for 18 and under. The Salmon River Canyon trip recommended for kids as young as 3 costs $600.

Idaho Afloat
P. O. Box 542
Grangeville, Idaho 83530
Telephone: 208-983-2414
Owner: Scott Fasken
Operating season: June–September
Trips in: Idaho

IN THEIR OWN WORDS: "As the owner and operator, I personally run each trip. I have a low guest to guide ratio of four to one so that, especially for families, the guides have time to spend with the guests leading hikes, organizing volleyball games, etc."

THE TRIPS: Fasken has logged 20,000 miles of safe rafting since 1969.

He recommends all of his midsummer trips, from late June to late August, for families. Kids should be at least 6 years old and know how to swim. Trips last from two to six days and are along the Snake River in Hells Canyon.

For families who aren't sure they're ready for camping out, Fasken has put together what he calls lodge trips, which offer the thrill of the rapids, great meals, relaxation in the riverside hot springs, plus the comfort of overnight accommodations at dude ranches along the river. At the ranches there's time for hiking, fishing, horseback riding, or just sitting on the porch. (This is ideal for the family that prefers both more privacy and real bathrooms.) For familes who want their whitewater trip more mild than wild, he offers three-day trips on the Lower Snake, which has great scenery but calmer rapids than the upper section. And finally, families can choose a horseback riding-river package that combines three days of riding and three to four days of rafting. Customized trips are also possible.

EQUIPMENT: Food, duffels, life jackets (minimum weight 35 pounds) are all provided. Participants either take their own sleeping bags and pads and tents or rent the whole set for $30.

RATES: Rafting trip costs range from $300 for a two-day trip to $760 for a five-day trip (the most expensive includes all transportation from Boise and back). The lodge trip is $1,300. Readers of *Great Vacations with Your Kids* are entitled to a special discount of 20 percent for children under 12.

Eastern River Expeditions
Moosehead Lake
Box 1173
Greenville, Maine 04441
Telephone: 207-695-2411, 207-695-2248, or 800-634-RAFT
Owner/operator: John Connelly
Operating season: April–October
Trips in: Maine, New York, West Virginia

IN THEIR OWN WORDS: "The most frequent (and fervent) comments we have are in appreciation of our staff. We are lucky to have mature staffers, who are experts about safety, knowledgeable about rivers and wildlife, and full of spirit and fun. Our files are filled with glowing letters praising individual guides as well as the company's 'esprit de corps.' We help each guest to discover all that Moosehead Lake has to offer: from easy worm-dunking to fishing."

THE TRIPS: Most of Eastern's trips are day trips, but they also have some overnight trips and trips for people who want to raft several rivers back-to-back. Summer water temperatures are fairly warm—in the 60s and 70s, and each trip usually includes swimming as well as paddling and floating. Kids between the ages of 5 and 12 who weigh at least 50 pounds join parents for floats down the calmer sections of the Kennebec Gorge. Called the Carry Brook Trip, this trip allows older children and adults to raft the "big" water and have younger children meet them downstream to enjoy the smaller waves and swimming. Kids 12 and over will enjoy either the Kennebec Gorge, the Big Eddy trip on the Penobscot River, or an overnight that explores the headwaters of the Kennebec River.

Custom kayak or canoe clinics allow families to paddle within the range of their interests and abilities with lots of games, swimming, and bountiful riverside picnics. Maine rivers are dam releases; this means you can depend on summer whitewater even when there's been little rain or spring snow. Because water is stored in massive lake systems and then released to generate hydropower, river recreation is always available.

The people at Eastern are also happy to help you and your family plan a trip to the north woods of Maine. They can tell you about canoe and boat rentals, backcountry camping and fire permits, the best trails for short family hikes, moose-watching opportunities, fishing services, floatplane rides, and lake cruises on a large and fascinating log-driving steamer. They'll also give you listings of reliable local baby-sitters and complete accommodations lists with everything from camping to lakeside cabins, modern motels, bed and breakfasts to full-service resorts complete with pools and restaurants. If you're interested in an extended stay in this part of the world, they'll refer you to a local cabin-finding service.

EQUIPMENT: All paddling gear is provided. For overnights, tents and cooking gear are provided, but you'll have to bring your own sleeping bags. Bring wool hats (even in summer) for the kids.

RATES: The price of raft trips vary. An example is $65 for an adult during the week on a one-day trip; $40 for kids. On weekends the day trip is $85; overnight trips are $180.

Wapiti River Guides
Summer/Fall: Box 1125, Riggins, Idaho 83459
Winter/Spring: Route 1, Cove, Oregon 97824
Telephone: 503-568-4663 in winter/spring; 208-628-3523 in summer/fall or 800-727-9998 (wait for dial tone and then dial 8352)
Owner: Gary Lane
Operating season: Year-round
Trips in: Oregon, Idaho, Alaska

IN THEIR OWN WORDS: "Enthusiasm generated by the river's magic is a highly contagious, fun disease to catch. It's the only malady we know of that gets better the more you have of it. . . . If you appreciate rare opportunities, extraordinary beauty, and exciting action, then come with us."

THE TRIPS: Lane tells us that he has lots of experience with kids and families on the river, "We consider it to be one of our specialties. Emphasis is given to customizing family interests to river difficulty." He's chosen five of his regularly scheduled trips as suitable for kids, some for kids as young as 3. The five he recommends are the Minam River; a combination horseback and float trip in the Eagle Cap Wilderness in Oregon (based at a ranch that used to belong to Lane's great-grandfather); the lower Owyhee River; the Lower Salmon; and another horseback-float combination in the Seven Devils Mountain Range in Idaho. Trips range from one to five days and many include side hikes "to places so awe inspiring that you will pinch yourself just to be sure it isn't only a dream." Nights are spent camping by the river at sites that have chairs, kitchen shelters, tables, utensils, and sometimes even a hot shower. Most trips have ten participants, maximum is 15.

EQUIPMENT: You'll need your own sleeping bag and tent or you may rent them, and you will be given waterproof bags for your personal gear and camera.

RATES: The combination horseback-float trip on the Minam River costs $649 for five days for adults. Discount rates for kids vary with the age of the children.

Wild Water Adventures
P. O. Box 249
Creswell, Oregon 97426
Telephone: 503-895-4465
Owner: Al Law
Operating season: Year-round
Trips in: Oregon, California

IN THEIR OWN WORDS: "We are a small outfit catering to families and small groups. We specialize in individual attention. Families often organize their own 'custom tours' with us so that they have their friends along on the trip."

THE TRIPS: Law recommends a number of his trips for families. The minimum age ranges between 4 and 6, depending on the trip. (Children should weigh 40 or 50 pounds to fit the life jackets.) Trips last from a half day to nine days and longer. Some of the possibilities: three to six days on the Deschutes River, which is fine for beginners age 6 and up; Grande Ronde for three or five days, good for age 6 and up; the Klamath River, good for age 5 and up with good swimming and lots of opportunities to take wildlife photos; the one-day trip on the McKenzie River, fine for age 4 and up; three days on the Rogue River for age 6 and up with lots of good fishing; five days on the Owyhee River for 10 and up with spectacular scenery; and three days on the John Day River for ages 5 and up that is both easy and scenic.

Some of the activities that will appeal particularly to kids on Wild Water's trips are supervised swimming in river pools; body surfing in rapids; inflatable-kayak lessons; Indian petroglyph tracing; fishing for trout, catfish, and bass; gold panning; hikes on hills out of camp; outdoor cooking lessons; photography lessons; and games such as frisbee and volleyball in camp.

EQUIPMENT: Everything is provided except tents and sleeping bags, but both can be rented for $20 for two people for a two-to three-day trip. Wild Water's menus have been featured in a camping book. Forget about burned hot dogs and canned beans. Wild Water offers pan pizza, lemon-herb chicken, "Guide's Stew," and peach-apricot crisp.

RATES: The trips mentioned above range from $30 for the one-day adventure to $420 for five days on the Owyhee River. There's a youth discount for ages 13 to 16 and a child's discount for those under 12.

Orange Torpedo Trips
P. O. Box 1111
Grants Pass, Oregon 97526
Telephone: 503-479-5061
Owner: Don Stevens
Operating season: May–September
Trips in: Oregon, California, Idaho

IN THEIR OWN WORDS: "Our follow-the-leader system allows first-timers and experienced paddlers alike the opportunity to enjoy the exhilaration of challenging major whitewater rivers in their own inflatable kayak. . . . Over ninety percent of our guests are return paddlers or have been referred to us by previous guests."

THE TRIPS: The folks at Orange Torpedo (they originated the sport of inflatable kayaking in 1969) suggest that families choose from any of the Klamath River trips (there are four that are three days each); the Rogue River trips—one to four days—or two of the Salmon River trips—one is four days, the other six. The minimum age is 6. Trips involve staying in tents, cabins, or lodges, depending on the trip you choose. One sample out of the many choices Orange Torpedo offers is the Klamath Lodge trip, three days with overnights spent at riverside lodges. Guides prepare dinner barbecues; there's one guide to every four people. If the idea of paddling your own kayak doesn't appeal to you, ask whether a passenger raft is available.

EQUIPMENT: All equipment is provided. If you'd like to do some fishing, bring your own collapsible rod.

RATES: As an example, the Klamath Lodge trip costs $335.

Anderson River Adventures
Route 2, Box 192-H
Milton-Freewater, Oregon 97862
Telephone: 503-558-3629 or 800-624-7583
Owners: Bob and Fran Anderson
Operating season: Year-round
Trips in: Oregon, Idaho

IN THEIR OWN WORDS: "Kids are welcome, . . . float trips are great for families. We spend five to six hours floating, then we may explore an old gold mine, Indian writings, old homesteads, hike, swim, take photographs, fish—there are lots of fun things to do."

THE TRIPS: The Andersons especially recommend two of their trips for families with kids 8 and over. The first trip is the one on the Grande Ronde in summer—one to three days on whitewater that "seems created just for gaining experience. We've even had kids as young as three on this trip." The second is their Hells Canyon adventure (kids should weigh at least 70 pounds), three to six days of thrilling whitewater rafting along with an as-you-float informal course in the history, geology, and wildlife of the canyon.

EQUIPMENT: The Andersons provide tents—one that's big enough for four for every two people—a camera box, waterproof bag, sleeping pad, sleeping bag, and utensils.

RATES: The Grande Ronde trip ranges from $49 to $269, depending on length; the Hells Canyon, from $395 to $630. Combinations of horseback riding and rafting trips can be arranged at a cost of $125 per day for the horseback riding portion. Kids 17 and under accompanied by two adults are entitled to a 10 percent discount.

Pocono Whitewater World
Route 903
Jim Thorpe, Pennsylvania 18229
Telephone: 717-325-3655
Owner/Operator: Doug Fogal, Sr.
Operating season: March–November
Trips in: Pennsylvania

IN THEIR OWN WORDS: "We love the rivers, and want to comfortably introduce them to children. It's great exercise and at day's end we have that pleasant tiredness that comes from fresh air and the thrill of adventure."

THE TRIPS: The Lehigh River in the Poconos is the backdrop for this group's operation. Although they offer lots of one-day trips, they've put together what they call "Combo Packages" that are good for families. Possibilities include two days of rafting the Upper and Lower Lehigh or a day of rafting and a day of mountain bicycling. Accommodations can be arranged in town houses with two or three bedrooms located just eight miles from the rafting center or at an inn nearby. Ten is the minimum age on most trips.

EQUIPMENT: All rafting equipment is provided.

RATES: The Paddling Plus trip—two days of rafting and one overnight—starts at $96 at the inn and $101 at the condo.

Outback Expeditions
P. O. Box 44
Terlingua, Texas 79852
Telephone: 915-371-2490
Owner/operator: Mark Mills
Operating season: Year-round
Trips in: Texas

IN THEIR OWN WORDS: "We're a small company with personalized service, an experienced and professionally trained staff. We have an impeccable safety record."

THE TRIPS: Guides are chosen for their "good humor and professionalism." The company has been organizing wilderness trips since 1971 and offers guided family adventures for kids 4 years and older on river trips, 12 and over on backpacking excursions. Wilderness backpacking or mountaineering trips run by Outback are half-day to seven days long. Families with kids 7 and over might want to check out a combo half-day horseback riding, half-day float trip—a quick riding lesson, a guided trail ride up and over Lajitas Mesa, a lunch by the Rio Grande and a float trip down the river and back to Lajitas.

EQUIPMENT: All equipment is provided except sleeping gear; rentals are possible.

RATES: Two-day trips on the Rio Grande are $150 per person; one-day trips are $55–$75; children under 12 get a 15 percent discount. The horseback riding–float trip combo costs $60.

Colorado River and Trail Expeditions
P. O. Box 7575
Salt Lake City, Utah 84107
Telephone: 801-261-1789
Owner: David J. MacKay
Operating season: April–October
Trips in: Utah, Colorado, Alaska

IN THEIR OWN WORDS: "River trips are for people of all ages and abilities who enjoy the out-of-doors. . . . If you rejoice in the sound of running water, the touch of sunny warmth, and the feel of gentle breezes, there's a river trip for you."

THE TRIPS: The MacKays offer a number of river trips, but the one they think is best for families is their five-day Desolation Canyon trip. It's got "fast water, lots of good rapids, lovely sandbar beaches, giant cottonwood trees and beautiful scenery." The minimum age is 6 to 8—it all depends on the swimming ability and maturity of your child. You can choose from a ride on a paddle raft with secure seating for the kids and a professional oarsman or, for the more adventurous and experienced, an inflatable kayak. This trip runs from the end of May through to Labor Day.

EQUIPMENT: They'll provide sleeping bags, ground cloths, and foam pads and will rent two-man tents if you don't have your own.

RATES: The Desolation Canyon trip costs $450; for kids under 16, deduct 10 percent.

PACK TRIPS

McGee Creek Pack Station
Route 1, Box 162
Mammoth Lakes, California 93546
Telephone: Summer: 619-935-4324
                Winter: 619-872-2434
Owners: Lee and Jennifer Roeser
Operating season: June 1–October 15
Trips in: California

IN THEIR OWN WORDS: "A majority of our wranglers are women; most families like that. We specialize in families, with no minimum age. We use home bred, raised and trained Morgan horses which are not only gentle, trustworthy, and sure-footed, but a real pleasure to ride. Ours is a family-run operation that knows how a family likes to be treated."

THE TRIPS: The Roesers recommend their High Sierra Weekend (three days) or their John Muir Wilderness Trail Ride (one week) for families. They'll also customize all-inclusive, everything provided trips as well as spot trips—trips that include getting you to the campsite and a horse and a mule per person. The setting is the eastern High Sierra's McGee Canyon. The canyon is uncrowded and colorful with multihued wildflowers and marbleized red slate and granite peaks.

EQUIPMENT: This depends on the type of trip. The all-inclusive trips include tents, foods, a guide, cooking gear, and packhorses.

RATES: Cost for an all-inclusive trip for riders is $140 per person per day for three to four people; $120 per day for five or more.

Telemark Inn and Llama Treks
RFD 2
Box 800
Bethel, Maine 04217
Telephone: 207-836-2703
Owner: Steve Crone
Operating season: Summer and fall for llama treks, inn open all year

IN THEIR OWN WORDS: "We have a casual but elegant turn-of-the-century Adirondack wilderness estate nestled in the White Mountain National Forest. It's a nature lover's paradise with llama trekking and canoe trips when it's warm and ski touring and horse-drawn carriage rides when it snows."

THE TRIPS: Crone's operation is a bit different from the others we describe here in this chapter. He operates an inn with wraparound mountain views all year round; and from that inn he also offers llama trekking and canoe trips in the Maine wilderness. According to Crone, his six-day Mountain and Lake trip, which takes place in July and again in August, is perfect for families. It combines three days of llama trekking, two days of canoeing, and one day of mountain biking in between. The llama trek goes along the Wild River into the heart of the White Mountain National Forest. For two nights, participants stay in a base camp that is set up by guides. On the third night, trekkers head back to the inn and spend the night there. The next day they can go out mountain biking or just spend the day relaxing at the inn with its wide front porch.

The next two days may be spent on a canoe trip on the remote Richardson Lakes: "Experience the tranquility of Maine lake canoeing where moose are frequently spotted and the echoes of loons serenade you to sleep." Recommended by a reader, a single parent of a teenage girl, the warm welcome combined with Crone's love of his surroundings make this a wonderful family experience.

EQUIPMENT: Camping equipment, except for sleeping bags, is provided for the llama treks and the canoe trips.

RATES: The six-day trip costs $599 for adults, $399 for kids under 12 and includes pre-trip lodging at the inn, meals, guides, instruction, and equipment. The three-day llama trip alone costs $299 for adults, $185 for kids. A stay at the inn costs $75 per night double occupancy.

Yellowstone Llamas
Box 5042
Bozeman, Montana 59717
Telephone: 406-586-6872
Owners: Will and Renee Gavin
Operating season: July 1–September 15
Trips in: Yellowstone National Park and Montana

IN THEIR OWN WORDS: "Our days start with the smell of coffee on a crisp mountain morning. As the sun climbs over the mountain peaks, a hearty breakfast gets you ready for a day of hiking through some of the most beautiful country in the United States. . . . Our hiking groups are friendly, casual and very relaxed."

THE TRIPS: Trips last from three to six days and vary in terrain; people in good shape should have no trouble with any of the trips, and kids 5 and over (some even younger have gone along) are welcome just as long as they can hike at least three miles at a stretch. Trips can be custom designed, groups are composed of four to eight people with flexible starting dates. The Gavins told us about three trips that they feel are especially suitable for families: the Campfire Lake trip—four or five days in all with a total of 18 miles of hiking, through deep forests, along a beautiful creek and over a high pass to the lake where hikers can relax, fish, take photos, or look for mountain goats; the Thorofare Region of Yellowstone trip—a hike through lodgepole pine forests, across meadows, to a camping site on the shores of Yellowstone Lake, where you can fish, follow animal tracks, or watch eagles; and the Black Canyon—perfect for a short trip, with only eight miles of hiking across large, open meadows and down into the canyon along the Yellowstone River. On longer trips, a base camp is set up so that you can explore, fish, climb a mountain, take photographs, or just relax.

Will is a geologist, so you are bound to learn a great deal about the area's geology and natural history from him. Renee, once an attorney and now a llama farmer, can tell you all you ever wanted to know about these gentle but sturdy animals.

EQUIPMENT: The llamas will carry virtually all the equipment. All you'll need to take is a light daypack for cameras and other personal items. Just about everything is provided—dome tents, all camping gear, and food. The Gavins pride themselves on their meals—"camping fare has never been better . . . delicious Indian curries, fresh salads from our garden and even a bottle of wine chilled in a cold stream." If you don't bring along your own sleeping bag, you can rent one.

RATES: For children under 12, the rate is $100 per day; for adults, $135. Private trips can be arranged for a minimum of $450 per day.

Holland Lake Lodge
Swan Valley
SR Box 2083
Condon, Montana 59826
Telephone: 406-754-2282 or 800-648-8859
Owners: Howard and Loris Uhl; outfitter Ken Mitchell
Operating season: July 1–September 1
Trips in: Montana

IN THEIR OWN WORDS: "We customize our pack trips to fit the individual needs. Scenic beauty, quality stock and tack, and a knowledgeable staff all add up to a memory of a lifetime."

THE TRIPS: Kids have to be old enough to sit on a horse alone and hang on; children under 6 years are probably too young. A good trip for families who haven't done a lot of camping is a five- to seven-day trip with a base camp about 20 miles from the lodge in the Bob Marshall Wilderness. The trip includes swimming, fishing, short hikes, and a seven-mile ride to the South Fork of the Flathead River. Custom trips can be arranged for four or more people. (See page 448 for information on the lodge.)

EQUIPMENT: Everything except sleeping bags, duffels, fishing gear, and life vests is provided. Food is home-cooked, not freeze-dried.

RATES: Customized trips cost $120 per day per person. A seven-day guided trip costs $840 per person and includes one night at the lodge.

Hurricane Creek Llamas
Route 1, Box 123, Dept. GVWK
Enterprise, Oregon 97828
Telephone: 503-432-4455
Owners: Stanlynn Daugherty
Operating season: May 15–September 15
Trips in: Oregon

IN THEIR OWN WORDS: "Llama trekking is the ideal family vacation. Parents are free from camp chores and are able to spend time with their children exploring all that nature has to offer."

THE TRIPS: According to Daugherty, llamas are natural hiking companions for adults and children alike because of their gentle nature. On these treks, llamas carry all food and equipment, and the staff takes care of the cooking and the camp chores.

The trips that are recommended for families with kids age 6 or over are the Upper Hurricane Trip in August—six days based at a campsite in an expansive meadow at the head of Hurricane Creek—and the six-day August astronomy trip, led by an astronomer and featuring a viewing of the Perseid meteor shower (or when the time is right, as in the summer of 1989, a total lunar eclipse) from a high wilderness point.

Trips can also be customized for any family group. All trips are limited to ten participants and take place against the backdrop of the Eagle Cap Wilderness in the Wallowa Mountains in northeastern Oregon. Participants must be able to walk four to ten miles per day over trails that range from easy to moderate.

EQUIPMENT: Hurricane Creek provides tents, sleeping pads (take your own bag), food, the llamas, and pack equipment. You may take up to 20 pounds of personal gear for the llamas to carry.

RATES: The cost is $88 per person per day, 20 percent less for children 6 to 11 years old. The Upper Hurricane Creek trip costs $525 for adults; the Astronomy trip is $595.

Big Buffalo Trail Ride, Inc.
P. O. Box 772
Gallatin, Tennessee 37066
Telephone: 615-888-2453
Owners: Fred and Mike McDonald and Tim Aston
Operating season: June, August, and October
Trips in: Tennessee

IN THEIR OWN WORDS: "Big Buffalo Trail Ride is for families who love horses and enjoy riding together. On our rides, families camp together, eat together, and ride together. The rides are for people who have their own campers and horses."

THE TRIPS: There are three rides scheduled each year—two rides in the summer and one foliage ride in October. The rides are a week long and follow trails that are old logging roads through the Tennessee hills: "sparkling streams, rugged hills, and secluded hollows." Participants stay in their own tents or campers; electrical hookups are available. Meals are provided at the dining hall. All ages are welcome—there is no minimum. When you're not riding, you can canoe, fish, tube, or swim in the Buffalo River, which borders the campground. Each night there's live country music and entertainment. Custom trips can be arranged, too.

EQUIPMENT: Guests take their own tents, campers, or trailers and horses. There are no horses for rent. Stalls are available for rent, and feed is available.

RATES: Adults pay $140 for the week; children aged 8 to 12 cost $115; kids 4 to 7 cost $90, and for those 3 years and under it is free.

WAGON TRAIN

Oregon Trail Wagon Train
Route 2, Box 502
Bayard, Nebraska 69334
Telephone: 308-586-1850
Owner: Gordon Howard
Operating season: May 15–September 15
Trips in: Nebraska

IN THEIR OWN WORDS: "Come with us to experience life as it was on the Oregon Trail in 1850."

TRIPS: You may choose from one-, three-, four- or six-day treks out on the prairie with a wagon train. You have your choice of riding in the wagon or on one of the scout horses. Along the way you'll search for pioneer and Indian artifacts, participate in muzzle loading, see a rifle demonstration, do prairie square dancing, enjoy campfire-cooked food, and sleep in the wagon, a tent, or under the stars. "Life is free and easy, simple and rugged—no phones, no radios, no modern pressures." These trips are not recommended for kids under 4 but are particularly good when your kids are learning about pioneer days. There's even the chance to get college credit for the six-day trek by enrolling in the "Westward Ho" living history graduate course offered at the end of June and taught by a professor from the College of New Rochelle.

THE EQUIPMENT: The Oregon Trail folks provide a trail bag, all meals, sleeping bags, and tents.

RATES: Three-day treks cost $289 for adults, $230 for kids under 12; six days are $479 and $384 respectively.

BIKING

NOTE: For an annual listing of bicycle tours, send for a copy of Bicycle USA's *Tourfinder* edition, which comes out every spring. The guide is available from the League of American Wheelmen, Suite 209, 6707 Whitestone Road, Baltimore, Maryland 21207, telephone 301-944-3399, and costs $4.

Cycle Tours (2007 39th Street, Des Moines, Iowa, 50310, 515-255-5352) acts as a clearinghouse for 60 bicycle touring companies. Tell them the kind of tour you want and they'll send you a free printout of the ones that best match your interests. They'll handle your travel arrangements, too.

Always ask about helmets: Does the operator provide them for free, does he rent them, or do you have to bring your own? Your kids shouldn't ride without them and neither should you!

Bike Arizona
7454 East Broadway
Tucson, Arizona 85710
Telephone: 602-722-3228
Owner: Bill Drum
Operating season: Year-round but mostly in fall and spring
Trips in: Arizona

IN THEIR OWN WORDS: "Experience Arizona on a bike. Our luxury tours are carefully planned for you. From the time you join us or we pick you up at the airport, until we bring you back, you can forget the pressures of daily life and relax and enjoy the beauty of Arizona and the good company of other bikers."

THE TRIPS: Bill offers six in all and recommends them all to families: A Grand Canyon to Ducson tour, White Mountain Summer tour, Arizona Historic tour, Hohokam Loop/Colossal Cave tour, Tombstone Territory Ghost Town tour, and Verde Valley Ghost Town Indian Ruins tour. Trips last from three to five or seven days and average about 25 miles per day; shorter tours can be combined. Tours are limited to 12 cyclists. The group's motor home and sag vehicle carries all luggage and food. Accommodations are in motels, and any tired bikers always have the option of riding in the motor home. Bill will also be happy to arrange a custom tour for groups of six or more—your family might qualify.

EQUIPMENT: Bill can arrange for bike rentals.

RATES: The cost of the White Mountain Summer tour, a four-day, three-night trip, is $275, which includes all meals, lodging, and full support from the sag vehicle. Call to ask about children's rates.

On the Loose Bicycle Vacations
1030 Merced Street
Berkeley, California 94707
Telephone: 415-527-4005 or 800-346-6712
Co-directors: Ed and Rebecca Tilley
Operating season: Year-round
Trips in: California, Oregon, Hawaii

IN THEIR OWN WORDS: "Past guests return again and again because they are assured of a vacation which enables them to meet new friends in a smaller group setting, explore scenic bicycle routes along carefully selected terrain and be pampered at first-class country inns or pristine campgrounds."

THE TRIPS: Although the Tilleys welcome kids on most of their trips—and there's a catalog full of tempting possibilities—they offer two trips that are specifically for families: the Russian River camping tour, routed through quiet inland roads sheltered by redwoods that eventually lead to the beaches, and the Folsom Lake tour, with rides along the American River and the secluded Green Valley Road toward Lotus. Both are weekend trips. Although both family trips involve camping, other tours in the catalog offer a choice of either camping or inns.

EQUIPMENT: Two-person tents are provided, but you are expected to bring your own sleeping bag. Bikes may be rented, and free helmets are provided.

RATES: The two family trips described above cost $169; kids 3 and under go for free. If mothers go along on Mother's Day or fathers on Father's Day, they pay only half-price. All of On the Loose's trips include discounts for kids.

Backroads Bicycle Touring
P. O. Box 1626
San Leandro, California 94577
Telephone: 415-895-1783 or 800-533-2573
Owner: Tom Hale
Operating season: Year-round
Trips in: California, Alaska, Colorado, Idaho, New Mexico,
  Washington, Oregon, Vermont, Virginia, Canada

IN THEIR OWN WORDS: "From the start, our goal has been clear and consistent: to create the ultimate bicycling vacation. We've built our reputation on three things: quality, service and a fervent belief that perfection is found through the utmost attention to detail."

THE TRIPS: Backroads' 50-page catalog is full of tantalizing possibilities. Two of the regular offerings have been adjusted for families. The first is a weekend trip in California's Point Reyes peninsula—"California's most dramatic meeting of land and sea." The second is a week-long trek in the Canadian Rockies. The Point Reyes trip has been changed a bit from the way it appears in the catalog to make it easy for children to cycle; the Canadian trip offers wide-shouldered roads for extra safe cycling between Banff and Jasper. "Besides the fun of family activities, both destinations combine fabulous scenery, intriguing wildlife, and opportunities for children to expand their perceptions of the outdoors and the wonders of nature."

EQUIPMENT: Sleeping bags, bicycles, and helmets may all be rented from Backroads. Tents and other camping equipment is provided. With Backroads, you won't need to carry anything at all on your bike because the company's trailer will carry all luggage, supplies, and food. It's nice to know that there's plenty of room in the van for anyone who wants to hitch a ride and that it serves as both a mobile repair shop and refreshment center. If you are going to use a child's seat on the back of your bike, you'll need to have your own. Also, keep in mind that children under 8 may not ride in the van by themselves, so if your little one gets tired, you'll have to go along.

RATES: The weekend trip costs $179 for adults with a 25 percent discount for kids 7–15, 50 percent off for 3–6, and 75 percent off for under 3. The Canadian trip costs $596 with the same youth discounts. Rates include accommodations for two in a four-person tent, all meals, use of a safety helmet, services of three tour leaders, and the use of the support van. There are youth discounts on other trips in the Backroads catalog. It's best to call them and consult on whether or not the trip that appeals to you is suitable for your child. And remember, too, that if staying in a tent is not your idea of fun, some of Backroads' trips include stays in inns along the route.

Michigan Bicycle Touring
3512 Red School Road
Kingsley, Michigan 49649
Telephone: 616-263-5885
Owners: Michael and Libby Robold
Operating season: May–October
Trips in: Michigan

IN THEIR OWN WORDS: "When Michigan Bicycle Touring (MBT) cooks up a vacation, the ingredients are clean, fresh air and sparkling waters; inviting accommodations and delicious food; secluded routes with incredible scenery; and warm, caring trip leaders. Set in the tranquil north woods of Michigan, MBT tours provide unsurpassed beauty amidst one of the country's most scenic regions."

THE TRIPS: Bicycle touring is the main focus of MBT's trips, but many of their outdoor vacations include combinations of bicycling and sailing on the Great Lakes, wilderness hiking, and easy canoeing. MBT assures us that they can accommodate any age group on any of their trips, but for families they particularly recommend the Betsie River Pedal and Paddle, Sleeping Bear Pedal and Paddle, Mackinac Islander (all two-day trips), or Straits Sightseer and Interlochen Sightseer (five-day trips). The first, the Betsie River, is MBT's easiest—each day's ride travels through level to gently rolling farmland with ample time set aside in the afternoon for golf, tennis, a hike, or a swim. The paddle part of the trip is an hour-and-a-half canoe trip on the Betsie River. The Sleeping Bear trip takes families to the Sleeping Bear Dunes National Lakeshore and also combines canoeing with cycling. If you want to spend more time on this kind of trip, MBT's Straits Sightseer is its easiest five-day tour and includes three nights on the beach of Mackinac Island. The Interlochen Sightseer is a bit more difficult and involves fairly hilly terrain on the first, second, and fifth days, so is probably best for families with kids who are pretty accomplished cyclists. Accommodations are always in inns or resorts.

EQUIPMENT: Bicycles may be rented; a helmet is free with rented bikes, and vests are provided on all canoe rides.

RATES: The Betsie River trip costs $249; the Sleeping Bear Trip is $259. In general, weekend packages cost from $205 to $265 and from $519 to $689 for five-day journeys. Children's rates are 75 percent off for kids under 3; 50 percent off for 3–6; 25 percent off for 7–12, and 15 percent off for 13–16 (this assumes that the children will share a room with parents). Rates include accommodations, tour leaders, support van, canoeing, boat rides, and, with a few exceptions, three meals a day.

Bikecentennial
P. O. Box 8308
Missoula, Montana 59807
Telephone: 406-721-1776
Program director: Michael McCoy
Operating season: April–October
Tours in: All over the U.S.

THE TRIPS: Bikecentennial, a not-for-profit membership organization, offers three categories of trips. First are very long self-contained camping trips that last ten to 90 days; second are mountain bike adventures, fat-tire outings based out of resort communities, and third, the ones most suitable for families, Light Touring, which combines bicycling with stays in country inns. Three of the Light Touring offerings are seven days in Glacier Park; the Northwest Islander (Seattle to the San Juan Islands and back in six days); and Door County Fall Foliage (round-trip from Sturgeon Bay Wisconsin in five days).

EQUIPMENT: Bicycles may be rented on some of the Light Tours.

RATES: The Light Tours listed above range from $595 to $795. No sag wagon is provided.

Country Cycling Tours

140 West 83rd Street
New York, New York 10024
Telephone: 212-874-5151
Directors: Peter and Sherry Goldstein and Gerry and Arlene Brooks
Operating season: Year-round
Trips in: Northeastern states, Louisiana, Maryland

IN THEIR OWN WORDS: "We offer a unique variety of bicycling and walking tours for adults and families who enjoy discovering the countryside in comfort and style. The CCT experience appeals to singles, couples and families of all ages. . . . You cycle at your own pace, in groups or alone, . . . selecting the distance you want to ride."

THE TRIPS: Sherry recommends any of the group's one-day, weekend, or week-long trips. The Goldsteins have two of their own kids and are very enthusiastic about biking with children, particularly ones under 3 and over 9. Sherry explained that in the in-between ages, the kids aren't old enough to bike by themselves and are too old to be carried in a bike seat. This makes them a bit of a disadvantage on a bike trip. The CCT catalog is full of possibilities. Just a few examples include a weekend in Pennsylvania Dutch country or in Southwestern Vermont, a midweek combination cycle and sail vacation along the Maryland shore, and a week-long tour of the Mississippi shore, called the Great River Road and New Orleans tour. All CCT trips provide accommodations in inns.

EQUIPMENT: Bring your own bike or rent one from CCT—they have lightweight 12-speeds available. Helmets are also available to rent.

RATES: As an example, the weekend Pennsylvania Dutch tour costs $225; the Great River Road adventure costs $725. Discounts of 25 percent are available for children 6–12; 50 percent for children under 6 sharing a room with their parents. Lodging, breakfasts, some lunches and dinners, the services of two guides, and a sag wagon are included in the rates.

Four Seasons Cycling

P. O. Box 203
Williamsburg, Virginia 23187
Telephone: 804-253-2985
President: Allen Turnbull
Operating season: Year-round

Trips in: Maryland, Virginia, Florida, South Carolina, Pennsylvania, Georgia

IN THEIR OWN WORDS: "We feel . . . that this great big world of ours is best understood through exploration by bicycle. The unexpected discoveries you make during these journeys are lifetime treasures which cost no more than your sense of adventure. Our never-changing ingredients for success are straightforward—superb inns, wonderful food, tranquil backroads, outstanding guides, total van support, and small groups of interesting cyclists and new friends all sharing laughter."

THE TRIPS: Turnbull has selected four of his tours as best for families. The first, Bike Virginia, is an annual event in June that starts in Charlottesville and crosses the state, ending in Williamsburg for a weekend of dayrides. The event is open to all kinds of riders; rest stops are set up every ten miles. Cyclists who aren't able to ride the average daily 75 miles can hitch a ride at any of these spots. The other three trips that Turnbull suggests for families are Colonial Williamsburg, a week that includes time to explore Williamsburg and a sail on a 40-foot trimaran on the James River; Pennsylvania Dutch, a weekend in Amish country where the pace is slow and peaceful; and the Eastern Shore of Maryland, another easy weekend trip where bicycling can be combined with sailing and swimming. For the Bike Virginia trip participants may choose to camp or stay in motels along the way; for all other trips, nights are spent in country inns. As you read through the Four Seasons' catalog you'll notice that each trip has a variety of mileages listed for each day: Participants choose the mileage that's right for them. Two guides go along on each trip to serve as "historians, mechanics, leaders, entertainers, and gourmet picnic providers."

EQUIPMENT: If you do not have your own bicycle, Four Seasons will rent you a 12- or 18-speed lightweight bike and will give you a helmet at no extra cost.

RATES: The Pennsylvania Dutch and Eastern Shore weekend trips cost $239 per person, which includes accommodations (two per room), meals, two guides, van support, and admission to historic sites and other special attractions. The six-day, five-night Williamsburg trip costs $699. Rates for kids under 12 may be lower, but this varies with the policy at the individual inns—call Four Seasons for details.

The Wayfarers

P. O. Box 73408
Washington, D. C. 20056
Telephone: 202-265-1418
Owner: Tom Pendleton
Operating season: late March–mid-November
Trips in: New Jersey, Maryland, Pennsylvania

IN THEIR OWN WORDS: "I have lots of experience with kids bicycling. In fact, I've led workshops on bicycling with kids several times at national bike events. Perhaps the key to my operations is that I treat everyone—adults and kids—as individuals."

THE TRIPS: As you can tell by the above, Tom is gung ho about traveling with kids. In fact, he encourages kids to come along on all of his trips and doesn't have any official minimum age for participation. Kids under 15, though, must be accompanied by an adult ("The adult need not be a relative, and need not bike with the kid, but they must be able to find each other for emergencies—like lunch!). In general, if kids are going to bike by themselves, they should be able to ride at least 25 miles per day. One trip that Tom designs especially for families is his Cycling Jersey trip, 250 miles in six days in August. The route of the tour runs along the New Jersey shore. Highlights include High Point State Park, mountain valleys, old railroad trails, the Delaware and Raritan Canal, Allaire Village, the Hindenburg hangar, the Pine Barrens, the Ocean Highway, and the glories of Cape May. As for the ages of participation—"we have had bikers as old as 75 and as young as 3. On the last trip, the 3-year-old got everyone's attention, the 7-year-old bustled into everyone's attention, and the 11- to 17-year olds formed three or four fluid groups and paid attention to each other."

EQUIPMENT: Participants camp each night in a variety of sites along the route—one night it might be a school, another a church, a park, or commercial campsite. "We try to have showers each night, but cannot guarantee them. At least one site will be primitive, that is, no flush toilets." If roughing it is not for you, you may arrange to stay at nearby motels—Tom will send you a list. You'll need to bring your own bicycle (one with at least ten gears is advisable), and each biker should carry basic tools. Helmets are required. Meals, except for a group dinner near the end of the trip, are not included in the cost, but where there are not adequate restaurants, Tom will try to arrange to have a local group come in to fix supper and breakfast for the cyclists.

RATES: The cost of the trip is $75 for the first in a family; $65 for each additional person in the same family; $55 for kids under 15; $30 for kids under 6. The fee covers seven nights of camping, limited sag service (that's the backup van); baggage transport, a cycling jersey, and an administrative fee.

Off the Deep End Travels
P. O. Box 7511
Jackson, Wyoming 83001
Telephone: 307-733-8707 or 800-223-6833
Director: Tom Sheehan
Operating season: May–September
Trips in: Wyoming

IN THEIR OWN WORDS: "It's your vacation and we want you to help shape it. Flexibility is our hallmark. You don't have to adhere to a strict schedule or race down the road in a pack. . . . [Our] genial guides are always there with suggestions and ideas."

THE TRIPS: The two that Tom picked out as most suitable for families are two of his American Safaris: one called Beyond the Grand Tetons, the other, Yellowstone. Both are seven-day trips beginning on Sundays. The first combines a rafting trip through the Grand Canyon, bicycling around the Teton mountain range ("We have the roads virtually to ourselves all the way"), and two days of hiking with pack-llamas. The Yellowstone trip can be taken as an extension to the Grand Teton adventure. It also combines rafting, cycling ("Yellowstone's 2.3 million acres of wild grandeur are perfectly suited to the lazy pace of cycling"), and hiking and features a horse-drawn wagon trip to an Old-West-style cookout under the stars. "Each night, sitting around a campfire, we'll make short shrift of our sumptuous dinners, listen to the wind that smells of the high mountain air, then sleep the full sleep of early childhood while cocooned in our comfortable tents." When asked about the appropriate age for kids to go along on these trips, Tom replied that he doesn't like to specify an age limit: "Rather, we discuss the tour with the parents, its difficulty and its activities and size. Then we jointly decide if the program is suitable for their children."

EQUIPMENT: Tents and cots are provided, sleeping bags may be rented as well as bicycles. Helmets must be brought by participants, and backpacks can be borrowed at no extra charge.

RATES: The cost of the Teton trip is $525; the Yellowstone,

$475. Special rates for really young children are available; call Tom for specifics.

SAILING

Adventure Sailing Escape
Royal Palm Tours, Inc.
P. O. Box 06079
Fort Myers, Florida 33906
Telephone: 813-489-0344
Owner: Ron Drake
Operating season: Year-round
Trips in: Florida

IN THEIR OWN WORDS: "The shared responsibility of sailing, cruising, docking, mooring, anchoring, and navigating brings families much closer together than a typical hotel stay. Limited to sailings of no more than five boats, sailing 'in company' for a week creates a second family, flotillawide, every time out."

THE TRIP: Royal Palm's sailing program is for people whose only sailing experience is wearing boat shoes. It gives families the chance to sail without hiring a captain. The "Escape Package" is seven days and six nights long and begins with a day-long Skipper School for novices. After that, it's hands-on skippering, navigating, crewing, docking, mooring, and anchoring with coaching by radio as needed: "Rarely does a flotilla look like ducks in a row." The captain of the flotilla is a 50-year-old Dutchman named Jacques. Anyone who wants to spend extra time at the end of the flotilla week with Jacques can qualify for American Sailing Association certification. The protected Intracoastal Waterway, Pine Island Sound, Charlotte Harbor, and the Gulf of Mexico are the flotilla's cruising grounds. Stops along the way include some of the undeveloped islands of the Florida coast, Cabbage Key, and South Seas Plantation. The folks at Royal Palm can also arrange coastal houseboating "not on a box on pontoons but on a seaworthy coastal cabin cruiser."

EQUIPMENT: Sailing yachts are 25 to 43 feet in length. Participants sleep on board at a different marina or resort each night. Included in the cost of the package are the yacht charter, dock rentals, all linens, most meals, sea bags, charts, and the supervision of the fleetmaster.

RATES: The price of the package varies with the number of people. A family of four would cost $780 per person for each adult and $680 per child under 12. Royal Palm rents three-level, 38-foot coastal cabin cruisers with four double beds and one single, including a refrigerator, propane range, full galley, shower, and tub—ideal for six people. Captains are available on request. Rental fees range from $225 for an eight-hour day to $1,344 a week.

Steve Colgate's Offshore Sailing School
16731 McGregor Boulevard
Fort Myers, Florida 33908
Telephone: 813-454-1700
Owners: Steve and Doris Colgate
Operating season: Year-round
Trips in: Florida, New York, New England

IN THEIR OWN WORDS: "There's nothing else like it. No other sailing school offers this opportunity, this unforgettable mix of instruction and vacation."

THE TRIPS: Offshore is the largest sailing school in the world: more than 50,000 students have taken courses there. Offshore's headquarters is Fort Myers, but it has schools in some popular vacation spots—on Captiva Island on Florida's Gulf Coast, Tortola in the British Virgin Islands, and Cape Cod, Massachusetts. Offshore runs the school and arranges for the accommodations at resorts at the various sites. A good choice for families is the school on Captiva Island, where guests stay at South Seas Plantation, a 330-acre tropical paradise that offers year-round children's programs for family members who are too young for sailing lessons. Children's programs begin at age 3. A well-traveled, savvy 8-year-old recently told us this program was "the best ever." (Twelve is the official minimum, but exceptions can be made.) "Learn to Sail," "Advanced Sailing" and "Bareboat Cruising Preparation" are some of the course choices. Family members can sign up for different courses and can sail at the same time, go to class at the same time, and have free time together. Offshore has its own travel agency, Offshore Travel Inc., which can make any and all arrangements.

EQUIPMENT: On Captiva Island you'll learn on 27-foot Olympic class Solings. "Advanced Sailing" is taught on Laser 28's, and "Bareboat" is taught on 36-foot S2's.

RATES: Costs vary from place to place. A sample: "A Learn to

Sail" course on Captiva Island with accommodations in a one-bed-room beach villa costs $975 per person from mid-October to mid-December for a full week, Sunday to Sunday.

Annapolis Sailing School
Box 3334
Annapolis, Maryland 21403
Telephone: 301-267-7205 or 800-638-9192
Owner: Jerry Wood
Operating season: Year-round
Trips in: Florida, Maryland

IN THEIR OWN WORDS: "We are the first and largest sailing school in the nation. . . . It's hard to imagine a family activity as rewarding as sailing."

THE TRIP: Annapolis offers a seven-day Family Sailing Vacation package at two of its locations, in Annapolis on Chesapeake Bay and in St. Petersburg, Florida, on Tampa Bay. The vacation (for families of two to six people) begins with a Weekend Beginners course. While taking the course, the family spends nights on shore in Annapolis, on board in Florida. The optimum minimum age for participants is 12, although special arrangements may be made for younger children. Once the essential skills have been mastered, you and your family take off on a five-day live-aboard cruise in a 26- or 30-foot cruising auxiliary sailboat that sails as part of a fleet accompanied by Annapolis instructors on their own lead boat. A friend of ours, a single mother with a teenage son, claims this was the most fun they've ever had together. This was partly because they spent enough time in different classes, so their time together was spent sharing and comparing their similar yet different experiences.

EQUIPMENT: Beginning students learn to sail on a 24-foot Rainbow (built as a teaching boat), and in Annapolis the live-aboard portion of the package is on either an Annapolis 26 or a Newport 30. In St. Petersburg, students live and learn aboard an Annapolis 26 for the entire trip.

RATES: A beginner's course plus a cruise based in Annapolis is $1,605 for a family of four; in St. Petersburg it's $1,235. Participants must provide their own linen, food, and other equipment; a list is supplied.

Lyric Enterprise
5119 23rd Avenue West
Everett, Washington 98203
Telephone: 206-355-9066
Owner: Charles W. Guildner
Operating season: Year-round
Trips in: Pacific Northwest

IN THEIR OWN WORDS: "We are interested in encouraging and promoting sailing as a family activity and have been operating such programs for the past eight years. Most of our passengers have been in the learning stages, and teaching and communicating safe boating is one of our most highly regarded services."

THE TRIP: The Guildners' own *Lyric,* a custom-built 44-foot boat that accommodates up to six people. One crew person comes along for each trip. Trips can be arranged for just a day or for a week or two.

EQUIPMENT: Passengers must buy their own food, but the Guildners supply suggested menus and shopping lists. Cribs can be provided with advance notice, but passengers must bring their own sleeping bags. Their enthusiasm for sailing is contagious—one phone call and you'll be ready to pack up.

RATES: A day out on the *Lyric* will cost $250; six days, from Sunday noon to Saturday noon, costs $1,400.

7

CITY VACATIONS

Cities are great places to go for vacations with kids. There are lots of things to do and lots of resources to count on. Obviously one couldn't cover every city that would be fun for you and your kids, so we've chosen ten of the most popular. Next time around we'll add more. Just tell us which ones you'd like covered.

Cities offer incredible pleasures; many virtually pulsate with excitement, are crammed with culture, and packed with playgrounds and parks for you to enjoy.

Now there are more resources around than ever before for families heading for a city vacation. New books are popping up all over the place, books that are written especially for families (e.g., *The Candy Apple: New York for Kids,* see page 184) and books written for the kids themselves (e.g., the new Gulliver Travels series by Harcourt Brace Jovanovich and the *Kidding Around* series by John Muir Publications). Another great resource are the parents' newspapers that are mostly tabloid-style, monthly papers filled with wonderful information and resources—the same resources that local parents use. Most contain a current calendar of events, highlighting the best the city has to offer from museum workshops to parent and toddler nature hikes at local parks, plus childcare services, family-friendly restaurants, and more. Most are free. A little further on we give you a list of these publications, a list you won't find anywhere else.

Before we begin our city-by-city rundown, let's begin with a few words about getting ready for a city trip with kids. First, call or send for all of the maps and brochures the city tourist office has to offer. Go to the library or bookstore for a good guidebook—we have some suggestions in our individual city sections. At the library it's a nice idea to take out a few children's books that have as their setting the city you're about to visit (like *Eloise* if you're New York–bound or *Make Way for Ducklings* for Boston or *The Cable Car and the Dragon* for San Francisco). A good source of suggestions for this type of book is *Family Travel Times,* the newsletter we mention on page 8. Write for an advance copy of one of the parent publications mentioned below (be sure to enclose $2 to cover postage and handling). And, as we've said before, try to get everyone in the family involved in the planning.

When it comes time to decide where you are going to stay, the choices can be mind-boggling. Budget to deluxe hotels are always possibilities and don't overlook the extra space of an all-suite hotel, an apartment rental, or even an urban bed and breakfast spot where the hosts may have kids close to the age of your own. Staying out of town may be less expensive but consider the added cost of getting to the city each day. Check out weekend specials. Even the most expensive hotels drop their rates dramatically from Friday to Sunday.

Once you've gotten to your destination, you may want to start out by taking a half-day guided tour (best with kids 7 and over) to give you all an overview of the city. Then, on your own, you can return to the places that most interested you.

Underplan. Don't try to cram too much into one day. Allow time for eating, souvenir shopping, bathroom stops, and unexpected pleasures. List what you'd like to do in the order of importance, visiting the most important places first. Sightsee in the morning, when energy levels are at their highest, and save the afternoons for more leisurely pursuits and kid-oriented sights such as nearby parks or a zoo, or a swim in the hotel pool. Try to find a nice balance between the sidewalks and skyscrapers.

We'll repeat some advice from Chapter 5 here because it's so important for city travel: Schedule at least one activity each day especially for the kids and make it in the afternoon. Then, if they get cranky, you can tempt them with the next stop—theirs.

Cluster your sightseeing, picking one neighborhood at a time to explore. In our city chapters we've done the clustering for you. In each area, seek out a restaurant to retreat to and an open space to run and play and even to picnic. Consider separating every once in a while—mom with one of the kids, dad with another. It can be lots of fun and a nice break to a bit too much togetherness.

Finding the right restaurants for dining with the whole family is easily accomplished by picking up a copy of the Zagat Restaurant Survey for the city you're visiting. The index lists places that are particularly child-friendly and includes special choices for teenagers. Zagat Guides cost $9.95; to reach the publisher write to Zagat Survey, 45 West 45th Street, Suite 609, New York, New York 10036, 212-302-0505.

Here's the list of parenting publications we promised. Parenting Publications of America, 12715 Path Finder Lane, San Antonio, Texas 78230, 512-492-9057 will be able to tell you about publications for the area you're visiting in case it is not listed here (new ones appear all the time). Parenting publications for the cities we cover individually will be found under that city's listing.

Parent's Press
1454 Sixth Street
Berkeley, California 94710
415-524-1602

Peninsula Parent
(covering San Francisco and the peninsula)
P. O. Box 89
Millbrae, California 94030
415-342-9203

San Diego Family Press
P. O. Box 23960
San Diego, California 92123

Bay Area Parents News
P. O. Box 2277
Saratoga, California 95070
408-358-1414

Denver Parent
818 E. 19th St.
Denver, Colorado 80218
303-832-7822

Connecticut Parent
8 Glastonbury Avenue
Pomfret, Connecticut 06067
203-721-7455

Fairfield County Parent
315 Peck Street
New Haven, Connecticut 06513
203-782-1420

The Mother's Network
P. O. Box 38253
St. Petersburg, Florida 33702
813-522-3175

Tampa Bay Parent
5700 Memorial Highway, Suite 211
Tampa, Florida 33615

Atlanta Parent
35 Executive Park Drive, Suite 3513
Atlanta, Georgia 30329
404-325-1763

Youth View News Magazine
1401 West Paces Ferry Road
Suite A-217
Atlanta, Georgia 30327
404-231-0562

Indy's Child
8888 Keystone Crossing
Suite 538
Indianapolis, Indiana 46240
818-846-0400

KC Parent
(serving Kansas City)
6400 Glenwood
Suite 300
Overland Park, Kansas 66202
913-262-3635

Baltimore's Child
11 Dutton Court
Catonsville, Maryland 21228
301-367-5883

Child's Play
401 Dickinson Street
Springfield, Massachusetts 01106
413-733-8055, ext. 10

Metropolitan Parent
140 Madison SE
Grand Rapids, Michigan 49503

All Kids Considered
(Detroit area)
4000 Town Center, Suite 710
Southfield, Michigan 48075
313-443-0990

Minnesota Parent
100 W. Franklin
Number 212
Minneapolis, Minnesota 55404
612-874-1155

St. Louis Parent
P. O. Box 13087
St. Louis, Missouri 63119
314-968-1969

Suburban Parent Magazine
575 Cranbury Road
East Brunswick, New Jersey 08816
201-390-0566

Considering Kids
P. O. Box 24D
Cincinnati, Ohio 45224
214-960-8474

SKIP
(serving the Philadelphia area)
P. O. Box 404
Bala Cynwyd, Pennsylvania 19004
215-664-1952 or 668-4000

Pittsburgh's Child
Box 418
10742 Babcock Boulevard
Gibsonia, Pennsylvania 15044
412-443-1891

Dallas Child
3330 Earhart Drive, No. 102
Carrollton, Texas 75007
214-960-8474

Houston Kid Times
P. O. Box 272351
Houston, Texas 77227
713-529-3365

Our Kids
6804 West Avenue
San Antonio, Texas 78213
512-349-6667

Parents' Express
347 Pierpont Avenue
Salt Lake City, Utah 84104
801-363-1336

Wednesday's Child
P. O. Box 35612
Richmond, Virginia 23235
804-745-0498

Seattle's Child
P. O. Box 22578
Seattle, Washington 98122
206-322-2594

BOSTON

Boston's a great place for families. It's a manageable size, has lots of child-oriented sights and activities, has a good public transportation system, is full of history come-to-life, and is fun besides.

For Information

Before you go, call the Greater Boston Convention and Visitors Bureau toll-free number, 800-858-0200. You'll get a recording, but if you leave your name and address they'll send you basic information about sights, events, and accommodations. Send, too, for a copy of *Boston Parents Paper*, Box 1777, Zip: 02130. There are a number of Boston guidebooks that you'll want to check out. (If you wait until you get to the city to buy one, stop in the downtown area at the historical Globe Corner Bookstore, 3 School Street, which once was the center of literary America and now has a large section just for travel books.) Some of the best for families are: *In and Out of Boston With (or Without) Children* by Bernice Chesler ($10.95), published by Globe Pequot Press. This is a well-researched, well-organized guide to the city with museums, parks, historic sites, nature centers, nearby beaches and ski areas, and all kinds of other helpful information.

Car-Free in Boston: A User's Guide to Public Transportation in Greater Boston and New England (Association for Public Transportation, Inc., P. O. Box 192, Cambridge, Massachusetts 02238, $3.95) add $1.25 if you order by mail. This book includes everything you need to know about getting around Boston on public transportation, maps, schedules, and routes included.

The operators of the Uncommon Boston tour, mentioned a bit later (Susan Berk and Jill Bloom), have put together a collection of their tours in a 242-page paperback, *Uncommon Boston* ($7.95). Two chapters are especially for families and kids; other chapters present special tours for book lovers, architects, history buffs, and nature lovers. *Uncommon Boston* is published by Addison-Wesley.

Other books worth a look are *The Greater Boston Parks and Recreation Guide* by Mark Primack, published by Globe Pequot Press ($9.95); *Historic Walks in Boston* by John Harris ($9.95), also from Globe Pequot Press; *Frommer's Guide to Boston* ($5.95), Simon & Schuster; and *The Blue Guide to Boston*, distributed by W. W. Norton ($15.95).

Once you get to Boston, call the Events Line—267-6446—and/ or visit one of the Greater Boston Convention and Visitors Bureau's two offices and be sure to pick up a copy of the Bureau's free *Boston: The Official Guidebook*. The Prudential Visitor Center, 617-536-4100, open 9:00 A.M. to 5:00 P.M. daily, has brochures on many city sites. It's on the west side of Prudential Plaza, near the Copley T and Prudential T subway stations. Parking is available at the Prudential Center Parking Garage.

The Boston Common Information Kiosk is downtown, on the Tremont Street side of Boston Common, and it's the first step on Boston's historic Freedom Trail. *No* public phone number here— visit them in person for information on the city and state. For access, use the Park Street T station or park at the Boston Common Underground Parking Garage.

The National Park Service Visitor Center, 15 State Street, Zip: 02109, 617-242-5642, opposite the Old State House, offers information on the Freedom Trail and Boston, restrooms, and phones. It's open 9:00 to 5:00 daily and is near the State Street T stop.

The Bostix Ticket Booth at Faneuil Hall, near the Government Center T stop and the Government Center Garage, is the city's official entertainment and cultural information center. You'll find information on theater, music, dance, historic sites, and special visitor attractions. It's open 11:00 to 6:00 Monday through Saturday, Sunday noon to 6:00. Half-price tickets are available on the day of performance.

Tours of the City

Brush Hill's Beantown Trolleys, 109 Norfolk Street, Zip: 02124, 617-287-1900 or 800-647-4776, or 1-800-343-1238 in Massachusetts. You can travel the historic Freedom Trail on a trolley. With a ticket you can ride all day, get off at important landmarks, visit at your own pace, and rejoin the continuously narrated shuttle service at any time. The trolley leaves from the Visitors' Information Booth on Tremont Street at Boston Common, and from Copley Square in the Back Bay, seven days a week, starting at 9:20; the last trip leaves at 4:20. Tickets for children 5–12 are $5; adults pay $8; under 5 free.

Uncommon Boston, Ltd., 437 Boylston Street, Zip: 02116, 617-731-5854, gives visitors an insider's view of Boston Gardens, galleries, clubs, and libraries and plans special tours for children.

The Gray Line of Boston, 367 Dorchester Avenue, South Boston, Zip: 02127, 617-426-8800, offers fully narrated bus tours of Boston. Children, up to three per family, are free.

New England Sights, Inc., 25 Mt. Auburn Street, No. 204, Cambridge, Zip: 02138, 617-492-6689, operates custom car tours for families.

Children will enjoy Make Way for the Ducklings, a walk through Beacon Hill along Mrs. Mallard's route; A Kid's View of the North End; Chinatown and Waterfront Tours, all run by the Historic Neighborhoods Foundation. Tours are recommended for kids 5–9, cost $4, and run at varying times throughout the year. Call 617-426-1885 for details.

The Freedom Trail

Think Boston and you think history. And in fact, a lot has happened here, much of which you can learn about along the Freedom Trail.

The trail isn't a straight path you can take from start to finish. Instead, it's a historical tour of Boston winding in and out of the heart of the city, and most of the stops along the way are free.

The best place to start is at the National Park Service Visitors' Center at 15 State Street, Zip: 02109. You can grab a map and walk on your own, or join one of the free guided walks offered several times a day from April through November that give you an earful of history from the Revolution through 1812. Stops along the Freedom Trail include the following:

The State House
The Park Street Church
Granary Burying Ground
King's Chapel
Benjamin Franklin Statue
Old Corner Bookstore
Old South Meeting House
Old State House
Faneuil Hall
Quincy Market
Paul Revere House
Old North Church
Copp's Hill Burying Ground

The Charlestown Navy Yard (USS *Constitution*, USS *Constitution* Museum, USS *Cassin Young*)
Bunker Hill Monument and Museum

A good way for kids to see part of the trail is with Boston By Little Feet, an hour-and-a-half tour given on Sundays at 2:00 P.M. from May through October. It is suggested for kids from 8 to 12 with an accompanying adult and is led by an enthusiastic local historian who knows when the kids have had enough. Call 617-367-2345 for details.

Recommended for stops along the trail for kids 5 and over is "The Whites of Their Eyes," a multimedia presentation that recreates the battle of Bunker Hill and the events that led up to it. For kids 6 or over, a stop at the USS *Constitution* Museum is also fun. The museum presents the story of how the famous ship was built and how her crew of 450 men and boys lived while at sea—what they ate, how they slept and worked together, and how they often fought among themselves. Kids can try out an 18-inch hammock, climb to the ceiling on an actual fighting top, or match their decision-making skill with those of the *Constitution*'s captains as they sailed into battle. Strollers are allowed, and there are guided tours (with advance notice) and self-guided tours available. There is a playground next to the museum and another across the street.

Back Bay

The Back Bay area used to be a shallow mudflat until it was filled in back in the mid-19th century. Today it gleams with elegant townhouses—look up for details on chimneys, gables, and balconies on houses on Commonwealth Avenue and Marlborough Street. Boutiques and outdoor cafés give the area a cosmopolitan flavor.

Copley Square is an architectural delight, with several chu and antique buildings, but kids will have more fun at the Bo an Public Library (the oldest free municipal library in the world), where, with an adult in tow, they can look up the newspaper for the day they were born. The children's room has special programs all the time. And you can add a touch of class by stepping over to the Copley Square Hotel for tea and crumpets among the palms between 2:00 and 5:00 P.M.

For a wide-angle view of the city, head for the John Hancock Observatory at the John Hancock Tower, Copley Square. Special exhibits and a sound-and-light show describe how Boston has changed from a Revolutionary period town to a modern city; a short film gives you a helicopter peek, and kids will like the telescopes that bring landmarks closer. Admission is $2.75 for adults; kids under 5 are admitted free.

Also fronting on the square is the new glass and chrome shopping mecca, Copley Square Plaza, with high-priced shops, movies, and restaurants. A good snack spot here is Au Bon Pain, best for soup, croissants, and special coffee.

Walk out of the Plaza and over the pedestrian walkway to the Christian Science Center. Children may lose patience with a detailed tour of the center, but they'll be awed by the Mapparium. You enter via a glass catwalk and find yourself encircled in the world as it was politically divided in 1932. It's fashioned from 608 individual sections of colored glass, each a quarter of an inch thick, and brilliantly lit with electric lights. Because glass doesn't absorb sound, you can hear whispers from every part of the room. Telephone 617-262-2300 for hours.

Boston's landmark for kids—the swan boats—grace the Boston Public Garden from the first Saturday before April 19 until the last Saturday in September. Take bread to feed the ducks during the 12-minute ride. Flowers and meandering paths make this a good spot for a picnic and unwinding.

Nearby is the Gibson House at 137 Beacon Street (Zip: 02116). Four floors of this townhouse are filled with Victoriana just as the last Gibson left them in 1954. It's open May through October, Wednesday through Sunday, 2:00 to 5:00 P.M., and weekend afternoons in winter. Call 617-236-6338. The Gardner Museum and the Museum of Fine Arts (this is a favorite of the publisher of the *Boston Parents Paper* and her kids) are also in this area.

Try Legal Seafoods for fresh fish (Boston Park Plaza Hotel, Columbus Avenue and Arlington Street) and children's specials or the Magic Pan, 47 Newbury Street, with crepes geared to kids.

For some modern-day excitement, try The Skywalk at the Prudential Tower, 617-236-3318. A speedy elevator whisks you up 50 floors in seconds for a wonderful view of Boston.

Beacon Hill

The "Hill" used to be 60 feet higher than it is today, but even though it's flattened some, the area's still the most prestigious spot in town. It's dominated by the Massachusetts State House, a gold-domed building that makes for an interesting tour, and fronts Boston Common and the Public Garden.

The first Bostonian built a house on Beacon Hill in 1622, and the area has held its cachet through the years. The streets are cobblestoned and narrow, and the houses have lots of period architectural detail. Louisburg Square is a lovely, tree-lined spot bound by elegant brick townhouses and is an inviting place to stroll any time of year.

There are a few museums and antique houses to visit here, but they aren't interesting to most children. They'll probably be more thrilled by the Hampshire House at 84 Beacon Street, the prototype for the TV show "Cheers." It's oak-paneled and properly Bostonian and overlooks the Public Garden, a nice spot for a civilized brunch on Sunday.

On Charles Street, you'll find several reasonably priced restaurants and delis, with menus posted in the windows. Rebecca's at 21 Charles Street has a fine reputation as a gourmet food restaurant with an informal setting, where kids can find something good to eat, too.

In the summer, free concerts at the Hatch Shell on Storrow Drive are local traditions. It's best to park in the Underground Garage at Boston Common and walk from Beacon Street over the Arthur Fiedler Footbridge and plant a blanket on the lawn. Also in the summer, but not free, are Concerts on the Common, where pop singers play to thousands on warm nights. Check the *Boston Globe* for the schedule.

Downtown and Chinatown

Bostonians say the busiest intersection in New England is at Washington and Summer Streets, called Downtown Crossing. Six major department stores, including Filene's with its famous basement converge at this pedestrian mall, where street musicians and mimes entertain in all kinds of weather. Within a few blocks you'll find lots of stops on the Freedom Trail, such as Ben Franklin's birthplace marker and the Old South Meeting House. A little of these goes a long way with kids.

Between Downtown Crossing and Back Bay sits the third largest Chinatown in the country, which you enter officially through the Chinese Gate, a gift from Taiwan, at Beach and Edinboro Streets. The area is rough around the edges, filled with markets and shops catering to the community, and many restaurants, all run by Chinese. The best time to visit is Sunday mornings, when many of the restaurants offer *dim sum,* the Chinese brunch that's especially fun for kids. Waiters take trolleys of nibbles around, and you pick what you want while the waiter keeps a running tab. The Imperial Tea House, 70 Beach Street, is a local favorite, so be prepared to wait in line. The festivities during the Chinese New Year feature a day-long parade with firecrackers and dancing dragons.

Boston's theater district, which has shrunk in recent years, is squeezed between these two parts of town. Look in the *Boston Globe's* Thursday calendar section or consult Bostix at Faneuil Hall for what's going on when you're in town. Most of the restaurants here aren't worth a stop.

North End and Haymarket

The North End, Boston's Little Italy, is quickly becoming yup-pified, but it's still a colorful place to visit and to eat in. You can walk there from the Faneuil Hall Marketplace, along Haymarket to Blackstone Street, parking is difficult at best.

Haymarket, along the way, is a venerable Boston tradition, a colorful produce market open Fridays and Saturdays until early evening. Vendors crowd the streets hawking fruits and vegetables from pushcarts, and bargaining is acceptable behavior. Kids will be amazed at the wholesale meat markets housed in small storefronts along the street. Other stores are crammed with cheese, fish, and specialty foods that are hard to find in other places. Haymarket's appealing because it's still real, not a contemporary version of an upscale market, like Faneuil Hall.

The North End has been home to generations of European immigrants, most recently to Italian families, and although the area is changing, there's still a strong neighborhood flavor in the narrow streets, bakeries, and restaurants, where you'll hear as much Italian as English. The stores are fun for browsing, and there are so many restaurants the best bet is to look at posted menus before you make a choice. The European, at 218 Hanover Street, has a children's menu and offers all Italian dishes, with pizza a favorite. Regina Pizzeria at 11½ Thatcher Street, the original restaurant in what is now a chain, serves pizza only in a plain atmosphere. You'll probably have to wait for a booth.

After lunch or dinner, stop in one of the cafés featuring Italian bakery items and cappuccino and feel like you're in Europe for a while.

Several points on the Freedom Trail are here in the North End, including Rose Fitzgerald Kennedy's birthplace, the Paul Revere House, and the site of Benjamin Franklin's boyhood home.

Italian feast days are still celebrated here with parades, and they draw huge crowds from all over the city.

Kids in need of a rest would enjoy a stop at the North End branch of the Boston Public Library. There are a nice children's area and a diorama of the ducal palace in Venice.

The Waterfront and Faneuil Hall Marketplace

You can spend several days in Boston with children and never leave this area, because it's chock full of things to do with kids. The big attractions are all the museums and dozens of eating spots.

Durgin Park, a Boston eating institution, is in this part of town. The atmosphere's rough and rowdy, you share tables covered with checkered cloths, and the portions, of favorites such as prime ribs and Indian pudding, are huge. Prices are reasonable, but you'll probably have to stand in line for a table.

First, the museums. On the waterfront, start with Museum Wharf, where you'll find the Children's Museum, the Computer Museum, and the Tea Party Ship and Museum, all accessible via the South Station or Aquarium T stop and within a few blocks of each other.

THE CHILDREN'S MUSEUM (300 Congress Street, Zip: 02210, 617-426-8855). A fabulous place. It is an example of participation learning at its very best. Toddlers can jump and slide in Playspace while older kids run up and down the Climbing Sculpture. Our kids loved "Mind Your Own Business, an Exhibit about You and Your Body" and "The Estimating Game." There are changing tables, strollers, a restaurant (a McDonald's branch), and small-size drinking fountains. Leave enough time for kids to go back to their favorite exhibits; there will be many. And try to participate in a workshop (there are even overnights once in a while!).

BOSTON TEA PARTY SHIP AND MUSEUM (Congress Street Bridge, Zip: 02110, 617-338-1773). Where Boston's most notorious protest is re-created. You can explore a replica of the original ship and even toss some tea overboard. Older kids especially like the "Where Do You Stand?" exhibit, which explores the issue of protest. Strollers are allowed.

THE COMPUTER MUSEUM (300 Congress Street, Zip: 02110, 617-426-2800). As the world's only museum devoted solely to computers and their impact on society, it has the finest collection of vintage robots and computers ever assembled. Sixty dynamic hands-on exhibits invite adults and kids alike to make friends with the future. Kids can play with robot toys, tryout an antique keypunch machine or the Apollo Guidance Computer. After watching robot and computer animation shows, they can design a car, "fly" a plane, create an animated movie, play with an image of their face, or talk with a computer. Strollers are allowed, and there are guided tours every Saturday and Sunday at 1:30 and again at 3:00.

For older children, the John F. Kennedy Library across the bay at Columbia Point is an exciting stop. Walk up to Central Wharf to get to the Aquarium.

NEW ENGLAND AQUARIUM (Central Wharf, Zip: 02110, 617-973-5200). Its center is a 187,000-gallon ocean tank that spirals to the ceiling. As you walk up the ramp alongside the tank, sharks, huge sea turtles, and moray eels watch your progress. In all, there are more than 70 exhibits that feature marine life from as far as India and the Amazon and as near as the waters of New England. The "Edge of the Sea" tidepool exhibit, where kids are encouraged to pick up and touch a variety of creatures, is popular with the littlest visitors. The dolphin and sea lion show is another kids' favorite. Facilities include a snack bar, ramps, and small-size drinking fountains; strollers are allowed.

In the summer, you can get to the Boston Harbor Island via ferries from Long Wharf. The free service, run by the Boston Harbor Island State Park, stops at six islands, where you can picnic, camp, swim, and explore historic ruins. Ferries run from May 30 to September 30.

The playground and the view from Waterfront Park (or Christopher Columbus Park) are worth a stop.

After the museums, cross over Atlantic Avenue to get to Faneuil Hall Marketplace, a complex of three 500-foot-long buildings dating back to 1826. The copper-domed central building houses stand-up food spots featuring everything from frozen yogurt to gourmet potato chips to every kind of ethnic food you can imagine. Across the street from Faneuil Hall is equally popular Quincy Market.

Let kids pick what they want to eat, and picnic on a bench outside on the cobblestoned, traffic-free mall, where street entertainers and special events keep the place hopping all year long. This is also a good place to let kids go free with a few dollars in their pockets, because pushcarts sell all the little things they like to buy. Lots of specialty shops and trendy boutiques mix with the restaurants.

Another Boston Feature

The Boston Museum of Science, located in Science Park along the Charles River, is 200 yards away from the MBTA's Science Park Station on the Lechmere Green Line, 617-723-2500. This is an "interactive, participatory" museum with more than 400 exhibits and live animal shows, demonstrations, and special weekend presentations. One of its most popular features is Omnimax, a movie with images that fill a seven-story-high dome. The museum includes a popular dinosaur exhibit, planetarium shows, Computer Place, the Theatre of Electricity, and more. It is a wonderful place. For changing diapers or nursing you can use the first-aid room; there are two restaurants with high chairs, a children's gift shop, and small-size drinking fountains.

Time Out

For baby-sitting contact Parents in a Pinch, 45 Bartlett Crescent, Brookline, Massachusetts 02146, 617-739-KIDS. Sitters are trained, screened, Red Cross–certified child care professionals and available for days, evenings, weekends, and overnights. The co-owners Barbara Marcus and Davida Manon say that it's best to call at least 24-48 hours in advance. The rates are $12 per hour for one child, with a four-hour minimum, 50 cents extra for each additional sibling. Transportation costs are additional. Most hotels also provide baby-sitting; some at substantially lower prices.

Accommodations

Bed and Breakfasts

For a free guide to bed and breakfast accommodations and guest houses in Massachusetts with some in Boston, call 800-343-9072 and ask for *The Spirit of Massachusetts Bed and Breakfast Guide*, or order by mail from the Massachusetts Division of Tourism, 100 Cambridge Street, Boston, Massachusetts 02202. Remember, too, to check the bed and breakfast books listed in Chapter 4.

Two bed and breakfast services that specialize in rooms in the Boston area are New England Bed and Breakfast, Inc., 1045 Centre Street, Newton Centre, Massachusetts 02159, 617-244-2112 or 498-9819; and Greater Boston Hospitality, P. O. Box 1142, Brookline, Massachusetts 02146, 617-277-5430. The latter sent some sample listings: A four-story townhouse on Beacon Hill with rooms with private bath and an English breakfast served in a Queen Anne style dining room for $50 for two; $15 for a child in an adjoining room; a 1940 custom-built home in Brookline with play areas for kids, a sun deck, and free breakfast for $35 to $60 per night, no charge for children under 1 year.

Hotels

FOUR SEASONS (200 Boylston Street, Zip: 02116, 617-338-4400 or 800-332-3442). This beautiful hotel, right on the Commons, provides lots of nice extras for kids. One of the nicest is the duck food that the staff will give you at check-in time so that you can go right over to the Commons to feed the ducks that were immortalized in *Make Way for Ducklings*. At bed time, the kids will find snacks waiting for them; baby blankets, bottles, and lotion are all available, and if you've forgotten your stroller, they'll supply one. A special family rate allows you to rent two rooms for the single rate—a room with king-size bed costs $195 and connects with a room with two twins for $215.

GUEST QUARTERS SUITE HOTEL (400 Soldiers Field Road, Zip: 02134, 617-783-0090 or 800-424-2900). All of the one-bedroom suites include a living room, bedroom, bath, refrigerator, wet bar, two color televisions, and three telephones. All of the suites overlook a skylit atrium. A complimentary continental breakfast is included in the rate, and the hotel has an indoor pool, a whirlpool, and a sauna. Rates are $123 for Friday or Saturday night; $165 and up on weeknights. The hotel is located on the Charles River, on the Boston/Cambridge line, and there's a free shuttle service to central sites in Cambridge and Boston. Baby-sitting can be arranged, and special weekend packages, including full American breakfasts are available. Our friends spent a weekend at Guest Quarters and loved it. Their kids were crazy about the pool. One suggestion, though: It's best to have a car, since the location is a bit off the beaten tourist path.

THE MIDTOWN HOTEL (220 Huntington Avenue, Zip: 02115, 617-262-1000 or 800-343-1177). The basic rate is $79 for a double room, and kids under 18 stay free with their parents. Free underground parking is a plus, and in nice weather, the outdoor pool is fun. This hotel is conveniently located not far from Boston Common.

THE RITZ-CARLTON (15 Arlington Street, Zip: 02117, 617-536-5700). Right by the Boston Public Garden, this elegant hotel offers "a weekend of social savvy" for kids several times during the year—"Children should be seen and heard at this refined and recreational weekend designed to practice and polish their social skills." There aren't many other programs like this one; it includes a grand tour of the 60-year-old hotel, and instruction and demonstration in table setting, table manners, food preparation, grooming, and dancing in preparation for a Saturday night dance. Kids stay in twin-bedded rooms; the fee is $200. The suggested ages are 8 to 12. Parents staying at the hotel while their kids participate in the social savvy weekend pay a special rate of $150 for a room. These weekends are held throughout the winter on seven different dates.

SHERATON BOSTON HOTEL AND TOWERS (Prudential Center, Zip: 02190, 617-236-2000 or 800-325-3535). The lowest rate is $55 per person; kids under 17 always stay free in their parents' room. The hotel has a glass-covered indoor pool and its own health club. Cribs are provided free, and baby-sitting is available through the House-keeping Department for $4.75 per hour with a three-hour minimum.

There's no Hyatt property in Boston but there is one in Cambridge, at 575 Memorial Drive, 02139. See page 50 for what Hyatt offers families; call 800-233-1234 for details on the Cambridge location.

CHICAGO

Chicago is a spectacular-looking city, with its lakefront its most striking feature. Scattered along the shore are playgrounds, picnic sites, and marinas—all wonderful places to stop to rest or play. Lake Michigan is almost always within walking distance of wherever you are. You can visit a museum in the morning, sail on a lake, and take a swim in the afternoon, depending only on your own two feet for transportation.

For anyone with an interest in architecture, Chicago is a dream—you'll find the works of Louis Sullivan, Frank Lloyd Wright, and Mies van der Rohe and two outstanding examples of the architecture of the 1970s, the Sears Tower and the John Hancock Building. To see some spectacular outdoor sculpture, walk from the Archicenter (330 South Dearborn) north on Dearborn to see Calder's "Flamingo" on the Federal Center Plaza; Chagall's "Four Seasons," a mosaic, on the First National Bank Plaza (be there at lunchtime in summer for free entertainment); Miro's "Chicago" and Picasso's "Lady" facing each other on Daley Plaza across from City Hall; and Dubuffet's "Monument with Standing Beast" in front of the State of

Illinois Center, where you can wander in, explore the atrium, and ride the glass elevators. Chicago starts to celebrate every year as soon as the weather gets nice. From June to August there are concerts by the Chicago Symphony Orchestra at the Ravinia Festival in Highland Park (easily reached by special train at concert time) and free concerts in Grant Park; take a picnic supper and make yourself comfortable on the lawn. For information on these special events, call 312-744-3315.

The best guidebook to the city for families is not available at bookstores—it's called *Chicago: A Child's Kind of Town* and is published by the Department of Child Psychiatry, The Children's Memorial Hospital, 2300 Children's Plaza, Chicago, Illinois 60614. It costs $4.50, is available by mail, and is an excellent guide to everything the city has to offer that is of special interest to kids, with good advice on taking excursions with kids, and even some connect-the-dot activity pages to keep the kids busy while on line or in buses. We wish they'd update this one—it hasn't been revised for quite a while.

A more standard source of information on the city is the Chicago Tourism Council located at the Water Tower, Michigan and Chicago Avenues, 312-280-5740. Call to order information on Chicago or, if you wait until you're in the city, stop at their Visitor's Center, across the street at 163 East Pearson in the Pumping Station. (The phone number's the same.) Be sure to tell the folks at the Council that you are coming with your kids and they will send, besides the regular tourist information, a list of attractions for kids and restaurants that especially welcome kids. They'll also enclose a two-for-one coupon for Here's Chicago (see below) and a combination coloring/guide book to the city called *A Kid's Guide to Chicago,* which has been put together by the people at the Sheraton Plaza hotel.

The Tourism Council also offers two special vacation packages each year—one in summer called "Summer in Chicago" and the other at holiday time called "Wrap up a Holiday Package." Both include discounts at any of 38 hotels, 40 coupons with special deals for a variety of tourist possibilities—museums, dinner theaters, sightseeing tours, and jazz clubs—and a special rate on Midway Airlines.

For general information on the city, pick up a copy of *Chicago Magazine,* a monthly that you'll find at newsstands all around town. But, for more child-oriented information, get a copy of *Chicago Parent,* a monthly available free in family-type locations. Call them at 312-508-0973 if you're having trouble finding a copy. (Their address is 7001 North Clark Street, Chicago, Illinois 60626; send them $2 for a current issue.) Another Chicago-based publication just for parents is called *Mother's Network News* and is designed specifically for kids 4 years old and under. It includes events such as storytelling, classes for kids, and workshops. Copies are $3 each and are available by mail from P. O. Box 11569, Chicago, Illinois 60611, or by phone, 312-642-3022. A year's subscription, six issues and three "Special Reports," costs $20.

Tours and Overviews

A good starting point for your Chicago adventure is "Here's Chicago," a multiimage show about the city that's located in the Water Tower Pumping Station. The first show starts at 10:00 A.M. and shows run continuously every half-hour. Admission is $4.75 for adults, $2 for kids 12 and under. Call 312-467-7114 for details.

And for kids who like to get a view from the top, we suggest the 39-second elevator ride up to the Observatory of the John Hancock Center. From the observatory you'll be able to see Chicago, Lake Michigan, and the three-state surrounding area, 80 miles on a clear day. By renting an "audio wand" for $1.50 you can hear all about Chicago and the observatory while you're up there. The admission is $3.50 for adults, $2 for kids 5 to 15, and free for kids under 5.

Another spectacular view from the top is possible from the 103rd floor Skydeck of the Sears Tower. Call 312-875-9696 for details.

If a boat tour on Lake Michigan appeals to you, call Wendella Sightseeing Boats, 312-337-1446. One- and two-hour tours are available. The boats operate from May 30 through Labor Day. And Mercury-Skyline Tours, across the lake from Wendella, 312-332-1353, offers regular tours as well as a special one for kids called "The Wacky Pirate Cruise" on weekends.

And for those who prefer to remain on dry land, consider the Chicago Transit Authority's Culture Buses. The three routes all start at the Art Institute and stop along the way at all the museums and other points of interest in town. You can hop on and off whenever you want. The culture buses run from mid-May to the end of September, and they leave every 20 to 30 minutes. Call 312-836-7000 for information.

Things to See and Do

We've grouped Chicago's attractions from north to south in walkable clusters. Parks are always nearby. You can get to almost all the places listed here by riding the CTA's Culture Bus.

Navy Pier

This is where lots of Chicago's special events are held. It's a popular spot for families out for a picnic on a weekend afternoon.

EXPRESS-WAYS CHILDREN'S MUSEUM (435 East Illinois Street, Zip: 60611, 312-527-1000). This is a relatively new location for the museum with 21,000 square feet—more than three times the space of its former Lincoln Park location. Preschoolers can crawl through the tunnel at "Touchy Business," explore the home of the Three Bears, and have fun learning about the "Art and Science of Bubbles." Older kids (up to 12 generally) like "Magic and Masquerades"—an exhibit of West African art and tradition; "City Hospital" complete with an ambulance, wheel chair obstacle course, and plaster casting room; "Quilts Tell Stories" with a changing array of quilts from all over the world; and "Amazing Chicago"—a mini-metropolis with architectural treasure hunts. The museum sponsors workshops every weekend with a different theme each month for kids from 3 to 14 (ages vary with workshops). Special events are also held throughout the year. Admission is $3 for adult and $2 for kids. You'll find changing rooms in both the men's and the women's restrooms and there's a quiet spot set out in the "Touchy Business" exhibit for nursing mothers.

Lincoln Park

LINCOLN PARK ZOO (2200 North Cannon Drive, Zip: 60614, 312-294-4660). The zoo is home to 2,000 animals. Guided tours, films, and talks about animals are scheduled daily. You can watch the elephant workout or check out the nation's largest polar bear pool. The younger kids will like the Farm-in-the-Zoo and the Children's Zoo, which encourage real close-up observation. The zoo is free, and we recommend it. It's compact and easy to navigate with kids.

Grant Park Area

The following five places of interest are all close to the greenery of the lakefront and Grant Park—perfect for stretching out and having picnics or boat rides.

THE FIELD MUSEUM OF NATURAL HISTORY (Roosevelt Road at Lake Shore Drive, Zip: 60605, 312-992-9410). One of the largest and most famous museums in the world, The Field is a favorite of kids. There are nine acres of exhibits and special displays: dinosaurs, Egyptian mummies, and a "Place for Wonder," a treasure room full of touchable displays for all ages. At the "Pawnee Earth Lodge" you can hear songs and stories of Indian life, and on weekends there are often family programs and tours. The museum is open 9:00 A.M. to 5:00 P.M. Admission is $3 for adults, $2 for kids 2 to 17, free for kids under 2 and $10 for families. Thursdays are free for everyone.

THE ADLER PLANETARIUM (1300 South Lake Shore Drive, Zip: 60605, 312-322-0300). The Sky Show is for kids 6 and over; the younger ones have a special children's version on Saturdays and Sundays at 10:00 A.M. The planetarium is open every day. Boat rides depart from the planetarium, so when you've finished looking around inside, why not get some fresh air out on the lake? The admission to the planetarium is free; the Sky Show costs $3 for adults, $1.50 for kids 6 to 17. Special astronomy and space science workshops are held on Saturday mornings throughout the year.

JOHN G. SHEDD AQUARIUM (1200 South Lake Shore Drive, Zip: 60605, 312-939-2438). They call this Chicago's "Ocean by the Lake." It contains 7,000 animals of more than 700 species. The six major galleries take the visitor on a journey through six major aquatic areas, and there are more than 160 exhibits in all. Kids especially like the Coral Reef Exhibit, where the diver enters, feeds the animals, and then talks to visitors through a microphone in the dive mask about the sharks, sea turtles, money eels, and other colorful reef fish in the exhibit. "Tributaries," an area with smaller tanks, and the "Shark Exhibit" are kid pleasers, too.

Workshops are offered all year long for kids 3 to 4 and 5 to 16; kids under 4 must be accompanied by an adult. Behind-the-scenes tours for kids 8 and up can be arranged. There are infant changing tables in the men's and women's rooms, and a gift shop, and strollers are allowed at all times. Admission is $3 adults, $2 kids 6–17.

JUNIOR MUSEUM OF THE ART INSTITUTE (Michigan Avenue at Adams Street, Zip: 60603, 312-443-3600). The Junior Musuem of this larger, world-famous museum features exhibitions designed especially for kids, focusing on works in the museum's permanent collection or related to special exhibitions. Workshops are available throughout the year. Kids 4 to 6 with their parents have their own Early Bird Workshops, and kids 7 and older and their parents have

Family Workshops that include a gallery visit and related art activity. Gallery walks are available to kids 9 and older and their parents on Saturdays, and storytelling and drawing in the galleries are scheduled on Sundays. Each month a different artist works in a different medium while people of all ages look on, and every day there are gallery games and self-guides available. Just check at the Little Library for scheduling. Special holiday workshops are held during the week between Christmas and New Year's Day. The museum offers many services to families: There are infant changing tables in the women's restroom. Strollers are generally allowed (a few special exhibits are exceptions). There are a cafeteria complete with booster seats, a children's gift shop, small-size drinking fountains, and self-guided tape tours for special exhibits.

CHICAGO PUBLIC LIBRARY (Cultural Center, Thomas Hughes Children's Library, 78 East Washington Street, Zip: 60602, 312-269-2835). This library schedules programs for kids from preschool age through eighth grade. During the school year, programs generally take place on Saturday mornings at 11:00. Children's programs are listed in the Cultural Center Calendar of Events and are all free of charge. In summer, the library and the Council on Fine Arts combine to present a series of kids' programs, including puppet shows, drama, music, storytelling, book talks, and appearances by authors and illustrators.

A permanent display in the library may interest your kids, too; it's a storybook dollhouse that contains clues to over 60 children's stories, poems, and nursery rhymes. A nice idea!

Hyde Park Area

MUSEUM OF SCIENCE AND INDUSTRY (57th Street and Lake Shore Drive, Zip: 60637, 312-684-1414). Admission and parking are free for this, the oldest, largest, and according to their staff, most popular contemporary science and technology museum in the nation. Every year 4 million people visit! Most of the exhibits are three-dimensional and participatory; visitors push buttons, turn cranks, operate computers, lift levers, and activate recorded messages. There's nothing passive about a visit to this museum. Younger kids like "Curiosity Place," a preschool science exhibit, and they're always fascinated by the hatching chicks in the "Food for Life" exhibit. The older kids seem to like the World War II German U-505 submarine, Colleen Moore's fairy castle, a full-scale replica of an underground coal mine, the Henry Crown Space Center with the actual *Apollo 8* capsule, the Omnimax Theater, and the National Business Hall of Fame. Call and ask about workshops and summer camp for kids.

The museum offers infant changing tables, a restaurant, and small-size drinking fountains. It allows strollers at all times.

DU SABLE MUSEUM OF AFRICAN AMERICAN HISTORY (740 East 56th Street and Cottage Grove, Zip: 60637, 312-947-0600). Not far from the Museum of Science and Industry, you'll find demonstrations of African instruments, films, lectures, and guided tours for all ages. Workshops are held throughout the year to supplement special events such as the Heritage Book Festival, the Kwanzaa Celebration, and the Martin Luther King, Jr. holiday.

Reflecting the polyglot character of Chicago are a number of other ethnic museums scattered throughout the city that may interest you and your kids. We've already mentioned the Du Sable, but there are more: The Balzekas Museum of Lithuanian Culture, 6500 South Pulaski Road, 312-847-2441, includes a children's museum with Lithuanian artifacts, hands-on exhibits, and arts workshops; the Polish Museum of America, 984 North Milwaukee Avenue, 312-384-3352, features folk art and costumes with one-hour tours available; Spertus Museum of Judaica, 618 South Michigan Avenue, 312-922-9012, the Midwest's best and most complete Jewish museum with a wonderful new Artifacts Center where kids can participate in a make-believe archaeological dig; Swedish-American Museum of Chicago, 5248 North Clark Street, 312-728-8111, features exhibitions demonstrating the contributions of Swedes to American culture (hours vary, so call ahead for details); Ukrainian National Museum, 2453 West Chicago Avenue, 312-276-6565, has exhibits of ceramics, wood and metal carvings, Ukrainian Easter eggs, and costumes. The hours of many of these ethnic museums are erratic, so be sure to call ahead for details.

And one more possibility: The Children's Theater of Second City performs a show for kids at 1616 North Wells every Sunday at 2:30 P.M. The shows are either original scripts written by the director or created by the cast through improvisation. After the show, kids can go onto the stage with the actors and participate in theater games. For information, call 312-929-6288.

Time Out

ART RESOURCE STUDIO (2828 North Clark, Zip: 60657, 312-975-1671). Located on the lower level of the Century Mall, a onetime vaudeville theater. On weekends the studio offers what they call Child-Free Shopping—from 1:30 to 6:30 on Saturdays and 1:30 to 4:30 on Sundays they'll entertain your kids (3 to 10) while you shop. The cost is $6 per hour. During the week the studio offers a variety of one- to two-hour arts and crafts workshops for kids 3 to 16. Drop-ins are fine. Call for details.

AMERICAN REGISTRY FOR NURSES AND SITTERS (3921 North Lincoln, Zip: 60613, 312-248-8100). A more conventional way of entertaining your kids while you're off doing grown-up things is this service that is open from 9:00 to 5:00 Monday through Fridays, 9:00 to 1:00 on Saturdays. It's been operating since 1950 and is bonded. The rate is $7 per hour, 25 cents more each hour for additional children, with a four-hour minimum plus cab fare after 9:00 P.M. Advance notice is recommended, but "don't hesitate to call the same day."

Accommodations

Bed and Breakfast

BED AND BREAKFAST, CHICAGO, INC. (P. O. Box 14088, Zip: 60614-0088, 312-951-0085). This reservation service offers accommodations in private homes or in what they call "self-catering" apartments. For families, the owner of the service, Mary Shaw, recommends self-contained units. During holiday and vacation times, she often has vacant homes available, many complete with toys, cribs, and so on. Apartments start at $65 per night, with weekly and monthly rates available. We discovered two tempting possibilities: a self-contained, twin-bedded garden apartment with a sofa sleeper in the living room located in the heart of Old Town for $65 per night; and a two-bedroom, two-bath apartment with a wood-burning fireplace, a greenhouse, and a backyard with play equipment for $150 per night or $1,500 per month.

Hotels

DAYS INN (644 North Lake Shore Drive, Zip: 60611, 312-943-9200 or 800-325-2525). Located opposite the Navy Pier (that's where the Express-ways Children's Museum is) eight blocks from the Water Tower and two blocks from McCormick Place, this urban property of the budget chain offers rates as low as $49 per night double occupancy. The rate is called the Super-Saver and requires a 29-day advance reservation. Other special rates of $75 are available on shorter notice; kids under 18 stay free. There's an outdoor pool and nice views from every room. Baby-sitting is available for $8 per hour.

THE DRAKE (140 East Walton, Zip: 60611, 312-787-2200 or 800-445-8667). The Drake welcomes kids and lets them stay in their parents' room at no extra charge. Across the street from the hotel are a playground and a place to swim at the Oak Street beach. In the Drake's Oak Terrace Restaurant, kids 6–12 pay half-price for their meals, kids under 6 are free. Baby-sitting can be arranged through the Housekeeping Department. Regular room rates begin at $180 for a double, but weekend packages start at $125.

RITZ-CARLTON (160 East Pearson Street, Zip: 60611-0142, 312-266-1000 or 1-800-621-6906). Kids are treated to special services at the Ritz, and they're all listed on an information card, "Ritz-Carlton Services Especially for Kids." The concierge will tell you what's happening especially for kids while you're in Chicago; strollers are available at no charge to hotel guests, and baby-sitting is available for $4 per hour for a four-hour minimum. The housekeeping staff will supply games, coloring books, and crayons for the kids and some very practical baby supplies such as bathtubs, shampoo, bottle warmers, cribs, cots, diapers, and high chairs. The café has a special menu for kids under 12, and just across the street from the hotel there's a fenced-in playground, and only three blocks away is the Oak Street Beach.

The Ritz "Family Package," which includes two rooms, one with a king-size bed and one with two twins, costs $325 per night. Weekend packages called "Adventure Chicago" cost $155 per night for a queen-size or twin-bedded room and includes use of the hotel's health club. Kids can stay free in the room with parents. These packages are available Thursday, Friday, and Saturday nights only.

There are two Hyatts in Chicago—one at 151 East Wacker Drive, 60601, the other at 800 North Michigan Avenue, 60611. See page 50 for what you can expect for the family from Hyatt, and call 800-233-1234 for details and prices on these two properties.

LOS ANGELES

Another city that's fun for kids, Los Angeles has a sprawl that needs some getting used to. Good planning is the key to your vacation in L.A. Plan your sightseeing around a car; take your own or rent one. We've arranged the section on things to do and see here by area so that you can avoid the traffic as much as possible.

For Information

You should most definitely have a copy of *L.A. Parent,* a tabloid-size newspaper published monthly and distributed at places that cater to families. The day-by-day calendar of events in every issue is invaluable for planning your stay. Reprints from back issues on subjects such as "The Best Baby-sitting Agencies," "Child's View of Chinatown," and "Daytrips for Toddlers" are available from the publisher for $2. Write to Box 3204, Burbank, California 91504, or call 818-846-0400. A guidebook we recommend is *Places to Go with Children in Southern California,* by Stephanie Regan, published by Chronicle Books ($9.95). The book will help you have fun in L.A. and beyond.

A new and welcome addition to the library of books on travel with kids is *Frommer's California with Kids* by Carey Simn and Charlene Marmer Solomon (Prentice Hall, $4.95). The book is well-organized, thoroughly researched, and written in an easygoing style. From San Francisco and the North Coast right down to Tijuana, the guide covers a wide range of family-tested activities, attractions, accommodations and restaurants in all kinds of settings, all kinds of price ranges. It is especially handy because it follows our theory of cluster sightseeing whether in the city or out on the road. The authors, both parents, provide information, too, that other books often overlook: whether restaurants have booster seats, high chairs, and children's menus; which will warm bottles and baby food, children's rates and more.

Happily, one of Harcourt Brace Jovanovich's Gulliver Travels series is *A Kid's Guide to Southern California,* which obviously includes lots of material on Los Angeles and its surrounding area. This is a terrific new series of guides for kids, and we applaud the publisher and compilers for giving such good and interesting background on the area, games to play, and suggestions for what to see and do. Get a copy of this one ($6.95) before you set out on your trip so that the kids have plenty of time to read it and pick out what they want to do while they're in L.A.

And for good, general guides to L.A., we like Tom and Karen Horton's *Dolphin Guide to Los Angeles,* which also tells you what kids might like to do in that town and *Hidden Los Angeles,* published by Ulysses Press ($12.95).

For general tourist information, maps, and advice on what's worth doing and seeing, contact the Greater Los Angeles Visitors and Convention Bureau, 515 South Figueroa Street, 11/E, Los Angeles 90071, 213-624-7300.

To plan for side trips from Los Angeles, take a look at Mike Michaelson's *Weekends Away: Los Angeles,* published by E. P. Dutton ($9.95), which lists 120 trips to take within 200 miles of the city. Michaelson's suggestions go as far south as Ensenada, north to Fresno, and east all the way to Las Vegas. They're coded to show you which trips are best for families.

An interesting possibility: For those of you whose kids are TV or movie fans, we've come across an unusual way for you to explore while you're in Los Angeles. The folks at "Hollywood on Location" can tell you exactly where and when you can find the stars of television, movies, and music videos filming around Los Angeles. Each weekday at 9:30A.M. they publish a new "Location List" telling you what's being filmed where, who is involved, and the address and times of location sites. On a typical day, there's an average of 35 different locations, almost all within a ten-mile radius with filming going on until dawn. For $29 you and your family get a Location List and a large map pinpointing locations. According to our contact at On Location, there are no age restrictions when filming is on location, but there are limits for studio tapings. For a brochure, a sample list, and map, send a self-addressed envelope to 8644 Wilshire Boulevard, Suite 204V, Beverly Hills, California 90211, or phone 213-659-9165.

Things to See and Do

Downtown

LOS ANGELES CHILDREN'S MUSEUM (310 North Main Street, Zip: 90012, 213-687-8800). This ten year old museum offers a hands-on environment for kids aged 2 to 12. This is a place full of energy and excitement with a recording studio that kids can use; "Ethnic L.A.," a Mexican-American and a Japanese-American environment; "Zoetrope," the animators' workship with a neon Mickey Mouse to oversee the activities; "H.E.L.P.," the Health Education Learning Project, which depicts a doctor's office and an emergency room; "City Street," where kids have a chance to drive a bus, ride a policeman's motorcycle, and pretend to be a fireman; and one of the favorite exhibits of all, a working television studio. The littlest kids—

3 and under—also love the "Softspace," lots of cozy foam for crawling. Throughout the year there are special workshops and performances, with folk singers, puppet shows, preschool arts and crafts classes, improvisational theater, and a how-to-make-sushi demonstration. During the summer, the museum operates wonderful "Inside L.A." tours that require advance registration. Last summer the excursions included trips to a drum factory, Dodger Stadium, a toy factory, a shipyard, and a tortilla factory. Costs are $7 to $10, and tours last from one to two hours each. The Children's Museum has infant changing tables in the men's and women's rooms, strollers are allowed, and there are small-size drinking fountains.

Right near the Children's Museum is Olvera Sreet, the oldest street in Los Angeles. Now it's a touristy Mexican-American area with lots of shops and restaurants. Little Tokyo's not far from here either, located between Alameda and Los Angeles Streets and First and Third Streets.

LOS ANGELES PHILHARMONIC SYMPHONIES FOR YOUTH (135 North Grand Avenue, Zip: 90012, 213-972-0703). The Philharmonic presents six specially designed concerts for kids throughout the school year. The fun begins one hour before performance time in the lobby with a workshop presented by the staff of the Children's Museum. Lobby activities begin at 9:00 A.M., concerts last from 10:15 to 11:15 A.M.—just the right amount of time for kids.

In summer the symphony sponsors a six-week multicultural performing arts festival for kids 5 and up. A performing arts or crafts workshop follows an Open House performance of a music, dance, or theater piece. You can also sit in on a rehearsal of the Philharmonic and picnic in one of the Hollywood Bowl's areas set aside for just that purpose. Call 213-850-2077 for information.

South Central Los Angeles

NATURAL HISTORY MUSEUM OF LOS ANGELES COUNTY (900 Exposition Boulevard, Zip: 90007, 213-744-DINO or 213-744-3414). This is the third largest museum of its kind in the United States with what you'd expect—collections of fossils, exhibits of earth sciences and life sciences, and areas devoted to archaeology, gems and minerals, mammals, marine biology, and, of course, dinosaurs. Younger kids love the dinosaurs, the La Brea fossils, and the Discovery Center best. Older kids like the antique autos, the gems and minerals, and the Discovery Center too. Children's workshops are scheduled throughout the year. One recent one was called "Dinosaurs and Their Kin: From Allosaurus to Zanclodon." In June, the museum presents it Festival of Folk Art; in December, it holds a Native American Indian Festival and at Christmas vacation time, special films and activities are featured. Strollers are always allowed; it has a restaurant open from 10:00 A.M. to 4:00 P.M. and a Children's Gift Shop. Museum hours are 10:00 A.M. to 5:00 P.M. Tuesday through Sunday; Discovery Center hours are 11:00 A.M. to 3:00 P.M. Admission is free on the first Tuesday of the month; otherwise it's $3 for adults, $1.50 for students 12–17; 75 cents for kids 5–12; and free for under 5.

Los Feliz and Hollywood

Griffith Park is the largest municipal park in the United States with 4,000 acres of picnic areas, playgrounds, hiking trails, bridle paths, a miniature railroad, pony and stage coach rides, a nature center, and a carousel. Travel Town is an outdoor museum in the park where kids can climb on the transportation. You can easily spend a whole day and evening here.

GRIFFITH OBSERVATORY (2800 East Observatory Road, Zip: 90027, 213-664-1191). The planetarium transports you to times and places way beyond the realm of everyday existence—to all parts of the solar system, to Stonehenge or ancient Egypt or beyond the Milky Way. Shows last an hour and change several times a year. Admission is $2.75 for kids 16 and over and $1.50 for those 5 to 15. Kids under 5 are admitted only to the 1:30 show and other special children's shows.

In the observatory's Hall of Science, exhibits include the Foucault Pendulum, the Solar Telescope, six-foot earth and moon globes, and meteorites; tours are given throughout the day.

LOS ANGELES ZOO (5333 Zoo Drive, Zip: 90027, 213-666-4090). Located in Griffith Park, the zoo costs $4.50 for adults and $2.00 for kids 2–12, and is free for kids under 2. Here you can see 2,000 animals in natural settings, ride an elephant or camel, see the "World of Birds" or "Meet the Elephants" shows. The new children's zoo, Adventure Island, includes a hacienda farmyard with pettable animals, baby animal nursery, and a theater with shows for kids year-round.

Strollers may be rented for $2. Give yourself two to four hours to "do" the zoo.

Mid-Wilshire

GEORGE C. PAGE MUSEUM OF LA BREA DISCOVERIES (5801 Wilshire Boulevard, Zip: 90036-4596, 213-936-2230 for a recorded message; 857-6311 during msueum hours). The Page Museum was built to house a heritage of over 1 million Ice Age mammals, birds, and plant specimens recovered from the world-renowned La Brea asphalt deposits or "tar pits," as they're more commonly called. The museum features more than 30 separate exhibits, including reconstructed skeletons of sabertooth cats, mammoths, wolves, and other animals. The "La Brea Story," a 15-minute multimedia introductory film, is a favorite of kids who visit, and the older ones especially like the glass-walled paleontology lab. Admission is $3.00 for adults, 75 cents for kids 5 to 12, $1.50 for students, and free for under 5's and on the second Tuesday of each month. The museum is located right in Hancock Park. Strollers are okay; there are a children's gift shop and small-size drinking fountains. Although there's no restaurant at Page, there's a refreshment stand in front of the museum, and Hancock Park, where the museum is located, is perfect for picnics. Hours are 10:00 A.M. to 5:00 P.M. Tuesday through Sunday.

BOB BAKER MARIONETTE THEATER (1345 West First Street, Zip: 90026, 213-250-9995). This theater has been in the same spot for over 25 years and is the country's oldest marionette theater in continuous operation. Showtimes are usually Saturdays and Sundays at 2:30; extra performances are scheduled during Easter, summer, and Christmas vacations. Admission is $7 and includes the performance, a tour of the group's workshop, and refreshments. Reservations are a must.

Beyond the City

If you have the time to venture beyond city limits, here are some possibilities your kids should like:

NBC STUDIOS (3000 West Alameda Avenue, Burbank, California 91523, 818-840-3537). This is the only network that opens its doors to you. Tours give you a look at the largest TV studios in the world, where the "Tonight Show" and many daytime game shows are filmed. Admission is $6 for adults, $4 for kids. You'll learn how a show is put together and how it goes from an idea all the way to television sets all over the United States. The 75-minute walking tour goes off every half-hour from 9:00 to 4:00 on weekdays, 10:00 to 4:00 on Saturdays, and 10:00 to 2:00 on Sundays. For free tickets to any of the shows, go the ticket counter, which is open 8:30 to 4:00 weekdays; 10:00 to 4:00 Saturdays and 10:00 to 2:00 Sundays. The minimum age limit is generally 8 years old, but to be in the audience of the "Tonight Show," kids have to be at least 16. You can write in advance of your visit to "Tickets" at the address listed, giving the name of the show you want to see and the number of tickets you need and enclosing a self-addressed stamped envelope.

UNIVERSAL STUDIOS HOLLYWOOD (100 Universal City Plaza, Universal City, California 91608, 818-508-9600). Set aside a full day for a behind-the-scenes look at the world's biggest and busiest motion picture and television studio. A seven-hour excursion through Universal's well known 420-acre front and back lots has lots of highlights for kids: an encounter with the 6½-ton, 30-foot King Kong, plus Jaws, the Parting of the Red Sea, the Collapsing Bridge and Flash Flood as well as sets from hundreds of classic movies and television shows. "Streets of the World," motion picture sets accessible to the public, are always fun for kids. Visitors get to participate in special effects on a soundstage plus "live" special effects shows which include the Star Trek Adventure, Miami Vice Action Spectacular, Animal Actors Stage, Conan: A Sword and Sorcery Spectacular, and the Western Stunt Show. The newest attraction of all is Earthquake—The Big One, where movie magic brings you the experience of an earthquake that would measure 8.3 on the Richter scale (described as "awesome" by the 10-year-old son of a friend of ours). Universal Studios is open daily and costs $18.95 for 12 and over; $3.95 for 3–11; and free for kids 3 and under. More than four million people a year visit this attraction—it is enormously popular.

KNOTTS BERRY FARM (8039 Beach Boulevard, Buena Park, California 90620, 714-827-1776 or 714-220-5200 for recorded information). This, the nation's oldest theme park, really did start off as a berry stand on ten acres of rented land along the dusty roadside of Buena Park. Now it boasts 150 acres with five theme areas, nonstop entertainment, rides, and 60 eating spots. Only in America! Knott's is 30 minutes south of Los Angeles, and it features a Ghost Town complete with cowboys, can-can-girls, and gold panning; Camp Snoopy, six acres of rides and shows, Fiesta Village, Roaring 20's and Wild Water Wilderness, a turn-of-the-century California river wilderness park featuring a thrilling whitewater raft ride— Bigfoot Rapids. The park is open year-round, and admission, which includes unlimited rides, shows, and attractions, costs $18.95 for adults, and $14.95 for kids 3 to 11 (under 3 is free).

DISNEYLAND (1313 Harbor Boulevard, Anaheim, California 92802, 714-999-4565). The world according to Disney, about 30 miles from Los Angeles. Seven theme lands, heaven for kids. To avoid long lines, visit the most popular attractions (Matterhorn, bobsleds, Space Mountain, and Star Tours) when the park opens, and in summer come later and stay into the evening to enjoy the fireworks. For the complete scoop on Disneyland, we recommend the books mentioned on page 83.

Accommodations

Bed and Breakfasts

EYE OPENERS BED AND BREAKFAST RESERVATIONS (P.O. Box 694, Altadena, California 91001, 213-684-4428 or 818-797-2055). The owners, Ruth Judkins and Betty Cox, tell us that about 30 percent of their hosts accept children. Rates start at $40 and go to $80 for double occupancy and they have b and b's all over California.

BED AND BREAKFAST OF LOS ANGELES (32074 Waterside Lane, Westlake Village, California 91361, 818-889-8870 or 805-494-9622). Approximately half the hosts in this network are happy to have families. A particularly tempting one is a house overlooking the Pacific Ocean: it has two bedrooms and a bath and rents for $80 for the night. Another good bet for families is a guest suite in a private home with queen-sized bed, mini-kitchen, private bath, and living room with a fireplace and a sofabed. It costs $45 for 2, $5 for each extra person with full breakfast besides. If you have a big family, there are two other rooms downstairs with double beds that cost $35 a room.

Hotels

Although not actually in Los Angeles, the following two hotels are great bases for Disney visits.

ANAHEIM HILTON AND TOWERS (777 Convention Way, Anaheim, California 92802, 714-750-4321 or 800-222-9923). Two blocks from Disneyland and 28 miles south of downtown Los Angeles, this hotel offers a "Kids Klub" from June to September for children 5 to 15. It operates from 10:00 A.M. to 3:00 P.M. on the one-acre sun deck near the pool, and it includes whiffle ball, volleyball, arts and crafts, team sports, and board games. The Anaheim Hilton is the largest hotel in Southern California, with a staff of 1,300. The concierge keeps a file of activities for families. There are lots of high chairs and booster seats, a Kids Menu, and 50 percent off on items on the room service for kids. Baby-sitting is available for $5 to $6 per hour, and cribs are provided free. Children stay in the same room as their parents free, or, if you prefer two rooms for more privacy, the price is based on two singles, rather than two doubles. A "Disneyland Family Fun" package—two nights and three days for two adults and two kids—costs $303 and includes breakfasts and all-day passports to Disneyland.

DISNEYLAND HOTEL (1150 West Cerritos Avenue, Anaheim, California 92802, 714-778-6600 or 800-854-6165). Our kids went crazy just looking at the brochures for this, the "official hotel of the Magic Kingdom." It's linked to Disneyland via monorail, has three swimming pools, a white sand beach, ten tennis courts, and "Seaports of the Pacific," a mini-amusement park of its own with a video game center, remote-controlled boats, and two-seat pedal boats for rides on the marina. There's free entertainment day and night and 16 restaurants and bars. There's even a children's program in the summer and during holiday times. Kids 5 to 12 meet with counselors at the Yukon Klem Club from 6 to 10 every evening for dinner and games ($15 per kid). Kids 3 to 12 have a crafts workshop every Sunday for two hours. Baby-sitting is available for $26 for four hours. Rates are $99 to $190 per night for a double, with no charge for kids under 18; roll-away beds are $12 extra; cribs are free.

THE RITZ CARLTON, LAGUNA NIGUEL (33533 Ritz Carlton Drive, Laguna Niguel, California 92677, 714-240-2000 or 800-241-3333). Located on a 150-foot bluff above the Pacific Ocean, this Mediterranean-style hotel has the feel of a fine home, albeit a rather large one, with 393 rooms. Midway between Los Angeles and San Diego, it has four tennis courts, a nearby 18-hole golf course, and two miles of unspoiled beach at its doorstep. All rooms have refrigerators, VCRs with a children's video selection, and cable television with the Disney Channel. From mid-June through Labor Day, kids from 6 to 11 can participate in a supervised program Thursday–Monday from 12:30 P.M. to 3:30 P.M. at a cost of $20 per day. Cribs are available. There's a children's menu, which is also offered through room service. Baby-sitting can be arranged for $6 per hour through the concierge with a minimum of one day notice. Rates range from $185 to $350 per night, depending on your view.

MARINA PACIFIC HOTEL AND HOTEL SUITES (1697 Pacific Avenue, Venice, California 90291, 213-452-1111 or 800-421-8151).

Located 30 minutes from downtown L.A., 15 minutes from the airport, this hotel is only 500 feet from the Venice Beach Boardwalk. Suites with living room, kitchen, and bedroom are available for families. Rates begin at $85 for a double. One- and two-bedroom suites are $135 and up.

THE WESTIN BONAVENTURE (404 South Figueroa Street, Los Angeles, California 90071, 213-624-1000 or 800-228-3000). Located in the heart of downtown Los Angeles, the hotel's five towers are a city within a city: a five-level shopping gallery, a heated pool, tennis next door at the YMCA, even a lake right in the atrium lobby. The Bonaventure offers a weekend special—50 percent off the regular rate. Kids under 18 stay free of charge in the same room as parents. Regular double occupancy rates range from $150 to $159. Specialty Suites are available for $250 to $905 per night. Baby-sitting is available.

Hyatt has two properties in Los Angeles: one at 711 South Hope Street, 90017; the other at 3515 Wilshire Boulevard, 90010. See page 50 for what to expect for the kids, and call 800-233-1234 for details.

NEW ORLEANS

The minute we arrived at the airport in New Orleans we could tell that we were going to love the city. By now, we've developed a kind of radar, an instinct that gives us instant feeling about a city. The next few days in New Orleans proved that we'd been absolutely right—that our instincts were still in working order. New Orleans is a fabulous place to visit with kids. It's a fascinating, vibrant city. Because of 250 years of French, Spanish, Italian, West Indian, and finally American influence, New Orleans is probably the most European city in all of North America. Its narrow streets, splendid antebellum mansions, old-time jazz, Creole culture, and the wonderful Mississippi River are all reminiscent of another time—of Mark Twain, William Faulkner and Tennessee Williams. In spite of the new buildings, the space-age Superdome and the towering office buildings in midtown, many of the old ways are alive and well in this city. In the past few years, New Orleans has developed a number of tourist attractions just right for kids—a Children's Museum, a wonderful zoo, and a riverfront area that vibrates with music and activities from early morning to late at night.

This is very obviously a city that likes a good party, and the festivities around Mardi Gras time are of course legendary. But Mardi Gras is only one of the festivals that the city hosts each year. You may want to schedule your visit for the Black Heritage Festival, the Tennessee Williams Literary Festival, Spring Fiesta, the French Quarter Festival, the New Orleans Jazz and Heritage Festival, La Fete—the National Festival of Food and Cookery, the Italian Festival, or the Louisiana Heritage Festival. For dates and details, contact the Tourist and Convention Commission—the address is below.

Even when there's not a special festival going on, New Orleans invites you to explore its old streets, to wander through its French Quarter, to look for little architectural surprises, little bits of history, and to listen for the wonderful sound of jazz that really does permeate the city. And its not just your sense of sight and sound that are given a treat in New Orleans—your sense of taste is in for some great surprises. Be sure to have as many cups of café au lait as you can manage, try the blackened fish, the gumbos, the jambalaya, and the "beignets."

For Information

Two general guides to New Orleans are *Frommer's New Orleans* ($5.95) or *Fodor's Guide to New Orleans* ($8.95). Both provide a good overview of the city.

There are three books just for kids visiting New Orleans. One, *New Orleans for Kids,* was put together by the Greater New Orleans Tourist and Convention Commission. It costs $3.95 and is available in most bookstores in the city. It was written in 1984, though, and is pretty out of date. Two other books meant to introduce kids to the city are *Here We Are in New Orleans* by Joann Yockey and *A Visit to New Orleans: Pictures to Color and Verses to Read.* The first, published by Banana Books, P.O. Box 6434, Metairie, Louisiana 70009 ($8.75 plus 50 cents for postage and handling), combines interesting information about the city with some clever things to do (e.g., crossword puzzles and a page set aside to record a description of someone who made the trip pleasant). The author encourages kids to observe the city and organize their thoughts about what they see and do. Try to get a copy before you go. The second book, *Pictures to Color* (published by Carvin Publishing, $3.50), is fine for really young kids.

Another excellent source of information on the city is the

Greater New Orleans Tourist and Convention Commission, which will send you a hefty packet of brochures, maps, and information sheets. Write to their main office in advance at the Louisiana Superdome, Sugar Bowl Drive, New Orleans, 70112, 504-566-5011. Once you've arrived in the city, stop at the Visitor Information Center, 529 St. Ann Street, 504-566-5011.

Getting Around

One of New Orleans' most appealing features is the ease with which you can get around the city. Shaped like a crescent along a gentle bend in the Mississippi, the city is simple enough to navigate. In the lower right of the crescent is the famed French Quarter, where the streets are laid out in a perfect square. A do-it-yourself walking tour map of the Quarter (available at most hotels) is particularly helpful, since Orleanians don't use compass points as directions. Instead, lakeside (North Rampart Street boundary), riverside, uptown (beginning at Canal Street), and downtown (the Quarter itself) are the sometimes confusing references. The Central Business District, with high-rise buildings, plazas, parks, and luxury hotels, lies directly above Canal from the river. Much of what you'll want to see is within walking distance—in fact, New Orleans seems made for strolling. But when you need to go too far to walk, the public buses and streetcars are easily accessible and inexpensive. Fare for both buses and street cars is 60 cents—exact change is required.

The second-best-known New Orleans streetcar (the first is most definitely the one named *Desire,* which is no longer in operation) is the one that goes up and down St. Charles Avenue. This trolley is more than just a way to get from one point to another—it's a tour in itself, a kind of movable museum. Just board at Canal and Carondelet Streets, sit back and enjoy a wonderful ride past Lafayette Square, Lee Circle (where the general's statue faces north so that his back will never be to the enemy); the Garden District (you may want to get off here to wander and then get back on); and on up St. Charles, past beautiful antebellum homes in lovely garden settings, Tulane and Loyola Universities and all the way on up to Audubon Park, the home of the zoo. If you ride round-trip you'll cover about 13 miles; give yourself at least an hour and a half for the ride.

Another streetcar that's fun to take is the one along the Riverfront, the newest line. A good deal for tourists is the Regional Transit Authorities VisiTour Pass which is available for $2 for unlimited travel for one day or $5 for three days on any bus or streetcar line. Call 569-2700 to find out where you can get the pass; for route and schedule information, call the RTAs RideLine at the same number.

Tours

Sometimes it's fun to sit back and let someone else show you around. New Orleans offers a variety of tours. Here are some possibilities that you and the kids might like:

New Orleans Tours and Convention Services, Inc. 7801 Edinburgh Street, 70125. We took the half-day city tour and found it to be a perfect introduction to the city. Our guide, a Mr. Winkle who said, "Just call me Rip," was knowledgeable and friendly and gave us lots of information about the city we were about to explore on our own. The same outfit offers tours to plantations, river and city combinations—14 tours per day in fact. They'll pick you up at your hotel and drop you off again, which makes it all nice and convenient. The City Tour we took costs $15 for adults and $8 for kids 3 to 12. Call 504-482-1991 or 800-543-6332 for information.

Gray Line of New Orleans, 2345 World Trade Center, 70130. Here's another tour operator that will give you a combo city and riverboat tour, a River Road plantation tour, a trip to Longue Vue House and Gardens and a lot more. Call 504-587-0661 or 800-535-7787 for details.

Honey Island Swamp Tours, 106 Holly Ridge Drive, Slidell, 70461. Twice a day Dr. Paul Wagner, a well-known wetland ecologist, takes groups on an interpretive nature tour of one of America's least altered, wildest river swamps about 45 minutes from the city. This two-hour tour takes you through narrow backwater bayous lined with ancient cypress trees. Probably best for families with older kids, it's a dream for anyone who likes wildlife photography. The cost of the tour is $17.50 per adult and $10 for kids under 12; with transportation from New Orleans the price goes up to $35 and $20. Call 504-641-1769.

Creole Queen, Poydras Street Wharf, 70130. Since so much of New Orleans' history centers on the Mississippi River and since traveling on a paddle wheeler is so much fun, you really should be sure to spend some time on the river with your kids. We took the *Creole Queen's* Jazz Cruise—from 8:00 to 10:00 P.M. complete with a buffet dinner and lots of good jazz. Some kids might not be that interested in the music, so for them, we'd recommend instead one of the *Queen's* daytime trips—called the River, Plantation and Battlefield Cruise. It lasts three hours, departs twice a day, and costs $12 for adults, $6 for kids 6–12, and free for kids under 6. The tour takes you past the working harbor and old New Orleans neighborhoods, to the site of the Battle of New Orleans, and includes a visit to the old Beauregard House, a plantation built 17 years after Jackson's victory in 1815. Call 504-529-4567.

Cotton Blossom Paddlewheeler, 2340 World Trade Center, 70130. This boat leaves right from Riverwalk three times a day for the Audubon Zoo. The trip to the zoo, narrated as you go, takes about an hour. The return trip can be made on the boat or, as we chose, by the St. Charles Avenue streetcar. There's a free shuttle that takes you from the zoo to the streetcar. The round-trip cruise is $8.50 for adults, $4.25 for kids 2–12, and free for under 2. A one-way fare is $5.50 and $3.25, and reduced zoo admission tickets are available to passengers. Call 504-587-0740 or 800-233-BOAT.

Jean Lafitte National Historical Park, French Quarter Unit, Folklife and Visitor Center, 916-918 North Peters Street, 70130. Free, regularly scheduled walking tours are offered by the park rangers seven days a week. The walks include "The City of the Dead," 90 minutes in the amazing St. Louis Cemetery No. 1, the oldest in the city; "Faubourg Promenade," two hours, including a streetcar ride and views of lush greenery and magnificent homes; "History of New Orleans," 90 minutes around the French Quarter with emphasis on the history and ethnic and cultural diversity of the city; and the Tour du Jour, 90 minutes on a topic that changes daily. Although there's no minimum age, one of the rangers told us that kids under 10 might get a bit fidgety. For more information, call 504-589-2636.

Sound Promenades, Inc. P.O. Box 8876, 70812. For anyone who prefers the do-it-yourself tour, this company produces two 90-minute cassette recordings ($19.95 for both) that lead you step-by-step through the French Quarter. You can order the tapes before you leave on your trip or, if you wait until you're in New Orleans, just call 504-282-1932 to find out where you can get one.

Things to See and Do

In and Around the French Quarter

First of all, put on your walking shoes and get ready to stroll. This is a wonderful area for exploring on foot. Going to and from the places you've chosen to visit, you'll find lots of surprises—lovely balconies, gracious gardens and courtyards reminiscent of the city's gracious past.

JACKSON SQUARE. Begin here at the heart of the French Quarter, bounded by Decatur, Chartres, St. Peter, and St. Anne Streets. Since 1721 it's been a focal point of life in the city. (Originally called the Place d'Armes, its name was changed in the 1850s to honor the hero of the 1815 battle.) The kids will love seeing the mimes and jugglers, artists, and other street performers that line the fence that surrounds the park. While you're in the area of the square, be sure to stop in at Oh Susannah at 518 St. Peters Street. We walked in quite by chance and found a fabulous collection of dolls, which included a bride of the seventies, Pierrots, and even a Lady of the Lake, all in blue with blonde hair to her knees. Almost three-quarters of the dolls here are made by local artists. Although lots of the dolls are quite expensive, it is possible to buy a treat for the kids or for someone back home for $5 or $10. Ask about children's workshops at the Cabildo (part of the Louisiana State Museum, 568-6968) and visit the Presbytere, both along the square.

THE FRENCH MARKET. Just across from Jackson Square, the French Market begins. It runs for about six blocks along the Mississippi and is a must-see. You'll find fruits and vegetables, souvenirs, fish, meat, and on Saturdays and Sundays, a flea market that's a big tourist attraction. While you're in the area you must stop for café au lait, beignets (square doughnut-type pastries), and people-watching at the Café du Monde, 800 Decatur Street. Walking uptown along the river from the Café du Monde you'll come to the Jackson Brewery, once in fact just that, but now a shopping mall.

MUSEE CONTI—THE WAX MUSEUM OF LOUISIANA LEGENDS (917 Conti, 504-525-2608). Wax museums are not often one of our favorite things—but this one was great. The concierge at the hotel had told us that she was brought up in New Orleans and that one of her favorite weekend outings with her family was to the Musee Conti. We spent part of an afternoon there and found out why. The guide was terrific—he taught us an enormous amount about the history of the city, and the learning was fun. The kids had a chance to ask lots of questions. The museum features a number of tableaux of events in the history of New Orleans and honestly does bring it all to life. We saw the likes of Andrew Jackson, Jean Lafitte, Mark Twain, and even Marie Laveau, the voodoo queen. Since there isn't always a guide available, and the experience wouldn't be half as interesting without one, be sure to call before you go.

PRESERVATION HALL (726 St. Peter Street). As we said before, jazz is everywhere in New Orleans but there's no better place to go for real authentic New Orleans jazz than this old, run-down hall with torn burlap on the walls, a splintered wooden floor, and just a few benches. We sat up front on the floor and heard some of the best jazz we've ever heard. The music starts at 8:00 P.M. and goes on until 12:30 A.M. every night. At Preservation Hall jazz is everything—$2 in the basket gets you in—so don't expect any food, drinks, or air-conditioning. Don't miss it; the kids will love it as much as you do.

HERMANN-GRIMA HISTORIC HOUSE (820 St. Louis Street). This home is one of the earliest and best examples of American architecture in the French Quarter with an 1830s Creole kitchen, authentically restored interiors and gardens, and the last private stable in the Vieux Carre. If your kids are old enough, you might all enjoy the 40-minute tour. Call 504-525-5661 for details.

If you have the time, visit the relatively new Ripley's Believe-It-or-Not exhibit, 501 Bourbon Street, 529-5131, and try to see a children's show at Le Petit Theatre, 616 St. Peter Street, 522-4958.

On the western edge of the quarter, you'll find the Aquarium of the Americas and Woldenberg Riverfront Park. When we were in New Orleans, all we could see of the aquarium was a crane and a sign announcing its coming, but by the time you read this, the aquarium, built right on the river, should be complete. On the eastern edge, visit the Old U.S. Mint, now home to the Louisiana State Museum Library and Jazz and Carnival Museums, 568-6968.

Beyond the French Quarter

There are a number of places not right in the French Quarter that are just perfect for families. All of them, however, are easily accessible from the Quarter.

We've already mentioned the Riverfront Trolley. You can take it from the French Market district to a stop on Julia Street, where you'll find the Louisiana Children's Museum. (Just walk a few blocks away from the river to the museum once you get off the streetcar.)

Then, if you decide to take the Riverfront Trolley back to the French Quarter area, you can take some time to go into the River-walk—an enclosed mall that stretches along the river and includes lots of shops, places to get a quick meal and an occasional clown or mime. The Riverwalk's a lively spot and will be fun for kids—in small doses.

LOUISIANA CHILDREN'S MUSEUM (428 Julia Street, Zip: 79130). This is one of New Orleans' newest treats for families. It's a dynamic environment where children and their families learn together by playing together. Exhibits include a Bubbles Exhibit, where kids can make a bubble taller than they are, an Eyewitness News Kid Watch Studio, where kids can make their own news broadcast, a Model Supermarket complete with carts and cash registers, and a model of a big city port. Although the staff at the museum recommends the place to kids 2 to 12, we recommend it most for kids up to 9. Each month the museum offers workshops and special programs—usually three per month—that may involve cooking, animation, magic, or more. Call 504-523-1357 for current information.

AUDUBON PARK AND ZOOLOGICAL GARDENS (6500 Magazine Street, Zip: 70118). You can reach the zoo on the Paddlewheeler Cotton Blossom (see above) or by way of the St. Charles Avenue Streetcar. It's a great zoo, ranked as one of the top five in the U.S. There are more than 1,500 animals, all living in their natural hab-itats. We espcially liked the Louisiana Swamp Exhibit (which in-cluded extremely rare white alligators), the white tiger, the elephant show, the playground, and what the zoo likes to call its state-of-the-art, climate-controlled Reptile Encounter. The zoo is big—but not too big—with lots of nice places to stop and rest along the way and places to get inexpensive snacks in case you didn't get a picnic together. The zoo rents big wooden wagons large enough for a few small kids—more fun than a stroller for the little ones. For informa-tion, call 504-861-2537.

CITY PARK. Originally a sugar plantation, this beautiful park is home to the New Orleans Museum of Art. It's located straight out Esplanade Avenue, about 20 blocks from the Quarter. The park is a great place for the kids to work off some of their energy. Here they can play in Storyland, a children's theme park, open Wednesday through Sunday, and in the Carousel Gardens, where, on weekends, an antique carousel and a children's train called the General P.G.T. Beauregard are popular attractions as are the bumper cars and a Ferris wheel. Storytelling and puppet shows are scheduled throughout the year. For up-to-the-minute information, call 504-482-4888.

LOUISIANA NATURE AND SCIENCE CENTER (in Joe W. Brown Memorial Park, 1100 Lake Forest Boulevard, 504-246-9381). For a bit of the outdoors in eastern New Orleans, not far from the middle of town, take a trip to the Center. You'll find three nature trails for exploring, hands-on exhibits, a Discovery Loft in the Interpretive Center (where you can fondle bones and skulls, animal pelts and skins), and a planetarium. Admission is $3 for adults, $1 for kids 3–14, kids 2 and under free. A special family rate is $6 during the week; $10 on weekends.

Time Out

DEPENDABLE NURSING AND FAMILY CARE, INC (5862 General Haig Street, Zip: 70124, 504-486-5044). The concierge at our hotel told us that this is the service that President Reagan used for his grandchildren during the Republican convention, so obviously, the Secret Service thinks it's quite reliable. Baby-sitters are available 24 hours per day and rates are $25 plus $5 for parking for five hours of service and $4.50 for each additional hour. Add 50 cents per hour for additional children or $15 extra if the child is from a different family. You should call at least four hours in advance and much more than that during holidays, Super Bowl time or Mardi Gras.

Accommodations

Bed and Breakfast

Bed and Breakfast, Inc., 1360 Moss Street, Box 52257, Zip: 70152, 504-525-4640 or 800-228-9711 dial 184. Hazell Boyce, the woman in charge of this operation, assured us that "most of our hosts love children and will line up baby-sitters if desired." Hazell has some wonderful places to offer, including—along the St. Charles Avenue streetcar line—a Victorian home recently renovated by its interior decorator-owner; a quaint guest cottage that looks onto a patio with an antique swing; a house on Napoleon Avenue that has a "tropical" feel; and right in the French Quarter itself, a Creole cottage and guest house with a lush patio full of native plants that has been restored by the architect-owner. All homes are air-conditioned. "Hosts will help you locate and plan what interests you. They willingly point out the secret nooks and crannies, along with famous restaurants and sightseeing treats."

Hotels

DAUPHINE ORLEANS (415 Dauphine Street, Zip: 70112, 504-586-1800 or 800-521-7111). This wonderfully quaint hotel, right in the heart of the French Quarter, has lots of charm and a thoughtful staff. Along with your room at the Dauphine Orleans you're entitled to an impressive list of extras: a breakfast in a cheerful dining room right by the pool (cereal, fruit, pastry, coffee, juice); a welcome drink at the hotel's Bagnio Lounge (that can include a Coke for the kids); a morning newspaper delivered to your door, free parking, and free transportation within the French Quarter and central business district in the "Dauphine Jitney" every day from 8:00 A.M. to 8:00 P.M. Rooms are spacious, clean, and nicely furnished. Some even have their own little balconies with two chairs and a table that overlook the quarter. Rate for a room with a patio and a queen-sized bed for two costs $105; kids under 12 are free (remember, too, that breakfast is included). Baby-sitting can be arranged for $5 per hour for a minimum of four hours.

WESTIN CANAL PLACE HOTEL (100 rue Iberville, Zip:70130, 504-566-7006 or 800-228-3000). This is New Orleans at its most modern. Perched right on top of the Canal Place Shopping Centre and the Canal Place Office Tower, the Westin is located right by the French Quarter and at the gateway to the riverfront renaissance area. The hotel's lobby, on the 11th floor overlooking the river, is splendid—a blend of marble, fresh flowers, and antiques. The rooms are large and comfortable with fully stocked refrigerators and expansive views of the river. Amenities include concierge service (the head concierge keeps a list of children's activities), a heated rooftop pool, a putting green, 18-hole golf privileges, and the use of a health club and fitness room. At holiday time—from just before Thanksgiving to after New Year's—the Westin has a special children's tea in its lobby from 3:00 to 6:00 P.M. every day. Overnight rates begin at $195 for a double room; kids 18 and under are free in their parents' room.

QUALITY INN/MIDTOWN (3900 Tulane Avenue, Zip: 70119, 504-486-5541 or 800-228-5151). Although it's not right in the middle of things, this Quality Inn is still only a few minutes from the business district. There's a pool, all rooms have balconies, and parking is free. Rates for a room with two double beds range from $59 to $85; kids under 16 are free.

There's a Hyatt in New Orleans on Poydras at Loyola Avenue, Zip: 70140. See page 50 for all of the great things Hyatt has to offer families, and call 800-233-1234 for details.

NEW YORK

We live in New York City and we love it. Forget that old cliché about New York's being a great place to visit but "I wouldn't want to live there." Living here is great; visiting is exciting, too. There's so much to do here that you could easily go on sensory overload, so we've sorted through the possibilities and chosen the places we like best. We've arranged them geographically so that you can digest the Big Apple in small bites. Take time to appreciate our city by not rushing through it. Include a playground, picnic, or sky-high view each day to balance all the concrete and tall buildings. New York is a great city for walking. Every street is another adventure from the mosaic on the side of a building to the people walking behind you speaking a language you've never heard before. Although our public transportation is efficient—our subways and buses take you any place you want to go—walking is the best way to enjoy the city.

To help you get ready for your trip to New York, there is a lot of good information available. Here we include books, information offices, organizations, and even tapes that will help you make your family's trip as good as you want it to be.

Books

You'll have no problem finding plenty of general guidebooks to New York. But if you're coming with the kids, we recommend *Candy Apple: New York for Kids* by Bubbles Fisher, a grandmother who's discovered 600 things to do and written them all down. The new edition includes hotel possibilities as well. A Frommer book, published by Prentice Hall, it costs $11.95. For general guides, we like *Frommer's New York on $45 a Day* (Simon & Schuster, $9.95) and the *I Love New York Guide* by Marilyn Applesberg (Collier/Macmillan, $4.95). A great book that's just recently appeared is called *A Kid's Guide to New York City* ($6.95) and is part of Harcourt, Brace Jovanovich's Gulliver Travels series. Try to get a copy in advance of your trip so that the kids can have a chance to absorb some of the fascinating facts. The oversize paperback has travel diaries, puzzles, maps, lots of photos and drawings, calendars of events, and useful suggestions of what to see and do.

Another book we've dicovered since our last edition is Sylvia Carter's *Eats: The Guide to the Best Little Restaurants in New York* ($9.95, New American Library). Carter is a New York restaurant critic who shares her favorite finds in this book. She doesn't forget the other boroughs, either, and so far, we've never been disappointed by her recommendations.

When you're ready to get out of town, pick up a copy of *Weekends Away: New York* by Mike Michaelson, published by E. P. Dutton, which lists 120 trips to take within 150 miles of New York City. The book costs $9.95, and for each excursion noted, there's a rating on whether the trip is best for romance, for families, or, in some cases, for both.

For the most up-to-the-minute information on what's going on in town for kids, you should know about seven magazines/newsletters that are published here especially for parents. Each one is a gold mine of ideas for what to do with the kids and where to go for help if you need it.

- *New York Family* magazine is now in its third year of publication. Published by Susan Ross and Felice Shapiro, it is available by mail for $3.50. It, too, has a calendar of family events. For information, contact the publisher, 420 East 79th Street, Suite 9E, New York, New York 10021. Subscriptions are available for $30 per year. A spin-off of *New York Family* is *Westchester Family* magazine, which does for the northern suburbs what the original does for the city.

- *New York City Family Entertainment Guide* is a seasonal listing of entertainment, party services, museums, theater, and other activities for kids that's available in child-oriented shops. If you'd like to order one before your trip, send $1 and a stamped, self-addressed envelope to Family Publishing, 37 West 72nd Sreet, New York, New York 10023.

- *Parents and Kids Directory,* published by Marquee Communications, P.O. Box 1257, Peter Cooper Station, New York, New York 10276, also lists special events, shops, and services for the whole family. It is published four times a year; six issues cost $14.95; single copies are $2.50.

- *Children's Focus: A Cultural Newsletter* is a monthly publication that focuses on arts and cultural events geared to children between the ages of 5 and 12. A recent issue included a notice about a rock musical for kids, workshops at the Bronx Zoo, a puppet festival, and free films at libraries. Single copies are available for $1 from Myra Henry, Children's Focus, P.O. Box 7196, Flushing, New York 11355. A year's subscription is $12.

- *PARENTGUIDE News* is available from Parentguide Inc., 2 Park Avenue, New York, New York 10016, 212-213-8843 ($11.90 for a year's subscription; $21.90 two years), or on newsstands for $1.50 per copy.
- *The Big Apple Parents' Paper* is a monthly paper published by Buffalo-Bunyip, Inc., 67 Wall Street, Suite 2411, New York, New York 10005. It costs $15 for one year; $25 for two and can be picked up all over town in 700 different spots. This paper, too, has a calendar of events for the month as well as regular features.
- *Long Island Parenting* is the tabloid you'll want if you'll be spending time in Nassau or Suffolk counties. You'll find a calendar of events and parenting advice in this publication, which appears monthly. For a sample copy, send $2 to the editor, Pat Simms Elias, at Box 214, Island Park, New York 11358; a year's subscription costs $15.

The most obvious but sometimes overlooked source of information on New York is the city's Convention and Visitors Bureau, 2 Columbus Circle, New York, New York 10019, and 158 West 42nd Street, 212-397-8222. Everything's free—from maps to calendars of events to an occasional ticket for a television show. And for information on what's happening in the parks of New York—and there's always something—simply dial 212-360-1333.

Tours

If you prefer to have someone else arrange your tour of the city, or at least a part of it, consider these possibilities.

Joyce Gold Tours

Joyce Gold is a historian and teacher who has given walking tours of New York for 15 years. She's also described her tours in two books she calls *From Windmills to the World Trade Center: A Walking Guide to Lower Manhattan* and *From Trout Stream to*

Bohemia: A Walking Guide to Greenwich Village History (available by mail for $4.75 and $6.20, respectively, from Gold at 141 West 17th Street, New York, New York 10011, 212-242-5762). Tours begin in the spring and run through the fall. There are five different tours in all, always on Sundays. She walks her groups through the Financial District, Greenwich Village, Chelsea, the East Village, and Ladies' Mile and condenses what she's learned from the 800 books she's read on the subject of New York. Tours last two to three hours and cost $8 per person. Kids should probably be at least 10 years old to be able to appreciate the tour.

The Museum of the City of New York

The museum offers a season of Sunday walking tours in spring and fall, exploring various parts of Manhattan and Brooklyn. The cost is $10 per person. Call 212-534-1034 for information.

Circle Line Cruise

The Circle Line Cruise is a classic great for kids, especially on a nice day. The cruise takes three hours and is a great way to orient yourself and the kids to what New York looks like. Boats sail from March to November. The first boat leaves at 9:30 A.M., and there's a sailing every 45 minutes. The ride costs $15 for adults, $7.50 for kids under 12. Call 212-563-3200.

Staten Island Ferry/Statue of Liberty

For 25 cents, round-trip, you can take a cruise across New York Harbor. You'll pass the Statue of Liberty en route, but for a visit to the Statue you'll have to take the Statue of Liberty Ferry from South Ferry. The round-trip costs $3.25 for adults, $1.50 for kids 11 and under, and includes a visit to the Statue. Call 212-269-5755 for information.

Pioneer

The schooner *Pioneer* is a part of the South Street Seaport, which also offers cruises of the harbor for two or three hours at a time. The two-hour cruise is $15 for adults, $10 for kids; the three-hour cruise is $22 and $16. The *Pioneer* is docked at Pier 16 and cruises from early May to mid-September. Call 212-699-9416 for information and days, since at certain times of the year cruises are on weekends only.

I See New York by Helicopter

I See New York is a sightseeing option run by Island Helicopter, based at 34th Street and the East River. Tours run every day, 9:00 A.M. to 9:00 P.M. (except from January to March, when they're until 5:00 P.M., and there are five itineraries to choose from. The shortest is a 160-mile flight over the river that costs $35 per person (children must pay full fare because safety regulations require that they occupy their own seat). Call 212-683-4575 for information.

Talk-a-Walk

For do-it-yourself walking tours of Lower Manhattan, consider the four cassettes created by Sound Publishers, Inc.: World Trade Center to Bowling Green, Customs House to Seaport Museum, Seaport Museum to World Trade Center, and across the Brooklyn Bridge. All are suitable for interested kids 6 years old and over and cover history, culture, architecture, and legend. Tapes are $9.95 each and are available from Sound Publishers, 30 Waterside Plaza, Suite 10D, New York, New York 10010, 212-686-0356.

Things to See and Do

Before we begin, here's a quick geography lesson. Fifth Avenue divides Manhattan into the East and West sides. Cross streets are numbered from 8th Street north. The lower the address on the cross streets, the closer it is to Fifth Avenue. Between 60th Street and 110th Street, Central Park intervenes and the distance between East and West widens substantially but is still walkable (avoid the park after dark; during the day it's a fine place to be).

To help you cluster your sightseeing, we've listed places in geographical groups. Each day, pick a neighborhood and go exploring. Don't try to cover everything we list. It's taken us 20 years! Walk whenever you can. If you want to ride, get a subway or bus map (supposedly available free at token booths, definitely available at the Visitors Bureau). Don't be afraid to ask New Yorkers how to get around: They really are very helpful as a rule. Kids under 6 ride free, and exact change is always necessary. Stock up on tokens ($1) at a subway booth at non-rush hour. Let us begin:

Museum Mile

Museum Mile is a wonderful stretch of Fifth Avenue from 104th Street south to 81st Street. When planning, remember that most museums are closed Mondays with the exception of the Jewish Museum. Here we begin at the north end, or the uptown end, of the "Mile."

THE MUSEUM OF THE CITY OF NEW YORK (Fifth Avenue at 104th Street, Zip: 10029, 212-534-1034). Start by watching "The Big Apple," a multimedia history of New York City that kids love. Then go on up to the Toy Gallery and Dolls' House Gallery; then on to the Dutch Gallery, complete with a fort that kids can explore; and the Fire Gallery, full of antique fire engines and firefighting equipment. Older kids like the six period rooms, peopled with mannequins portraying New Yorkers from the 17th to the 20th century. Throughout the year, on most Saturdays the museum sponsors family workshops led by instructors who explore a special topic and then tour the galleries. Some possibilities: "All Children Play" which focuses on old and new street games, and another called "Native New Yorkers," all about the people who lived here before the Dutch and English settled. Each month, on a Sunday, the museum presents a special performing group—puppets, storytellers, actors and actresses—who bring to life the stories of America's past. Right across from the museum, at 105th Street, is the extraordinarily beautiful Conservatory Garden in Central Park. We spent an hour at the museum, went out for 30 minutes in the park, and back for another hour and one-half. It was a perfect break. The Museum of the City of New York has changing tables, allows strollers, has an excellent gift shop and small-size drinking fountains, and officially charges no admission fee but suggests $5 for families and $3 for adults, $1 for kids.

THE JEWISH MUSEUM (5th Avenue at 92nd Street, Zip: 10128, 212-860-1889). This is a lovely, small museum, located in the former Warburg Mansion. Main exhibits change two or three times a year, but "Israel in Antiquity," all about archaeology, is permanent and a favorite with kids 8 and over. Throughout the year the museum presents "Family Programs" (we've been to lots and they've been terrific) on Sunday afternoons. Remember that this museum is closed on Fridays and Saturdays. Admission is $4 adults, $2 for kids, and under 6, free.

THE COOPER-HEWITT MUSEUM (2 East 91st Street, Zip: 10128, 212-860-6898). This is another gem of a museum—nice and small and manageable. It's a part of the Smithsonian, actually, and is devoted to historical and contemporary design. On Saturdays, there are often workshops for kids. Call for details. No strollers are allowed, but free backpacks are available. Admission is $3, free for kids under 12.

THE GUGGENHEIM MUSEUM (1071 Fifth Avenue, Zip: 10128, 212-360-3513). The giant snail up ahead is the Guggenheim. The design is great for kids, who like to spiral down the ramps. Our kids are always happy to visit—the art is eclectic and easy to view; the gift shop's great, too. On Tuesday evenings from 5 to 8 admission is free. Admission is $4.50, kids under 7 are free.

METROPOLITAN MUSEUM OF ART (82nd Street and Fifth Avenue, Zip: 10028, 212-879-5500). You already know all about this one; it is New York's number one tourist attraction. The kids will love the sculpture gallery, the armor, the mummies, and, depending on the theme, the exhibit in the Costume Gallery. Every weekend there are programs for kids 5 to 12 years old and their parents that include gallery talks and sketching, slide talks, and gallery hunts. Call for specifics. On Sundays from 1:30 to 3:00 there are drawing classes in the galleries; for those who prefer do-it-yourself, there are written gallery hunts available at the Great Hall Information Desk. Suggested admission is $5 for adults, free for kids under 12.

Playgrounds and Other Treats Along the Way

Along Fifth Avenue, at 100th, 95th, 84th, and 79th and below at 77th, 71st, and 67th Streets there are playgrounds in Central Park that make perfect diversions for the kids. The newly renovated Central Park Zoo is further south at 64th, and the Carousel, a wonderful treat for kids at 75 cents a ride, is in midpark at 64th Street. Not far from both attractions is the Dairy, a beautifully restored building where kids get a good introduction to the park via a short video, and where you can pick up lots of free material on what's happening where in magnificent Central Park. After your Museum Mile meander, both the Dairy and Belvedere Castle in Central Park offer fun workshops—some just for kids, some for the whole family. Many are led by Park Rangers. For Belvedere, call 772-0210; for the Dairy, 397-3156. To reach the Urban Park Rangers, call 860-1351.

If you're still going strong after your Museum Mile trek, you can walk east to Madison and visit the Whitney Museum (at 75th Street)—kids like the Calder Circus in the lobby and the giant elevator. This is another favorite of our kids. Both the permanent and changing exhibitions are exciting and appealing. We sometimes actually argue about visiting here or the Guggenheim. Did someone say museums aren't for kids?

Toys and Other Good Things

F.A.O. SCHWARZ (767 Fifth Avenue at 58th Street in the General Motors Building, 212-644-9400). Spend some time in this kids' paradise. They're good about letting kids play with display toys and from time to time have special events for kids.

TRUMP TOWER (Fifth Avenue and 56th Street). For a look at affluence on parade and for a place to rest your feet, this is a convenient stopping point with a spectacular waterfall.

IBM GALLERY (56th Street and Madison Avenue, 212-745-6100 for a recorded announcement). Exhibits vary, but often they're great for kids. No admission fee; call ahead for details.

MUSEUM OF BROADCASTING (1 East 53rd Street, Zip: 10022, 212-752-4690). This unique institution is like a library of television and radio programs. Its collection spans 60 years of broadcasting: in all, 25,000 radio and television programs. Visitors may come by and watch or listen to their favorite program from the past for an hour at a time. Possibilities include "Howdy Doody," inaugurations of presidents since Truman, Watergate hearings, *The Nutcracker* with Baryshnikov, and on and on. Admission is $4 for adults, $3 for students, and $2 for kids under 13.

MUSEUM OF MODERN ART (MOMA) (11 West 53rd Street, 212-708-9400; program information, 212-708-9480). You decide whether your kids are going to enjoy the art. Children under 16 are free. Every once in a while there are parent-child workshops that involve a Thursday evening session for adults only followed by a Saturday morning session for adults and kids 5–10. Call for dates.

ROCKEFELLER CENTER (from Fifth to Sixth Avenue, 48th to 51st Street). This favorite for tourists has great appeal in both summer and winter. In the warm weather, admire the Channel Gardens; in winter watch (or join) the ice skaters. While you're in this part of town, stop at A.T. and T.'s Infoquest at 56th Street and Madison for "an interactive exhibition of the information age." Our kids had fun fooling with the computers and robots and creating their own music video. Call 212-605-5555 for information.

Midtown—On the West Side

EMPIRE STATE BUILDING (34th Street and Fifth Avenue). Has a great view from the 102nd floor. It costs $3.50 for adults, $1.75 for kids under 12. Call 212-736-3100 for hours. In the concourse of the building is the Guinness World Records Exhibit Hall, for people who like to find out about the "best," the "greatest," and the "largest."

INTREPID SEA-AIR-SPACE MUSEUM Pier 86, (46th Street and 12th Avenue on the Hudson River, 212-245-0072). This was a great surprise to us. We resisted going at first but actually liked it as much as the kids did. The museum is actually in and on an aircraft carrier built in 1943 and decommissioned in 1974. The kids are free to climb and explore. Open Wednesday through Sunday, 10:00 A.M. to 5:00 P.M., $4.75 for adults, $2.50 for kids under 12.

AMERICAN CRAFT MUSEUM (40 West 53rd Street, between Fifth and Sixth Avenues, Zip: 10019, 212-956-3535). Not long ago the museum abandoned its cramped brownstone for a new home in the E. F. Hutton building. The new space is beautiful, with lots of room to show off the exhibits of hanging sculpture, ceramics, furniture, or, the last time we were there, a fabulous show of art made from candy. The kids went wild over the full-size table and chair made of chocolate and still talk about the incredible cakes, especially the one made to look exactly like the White House. The museum has occasional workshops for kids and down on the lower level a space for hands-on activities, whether there's a workshop on or not. Admission is $3.50 for adults, free for kids 12 and under.

Consider taking your kids, especially any baseball fans, to Mickey Mantle's at 42 Central Park South (perfect for a lunch stop on a day you visit the park). Filled with baseball memorabilia, a small gift counter, and TVs turned on to sporting events, it's loud and fun—but not cheap. Food is quite good, and there's a children's menu. If Mickey's in town, he usually stops by.

Another good spot for lunch or dinner is Hamburger Harry's at 145 West 45th Street or the high-tech McDonalds on 57th Street, which author Bubbles Fisher so appropriately calls "The State of the Arch."

Midtown—On the East Side

CITICORP CENTER (153 East 53rd Street, 590-2330). This city version of a shopping mall has tables for picnics and a Saturday Kids Corner at 11:00, where you may find magicians, puppets, or musicians.

THE UNITED NATIONS (First Avenue and 45th Street, Zip: 10017, 212-754-7713). Children 6 or over may like the tours of the UN given every 15 minutes from 9:15 A.M. to 4:45 P.M. every day of the week. Most kids have seen or heard references to the UN on television, so a visit will help make future news much more meaningful. Free tickets to open sessions of the General Assembly are also available on a first-come, first-served basis. The tour costs $2.50 for students and $4.50 for adults. Be sure to visit the gift shop with a large selection of pretty things from all over the world. The UN, situated along the East River, is a nice, cool spot in the summer. You can stroll along the river's edge and enjoy the breeze; unfortunately, no picnics are allowed in this inviting space.

Way, Way Downtown

See page 187 for information on a visit to the Statue of Liberty.

Start off this tour at the World Trade Center. On the 107th floor of Tower 2 you can take a look at a view you won't soon forget. It costs $3.50 for adults, $1.75 for kids 6 to 12, and is free for 6 and under. Call 212-466-7377 for information. If you walk north of the Trade Center, there's a lovely park on Chambers Street between Independence Plaza and Manhattan Community College. A good lunch spot is Hamburger Harry's at 157 Chambers Street, with booster seats, a children's menu, and all. As you go downtown after lunch, decide whether you want to head for the Financial District and Wall Street—for the older kids, a look at tours of the American Stock Exchange, 212-623-3000, may be fun—or go crosstown to South Street Seaport.

SOUTH STREET SEAPORT (212-669-9424). This is a mix of restored seaport buildings reminiscent of the area's 19th-century glory and chic restaurants, boutiques, malls, and public terraces with spectacular views of New York Harbor and the Brooklyn Bridge. There's always something going on down here; often free performances on weekends out in the open. We've seen some great magicians and jugglers, some carolers at holiday time, and two comedians who were very, very funny. Boat rides leave from the Seaport and food halls, and you'll find shops, reminiscent of Faneuil Hall in Boston but with an unmistakably New York flair. A multiscreen film presentation, "The Seaport Experience," is shown every day. It's $4.75 for grown-ups, $3.00 for kids under 12.

THE SEAPORT MUSEUM (207 Front Street, Zip: 10038, 212-669-9400), is not one building but actually an 11-block landmark district that includes daily tours, films, and special programs; galleries; a children's center with hands-on programs; a re-creation of a 19th-century printer's shop; the lightship *Ambrose;* the great four-masted bark *Peking;* and a harbor excursion line. Admission of $5 for adults, $2 for kids under 12 allows you to see it all. There's an occasional program that includes an overnight on the ship where you and your kids take turns with other participants on "evening watch." This is great fun if your kids are 8 and over.

More Downtown

New York is a conglomeration of ethnic neighborhoods, and two that are especially fun to explore are Chinatown (Canal Street going west from the Manhattan Bridge to Centre Street, south to Chatham Square and some blocks north of Canal to Grand Street) and nearby Little Italy. We suggest walking around Chinatown—there are lots of little stores where you can buy inexpensive gifts to take back home with you—having lunch or dinner in Chinatown, and then going on to Mulberry or Grand Street for an Italian ice or pastry.

Not far away are Greenwich Village and Soho, filled with boutiques, galleries, and lots of food treats. In this area, too, you'll find:

THE LOWER EAST SIDE TENEMENT MUSEUM (97 Orchard Street, 212-431-0233). This new living history museum is meant to tell the story of the Lower East Side during the time of mass immigration in the 19th century (from 1850–1910, specifically). At press time, the staff was trying to raise the money to re-create apartments that would be typical of those lived in by blacks, Germans, Chinese, Italians, Irish, and East European Jews. While the museum is being put together, its staff offers a number of exhibits and programs for families. Call to find out just what's available and how far they've gotten by the time of your visit.

If you're in this part of town on a Sunday, call the Henry Street Settlement, 212-598-0400, and ask whether they have one of their excellent "Arts for the Family" series going on—performances begin at 2:00 P.M. and cost $2.50 for adults, $1 for kids.

MUSEUM OF HOLOGRAPHY (11 Mercer Street, Zip: 10013, 212-925-0526). It's in the middle of Soho and has two floors of exhibits on holography, three-dimensional images created with laser light. Strollers are allowed; admission is $3 for adults, $1.75 for kids 12 and under. (Not recommended for the littlest—the exhibits are too high for them to see, and no stools are provided.)

FORBES MAGAZINE GALLERIES (62 Fifth Avenue, near the corner of 12th Street, Zip: 10011, 212-206-5548). In Greenwich Village and known as "the best museum" to one of our kids who's been visiting it and loving it since he was 3 years old. Kids will like the collection of toy boats in an oceanlike environment, the Fabergé eggs, and the 12,000 toy soldiers. Open on Tuesdays, Wednesdays, Fridays, and Saturdays only. Admission is free.

While you're in the village, there are lots of parks for you and the kids: Washington Square Park at the downtown end of Fifth Avenue has playgrounds and impromptu entertainment in all seasons; the Mercer Street Park north of Houston Street next to the New York University Coles Sports Center has a fountain to cool you off on those hot, steamy New York days; and Abingdon Square Park, good for all ages, with a big sandbox and new large climbing and play equipment.

And for kids 4 years and over in search of entertainment in this same neighborhood on Saturdays and Sundays there are musical adaptations of fairy tales at the 13th Street Theater, 50 West 13th Street, 212-675-6677. Tickets are a real bargain at $3. Or, call the Little People's Theater Company, 39 Grove Street (212-765-9540) for their Saturday and Sunday schedule.

Upper West Side

We define the Upper West Side as the area that begins at Central Park South, heads west to the Hudson River and Riverside Park, and up beyond Columbia University at 117th Street and Broadway. Its eastern border is Central Park, and wherever you are on the Upper West Side you're never far from the glorious park and all it has to offer you and your kids. If you're going to picnic in this neighborhood—and we think you should if the weather is nice enough—stop first at Zabar's, a food emporium that defies description. It's at Broadway and 80th Street, just a short walk from Central Park or even shorter walk to Riverside Park. Also in the park, on the west side, are the Swedish Cottage Marionette Theater at 79th Street (call 212-988-9093 for schedule), Heckscher Puppet House and Playground at 62nd Street (same phone number above), and playgrounds at 93rd Street, 91st Street, and two particularly exiciting ones at 85th and 67th Streets just off Central Park West. Lincoln Center is in this part of town; there, depending on the season, you'll find dance, opera, symphony, or theater. The Lincoln Center Library has a children's section with special exhibits from time to time.

THE AMERICAN MUSEUM OF NATURAL HISTORY AND THE HAYDEN PLANETARIUM (79th–81st Streets and Central Park West, 212-769-5900 for museum, 212-769-5920 for planetarium). These two need no introduction. Favorites at the museum include the diving whale; the dinosaurs, of course; the 94-foot dioramas with mammals of three continents; the Minerals and Gems Hall; and the Discovery Room for ages 5 to 10 on Saturdays and Sundays from 12 to 4:30 P.M. You won't want to leave without seeing the Nature Max Theater, a four-story screen presentation that's thrilling. Kids of all ages like the museum. The planetarium is best for school-age kids, with its sky show using the world's largest computer automation system and over 100 special effects projectors plus two floors of exhibits, including one of the world's largest meteorites, the Hall of the Sun, and "Your Weight on Other Worlds." Strollers are allowed; there are a nice children's gift shop and small-size drinking fountains.

Right next door to the planetarium and museum is the New York Historical Society, 170 Central Park West, 212-873-3400. From time to time they have an exhibit of interest to kids and programs especially for them. Call to check.

Two museums that used to be in midtown have moved to the Upper West Side since the last edition of our book; the Museum of American Folk Art and the Children's Museum of Manhattan.

THE MUSEUM OF AMERICAN FOLK ART 2 Lincoln Square, on Columbus Avenue between 65th and 66th Streets, Zip: 10023, 212-977-7298). This museum (which does not charge admission) is dedicated to preserving the rich folk heritage of America and often has exhibits that will appeal to kids—things like whirligigs and weathervanes, toys, scrimshaw, quilts, and folk paintings—especially the ones with animals and children as their subject. At press time the education department of the museum hadn't been set up in its new location, but we were promised that workshops would be scheduled and would include families. Call the number above to see what's available.

THE CHILDREN'S MUSEUM OF MANHATTAN (212 West 83rd Street, Zip: 10024, 212-721-1234). As we write this, the museum has not moved to this new location, so we can't give you a first-hand account, but we can tell you what you should be able to expect in the new spot. The centerpiece of the new museum's exhibit and education center is a walk-through model of the brain called "The Brainatarium," a domed theater that introduces kids to their most powerful possession through an animated sound, light, and laser show. From there, the kids enter an exhibit called "Magical Patterns," a multicolored kaleidoscopic exhibit where they write their names and record their fingerprints, giving them access to a network of brain games that provides personal information about themselves. "City Patterns," a working model of the cityscape and of underground New York, invites kids to explore and wander, and a "Toddler Center" will make the littlest visitors happy. Frequent performances and workshops are planned for the new space; call for details. It's guaranteed to make for a fun-filled visit with any age child—even teens have been considered in the thoughtfully designed space.

For good children's theater in this part of town, call New Stagings for Youth of the Open Eye Theater, 212-769-4141 and see what's scheduled. We saw a work-in-progress, about Old New York and were impressed with the high quality of the production.

Check, too, with Symphony Space at 95th Street and Broadway (212-864-5400) to see whether the Paper Bag Players, one of the most creative companies ever, are scheduled. You and the kids will love the show.

Harlem

For a brochure about the area with information on tours and special events, contact the Harlem Visitor and Convention Association, 310 Lenox Avenue, New York, New York, 10027, 212-427-3317. Some of the highlights of a visit to this area follow.

THE MUSEUM OF THE AMERICAN INDIAN (Broadway at 158th Street, Zip: 10032, 212-283-2420). This museum is devoted to collecting, preserving, studying, and exhibiting everything connected with the anthropology of the aboriginal peoples of the Americas and is well worth a visit. Demonstrations by visiting Native American artists and artisans—in the past they have included basketry, bead work, doll making, and silver work—take place in the first-floor exhibit area. Call for details on music and storytelling programs held on weekends throughout the year.

THE STUDIO MUSEUM (144 West 125th Street, Zip: 10027, 212-864-4500). This museum celebrates contemporary and historical African, Caribbean, and American art. Special events include puppet shows, storytelling, and concerts.

AUNT LEN'S DOLL AND TOY MUSEUM (6 Hamilton Terrace, on 141st Street between Convent and Saint Nicholas Avenues, Zip: 10031, 212-281-4143). Call ahead to make an appointment to see

Aunt Len's collection of over 3,000 dolls, dollhouses, and antique toys.

As long as you're uptown, go all the way up to the Cloisters, a branch of the Metropolitan Museum of Art dedicated to medieval art, located in Fort Tryon Park, overlooking the Hudson. Call 212-923-3700 for information on special children's programs which are held one weekend a month and daily at holiday times for kids 5–12.

The Other Boroughs

If you have a day to spare, why not spend it in one of the other boroughs—Queens, Brooklyn, Staten Island, or the Bronx? There are lots of special things to do in each, and most are easy enough to reach by public transportation. Just call the numbers listed here for directions.

Staten Island

Start off your day with a ride on the Staten Island Ferry. You'll see Governor's Island, the Statue of Liberty, Brooklyn, New Jersey, The Verrazano Bridge, and the Manhattan skyline. The ferry runs seven days a week, 24 hours a day. Call 212-806-6940 for information. When you get off the ferry, you can take the new Snug Harbor Trolley to Snug Harbor Cultural Center, 26 landmark buildings overlooking New York Bay. On Sundays there are free guided tours; call 718-448-6166. The highlight of a visit to this area will be a stop at the Staten Island Children's Museum. The museum is full of hands-on environmental exhibitions, really creative offerings that kids love. For the price of museum admission ($2 for adults, and kids under 3 are free) you may catch a special performance—music, dance, theater, or puppetry—usually on Saturday mornings. Every spring the museum sponsors Meadowfair, an outdoor arts festival for the whole family. The Children's Gift shop is a nice place to buy souvenirs or presents for friends back home. You'll like the small botanical garden and the duck pond—perfect for a background to a picnic. Call 718-273-2060 for information. From here you can drive or take a cab to the comfortably sized Staten Island Zoo, where the kids can have a pony ride and feed the animals. As we write this, we've been told that the trolley mentioned above may go to the Zoo from Snug Harbor—call to check. Call 718-442-3100 for details.

Admission is $1 for everyone over 3; children under 3 are admitted free, and Wednesdays are free for everyone.

Richmondtown Restoration, a re-creation of life in Staten Island over the past 300 years, is another good destination for adventurous families. There are 26 historic buildings on 20 acres, and 12 are open to the public. Your kids will want to see the 17th-century school, the antique doll and toy exhibit, and the old fire engines. Outdoor demonstrations of gardening, domestic chores, woodworking, harness making, and so forth, take place during the summer season. Tours for kids 3 and up and their parents are available. Call 718-351-1611 for information on daily events.

For an idea of what's happening on Staten Island on the day you decide to go, call the Staten Island Council on the Arts hotline, 718-720-1800.

Brooklyn

If you begin your visit in the historic landmark section of Brooklyn Heights, you'll enjoy the most spectacular view of lower Manhattan from the Promenade. One of our favorite playgrounds is at the end of Pierrepont Street at the Promenade. Prospect Park— large and lovely with wooded hills, lakes, and open meadows—has a zoo and a Children's Farm (open from spring through the fall). Call 718-788-0055 for events in the park, 718-965-6560 for zoo information, and 718-965-6586 for the Children's Farm. A short walk from the park is the Brooklyn Museum (Eastern Parkway at Washington Avenue, Brooklyn, 11225), an imposing building where special programs for kids are often scheduled. The gift shop here is excellent and there's a separate one just for kids. Call 718-638-5000 for information.

THE BROOKLYN BOTANICAL GARDEN (1000 Washington Avenue, Zip: 11225, 718-622-4433). Fifty-two acres of everything from a replica of a Japanese mill-and-pond garden to a children's garden planted and harvested by New York's school kids is right next door to the museum. The newest addition to the grounds is the Steinhardt Conservatory Complex, which includes a Discovery Room just for kids. Ask about their children's videotape and the booklet *Ready, Set, Grow.*

BROOKLYN CHILDREN'S MUSEUM (145 Brooklyn Avenue at Saint Mark's Avenue, Brooklyn, New York 11213, 718-735-4432). The museum is a wonderful stop in Brooklyn. This is the world's first children's museum. There's always something exciting happening, from the permanent exhibits that include a three-foot-wide river that flows by the entrance to lots of other things to be manipulated, played with, and enjoyed. On weekdays after school and on weekends there are all kinds of great workshops and activities: helping to make a mural, listening to stories, and so on. Call for exact dates and times. The kids' gift shop has inexpensive souvenirs, and the whole experience is one we recommend.

BROOKLYN MUSEUM (200 Eastern Parkway, Brooklyn, Zip: 11238, 718-638-5000). The permanent collection includes a sculpture garden, Islamic, Oriental, and Egyptian art, costumes, textiles, period rooms, American and European painting. Every Saturday at 11:00 A.M. kids 4–12 may join "Arty Facts," a tour of one of the galleries followed by a craft workshop, and on Saturdays and Sundays at 2:00 P.M. kids 6–12 are invited to a similar program called "What's Up?" The museum has a terrific gift shop and one just for kids called Art Smart. Suggested admission for adults is $3, kids 12 and under are free.

THE NEW YORK AQUARIUM (on Coney Island at West 8th Street off Surf Avenue, Brooklyn, New York 11224, 718-265-FISH). This is another Brooklyn offering that's great for kids. Indoor and outdoor exhibits are fun, and as long as the weather is not too bad, there are performing sea lions and dolphins in the summer and whales and sea lions in winter in the outdoor aquatheater. Our kids loved the show. The aquarium sponsors many weekend programs for kids and their parents throughout the year. Call for specifics.

If you're going to be in Brooklyn, consider seeing a performance of a most unusual and creative group called the Shadow Box Theater. With an office in New York (212-724-0677 or 877-7356) but with a theater at the Brooklyn YWCA at 30 Third Avenue (across from the Brooklyn Academy of Music), the group presents wonderful plays for kids that combine shadow puppetry, body and hand puppets, live performers, and original music. All of Shadow Box's presentations have a message (one recent presentation, "Little Is Big," illustrated how it is possible to settle differences peaceably). From time to time the folks from Shadow Box perform at the Museum of Natural History or in other spots around New York—it's best to call and see where they're going to be while you're in the city.

The Bronx

THE BRONX ZOO (185th Street and Southern Boulevard, Bronx, New York 10460, 212-220-5100). Everyone's heard of this zoo. This is a full day's excursion and fun for all ages. Pack a picnic (the lines can be long at the snack bars) and take your time seeing all there is to see—the new Jungle World, the World of Darkness, the World of Birds, Wild Asia, and best of all, for kids, the Children's Zoo. Here the little ones can explore a prairie dog tunnel, try on a turtle shell, or climb on a rope model of a spider's web. Our kids—from the 3-year-old all the way up—love it. The zoo is a lovely place with all kinds of special events at different times of the year. Don't rush a visit to the zoo, and if you can, bring a picnic with you, the food choices are okay but far from terrific.

THE BRONX CONSERVATORY AND BOTANICAL GARDENS (Southern Boulevard and 200th Street, Bronx, Zip: 10458, 212-220-8700). These are right across from the zoo and are very beautiful, but it's doubtful that you'll have the energy left over after the zoo trip. Perhaps another day when you can take your time and enjoy the beautiful gardens; have lunch alongside the Bronx River; wonder at the 60-foot palms, tropical ferns, and desert cactus all under the glass roof of the beautiful Enid A. Haupt Conservatory. If you're going to be in New York for an extended stay, your kids can learn to grow their own vegetables in a class at the Children's Garden.

Queens

One of the most neglected boroughs, Queens has some wonderful offerings for families:

THE NEW YORK HALL OF SCIENCE (47-01 111th Street, Flushing Meadows, Corona Park, New York 11368, 718-699-0005). Here's a hands-on science museum, a place where the worlds of science and technology are close enough to touch. Exhibits dealing with color and illusion, investigation of atoms, and self-sensing feedback are all staffed with "Explainers"—college students, majoring in sciences and communications, who explain, demonstrate, and discuss. These "Explainers" also lead on-floor demonstrations and workshops. On weekends there are family workshops for kids 5 years and up. We saw a laser demonstration, watched the dissection of a cow's eye, and spent some time at a color and light workshop. The museum provides backpacks for small children and has an area for changing and nursing babies, small-size drinking fountains, and a "snack-a-mat" for sandwiches, drinks, and snacks.

THE ALLEY POND ENVIRONMENTAL CENTER (228-06 Northern Boulevard, Douglaston, New York 11363, 718-229-4000). If the crowds and quick pace of New York get to you, consider a retreat here. Alley Pond is a nature center located on the northern fringe of a park. It is home to rabbits, snakes, turtles, fish, frogs, and a dove and includes exhibits of taxidermied animals and a please-touch display. The center's backyard consists of woodlands, a meadow, wetlands, and Alley Creek, a tidal waterway that attracts migrating birds in the fall and spring. On any day of the year you're likely to find an educational program in progress that you can attach yourself to. The center also schedules walks with their naturalists, stargazing, macramé snowflake workshops, and lots of other activities. Call for schedules. The gift shop has treats for as little as 25 cents, picnic benches are available, and admission is free.

SHEA STADIUM (Flushing, Zip: 11368). For Mets games, call 718-507-8499; for Jets games, 212-421-6600.

Time Out

For the times you want to do grown-up things here are some people who can help with the kids:

BARNARD COLLEGE (212-280-2035). Barnard students are available to baby-sit for $4 per hour; 50 cents extra for more than two kids. You'll have to provide transportation for your sitter after 9:00 P.M. Remember that the students are unavailable during vacation times.

GILBERT CHILD CARE AGENCY, INC. (115 West 57th Street, Suite 3R, Zip: 10019, 212-757-7900). This agency charges according to the age of the child—newborn to 2 months is $7.00 per hour, 2 to 9 months is $6.10, 9 months and over is $5.50. There are a four-hour minimum and a $3.00 transportation charge during the day and $6.00 after 8:00 P.M. Arrange sessions by 3:00 P.M. the day before you want a sitter. For the same charge, sitters will take kids to any events the parents request—the Circle Line, Radio City, and so forth. The agency is licensed and bonded and has been operating since 1980.

Accommodations

Bed and Breakfasts

Although New York may not be the kind of place that suggests "bed and breakfast," there are three bed and breakfast agencies just waiting to find you a room in an apartment or private house, or, better still for families, an entire unhosted apartment.

URBAN VENTURES, INC. (P.O. Box 426, New York, New York 10024, 212-594-5650). Mary McAulay has been placing visitors in New York homes since 1979. Possibilities range from penthouses to walk-ups, entire apartments with no host, or bed and breakfast with a host who can "offer advice and an umbrella." Prices range from $38 to $85 per night, and for entire apartments, $65 per night or up. One apartment that they have listed is a two-bedroom, two-bath on the Upper West Side that comes complete "with dishes, sheets, towels, and umbrellas" and costs $160 per night; another, a one-bedroom on East 54th Street has room for four and costs $140. A relative from Norway used this service and was delighted with her room in an apartment near NYU.

CITY LIGHTS B AND B, LTD. (P.O. Box 20355, Cherokee Station, New York, New York 10028, 212-737-7049). According to the owner, most of this agency's hosts are happy to take families. Many have a spare room, cots are provided for kids, and cribs are available at a small additional cost. Unhosted apartments are available as well. Rates range from $50 to $85 per night; unhosted apartments range from $85 to $180 per night. Accommodations are primarily in Manhattan, but there are some spacious town houses in Brooklyn Heights and Park Slope that welcome guests and there are places in the other boroughs as well. In most cases there's a two-night minimum stay required.

AT HOME IN NEW YORK (P.O. Box 407, New York, New York 10185, 212-265-8539 or 956-3125). This is a relatively new addition to the b and b network in New York with hosted and unhosted apartments to rent in Manhattan, Brooklyn, Queens, and Staten Island. According to owner Lois Rooks, her hosts and hostesses are from varied backgrounds and careers. One with an interesting duplex in Greenwich Village is a research scientist who conducts walking tours of his neighborhood, another is an actor-magician who will pick guests up in Manhattan and drive them to his rustic Staten Island home. Rates for a hosted b and b range from $60 to $75 per night double occupancy and from $75 to $250 for unhosted apartments.

Hotels

LOEW'S SUMMIT HOTEL (Lexington Avenue at 51st Street, Zip: 10022, 212-752-7000). All rooms have refrigerators; cribs are available at no extra charge. Children 14 and under stay free with parents, and baby-sitting is available for $8.50 per hour. The hotel has a health club with Nautilus equipment, exercise cycles, jacuzzi, and sauna, too, but it's for adults only. Regular rates range from $150 to $180 per night for double rooms; weekend packages are available.

MANHATTAN EAST SIDE HOTELS (505 East 75th Street, Zip: 10021-3103, 212-772-2900, 800-ME-SUITE). This all-suite group manages nine properties in all—the Beekman Towers, Dumont Plaza, Eastgate Tower, Lyden Gardens, Lyden House, Plaza Fifty, Shelburne Murray Hill, Southgate Tower, and Surrey Hotel—and all but one of these are on the East Side. There are studios, one- and two-bedroom suites, and at the Plaza Fifty, even a three-bedroom. All have kitchens. Regular rates average just under $200 per night for a one-bedroom suite, but special promotional deals are offered throughout the year. Weekend and summer rates are usually much lower, too, as low as $120 per night for a one-bedroom suite, $93 for a studio suite. Baby-sitting can be arranged for $8.50 per hour.

OMNI PARK CENTRAL HOTEL (Seventh Avenue at 56th Street, Zip: 10019, 212-247-8000 or 800-THE-OMNI). We like the way the people who make the policy at the Omni think. They've worked out a great deal for families that offers them two rooms for the price of one at a rate of $169 per night during the summer and some holiday periods. We don't have to tell you how nice it is not to have to be crammed into the same room with your kids on a vacation and also how expensive two rooms can be, especially in a big city hotel. The Omni is ideally located in midtown within walking distance of lots of attractions and even Central Park. Besides this great two-for-the-price-of-one deal, the Omni also employs a "Concierge for Kids" who is available to provide information on kid-oriented activities, help plan family outings in and around Manhattan, arrange for baby-sitting, make recommendations for family-friendly restaurants, and provide help in case of an emergency. And there's more: The hotel provides half-price children's portions at Nicole, their restaurant, and will pack a picnic lunch for a family of four to enjoy in the park.

HOTEL BEVERLY (125 East 50th Street, Zip: 10022, 212-753-2700 or 800-223-9045). This is a small (by New York standards), European-style hotel which is a short walk to the United Nations, Fifth Avenue shopping, and Radio City Music Hall. The Beverly has 100 one-bedroom suites with sofa beds in the living rooms and complete kitchenettes. A weekend double rate for a one-bedroom suite is $110; $10 extra for each additional person.

The Hyatt has a hotel right by Grand Central Station at Park

Avenue and 42nd Street called the Grand Hyatt. See page 50 for what you can expect in the way of special services for families at this Hyatt as well as the others around the country. For details on this one in particular, call 212-883-1234 or 800-233-1234.

PHILADELPHIA

Philadelphia was a big hit with our kids. It's a vibrant, friendly place with loads of attractions that are just right for families. As any school-age child knows, the City of Brotherly Love is chock full of history, so what better place for a family to see their social studies lessons come to life? In the material that follows, we've given you a few ideas for your trip to Philadelphia and a few on places to go just a bit beyond the city. Remember, too, to be sure to have at least one soft pretzel, a Philly cheesesteak, and a tastykake (this city's version of a cupcake) before you leave.

For Information

Begin by contacting the Philadelphia Convention and Visitors Bureau, 1515 Market Street, Suite 2020, Philadelphia, Pennsylvania 19102, 215-636-1666. Ask them for their Philadelphia Visitors Guide, filled with useful information.

One excellent source of information on the city from its historical perspective is the Visitors Center at Independence Park, Third and Chestnut Streets, 215-597-8974. Their half-hour film, "Independence," is a fascinating attention-grabbing introduction to the city and is shown throughout the day. The Center also houses an exhibit called "A Promise of Permanency," which uses state-of-the-art computer technology to explore key Constitutional issues and milestones. Admission is free and hours are 9:00 A.M. to 5:00 P.M.

If you decide to see a play while you're in town, you can take advantage of half-price tickets available on the day of the performance. Just stop by the Cultural Connection TixStop booth in the Convention and Visitors Bureau's office at 16th Street and JFK Boulevard. Hours are Tuesday through Thursday 11:30 A.M. to 3:30 P.M., and Fridays and Saturdays until 5:00 P.M.

You'll find lots of guide books available on Philadelphia in general, but one written especially for families is *Philadelphia with Children* ($9.95) by Elizabeth S. Gephart and Anne S. Cunningham, published by Starrhill Press, P.O. Box 32342, Washington,

D.C. 20007. The authors and their four children spent a year visiting places from historical sites to zoos to amusement parks. They've come up with lots of adventures for kids in and around Philadelphia—from milking cows to tubing to children's theater.

And finally, if you are going to be getting around Philadelphia by public transportation, you will be using the Southeastern Pennsylvania Transit Authority (SEPTA) buses, subways, and trolleys. For information on how to get around on the SEPTA system, call 215-574-7800.

Tours

Centipede Candlelight Tours was voted "Best in Philly" by *Philadelphia* magazine. Tours begin at 6:30 P.M. from City Tavern at Second and Walnut Streets every Wednesday, Friday, and Saturday and include a stroll through the hidden gardens and courtyards of Society Hill or a walk past the same sites that our founding fathers visited. The tour costs $5 for adults, $4 for kids under 12. For information and reservations, call 215-735-3123.

Seventy-six Carriage Company offers 20- and 35-minute tours by horse-drawn carriage so that you can sense the feeling of the city 200 years ago. The sounds of the hoofbeats and iron wheels on the cobblestones help make the "most historic square mile in America" come to life. The 20-minute tour is $10 for up to four people, $2.50 for each additional person; the 35-minute tour goes up to $20 and $5 respectively. Call 215-923-8516 to arrange a ride.

American Trolley Tours offers a three-hour tour on a Victorian trolley bus lead by a guide dressed in 18th-century costume. The tour begins at the Visitors Center at 16th Street and JFK Boulevard and includes Center City, Independence National Historic Park, the Betsy Ross House, and Elfreth's Alley. Tours run twice a day year-round; admission is $14 for adults, $8 for 3 and over, and free for under 3.

Fairmount Trolleys run tours on Saturdays and Sundays at 10:00 A.M. and again at 2:00 P.M. The two-and-a-half-hour tour includes stops at the Betsy Ross House, the Historic District, and Fairmount Park. While in the park, everyone gets a chance to visit one of the colonial homes. The tour begins at the Visitors Center, 16th and JFK Boulevard, and costs $5.50 for adults and $4.50 for kids. Call 215-636-1666 for information.

Talk-A-Walk, a company based in New York, has put together a do-it-yourself cassette tour of Independence Park—75 minutes of history and commentary that you can follow at your own pace. The tour begins at the Visitors Center and ends at Independence Hall. The tape may be ordered directly from 30 Waterside Plaza, New York, New York 100010, 212-686-0356; it costs $9.95.

Things to See and Do

East Philadelphia/Old City Historic District

INDEPENDENCE NATIONAL HISTORIC PARK (313 Walnut Street, Zip: 19106, 215-597-8974). "The most historic square mile in America" contains the Liberty Bell, Independence Hall, Congress Hall, Old City Hall, Graff House, Second Bank of the U.S., Franklin Court, the Army-Navy Museum, Marine Corps Memorial Museum, Carpenter's Hall, City Tavern, the Todd House, and the Bishop White House. Don't you dare leave Philadelphia without seeing the following:

LIBERTY BELL PAVILION; (Market Street, between Fifth and Sixth Streets, Zip: 19106). Without a doubt, this is one of the most cherished symbols of American freedom and is housed in its own glass-enclosed building right across from Independence Hall. It's on view from 9:00 to 5:00 every day for free.

INDEPENDENCE HALL (Chestnut Street between Fifth and Sixth Streets, Zip: 19106). Here is where the Declaration of Independence was adopted and the U.S. Constitution was written. It's open daily from 9:00 A.M. to 5:00 P.M. and is free with a 20-minute tour provided.

FRANKLIN COURT (between Third and Fourth Streets, Chestnut and Market, Zip: 19106). Benjamin Franklin lived here and now it stands as a tribute to this extraordinary man. Kids love the mirror hall with flashing neon signs and the telephone hotline that lets them chat with famous people from America's past.

CITY TAVERN (Second and Walnut Streets, Zip: 19106, 215-923-6059). This working restaurant is a reconstruction of the famous Revolutionary War Tavern, where delegates to the First and Second Continental Congress gathered for informal discussion. It's open from 11:00 A.M. to 11:00 P.M. daily.

GRAFF HOUSE (Seventh and Market Streets, Zip: 19106). You'll want to visit the reconstructed house where Thomas Jefferson lived while he was writing the Declaration of Independence.

HOME OF BETSY ROSS (239 Arch Street, Zip: 19106). Of course your kids are going to want to see the house where Betsy Ross, seamstress, upholsterer, and patriot, lived. This was her home from 1773 to 1786 and where she was supposed to have made the first American flag, following a sketch by George Washington.

ELFRETH'S ALLEY/THE ELFRETH'S ALLEY MUSEUM (126 Elfreth's Alley, Zip: 19106, 215-574-0560). This 18th-century thoroughfare is the oldest continuously residential street in America. The 30 houses that line the alley were built between 1728 and 1836 and occupied by middle-class craftspeople and shopkeepers. The privately owned homes are open to the public once a year—the first weekend in June. The museum is open daily from 10:00A.M. to 4:00 P.M. except in January and February, when it is open only on weekends. Admission is free.

U.S. MINT (Fifth and Arch Streets, Zip: 19106, 215-597-7350). The first mint was started by George Washington not far from here; this is the city's fourth mint building. The first part of the exhibit illustrates the history of coinage and the second part lets you see how pieces of metal become coins. Plan to spend about an hour here.

Center City

PLEASE TOUCH MUSEUM (210 North 21st Street, Zip: 19103, 215-963-0667). This was the first museum in the country designed specifically for kids who are 7 years and under. Our kids, even one who exceeds the 7-year limit, loved it. "All of the exhibits are designed to delight children and their families. It's best to allow the child to chart his or her own course through the museum." The museum is set up to encourage hands-on exploration with tantalizing exhibits such as "The Doctor's Office," "The Grocery Store," a mini-television station, and the "Show and Tell Gallery." The Resource Center is geared to kids 5 to 7 and is a place where they can examine fossils and rocks, experience the world of computers, learn about dinosaurs, create their own stories with puppets, and explore different cultures by means of "discovery boxes," treasure chests filled with a variety of please-touch artifacts.

The Tot Spot is an area especially designed for the youngest visitors with space to crawl, climb, and explore.

Workshops for adults and kids together are offered throughout the year on Saturdays. You can expect topics such as "Dad and Me: Cooking for Kids"; "Fairy Tale Favorites"; "Create-a-Castle"; or "Create Your Own Folktale." On your way out of the museum, you'll want to be sure to stop at the store—just full of interesting and educational goodies for kids.

ACADEMY OF NATURAL SCIENCES MUSEUM (19th Street and Benjamin Franklin Parkway, Zip: 19103, 215-299-1000). Your kids will love being greeted by the roaring dinosaur who guards the lobby entrance. The museum's "Discovering Dinosaurs" is enormously popular and features Tyrannosauras Rex and more than a dozen other dinosaurs and their assorted prehistoric relatives; a high-tech video presentation; a prize-winning multimedia show; a computer quiz; and a drawer full of fossils. It's great fun.

Outside-In is a mini-museum designed for kids 12 and under. It brings the great outdoors down to kid's scale and includes a live beehive, a fossil cave with dinosaur footprints, aquariums, and an insect zoo.

Try to schedule your visit to coincide with one of the museum's Saturday Aventures, workshops on science and nature for kids 3–12 with topics such as "Animals with Bad Reputations," "Trees are Terrific," and "Animals in Myth and Legend."

EDGAR ALLAN POE NATIONAL HISTORIC SITE (532 North Seventh Street, corner of Seventh and Spring Garden Streets, Zip: 19123, 215-597-8780). This site is the only remaining Philadelphia home of this great American poet and writer. It serves as our nation's memorial to him; tours, a slide presentation, and exhibits focus on his life and works. The tour raises some intriguing questions about the author and would be quite interesting to older kids who are somewhat familiar with his work. Admission is free, and you might want to take advantage of the pleasant picnic area right on the site.

THE FRANKLIN INSTITUTE (20th Street and Benjamin Franklin Parkway, Zip: 19103, 215-448-1200). This is one of the country's leading science museums. It's a fabulous place to learn all about science through an ingenious array of hands-on exhibits. Our kids still talk about crawling through the throbbing corridors of the giant human heart. Other exhibits let them feel their hair stand on end because of static electricity and let them create their own rivers and mountains. Family workshops are held on Saturdays. We spent one Saturday morning mesmerized at one on semiconductors that was presented by a Mr. Wizard–type scientist with a wonderful sense of humor.

The Institute's Fels Planetarium offers sky shows every day, and on weekends at 11:00 A.M. there's a special show for kids 7 and younger. Admission to the Institute is $5 for adults, $4 for kids 4–11, and free for kids under 4. The Planetarium costs an additional $1.50; the children's show is $1.

Fairmount Park

Fairmount Park is the largest landscaped city park in the world, with more than 8,700 acres of trails, creeks, and jogging and bike paths. A good way to get there is to take the Fairmount Park Trolley Bus that leaves every 20 minutes from the Philadelphia Visitors Center, 16th and JFK Boulevard, from 10:00 A.M. to 4:20 P.M. and from Independence Park Visitor Center, Third and Chestnut, from 11:00 A.M. to 5:00 P.M. Fare is $2 adults, 50 cents for kids.

Once in the park, you can rent a bike at 1 Boat House Row (236-4359). Bike maps are available at the Park Office (868-0001). The whole family will get a kick out of seeing the Boat House Row at night when all of its Tudor Houses are outlined with white lights. Kids like the Andorra Natural Area, a rustic nature center where they can touch antlers and porcupine quills and handle turtles, snakes, and rabbits.

PHILADELPHIA MARIONETTE THEATER AND MUSEUM (Belmont Mansion Drive, Zip: 19131, 215-879-1213). Magical marionette productions of "Pinocchio," "Jack and the Beanstalk," the "Reluctant Dragon," and other classics feature traditional, European-style marionettes. All are wonderful for the entire family to see but because of their enormous popularity, reservations are an absolute must. Weekday performances are at 10:00 A.M.; Sunday performances at 2:00 P.M., and admission is $4 per person.

ZOOLOGICAL SOCIETY OF PHILADELPHIA (34th Street and Girard Avenue, Zip: 19104, 215-243-1100). America's first zoo features 1,600 mammals, birds, and reptiles from around the world. Exhibits include the World of Primates, Bear Country, and a Bird House. The George D. Widener Memorial Treehouse is a great favorite with kids—they get a chance to climb a giant beehive, feel what it's like to hatch from an egg, ride a dinosaur, emerge from a cocoon, investigate life inside a blossom, and explore a four-story tropical tree to get a look at life from an animal's-eye view. The youngest kids will love the Children's Zoo with its live animal shows, cavorting sea lions, pony rides, and petting pen. A Victorian picnic grove makes a nice place for a rest stop.

Zoo hours are usually 9:30 A.M. to 5:00 P.M. during the year and until 6:00 P.M. during the summer. Admission is $4.50 for adults; $3.50 for kids.

Beyond the City

At the city line, separating Philadelphia from Bucks County is the world's largest shopping mall, Franklin Mills, with more than 230 stores. Here you'll find great outlet shopping plus lots of family entertainment. If you enter at the 49th Street Galleria you'll find such places as Casey's Dugout with their softball and batting cages, Rollertowne USA, Bowling Green, Miniature Golf and Chase, a state of the art laser game. This is in addition to numerous music, magic, juggling and puppet shows, special children's activities and perhaps the largest video game room around. There's even a babysitting service for children 3 and older at Kids Corner, open Monday to Saturday from 10:00 A.M. to 9:00 P.M. and Sundays from 11:00 A.M. to 6:00 P.M., staffed by experienced YMCA personnel. The cost is $3 per hour per child with a three hour maximum. For more details call 215-632-1500.

SESAME PLACE (100 Sesame Road, Langhorne, Pennsylvania 19047, 215-752-7070). Just 30 minutes from Philadelphia, Sesame Place is really lots of fun for the kids and parents, too. (See Theme Parks, page 86.) The best thing about this park is that time spent there is anything but passive—kids and grown-ups alike get to jump, climb, and get involved in all sorts of fun exhibits. My kids' favorites were the water rides—be sure to bring a swim suit and try to go on a nice day. Younger kids like to splash around in the Count's Fount and Little Bird's Bird Bath; the older ones head for the Runaway Rapids and Slippery Slopes. Kids also love the regular guest appearances by Jim Henson's muppet favorites—Bert, Ernie, the Honkers, Cookie Monster, Grover, and Prairie Dawn. Another big favorite with the kids and adults as well is the Computer Gallery with more than 50 especially designed activities that make learning fun. To prove just how enlightened the designers of the park were, there are changing tables in both the men's and women's rooms, and the food in the restaurant is actually good for you. Admission is $12.95 for adults, $14.95 for kids 3–15, and free for kids under 3. A special twilight rate of $9.75 goes into effect after 5:00 P.M. Since hours vary with the season—the park is open only from May through October—it's best to call ahead for information on the time you will be going.

If you decide to overnight near Sesame Place, we highly recommend the Royce Hotel, located directly across the street. If you or the kids get tired or cranky you can cool off in their indoor pool, take a nap and then return to the park later in the day. They can be reached at 215-547-4100 or 800-23-ROYCE.

VALLEY FORGE NATIONAL HISTORIC PARK (North Gulph Road and Route 23, Valley Forge, Pennsylvania, 19481, 215-783-7700). Valley Forge was the site of the American army's winter encampment during the Revolutionary War. Within days the once peaceful farmland just 18 miles from Philadelphia was transformed into a busy military operation. For six months the men drilled here and supply problems eventually improved. On June 19, 1778, the army marched out of Valley Forge as a solid, unified fighting force. You can explore the area by car, bicycle, or on foot—there are 2,788 acres in all.

LONGWOOD GARDENS (Route 1, P.O. Box 501, Kennett Square, Pennsylvania 19348, 215-388-6741). Just 30 miles from the city, Longwood is one of America's first tree parks, with 350 outdoor acres and four acres of glass-enclosed gardens. The children's garden offers youngsters an opportunity to play in a garden designed just for them. They're welcome to splash in the fountains, smell the flowers, walk through the maze, and play in a treehouse. Special programs for kids—comedy theater and folksinging, to name two—are held on weekends throughout the year. Call for details.

BRANDYWINE RIVER MUSEUM (Box 141, Chadds Ford, Pennsylvania 19317, 215-388-7601). This is the home of the largest collection of paintings by one of America's best known artists, Andrew Wyeth. It also exhibits the work of N. C. Wyeth and Jamie Wyeth, Andrew's father and son. The museum's Christmas exhibit of dolls and trains is something you won't want to miss if you are in the area at holiday time. In nice weather, consider combining a trip to the museum with a trip on the river—in a tube or a canoe.

POINT PLEASANT TUBE RENTALS (Route 32, Point Pleasant, Pennsylvania 18950, 215-297-8181). Just a little over an hour from the city, you and your family can kick your shoes off and take a tube or raft ride down the Delaware River. Call ahead for reservations; don't forget your bathing suits and sunscreen.

Time Out

ROCKING HORSE CHILD CARE CENTER (Sixth and Walnut Streets, Independence Square West, Zip: 19106, 215-592-8257). This day-care center is open Monday through Friday from 6:45A.M. to 6:00 P.M. and staff is ready and willing to have your kids join the fun at any point during the day. During the school year, the ages are 6 weeks to 5 years, but in summer, when Rocking Horse runs a summer camp, kids up to 12 may be accommodated.

Accommodations

Bed and Breakfasts

SOCIETY HILL HOTEL (301 Chestnut Street, Zip: 19106, 215-925-1919). This well-known bed and breakfast inn is happy to accommodate families. The owners describe their place as an "eclectic, fun-loving place with antiques, brass beds and a great, relaxed restaurant specializing in the best Philadelphia cheese steaks." Rates range from $77 to $130 per night, which includes breakfast delivered to your room each morning. Special packages combining dinner at a local restaurant or tickets to a comedy club can be arranged. It's located just two blocks from Independence National Historic Park.

LA RESERVE BED AND BREAKFAST (1804 Pine Street, Zip: 19103, 215-735-1137). This bed and breakfast is located in the Victorian Rittenhouse Square section of Center City. The owners of the 140-year-old private mansion have eight rooms available, with names like Le Beaudelaire, Le Mallarmé, and Le Stendahl. Rates begin at $40 for a double and go up to $75.

Hotels

THE HERSHEY PHILADELPHIA HOTEL (Broad and Locust Streets, Zip: 19107, 215-893-1600 or 800-533-3131). The Hershey people really know how to make families happy. Their hotel is within walking distance of just about everything, has a four-story atrium lobby, indoor pool, racquetball courts, a roof garden with sundecks, and a complete health spa. Special weekend rates are impressive: $90 for a double room, kids 18 and under in the room for free. These rooms are large, too, with plenty of room for a family of four. On holiday weekends (Presidents' Weekend, Easter, Labor Day, etc.) a special three-nights-for-the-price-of-two is available. All packages include use of the indoor pool and health spa. Our kids loved topping a day of sightseeing off with an hour in the pool. Another nice feature for families is the concierge service at the hotel, where you can get lots of advice on kid-oriented activities and help in arranging babysitting.

THE LATHAM HOTEL (17th Street at Walnut, Zip: 19103, 215-563-7474 or 800-528-4261). The Latham is within a three-block radius of 136 restaurants, 19 art galleries, and over 300 boutiques—but who's counting? Regular rates range from $138 to $400 for a double, but what the hotel calls its Irresistible Weekend rate is much lower and great for families—$89 for a double with a full breakfast and valet parking.

FOUR SEASONS HOTEL (One Logan Square, Zip: 19103, 215-963-1500). Since this hotel is located on the Benjamin Franklin Parkway, it is ultra-convenient for visits to the Please Touch Museum, the Academy of Natural Sciences, and the Franklin Institute. The hotel has an indoor pool and a health spa, nice extras. At Christmastime, the Four Seasons schedules a special event called "Tea Time in Wonderland"—Alice in Wonderland and the Mad Hatter greet kids and sit them down to an extravagant tea of scones with double devon cream, sandwiches, and cakes plus entertainment. Double rooms on weekends begin at $130; with a special Family Plan it's possible to arrange for two double rooms—one for the kids, one for the parents—with a 50 percent reduction on the second room. If you don't mind sharing a room with the kids, there's no extra charge as long as they're under 18.

GUEST QUARTERS SUITE HOTEL (Philadelphia International Airport, One Gateway Center, Zip: 19153, 215-365-6600 or 800-424-2900). This all-suite hotel is located at the airport, about 15 minutes from the center of Philadelphia. Suites overlook a plant-filled, eight-story atrium. The kids will love the indoor pool, and you'll appreciate the whirlpool and sauna. Parking is free, and a complimentary breakfast is included in the room rate. Rates vary; special weekend packages may be as low as $89 for a suite with a king-size bed and a pull-out couch. Kids 18 and under may stay with their parents at no extra charge. Guest Quarters has two other properties not too far from Philadelphia that you may want to consider if you are going to have a car: one in suburban Philadelphia at 640 West Germantown Pike, Plymouth Meeting, 19462, and the other in Chesterbrook Corporate Center, overlooking Valley Forge National Park at 888 Chesterbrook Boulevard, Wayne, 19087. The 800 number for both of these properties is the same as the one above.

The Hyatt has a hotel five miles from down-town Philadelphia in Cherry Hill, New Jersey, 2349 Marlton Pike, 08002. For details on all of the great things Hyatt has to offer your family, see page 50 and call 800-233-1234.

SAN ANTONIO

San Antonio is a big city with a slow pace—the best of both worlds for vacationing families: there's lots to do and the doing is easy. The warm weather, a "South of the Border" ambience, and the scenic River Walk are enough to delight visitors of all ages. But there's much more—remember the Alamo?

Getting Organized

Before you arrive write to the San Antonio Convention and Visitors Bureau, P.O. Box 2277, San Antonio, Zip: 78298, 800-447-3372, to request a free information packet about the city's sights and events.

Once in town, your first stop should be the Visitor Information Center at 317 Alamo Plaza, directly across from the Alamo, for listings of special events, restaurants, maps, and directions to local and area attractions. While you're there, pick up a free map of the Texas Star Trail, a self-guided, three-mile walking tour of the historic points of interest in downtown San Antonio. You can call them at 512-299-8155.

The best monthly calendar of local events for families is published in *Our Kids Magazine* (6804 West Avenue, San Antonio, Zip: 78213). It contains great ideas for outings with child-appeal. Send for a copy ($2 includes postage) or buy one on the newsstand upon arrival. Call 512-349-6667 if you have trouble finding a copy.

A high-quality softcover book, the *Texas Monthly Guidebook to San Antonio,* by Nancy Haston Foster and Ben Fairbank, Jr. (Texas Monthly Press, 1988, $9.95), lists restaurants, shops, museums, missions, parks, and other helpful information, including a "Kids' Stuff" section.

The best guide for taking the kids camping, hiking, biking, or simply out to enjoy nature in the area is the Sierra Club's *Outdoor San Antonio and Vicinity* (1986, softcover, $7), available at most bookstores.

Tours and Overviews

An ideal way to see the downtown area—guaranteed not to bore even your youngest children—is to hop aboard one of VIA San Antonio streetcars. "Travel back in time for one thin dime," as VIA Metropolitan Transit says, on authentic reproductions of the old rail streetcars that traveled the streets 50 years ago. Now on rubber tires, the streetcars pass by all major sights of interest downtown on five different routes. Fares are adults, 10 cents; children 5 to 11, 5 cents; under 4, free. Look inside the streetcar for a route map or call 512-227-2020.

One view of San Antonio your kids won't *let* you miss is from the top of the Tower of the Americas at HemisFair Plaza. In a glass elevator, you'll zip up 750 feet to the observation deck in 52 seconds. If you're not too dizzy, it's the best view in town. There's also a revolving restaurant at the top which completes a 360 degree revolution in about one hour. Open seven days per week from 9:00 A.M. to 11:00 P.M.; admission is adults, $1.75; children 4 to 11, $1; under 4, free.

Now that you've had a land tour (the streetcars) and an aerial view (the Tower), your next excursion should take you 20 feet below the street level for a riverboat tour. Colorful barges ply the San Antonio River as it loops through downtown, giving you the best shoreline look at the River Walk shops, restaurants, hotels, and nightclubs. You'll float for about 45 minutes by the lush, tree-shaded banks of the river. Embark at the "dock" at the Market Street Bridge, across from the Hilton Palacio del Rio. For adults, fare is $1.75; children 2 to 11, 50 cents; under 2, free. Barge rides run seven days per week, 9:30 A.M. to 9:30 P.M., slightly longer from April 1 to October 1, and are operated by the P.D.R. Boat Company, 512-222-1701

A horse and carriage ride, always popular with the kids, is another leisurely way to see the city. Since at this writing, routes have been detoured because of major street renovation, the best bet is to check with the Visitor Information Center (512-299-8155), or find one waiting near the Alamo. Be sure to ask about fares in advance. The price adds up for families, since the charge is per person.

VIA Gray Line offers a variety of guided tours, all of them leaving from the Alamo for different parts of San Antonio. Brochures and tickets are available at most hotels. Call 512-227-5371 or write to Gray Line, P.O. Box 12489, San Antonio, Zip: 78212.

Getting Around

Most of the attractions in downtown San Antonio are located within walking distance of each other. Streetcars, buses, and taxis

($2.45 first mile, $1 each additional mile) are plentiful. If you don't have a car, the easiest way to get to Sea World, 18 miles northwest of downtown San Antonio, is on one of the VIA Express buses which leave the corner of Alamo and Houston Streets every 45 minutes starting at 9:00 A.M. until approximately 6:20 P.M. (later during holidays and summer). The bus returns from Sea World every 45 minutes. There is also bus service to other attractions; call 512-227-2020 for information.

Having a car, however, is a convenience for families, unless you plan to stay downtown. Parking is easy to find and free or inexpensive in most places.

Things to See and Do

Paseo del Rio

Better known as the River Walk, the Paseo del Rio is San Antonio's top attraction for visitors and natives alike. This natural waterway, part of the San Antonio River, winds through the middle of the central business district, 20 feet below street level. The river itself may be unimpressive in size, but the banks, lined during the Depression by the WPA in rough-cut limestone, and lavishly landscaped with tropical plants, are lovely. It's a unique, quaint, and quiet setting for enjoying whatever: boat rides, shopping, dining, strolling, listening to music, or joining in the local celebrations, of which there are many.

Kids will have the most fun negotiating the many stairs, footbridges, stepping stones, and waterfalls, or watching aquatic life in the river. Because of the uneven rock walks, stroller pushing is a big effort. Back carriers or Snugglis may be the best choice for infants. Handicapped access is limited.

Rivercenter, a major shopping mall located on the Paseo del Rio, is also worth a stop on your stroll along the river. The whole family will enjoy the pause to refresh at the sidewalk tables in front of the river square where the boats and barges turn around. There's also an IMAX Theater at Rivercenter Mall with a six-story-tall movie screen. "Alamo . . . The Price of Freedom" is a 45-minute docu-drama that will make your children's visit to the Alamo all the more meaningful. Hours are 10:00 A.M. to 9:00 P.M. daily, and admission is adults, $5.25; children, $3.75. Call 512-225-4629 for information.

Summer brings added attractions to the river. At the outdoor

Arneson River Theater, a musical revue with a Spanish flavor called "Fiesta Noche del Rio" is presented every Tuesday, Friday, and Saturday at 8:30 P.M. Call 512-226-4651. Admission is adults, $7; children aged 6–14; $3; under 6, free. And each Sunday evening, during June, July, and August, the Ballet Folklorico de San Antonio performs. Tickets are $7 for adults; $1 for children; under 6, free. Call 512-558-7787. Both of the above are great entertainment for families with restless children because the seating is on grassy steps overlooking the stage across the river.

Another special time in San Antonio is the second weekend in December—La Posadas—when everyone joins in a huge procession, carries candles, and carols. After the march, there's mariachi music, a piñata party, and hot chocolate for the kids.

La Villita

If you continue to the top of the Arneson River Theater's steps, you'll discover La Villita, a historic restored little village which was the center of revolutionary activities in Texas in 1835 and 1836. Today, it's a National Historic District that houses shops and craftspeople. Children will delight in watching the glassblower, spinners, weavers, potters, painters, candlemakers, stained glass artist, and jeweler at work. For information on La Villita, contact the Texas Connection at 512-227-2FUN.

There's a bewildering array of restaurants in the River Walk and downtown area. Two we think are a cut above the rest for lunch are the Calico Cat Tea Room, 304 North Presa, 226-4925, for delicious salads, soups, quiches, and the like, or Schilo's Delicatessen, 424 East Commerce Street, 512-223-6692, an old German-style restaurant that serves great homemade root beer and hearty sandwiches. Close to the river (but not on it) is a one-of-a-kind cafeteria—perfect if you have tired and hungry kids in tow. Luby's, 911 North Main, 512-223-9155, serves very tasty, home-style food in an opulent building that was formerly a bank.

The Alamo

Whether you find it fascinating or disappointing, you have to see "The Cradle of Texas Liberty." In 1718 the Alamo was the first mission to be established in San Antonio. Called San Antonio de Valero, it became the stronghold from which 188 men and women fought and were defeated by a Mexican army of over 2,500 in 1836. What remains, the chapel, has been made into a shrine to the Texas heroes.

An interesting way to approach the Alamo, located in Alamo Plaza at Alamo Street, is via the Hyatt on the River Walk. Walk through the lobby past some lovely waterfalls and up through the Paseo del Alamo. The Alamo will suddenly loom in front of you. On the left, as you enter, is a small room with a free film describing the monument. It's short enough to hold the attention of most kids.

Elementary-age children and up will probably be most interested in Alamo history, but smaller children will be able to stretch their legs in the enclosed courtyard surrounding the Alamo. Hours are Monday–Friday 9:00 A.M. to 5:30 P.M.; Sunday 10:00 A.M. to 5:30 P.M. It's free. Call 512-225-1391.

If you're hungry after your Alamo visit, head for the Cocula Restaurant, 329 Alamo Plaza, 512-223-2281 (directly across the street from the Alamo), where they serve delicious Mexican food.

HemisFair Urban Water Park

HemisFair, at 200 South Alamo Street, is the revitalized site of the 1968 World's Fair. The area around the Tower of the Americas has been relandscaped with water flowing in cascades everywhere. On a hot day, the children might even be tempted to run through some of the fountains—be on guard or bring dry clothes. It's a lovely walk from La Villita through the Water Park to the Institute of Texan Cultures.

Institute of Texan Cultures

The University of Texas Institute of Texan Cultures, Bowie Street at Durango Boulevard in HemisFair Park (512-226-7651), has a fine display of exhibits highlighting the many ethnic and cultural groups of Texas, focusing on their experiences, customs, history, and cultural life; it is a real must-see. Visitors are invited to participate in hands-on interpretive areas depicting the life of the Texas Indians. You can climb into a tepee, learn how Indians prepared their meals, and try your hand at weaving. Don't miss the Dome Show, a multi-image audiovisual presentation, the "Faces and Places of Texas," shown several times daily. Guided tours are available. Infant changing tables are located in the women's restroom on the lower level. Wheelchairs are provided, and strollers are allowed at all times. Most of the exhibit area is located on the ground floor, and there are elevators. The gift shop carries unusual specialty items for children, plus the Institute's Young Reader's Series publications. Hours are 9:00 A.M. to 5:00 P.M., Tuesday through Sunday, closed Mondays, Thanksgiving, and Christmas. Admission is free, but donations are accepted. The first weekend in August, the Institute of Texan Cultures hosts the Texas Folklife Festival, a four-day event celebrating the state's ethnic diversity and pioneer heritage. Nearly 6,000 participants share the music, dance, food, crafts, and traditions of their ancestors.

The Downtown All-Around Playground

A short walk from the Institute is a brand-new children's playground that's the perfect place to stop to let the kids romp around after their museum adventure. Designed by architect Robert Leathers with the input of local children, it even has a rubber surface and play equipment for handicapped children.

Tower of the Americas

See our description under Tours and Overviews.

Market Square

Market Square at 514 West Commerce (512-299-8600) is a unique shopping and entertainment area. Patterned after an authentic Mexican market, there are 33 specialty stores selling everything from piñatas to ponchos at bargain prices. A piñata that would be $30 in New York was $4 here. Farmers peddle their produce early in the day at the Farmer's Market. If hunger strikes, you can always eat at one of several good Mexican restaurants in the Square. Mi Tierra Café and Bakery, 218 Produce Row (512-225-1262) and La Margarita Restaurant and Oyster Bar, 120 Produce Row (512-227-7140) are local favorites that welcome kids. If you feel indulgent, let your kids sample some of the special Mexican candies in the panaderia at Mi Tierra, sit a spell, and enjoy the mariachi band. Market Square is directly on one of the streetcar routes.

Brackenridge Park

Families can spend an enjoyable day or more in and around beautiful Brackenridge Park. Enter at Tuleta Avenue, left off Broadway, five minutes north of the downtown area. This 343-acre park, established in 1899, is situated among fine old trees on the San Antonio River. In the park you can picnic and relax and take in the San Antonio Zoo, a miniature railroad, an aerial skyride, horseback riding, the Japanese Sunken Gardens, or the Witte Museum. The setting and scenery are green and pleasant.

On your way to the park, plan a stop at the San Antonio Museum of Art (200 West Jones Avenue, Zip: 78215,

512-226-5544). This museum was once a brewery, and the renovation is spectacular. Riding the giant glass elevators makes all of the galleries look so appealing. For kids, the highlight here is the museum's collection of over 8,000 pieces of folk art (many from the collection of Nelson Rockefeller), which will intrigue any age group. The place to begin your visit to this wonderful museum is the "Start Room," designed with kids in mind, where children's workshops are often held. Take the Start Gallery Scavenger Hunt to begin an exciting adventure through a fascinating space. The museum is open daily, and admission is $3 for adults, $1 for children 5–12.

SAN ANTONIO ZOO (in Brackenridge Park on North St. Mary's Street, 512-734-7183). San Antonians are justifiably proud of their zoo, which is often rated one of the top ten in the country. It houses 3,612 animals of 674 species and has gained recognition for captive breeding success. Equally impressive is the natural habitat, which ranges from nearly tropical along the river to semi-arid. The animals are surrounded by limestone cliffs and shaded by native oak, pecan, and cypress trees.

The children's zoo features a Tropical Tour with a boat ride, a playground, an Everglades exhibit with alligators and water birds, and an animal nursery. Elephants await riders just outside the children's zoo. Animal-shaped strollers can be rented at the gate. Snack and souvenir stands are scattered throughout the grounds.

The zoo is easily reached by car, taxi, or bus from downtown. Hours are 9:30 A.M.–6:30 P.M. and admission for adults is $5; children 3–11, $3; under 3, free.

THE WITTE MUSEUM (3801 Broadway, at the entrance to Brackenridge Park at Tuleta and Broadway (512-226-5544). This museum is chock-full of collections of interest to families. Permanent exhibits relating to Texas history, natural science, and archaeology include "Texas Wild: Ecology Illustrated," "Animal Sense," where children use advanced technology to experience how animals perceive their world, "Dinosaurs: Vanished Texans," and more. Major traveling exhibits and the Witte grounds, which include historic houses and a butterfly and hummingbird garden, are other family-oriented attractions. Saturdays and Sundays, all year around, the Witte offers the Museum Un-School, a series of workshops for all ages, from preschoolers to adults. Topics cover art, animal ecology, and folk art, and field trips are offered to explore, among other things, stars, fossils, bat caves, and wildlife preserves. Times and fees for the workshops vary, and participation is limited in number.

The Witte gift shop has a nice selection of quality children's souvenirs and educational toys. Changing tables for infants, and easy access for strollers and wheelchairs are available. Hours are Monday to Saturday 10:00 A.M. to 5:00 P.M.; Sunday, noon to 5:00 P.M. (6:00 P.M. in June, July, and August); Tuesday, 10:00 A.M. to 9:00 P.M. Admission is adults, $3; children 6 to 12, $1; children 5 and under, free. On Tuesdays from 3:00 P.M. to 9:00 P.M. admission is free for everyone.

San Antonio Missions National Historical Park

The Alamo, or Mission San Antonio de Valero, established in 1718, was the first of five missions established by the Spanish Franciscan friars along a nine-mile stretch of the San Antonio River. All, except for the Alamo, are active parish churches today and part of the San Antonio Missions National Historic Park. Children— especially older kids—will enjoy visiting all of them. If you are pressed for time, however, Mission San Jose, "Queen of the Missions of New Spain," having at one time been the most beautiful, most prosperous, and best fortified of all the missions, is still noted for its Spanish Colonial ornamentation (including the famous "Rosa's Window") and for its fully restored compound surrounding the parish church. The fortified tower (fort), a granary, Indian compartments, and restored mill will especially interest the children. Visitors are welcome at noon on Sunday to hear a mariachi mass, which is bilingual and filled with families. Mission San Jose is located at 6529 San Jose. The National Park Service office, at 2202 Roosevelt Drive, 512-229-5701, has tour information. Admission is free, but donations are accepted. Hours are 9:00 A.M. to 6:00 P.M. daily.

Sea World

The newest location of the world's largest marine life park is in northwest San Antonio. Far from the sea, yes, but you would never know it as you spend the day watching the spectacular performances by killer whales, dolphins, sea lions, and penguins. This is family entertainment at its best, but be prepared to walk; the attractions are spread out, making foot traffic less congested, but requiring quite a bit of hiking. You may prefer to push toddlers in a stroller or rent the park's own conveyances. Electric carts can also be rented. Don't forget hats. The sun is very hot, and there are huge areas that are still unshaded.

Star performances are put on daily by Shamu the killer whale and his friends in 4,500-seat Shamu Stadium. Daring kids sit in the "splash zone" for a ringside view of the acrobatic action. Another show, "New Friends," stars several species of whales and dolphins. (We saw this in Orlando and didn't think it was worth the wait). For comic relief, try the "Spooky, Kooky Castle" show where walrus, sea lions, and otters goof around. Humans perform feats of skill on wheels and water skis. Allow at least a full day, perferably two days if you have small children, to see everything.

Children under age 14 will enjoy Cap'n Kid's World, a nautically themed four-acre playground. The 16 creative play areas are supervised and even include huge water guns plus a large galleon great for climbing.

Penguin habitats, a Sharks and Coral Reef exhibit, a Marine Mammal Touching and Feeding Pool (a favorite), and other aquariums are exciting to visit between shows.

With all that, you may not have time to shop, but there is plenty to buy—educational toys, games, puzzles, and books, as well as an assortment of souvenirs. Various restaurants, fast food, and snack stands keep all well fed.

Sea World is located 18 miles northwest of downtown San Antonio, between Loop 410 and Loop 1604, at the intersection of Ellison Drive and Westover Hills Boulevard, off State Highway 151. It is open daily from 9:00 A.M. to 7:00 P.M., longer during summers and holidays. For bus service, see Getting Around on page 217. Admission is adults, $20.95 plus tax; children 3 to 11, $17.95 plus tax; children under 3, free. Tickets can be purchased at the Sea World entrance. Call 512-523-3611 for current hours and prices.

Time Out

NORTHSIDE SITTERS CLUB PLACEMENT SERVICE (2500 Jackson Keller, No. 206, San Antonio, Zip: 78230, 512-341-9313). Established over 60 years ago, Northside Sitters is a reliable, 24-hour service that can usually provide a sitter whenever needed. Rates are $4 per hour with a 4-hour minimum, plus $7 for transportation and any parking fee. Expect an additional charge for sitting for more than one family ($2 per hour per child). The agency may be able to arrange for the same sitter for the length of your stay.

Accommodations

Bed and Breakfasts

Bed and Breakfast Hosts of San Antonio (166 Rockhill, Zip: 78209, 512-824-8036) lists host houses throughout the city with rates starting at $62 for double occupancy. In the King William area, a downtown residential district of restored Victorian houses, there are several b and b's that are charming and especially suitable for families. King William is a quiet neighborhood, yet it's close to all the action and is even on the streetcar line.

Molly Sorrel (320 Adams Street, Zip: 78210, 512-824-8036) welcomes guests to her 100-year-old Victorian home, which is painted a cheerful yellow. Two bedrooms and a TV sitting room in the main house accommodate a family, and a guest cottage on the property has a kitchen, bedroom, bath, and sitting room with a sleeper sofa. A crib is available. The owner, formerly in the childcare business, loves children and sometimes even provides snacks for the small set.

The Bed and Breakfast Sartor House (217 King William, Zip: 78204, 512-223-9180) has a three-room suite (complete with kitchenette) that is furnished in antiques and Mexican folk art. The owner is a most gracious lady who offers the use of her extensive library and is eager to point families in the direction of a nearby playground, the River Walk (two blocks away), or the Institute of Texan Cultures, also close enough to walk to. She welcomes even the youngest infant or toddler, but cautions that the house is not suitable for rough play. The suite sleeps five comfortably. Rates start at $85 for double occupancy; $100 for a couple with two children. Special rates are available for weekdays and non-holiday weekends; a minimum two-night stay is required.

Hotels

LA MANSION DEL RIO (112 College Street, Zip: 78205, 512-225-2581 or 800-531-7208). This wonderful hotel overlooks the Paseo del Rio or Riverwalk, and we fell in love with it. The rooms are enormous and pretty, hallways are extra wide and spacious, the food is excellent, and the location, just three blocks from the Alamo and the center of town, made touring a breeze. Manager Mark Fallon, father of three himself, is very much attuned to the needs of families. Double occupancy rate is $130 per night.

EMBASSY SUITES HOTEL—AIRPORT (10110 Highway 281 North,

Zip: 78216, 512-525-9999 or 800-EMBASSY). Having a kitchenette and a separate room for the children to sleep in has made this moderately priced hotel popular with traveling families. A full complimentary, cooked-to-order breakfast, an indoor pool, and lovely atrium add to the family appeal. The hotel is convenient to the airport and is an easy ten-minute ride to downtown attractions. Rates for double occupancy are $104. No charge for children under 18. Check for special family rates.

ECONO LODGE AIRPORT (333 Northwest Loop 410, Zip: 78216, 512-344-4581). Formerly a Ramada Inn, the Econo Lodge near the airport and North Star Mall offers families a clean, simple hotel at very reasonable rates. It is an easy drive along Loop 410 to Sea World. A large, heated pool in the outdoor courtyard is well kept.

The restaurant features a children's menu and booster seats. Rates for double occupancy are $35–40; children 18 and under stay free. Cribs (no charge) and roll-aways ($8) are available.

AMERISUITES—SAN ANTONIO (11221 San Pedro Avenue, Zip: 78216, 512-342-4800 or 800-654-2000). This is another all-suite possibility, run by the Howard Johnson people. Complimentary continental breakfast is served, and suites have kitchenettes with microwaves and refrigerators, living rooms, and bedrooms (separated by a half-wall, no door) with two double beds. Rates are $53 per night; a seven-night stay is less. This hotel is adjacent to the airport, a ten-mile drive to downtown.

PLAZA SAN ANTONIO (555 South Alamo, Zip: 78205, 512-229-1000, 800-421-1172). Of all the luxury hotels in the downtown area, Plaza San Antonio has the most to offer families—quiet, spacious grounds with pheasants strutting about, bicycles, croquet, tennis courts, a heated swimmming pool, and a wading pool for babies. You can even bring your pet. The interior is beautifully appointed. There is a full range of luxury-class services, including an excellent restaurant and high tea in the Palm Terrace. The hotel uses a bonded baby-sitting agency. Hotel rates are $120 to $160 for double occupancy; no charge for children under 18, and in summer rates are lower.

The Hyatt has a hotel right on the Riverwalk at Paseo del Alamo: the Hyatt Regency, 123 Losoya Street, Zip: 78205. See page 50 for all that Hyatt has to offer you and your family, and call 800-233-1234 for details.

SAN DIEGO

San Diego, in the words of one native, is "a city that seems to have been designed by parents with family vacations in mind." Historic sites—California began here—and natural beauty—beaches, parks, mountains, and the desert—all make the city a visual, recreational, and educational experience with activities varied enough to satisfy everyone. And, let's not forget the temperate climate that makes it a pleasant destination whatever the season.

Activities for children and parents alike abound—a world-class zoo, Sea World, miles and miles of beaches, windsurfing, skateboarding, roller-skating, museum-hopping are just a few of the diversions for families. Down at the waterfront you can cruise around the harbor or picnic at Marina Park; bike, fish, swim, and play at Mission Bay Aquatic park; or see the city by following along its 52-mile scenic drive, clearly marked so that you can't get lost with the symbol of a blue and yellow seagull every quarter of a mile. If you're in a hurry, you can do the tour in three hours; if you have more time, stretch it out to a full day.

Since San Diego is so strategically located, south of Los Angeles, just north of Mexico, and to the west of mountains and desert, lots of interesting day trips are possible, too.

For Information

Some of the most informative guidebooks on San Diego are Carol Mendel's *San Diego City and County* and *San Diego on Foot,* $3.95 each. Fodor's *San Diego* is a good, reliable guide, but for an everything-you-wanted-to-know type of book that goes beyond just tourist information, take a look at *San Diego—Where Tomorrow Begins* by Dan Berger and Peter Jensen ($29.95). For background on your vacation spot, pick up a copy of *A Short History of San Diego* by Michael McKeever ($9.95). (See also Gulliver Travels *Kids' Guide to Southern California* and Frommer's *California for Kids* described in the Los Angeles section). San Diego is the kind of city where it's best to have a car. Maps to help you get around are widely available at gas stations and convenience stores. If you plan to do some biking during your vacation, there are dozens of bike routes throughout the county. For a bicycle route map, just call 619-231-BIKE.

For tourist information, contact the International Visitor Information Center at First Avenue and F Street, 619-236-1212, or the Convention and Visitors Bureau, 1200 Third Avenue, Zip: 92101, 619-232-3101. Another handy reference is the *San Diego Family Press,* which features, along with articles of interest to parents, a monthly calendar of events of family happenings throughout the county. This tabloid-size magazine is free and widely available in supermarkets and libraries in the area. If you have a problem finding a copy, call them at 619-541-1162.

Tours

Gray Line Tours, 619-231-9922, offers a variety of sightseeing packages, including "The city of San Diego, La Jolla and Old Town"—a half-day tour that costs $21 for adults, $12 for kids 3–11. Other tour possibilities include the zoo, a harbor excursion, and a shopping spree to Tijuana. And, from December to March, the tour company offers a two-and-a-half-hour narrated boat trip that will give you a chance to see the impressive migration of the mammoth California gray whales. The cost is $18 for adults, $13 for kids.

The Molly Trolley, 619-233-9177, gives you a two-hour narrated circle tour through the city on an old-time trolley. It runs from 9:00 A.M. to 7:00 P.M. seven days a week, and for $5 you can ride it as long as you'd like, getting on and off anywhere along the way.

San Diego Mini Tours, 619-234-9044, offers bus tours to lots of the more interesting places in and around the city, like La Jolla, Coronado, Old Town, and the Gaslamp Quarter, all in one afternoon. The cost is $22 for adults, $16 for kids under 12.

San Diego Harbor Excursions offers a one-hour narrated tour of San Diego Bay every day of the week. Tours begin four times per day and cost $8 for adults, $4 for kids 3–11. A two-hour tour of the harbor leaves at 2:00 P.M. every day and costs $11.50 for adults, $5.75 for kids. The ticket office is located at 1050 North Harbor Drive; the phone is 619-234-4111.

The Star and Crescent Ferry will take you over to Coronado. Before the Coronado Bay Bridge was built, this was the only way to get to the island. The ferry leaves from 1050 North Harbor Drive on the hour from 10:00 A.M. to 10:00 P.M. Once you're in Coronado you can visit a variety of shops and places to eat along the ferry landing. Tickets are $1.50 each; an additional 50 cents if you want to bring your bicycle.

Things to See and Do

Balboa Park Area

This should probably be the first stop for visiting families. There's more to see and do here than can be packed into one, even two days, with the San Diego Zoo, lots of museums, theaters, kiddie rides, and weekend street entertainment with anything from mimes to tightrope walkers to saxophone players to native Indian dancers.

THE SAN DIEGO ZOO (2920 Zoo Drive, Zip: 92103, 619-231-1515). This is one of the major tourist draws in San Deigo, and for good reason. It's known as one of the best zoos in the world, where 777 species of animals live in a sprawling, 1,000-acre tropical garden, roaming in moated exhibits free of bars. The newest addition to the zoo is the Tiger River exhibit, a walk-through tropical forest with sweeping views of tigers at rest and at play. Don't miss the children's zoo, which is perfect for toddlers and preschoolers who love the petting zoo, walk-through bird house, and zoo nursery.

A nice, relaxing way to see the zoo is via the 40-minute bus tour or the skyride. Strollers are available for rent at the gate. General admission is $8.50 for adults, $2.50 for kids 3–15, and free for kids under 2. A "deluxe ticket package" which includes admission, the bus tour, sky ride, and admission to the children's zoo is $13 for adults, $6 for kids 3–15.

Besides the zoo, there are a number of museums in the park. If you plan to visit a few of them consider buying a Passport to Balboa Park, which entitles you to admission to up to four of the park's museums for a reduced rate of $9. Passports are available at any one of the participating museums or at the Information Center in the House of Hospitality, 1549 El Prado. Some of the museums in the park that your kids should enjoy are:

THE MUSEUM OF MAN (1350 El Prado, Zip: 92101, 619-239-2001). Here's where you and the kids can explore the development of mankind through a series of exhibits, including what the museum calls its "living displays"—weavers demonstrating their craft and a Mexican woman making tortillas in the traditional fashion. Although the museum is meant to trace the cultural and physical development of man in general, the emphasis is on the people of the Western Americas. Call to find out about special weekend programming. The museum is open seven days a week from 10:00 A.M. to 4:30 P.M.; admission is $3 for adults, $1 for kids 6–11, and free for anyone under 6.

THE SAN DIEGO MUSEUM OF ART (1450 El Prado, Zip: 92101, 619-232-7931). Although it's more likely that this museum, with its fine collection of Italian Renaissance and old master paintings, would appeal to an adult audience, a new "Young Art" exhibit might please the kids. The exhibit shows off the work of some of the kids from the local schools, kindergarten through 12th grade. And, if your budding artists are going to be in San Diego for an extended time, you might want to check into the month-long classes for kids with titles such as "Arts and Crafts for the Young Artist." Open Tuesday through Sunday, 10:00 A.M. to 4:30 P.M., admission is $5 for adults, $2 for kids 6–18, and free for 5 and under.

REUBEN H. FLEET SPACE THEATER AND SCIENCE CENTER (1875 El Prado, Zip: 92101, 619-238-1168). The whole family will thrill to the film in the Space Theater that gives you a spectacular "you are there" feeling, and the science center offers lots of "hands-on" learning experiences. During the summer the museum is open every day, the rest of the year it's closed on Fridays. Admission is $5 for adults, children 5-15, $3, and kids under 5, free.

THE SAN DIEGO NATURAL HISTORY MUSEUM (1788 El Prado, Zip: 92112, 619-232-3821). This is a big favorite with kids because of its impressive dinosaur exhibit. The accent here is on "hands-on" experiences with a Desert Hall, complete with live desert creatures, and a Discovery Lab, a "please touch" area all about threatened and endangered species. Older children and adults, too, will find it fascinating to watch volunteers clean million-year-old skeletons in the Fossil Prep lab; questions are welcomed. During many weekends, the museum offers workshops for parents and kids together, from kindergarteners to fourth graders; the cost varies from $10 to $20 per workshop. The museum is open from 10:00 A.M. to 4:30 P.M. and until 5:00 P.M. in the summer. Admission is $4 for adults, $1 for kids 6–18, and free for 5 and under.

SAN DIEGO AEROSPACE MUSEUM AND INTERNATIONAL AEROSPACE HALL OF FAME (2001 Pan American Plaza, Zip: 92101, 619-234-8291). Here you can explore the history of aviation right up to the present. Kids will get to see an impressive array of aircraft and spacecraft while they learn about the men and women who guided the planes. Some of the exhibits that have been favorites with older children include the circus display, the air mail exhibit, and the section all about the Wright Brothers. Although there are no displays geared specifically for young kids, any with a love of planes will be wide-eyed at the exhibits. According to the staff, "Young children whose parents are enthusiastic and willing to spend time telling aviation stories enjoy most of our exhibits." Open from 10:00 A.M. to 4:30 P.M. daily, the museum charges $4 for adults, $1 for kids 6–17.

The Casa de Balboa is home to the Hall of Champions, a sports museum and a good stop for kids who want to get a look at some of San Diego's hometown heroes. The Museum of Photographic Arts has exhibits that are, for the most part, most appropriate for adults.

Then, when the kids are museumed out—and that's inevitable—take them for a spin on the carousel, for a ride on the miniature railroad, or let them release some of their excess energy at the Balboa Park playground on Sixth Avenue.

The Beaches

It wouldn't be a visit to San Diego without some time spent on one of the many beautiful area beaches. San Diego's beaches vary like the waves in the sea, running from the funky Pacific and Mission beaches where you can grab a fish taco, roller-skate on the boardwalk, rent a boogie board, and have a rollicking good time, to the windswept bluffs at Torrey Pines State Park, to Ocean Beach, a somewhat honky-tonk spot where at one end people like to run with their dogs along a stretch called, appropriately enough, "Dog Beach."

Mission Bay Area

Mission Bay Aquatic Park is 4,600 acres of boating, fishing, water skiing, swimming, and picnicking. If it's exercise you're seeking, walk through the park, take the kids to one of the many playgrounds, rent a bicycle, or try some roller-skating. You'll find a golf course and a campground here, too. For more information, call 619-276-8200.

SEA WORLD OF CALIFORNIA (1720 South Shores Road, Mission Bay, Zip: 92109, 619-226-3901). No visit to San Diego would be complete without a stop to say hello to that most famous killer whale, Shamu. Shamu's popularity has been somewhat eclipsed recently by the arrival of Baby Shamu, who is now rehearsing her own show. At Sea World, kids get to pet dolphins, whales, and a baby walrus in special "petting pools." They also love the Penguin Encounter, which recreates the South Pole, the shark exhibit ("a nice place to visit but you wouldn't want to live there"), the sea lion and dolphin shows, and Cap'n Kids' World, a two-acre playground where they can swing, climb, and play to their hearts' content while parents look on from an observation station. Sea World is open from 9:00 A.M. to 5:00 P.M. in winter and until 11:00 P.M. during the summer. Tickets are $19.95 for adults, $14.95 for kids 3–11, and free for 2 and under.

Old Town

Here is where you'll find a little piece of Mexico transported to the heart of San Diego. This was the center of town in the 1800s, and the area makes a perfect afternoon stop with Mexican restaurants every few yards—most with outdoor tables and strolling bands—and lots of gift shops. Take some time to watch women making fresh tortillas in the window of the Old Town Mexican Café, a favorite among locals, and then head to Washington Square to relax and enjoy the passing crowd. If you're in the mood, try a horse-drawn carriage tour of the area or join one of the ranger tours available across from the Plaza (call 619-237-6770 for times and information). Since Old Town is where San Diego began, its history is preserved in a museum called the Father Junipero Serra Museum on Presidio Hill, a pretty park right next to Old Town.

Harbor Area

The harbor tours described above give tourists a splendid view of the city from the bay. Children and adults with any kind of love of the sea—and that's most—will want to visit the Maritime Museum, 1492 North Harbor Drive, Zip: 92101, 619-234-9153. This museum is actually three floating exhibits—the *Star of India,* built by hand in 1863 and the oldest merchant sailing vessel still afloat; the San Francisco ferryboat *Berkeley* built in 1898; and the English luxury yacht *Medea,* which dates from 1904. The *Star of India* has a below-deck museum and nautical videos that are bound to interest the kids. Open every day from 9:00 A.M. to 8:00 P.M., admission is $5 for adults, $4 for kids 13–17, and $1.25 for kids 6–12.

In the same area you'll find Seaport Village, a shopping and dining complex designed to look like an old-time fishing village. The kids will like the turn-of-the-century carousel, the old-fashioned popcorn wagon, and the street performers—bands, puppeteers, and mimes. For more information, call 619-235-4013.

Marina Park is adjacent to the village and has plenty of space for picnicking and catching breathtaking views of San Diego and its harbor. Just walk along Embarcadero across the bay and watch the vast array of sailing vessels. Cabrillo National Monument, at the tip of Point Loma, commemorates the discovery of California by Juan

Rodríguez Cabrillo in 1542. Nearby are the Old Point Loma Lighthouse and a free whale-watching station, with a glassed-in observatory from which you can spot whales from mid-December to March.

Gaslamp Quarter

Between downtown and the harbor areas, this 16-block area, a National Historic District, is filled with art galleries, antique shops, and restaurants, all in beautifully restored Victorian, Florentine, Romanesque, and Italianate buildings. In this area you'll find a restaurant that's a favorite with kids—The Old Spaghetti Factory at 275 Fifth Avenue. Don't expect much besides spaghetti on the menu, but it's good, and the Victorian building that houses the restaurant is inviting and always teeming with families.

Short Jaunts and Day Trips

La Jolla

La Jolla, aptly named "the jewel," is located about fifteen minutes north of the city off Interstate 5. It boasts several gorgeous stretches of beach, including La Jolla Shores, a great family place with an inviting picnic area, and La Jolla Cove, known for its impressive array of sea life. Snorkeling, swimming, and cave exploration are all popular in this area.

While in La Jolla, you must be sure to visit the Scripps Aquarium, with its 22 tanks of sealife from the waters of Southern California, Mexico, and Micronesia. Call 534-FISH to find out when the fish are being fed.

In La Jolla, too, you'll find the popular Children's Museum of San Diego (8657 Villa La Jolla Drive, La Jolla, California 92037, 619-450-0768). Kids from babyhood to 12 can easily spend hours in this "hands-on" environment, painting with watercolors in the art room, dressing in costume and performing in their own show, acting as dee-jay in the KKID newsroom, or playing wheelchair basketball. Workshops and special events are planned throughout the year; just call for details.

Downtown La Jolla is like a mini Rodeo Drive, with a variety of exclusive shops and enough cookie shops and upscale T-shirt emporiums to keep kids happy. Teens will want to have a burger at the Hard Rock Café on Prospect Street with its rock and roll memorabilia, blasting music, and great milk shakes.

Tijuana

Take the bright red San Diego trolley the 16 miles to the border of Tijuana for a day of bargain hunting in another country. Once you're there, souvenir gathering is a required activity. Photos of the kids on burros painted to look like zebras are great favorites. Besides shopping, the city is known for its bullfights, jai alai, and horse races. For information on the trolley runs and ticket prices, call 619-231-8549. (One word of caution: Once in Tijuana you can expect to be approached often by beggars. We'd suggest explaining this to your children before they go.)

Julian

How about a visit to a country mountain town where you can pull up a stool at an old-time drug store and enjoy a chocolate malt? The old gold-mining town of Julian is just about an hour east of San Diego off Interstate 8. Julian is best known for its apple crop, and in the fall visitors come from all over for the apple harvest festival. But apple pies, the main attraction here, are sold year-round, and more often than not you'll find a line outside Mom's Apple Pie Shop. Julian is a small town, but with its restored gold mine, antique shops, and local store where you can watch bees making honey, there's plenty to do for a day's trip.

Just east of Julian is the Anza Borrego State Park, 550,000 acres of desert. It is spectacular, especially in the spring when the desert flowers bloom. The drive to the park from San Diego takes you past Palomar Observatory. For information on the park, call 619-767-5311.

Escondido

This is the site of the Wild Animal Park, just 30 miles north of San Diego. The park is part of the San Diego Zoo—it handles the tough job of breeding endangered species. Animal shows, elephant rides, and a petting area are favorites with kids. Take a narrated monorail tour and watch as animals roam in natural habitats. You can walk through a Nairobi Village and the park's version of a rain forest. The park is open from 9:00 A.M. to 4:00 P.M. and until 6:00 P.M. during the summer. Tickets are $12.95 for adults, $6.20 for children 3–15, free for kids under 2.

Time Out

For the times when you'd rather do something without the kids, here are some sources of childcare in the area:

The San Diego YMCA Childcare Resource Service, 619-275-4800, will provide a list of baby-sitting services as well as childcare centers that will accept drop-ins. When calling, it helps to know the zip code where you'll be staying, since lists are arranged by zip.

Kindercare, 6150 Agee Street, University City (near La Jolla), will take drop-ins on a space-available basis. Rates for kids 3 and older are $26 for a day or $3.75 per hour; for infants and toddlers it's $4 per hour, $33 per day.

Palo Alto Preschool at University Town Center in La Jolla also allows kids to drop in and is open from 9:00 A.M. to 6:00 P.M. for kids 2½ to 8. No diapers allowed. Rates are $3 per hour; call 619-452-9732.

Kid's Day Out, Educational Safaris for Children, is a children's-only tour company for ages 5–15. From Tuesdays through Saturdays, they will pick up your kids between 9 and 10 A.M. (returning between 3 and 4 P.M.), take them to such sights as the Aerospace Museum, the Zoo, Wild Animal Park, etc. There's a new excursion each day and the $55 per child price includes pick-up and delivery, a nutritious lunch and snack and all entrance fees. Contact them at P.O. Box 3804, San Diego, CA 92103-0260 or call 619-299-6069.

Accommodations

Bed and Breakfasts

Two of the bed and breakfast establishments in the San Diego area that welcome kids are owned by Jeri Grady: The Surf Manor and Cottages, 619-225-9765, are quaint beach cottages just a few blocks from Mission and Ocean Beaches. The three one-bedroom cottages are in South Mission Beach, a short walk from the bay and beach. The cottages have brick patios, double beds, and a pull-out couch. Portacribs are available. Grady stocks the refrigerator with a serve-yourself breakfast. Rates are $60 per night and $550 per week in July and August. Grady's second property is Surf Manor in nearby Ocean Beach: seven one- and two-bedroom apartments that rent for $90 per day or $750 per week with breakfast included in July and August.

Hotels

SAN DIEGO PRINCESS (1404 West Vacation Road, Zip: 92109, 619-274-4630 or 800-542-6275). This is a true getaway resort that warmly welcomes children. Stay in a cottage-style guest room in a tropical setting. Located in the Mission Bay area, the resort has 450 rooms, including suites, that range in price from $105 to $265 per night. The hotel offers a special "Sunshine Getaway Package" of three days and two nights for $98 per person. Cribs are available for $15 per night. The Princess offers guests tennis, sailing, windsurfing, and a swimming pool. Baby-sitting is also available at $18.50 for three hours for up to three kids.

HOTEL DEL CORONADO (1500 Orange Avenue, Coronado, Zip: 92118, 619-435-6611 or 800-522-1200). This Victorian hotel is a national historic landmark located on the Pacific Ocean, a short ride across the Coronado Bay Bridge from San Diego. This is where Marilyn Monroe filmed her movie "Some Like It Hot." The hotel's 750 rooms in the main building and a newer annex is actually like a little city in itself, with three restaurants, a variety of shops, a hair salon, six tennis courts, an Olympic-sized pool, health spa, and bike rental service. Rates are $135 for a room on up to $750 for a two-bedroom apartment. Cribs are available free of charge, and baby-sitting can be arranged for $27 for the first three hours. The hotel also offers a number of children's programs during the summer and Christmas vacation period, including a "Kids Summer Jamboree," three nights a week from 6:00 P.M. to 9:00 P.M., where kids 6–12 play games, watch movies, and have snacks while parents enjoy an evening to themselves. The cost is $12. During the summer, Camp Breaker operates from 1:00 to 4:00 P.M. for kids 6–12, and Camp Oz offers the same hours for kids 3–5.

BAHIA RESORT HOTEL (998 West Mission Bay Drive, Zip: 92109, 619-488-0551 or 800-288-0770). This is a 14-acre resort on Mission Bay, just two blocks from the beach. It's a perfect family place, with a seal pond, playground, outdoor heated pool, and game room. The hotel has 325 rooms, including family suites with a separate bedroom and living room. Rates range from $85 to $185 per night, and children under 12 stay free with their parents. Cribs are free.

CATAMARAN RESORT HOTEL (3999 Mission Boulevard, Zip: 92109, 619-488-1081 or 800-288-0770). Having recently completed a $25 million renovation and being in a prime location just minutes from Mission Bay, one block from the Pacific, this hotel is a perfect spot for families who enjoy water sports. It has a heated pool, whirlpool spa, and a lobby waterfall complete with birds and fish. Kids under 12 stay for free in their parents' room, and rates are $120–$205 per night.

BEST WESTERN BLUE SEA LODGE (707 Pacific Beach Drive, Zip: 92109, 619-483-4700 or 800-BLUE SEA). This family-type motel with 100 rooms is located right on the beach, offering guests an outdoor pool, sailing, windsurfing, water skiing, scuba diving, and bike rentals. Children under 18 are free in a room with parents, and there's no charge for cribs. Rates range from $100 to $125.

HOLIDAY INN ON THE BAY AT THE EMBARCADERO (1355 North Harbor Drive, Zip: 92101, 619-232-3861 or 800-HOLIDAY). Just a few minutes from the airport, this hotel is also near Seaport Village and downtown. Kids under 19 are free, and rates vary from $115 to $138 per night.

DANA INN AND MARINA (1710 West Mission Bay Drive, Zip: 92109, 619-222-6440 or 800-445-3339). This pleasant inn is right on Mission Bay Aquatic Park and next door to Sea World. The staff welcomes kids. Those under 18 stay for free, and most rooms have double beds. The inn offers shuffleboard, ping-pong, tennis, and a heated pool and spa. Jogging and bicycle paths wind through the property and out around the park and bay. Rates range from $69.50 to $129.50, highest from May to September.

If you'd like to combine a trip to San Deigo with a stay at a much-praised resort, consider the Rancho Bernardo Inn, listed in our Tennis and Golf chapter.

The Hyatt has a property in San Deigo called the Hyatt Islandia, 1441 Quivira Road, Zip: 92109. See page 50 for all of the good things Hyatt offers families, and call 800-233-1234 for details.

SAN FRANCISCO

A lovely city, San Francisco. Somerset Maugham called it "the most civilized city in America," and it just may be. Two advantages that San Francisco has for visiting families are that it's scenic and at the same time, compact. It's an easy place to visit. The public transportation makes getting around a cinch.

San Francisco is a city where the setting is as important as streets and museums. Nature plays a significant role in the goings-on and activities of the people who live and work here. The westernmost boundary of the city, extending from the ocean to the bay, is part of the Golden Gate National Recreation Area; under its management are museums, islands (including Alcatraz), beaches, and even a working pier with theaters and restaurants. Taking a walk in this city affords continually changing vistas of bridges, coastal ranges, bays, and the ocean in endless variations. The best way to enjoy San Francisco with children is to take them out into this urban wilderness where nature and civilization come together in a unique way, almost unknown to the rest of the United States.

For Information

The San Francisco Convention and Visitors Bureau at the Powell Street BART Station has a Dial-an-Event phone line (415-391-2000) with tapes in several languages. The staff is helpful and hands out maps and other information on the city. The address is 201 Third Street, San Francisco 94103, 415-974-6900.

Two periodicals especially for kids and parents that are available free at children's stores and other child-oriented spots are *Parents' Press* (1454 Sixth Street, Berkeley, California 94710) and *San Francisco Peninsula Parent* with a special San Francisco supplement (P.O. Box 89, Millbrae, California 94030). Check the pink entertainment pages of the *San Francisco Examiner* for a special kids' section every Sunday, and when you're looking for a guidebook, consider these:

> *Places to Go with Children in Northern California* by Elizabeth Pomada, published by Chronicle Books ($9.95)
>
> *Eating Out with the Kids in San Francisco and the Bay Area* by Carole Terwilliger Meyers, published by Carousel Press ($7.95)
>
> *Weekend Adventures for City-Weary People: Overnight Trips in Northern California* by Carol Terwilliger Meyers, published by Carousel Press ($11.95)
>
> *San Francisco at Your Feet: The Great Walks in a Walker's Town* by Margot Patterson, published by Grove Press ($5.95), is useful, though not written specifically for families.
>
> *The Best of San Francisco* by Don and Betty Woo Martin, published by Chronicle Books ($7.95) uses the "top ten" approach to save tourists from wasting their valuable time on anything uninteresting.
>
> *Kidding Around San Francisco: A Young Person's Guide to the City,* by Rosemary Zibart, published by John Muir Publications ($9.95) is part of a terrific new series written especially

for kids 8 and older and includes information on some of the more familiar sites mixed in with some of the lesser known.
Adventures on and off Interstate 80 by Eleanor Huggins and John Olmsted, published by Tioga Publishing Company, P.O. Box 98, Palo Alto, California 94302 ($12.95). This fascinating book offers a look at natural and human history along the pioneer and Gold Rush corridor from San Francisco's Pacific shore to Nevada's desert. It is based on the California Institute of Man in Nature's trips along the I-80 corridor that were designed for students, parents, and teachers. A tape with the same title as the book, a 90-minute talking tour of the route from San Francisco to Reno, is available from the same publisher for $9.95.

Things to Do and See

Getting Around

As we said before, San Francisco's public transportation system should be the envy of most of our major cities. MUNI runs the buses, the electric cars, the cable cars, and the underground trains or MUNI metro. Bus maps are available for $1.50 at stores, at some ticket booths of the underground, and at the Convention and Visitors Bureau. Wall maps in the MUNI Metro Stations are a big help, and if you're ever lost, just call 415-673-MUNI for directions. MUNI fares are reduced for kids ages 5 to 12; kids under 5 ride free. There are two cable car lines: from Union Square to Fisherman's Wharf and from Embarcadero to Van Ness Avenue.

If you travel with your kids on MUNI, be sure to have a collapsible stroller. Be prepared for lots of escalators and architectural impediments. Try to travel in the off-hours, after the morning rush and before the evening commute. The other underground system running in the Bay area is Bay Area Rapid Transit (BART). BART takes commuters between San Francisco and the East Bay; each station has easy-to-read wall maps and fares listed prominently. Elevators that take you to the train platforms may be summoned via a white courtesy phone; meant primarily for the handicapped, these elevators can be used for people with strollers. The BART information number is 415-788-2278.

Sam Trans connects San Francisco with the South Bay, 415-872-6748; to the North Bay it's the Golden Gate Transit System, 415-332-6600. A great way to go to Sausalito and the Larkspur terminal is by ferry from the Ferry Building at the foot of Market Street and Embarcadero. There's food service on board, and you can sit inside or outside. The trip takes one-half hour; for information call Golden Gate Transit, 415-332-6600. (There's a limit of two children per adult for the ferry; kids under 5 ride free.)

Now, let's start our exploration of San Francisco. Our listing is geographical, starting with Union Square, the downtown magnet shopping area.

If you can convince your kids to do some shopping with you, you can hit Macy's, Neiman Marcus, and Saks Fifth Avenue, and when they get tired and cranky, head out to Union Square to feed the pigeons. (We like to save our shopping for the North Beach and Fisherman's Wharf area.)

Union Square Area, South of Market

Within walking distance of the Square is the Old Mint, Fifth and Mission Streets, where the admission is free and you get a glimpse into the Victorian past of the city and a look at a famous gold collection.

The Old Mint is in a part of town that is now being called SoMa for South of Market, which is reminiscent in more than just name to New York City's SoHo. The area is an old industrial district that is being gentrified; its boundaries are Market Street, the Embarcadero, China Basin, and Division Street. Although industry hasn't disappeared from the area, what's arrived lately are restaurants, night clubs, galleries, museums, experimental theaters, and lots of discount clothing shops. Some of the museums that are here already are the Cartoon Art Museum, which features the actual artwork from which cartoons are made, the Museum of Modern Mythology, the world's only museum of advertising characters and other mass media phenomenon, and the Telephone Pioneer Communications Museum, which traces the beginning and evolution of communications. Coming in 1993 will be the San Francisco Museum of Modern Art. Obviously, the city has great plans for this area.

Chinatown

Still within walking distance of the Square in the opposite direction from SoMa is the city's Chinatown. The entrance gates stand out prominently at the intersection of Bush and Grant streets; for blocks proceeding toward the bay and in several directions are restaurants, stores, and markets. Some advice for parents: The sidewalks are always congested, so manuevering a stroller is difficult.

The best time to visit Chinatown is early morning, when fresh produce and fish are being delivered. When all the crowds and noise become too much, stop at St. Mary's Square on Pine Street between Grant and Kearny. It is a restful park with large shade trees and offers a pleasant break from the congestion. Don't miss a *dim sum* Chinese pastry lunch—a quick and fun way to eat. On Pacific Avenue, try Asian Garden, Hong Kong Tea House, or Tung Fong.

THE CHINESE CULTURE FOUNDATION (750 Kearny Street, Zip: 94108, 415-986-1822). A visit here provides an alternative to Chinatown shopping. The changing exhibits feature Chinese culture and art. The foundation offers two walks through Chinatown that take you to the less well known parts of the area: "The Culinary Walk" includes a *dim sum* lunch, and the "Heritage Walk," which lasts about two hours and covers the history of the area, for $9 and $2, respectively.

To see how fortune cookies are made, stop at 23 Ross Alley at the Golden Gate Fortune Cookie Company.

North Beach

If you continue toward the Bay from Chinatown, you will arrive at Washington Square, the heart of North Beach. Along the way, you will pass the Wells Fargo History Museum at 420 Montgomery Street (415-396-2619). The surrounding area is the traditional Italian neighborhood of the city. Although Chinatown continues to encroach on its boundaries, plenty of Italian bakeries and restaurants can still be found. Dominating the square are the spires of the church of Saints Peter and Paul, bringing a European feeling to the whole scene. For kids, there's a good playground on the square where they can unwind from all the walking and shopping. Overlooking Washington Square, off to the east, is Coit Tower, on Telegraph Hill between Lombard and Greenwich streets. Coit Tower was built by Lillian Coit to commemorate the heroics of the San Francisco firemen; take a number 41 Union MUNI bus, as the climb is quite steep. Inside the tower are frescoes painted by WPA artists, but it's the almost 180-degree view of the bay from the East Bay to the Golden Gate Bridge that makes the visit worthwhile.

It's a logical jump from North Beach to Fisherman's Wharf, Pier 39, Ghirardelli Square, and the Cannery. Here again is endless shopping. You'll find anything and everything.

PIER 39. Pier 39 is a large shopping complex that juts out into the bay. For children, there is a two-tiered carousel.

From here you can take the Red and White Fleet Boat to

Marine World in Vallejo (call 415-546-2986) or the Blue and Gold Fleet Bay Cruise. The one-and-a-quarter-hour cruises leave from the west marina (415-781-7877).

Another thing kids like to do in this area is visit the Maritime Museum and the Hyde Street Pier, where vintage ships are moored for the public to visit.

THE MARITIME MUSEUM (mailing address: Building 201, Fort Mason, Zip: 94123, 415-556-3002). The museum has exhibits centering around the Gold Rush days at sea. Parts of seafaring vessels are on view with other artifacts. Five ships are on view at the pier and within walking distance of the museum. Admission is $3; free for 16 and under.

The *Balclutha,* Pier 43, a Cape Horn sailing ship dating from 1886

C. A. Thayer, Hyde Street Pier, one of two survivors of a fleet of 900 that carried lumber from the Pacific Northwest to California cities

The *Eureka,* Hyde Street Pier, a sidewheel ferry that carried passengers and cars daily across the bay from 1921 to 1941

The *Hercules,* Hyde Street Pier, one of a few tugs that made the journey through the Straits of Magellan

Jeremiah O'Brien, located at the Fort Mason pier, the last unaltered survivor of 2,751 Liberty Ships built during World War II

GHIRARDELLI SQUARE. This was once a chocolate factory but is now a potpourri of shops and restaurants across from Victorian Park. You can still see chocolate being made at the Chocolate Manufactory, 415-771-4903. The Cannery—more shops—is across the street from the American Carousel Museum, 633 Beach Street, 415-928-0550.

West of Fisherman's Wharf are the Fort Mason Center and the Marina Green. Fort Mason Center at Laguna and Marina Boulevards is composed of renovated piers that house theaters, galleries, and restaurants.

THE MEXICAN MUSEUM (Fort Mason Center, Building D, Zip: 94123, 415-441-0404). While you're at Fort Mason Center, you may want to visit this museum. Admission is $1, and children under 6 enter free at this excellent, small museum with a folk art collection inherited from Nelson Rockefeller. There are also changing exhibits centered on Mexican artists and themes. Children delight in all the fanciful colors associated with the arts of this region, and the atmosphere is casual. It's just large enough to keep you interested, but not big enough to give you a case of "museum feet." There's a museum store that has some very affordable and interesting pieces for sale.

THE MUSEO ITALO AMERICANO (Fort Mason Center, Building C, Zip: 94123, 415-673-2200). This small museum has a changing exhibition program devoted to Italian-American artists. Admission is free.

Another museum possibility here is the San Francisco Craft and Folk Art Museum, Building A, 415-775-0900.

Walking further west, next to the Palace of Fine Arts is:

THE EXPLORATORIUM (3601 Lyons Street, Zip: 94123, 415-563-3200). The museum costs $5 for adults, $1 for 6–17, and free for kids 6 and under. It's a must-see for all families visiting San Francisco: the country's first hands-on scientific museum. Housed in a turn-of-the-century warehouse building erected for the San Francisco Exposition, it's filled with experiments to keep you busy. Older children will benefit most from this experience, but younger ones won't be bored. "Explainers," teenagers trained to assist you with the experiments, are helpful and interested in the needs of the children. The Tactile Dome is a by-reservation-only experience that will have you and the kids groping by your wits and senses through a maze constructed by museum experts. Whatever you do, don't miss this one and be prepared to have the kids ask for a second visit.

When hunger strikes and you're in this part of town, consider this for a pit stop:

GREEN'S AT FORT MASON (Bay at Laguna, Building A, 415-771-6222). Best for family brunch, this vegetarian restaurant is one place where meat eaters are rarely disappointed. Run by the Zen Center, this restaurant serves up only the freshest of foods. The interior abounds with modern art, and the views of the bay from the large windows are a great source of pleasure. The menu includes choices just right for the small eater, such as muffins and yogurt. Dinners tend to be a bit expensive, so keep to the early hours for family meals.

Golden Gate Park

This is the place in San Francisco where there really is something for everybody. To start with, on the Museum Concourse, off Eighth Avenue and Kennedy Drive, there are three museums and the Japanese Tea Garden.

THE DE YOUNG FINE ARTS MUSEUM (415-750-3659). The museum is open Wednesdays through Sundays. The highlights for children here are the Primitive Arts Galleries and on Saturdays at 1:00 P.M. docent-led tours that introduce children to this collection. The tours are geared to children 6 and older and incorporate the Art for Touching Gallery, where children are allowed to touch art pieces.

THE ASIAN ART MUSEUM (Housed in the same complex as the De Young Fine Arts Museum). This museum houses a collection devoted to the arts of Asia, including India, China, Tibet, Nepal, Japan, and Iran. The sculpture seems to captivate children, especially the statue of Ganesha, the Indian elephant god.

THE JAPANESE TEA GARDEN. The Japanese garden is adjacent to the De Young Fine Arts Museum on the Concourse. It's fun to walk with children (accessible with strollers) through an authentic Japanese garden with temples and bridges. There is a teahouse in the garden where you can drink green tea and eat cookies, even when it rains. The garden is at its best in the spring when the cherry blossoms are in bloom.

THE STRYBING ARBORETUM (Ninth Avenue at Lincoln Way, Zip: 94122, 415-661-1316). The arboretum is free and is several gardens all mapped into one, including a duck pond and roaming geese. There's a scent garden where children can smell their way through the flowers, and tours for children are scheduled from time to time. Call for information.

THE CALIFORNIA ACADEMY OF SCIENCES (415-750-7145). This is home to the city's natural history museum. It's sure to delight your kids with its walk-through dioramas of the African veldt, an earthquake exhibit that simulates the feel of the real thing, and a solar system hung from the ceiling.

THE STEINHART AQUARIUM (415-221-1311). Every kind of fish imaginable is here, plus penguins, dolphins, and the Fish Roundabout, a special gallery where the fish swim around you. Bring sandwiches and eat them in the open courtyard with a pretty central fountain.

MORRISON PLANETARIUM (415-750-7141). Featuring sky shows in tune with the time of year and the location of the stars, the planetarium offers shows daily at 2:00 P.M. and hourly from 1:00 to 4:00 P.M. on weekends.

THE LASERIUM (415-750-7138). This combines lasers and loud music. It's not recommended for younger kids (or older parents) since the music is of the Pink Floyd to Springsteen variety.

THE BUFFALO PADDOCK (just off Kennedy Drive on the way to

the ocean). The paddock is where the buffalo roam, over several acres.

THE MARY B. CONNOLLY PLAYGROUND (at the east end of the park off Lincoln Way). This is the oldest park/playground in the country and the finest playground in the city. A turn-of-the-century carousel and a barnyard of petting animals are just some of the highlights.

The Ocean Side of San Francisco

The perimeter of San Francisco is almost all a part of the Golden Gate National Recreation Area, and under its aegis these lands are well kept and overseen by park rangers.

Ocean Beach

The long expanse of beach from the San Francisco County line to the renowned Cliff House is a windy but impressive beach. It can sometimes get a little dirty from its city patrons and is not a very good swimming beach, even if the San Francisco weather cooperates.

THE SAN FRANCISCO ZOO (45th Avenue and Sloat Boulevard, Zip: 94176, 415-661-4844). Outstanding exhibits are the Primate Discovery Center with a small hands-on gallery and large airy cages that give the effect of the animals' watching you, instead of the other way around. There are also Gorilla World and the Koala Crossing. A beautiful carousel is located outside the children's zoo. There are plenty of different food cafés and even a large playground area at the entrance to the park. Strollers are available for rent at the Sloat Boulevard entrance. Admission is $5 adults, $2 for 12–15, and free for under 12. The first Monday of every month is free to all.

For a really detailed look at this part of the city, check a copy of the *The Complete Guide to the Golden Gate National Recreation Area* by Karen Liberatore, published by Chronicle Books ($7.95). One of the book's nicest features is its listing of kids programs in the area.

If you're looking for San Francisco's best beach, a friend who's a native thinks it's the one at 25th Avenue and Lincoln Boulevard, part of the Recreation Area that sits just inside the entrance to the bay. It's a lovely beach with picnic facilities, views of the Golden Gate Bridge, and the Marin Headlands. Few if any beaches in San Francisco are warm enough for swimming, but if the weather happens to cooperate, this is the place to be.

All Around the Town

Here are some museums, performances, and playgrounds in other parts of town that are worth a look.

The Cable Car Museum (1201 Mason Street, Zip: 94108, 415-474-1887) is free and full of memorabilia and cable car lore.

The Fire Department Museum (665 Presidio between Pine and Bush, Zip: 94115) is also free and features vintage fire trucks and other firefighting equipment.

Fort Point National Historic Site (Presidio, beneath the Golden Gate Bridge) is a 19th-century fort built on the site of a Spanish fort and finished in 1861.

The Randall Museum (199 Museum Way off Roosevelt, Zip: 94114 415-863-1399 is free, is hidden away in a quiet corner of the city, and features a live animal exhibit.

Julius Kahn Playground (West Pacific Avenue and the Presidio) is nestled in the Presidio near the army base of the same name. It's warm when the fog rolls in, protected by the grove of trees that surrounds the park area.

Mountain Lake Park (at Ninth Avenue and Lake) has imaginative play equipment and is almost always filled with kids; there's also a lake with ducks, just right for a quiet walk.

Pickle Family Circus: This vaudevillian circus is the best. With its troupe of performers, there is no need for animals; they are all the entertainment you could need. Sometimes you can catch their performances free in the city parks, but recently they have begun a series of paid events. Watch the pink section of the Sunday *San Francisco Examiner* for dates.

Make-A-Circus: Another group troupe of performers, whose emphasis here is on juggling and acrobatics. After the performance, children are invited to meet the performers and learn a few tricks for themselves. Usually they perform free in the city parks; again, check the pink entertainment section of the *San Francisco Examiner*.

Levi Strauss and Company: This is a cluster of buildings at the base of Telegraph Hill with a "soft" park, fountains, a restaurant, and retail facility. Wednesday tours of the factory book up well in advance. Call 415-565-9153.

Stern Grove Concerts (19th Avenue and Sloat Boulevard) are a Sunday summer concert series that runs the gamut from ballet to jazz. The Ethnic Dance Festival segments are colorful and fun for everyone. Surrounded by a grove of eucalyptus trees, children are happy to be outdoors, and the feeling is casual. If the concert becomes a bit boring for the kids, there's a playground right off Sloat Boulevard to revive tired spirits.

New Conservatory Children's Theater Company: Here you'll see plays acted for and by children at the Zephyr Theater Complex, 25 Van Ness at Market Street, 415-861-4914.

Walks in Your Parks Next Door: These park ranger tours can be found all over the city, sponsored by the National Park Service. For details, call 415-556-8642.

Tours: Free walking tours of the city are offered by the Friends of the San Francisco Library. Schedules are available at the branch libraries or by calling 415-558-3981.

Beyond San Francisco's City Limits

Two easy journeys, filled with excitement, especially the getting there part, are to Alcatraz and Angel Island. There's also a short cruise departing from Pier 39 or Fisherman's Wharf for those who don't want to take the longer trips.

ALCATRAZ. Ferries leave Pier 41 daily from 8:45 A.M. to 2:45 P.M. for the trip to Alcatraz. In all, it's about a half-hour journey. Food service is available on the ferry, but there is no food on Alcatraz. On Alcatraz, park rangers from the Golden Gate National Recreation Area lead informative tours of the famous prison. Tickets must be purchased in advance because tours fill up quickly. Call 415-556-0560 for information. Everyone knows Alcatraz as the famous prison, but few are aware that from 1853 until 1933 this was also an army post. Older children will delight in the tales of the notorious, and they like experiencing the feeling of confinement in the cells. Trails on the island are steep, so this is an excursion set aside for those who are sturdy. Always take warm jackets for bay excursions.

ANGEL ISLAND STATE PARK. You can get there by ferry (call 415-435-2131 or 415-546-2815) from Pier 43½. This is San Francisco's Ellis Island. The original barracks remain and can be visited. The other attractions include plenty of hiking trails and several lovely beaches. The ferry docks at Ayala cove; there are picnic tables and a wading beach. This was an army base, as well, and you can visit these historic buildings while you're on the island.

For information on bay cruises that leave from Fisherman's Wharf or from Pier 43½ and last just over an hour, call 415-546-2810 or 415-781-7877. The cost is $8.95 for adults, $5.95 for children 11 to 17, children $3.95 for ages 5 to 11, and free for kids under age 5.

The North Bay

Just off Highway One, across the Golden Gate Bridge, is Muir Woods, a pristine grove of redwoods with a gentle trail that is easy for toddlers and grownups alike. Mount Tamalpais is another popular hiking spot for families, with trails of varied lengths and steepness. Plays and concerts are scheduled often at an amphitheater nestled in the woods.

POINT REYES NATIONAL SEASHORE (30 miles north of San Francisco on Highway 1, 415-669-1539). This beautiful national park is almost in San Francisco's backyard, with many beaches and lots of wilderness.

BEAR VALLEY VISITORS CENTER AND MUSEUM (415-663-1092). You can whalewatch from the historic lighthouse set out on the promontory. Some trails are easy enough for young children, for instance, the self-guided trails to the reconstructed Miwok Indian Village and the Earthquake Trail, where you can see the effects of the San Andreas fault. As always, be prepared for cool weather.

The East Bay

THE LAWRENCE HALL OF SCIENCE (Centennial Drive at the University of California at Berkeley, Zip: 97420, 415-642-5132). After visiting the University of California at Berkeley campus, take the kids here. Lively hands-on exhibits, a biology lab that is a must for young children, and a planetarium make this a delightful destination. Plan to take in the latest performance of the Science Discovery theatre, where science meets the dramatic arts with wonderful results.

THE OAKLAND MUSEUM (Tenth and Oak Streets, Zip: 94607, 415-273-3401). Accessible by BART at Lake Merritt Station, here's a fun museum devoted to the arts, science, and history of California. Housed in an award-winning building, its gardens are stacked one on top of the other, a great place for a children's picnic. Workshops are held all through the year; call for details.

CHILDREN'S FAIRYLAND (Lakeside Park near Lake Merritt, Oakland). Open weekends and holidays 10:00 A.M. to 4:30 P.M.,

Fairyland offers storybook rides, park, and puppet shows at 11:00 A.M., 2:00 P.M., and 4:00 P.M.

Time Out

TOURS FOR TOTS THROUGH TEENS (P.O. Box 504, Corte Madera, California 94295, 415-924-1795). Tours (they may include the zoo, Golden Gate Park, the Presidio, Angel Island, and the beach) are scheduled weekly or may be custom-designed. Kids of all ages are welcome and the owner, Carol Dodds, will also arrange baby-sitting and overnight care. We've been recommending Carol to San Francisco-bound friends for years and have always gotten great reports back. Carol also runs childcare programs for San Francisco conventions and offers to arrange fun-filled birthday outings.

BRISTOL-HARAN AGENCY (1724 Sacramento, Zip: 94109, 415-775-9100). This agency is bonded. Rates start around $5 an hour, depending on the age and number of children, with a four-hour minimum. Rates increase to $8 after 9:00 P.M., and you are responsible for the sitter's transportation, day and night.

ENTERPRISE FOR HIGH SCHOOL STUDENTS (415-921-6554). They'll supply you with names of students willing to babysit who live near your hotel.

Accommodations

Bed and Breakfast

BED AND BREAKFAST INTERNATIONAL (1181-B Solano Avenue, Albany, California 94706, 415-525-4569). This bed and breakfast network was the first set up in the United States. It's run by Jean Brown, a former nursery school teacher, who explains that the best kind of facility for a family is an "in-law" apartment: "The advantage to these apartments is the ability to keep snacks in the refrigerator or even have a pizza in the dining room. And families can have breakfast without going outside to a restaurant." Ms. Brown is careful to put families with people who are warm to the idea. Ms. Brown warns her clients with kids, though, that virtually every home in San Francisco has one or two flights of stairs so kids must be able to navigate.

BED AND BREAKFAST SAN FRANCISCO (P.O. Box 349, Zip: 94101-0349, 415-931-3083). This bed and breakfast service has a limited number of accommodations for families. One example is a family room for three for $75, which includes a full breakfast and a crib if you need it.

Hotels

THE FOUR SEASONS CLIFT HOTEL (495 Geary Street, Zip: 94102, 415-775-4700 or 1-800-332-3442). This one's a bit pricey, but they go out of their way for kids. There are puzzles, games, bedtime milk and cookies, and a send-off with popcorn, soda, and balloons. Cribs and roll-away beds are available, and all rooms have wet bars. Diapers, bottles, baby bathtubs, and strollers are available on request; they've even thought of aspirin, thermometers, and humidifiers if a cold strikes. The French Room restaurant gives kids a toy and a snack just as soon as they're seated. Baby-sitters are available through the concierge. The hotel is located a block and a half west of Union Square and offers families two adjoining rooms at the single rate, for example, a room with a king-size bed would be $175; with an adjoining room with two twins, the total charge would be $215.

PACIFIC HEIGHTS INN (1555 Union Street, Zip: 94123, 415-776-3310 or 800-523-1801). A room with two queen-size beds, a kitchenette, and continental breakfast costs $59–$95 per night. Kids under 12 are free and parking is, too. All rooms have refrigerators, even if they don't have a kitchenette, and coffee and tea are always available. The inn can arrange baby-sitting for you. From the Inn you can walk to Ghirardelli Square and Fisherman's Wharf.

THE SHERATON AT FISHERMAN'S WHARF (2500 Mason, Zip: 94133, 415-362-5500 or 800-325-3535). Close to the bay, with Fisherman's Wharf right outside your door. The kids will like the outdoor pool. Regular rates range from $145-$205, but special packages bring the rate down as low as $105. Kids under 17 are free.

Five hotels operated in San Francisco by the Hotel Group of America offer reasonable rates starting at $55 per night for a double room with two queen-sized beds. Kids 12 and under stay for free. The hotels are small (about 100 rooms), most offer complimentary continental breakfasts, and one even has McDonald's room service. The hotels are: the Hotel Union Square, 114 Powell Street, Zip: 94102, 415-347-3000; Hotel Diva, 440 Geary Street, Zip: 94102, 415-885-0200; Kensington Park, 450 Post Street, Zip: 94102, 415-788-6400; Oxford-Cambridge Inn, 16 Turk Street, Zip: 94102, 415-775-4600; and the U.N. Plaza Hotel, 46 McAllister Street, Zip: 94102, 415-626-5200.

In San Francisco, the Hyatt has three properties—the Park Hyatt at 333 Battery Street, Zip: 94111; the Hyatt Regency at 5 Embarcadero Center, Zip: 94111; and the Hyatt on Union Square, 345 Stockton Street, 94108. See page 50 to know what to expect for you and your family at the Hyatt and call their toll-free number, 800-233-1234, for details.

WASHINGTON, D.C.

You can visit Washington with your family now or wait until your kids' teacher takes them on a school trip. We suggest the former because Washington is fun and full of family-type activities.

Before you plan your trip, we suggest first writing to the Washington D.C., Convention and Visitors Association, 1212 New York Avenue, N.W., Washington, D.C. 20005, 202-789-7000, and asking for a packet of their excellent brochures and maps.

The second place to contact is less well known; it's an independent school just outside Washington that publishes a book called *Going Places with Children in Washington, D.C.* It began in mimeographed form and has grown to a full-fledged book, still written and edited by parent volunteers. The book is available in its 12th edition for $8 (includes postage and handling) from Green Acres School, 11701 Danville Drive, Rockville, Maryland 20852. Every sight listed in the book has been visited by Green Acres' parents. In the book, you'll find sightseeing attractions, historic sites, parks, sports, entertainment, restaurants—all geared to kids. In the beginning of the book, the Green Acres people outline a three-day tour that includes the top tourist attractions but promises not to exhaust the family. It includes on the first day a trip to the Washington Monument, a walk to the National Museum of American History, lunch at the Post Office Pavilion, and back to the National Museum of American History. After dinner they recommend a visit to the Lincoln and Jefferson memorials, so beautifully illuminated at night. (We recommend a visit to the Vietnam Memorial, next to the Lincoln Memorial. Our kids were noticeably moved by the crowd and were struck by the fact that the memorial represented such recent history; it was not as remote as the other two memorials we visited.) On the second day, they suggest an FBI tour, a walk to the National Archives, and then a visit to the National Air and Space Museum. For families with younger kids, they recommend a morning at the zoo instead, with the Air and Space Museum on the third day. The second day can wind up at Arlington National Cemetery. For the third day they recommend a tour of the Bureau of Engraving and Printing (weekdays only), the White House (a tour is not even necessary, just seeing the familiar façade is fun for kids), on to Capitol Hill, lunch in the Supreme Court cafeteria, followed by a tour of the Capitol. For younger kids, skip the Capitol, buy lunch from a vendor on the Mall, and spend the afternoon at the Air and Space Museum or take a taxi to the Capital Children's Museum. Or, for little ones, consider a boat ride on the Tidal Basin (pedal boats for rent, 202-484-3475).

A book we discovered through a friend who is always coming up with little-known travel gems is published by a small press called Noodle Press and is a wonderful guidebook just for kids. Called *Washington, D.C. for Kids*, it's written by Carol Bluestone and Susan Irwin and is filled with fun facts, sightseeing suggestions, games, puzzles, and maps. This is an excellent piece of work, best to get before you set out on your trip so that you can use it in your planning phase. Copies may be ordered from the publisher at P.O. Box 42542, Washington, D.C. 20015 for $5.95. Our kids used this book to plan a wonderful Washington visit.

Washington, D.C., is another title in the Gulliver Travels series we've mentioned before: *A Kid's Guide to Washington, D.C.* (published by Harcourt Brace Jovanovich, $6.95) should be read a few weeks before the trip. It covers history, places to see, things to do, and lots of fascinating and little-known facts about Washington—all written just for kids 7 or 8 or older.

Another book with the same idea is *Kidding Around: Washington, D.C.* (John Muir Publishing, $9.95) meant for kids 8 and over. We like this one a lot, and we're sure your kids will, too. For younger children, we recommend Jill Krementz's book of photos, *A Visit to Washington, D.C.* Sit down and read this to your little ones, talk about the pictures, and use it to help plan what you all want to see. Published by Scholastic, Inc., it costs $13.95.

Yet another source of information on interesting programs for kids in the Washington area is the National Park Service. For up-to-the-minute information on park activities—such as hikes through Fort Washington Park looking for signs of whitetail deer, holiday storytelling, or a harvest celebration—call 202-485-PARK or 485-9666. Or write to the Editorial Office of Public Affairs, National Capitol Region, 1100 Ohio Drive, S.W., Washington, D.C. 20242, and ask for a copy of *Kiosk*, a monthly guide to events.

And, before your trip, be sure to get a copy of *Potomac Children* from Box 39134, Washington, D.C. 20016. It's one of those excellent parent publications we talked about in the introduction to this chapter; it has a comprehensive calendar of events just for families.

A somewhat newer parent publication that covers the Metropolitan Washington area, including the Maryland suburbs and Northern Virginia, is *Parent and Child.* This magazine contains a detailed calendar of events and is available from 7048 Wilson Lane, Bethesda, Maryland 20817.

And, if you'll be in the area long enough to plan weekend trips away, take a look at Eleanor Berman's *Away for the Weekend,* published by Clarkson N. Potter, Inc. ($11.95). (Berman gives you 52 getaways from the city, arranged by season. Another book on the same subject is *Weekends Away: Washington,* part of a series published by E. P. Dutton and edited by Mike Michaelson ($9.95). Each excursion is rated as suitable for romance or for family fun, and lots are deemed fine for both.

Two other guides to the area around Washington are Robert Shosteck's *Weekender's Guide to the Four Seasons,* published by Pelican Publishing Company, 1101 Monroe Street, Gretna, Louisiana 70053, which lists places to see and things to do within 200 miles of Washington, Baltimore, and Richmond; and *One-Day Trips through History: 200 Excursions within 150 Miles of Washington, D.C.,* by Jane Ocershausen Smith, published by EPM Publications, 1003 Turkey Run Road, McLean, Virginia 22101 ($9.95).

A book that's meant for families who live in Washington or are going to spend at least a few months there is *Serious Fun* by Amity Kaye Horowitz. This book is a wonderful resource to all that Washington has to offer kids; there are listings on dance classes, art workshops, how to produce a family history, where to go to play just about any sport you can imagine. Copies are $14.95 and are available from the publisher, EPM Publications, 1003 Turkey Run Road, McLean, Virginia 22101.

Getting Around

Washington is an easy town to get around. Public transportation is excellent; don't bother to take your car touring downtown: parking is too expensive and hard to find. Metrobus and Metrorail routes link all parts of the city, and riding the Metro is a real adventure for kids. Children under 5 ride free. Families may buy a Metro ticket for unlimited travel on Saturday and Sunday for $5. For Metrorail/

Metrobus information, call 202-637-2437. Another great boon to tourists is the Tourmobile, 202-554-7950, which operates tours to 18 historic sites aboard shuttles. Guides on board give background information, and one ticket (adults, $7, kids 3 to 11, $3.50) allows you to get on and off whenever you'd like. (The Arlington portion costs another $2.50 and $1 respectively.)

We recently took the Old Time Trolley Tour (202-269-3020), which is similar in concept to the Tourmobile, and loved it. Tickets are available at hotels and are $12 for adults, $5 for kids 5 to 12, and free for kids under 5. A great map is included in the price of the ticket. The trolley stops at most of the Washington hotels and all of the major sights, and its route is more extensive than that of the Tourmobile.

Things to See and Do

Some of the places we like best in Washington follow. All are in the area of The Mall, which is one reason that touring Washington is so easy. The first listing, the Air and Space Museum, is part of the impressive Smithsonian Institution Museum group, the world's largest museum complex, where admission is always free. Most of the Smithsonian buildings surround the Mall, which is within a five-minute walk of the Capitol on one side and the Washington Monument on the other. On The Mall, other attractions that interest kids are the Hirschorn Museum and Sculpture Garden, the Arts and Industry Building, the Freer Gallery, the Museum of Natural History, and the Museum of American History (the last two are right next door to each other). While waiting to go into the White House—tour times are assigned at a booth on The Ellipse—we spent a delightful two hours at the Museum of American History and recommend it for your family. When we got hungry, we went to the cafeteria in the East Building of The National Gallery of Art for a quick, tasty lunch.

For recorded information on Smithsonian daily events, call 202-357-2020; for general information, 202-357-2700. For information on presentations given in the Smithsonian's Discovery Theatre by the Institution's Resident Associate Program, call 202-357-1500. Performances are held from October to June, either at the Arts and Industries Building or at the National Museum of Natural History during the week and/or on weekends. Performances all relate to a specific museum or exhibition, and tickets are $3 for adults, $2.50 for kids 12 and under. Some past productions included "Music and the Underground Railroad," with music, story and songs, and a marionette production of "Jack and the Beanstalk" set in the mountains of Appalachia; call for current information.

NATIONAL AIR AND SPACE MUSEUM (Sixth and Independence Avenues, S.W., Washington, D.C. 20560, 202-357-2700). The grown-ups among us resisted this one at first, but we ended up loving it. Go early in the day if you can. Take a highlight tour at 10:15 A.M. or at 1:00 P.M. See the "Milestones of Flight" gallery, from the Wright brothers to the command module of the Apollo 11 moon-landing mission. And the films presented in the IMAX theater are truly spectacular. Don't leave without seeing them. The museum includes lots of conveniences for families—infant changing tables, strollers allowed, an area for nursing mothers, self-guided tape tours, and a cafeteria and full-service restaurant.

NATIONAL ARCHIVES AND RECORDS SERVICE (Constitution Avenue between Seventh and Ninth Streets, N.W., Zip: 20408, 202-523-3000; one block off the Mall). Older kids who have studied the beginnings of American government may want to take a look at the Declaration of Independence, the Constitution, and the Bill of Rights. If you and your kids are really interested, you can arrange a behind-the-scenes tour given by docents at 10:15 A.M. and 1:15 P.M. each day. During the summer, special children's programs are offered. Call 202-523-3347 for information.

FBI BUILDING (E Street between Ninth and Tenth Streets, N.W., Zip: 20535, 202-324-3447; a 5-minute walk from the Mall). The FBI tour is one of the most popular shows in town for kids. Our teenager thought it was terrific. They love all the exhibits on crime detection, fingerprinting, blood typing, reminders of some of our more notorious law breakers, and, at the end of the tour, the firearms demonstration. Tours run Monday to Friday from 9:00 A.M. to 4:15 P.M., every 20 minutes or so. Up to 5,000 people per day take this tour! If you contact your congressman's office for advance reservations, you can avoid long lines.

BUREAU OF ENGRAVING AND PRINTING (14th and C Streets, S.W., Zip: 20228, 202-447-1391; one block off the Mall). Here's where our money and our postage stamps are printed. Continuous free self-guided tours, about 20 minutes long, run Monday through Friday from 9:00 to 2:00. (They're closed the week between Christmas and New Year's, though.) Get on line early—the wait averages an hour and a half during high season. At the end of the tour you'll stop at the Visitor Center, where you can see uncut sheets of currency and engraved prints. Kids love to buy little bags of shredded currency to take home with them.

Following are other worthwhile Washington sights:

ANACOSTIA MUSEUM (1901 Fort Place, S.E., Zip: 20020 202-287-3369). This is one of the smaller branches of the Smithsonian, and it is devoted to presenting programs and exhibits that relate to black history and culture. The museum offers free, self-guided audiocassette tours and, periodically features special demonstrations, storytelling, and hands-on activities. There's no restaurant, but a picnic area is adjacent to the museum.

CAPITAL CHILDREN'S MUSEUM (800 Third Street, N.E., Zip: 20002, 202-543-8600). Here your kids (most of the exhibits are geared to ages 5 to 12) can paint with a computer, bake a tortilla, launch a satellite, crawl through a manhole, print a poster, or read an electronic newspaper. The four major exhibit areas are Communications, Mexico, Future Center, and Changing Environments. From time to time, the museum also presents musical plays. Every weekend, there are arts and crafts activities—a special workshop on mask making or string painting or thumb pottery are examples. Admission is $5 for anyone over 2.

KENNEDY CENTER FOR THE PERFORMING ARTS/PROGRAMS FOR CHILDREN AND YOUTH (Washington, D.C. 20566, 202-254-7190). The Kennedy Center presents free programs for young people during their fall session of performances, which includes contemporary adaptations of well-known tales from September to December; a Cultural Diversity Festival in February featuring poetry, African folktales, and international folk dance; and their Imagination Celebration in April, which involves drama, music, and puppetry at a children's art festival. All of these are held in the theater of the center, or the Terrace Theater. Call for details.

EXPLORERS HALL, NATIONAL GEOGRAPHIC SOCIETY (17th and M Streets, N.W., Zip: 20036, 202-857-7000). This small museum is nice for kids. It is just four blocks north of the White House. A new hands-on interactive science center features "Geographica: A New Look at the World," where you can touch a tornado or walk under the wingspan of a giant dinosaur. The big feature here is the world's largest unmounted globe: 11 feet from pole to pole and 34 feet around its equator. It usually rotates on its axis, just like the earth. Globe demonstrations can be arranged in advance by calling 202-857-7689.

THE WASHINGTON POST (1150 15th Street, N.W., Zip: 20071,

202-334-6000). If you have kids 11 or older (or fifth grade and up), you can arrange for a tour of the *Post's* facilities. The news department and all of the production facilities are included, so if your kids are interested in a behind-the-scenes look at a newspaper, call 202-334-7969.

NAVY MUSEUM (Washington Navy Yard, Ninth and M Streets, S.E., Zip: 20003, 202-433-4882). We chose this because it's a little like an indoor-outdoor playground. The point of the museum is to present a chronological and thematic overview of the Navy's history in the United States from the Revolution to the 1980s. What the kids love is the chance to climb on cannons, tanks, and missiles and turn periscopes. Going on board the decommissioned destroyer *USS Barry* is fun, too. For kids, the museum has put together a *Scavenger Hunt* booklet and an activity sheet that would be good even for the smallest children. There are strollers allowed always, free guided tours, tours self-guided geared for kids 5 to 7 and 8 to 14, and a park with picnic tables right across the street. Admission is free.

NATIONAL ZOOLOGICAL PARK (3000 Block of Connecticut Avenue, N.W., Zip: 20008, 202-673-4817). This is yet another section of the Smithsonian. Admission is free, but parking costs $3. What a zoo! We spent three hours there recently with kids aged 3 to 16 and we all had a good time. Don't miss the white tigers, the pandas, the giraffes, the hippos, and the reptiles. We picnicked on a bench and avoided the long, long lines at the snack bars. Strollers are available for rent on weekends except in the summer, when they're available every day.

Time Out

SITTERS UNLIMITED (10681 Oak Thrush Court, Burke, Virginia 22015, 703-250-5250). The office is open from 9:00 A.M. to 5:00 P.M., otherwise you'll have to leave a message on the machine. The hourly rate is $7 with a four-hour minimum plus a parking fee at the hotel or $4 for transportation, whichever is greater. Overnight rates are $75 for a full 24 hours plus $10 a day extra for each sibling. If you'd like a sitter to take your kids out on tour, the cost will be $8 per hour plus all expenses for the sitter. There's a 35 percent cancellation fee, and sitters must be paid in cash.

Accommodations

A bed and breakfast venture that specializes in accommodations in the city's historic districts is Bed and Breakfasts of Washington, D.C., P.O. Box 12011, Washington, D.C. 20005, 202-328-3510. Rates vary from $45 to $85 for doubles, with $10 to $20 for each additional person. Unhosted apartments are available and great for families; expect to pay $75–$90 for a family of four.

Hotels

Many Washington hotels have special family plans or, even more likely, special weekend rates. Often weekend rates are available every day during the summer.

For a free, one-stop reservation service offering discounts for families, just call 800-VISIT-DC. The system represents 70 hotels in downtown Washington and nearby Virginia and Maryland. It's operated by Capitol Reservations, 1201 K Street, N.W., Washington, D.C., 20005. The following hotels assured us they "warmly welcome" families with kids under 12.

LOEWS' L'ENFANT PLAZA HOTEL (480 L'Enfant Plaza, S.W., Washington, D.C. 20024, 202-484-1000 or 800-223-0888). This one is within walking distance of the Air and Space Museum, the Washington Monument, and the Capitol, and there's a Metro station right under the hotel. The hotel has an open air swimming pool, and there's a playground one block away at the Mall. Rooms all have refrigerators, televisions, minibars, and individual climate controls. Regular room rates are $165 to $205 for a double, but special weekend rates are much lower, for instance, $62.50 per person per night for their "Star Spangled Special." Kids 14 and under stay free in the same room with parents. Cribs are free. Baby-sitting can be arranged through the concierge for $6 per hour. Ask, too, about their two-night "Great Washington Family Getaways" package.

STOUFFER CONCOURSE HOTEL (2399 Jefferson Davis Highway, Arlington, Virginia 22202, 703-979-6800 or 800-HOTELS-1). Don't let the address put you off. This hotel is adjacent to the Washington National Airport and 10 minutes from D.C. There's a Metro station three blocks from the hotel. There are a rooftop swimming pool, an exercise room, saunas (the health club is reserved for people 16 and over), and a game room. Family suites are available. A special family weekend rate of $79 per night includes one free meal per day for kids under 12, complimentary coffee and newspaper with a wake-up call, and in-room movies. For a bit more, your family can stay on the Club Floor, where the rooms are larger and include a complimentary breakfast. Cribs are free, baby-sitting is available, and kids under 18 stay for free.

THE NEW HAMPSHIRE SUITES (1121 New Hampshire Avenue, N.W., Washington, D.C. 20037, 202-457-0565 or 800-762-3777). This all-suite hotel in Washington's west end offers complimentary "English sideboard breakfasts" every morning of the week and wine and cheese receptions from Monday to Thursday evenings. All of the suites have a separate living and sleeping area, kitchenettes with microwaves and coffeemakers with complimentary coffee. The weekend, summer, and holiday special rate is most attractive to families—$79 (regular rates range from $109 up to $145). Kids under 12 stay for free with parents, and cribs are available for $15 per night.

THE BEST WESTERN SKYLINE INN (10 I Street, S.W., Washington, D.C. 20024-4299, 202-488-7500 or 800-458-7500). Within walking distance of the Capitol and many of Washington's museums, this hotel has an outdoor pool and a park across the street with a basketball court and free tennis courts. Rates range from $70 to $105 per night, depending on season, and one-bedroom suites are $125 to $180. Ask about weekend rates—they were suspended when we went to press but we were told that they might be reintroduced. Kids under 18 stay for free with parents, and cribs are available at no extra charge.

HOTEL ANTHONY (1823 L Street, N.W., Washington, D.C. 20036, 202-223-4320 or 800-424-2970). Another all-suite hotel near the White House and the museums and monuments on the Mall. The Metro is one block away. Most suites have a full kitchen or wet bar, a living area, dressing room, and free movies, coffee, and the *Washington Post*. Facilities of the health club are available at no extra charge to guests. Weekend rates are as low as $59 in summer, $69 the rest of the year. Kids under 16 are free with parents, and cribs are free.

There are three Hyatt properties in Washington, D.C.: the Grand Hyatt at 1000 H Street, N.W., Zip: 20001; the Hyatt Regency at 400 New Jersey Avenue, N.W., Zip: 20001; and the Park Hyatt at 24th and M Streets, Zip: 20037. For an explanation of all that Hyatt has to offer you and your family in these hotels, see page 50, then call 800-233-1234 for details on these specific hotels.

8

RESORTS

Some people like to go to one spot and stay there until their vacation is over. They like their meals, their sports, their entertainment all within walking distance. For these people we offer this chapter: resorts with activities galore and children's programs besides. Remember, too, that there are other resorts throughout the book, in the ski, golf and tennis, and dude ranch chapters. Check them out, too. Two books on the subject we recommend are *What to Do with the Kids This Year* by Jane Wilford with Janet Tice, published by Globe Pequot Press ($8.95). The book lists 100 places to stay, all with activities for kids, and *Super Family Vacations* (see page 13).

Our listings are alphabetical by state; as in everything else in the book, the emphasis here is on the facilities for kids.

Marriott's Grand Hotel
Scenic Highway 98
Point Clear, Alabama 36564
Telephone: 205-928-9201, 800-228-9290 or 800-544-9933
General Manager: John Irvin

IN THEIR OWN WORDS: "An exciting yet relaxed atmosphere for all age groups, . . . strolling by the lagoon, you can stop to feed the ducks or savor the breathtaking landscaping and gardens . . . . The hotel is located in a residential community, away from busy traffic.

All activities are available on property, and parents can feel safe letting their children roam around the grounds."

DESCRIPTION: The hotel's 550 acres of moss-draped oaks, lagoons, and gardens are located right on Mobile Bay. Since 1847, this resort has been seducing guests with the pleasures of tennis, golf, badminton, croquet, jogging, horseback riding (Point Clear Stables is a picture-book thoroughbred breeding and training farm right next to the golf course), boating, fishing from a charter boat or the Grand Pavilion Wharf, and swimming at the beach or in the enormous 750,000-gallon Grand Hotel pool.

FOR KIDS: Kids 5 to 12 can join the Grand Juniors Program, which operates from 10:00 A.M. all the way to 10:00 P.M., Monday through Saturday in summer and during vacation periods. Every day is different for the Grand Juniors—beach fun, biking, pool play, fishing contests, after-dinner movies, dance contests, and more. Kids can register for a full day of Grand Juniors or for any part of the day; there's no charge for the program. Lunch and dinner can be included for an additional fee. Kids are supervised by Grand Junior Hostesses, who are always available to discuss the program and any special needs you or your child may have.

Baby-sitting for younger kids is available by contacting housekeeping. Expect to pay about $3.50 per hour.

ACCOMMODATIONS: All of the 307 rooms have views of the bay, marina, or lagoon; most have balconies. A typical room has two double beds and a sofa bed. Cribs are available at no extra charge.

RATES: In winter rates average $125 per room; they range from $99 up during the summer. Kids under 18 stay free. Various packages are also available, so be sure to ask.

Hyatt Regency Scottsdale
7500 East Doubletree Ranch Road
Scottsdale, Arizona 85258
Telephone: 602-991-3388 or 800-233-1234
General Manager: James K. Petrus

IN THEIR OWN WORDS: "Our beautiful weather plays an important part in making this the perfect destination resort. And continuous sunshine means there's no end to the possibilities."

DESCRIPTION: The sunshine that they refer to above was glorious when we arrived at the Hyatt, refugees from a grim, gray New York winter. But the sun is not all that dazzled us. Just a few years old, the Hyatt is set against the McDowell Mountains in the Sonoran Desert—it is a gorgeous spot, a never-never land for vacationers. One of its most striking features is its "water playground," a half-acre ten-pool complex which includes a sand beach (with sand toys for the kids), a three-story waterslide inside a clock tower, and a 14-foot high water aqueduct which traverses above six pools. At the adjacent Gainey Ranch Golf Club, guests have access to 27 holes of championship golf, and tennis players can choose from eight laykold-surfaced courts, four of which are lit up for nighttime use. Not far from the resort there are some wonderful possibilities: horseback riding, desert jeep tours, hot air ballooning, and whitewater rafting. Biking is fun and easy at the Hyatt—bicycles are available for free—and the terrain is flat. We found that one of the most striking features of the resort was the art that we encountered as we explored the place. It seemed that around every turn there was a surprise—a beautiful clay bowl, a lovely watercolor painting, gaily painted outdoor sculptures.

FOR KIDS: This is one resort that has put an enormous amount of energy and care into organizing its children's programs. Over and over again, we heard parents raving about how much their kids loved the program. Our 8-year-old was no exception: "The best," he says.

One day, when we went to pick our kids up, we found them in the resort's kitchen, donning chef hats and concentrating all their energies on baking cookies. There's nothing passive about the children's program here—even when we picked ours up at 9:00 P.M. one night, the counselors were still playing games and jumping around with the kids. The Hyatt people call their program Kamp Kachina, and it operates on weekends, at holiday times, and during the summer for ages 3–15. On weekends, it begins with dinner and a movie on Friday night and continues on Saturday from 10:00 A.M. to about 9:00 P.M. and on Sundays until 5:00 P.M. At holiday times, and during the summer, it runs from 9:00 A.M. to 9:00 P.M. and often on until 11:00 P.M. The program costs $25 per day or $5 per event. During the summer a full-fledged camp operates at the resort, and kids from the area as well as guests of the resort participate. Kids who participate in the Kamp Kachina program get to do all sorts of interesting things—they bake; make T-shirts, socks, and hats; play lots of games; go horseback riding; participate in scavenger hunts; go bowling; and even get a lesson in nonalcoholic bartending.

The staff of the Kamp, led by the energetic Randy Babick, is cooperative and flexible; you can drop your kids off and pick them up whenever you please—a very convenient option. Although the program is open to kids ages 3–15, those under 5 may not take the off-property excursions (e.g., to a riding stable or to Rawhide, a nearby reconstruction of a southwestern cowboy town). Occasionally, during extremely busy periods, Kamp Kachina does not include swimming. Babick notes that this is "only when it is so crowded with guests that we have a tough time keeping a close eye on the kids."

ACCOMMODATIONS: In all, there are 493 guest rooms on four floors. All are spacious, decorated with a contemporary, southwestern feel and all have balconies that overlook one of five courtyards, the golf course, the mountains, or the lake. For real luxury, guests may stay in one of seven separate casitas that sit at the edge of the lake. Designed to feel like a private home, each has from one to four bedrooms plus a wet bar, refrigerator-freezer, private patio, fireplace, and two Jacuzzi-style spas.

RATES: Regular rates vary dramatically with the season. A deluxe room costs $230 per night from January 1 to May 21; $205 from September 16 to December 31, and $95 from May 22 to September 15. Families traveling with their kids may have two rooms, one at full price and the other at half-price, subject to availability at the time of booking. Kids 18 and under are free in the same room with their parents. An add-on of about $70 per night entitles guests to the privileges of the Regency Club—concierge services, an hour of court time for each day of the stay, and a special lounge where complimentary breakfast, afternoon tea, late afternoon cocktails, and evening cordials are served. (We had breakfast in the Regency Lounge one morning of our stay—it was both bountiful and delicious.) The resort offers a number of special packages, too, with names like "Desert Adventure," "Summer Splash," and "Golfer's Challenge." There's a children's menu for kids in the resort's more casual dining spots, and half-price portions are available in the specialty restaurants. Ask about special family packages.

The Broadmoor Hotel
P.O. Box 1439
Colorado Springs, Colorado 80901
Telephone: 719-634-7711
General Manager: Douglas C. Cogswell

IN THEIR OWN WORDS: "Each year tens of thousands of people from across the United States and scores of foreign countries converge on the Colorado Rockies. To the Broadmoor. Because the Broadmoor has never changed what it started out to be—a grand resort hotel reminiscent of the finest European traditions."

DESCRIPTION: The Broadmoor has been called the "Riviera of the Rockies" because of its pale pink buildings with red-tiled roofs set on the rim of a large lake. The theme is Mediterranean, and many of the adornments of the hotel were imported from the art centers of Europe and other parts of the world. In June 1918 the Broadmoor opened with a glittering, gala event that had all of Colorado Springs excited. Over the years, the hotel has expanded, built more golf courses and tennis courts, and won 26 years' worth of Mobil Five Star awards. This is one of those grand old hotels with a long-standing reputation for elegance that manages to avoid any feeling of snobbishness. Instead, it offers a gracious and warm welcome to families. Besides being a beautiful place—the Broadmoor is built against a breathtaking mountain backdrop—the list of activities at the Broadmoor is mind-boggling. Try to include high tea in your stay at the Broadmoor; the old-world elegance of the experience was great fun for us and the kids. The staff is incredibly nice, something we almost began to take for granted on our recent trip through Colorado. In short, we loved it.

A day at Broadmoor can include golf (54 holes in all), tennis (16 plexipave courts), skiing, year-round ice-skating, swimming, and biking. The surrounding Colorado Rockies are a major attraction. Sightseeing in the Pikes Peak region, making a trip to the Pikes Peak Cog Railway and the Will Rogers monument are all easy excursions from the hotel. Scenic tours can be arranged easily through the hotel.

FOR KIDS: We were impressed with the children's program and the care that the management takes in setting up activities for kids. The children in the program are kept active either on the grounds of the resort or on excursions to the nearby Cheyenne Mountain Zoo. The program is flexible—the way we like it—so that parents can drop their kids off and pick them up at just about any time during the day. Kids 5 to 12 can join the Bee Bunch Mondays through Saturdays during June, July, and August from 9:00 A.M. to 4:00 P.M. and again from 6:00 P.M. to 10:00 P.M. Mornings are filled with games, paddleboating, tennis, and golf clinics, trips to the zoo, swimming and lunch at the pool. At night, after dinner (the kids eat together), the Bee Bunch does crafts, plays games, ice skates, or sees a movie. Four nights of the summer are set aside for a family steak fry at Rotten Log Hollow, and the Bee Bunch goes along. The fee for the program is $25 per day, which includes all activities, lunch, dinner, and sports clinics.

Baby-sitting is available for younger kids at $4 per hour with a three-hour minimum. The concierge will make arrangements.

ACCOMMODATIONS: There are 560 rooms in all, divided among three facilities—Broadmoor Main, Broadmoor West, and Broadmoor South. The first was built in 1918, the second in 1961, and the third in 1975. There are 60 suites available.

RATES: Rate for a family of four with one room and two double beds in high season (beginning May 1) is $180 to $210; in low season (beginning November 1) it's $115 to $165.

Sunrise at Frank Davis Resort
Route 151, P.O. Box 415
Moodus, Connecticut 06469
Telephone: 203-873-8681
Owners: The Johnson Family

IN THEIR OWN WORDS: "Couples, moms and dads, tots, in-betweens, teens, aunts, uncles, old friends and groups can frolic day and night between May and October . . . We are a unique full service resort—affordable to the average working family."

DESCRIPTION: The activity at Sunrise is nonstop. A sample daily program starts with aerobics classes and includes acrylic painting, practice for a staff vs. guests softball tournament, a kite-flying contest, water exercises, a trip to a nearby state park, a miniature golf tournament, a demonstation of summer skin care, scuba lessons in the pool, a basketball game, a luau, an after-dinner movie, dancing to music of the '50s to '80s. Tennis is available on floodlit courts, and there are horseshoes, volleyball, canoeing, rowboating, and daily ballroom dance lessons.

FOR KIDS: All summer long, activities for kids from 3 to 11 are available from early morning until late at night. A counselor is on duty from 10:00 A.M. to 5:00 P.M. at the enclosed playground and wading pool, and the youth director schedules activities all through the day and evening—piñata parties, treasure hunts, magic and puppet shows, arts and crafts and more. For teens, the Johnsons schedule at least one daytime activity so that the kids will get to know each other, while evening events might include a pizza or deejay party, a dance contest, a hayride followed by a scary movie, or a game of miniature golf by flashlight.

ACCOMMODATIONS: Rooms vary from "homey and rustic to new and modern." You'll have a choice of a cottage by the water, near the tennis courts, or in what they call the "mid hill" area. Single cabins offer privacy; the rustic cottages are more centrally located. Motel-style rooms are also a possibility and adjoining rooms are available for families. There are plenty of cots and cribs with no extra charge for either. Or, you can bring your own room—the resort has camping sites for RVs and tents with shower rooms and water and electrical hookups.

RATES: The daily rate for all meals, entertainment, and use of all facilities ranges from $66 to $92 per person. Campers pay $44, and special package plans let you stay a full week and pay for only 5-1/2 days. Children 14 and under get a one-third reduction, and 4 and under, two-thirds.

South Seas Plantation Resort and Yacht Harbour
P.O. Box 194
Captiva Island, Florida 33924
Telephone: 813-472-5111; for reservations, 800-237-3102
General Manager: Austin L. Mott III

IN THEIR OWN WORDS: "An enclave of tropical tranquility, . . . 330 acres of barefoot elegance where not a single tree or shrub was unnecessarily disturbed. . . ."

DESCRIPTION: As you'd expect, all kinds of water sports are possible—sailing, cruising, racing (this is one of the sites of Steve Colgate's Offshore Sailing School; see Chapter 6), jet skiing, kayaking, windsurfing, snorkeling, and charter boat fishing. The resort's two-mile stretch of private white beach is where you'll find some of the best shelling in the world. When you want to get away from the shore, there are nine holes of golf at the resort, 18 more on neighboring Sanibel Island, 22 tennis courts, and 18 (!) swimming pools.

FOR KIDS: From Memorial Day to Labor Day, and in February, March, and April during school vacations, South Seas offers children's programs, usually five days per week. Kids 3 to 18 are eligible. The program for the 3–5-year-olds runs all year.

Pelican Pals is a program for kids 3 to 5 (no diapers) held from 9:30 A.M. to noon. Activities include swimming, sing-alongs, nature crafts, and sometimes, in the evening, a cookout followed by an evening of cartoons, games, and stories. The program costs $13 per day with a T-shirt, $7 without.

Captiva Kids is for kids 6 to 8, from 9:30 A.M. to 2:00 P.M., which includes games, crafts, picnics, and swimming. It costs $15 per day with a T-shirt, $10 without, or $45 per week. "This is the best program ever" says one well-traveled non-joiner we know.

Club Captiva is for 9–12-year-olds and has the same hours as Captiva Kids. Participants canoe, play ball, do sand sculpture, go on beach picnics, do nature crafts, have scavenger hunts, sail, and cook. The cost is $15 per day with a T-shirt, $10 without. Weekly rates are $45.

Tropical Adventure is especially for teens: it offers sailing and windsurfing lessons, biking, jet skiing, and cookouts. The rate is $25 per day, which includes lunch. At night, special teen-oriented activities are also planned, all at additional cost. Expect dive-in movies (movies by the pool), a beach party or "fright night" movies.

Baby-sitting can be arranged through Guest Services for $5 per hour with 24 hours advance notice.

ACCOMMODATIONS: You can choose anything from hotel rooms to four-bedroom beachfront homes. Portable and full-size cribs are available for $5 per night. Many of the accommodations have kitchenettes.

RATES: There's a great variety of rates, depending on the accommodations you choose. For a sample, a beach villa with two bedrooms for two people would cost $180 to $260 per night depending on season. Kids 12 and under stay free when sharing with parents from mid-April to mid-December. Lower package rates are available; ask about them.

Hawk's Cay Resort and Marina
Mile Marker 61
Duck Key, Florida 33050
Telephone: 305-743-7000 or 800-432-2242 in Florida,
    800-327-7775 outside of Florida
General Manager: Tom Cherniavsky

IN THEIR OWN WORDS: "A vacation in the Florida Keys can mean many things to different types of travelers. Active travelers come here to fish, scuba dive and swim. For others, unwinding with a piña colada on the beach may be the order of the day. At Hawk's Cay, we offer something for almost everyone. We are the only completely self-contained resort in the Keys. Dad can spend the day fishing; Mom can read a book on the beach; and both are assured that the kids will be well cared for in our popular Kid's Club. All this set on a private island hideaway midway down the Florida Key chain."

DESCRIPTION: We just returned from a visit here and it's true— there's something for everyone. The hotel itself comprises blush-pink low-rise interconnected buildings with most of the rooms having some type of water view. Hawk's Cay has recently been refurbished and renovated with very pleasing results. This informal resort overlooks a swimming pool with two jacuzzis, a poolside café, and two bars. Just beyond is a lagoon rimmed by a sandy beach; beachside you'll find kayaks, floats, and other seaworthy fare to play with. Adjacent to the lagoon are the dolphins. The excitement of actually swimming with and being pulled by these delightful sea mammals is indescribable. Our 8-year-old was a bit nervous, but we couldn't wipe the smile off his face for days afterward. The encounter costs $40 per person, child or adult, requires advance reservations (make them when making room accommodations, as they fill up way in advance). Children 18 months and older may participate; those under 8 must go with a parent and pay for both parent and child.

We also joined "Doctor Dan" for a knock-your-socks-off ecology tour which took us reef-hunting, beachcombing, and exploring the mangroves and other flora and fauna of the area via a Zodiac raft. Our group of adults loved it as much, if not more, than the kids! Scuba divers have a choice of up to three dives a day, snorkel trips are offered, and a boomless catamaran sailboat goes out several times a day; deep-sea fishing is steps away at the marina, from which sunset cruises and glass-bottom boat rides also depart. Tennis is best early in the day or late in the afternoon when the sun isn't as strong and lessons are offered for adults and youngsters. Bicycles are available at the tennis courts as well.

There are several dining possibilities for guests. In addition to the huge complimentary buffet breakfast, the three restaurants all have children's menus and a casual atmosphere; food runs from simple to gourmet.

FOR KIDS: Hawk's Cay Kid's Club has been operating for several years and is open to children from 5 to 12; the program runs from 10:00 A.M. to 5:00 P.M. There is a charge of $10 per child per day, which includes lunch. Children may come and go as parents wish; however, the $10 per day charge is the same. Activities are scheduled hourly and include glass-bottom boat rides, the ecology tour, a dolphin show, supervised pool time, theater arts, crafts, fishing, lagoon fun with complimentary use of the boats, lawn games, and more. Our kids made fabulous T-shirts one day and took a tennis clinic the next. The program runs daily from mid-June to mid-September, and during all major school holidays, including Easter, Thanksgiving, and Christmas and weekends from Memorial Day through mid-June. Occasional evening programs, "No Parents Allowed Parties" with dinner, and movies are also on the agenda.

Baby-sitting is possible at $6 per hour by contacting the front desk. The cheerful, energetic team of counselors may be available for evening sitting as well.

ACCOMMODATIONS: There are a total of 177 rooms and 86 apartments. We especially like the water-view rooms that open up onto the pool or lawn area with steps down from a private balcony. Rooms have either two double beds, a queen- or a king-sized bed. The apartments are great for families but are not as centrally located. Adjoining rooms are possible. Cribs are available at no extra charge.

RATES: From mid-June to mid-September, excluding the week of the Fourth of July, a Family Fun package features accommodations, a souvenir T-shirt for the kids, daily breakfast buffet, Kid's Club for children 5–12, daily dolphin and sea lion training shows, dinner for four at the Ship's Galley, one hour of tennis and tiki boat rentals per person per day. A five-night package, Sunday through Thursday, is $737 for two adults and two children sharing a room. Additional children cost $81 for those over 12, $109 for ages 5 to 11, with kids four and under, free. A second room, if required, is $90 per night.

Sonesta Sanibel Harbor Resort
17260 Harbour Pointe Drive
Fort Myers, Florida 33908
Telephone: 813-466-4000 or 800-343-7170
General Manager: Peter Eyssens

IN THEIR OWN WORDS: "This is truly one resort where you may do as much or as little as you wish."

DESCRIPTION: The centerpiece of this resort is the tennis center—12 lighted clay composition courts, a 5,000-seat stadium, a teaching pro staff and state-of-the-art video teaching aids. Guests can also work out at the spa and fitness center—40,000 square feet of exercise equipment, a pool, four raquetball courts, Swiss showers, whirlpools, saunas, steam baths, and tanning beds, and a staff of manicurists, pedicurists, and people ready to pamper you with herbal wraps, cellulite wraps, and loofah scrubs. Not far away guests find golf, boats to charter, and a beach just perfect for shelling.

FOR KIDS: At this writing, the complimentary "Just Us Kids" program operates from 10:00 A.M. to noon and 2:00 to 3:30 P.M. for kids 5–12 year-round, but the plan was to offer a full day of events "in the near future." We suggest you call to check. Activities include picnics, treasure hunts, nature hikes, pool games, arts and crafts, limbo contests, face painting, and pizza parties.

ACCOMMODATIONS: Your choice is a hotel room or a condo. Condos have one or two bedrooms, with full kitchens, a living/dining room, and a private balcony that looks out over the waters of San Carlos Bay and Sanibel Island.

RATES: A Condo Holiday package for 7 days and 6 nights is $960 for one bedroom and $1,170 for two from January 3 to January 31, April 16 to May 30, and right before Christmas. A one-bedroom condo sleeps four; the two-bedroom accomodates six. Daily maid service is included. The people at Sonesta offer a nice service, too, that they call the Condo Starter package: for $35 they'll stock your condo with all the basics and some not-so-basics, like eggs, bread, juice, coffee, beer, wine, and soda.

Hotel rooms are part of the Tennis Getaway package, which costs $280 per person double occupancy for three days and two nights with children under 18 free in the same room as a parent. Included in the package price are two lessons, unlimited court time, and one day free entrance to the spa and fitness center.

Cheeca Lodge
U.S. Highway 1,
P.O. Box 527
Islamorada, Florida 33036
Telephone: 305-664-4651 or 800-327-2888
General Manager: Herbert Spiegel

IN THEIR OWN WORDS: "Cheeca Lodge recently reopened after 18 months of refurbishment and expansion. We are a longstanding Keys tradition, newly inspired."

DESCRIPTION: Cheeca Lodge is a 25-acre hideaway that's adored by sun worshippers and people who love all kinds of water sports. The setting is beautiful—lush palm trees, oleander and hibiscus, salt water pools, man-made lakes and a 1,000-foot stretch of golden sand beach. Every water sport you can imagine is here—deep sea fishing, boating, windsurfing, scuba diving, and snorkeling. A Jack Nicklaus-designed par three golf course entices golfers. Six lighted tennis courts provide another possibility for fun. In all, there are three pools—one for family play, one for kids, and one free-form pool plus bar reserved for grown-ups only.

FOR KIDS: The relatively new children's program is a winner, supervised by Jennifer Fisher, an enthusiastic young woman who is formally trained in recreational management and is extremely interested in ecology. The program reflects Jennifer's interests and combines sports with instruction in the unique natural environment of the Keys. The program is for kids 5–12 and runs during the summer and at school break time from 8:30 A.M. to 4:30 P.M. Kids may sign up for a full day ($25), or half day ($9), either in the morning or afternoon. Lunch is included in the full day fee; kids staying only half day may have lunch for an extra charge of $7. Two counselors are on duty morning and afternoon. In the morning, kids may take a nature hike, go out on a marine-collecting walk or go fishing (the resort has its own 525-foot lighted fishing pier). "We try to make the kids understand what makes the Keys so special. While they're having fun we teach them why this area is so unique." The second part of the morning is spent in the water—perhaps snorkeling lessons or swimming instruction in the pool. The afternoon is time for the "Aquatic Wild Lab," which might involve making fish prints or taking a walk called "Plastic Jelly Fish" which teaches the kids all about the dangers of plastics in our oceans. The rest of the afternoon is spent swimming and playing water games. On weekends the resort adds movie nights, poolside barbecues, and special presentations by park rangers.

Baby-sitting is available for kids not old enough for the supervised program.

ACCOMMODATIONS: Scattered throughout the property are 155 villa rooms and 49 traditional guest rooms. All have private balconies with a view of either the ocean, the resort gardens, or Florida Bay. In addition, 64 suites have fully equipped kitchens, master bedrooms, bath, living room, and porch.

RATES: Per night rates (room only) are $195–$275 for lodge rooms; villa rooms and suites are $210 to $285 from December 23 to April 1. Kids 16 and under are free in their parents' room, and families who want a two-bedroom suite may subtract $50 from the regular rate.

Radisson Suite Beach Resort
600 South Collier Boulevard
Marco Island, Florida 33937
Telephone: 813-394-4100 or 800-333-3333
General Manager: Dennis Walker

IN THEIR OWN WORDS: "At our resort the room next to yours is yours! . . . The only thing we overlook is the Gulf."

DESCRIPTION: This high-rise resort sits on the Gulf of Mexico, not far from the Everglades. What's doing? Try tennis, sailing, swimming, windsurfing, parasailing, snorkeling, and shelling. Golf is available at a nearby course and there's a health club right in the hotel. Throughout the week, activities are scheduled for adults (beach crafts, aerobics, water volleyball, etc.) and for families (bingo night, a day cruise to explore the island, and shell crafts).

FOR KIDS: Children 3–5 join Marco Munchkins, which operates from 9:00 A.M. to 11:00 A.M. and involves beach walks, sand-castle building, coloring, drawing, games, and what the resort calls "no-cook cooking." The two-hour session costs $5. The older kids, ages 6–12, can sign up for Radisson Rascals, three hours in the afternoon of relay races, beach walks, pool games, and crafts; the cost is $7. These differing hours can be inconvenient if you have kids in both age groups. Once a week the kids have a pizza and movie night, and for teens, one night is set aside for movies. Baby-sitting may be arranged with the concierge a day in advance for $5 per hour for the first child and $1 more for each additional child.

ACCOMMODATIONS: The 222 suites all have fully equipped kitchens and private balconies with views of the Gulf from both the bedroom and living room areas. The one-bedroom suites are large enough for five people, the two-bedroom suites have enough room for seven.

RATES: From February 1 to April 2, a one-bedroom, beach-view deluxe suite costs $170, a two-bedroom, $240, no matter how many people are staying. From May 1 to December 21, the same accommodations are $99 and $129 respectively. Packages are available year-round.

Port of the Islands Resort and Marina
2500 Tamiami Trail East
Naples, Florida 33961
Telephone: 813-394-3101 or 800-237-4173
General Manager: E. S. Hightower

IN THEIR OWN WORDS: "We run a casual and relaxing 500-acre resort. It's very peaceful and tranquil here since we're surrounded by state and national parklands right at the gateway to the Everglades."

DESCRIPTION: This is Florida at its most natural. Port of the Islands is located right on the boundary between Florida's Everglades—the Sea of Grass—and the 10,000 islands. Surrounded by thousands of square miles of state parks and environmentally protected lands, the resort is a favorite of fishermen, naturalists, writers, and artists—"an ideal place to escape urban pressures and renew the soul." Although there's a great deal to do right within the resort's 500 acres—fishing, boating, tennis, two heated pools, a spa, bicycling, volleyball, and more—the real attraction here is the surrounding wilderness. This is one of the great remaining wilderness areas of the U.S., and in it you'll find a rich variety of fish, who feed among the mangrove roots, and birds—over 300 species have been spotted. You may see bald eagles, egrets, deer, racoons, even an occasional black bear. A freshwater river flows right through the resort property and feeds a harbor which has been designated a manatee sanctuary. From the resort, waters lead through the 10,000 islands to the Gulf of Mexico via a clearly marked channel. Guests may sign up for a two-hour cruise on the resort's 49-passenger catamaran for a ride through the 10,000 islands, and they can arrange to visit Briggs Nature Center, the Conservancy Nature Center, or the Miccosukee Indian Village.

FOR KIDS: Camp Kid is an honest-to-goodness overnight camp with five week-long sessions in June, July, and August. Kids sleep with the other campers, not with their parents, and live a typical camp life. During the school year director Art Ogden is the football, wrestling, and tennis coach at Naples High School. Campers—boys and girls from 8 to 14—learn about boat and water safety, how to locate and catch fish, about marine life and knot tying; they leave camp knowing about the birds and animals of the area, conservation, and the history and archaeology of this part of the U.S. Parents may see their kids occasionally while they're at camp. Baby-sitting can be arranged with enough advance notice—one week is requested—but there are no special activities for younger kids other than Camp Kid.

ACCOMMODATIONS: You have a choice of either a hotel-type room, a two-room suite in the hotel, or efficiency apartments with either one or two bedrooms, cooking facilities, and a breakfast bar. Most of the rooms are on the first floor with direct access to the beautiful outdoors.

RATES: From December to April, the high season for the resort, a two-room suite costs $115 per night; the two-bedroom efficiency is $125. Kids under 15 are free with a maximum of two per room. Cribs are free. Special package plans with children's rates include accommodations, breakfasts, nature cruises, and bike and canoe rentals and are available year-round. The cost of a five-night, six-day stay at Camp Kid is $295 per child.

The Breakers
One South County Road
Palm Beach, Florida 33480
Telephone: 407-655-6611 or 800-323-7500
President: Stayton Addison

IN THEIR OWN WORDS: "A very Palm Beach tradition. . . . Architecturally, the Breakers is quite literally a design masterpiece—fashioned from the era of Italian Renaissance, inspired by the most notable villa in all of Italy. And artistically, it is perhaps a hotel without equal. Built by over 1,000 artisans, its ceilings were painstakingly hand-painted by 75 artists who were imported from all over Europe."

DESCRIPTION: The preceding may not sound like the kind of place that would encourage little ones to visit, but that's just not true. The management of the Breakers assures us that they "warmly welcome" families with children under 12 at their "palace by the sea." The Breakers has its own private beach, an oceanfront pool, two 18-hole golf courses, 19 tennis courts—both hard and clay—and a health club. Scuba diving and snorkeling are also possible in the warm Gulfstream waters. And on Wednesday afternoons, treat yourself to a tour by the staff historian, Jim Ponce (a descendant of Ponce de León).

FOR KIDS: Organized programs for kids 2 to 12 years are available, and teenagers have special evening activities planned during the summer, at school vacation time, and on weekends during the year. The two-to-four-year-olds meet from 9:00 A.M. to 11:00 A.M. daily for arts and crafts, storytelling, games, and other outdoor activities. Five- to 12-year-olds meet from 9:00 A.M. to 4:00 P.M. and participate in arts and crafts, swimming, games, sports, and golf and tennis clinics. Picnic lunches, excursions to the zoo, roller-skating trips, and jaunts to the science museum are all included in the $10 daily fee. At night teens can look forward to pizza parties, MTV Night, and Game Show Night; during the day they can participate in tennis and golf clinics and all kinds of beach activities. Kids 5–12 may have dinner with counselors or with their parents and may spend from 6:00 P.M. to 10:00 P.M. with the counselors.

Baby-sitting may be arranged for $5 per hour. Ask, too about the Breakers' money management camp for kids held in July and their etiquette camp, also in July.

ACCOMMODATIONS: Rooms and one-bedroom suites are available. Typically a room has two double beds, with a view of either the gardens or the ocean.

RATES: Room rates range from $85 per night in summer to $165 in high season—October to December and April to May. Packages are available during summer and "shoulder" season. Kids under 17 are free when sharing with parents. Breakfast and dinner are included for $37 per person plus $7 service; $22 for kids under 12.

The Dunes
333 Fort Pickens Road
Pensacola Beach, Florida 32561
Telephone: 904-932-3536 or 800-83-DUNES
General Manager: Beverly F. Hofer

IN THEIR OWN WORDS: "We recently polled our guests to ask them what they liked most about us. Seventy-eight percent said 'the friendly staff.' What makes us special is a staff that enjoys being hospitable."

DESCRIPTION: This hotel is right on the Gulf of Mexico, which means a sugar-white beach, clear blue water, and usually loads of sunshine. One of the main attractions here is the nearby Tiger Point Golf and Country Club, open to guests of the Dunes. Santa Rosa Sound has two courses, the newest designed by Jerry Pate, U.S. Open golf champion and the principal owner of Tiger Point. Guests also have tennis and raquetball privileges at a nearby club, and, as you'd expect, full use of the beach for swimming, scuba diving, sailing, windsurfing, and fishing.

FOR KIDS: The Beach Bunch is a program for kids 4–12 that operates from 9:00 A.M. to 2:00 P.M. Wednesday through Saturday from Memorial Day to Labor Day and on weekends from Easter through Memorial Day. The program costs $2 per day and includes lunch at the activities tent. "The first thing to remember about the Beach Bunch is that it is not a baby-sitting service, but a program of fun and new friends for vacationing children of similar ages." Some of the things the kids do as part of the program include art and beach activities, puppet shows, games, contests, and story hours. The ratio of kids to counselor is seven to one. When it rains, the program moves indoors to the Holiday Inn nearby. (The Dunes and the Holiday Inn run Beach Bunch together.) On Saturday nights, from 6:00 P.M. to 10:00 P.M. Beach Bunch staff supervises dinner, a movie, and games for the kids, so that the parents can have a night out. Baby-sitting may be arranged through the hotel, too—rates are $4 per hour with a minimum of six hours.

ACCOMMODATIONS: The Dunes has one hotel building that's eight stories high and one motel-type wing that's two stories—the architecture is typically Florida beachfront. It's possible to walk right onto the beach from the rooms on the first floor of the motel building.

RATES: Summer rates, from May 16 to September 6, range from $69 all the way up to $229. The less expensive rate is a standard inside room (no view); the most expensive is for a penthouse suite. Children under 18 are free; a rollaway bed is $5 more. A Golf and Gulf package during the spring and summer is $65 per person per day on weekends, $59 during the week and includes unlimited green fees and cart for 18 holes.

Club Med Sandpiper
Port Lucie, Florida
Mailing Address: Club Med, 40 West 57th Street,
New York, New York 10019
Telephone: 800-CLUB-MED

IN THEIR OWN WORDS: "This is the old, unspoiled Florida . . . a beautiful place . . . warm, friendly and hassle free, the most luxurious Club Med ever."

DESCRIPTION: Located 45 minutes north of Palm Beach, this resort was taken over by the Club Med people, who invested $10 million in changes. The result is a luxurious Caribbean-like resort with 45 holes of golf, 19 tennis courts, and five swimming pools, all along the banks of the milewide St. Lucie River. Although the golf is a major attraction (and is not included in the rates), the Club Med folks want to be sure that people understand that it's only one attraction. Others are sailing, waterskiing, pedal boating, a fitness center, basketball, volleyball, biking, tennis, circus, and the use of a Beach Club on the Atlantic that is accessible via a free shuttle bus. Lunch is also served at the beach for those who don't want to return to the club at noontime. Readers who have never been to a Club

Med need to know that (1) we love the Club and have visited several and (2) that Club Med offers lots—lots of sports, lots of instruction, lots of fun, but not lots of service. There is no room service, no televisions, no bellmen. Help is available for the asking as GOs (the Club Med name for staff) are people-pleasers by training; but this is not the kind of a place where you can snap your fingers and expect five people to hover around you. And, while the stated philosophy is to leave your watch at home, don't. All sports and lessons are given at specific times, so you'll need to know what time it is to take advantage of all that is offered.

FOR KIDS: The Sandpiper has a baby club and a mini-club, and the services are outstanding. The Baby Club is for kids 4 months to 2 years who are cared for by GOs from 8:00 A.M. to 6:00 P.M. six days a week. Kids can stay the entire time or part of the time or go in and out of the program, whatever best suits the parents.

A specialist on baby food is on staff to plan and make meals for the little ones, and babies can be fed lunch by the GOs. Parents are expected to feed them dinner, but staff will prepare it. Bottle warmers, bassinets, potty seats, strollers—all the equipment you might need for a baby—are available.

Kids 2 to 11 are eligible for the mini-club, which meets from 9:00 A.M. to 9:00 P.M. and is open six days a week. Kids are divided into groups ages 2–3, 4–7, and 8–11, each with its own meeting space where activities are listed so that kids can easily find their group and join them at any time. Mini-club members over 8 can come and go as they please; learn archery, tennis, golf, sailing, trampoline, and even circus stunts. Little ones can enjoy the mini-pool outside the air-conditioned mini-club house. Mini-club members put on shows for guests, go on picnics, and take excursions. Kids learn to waterski in one of the pools (there are five in all) before trying out their new skill on the river. Mini-club members have early lunch and dinner (special menus designed to appeal to kids along with the GOs and their fellow club members) or they may eat with their parents. All of this is included in the price of the stay. Baby-sitters are available at an additional charge for after 6:00 P.M. for the babies and after 9:00 P.M. for the older kids. Families may join organized excursions to Disney World at an extra cost.

ACCOMMODATIONS: Guests stay in small clusters of buildings with three stories, built around a courtyard and along the riverfront. Each room has two oversize beds, a sitting area with a couch and two easy chairs, full carpeting, terrace or balcony, bathtubs, and small refrigerators. All rooms are air-conditioned.

RATES: Weekly rates (without airfare or transfers) range from $800 to $1,180, depending on the week booked, for adults, and from $400 to $590 for ages 4 months through 11 years,. Adult daily rates run from $120 to $180; children's daily rates run from $60 to $90; kids under 6 stay in the same room as their parents. Two children, one of whom must be 6, get their own room. A $90 charge entitles guests to unlimited golf.

Don Cesar
3400 Gulf Boulevard
St. Petersburg Beach, Florida 33706
Telephone: 813-360-1881 or 800-247-9810
General Manager: Luis Marco

IN THEIR OWN WORDS: "Come to our award-winning, pink castle island resort on Florida's West Coast."

DESCRIPTION: Much of the Don's charm lies in its history. Originally built in 1928 by Thomas J. Rowe, the hotel is an eclectic mix of Moorish and Mediterranean architecture. On opening night, January 16, 1928, 1,500 elegantly dressed men and women danced and dined, all for $2.50. The hotel survived Black Friday in 1929 but when the country went to war in 1941, with no prospects for the next season, they were forced to offer their beloved resort to the Army to remodel as a hospital. By 1945, the Don was serving as an office of the Veteran's Administration, its once luxurious interior stripped and painted "government green." By 1967 the VA moved and the Don was padlocked. Before long the building was vandalized and seemed doomed. When Pinellas County began plans to tear the building down and replace it with a public parkland, a group called the Save the Don Committee went into action and by 1973 an investor had rehabbed the resort, adding a pool, balconies, and air-conditioning. Although the resort's history is fascinating, what attracts guests year after year is the splendor of the beaches on the Gulf of Mexico. Guests at Don Cesar can fill their days with sailing, windsurfing, parasailing, scuba classes, and dive charters, fishing, fitness center workouts, tennis (two lighted courts on the property and nine Hartru courts at the golf complex), and golf at the Isla del Sol 18-hole course just three minutes from the hotel by free shuttle. Day trips from the Don can be arranged to many of Florida's most popular attractions, including Busch Gardens, Cypress Gardens, Disney World and Epcot Center, Sea World, and the Ringling Museum.

FOR KIDS: Every day, year-round, Kids, Ltd. offers a supervised program for children 5–12. Available from 10:00 A.M. to 5:45 P.M., the program varies depending on the ages and interests of the kids who register. Theme parties and excursions beyond the hotel can be arranged if the group is large enough. Baby-sitting is available for $6 per hour; two hours advance notice is needed.

ACCOMMODATIONS: Probably most comfortable for families are the one- and two-bedroom suites. Standard double rooms have two double beds or one king-sized bed, furniture in French style, chairs and a table.

RATES: A double room with a view of the Gulf costs $180 per night in the high season—January to May; a one-bedroom suite is $270–$290. Rollaway beds are available for $15 per day, cribs are free, and kids 18 and under may stay with their parents for free. MAP programs are available for an additional $45 per person per day for adults, $37 for kids. All sports at the Don—sailing, tennis, golf, etc.—cost extra. A variety of packages is also available. The Island Break offers three days and two nights with a water-view room and a free hour of tennis time; it costs $332 from January to May and $250 from mid-September to mid-December based on double occupancy.

TradeWinds on St. Petersburg Beach
5500 Gulf Boulevard
St. Petersburg Beach, Florida 33706
Telephone: 813-367-6461 or 800-237-0707
General Manager: Chris Ezzo

IN THEIR OWN WORDS: "Revel on the beach. Seven miles of sugar-white sand invite limitless choices for leisurely pursuits. Explore."

DESCRIPTION: This new six-story resort (built in 1985) has something that not many others do: its very own gondolas that drift in and out of the waterways crisscrossing the property. Situated on 13 acres along the Gulf of Mexico, TradeWinds offers some other, somewhat more usual, features: four pools, beachfront whirlpools, sauna, pedalboats, a fully-equipped health center, tennis and racquetball courts, a putting green, sailing and windsurfing and nearby, parasailing, waterskiing, golf, and charter fishing. The resort has its own island called Picnic Island, where guests can use the instant-start gas grills for barbecues whenever they please.

FOR KIDS: Daily except Tuesdays and Thursdays year-round, the resort offers a free Kids Klub for children 5–12 from 1:00 P.M. to

3:00 P.M. On Tuesdays and Thursdays, Beach Adventure Camp takes over for the same age group, and runs from 9:00 A.M. to 4:00 P.M. Registration costs $12 with lunch included. Wednesday and Friday nights are reserved for "Kid's Night Out" with games and supper for kids from 5:00 P.M. to 8:00 P.M. for $8. Teens have special nighttime activities on Thursdays, Fridays, and Saturdays. Baby-sitting is available for $5 per hour.

ACCOMMODATIONS: In all, TradeWinds has 381 one-, two- and three-bedroom suites and hotel rooms. Rooms have two double beds, wet bars with refrigerators, coffeemakers, toasters, private balconies, and telephones and televisions in the bathroom. Suites have kitchens with full-size appliances and living rooms with a double sofa bed.

RATES: Two packages, especially for families, are in effect from April through mid-December. Family Favorites includes suite accommodations, two passes to Kid's Night Out or Beach Adventure Camp, one hour of sailing or one day of a beach cabana rental and two beach towers for $579 for four nights; Family Adventures includes four tickets to Busch Gardens (30 minutes from the resort), one hour of sailing, or one day of the cabana and two beach towels for $498 for three nights, $879 for six.

Casa Ybel Resort
2255 West Gulf Drive
P.O. Box 167
Sanibel Island, Florida 33957
Telephone: 813-472-3145 or 800-237-8906
General Manager: Hal Williams

IN THEIR OWN WORDS: "This is a lovely resort, nestled in a lush, tropical setting on Sanibel Island. The island is two-thirds wildlife refuge . . . . The light sea breeze off the Gulf stirs the pelicans, herons, and ibis from their roosts while contented guests watch them take flight."

DESCRIPTION: On the Gulf side of Sanibel Island, this resort offers lots of possibilities. You can follow their Sun-Day schedule activities for guided beach walks, tennis clinics, exercise classes, and so on, or go off on your own to play tennis, swim in the pool, sail a Hobie Cat, bicycle, or just relax. There's golf nearby.

FOR KIDS: "Tiny Tots" is for kids 3 to 6 years old, who have an activity scheduled for them four times per week for 1-1/2 or 2 hours at a time. Arts and crafts, beach walks, games, and a snack are all possibilities. Once a week this same age group has a puppet work-shop, "Storybook Wonder," swimming lessons, and more.

"Casa Kids" is a Monday through Thursday program for 7- to 12-year-old kids, which operates during the summer and during school holidays. Games, arts and crafts, beach hikes, swimming, and biking are included from 9:30 A.M. to 2:00 P.M.

"Craft Kids" is scheduled two to three times per week for kids 6 to 12 with a different project each session.

"Care Bear Cookout" is an evening combination of a cookout, games, and cartoons for 3-to-8-year-olds, offered once a week. For teens there are special cookouts, beach parties, pizza nights, and so on.

There's a fee for most of these programs. All through the week, too, are activities that are meant for kids and adults together—shell crafts, kite making, "Win, Lose, or Draw," poolside bingo, and more.

ACCOMMODATIONS: One- and two-bedroom condos are clustered along the beach. All have a living/dining room area with a fully equipped kitchen, bedrooms, and a screened-in balcony overlooking the Gulf of Mexico. Cribs—portable and full-size—are available for $5 and $10 per night.

RATES: A variety of packages is available. The Family Fun package, accommodations in a one- or two-bedroom villa for four days and three nights, a half day of bicycling, picnic lunch for four, one day use of a cabana, unlmited tennis and the kids programs, costs $375 for a one-bedroom villa, $465 for a two, for a family of four.

Pointe Santo de Sanibel
2445 West Gulf Drive
Sanibel, Florida 33957
Telephone: 813-472-9100 or 800-824-5442
General Manager: Deborah Lallo

IN THEIR OWN WORDS: "Pointe de Sanibel offers you the most relaxing, carefree vacation paradise on the island."

DESCRIPTION: Sanibel Island is about 30 miles west of Fort Myers on the Gulf of Mexico, and is famous for having the best shelling in the world. It's been carefully preserved with no high-rises allowed and a number of wildlife refuges where you'll be able to see lots of tropical birds and other interesting flora and fauna. Average winter temperature is in the 70s, spring and fall it's in the 80s, and in summer it's in the high 80s. At the resort you can golf at either of two island courses, play tennis, bicycle on some of the peaceful nature trails, windsurf, sail, fish, or, if you're feeling lazy, just lie around on your own piece of white, sandy beach.

FOR KIDS: Kids from 3 all the way up to 18 can participate in a Monday–Friday program based in the resort's clubhouse. It's open all year (except for a few weeks in September, when the director takes her own vacation) from 9:30 A.M. to 4:30 P.M. and offers a variety of beach equipment, games, shuffleboard, and tennis and organized activities such as shell and jewelry crafts, beach walks, scavenger hunts, bingo, and cartoons. Most of the activities, planned on an hourly basis, are free; for some there's a minimal cost, usually no more than $1.

ACCOMMODATIONS: All accommodations are condos with one, two, or three bedrooms, their own private screened-in lanais with views of the Gulf, and full kitchens.

RATES: At the most expensive time of year—during the Christmas break and again from January 29 to April 15, a two-bedroom Gulf-view condo costs $215 per night. From June to December 20 the rate is $120.

Indian River Plantation Resort and Marina
555 Northeast Ocean Boulevard
Stuart, Florida 34996-1620
Telephone: 407-225-3700 or 800-444-3389
General Manager: L. William Pullen

IN THEIR OWN WORDS: "One of our resort's best features is its versatility, making it appealing to all age groups . . . . It is one of the most desirable vacation spots in Florida, featuring a natural, clean and uncrowded setting in a climate influenced year-round by tropical trade winds."

DESCRIPTION: The Indian River separates Hutchinson Island from Florida's southeast coast and it is here, on a spot where a pineapple plantation once flourished, that you'll find this resort. Indian River has its own 77-slip marina, three pools, a 1,700-foot ocean beach, an 18-hole par 61 golf course, 13 tennis courts (seven are lighted), bicycle and jogging trails, waterskiing, deep-sea fishing, and boating. Most guests like to take a cruise on the 150-passenger *Island Princess* along the Intracoastal Waterway.

FOR KIDS: Kids from 6 to 12 may join the camp that operates

from June to September and again during Christmas and Easter vacations, from 9:00 A.M. to 5:00 P.M. on weekdays. The cost is $25 per day. Kids 3–5 can sign up for Tiny Tots, which operates 9:00 A.M. to noon three days a week, costs $15 per day, and involves beach activities, nature walks, arts and crafts, and boat rides. From time to time, special events are scheduled for teens—a night on the town, a party or dive-in movies (by the pool). Baby-sitting for kids under 3 may be arranged for $5 per hour.

ACCOMMODATIONS: Individual rooms are available, but best for families are the one- and two-bedroom suites. Suites have refrigerators, a wet bar, a sitting room, and a balcony with a view of either the pool, the golf course, or the river.

RATES: From June 4 to September 30, the rate for a one-bedroom ocean view suite is $150, kids under 17 are free; at Christmastime, the most expensive time of year, the same suite costs $175. The rate is for accommodations only—golf, tennis, boating, and so on are all extra.

Callaway Gardens Resort
Pine Mountain, Georgia 31822
Telephone: 404-663-2281 or 800-282-8181
General Manager: Ted Robison

IN THEIR OWN WORDS: "We try to give people a serene place with educational and inspirational qualities, plus all the recreational facilities. After they've visited Callaway Gardens, we want people to take home with them consolation for the heart, nourishment for the soul, and inspiration for the mind."

DESCRIPTION: Tucked into the foothills of Georgia's Appalachian Mountains, this resort is set among 2,500 acres of garden beauty. Owned and operated by the Ida Cason Callaway Foundation, a not-for-profit group, the resort's profits are returned to the Foundation to "maintain its horticultural and educational excellence." Guests may enjoy biking and jogging on a new trail, hiking, miniature golf, pedal boats, four golf courses, 17 tennis courts, fishing, horseback riding, skeet and trap shooting, and swimming in an indoor or an outdoor pool or at the largest inland, man-made white sand beach in the world, Robin Lake. But it's the garden part that makes Callaway so very different from other resorts. Each season at Callaway offers special beauty: More than 700 varieties of azalea grow along the drives and nature trails in spring, the plumleaf azalea bursts bright red in midsummer, fall brings splendid outdoor color, and a variety of holly colors the winter green and red. The centerpiece of the resort is the five-acre John A. Sibley Horticultural Center, which features a two-story outdoor waterfall and six major floral displays each year. Not long ago the Cecil B. Day Butterfly Center opened on the property—the largest free-flight, glass enclosed conservatory in North America exclusively for the display of living butterflies. And for vegetable gardeners, there's a 7-1/2 acre garden, which serves as the setting for the PBS television program "The Victory Garden South." In order to integrate the horticultural splendors of the area with the resort experience, the Education Department of the Gardens organizes workshops demonstrating cooking with wild plants, arranging dried flowers, and seminars on topics such as pruning, landscaping, and holiday decorating. A pioneer log cabin set in the woodlands of the resort is a perfect setting for visitors to learn about how people in the 1800s used nature as a source for shelter, food, and clothing. A series called "Music in the Gardens" is held at the Outdoor Pavilion area during the spring, summer, and fall, and art exhibits and special music programs are scheduled year-round. Waterskiing is big at Callaway, and on sunny afternoons, guests are treated to performances of Callaway Gardens' Water Ski Spectacular.

FOR KIDS: During the summer, the resort offers an impressive recreation program for kids as young as 3 all the way up to adults. Counselors are students at Florida State University and performers in the Flying High Circus at Callaway and the Callaway Gardens Water Ski Show. They teach enthusiastic kids and adults how to do some of the simpler circus acts along with more standard games and sports. Kids from 3 to 6 join the Early Childhood Center for a program that begins at 9:00 A.M. and ends at 3:00 P.M. on weekdays and includes music, art, free play, outdoor games, storybook skits, and so on. Kids from 7 to 12 participate in the Day Camp program, also from 9:00 A.M. to 3:00 P.M. Monday–Friday, where they get the chance to learn some circus tricks, swim, waterski, bicycle, and play beach games. The older kids, 13–15, get to sail, play golf, go waterskiing, do arts and crafts, have circus fun, enjoy nature study, and play tennis. Kids may have lunch with their groups; lunch tickets must be purchased in advance. Special teen activities include dances on Saturday, Monday, and Friday nights, a pool party and a beach party complete with volleyball and hot dogs. A Teen Center is open on nights when no special activity is planned. For the littlest kids in your family, 2 and under, there's an infant program Monday to Friday from 8:30 to noon that costs $5 per day or $20 per week.

For in-between hours, when the scheduled programs aren't in session, a game room is open from 3:00 P.M. to 11:00 P.M. (from 9:00 P.M. on, it's for teens only). PG-rated movies are shown every night starting at 9:00 P.M.; children's movies are shown every Tuesday and Thursday at 7:00 P.M. And, with all that, we've only just scratched the surface. In short, Callaway Gardens' summer recreation program is, if you'll pardon the cliché, "awesome."

ACCOMMODATIONS: The choices are the 345-room Callaway Gardens Inn, Mountain Creek Villas, and new Callaway Country Cottages, privately owned vacation homes available for guest rental. Of course, the cottages and villas are most comfortable for families. Each villa has one to four bedrooms, full kitchen, dining room, living room with stone fireplace, all set against a natural woodland backdrop. The country cottages have one or two bedrooms, living room with fireplace, kitchen/dining area, and a screened-in porch.

RATES: Probably of greatest interest to our readers is the Summer Family Recreation program, which offers a week of activities (a week is the minimum stay) including canoeing, hikes, golf clinics, evening bird walks, scavenger hunts, and performances at the LaGrange College Summer Theater. (Expect a fee for some of these activities.) The package costs $1,350 for the week for one family in a two-bedroom cottage—if a second family shares the cottage, add $150 per week. Inn rooms range from $69 to $120, depending on the season, and kids under 19 are free in a room with parents.

The Cloister
Sea Island, Georgia 31561
Telephone: 912-638-3611
General Manager: Ted Wright

IN THEIR OWN WORDS: "The Cloister is family-owned and family-oriented. Families visit every day of the year—there are always some children in the main dining rooms at night . . . . We don't even charge for children under 19—including their meals—at Christmas and New Year's and during the Summer Family Festival . . . . We get three and four generations of families these days, with parents who first came in 1928 or 29."

DESCRIPTION: Off the coast of Georgia, on sunny Sea Island, you can enjoy five miles of beach, championship golf and tennis, gardens, historic sites, and 10,000 acres of protected forests and serene marshes beside the sea. For golfers, there are 54 holes and complete teaching facilities; for tennis enthusiasts it offers 18 courts, all fast-dry clay composition; a staff of teaching pros; clinics; and guest round-robins. For nongolf/nontennis hours skeet shooting, biking, fishing, swimming, jogging, and horseback riding on the beach or trails are available. At night there are torchlit plantation suppers, after-dinner entertainment, and dancing nightly to the Cloister's own orchestra.

FOR KIDS: From June to September and during school vacation periods, the Cloister offers a program for kids 4 to 8 from 9:00 A.M. to 3:00 P.M. every day except Sunday. Junior staffers take the kids for the day, playing with them and leading them in a variety of activities. Throughout the week there are also a number of special events for kids. We spotted a cooking class for kids 6 to 12 and a course in manners for kids 7 through the midteens. There's no charge for tennis and golf for kids 19 and under, so there's plenty of chance for practice during the stay, and they may even get to be almost as good as you are. Kids 4 to 12 can spend 6:00 to 9:00 every evening with children's hostesses. Tennis lessons are available to kids as young as 5, and junior golf clinics are scheduled twice a week in summer.

Baby-sitters are available for small children, who may join play times and evening programs along with their sitters. The cost of baby-sitting is $5 per hour, day or evening.

ACCOMMODATIONS: There are several options: the main hotel, River House, guest or beach houses. Cribs are available at no extra charge. In addition to hotel rooms, the Cloister also offers a wide range of home rentals, from two to five bedrooms, which rent from $500 to $2,000 per week, with the price depending upon both the size and location of the home.

RATES: All prices are full American plan—three meals per day—and include use of the Sea Island Beach Club, nightly dancing, and other resort amenities. A sample rate is a tennis package that costs $136 to $193 per night per person from March to May. There's no room charge for kids 19 and under sharing a room with parents; for meals it is $26 for kids 6 to 12, $18 for 3 to 5, and no charge at all for 2 years and under. During the summer "Family Festival," kids' meals are free; the same deal applies at Christmastime.

Kahala Hilton
5000 Kahala Avenue
Honolulu, Hawaii 96816
Telephone: 808-734-2211 or 800-445-8667
General Manager: Louis J. Finamore

IN THEIR OWN WORDS: "We're located just 15 minutes from Waikiki on the other side of Diamond Head in the beautiful Kahala residential area. Our private 800-foot sandy white beach ensures privacy and safety."

DESCRIPTION: The ten-story hotel is located on the site where the Hawaiian King Kamehameha the Great landed with thousands of warriors to begin his conquest of the Island of Oahu in 1795. The resort sits at the edge of the lagoons of Maunalua Bay, against a backdrop of mountains and a cascading waterfall. Of all the activities available at the resort, the management is proudest of its tennis facilities at the Maunalua Bay Club, located five minutes from the hotel by complimentary shuttle. The club, on two acres of oceanfront land, offers six plexipave, night-lighted tennis courts and a fully stocked pro shop. Private lessons, video clinics and analyses and a computerized ball machine are all available. In addition to tennis, the club features a fitness spa and a swimming pool.

FOR KIDS: Kamp Kahala operates during Christmas, Easter, and the summer for kids 6–12 from 9:00 A.M. to 4:00 P.M. Kids build sand castles, go on treasure hunts, weave leis from real or paper flowers, learn games and sports of old Hawaii, dance the hula, and make collages from odds and ends gathered on the beach. Kids take a lunch break and eat with their parents. Except for an occasional off-property excursion, the program is free. For younger children, there's baby-sitting available for $4.50 per hour with a four-hour minimum. One unusual feature of this resort is the hotel's dolphin pool, where the resident dolphins give free performances three times a day. The kids will love it.

ACCOMMODATIONS: Rooms are spacious—520 square feet without a balcony, 620 with. All rooms have refrigerators and his and her dressing rooms and depending where they're situated, a view of either the beach, the lagoon, or the mountains.

RATES: Rates vary enormously—all the way from $180 for a first-floor, mountain-view room with no balcony to $1,700 for a two-bedroom deluxe ocean-view suite, with lots of options in between.

Kona Village Resort
P.O. Box 1299
Kaupulehu-Kona, Hawaii 96745
Telephone: 808-325-5555 or 800-367-5290
General Manager: Fred Duerr

IN THEIR OWN WORDS: "Very few maps show Kaupulehu. Like all Edens it's elusive, difficult to find . . . . Being remote . . . Kona Village has some rare qualities. Actually, its charm lies in what it does not have. Like shopping arcades, tour groups, or even sidewalks . . . . Other civilized blessings it does without include juke boxes, swinging discotheques, TV sets or radios or telephones in cottages[;] . . . after arrival . . . folks take off their wristwatches."

DESCRIPTION: Kona Village, on the secluded west coast of the island of Hawaii, is a re-creation of the legendary Kaupulehu, where in 1801 an erupting volcano chased natives from the coast. One small area around an emerald bay with coco palms anad white sand beaches was spared, and over 150 years later, the location was rediscovered and Kona Village established. The specialty of the house, according to the management, is leaving guests alone. The village, they say, is dedicated to laziness. But, if you want activities, there's no lack of things to do: snorkeling, a motor launch ride to a far cove, volleyball, tennis, fishing, sailing charters, and scuba diving. Guides are available to show guests the slopes of Hualalai and Mauna Kea volcanoes. One of the favorite activities of all is a hike over the nearby lava flows, among house sites, shrines, and shelter caves of centuries ago. There are five golf courses and horseback riding facilities nearby. Throughout the week, there are a variety of activities for grown-ups—botanical walks, lei-making lessons, floral corsage classes, and other island-related crafts.

FOR KIDS: Organized activities for kids are available four to six hours each day. Children 5 and under, accompanied by an adult, can take hula lessons, enter fishing contests, do finger painting, or watch net throwing, poi pounding, and coconut husking. Kids 6 to 12 learn about local marine life or learn to play the ukelele, hunt seashells, go fishing, fly kites, or stargaze. For teenagers, there are snorkeling tours, volleyball games, scuba and sailing lessons.

Baby-sitting is available for $6 per hour with 24 hours' notice. The cost of most of the children's activities is included in the resort's American plan rates.

ACCOMMODATIONS: One hundred twenty-five thatched-roof "hales" (bungalows), spaced for privacy, stand on stilts beside the ocean and lagoon and in gardens. They're meant to look like a Polynesian village of huts, like those of old Hawaii. Sandy paths lead from the cottages right to the beach. Inside the hales are king-size or extra long twin beds, a dressing room, and a bath. There are coffeemakers and small refrigerators in every room. Most hales sleep four people.

RATES: The cost of a hale, based on double occupancy and full American plan, ranges from $330 to $450 for two per day, depending on the setting and size. Kids 6 to 12 cost $70; 5 and under, $43.

French Lick Springs Resort
French Lick, Indiana 47432
Telephone: 812-936-9300 or 800-457-4042
General Manager: Gaston Correa

IN THEIR OWN WORDS: "The true charms of French Lick lie in the picturesque and historic setting and in the friendly, helpful attitudes of the many employees who have been reared in this resort community."

DESCRIPTION: In the late 1700s this area was still very much the "far west" for the American settlers who came to stay. By 1812, a government fort stood on the site of today's hotel and just 30 years later a hotel was built on the same spot. This first hotel, built of wood, burned down in 1897. The one that now stands was constructed in the early 1900s and quickly became a magnet for the rich, famous, and politically powerful. French Lick is now a large resort with room for 2,000 guests. Just as you'd expect of such a massive place, it offers golf—two 18-hole golf courses—and the largest tennis facility in the Midwest—eight indoor and ten lighted outdoor courts. Its spa provides massages, mineral baths, facials, body treatments, exercise classes—the choice is yours: hard work, pampering, or a little bit of both. Guests may swim indoors or out, bowl, horseback ride along 30 miles of trails, go boating and fishing on nearby Patoka Lake, water-ski, bicycle, or play badminton, volleyball, or croquet. From June to October, as long as the weather cooperates, guests can sign up for an overnight ride at the Equestrian Center—a four- to five-hour ride, a barbecue followed by a campfire program, a sunrise breakfast the next morning, and a return to the resort before lunch. (Kids under 16 must be accompanied by an adult.)

FOR KIDS: The Pluto Club is for kids from 3 to 11 and operates all summer long, at school break time, and on Saturdays throughout the year. The morning session begins at 9:00 A.M. and continues until 12:15 P.M. Kids have lunch either with counselors or parents and then resume supervised activities until 5:00 P.M. During holidays evening activities are also offered. Groups are divided by age— the 3- to 5-year-olds are in groups of five to ten with one caregiver; the 6- to 11-year-olds have a one to 15 or 20 ratio. There is an $8 charge for a full day, $5 for a half day. Kids under 3 may join the younger group if they have a caregiver with them. Baby-sitting services may be arranged for the little ones at a charge of $3 per hour for two kids. Each day has its own theme: on "Under the Big Top" day kids might start out by making circus animal name tags and circus puppets, playing parachute games, and joining in clown relay races in the pool. Afternoons might be spent learning magic tricks and, after dinner making clown masks to wear in the French Lick Circus Parade. Teens aren't forgotten at French Lick; activities just for them are scheduled throughout the week—scavenger hunts, coketail parties, volleyball tournaments, pizza parties, and a twilight bike hike. Some of the teen activities have a minimal charge—$1 to $2.50.

ACCOMMODATIONS: This is a huge place—485 guest rooms in all. Rooms have double or king-sized beds, televisions, air-conditioning, and private baths. One-, two- and three-room suites are also available. There's no extra charge for cribs.

RATES: A package called "A Week of Everything" costs $89 per person per night double occupancy. Kids 6–18 staying with parents are $59; 5 and under are free. The rate includes breakfasts and dinners, golf, tennis, use of the spa, a 45-minute trail ride, use of bicycles and all facilities at the resort. A similar "Everything Weekend" package costs $109 per night for adults; kids rates remain at $59. A package that includes accommodations, breakfast and dinner, use of the health and fitness facilities and the pool costs $49 per person per night for a seven-night stay.

New Seabury Cape Cod
Box B-1
New Seabury, Massachusetts 02649
Telephone: 800-222-2044

IN THEIR OWN WORDS: "Seabury is made up of 13 individual villages, three of which contain privately owned homes, managed by the corporation as 'hotel villas.' This carefully planned community and destination resort offers both guests and residents a first-quality, four-season vacation environment."

DESCRIPTION: As noted above, this second-home community is open to paying guests. Located between Falmouth and Hyannis, just 70 miles from Boston, the facilities include an 18-hole golf course (playable ten months of the year), 16 all-weather tennis courts, miles of jogging trails, bicycle paths, oceanfront pools, restaurants, a marketplace, and direct access to Cape Cod's beaches. Sailing, windsurfing, waterskiing, and fishing are all easily arranged.

FOR KIDS: From the end of June until the end of August, kids from 3 to 12 may participate in a program that operates from 7:00 A.M. to 5:00 P.M. The youngsters are divided into two groups: the 3- to 7-year-olds swim, go shelling, take nature walks, play games, and do arts and crafts; 8- to 12-year-olds swim, play tennis, golf, and sail. The rate is $35 per day, $140 for a week. Teens may participate in a leadership training group or a field hockey camp or, if they prefer, may arrange their own schedule, including lessons in tennis, golf, and sailing. For kids under 3, individual baby-sitting may be arranged for the evening at a rate of $6 per hour.

ACCOMMODATIONS: Villas have either one or two bedrooms and all have kitchens. They are all privately owned and some are set right along the beach. Location here is important because the resort is quite large—be sure you're near the facilities you will be using.

RATES: A summer rate for a two-bedroom, two-bath villa large enough for four people is $260 per night for a village view, $290 for an ocean view.

Grand Traverse Resort
Grand Traverse Village, Michigan 49610-0404
Telephone: 616-938-2100 or 800-678-1308
General Manager: James A. Gernhofer

IN THEIR OWN WORDS: "The Traverse City area has long been a popular vacation area for Midwesterners. In the past it was famous for lumber and agriculture. Now it is gaining recognition as a national resort destination."

DESCRIPTION: Set along the sandy shores of East Grand Traverse Bay, this 920-acre property offers indoor and outdoor tennis; four pools (two inside and two outside, one reserved just for swimming laps); a health club with aerobics, weight training, whirlpools, and saunas; a beach club with boat rentals; cross-country skiing in winter and 36 holes of golf, including "The Bear," designed by Jack Nicklaus. During the year, the resort sponsors lots of special events— a Halloween Ball weekend, "Soap Celebrities Weekend," and "Homecoming Homicide," which gives would-be detectives the chance to solve a murder mystery.

FOR KIDS: During the summer and on weekends the rest of the year, Grand Traverse offers a program of organized activities for kids 5 to 12. Kids do crafts, go on hikes, play tennis and kickball and swim. The program, called "Max Mania" runs Monday to Saturday from 9:00 A.M. to noon and costs $20. During the rest of the day, other activities are often scheduled for kids, but not on a regular basis. Three nights a week kids from 5 to 8 can join the Rainbow Supper Club, which includes dinner and games and crafts from 6:00 to 9:00, and for the 9–12s, Munchies and More offers more games, T-shirt design, and dinner. The cost for the evening programs is $25 per session. The tennis pro gives group lessons for 5- to 8-year-olds every Saturday from 9:00 A.M. to 10:00 P.M. Baby-sitting is available for $5 per hour for the first child, $1 for each additional child, with a minimum of three hours and a one-time finder's fee of $5.

ACCOMMODATIONS: In all, there are 750 rooms, suites, and condos. Hotel rooms are located either in the six-story low-rise or a 15-story glass tower. Tower rooms have two double or one king-size bed, refrigerators and wet bars, TV, telephones, and bathrooms equipped with a whirlpool.

RATES: A hotel room costs $135 per night, Tower rooms are $160–$175, and condos range in price from $110 to $270. The resort offers lots of package deals, too. A sample is the Carefree Getaway, two nights of accommodations, one dinner, breakfast, or lunch on two days, and use of the health club for $150 per person double occupancy in the Tower or one-bedroom condo. Kids of all ages stay free in their parents' room.

The Mount Washington Hotel and Resort
Route 302
Bretton Woods, New Hampshire 03575
Telephone: 603-278-1000 or 800-258-1000 or 800-258-0330 in the
    Northeast
General Manager: Manfred Boll

IN THEIR OWN WORDS: "We're a classic grand resort with an ambiance hard to find in today's brass and glass resorts. The building itself is magnificent and the service and style of the resort hark back to the golden age of the White Mountain grand resorts."

DESCRIPTION: The setting is spectacular, right at the foot of Mount Washington and the Presidential Range. The resort is on the National Register of Historic Places and has been named a National Historic Landmark by the National Park Service. In winter the focus is downhill skiing at Bretton Woods Ski Area (20 trails and four lifts) and the Bretton Woods Touring Center, 100 kilometers of trails headquartered in the riding stables. In summer, there's everything you'd expect from a grand hotel—golf, tennis, riding, (with lessons available), indoor and outdoor pools, jogging paths, fishing, and miles of beautiful hiking trails. Music is an important part of life at the resort—chamber music, jazz, and opera performances take place indoors, and the Mount Washington Orchestra plays for dinner and dancing each night. Outdoor concerts are a regular part of the summer schedule, featuring Big Band music, patriotic music, rhythm and blues, country, and soft rock. Special theme weekends—Great Gatsby, Aloha, Harvest Moon, and Oktoberfest—are part of the yearly schedule and come complete with costume rental.

FOR KIDS: During July and August kids 5 to 12 have a supervised program of activities Monday through Saturday. The daily schedule includes arts and crafts, treasure hunts, swimming, hikes, movies, tennis and golf clinics, and day trips to local attractions. There's no charge except for lunch, horseback riding, and admission to outside attractions. Kids 2 months to 4 years may spend from 8:30 A.M. to 4:30 P.M. in the year-round nursery. Rates are $3.75 per hour with a three-hour minimum.

In winter, the 4- to 12-year-olds enjoy their own Ski School, called Hobbit after the J. R. R. Tolkien character. Once enrolled, the kids are introduced to the winter environment and the sport of skiing through games and the use of characters from Tolkien's books. The costs are $30 to $35 per day (8:30 to 4:00), depending on day of week. Lunch is included, equipment and lift tickets.

As in the summer, baby-sitting is available for $3.75 per hour with a three-hour minimum.

ACCOMMODATIONS: The Mount Washington Hotel has 200 rooms, including family suites, two rooms with adjoining bath. Traditionally the hotel was open only from May to October but at this writing it was undergoing a complete historic restoration and winterization. Check to see whether it's been completed. The Lodge at Bretton Woods, part of the resort, offers year-round lodging with rooms that all have private balconies with spectacular views of the main hotel and the mountains. The Bretton Arms, another National Historic Landmark at the resort, reopened in 1987 after a two-year renovation. It's a luxurious inn, decorated to look like an English retreat house. For longer stays, Bretton Woods offers condominiums as well, such as the ski-in/ski-out Rosebrook Townhouse.

RATES: Hotel rooms cost from $95 to $175 per person double occupancy; kids under 5 are free; 6–12, $25; 13–17, $35; and over 17, $45. Rates include a full breakfast and dinner. The lodge rates for a room large enough to accommodate up to four people are $60 in midweek and $95 on weekends; meals are extra. At the Bretton Arms a quad is $130 to $155, no meals; condo rates vary depending on type, size, and number of people. Both summer and winter packages are available; call for details.

The Balsam Grand Resort Hotel
Route 26
Lake Gloriette
Dixville Notch, New Hampshire 03576
Telephone: 603-255-3400 or 800-255-0600
Managers: Warren Pearson and Stephen Barba

IN THEIR OWN WORDS: "This is a grand hotel in the New England tradition—15,000 acres on a private estate that's been operating since 1873 . . . high in the White Mountains . . . operating completely within the American plan tradition. . . . Under any analysis this resort would rate within the top 10 for completeness of facility, quality, service, style, and openness of hospitality."

DESCRIPTION: Travel writers have showered praise upon this grand old resort for years. In winter or summer, fall or spring, the resort offers lots of treats: When there's snow, skating, skiing, snowshoeing, and snowmobiling; when it's warmer, biking, hiking, boating, canoeing, fishing, golfing, swimming (lake or pool), tennis, or trapshooting. During the summer the resort hosts visiting craftspeople—a basketmaker one week, a weaver the next, a watercolorist the third. Evenings offer nightclub entertainment, films and dancing in the lounges, chamber music, and guest lectures on topics as diverse as life in Northern Ireland to the story of glaciers.

A new natural history program has been added with an in-house historian studying environmental, ecological, and archaeological phenomena of the area, complete with nine marked and annotated trails for guests. A "dig" has been created in the hotel's 100-year-old trash dump, and guests of all ages are welcome to participate and learn of the hotel's history from the artifacts uncovered.

FOR KIDS: During ski season, there's a Balsam's Wilderness nursery for kids "out of diapers" on up to 6-year-olds. It operates from 9:00 A.M. to noon and 1:00 to 4:00 P.M. Parents are asked to pick up their kids for lunch. For the diaper set, baby-sitting can be arranged at about $3.50 per hour. For the older kids, 5 and over, there's a fully supervised program from 9:00 A.M. to 4:00 P.M. that operates June 30 to September 1 and again December 20 through April 1. Counselors all have elementary education teaching certificates. Activities depend on the season, of course, and include arts and crafts, hikes, games, drama, swimming, skiing, and sports. Kids can eat with or without their parents; the choice is yours. Right off the main lobby is The Cave, a nonalcoholic "club" especially for teenagers, with videos, movies, games, music, and half-price refreshments.

ACCOMMODATIONS: All rooms are in traditional New England style. In all there are 232 rooms with space for 425 guests at a time. Family suites are available at no extra charge. Cribs, too, are available.

RATES: A double room with a private bath ranges from $90 to $150 per person including all meals and unlimited use of the facilities plus the children's program. The rate for kids in the same room as their parents is $6 times their age with a minimum of $30 per night.

The Sagamore
Bolton Landing, New York 12814
Telephone: 518-644-9400 or 800-358-3585
General Manager: David Boyd

IN THEIR OWN WORDS: "We think you'll find a paradise island vacation right here at the Sagamore on the shores of magnificent Lake George. Get away together, a real family vacation."

DESCRIPTION: Since the 1880s, there's been a resort sitting on this gorgeous piece of land by the shores of Lake George. The present Sagamore was built in the 1920, flourished, and then fell upon hard times, closing in the late 1970s. Before too long, it was rescued by a local family, completely refurbished, and reopened in the early 1980s. Activities, depending on time of year, include golf on an 18-hole, 70 par Scottish-style course, indoor and outdoor tennis courts, swimming pool, health spa (where you can sign up for fitness walks, low-impact aerobics, water exercises, or, for the more passive, body massages, shiatsu, or a European facial), exercise rooms, racquetball courts, jogging trails, cross-country skiing, ice skating, five restaurants, a lively nightclub, and a charming Tudor-style Adirondack lodge, all nice and cozy with a roaring fire and decorative mooseheads. In winter, a free shuttle takes guests to nearby Gore Mountain for downhill skiing.

FOR KIDS: When the folks who run the Sagamore decided they wanted to attract families, they went ahead and designed a children's program that keeps kids from 3 to 12 busy and happy from 9:00 A.M. until 4:00 P.M. and again from 6 to 9:00 P.M. The program runs all summer long and during school vacations. Our friend's 8-year-old daughter joined the older group (kids are separated into 3–5s and 6–12s) and spent the day swimming in the indoor pool, having a box lunch by the pool, enjoying a poolside ice cream social, and, since it was raining, doing crafts, playing games, watching videos. If the weather had been more cooperative, the kids would have played outside—probably sledding if there had been enough snow or at the resort's own playground. "When I picked up Rachel, she begged to stay just another minute to finish up a spirited game of Pictionary with her new friends and several counselors." The younger children have a similar program. In summer, the older kids go to the beach or on Saturday excursions to a nearby amusement park. The children's program is free, but there is a $5 charge for lunch and a $10 to $20 fee for excursions, which include lunch. Kids may also have golf and/ or tennis lessons at an additional cost—there's a resident pro for both sports. Special teen events are scheduled throughout the week as well.

ACCOMMODATIONS: The hotel itself has 100 rooms, including 47 suites; the 240-room lodge has 120 suites with fireplaces, private balconies, and wet bars. Rooms are spacious, with lots of amenities such as in-room movies and remote-control television sets.

RATES: Sagamore offers a number of packages—for tennis, golf, and spa vacations, for holidays, and for specialty weekends such as a three-day '50s rock and roll party, and a murder mystery weekend where they provide the crime and the clues and you get to unravel the mystery.

A family package in summer that includes two nights in a room in the lodge, breakfasts and dinner, a cruise on the resort's boat *Morgan,* and the children's program costs $584; accommodations in the lower lodge (bedroom, kitchenette, and living room with a queen-sized pull-out couch) cost $724.

The Pines Resort Hotel
Lavral Avenue
South Fallsburg, New York 12779
Telephone: 914-434-6000, 800-431-3124, or 800-36-PINES (in New York)
General Manager: Steven Ehrlich

IN THEIR OWN WORDS: "Every season is 'in season' at The Pines, where pleasing you means everything to us. We love kids and families."

DESCRIPTION: This is a classic Catskills resort with lots to do, lots to eat, and lots of activities planned for kids and adults alike. In summer there are tennis, paddleball, golf, and an outdoor pool: in cooler weather, ice- and roller-skating, an indoor pool, indoor tennis, a sauna and health club, and, in winter, skiing is offered. The nightly entertainment is an attraction for many would-be guests, and the resort offers a night patrol service for parents who want to participate: they simply fill out a card, place it on the doorknob of their room, and a counselor checks the room every half-hour from 9:00 until midnight.

FOR KIDS: Any child 2 years old or younger gets his or her own mother's helper at no extra charge. These private counselors are available from 8:30 A.M. until 4:00 P.M. and 6:10 P.M. to 8:15 P.M., while parents have dinner. The counselors supervise the little ones closely: If you give permission for your child to go into the pool counselors either sit on the steps with the child or hold him or her. Take your stroller to breakfast with you, packed with bottles, diapers, and some familiar toys.

Once children are 3 years old, they can join the day camp, which operates throughout the year on weekends, daily at holiday times, and every day during the summer. The camp begins at 8:30 and lasts until 4:00. The kids get together again at 6:00 P.M. for dinner in their own dining room and are dismissed at 8:15 P.M. Kids 2 and over may eat with parents in the dining room—high-chair-aged kids are not allowed. Some of the day camp activities are pony rides, arts and crafts, movies, and magic shows. The camp is free, but some activities such as the pony rides and ice-skating require an additional $3 or $4 fee.

Teenagers are offered a flexible program that wisely includes both group and individual activities. Teens go ice-skating, horseback riding, hiking, golfing, or hayriding. They have their own section of the Main Dining Room, their own Daytime Lounge and Evening Dance Club.

Baby-sitters are available each evening starting at 9:00 P.M. Sign up for sitters between 6:00 and 6:30 the same evening. Baby-sitters cannot be guaranteed; infants and younger children have priority. One child is $3.50 per hour, two are $4.00, and there is a three-hour minimum charge. Remember, there's a night patrol service (described earlier) for the older kids who may not require an individual sitter.

ACCOMMODATIONS: Rooms have two double beds, and cribs are available at no extra charge. All rooms have refrigerators. We've recently learned that some rooms are badly in need of a fluff-up. Be certain to ask if the room you're reserving has been renovated.

RATES: All kinds of packages are available, but as a sample, consider the Washington's Birthday three-night, four-day package, which costs $250 per adult and $80 for children under 9, with the first child free. The rate includes lodging, all meals, and facilities.

The Grove Park Inn and Country Club
290 Macon Avenue
Asheville, North Carolina 28804
Telephone: 704-252-2711 or 800-438-5800
General Manager: Herman Rivon Treskow

IN THEIR OWN WORDS: "Our inn was built in 1913 out of native boulders and set in the splendor of the Blue Ridge Mountains. It has a charming turn-of-the-century atmosphere and is listed in the National Register of Historic Places. During the early years Thomas Edison, Harvey Firestone, Henry Ford, the Rockefellers, and F. Scott Fitzgerald were our guests. After a major renovation and expansion in 1984, we became a year-round resort."

DESCRIPTION: Grove Park combines the grace and romance of the beginning of the century with up-to-the-minute amenities. You can take a horse and carriage ride through the pines or work out at the Sports Complex. Offered are swimming in one indoor pool and one outdoor pool; tennis on indoor and outdoor courts; a playroom adjacent to the indoor pool with video games, books, toys, and so on; a nature trail; an 18-hole golf course; exercise/aerobics rooms; and the latest Nautilus equipment.

FOR KIDS: There's an enclosed playground area adjacent to the Sports Center with seven decks, a corkscrew slide, horizontal ladder, swing, and bubble window. For the family together there are horse-drawn carriage rides, a practice putting green, and a Thursday night barbecue. From May 23 to September 1 (and on winter weekends and at Christmas break time), the inn offers a Monday through Saturday supervised kids' program from 9:00 A.M. to 5:00 P.M. for ages 5 to 12. Activities include crafts, movies, swimming, water games, visits to the Carriage Hose and Antique Car Museum, and fun in the playground. On Saturday night—Parents' Night Out—the kids see a movie and have a pizza party from 6:00 to 10:30 P.M. A full day's program is $18, half is $10, and the Saturday night program is $15. Baby-sitting for younger kids is available for $5 per hour.

ACCOMMODATIONS: There are 389 rooms in all, each decorated in turn-of-the-century style. Cribs are available at no extra charge, but advance notice is requested.

RATES: Regular room rates from November to April are $100 for a double, $230–$405 for a suite; the other months are $30 to $50 more. Kids under 12 stay free in their parents' room; those over 12 cost $15 per child. Special tennis and golf packages and ones that include meals are available year-round.

Sunriver Lodge and Resort
P.O. Box 3609
Sunriver, Oregon 97707
Telephone: 503-593-1221 or 800-547-3922
General Manager: Peter Phillips

IN THEIR OWN WORDS: "A whole 3,300 scenic acres in the sunny high desert country of Central Oregon are yours for the picking. Over 300 days of sunshine to do with as you wish. With spectacular view of snowcapped Mt. Bachelor, lush forests and velvety green fairways."

DESCRIPTION: Located on the sun-splashed side of Oregon's Cascade Mountains, this resort is equally appealing in winter and summer. In winter, guests use it as a base to ski at Mt. Bachelor, a 30-minute free shuttle ride away or they cross-country ski on the resort's 50 kilometers of groomed trails. In summer it's just perfect for golf—rated one of America's top 25 resort courses by *Golf Digest* with two courses to choose from—one designed by Robert Trent Jones, the other with the Cascades in the background. Tennis lovers are not forgotten, with 18 plexipaved outdoor courts plus a racquet club with three indoor courts, a pool, workout equipment, hot tubs, and saunas. More outdoor possibilities include two pool complexes, each with full-sized pools and either an adjacent diving pool or kids' wading pool, the nearby Deschutes River for whitewater rafting, horseback riding, jogging, hiking, and bicycling (26 miles of paved paths let you ride easily all over the resort). For us, one of the nicest features of all at Sunriver is the Nature Center, which is right on property and gives guests access to a resident naturalist and a terrific schedule of activities during the summer for both kids and adults.

FOR KIDS: In summer, the Nature Center offers crafts, camp songs, creative movement, and more in 45-minute sessions for 3- to 6-year-olds. For 7- to 12-year-olds, there are two-hour biking programs with topics such as reptiles, pond life, and orienteering. In addition, the resort offers a Kids Klub. The Klub's supervisor is a student of elementary education, and all counselors have experience working with kids: "Our goal is to offer a broad-based activities program for children that will encourage opportunities for discovery and creativity." Each day of the summer and at school vacation times, from Monday to Saturday, the Klub meets in three separate sessions: one from 9:00 A.M. to noon, a second from 1:00 to 4:00 P.M., and a third in the evening from 6:30 to 9:30. The cost of each session is $11, and lunch is an extra $5. Kids Klub participants play games, make puppets, put on puppet shows, have races, and work on a variety of crafts. Besides the supervised children's program, kids can sign up for lessons in swimming, tennis, horseback riding, golf, raquetball, fly-fishing, and windsurfing. A special program coordinator is on staff to develop teen activities and events that will be fun for the whole family. They've even got a Teen Dating Service: "A great way to meet someone new to take to the dance on Saturday night. Fill out a questionnaire and we'll match you up."

ACCOMMODATIONS: The possibilities include the newly remodeled suites and bedrooms in Lodge Village and a variety of private resort homes and condos. Daily maid service is provided in all except the homes and condos, where it costs extra.

RATES: Regular rates vary from season to season; most expensive is the summer and Christmas vacation period. A suite (large enough for up to six people in three queen-size beds) costs $135 at high season (based on double occupancy, add $5 for each additional person); a two-bedroom condo costs $145, and a three-bedroom, $185.

Skytop Lodge
Route 390
Skytop, Pennsylvania 18357
Telephone: 717-595-7401 or 800-345-7759 from Connecticut, New York, New Jersey, Delaware, Maryland, and District of Columbia
General Manager: William W. Malleson

IN THEIR OWN WORDS: "There's a wonderful sense of promise as you approach Skytop. When the great lodge appears on the horizon, you'll feel the exhilaration of having arrived at an exciting and magnificent world apart."

DESCRIPTION: We spent a wonderful winter weekend at Skytop. We were initially a bit wary, since the resort sounded as though it might be somewhat too refined and sedate a place. But we were absolutely wrong. Refined it is, but welcoming nonetheless to kids. Skytop is located in the Poconos and is in stark contrast to the heart-shaped-pool type resorts that dot the area. Skytop is dignified, beautiful, and serene—5,500 acres of unspoiled mountain woodlands. If you and your family like glitz, go someplace else, but if you like beautiful surroundings, attended to by a friendly, helpful staff, Skytop is for you. It's a resort for all seasons. In winter guests ski on Skytop's own gentle slopes, go cross-country skiing, ice-skate on a weather-protected rink, go sledding and tobogganing, and relax on horse-drawn sleigh rides. Inside, there's always a cozy fire in the lovely Pine Room, a library (where our daughter played librarian with a little girl she had met at dinner the night before), hot tub, indoor and outdoor swimming pool, exercise room, and a game room. In summer, the choices include an 18-hole golf course that "challenges the serious golfer without overwhelming the casual player," tennis on five Har-tru and two all-weather courts, fishing in the property's own stream amply stocked with trout (clinics on fly-fishing are held throughout the summer), lawn bowling, hiking, and boating. At night, there's usually some sort of entertainment planned—a movie, a dance, or a performer. One of the great surprises at Skytop was the quality of the food—we had an impressive list of choices on the menu at each meal and everything we chose was delicious and beautifully presented. After a few days at Skytop it came as no surprise at all to find out that close to 80 percent of the guests at any given time have been there before. What higher recommendation can there be?

FOR KIDS: During the summer the Camp-in-the-Clouds operates from 9:30 A.M. to noon and 2:00 to 5:00 P.M. every day except Sunday for kids from 5 through 11. Kids have the choice of having lunch with their counselors or their parents. "Our counselors get out and do things with the kids—tennis, golf, archery, arts and crafts, swimming, and more." Kids who are old enough may take off-property trips to matinee performances at the Pocono Playhouse. Teenagers have special activities planned for them throughout the week—sporting events, dances, moonlight hayrides, and nighttime pool parties, among other things. The children's program operates at holiday times, too—at Christmas, Easter, and Presidents' Weekend. The cost of the camp is $10 per child per day. Kids may also sign up for private lessons in swimming, tennis, skiing, and skating. Baby-sitting is available for $3.50 per hour just as long as housekeeping is given notice before 2:00 P.M. of the day the service is needed.

ACCOMMODATIONS: In all, there are 182 rooms at Skytop, and the manager makes it a point to inspect each one: "I check everything out, even lie on the bed to make sure the mattress is comfortable." Our room was typical: twin beds, a dresser, two comfortably upholstered chairs—not large, but a very comfortable, cheerful place to be.

RATES: Skytop's family plan allows up to two kids 17 and under to stay free in their parents' room and receive three meals per day for a $10 service charge. (There is a minimum two-night stay.) A double room with twin beds costs $174 to $204 during the week and $249 to $269 on weekends. This includes virtually all activities (except golf) on the property and all meals.

Seabrook Island Resort
P.O. Box 32099
Charleston, South Carolina 29417
Telephone: 803-768-1000 or 800-845-5531
General Manager: John Stagg

IN THEIR OWN WORDS: "We're a 2,200-acre resort located on the Atlantic Ocean, 23 miles south of Charleston. No one gets bored here!"

DESCRIPTION: Back in the days when plantations thrived, many local owners would retreat to Seabrook Island to escape the oppressive summer heat of the mainland. The resort, although thoroughly modern, has been built with a careful respect for nature, and the villas are all designed to harmonize with the landscape. The Beach Club is the hub of the island activity—this is where you'll find the golf shop, tennis center, and recreation pavilion (where you can rent bikes, fishing, and crabbing gear). For anyone who wants to see the island from the back of a horse, there's an equestrian center, and for people who don't necessarily like to spend all of their vacation in a resort setting, the charming city of Charleston is only a short ride away.

FOR KIDS: At Easter vacation time and during the summer, kids from 3 to 10 may particpate in the Children's Escapades program for a cost of $18 per day or $72 per week (snack and lunch included). The program operates rain or shine from 9:00 A.M. to 3:00 P.M. and includes face painting, pool and pizza parties, scavenger hunts, and more. (There have to be at least six children enrolled to hold the full program; if there are less than six, a half-day program is offered instead.) For those aged 11–19, there are special Teen Adventures from 3:00 to 5:00 P.M. every day and after dinner, from 9:00 to 11:00. A number of family activities are also scheduled—one day there may be poolside bingo, water volleyball, a limbo contest, or a barbecue complete with a deejay right by the pool.

ACCOMMODATIONS: Guests stay in 1-, 2-, or 3-bedroom villas in a choice of settings—behind the dunes and across from the Beach Club, by the golf course, or near the racquet club. All villas have fully equipped kitchens, washers and dryers, screened porches or decks. For meals, guests may eat at any of six restaurants, from elegant to carry-out, and, for those who prefer to cook for themselves, there's a Village Market that stocks all the necessities.

RATES: A special week-long family package includes accommodations, pony rides, crabbing and fishing equipment, and the children's program. It costs from $179 to $259 per night per two-bedroom villa in summer and from $209 to $319 for three bedrooms. (The variation depends on location—the ocean villas are the most expensive.)

The Tyler Place on Lake Champlain

Box AA
Highgate Springs, Vermont 05460
Telephone: 802-868-3301
General Manager: Freya Chaffee

IN THEIR OWN WORDS: "Here, at The Tyler Place on Lake Champlain, we care for 50 families each week. We've specialized in family vacations for over 40 years."

DESCRIPTION: The mood is informal, the atmosphere low-key. Located on 165 lakeshore acres, the Tyler Place offers tennis, fishing, golf (nearby), sailing, windsurfing, canoeing, or just plain sun worshipping. There are daily activities for adults, such as cookouts, staff-versus-guest softball games, water volleyball, and sing-alongs.

FOR KIDS: Every age group is taken care of. For the smallest, you can arrange for a parents' helper who can sit by the hour or even on a live-in basis. The sitters are chosen from a list of local high school girls, most of whom the staff at the resort knows personally. The cost is $2.50 to $5 per hour. The same girls are available to sit on an hourly basis during the day and at night. If you take your own parents' helper, you will be charged $10.50 for linen per week, with no extra charge for the sitter.

"Pre-Midgets" is a program for kids 1 month to 2 or 3 years old and can include live-in help. Helpers often get together with other helpers and their charges for picnics, playground fun, or indoor play in the carriage house.

"Junior Midgets" is an optional low-key variation of the Senior Midget program (described next) for kids 2 and 3 years old who want to participate in some group activities but want a parent's helper around to give individual attention when needed. The program operates form 8:30 A.M. to 1:30 P.M. and 5:30 P.M. to 8:30 P.M.

Both Junior (2- and 3-year-olds) and Senior Midgets (4-, 5-, and 6-year-olds) have a full-day—8:30 to 1:30 and 5:30 to 8:30—program, but kids can be picked up earlier. Activities include nature walks, motorboat rides, hayrides, arts and crafts, singing, and games. Evening entertainment involves parties, peanut hunts, and story-telling.

"The Juniors," kids 6 to 8 years old, have college-age counselors who supervise them from 8:30 A.M. until 1:30 and 5:30 to 9:00 P.M. The group decides what it wants to do—canoe, hike, swim, play volleyball, make arts and crafts, among the choices.

"Pre-Teens," 9- to 11-year-olds, have lots of pool and waterfront time. They play tennis, volleyball, softball, and soccer; go canoeing; have ice cream-making parties and at night see movies, dance, play bingo, and have special parties. The program runs from breakfast until after lunch and from before dinner to 8:30 or 9:00 P.M.

Junior and Senior Teens are groups 12 to 14 years old and 15 to 18 years old. They have lots of sports activities, a mix of independent and group activities (free waterskiing and windsurfing) and evening events such as pool parties and video dances. Teens are encouraged to structure their own day with the help of an entertainment director.

ACCOMMODATIONS: Cottages are located on or near the lake. Each has a wood-burning fireplace in the living room and two to four bedrooms. The inn is a hospitable sprawl of fireplaced lounges, screened porches, outdoor dining areas, and recreation rooms. Sleeping accommodations are in a separate wing. There's no charge for cribs.

Children usually eat with their peers, but if you'd like your school-age child to eat with you in the main dining room on a weekday, you may make a reservation for an early dinner and pay extra.

RATES: Package rates include lodging, nearly all meals—preschoolers are not allowed in the main dining room, many free sports, children's programs, daytime activities for adults, and the resort's "low-key" evening entertainment. During July and August accommodations range from $75 to $120 per person per day for the first two people and $50 to $60 for kids 2–17. For example, two adults in an average two-bedroom cottage with an 8-year-old and a 5-year-old would pay $265 per day or $1,855 per week. During June, prices are 15 to 40 percent lower.

Hawk Inn and Mountain Resort
P.O. Box 64, Route 100
Plymouth, Vermont 05056
Telephone: 802-672-3911 or 800-451-4109
General Manager: Jim Reiman

IN THEIR OWN WORDS: "Vermont's Green Mountains have always been a source of great beauty and inspiration. Here, amid our 1,200-acre natural environment, Hawk Inn and Mountain Resort has created one of the most peaceful and unspoiled resorts in the world, with luxurious homes, townhouses and an elegant country inn."

DECRIPTION: Here's a beautiful piece of the world, close to downhill skiing (Killington and Okemo are minutes away) and near a lake with its own fleet of boats for sailing and canoeing. In winter guests may go cross-country skiing, snow-shoeing, ice-skating, swimming in an indoor pool, or take horsedrawn sleighrides. All seasons are right for the glass-enclosed spa, and in spring and summer, guests get a chance to pan for gold. Tennis and horseback riding are fun in fair weather, and just about any time of year you can take advantage of the many miles of nature trails graded for beginners, intermediates, and advanced hikers. All the activities are complimentary for guests. For the one car family, the resort van shuttles family members to the activities of their choice.

FOR KIDS: Kids from 3 to 12 may take part in Hawk's Summer Adventure program, which operates during the week from June to September from 8:00 A.M. to 5:00 P.M. "We encourage children to participate, emphasizing enjoyment rather than competition." Three-to-five-year-olds take part in the Little Adventure program, which involves hiking, pony rides, boating, games, swimming, and arts and crafts; kids 6–12 focus their energy on outdoors sports— boating, sailing, horseback riding, and group games; and teens 13– 16 get the chance to meet other kids their same age and play tennis, go swimming, cycling, hiking, sailing, canoeing, and horseback riding. At night, there are often performances out on the lawn—magic shows, mimes, and folk singers—that are fun for kids and parents together. Baby-sitting may be arranged day or night for $5 per hour.

ACCOMMODATIONS: There are inn rooms, but probably the most desirable accommodations for a family are the condos and the homes at the resort. Both have two, three or four bedrooms; all have fireplaces, fully equipped kitchens, saunas, and jacuzzis. And how is this for the ultimate luxury? At dinnertime, if you'd rather not go out to eat, you can simply have a chef come to your home, prepare a multicourse meal for you, and then quietly slip away.

RATES: In winter, a two-bedroom town house costs $300 per night; in spring and fall, $170; and in summer, $240. Packages for weekends, holidays, and week-long stays are usually available.

Basin Harbor Club
Basin Harbor Road
Vergennes, Vermont 05491
Telephone: 802-475-2311 or 800-622-4000
General Manager: Robert H. Beach

IN THEIR OWN WORDS: "With the 1987 season we entered our second century of Beach family ownership and management. Throughout this time, children have always been warmly welcomed. There are families who have been vacationing here for four generations . . . . We provide a beautiful site where families can relax together. . . . Parents don't have to spend their entire vacation time being chauffeurs either, because all facilities are right here, not a couple of miles down the road."

DESCRIPTION: On the eastern shore of Lake Champlain with a view of the Adirondacks, the Basin Harbor Club is known for its "active tranquility," on well-groomed and inviting grounds. During the day it offers fishing, boating, waterskiing, swimming in the lake or pool, tennis, golf, jogging, or biking. After 6:00 gentlemen and young men over 12 are required to wear a coat and tie in the public areas of the resort; the guests seem to like this bit of formality and voted to return to the custom a few years ago.

We have friends from London who took a family vacation here with a 10-year-old son and a 13-year-old daughter. Not the green pants and yellow sweaters crew, they loved their time here. Both adults and kids found plenty to do and friends to enjoy it all with.

FOR KIDS: Children between 3 and 10 are welcome to participate in the activities at the Playground, from 9:00 A.M. to noon. The Playground is a bit like a day camp with swings, slide, sandbox, jungle gym, and a playhouse filled with games, books, and toys. Specific activities are arranged each week, according to the interests and ages of the kids at the Harbor at any given time. Some possibilities are nature walks, outdoor sports, cookouts, treasure hunts, fishing and boating, and arts and crafts. At dinnertime kids eat together with an adult to supervise. Kids gather at 6:45 P.M. and stay together until 9:00 P.M.

For the older children, the schedule is somewhat less structured—golf, tennis clinics, volleyball, softball, pool races, and all kinds of water sports are all available. Evening entertainment includes movies, bingo, teen parties, and trips to local events.

A list of baby-sitters is available at the front desk. Sitters are either staff members or local young people, and rates are approximately $3 per hour.

ACCOMMODATIONS: Cottages, each one different from the other in design, or rooms in the main lodge are available to guests. All accommodations are within walking distance of the dining room and other resort facilities. Some have a lake view; others overlook the golf course and tennis courts. Some cottages have screened porches, and about half of the total 77 have fireplaces; most have a pantry with a refrigerator and wet bar. Some cottages are equipped for handicapped access.

RATES: A typical cottage for four, with living room, two bedrooms and two baths, is $400 daily for two parents and two children. If there were three children and two parents, however, the charge for the third child would depend on age—$5 per day for 2 years and under, up to $55 for 15 and over. All rates include breakfast, lunch, and dinner as well as lodging and children's programs; most activities are extra.

The Homestead
Hot Springs, Virginia 24445
Telephone: 703-839-5500; 800-336-5771
General Manager: Clifford H. Nelson

IN THEIR OWN WORDS: "The Homestead brings you all that is finest and worth preserving in America's great resort heritage . . . . Washington and Jefferson strolled here . . . . The Homestead reflects a style and grandeur that—delightfully—may still be enjoyed in this day and age."

DESCRIPTION: As you can tell from the above, this is one of the grand old resorts of America. It is set among 15,000 acres of the Allegheny Mountains and offers guests three 18-hole golf courses, three pools (one indoor), 19 tennis courts, a three-mile-long trout stream, hiking trails, lawn and indoor bowling, horseback riding, and skeet and trap shooting. In winter, add ice-skating and skiing to the list. In any season, one of the most unique features of the Homestead is its spa, originally built in 1892 and owing its fame to the water from the nearby hot springs, which, when it gets to the spa, is a soothing 104 degrees. Hydrotherapy treatments, utilizing some of the practices of the more venerable European spas, are popular, along with the saunas, whirlpool, mineral wraps, massages, aerobics classes, and exercise room.

FOR KIDS: Right next to the spa is the children's playground, a place set aside just for kids aged 3 to 10. At the playground, kids can play in the sandbox, go wading in the pool, climb up into a tree house, play on the swings, merry-go-round, and enjoy their own little playhouse. On rainy days, the kids move indoors to a playroom right in the spa that's equipped with toys and games and has its own painting, crafts, and music areas plus a carpenter's shop. Both the playground and the playrooms are supervised daily from 9:00 A.M. to 5:00 P.M. Kids under 3 must have their own baby-sitters—baby-sitting may be arranged through the hotel. Swimming, golf, tennis, and skiing lessons are all available to kids. A summer children's program runs for ages 7–12, with instruction in a variety of sports during the same hours listed above.

ACCOMMODATIONS: The resort is massive, with 530 rooms in all. Although the building itself is old, rooms have all been recently renovated and have all the modern conveniences you want.

RATES: Daily rates, from April to November, are $140 to $185 per person double occupancy, based on the modified American plan. Children, sharing a room iwth parents are, 16 and over, $75; 5–15, $50; and under 4, free. The children's program is included in the rate, but many of the activities (e.g., golf, tennis, riding, bowling, and archery) are extra.

Cavalier Resort Hotel
42nd Street and Oceanfront
Virginia Beach, Virginia 23451
Telephone: 804-425-8555 or 800-446-8199
General Manager: John W. Hendriksen

IN THEIR OWN WORDS: We've been focusing on family activity since 1927 . . . . the grande dame of Virginia Beach is as fascinating as ever, and always ready to offer a warm welcome."

DESCRIPTION: The original 1920s-era building sits right behind a modern beachfront addition. Water sports are the most popular feature for families. Besides enjoying the beachfront, guests can swim in either an oceanside pool or an indoor pool and play tennis right on the premises. Not far away, you can play golf, go fishing, or take a tour of some of the nearby tourist attractions, such as a water theme park, Seashore State Park, the Virginia Maritime Museum, Williamsburg, and Busch Gardens (the last two are about 60 miles from the resort.)

FOR KIDS: Children 5–14 have their own program that operates seven days a week from mid-May to mid-September from 10:00 A.M. until 4:00 P.M. Activities are supervised by teachers from the

Virginia Beach school system and include sand-castle building, sand painting, games, and movies on rainy days. The program schedule is posted daily so that parents can drop off or pick up kids whenever it's convenient. The resort has two playgrounds on the property, and baby-sitting can be arranged during the day or evening for $4 an hour; just give the housekeeper 12 hours' notice.

ACCOMMODATIONS: All rooms have balconies with ocean views, and most have two double beds. Connecting rooms are available for families, and there are loads of cribs—55 in all—available at no extra charge.

RATES: In summer there are two special packages just for families. The first, the "Bed and Board Special" is $291 for three nights, four days for two adults, with kids 12 and under free; breakfast is included. For a longer stay, the resort offers its "Vacation Special": $679 for seven nights, eight days of accommodations and breakfasts.

Wintergreen Resort
Wintergreen, Virginia 22958
Telephone: 804-325-2200 or 800-325-2200
General Manager: Gunter L. Mueler

IN THEIR OWN WORDS: "We're a four-season resort high in Virginia's Blue Ridge Mountains. In summer . . . our weather is frequently 10 to 15 degrees cooler than most metropolitan areas. Built on the mountain, there are breathtaking 50-mile views of the surrounding countryside . . . . Wintergreen is one of only 5 ski resorts south of New York with a vertical drop over 1,000 feet."

DESCRIPTION: Located 43 miles from Charlottesville, and another three hours from Washington, D.C., Wintergreen offers a mountaintop golf course and 18 tennis courts, 20 miles of hiking trails, and a complete equestrian center for trail rides and lessons. For swimming, your choice is Lake Monocan or one of five pools.

FOR KIDS: Children 2-1/2 to 12 years old have their own program. In winter it operates from 8:30 A.M. to 4:30 P.M. and in summer from 10:00 A.M. to 4:00 P.M. In winter, the 2-1/2- to 5-year-olds combine playing and ski instruction. In summer, crafts, playground fun, and butterfly walks are scheduled. Kids 6 and older ski in winter and in summer have swimming lessons and participate in a water rodeo; "hands-on" nature activities; "kids in the kitchen" sessions; "horse sense," a program based at the stables; fishing; and canoeing. The cost of the children's program is $17 per day.

From time to time during the summer, Wintergreen sponsors a "Kid's Nature Camp" for guests' children and grandchildren who are 6–8 years old. Campers sleep out and study the natural treasures of the area—usually for two or three nights.

Baby-sitting is available for approximately $5 per hour by contacting the Activities Office 24 hours in advance.

ACCOMMODATIONS: All accommodations are either condominiums or homes. Studios and one-bedrooms include kitchens or kitchenettes; larger condos have full kitchens and separate living rooms. Some have fireplaces.

RATES: A sample of a peak season "Recreation Package" for three nights, four days, for four in a two-bedroom condo is $189 in nonpeak season and $243 in peak. This includes lodging, breakfast, children's programs, unlimited use of Wintergarden spa (their health club facility), and unlimited tennis Monday through Friday. Skiing is extra.

The Greenbrier
White Sulphur Springs, West Virginia 24986
Telephone: 304-536-1110 or 800-624-6070
Managing Director: Ted J. Kleisner

IN THEIR OWN WORDS: "For more than two centuries, The Greenbrier has meant ladies and gentlemen being served by ladies and gentlemen . . . . it still does."

DESCRIPTION: Here's another massive, in-the-old-style resort with 6,500 acres in the midst of the Allegheny Mountains. What's to do during the day? Choose from jogging, horseback riding on woodland mountain trails, cross-country skiing, fishing, trap and skeet shooting, garden walks, horse and carriage rides, golf on one of three courses, and tennis on one of 20 courts (five indoors, 15 outdoors). There are two heated and lighted platform tennis courts for year-round use, too; swimming in an outdoor or indoor pool; bowling; and working out on the par course fitness trail or at the fitness center. At tea time there's chamber music; and at night dinner and dancing, if you're not too tired.

FOR KIDS: From mid-June to Labor Day and during school vacation breaks, kids 6 to 12 (5 during holiday time) have their own program, the Greenbrier's Sports School, from 9:45 A.M. to 4:00 P.M. and 7:00 to 10:00 P.M. every day. The cost is $20 for a day session, $14 more for the evening portion. Some activities require additional fees. College-trained counselors give the kids a choice of sport they want to pursue with group lessons, and the kids help plan the day's activities. Possibilities include mountain hikes, movies, arts and crafts, carriage rides, and swimming. Kids eat together at 6:00 and then have an after-dinner movie until 10:00.

Kids from 3 to 5 join the Brier Bunch from 9:45 A.M. to 4:00 P.M. to do arts and crafts, hear stories, and to do things that are "educational but fun." The charge is $20.

For younger kids you may want a baby-sitter. Expect to pay just under $4.50 per hour and make arrangements with the household department at least two hours in advance.

ACCOMMODATIONS: This enormous hotel has 700 rooms, each individually decorated. Some suites are available, and there are also a variety of free-standing guest houses, cottages, and two estate houses. One, Valley View, is big enough to entertain 200 people. It has four bedrooms and includes the use of a Cadillac Seville; rental is $240 per person per day based on occupancy by eight people.

RATES: A double-bedded room in winter season costs $109 to $147 per person, including breakfast and dinner as well as lodging. Kids 10 and up are $70; 5 to 9, $40; 1 to 4, $25; and under 1 year, no charge. There's no extra charge for the use of a crib. All sports facilities are extra; golf and tennis packages are available.

LEARNING VACATIONS

What follows are places where you and your family can go to combine a vacation with learning something new or polishing up an old skill. Since our last edition, we've discovered a woman named Ann Waigand, mother of two young children, who operates the Educated Traveler, a travel consulting business that specializes in educational and special interest travel. Waigand's database contains thousands of listings of tours and destinations that offer chances to learn about a particular subject or pursue a hobby while you vacation. For a small fee, she will search the listings to find vacations that fit your special interests and the ages of your children, and will provide you with detailed information on each selection plus background reading materials for the trip. Write to her at 3262 White Barn Court, Herndon, Virginia 22071, 703-435-1281.

University of California at Santa Barbara
Alumni Vacation Center
Santa Barbara, California 93106
Telephone: 805-961-3123
Director: Jim McNamara

IN THEIR OWN WORDS: "You're on a bluff overlooking the Pacific Ocean. Nearby are downtown Santa Barbara, Lake Cachujma, the Santa Ynez Valley horse and wine country, and the quaint Danish village of Solvang. No wonder families return year after year. Probably the Vacation Center's most important charm is the staff. Time and again, vacationers let us know what a pleasure it is to have such wonderful role models for their children during their stay at the Center."

DESCRIPTION: One of our friends wrote: "My husband and two daughters (ages one and five) spent one week at the Center last summer and found it a perfect vacation for us . . . given the ages of our kids, our life-style, and our budget . . . . There were about 40 families there when we were—plenty of kids of all ages . . . . Vacationers can participate in any activity they choose or just relax, enjoy the beach and bike trails or roam around Santa Barbara. The Center isn't for people looking for a sophisticated time—the atmosphere is camp-like, family-oriented and generally wholesome."

The Center is tucked into its own corner of the campus, and it offers use of all the facilities of the school including the dining commons, 10 tennis courts, a swimming pool, an outdoor patio for dining, a playground, a fitness program, and education and entertainment programs for all ages.

Family activities include square dancing, carnivals, and campfires. For adults there are wine tasting, seminars by U.C. faculty, and tours of Santa Barbara. Tennis and swimming lessons are included in the cost of the Center's package. Ten week-long sessions are held each summer.

FOR KIDS: The children's programs are set up to be flexible, to allow parents to spend as much time as they'd like with their kids but to be able to do some things on their own as well. Kids are divided into age groups. "Small World" is for 2- and 3-year-olds with activities such as tumbling, making sand castles, music, and making ceramic star necklaces. Kids 4 to 8, 9 to 10, and 11 to 12 are grouped together, and for teens there's a program that includes local excursions and an overnight campout. Children's programs generally run from 9:00 A.M. to 9:00 P.M., excluding meal times. For kids too young for the organized children's programs, baby-sitting is available at $3 per hour (our friends traded off baby-sitting with other parents they had met).

ACCOMMODATIONS: Each family lives in a fully furnished suite including a living room, bath, and two to four bedrooms. Daily maid service is provided, and there's a refrigerator for snacks. Cribs are available for $20 per stay.

RATES: Adults (12 and over) pay $460, which includes all meals, lodging, children's programs, tennis and swimming lessons, and use of all campus facilities. The rate for kids 6 to 11 is $330; for 2 to 5, $290; for 1 to 2, $60; and for under 1 year, $20. Members of a U.C. alumni association and their immediate family are entitled to a slightly lower rate, but the Center is open to nonalumni as well.

Anderson Ranch Arts Center
P.O. Box 5508
Snowmass Village, Colorado
Telephone: 303-923-3181

IN THEIR OWN WORDS: "The purpose of the Anderson Ranch Arts Center is to provide a stimulating environment that promotes individual artistic development and excellence in the making and understanding of the visual arts."

DESCRIPTION: Anderson Ranch is a unique spot. Its beautiful, sylvan location is inspirational for the artists who attend. From what we saw on a recent visit, the people who sign up for a week at Anderson are quite serious about their art. In the children's workshop, kids can explore their creativity. It's open to local youngsters as well as the children of the folks who are attending classes at the ranch. We went to a slide presentation/lecture at the ranch (a combination potluck supper and lecture is scheduled weekly and is popular with the locals as well as guests) and were extremely impressed—creativity and scholarship flourish in this setting, which is exactly what the founders had in mind when they first envisioned it.

Set in the mountain resort of Snowmass Village at an elevation of 8,200 feet, the ranch is ten miles west of Aspen and 200 miles west of Denver, surrounded by the 14,000-foot peaks of the Elk Mountain Range. The workshops offered every summer are meant to be "catalysts for change and growth" for those who want to explore their creativity and develop skills with the help of the faculty—respected, working artists. There are 70 workshops in all—in ceramics, photography, woodworking, furniture design, painting, drawing, and interdisciplinary and critical studies. Anyone, from novice to professional, is welcome, as long as they are serious about their work. The "campus" of the ranch is a lovely mixture of historic log cabins and barns, modern studio facilities, and new buildings designed to complement the historical setting.

FOR KIDS: The ranch's children's program offers a wide variety of workshops for kids from preschool age to teens. Workshops are lively and focus on a range of materials and media, including clay, painting, printmaking, photography, and art history. Children's workshops meet three to five days per week for about three hours per day, and tuition costs $65 for one week. Kids 1–3 may be enrolled in daycare facilities in the Community Center next to the ranch, and kids 3 and older may join Snowmass Sunbunnies, a day-camp program that runs during the week from 9:00 A.M. to 5:00 P.M. Infant care can also be arranged.

ACCOMMODATIONS: Families attending the workshops are housed in nearby condominiums; prices range from $450 per week for a one-bedroom to $550 for a three-bedroom unit. Participants may eat at the ranch for an extra charge.

RATES: Workshop prices vary with length (one or two weeks) and subject matter. Samples are the two week class "Oil Painting—the Figure," which costs $350 with an additional $45 model fee; or the one-week ceramics workshop, "Acquisition of Pottery Skills," which costs $350 with a $75 materials fee. Scholarships are available. A car is definitely recommended.

Cornell University
Adult University
626 Thurston Avenue
Ithaca, New York 14850
Telephone: 607-255-6260
Director: Ralph Janis

IN THEIR OWN WORDS: "The young people come along with adults and all take courses. The children's program provides an exciting, safe growing experience for each child."

DESCRIPTION: Cornell Adult University (CAU) offers three possibilities: from the end of June to the end of July they have week-long sessions on the Ithaca campus, where adults can choose from seven seminars and workshops, with topics such as "American

Humor: A Sometimes Serious Survey" and "Jerusalem: An Idea in Time."

FOR KIDS: While the adults are in class, the kids have their own very special programming. For the ones who are under 3 years old, CAU arranges baby-sitting; the 3-to-5-year-olds have a full nursery school program from 8:00 A.M. to 4:30 P.M. that includes field trips and science projects; 5-to-7-year-olds take an ecology course from 9:00 to 11:00 each morning and in the afternoon swim and have cookouts, and participate in drama and music. Kids 8 to 12 choose morning courses such as horseback riding, producing a weekly newsletter, veterinary anatomy, or wilderness adventures, including a ropes course, canoeing, outdoor survival, and backpacking at local sites. Afternoons and evenings are spent visiting the science center, roller-skating, swimming, and playing games. Teens choose from courses such as "Getting Ready for College," "Board Sailing," "Sculpture and Art," and "Karate and Self-Defense." They live in their own supervised dorm, and participate in sports, roller-skating, movies, and other extracurricular activities.

CAU also organizes educational vacations off-campus in New Mexico and Maine. In New Mexico, the focus is "Cultures and Landscapes of the Sangre de Cristo Mountains" (kids should be at least 12). In Maine it's "The Art and Science of the Sea," field seminars at the Shoals Marine Laboratory in the Isles of Shoals (teenagers accompanied by adults are welcome).

ACCOMMODATIONS: At Cornell, participants stay in dorms; in New Mexico they stay in resort accommodations, and in Maine they stay in residence facilities at the lab.

RATES: The Ithaca program costs $320 for tuition for adults; housing and meals cost $230 (off-campus housing with no meal plan is also possible). For kids the prices range from $180 for the pre-kindergarteners to $290 for the teen program. The CAU program in New Mexico costs $985 for adults, $585 for teens rooming with two adults; CAU at the Shoals is $625–$675.

Dillman's Sand Lake Lodge
Box 98
Lac du Flambeau, Wisconsin 54538
Telephone: 715-588-3143 or 800-433-2238, Ext. 327
Owner: Sue Robertson

IN THEIR OWN WORDS: "We've been a family-owned and operated resort for 54 years. We own an entire peninsula on clear, spring-fed White Sand Lake . . . many families return into the third generation . . . . Family members really get reacquainted in these peaceful surroundings and cozy cottages."

DESCRIPTION: "Our lake is not heavily developed, so there is a feeling of beauty and spaciousness. We can see loons, ducks and eagles as well as enjoy the cleanliness of the lake for swimming and watersports." The lake is, in fact, the centerpiece of the resort—it is where you can fish for your dinner, sail, swim, canoe, scuba dive, or waterski (each weekday from 2:00 to 4:00 P.M. guests may take a free waterskiing lesson). There's lots to do on dry land, too—hiking on trails forged by Indians and pioneers, playing tennis (there are three courts), practicing golf on a driving range, and bicycling. You may be wondering why we've included this resort in the Learning Vacations section since, so far, it sounds like a regular summer resort. The reason is that over the past ten years, the Robertsons have developed their Creative Workshop programs "to coincide with the public's interest in a less static experience while away from home. While one family member is fishing, another can be attending a workshop with a well-known instructor." Sample workshop offerings include "Enjoying Watercolor," "Simplicity in Oil Landscapes," "Figures and Landscapes in Pastels," "Journal Writing: The Art of Self-Reflection," even one on "Getting Started in Duplicate Bridge." Workshops last one week, combining an informal studio environment with a chance for both individual and group instruction. Families of workshop participants are cordially invited to go along and enjoy the life of the resort as well. During each week of the summer, there are a number of regularly scheduled activities for all ages—a guided nature hike, a steak fry, a trip to the Indian powwow in town, and a boat trip to Picnic Point for a hot dog roast.

FOR KIDS: A social director meets with the kids from age 3 up during the week from 9:00 to 11:00 A.M. and again from 1:30 to 4:00 P.M. to do arts and crafts, have treasure hunts, make a piñata, give a puppet show, or waterski. Baby-sitting may be arranged for $2 per hour, day and night.

ACCOMMODATIONS: Most of the cabins have a view of the lake, seven have fireplaces, and all have refrigerators. Cabins have one to three bedrooms and come in a variety of sizes and layouts. Motel accommodations are also available in the lodge annex, but here you won't be able to enjoy a view.

RATES: Six nights including breakfast and dinner begin at $417 per person as a base price. Add-ons for workshops vary from $50 to $300. Kids 2–10 are half-price, and under 2 are free.

9

TENNIS AND GOLF

Lots of you are tennis or golf aficionados. You remember with pleasure the tennis- or golf-centered vacations you took B.C. (before children). In this chapter we want to show you how you can bring back those "good old days"—spend time mastering your sport and just plain enjoying it—while your children are off on their own, involved in supervised activities with kids their own age. It is likely, too, that any of you who love tennis or golf will want your kids to love it as well and that you're eager to get your kids involved. At some of the resorts we list here, kids as young as 4 years old can start lessons.

To get the scoop on introducing kids to tennis and/or golf we spoke to two experts. First, we had a conversation with Roy Barth, the director of tennis at Kiawah Island since 1975. Barth thinks that kids should start being exposed to tennis as a fun experience—and he emphasized the fun part—at 4, 5, or 6. At Kiawah, he explained, the kids in this age group never keep score; instead, they practice hitting balls at hand-painted animated targets: an alligator, a pelican, or a raccoon. They are given small racquets, are taught to make contact with the ball, and then are let loose to have fun for a half-hour. Anything longer might seem too much like work. "Kids get hooked by themselves," Barth explained. "Don't force them!"

"I'm a tennis pro and a parent of two kids 11 and 13. When I gave them instructions, they weren't interested. 'We want to have fun!' they told me. Now they come to me for help, and now they play in tournaments, but I laid low for two to three years and let it happen by itself."

We asked Barth what to look for when choosing a resort with a tennis program for kids. He gave us a lot of hints. For kids 10 to 18 he suggested you check to see whether there are possibilities for round-robin doubles. This is good not only for the kids to get practice but also so they meet other kids their age. Find out how often instructional programs are offered and what the ratio is of pro to student—1:4 to 1:6 is best. Ask whether there are ball machines for practice and try to find out something about the reputation of the pro and the program. Barth says it's important to check on the time of the clinics for the youngest kids. "I've experimented," he said, "and when we started late in the afternoon we had cranky, tired kids. Early morning is the best time." He also emphasized the importance of safety—once you're at the resort be sure to take a look and see how well supervised the group lessons are. Barth himself tells about getting hit by a racquet when he was 5 and being afraid to touch one again until he was 7.

After we spoke to Barth about tennis, we turned to the subject of golf and talked to Mike Cook, head teaching pro at Sea Palms Resort in Georgia. Cook likes teaching kids. "When kids listen and pay attention you can teach them so much and you know that the basics will stick with them all through life.

"I started at 4," he went on, "but that's too young. I think that 7 or 8 is better. It is too hard for kids much younger than 7 to really listen." We asked Cook what to look for when choosing a kids' golf program at a resort. He suggested checking on the reputation of the teachers and making sure that kids actually get a chance to play golf, not just hit balls around. "At Sea Palms, the kids have use of one of our courses every afternoon after 3:30. We like to play with kids." The golf clinics that kids attend should emphasize the fun of the game, not just the discipline. And, just as every expert has said before, whatever his or her sport, Cook warns parents against pushing kids. "Let them play other sports besides golf; let them get their feet wet, but don't force them into just one thing."

When it comes to equipment, "There is a real difference between junior clubs and cut-down adult ones," according to another expert, James A. Frank, executive editor of *Golf* magazine. "Unfortunately many places just cut down adult-size clubs. This is very unfair to children; it makes the clubs very hard to hit for them. If people are serious about golf, they should call ahead and see if the resort has real junior clubs." What about cleated shoes? Will your kids need them? "Probably not," according to Frank, but he does advise checking with the resort.

Good news for golfing families is a newsletter put together just for them by Cindy Gum and Noreen Christopher (Cindy's the one who writes the book on home exchanging listed in Chapter 4). The newsletter, called the *Golfer's Connection*, tells all about little-known golf hideaways, good values on golf packages and tours, timely travel tips, and includes a special section with listings from golfers who want to exchange or rent their homes or rental properties. A year's subscription to the newsletter costs $29 and is available from 101 Church Street, Suite 24P, Los Gatos, California 95032, 408-395-6939.

Many of the resorts listed here offer good tennis and golf. Here we give you only some possibilities; check Chapter 8 for other ideas and don't forget, too, that lots of the ski resorts metamorphose into tennis and/or golf resorts in summer (like Copper Mountain and Snowmass in Colorado and Bolton Valley in Vermont), so also look at Chapter 10.

The Westin La Paloma

3800 East Sunrise Drive
Tucson, Arizona 85718
Telephone: 602-742-6000 or 800-222-1252
General Manager: Andrew MacLellan

IN THEIR OWN WORDS: "Set in the foothills of the Santa Catalina mountains, the Westin La Paloma is a total destination resort, styled to reflect Tucson's Spanish heritage and southwestern luxury."

DESCRIPTION: Just over three years old, this luxury resort was built with "a sensitivity to the land, a desire to enhance not detract." The result is a haven for golf and tennis lovers. Jack Nicklaus designed the 27-hole golf course, named one of the ten best in Arizona by *Golf Digest*. The 12 competition-caliber tennis courts have qualified the resort for *Tennis* magazine's rating as one of the top 50 tennis resorts in the U.S. Besides tennis and golf, a free-form swimming pool with a waterslide and swim-up bar, three Jacuzzi spas, a sandy beach, a volleyball court, jogging and cycling trails, and a fully equipped health club are all available to guests.

FOR KIDS: The Westin offers two possibilities. The first, the Children's Lounge, located in the Tennis and Health Club is open year-round and is a place where kids ages 6 months to 12 years can be dropped off at any time from 8:00 A.M. to 5:00 P.M. during the week and until 10:00 P.M. on weekends. The Lounge is supervised by a childcare professional and equipped with cots for little ones, games, arts and crafts equipment, and so on. The cost of a stay at the Lounge is $3 per hour. A more organized program for kids 5 to 12 is the day camp, available at holiday time and during the summer. The camp is in session from 10:00 A.M. to 4:00 P.M. and offers campers lots of outdoor sports, field trips to places like Old Tucson, movies not far from the resort, and activities such as ice cream socials and treasure hunts. Kids may participate a day at a time or sign up for a longer session. The cost ranges from $14 to $20 per day (depending on season), and lunch is included.

Baby-sitting can be arranged, as well, through Guest Services for hours when the Children's Lounge is closed.

ACCOMMODATIONS: The resort's 487 guest rooms are spread out among 24 two-story complexes. Arranged to resemble a village, each building has its own courtyard landscaped with native saguaro cacti. Rooms are large, with a sitting room area, dual sinks, make-up tables, dry bars, and refrigerators. Rooms for nonsmokers are also available with advance notice.

RATES: During the summer, a deluxe double room costs $120; in high season, January through May, it's $245. Kids under 18 may share the room at no extra cost. Tennis and golf packages are available year-round.

Wickenburg Inn
P.O. Box P
Wickenburg, Arizona 85358
Telephone: 602-684-7811 or 800-528-4227
General Manager: Charles "Lefty" Brinkman

IN THEIR OWN WORDS: "Our Inn is in a very relaxed and beautiful setting—most of which is natural. The dress is casual, and the staff is very helpful and understanding. We offer programs in riding and tennis which enable guests to improve their skills and have a good time doing it."

DESCRIPTION: This resort could as easily have been listed under ranches, but we flipped a coin and decided to put it under "tennis" instead. If you like tennis and horseback riding, consider it carefully. The tennis is good—11 acrylic courts with a complete pro shop, instruction center, rebound walls, and ball machines. Clinics and private lessons are available; clinics are three hours of group instruction daily with a 3:1 ratio whenever possible. When you're not playing tennis, try horseback riding (instruction and clinics available) or swimming at the hilltop spa. Two particularly interesting features of Wickenburg are its nature study program and its arts and crafts center. Adults, as well as children, can spend time with the resident naturalist learning about Wickenburg's desert setting or sketching, painting, making pottery, or doing leatherwork, macramé, or weaving at the inn's art studio. There's golf not far away, at the Wickenburg Country Club.

FOR KIDS: During school vacation periods there are special children's programs organized for kids 4 to 12. Kids 4 to 6 and their counselor do arts and crafts, go on horseback rides, visit the Nature Center, take nature walks, and play games together. The program lasts from 8:45 A.M. to 4:00 P.M., with an hour break for lunch with parents.

Older kids 7 to 12 participate in trail rides, tennis clinics, square dances, and special trips. A special dinner hour for this age group begins at 5:00 P.M. (kids can eat later with their parents if they'd rather). At 6:00 P.M. the evening program begins; it runs until 8:30 P.M. The cost is $30 for the full day and evening, $25 for day only, and $15 for half-day. Arts and crafts supplies are extra.

Baby-sitting for younger children is available with 24- to 48-hour notice at $4 per hour with a four-hour minimum.

ACCOMMODATIONS: Spanish-style adobe "casitas" including fireplaces and wet bars are set apart from the Main Lodge so that families can enjoy some privacy and quiet. All have one bedroom, a porch, double sleep sofas in the living room, a powder room, and a bath. Cribs are available at no extra cost.

RATES: Rates are based on a full American plan. All meals, swimming, whirlpool, wildlife study, use of the art studio, tennis court privileges, horseback riding, and other "standard" ranch activities are included. A deluxe casita suite ranges from $190 to $270 double occupancy. Children 2 to 12 sharing the casita cost $25; those 13 and over are $40. Tennis clinics cost $100 extra per person for three days and $150 for five.

Rancho Bernardo Inn
17550 Bernardo Oaks Drive
San Diego, California 92128
Telephone: 619-487-1611 or 800-854-1065
General Manager: John M. Morton

IN THEIR OWN WORDS: "You are welcomed to the warmth, taste and style of a fine country home. Beautiful antiques and furnishings convey a spirit of honest, uncomplicated hospitality."

Don't let the talk of antiques and high style scare you—families are very welcome here and come often, which is what prompted the children's program. All generations will feel comfortable here—we did!

DESCRIPTION: The inn is located in the San Bernardo Valley, surrounded by the Pasqual Mountains, just 25 miles from downtown San Diego. Golf and tennis are featured at this resort: a 72 par course "that must be played with almost rifle-like accuracy," and for tennis aficionados, 12 courts in all—four lighted and two designed for tournament play.

FOR KIDS: The resort runs free children's camps during Easter and Christmas vacation and through the month of August until Labor Day. Kids from 4 to 17 are invited to participate with activities from 9:00 A.M. to 9:00 P.M. Kids from 4 to 11, divided by ages, participate in games, cookie making, arts and crafts, scavenger hunts, and other supervised activities; a program for the preteens and teenagers is more loosely designed to suit the participants' own needs and interests. Each evening, the teenagers set their schedule for the following day. Kids are allowed to go in and out of the program as they wish. Baby-sitting is also available at a rate of $22.50 for the first three hours (the minimum) and $3.50 per hour after that. All baby-sitters and counselors are CPR trained—a nice plus for anxious parents.

ACCOMMODATIONS: The inn is composed of eight red-tiled haciendas with room for 287 guests. The choice includes executive suites and one- and two-bedroom suites. A typical room has two queen-size beds, a refrigerator, and either a patio or a balcony. Ask for a room away from the parking lot adjacent to the golf club, which is cleaned daily in the early, early morning.

RATES: Children under 13 may stay free in their parents' room. During high season, from January 1 to March 31, one-bedroom suites cost $260, two-bedrooms, $445 per night. At low season, June 1 to September 30, the same accommodations cost $210 and $345, respectively. During the other two "seasons" expect something in between.

Sheraton Bonaventure Resort and Spa
250 Racquet Club Road
Fort Lauderdale, Florida 33326
Telephone: 305-389-3300 or 800-327-8090
General Manager: J. Philip Hughes

IN THEIR OWN WORDS: "Our setting is superb . . . tropical, lush and green. It is a magical place that has everything for your enjoyment—for shaping up, living it up or just plain relaxing."

DESCRIPTION: The Bonaventure offers you a chance to combine golf (two 18-hole PGA-managed championship golf courses) and tennis (24 courts, most of them lighted for night play) with the added advantage of what they describe as their "world class" spa and fitness center, which features a Paramount fitness room, aerobics classes, massages, loofah scrubs and herbal wraps, Swiss needle showers, pools, saunas, whirlpools, and more. If you have time left over you can try the roller-skating rink, bowling alley, basketball court, pedal boats, water volleyball, one of the three fresh-water pools, racquetball and squash (in air-conditioned courts), or even see a first-run movie. Horseback riding is also available at the resort's equestrian center.

FOR KIDS: During the summer—mid-June to September, Christmas vacation, Easter vacation, and on weekends year-round, the Bonaventure offers a children's program for kids 4–12 that operates from 10:00 A.M. until 4:00 P.M. The program involves a half-day away from the resort on a field trip (a typical example is a trip to Everglades Holiday Park) with the rest of the day back at the resort doing arts and crafts, playing board games, roller-skating, and bowling. The on-site portion is free; the field trip costs $12 with an additional $3.50 for lunch. Tennis, golf, and horseback riding lessons are all available to kids (extra charge) but baby-sitting is not.

ACCOMMODATIONS: Guest rooms—there are over 500 of them—feature balconies with views of either the lake or the golf course, and all come equipped with a wet bar and a refrigerator.

RATES: There are a variety of packages to choose from—spa plans, golf and tennis packages, and some spa and sport combinations. The Seven-Day Spa and Sport plan includes lots of treatments (aromatherapy, a thermal back treatment, facials, and more), exercise classes, a choice of golf or tennis, and meals. The price in high season, from January 1 to April 15 is $1,795 per person. A special holiday rate, valid at Labor Day and Christmas vacation time, of $59 per person based on double occupancy, room only, is also possible; kids 17 and under may stay with parents at no extra cost. Remember, though, that the $59 rate is for room only; all activities are extra.

Sonesta Beach Hotel and Tennis Club

350 Ocean Drive
Key Biscayne, Florida 33149
Telephone: 305-361-2021 or 800-343-7170
General Manager: Felix Madera

IN THEIR OWN WORDS: "We're tucked away on our own tropical island but we're still just twenty minutes from Miami's International Airport. Everything you could possibly want for the full life in the sun is right here on Key Biscayne. You can do as little or as much as you please."

DESCRIPTION: Golf is at the Key Biscayne Golf Course, less than two miles from the hotel, which has been ranked number one in the state of Florida. The tennis is played on ten laykold courts, three of which are lighted for night play. There are two full-time pros to help with your game, and clinics for six or more include video playback.

During the summer and at spring break time, special tennis camps are offered for children 6 and older from one to five days or more. Tennis is the highlight, but pool and beach fun is also included. Besides tennis and golf, Sonesta offer deep-sea fishing and a fitness center with massages, steambaths, and whirlpools. The white sand beach will entice you away from the large pool. The modern lobby is bedecked with splendid works of art easily viewed from the comfortable leather couches liberally scattered throughout.

FOR KIDS: The "Just Us Kids" program is for children 5–13 and runs seven days a week from 10:00 A.M. to 10:00 P.M. year-round. It is divided into three separate modules. The program is counselor supervised and free to guests, with a charge only for meals and field trips. Mornings are for field trips—visits to the zoo, bowling, the Parrot or Monkey Jungle, Miami Science Center and Aquarium. The afternoon is for supervised beach and pool activities, tennis clinics, and more. Every night, before our boys went to bed, they'd ask, "Where are we going tomorrow?" On our most recent visit, after a two-year hiatus, our kids were delighted to meet up with some of the same energetic counselors they had had before.

Kids eat lunch at the beach snack bar on their way back from the morning field trip. From 5:00 to 6:00 P.M. parents collect their kids, who later reconvene for dinner and an evening activity. There is no charge for on-property play (except materials for jewelry making), but you do pay for all excursions and meals. Each child receives a T-Shirt and other "Just Us Kids" goodies (such as Frisbees and shoelaces).

The daily activity sheet for kids, as full as it is, is rivaled by the one for teens. Special teen activities, their own disco room and parties, are combined with shopping trips, tours, and bicycling.

Younger kids have their own baby-sitters with 24 hours advance notice. A minimum of three hours is required; the rate is $5.50 per hour.

ACCOMMODATIONS: You can choose from a room, a suite in the hotel, or a one-, two-, three-, or four-bedroom villa adjacent to the hotel, complete with a fully equipped kitchen and a private heated pool. Cribs are available for $15 per night. For privacy and space, plus the conveniences of all hotel facilities and services, a villa with a private pool will be our choice on our next visit. If you share with another family—and there is plenty of room—the cost can be quite reasonable. They even stock the fridge for the first morning's breakfast.

RATES: Kids under 12 stay free in rooms with their parents. In high season (December to April) a three-night "Sonesta Spree" package, which includes unlimited tennis, use of the fitness center, breakfasts, the kids' program, and the adult activity program, costs $390 double occupancy; oceanfront rooms cost an additional $35 per night.

Bluewater Bay Resort
P.O. Box 247
Niceville, Florida 32578
Telephone: 904-897-3613 or 800-874-2128
Manager: Richard A. Lumsden

IN THEIR OWN WORDS: "This is a place for getting away from the hectic sights and sounds of the city . . . ideally suited for those who love the great outdoors."

DESCRIPTION: This is a combined residential/resort community on the shores of Choctawhatchee Bay. Besides the golf—a 6,850-yard layout designed by PGA pro Jerry Pate and architect Tom Fazio—there are tennis night and day on 21 courts, three swimming pools, sailing and fishing expeditions to the bay and Gulf of Mexico, and a 2,000-foot island beach within easy reach.

FOR KIDS: During the summer (beginning of June to the end of August) and during school vacation periods, there's a program for kids 3 to 14 that's free for families who participate in a family package. Kids 3, 4, and 5 have a program from 9:00 A.M. to noon

Monday through Friday. Activities include arts and crafts, nature hikes, treasure hunts, fingerprinting, and sand-castle building. Kids 6 to 11 are kept busy from 9:00 A.M. to 4:00 P.M. with movies, sailing, golf and tennis clinics, arts and crafts, picnics and field trips.

Teens have their own activities scheduled throughout the week—volleyball, beach parties, sailing clinics, and trips off the property. The whole family can enjoy potluck dinners by the pool, canoe trips, beach cookouts, ice cream socials, and so forth.

Baby-sitting is available for $3.75 per hour; just contact the Recreation Department to arrange it.

ACCOMMODATIONS: The resort refers to them as "full size vacation homes"—most have one or two bedrooms and are multilevel (the tallest are three floors). You can choose to be on the bay, at the Swim and Tennis Center, or at the golf course. Cribs ar available at no charge; all accommodations have kitchen facilities.

RATES: A "Summer Family Vacation Package" that includes accommodations in a two-bedroom, two-bath town house or patio home, and the kids' program costs $750 for seven nights.

Hyatt Regency Grand Cypress
One Grand Cypress Boulevard
Orlando, Florida 32819
Telephone: 407-239-1234 or 800-233-1234
General Manager: Jack Hardy

IN THEIR OWN WORDS: "In the heart of central Florida, the Hyatt Regency is an award-winning five diamond resort hotel. An elegant, tropical paradise of lush gardens and soft colors. Of refreshing pools and impeccable service. Of distinctive architectures and world-class art."

DESCRIPTION: As with most other Hyatt properties, you can expect a feeling of luxury at this Florida resort. Most spectacular of all is the hotel's lagoon pool with its grottos and rope bridge, a dozen tumbling waterfalls, an 80-foot water slide, and three whirlpools. Just beyond the pool is 21-acre Lake Windsong with a sandy beach, sailboats, canoes, sailboards, and pedal boats. Golf is a big attraction here, with a 45-hole Jack Nicklaus Signature Course, a nine-hole pitch and putt course, a complete pro shop, and the Jack Nicklaus Academy of Golf for state-of-the-art golf instruction. Guests can play tennis on tournament-quality courts, work out in the health and fitness center, rent bikes, jog along the five-mile trail, or ride at the

Grand Cypress Equestrian Center. The resort is not far from many of Florida's biggest family attractions: Busch Gardens and the Kennedy Space Center are 90 minutes away, Cypress Gardens is a 30-minute drive, Sea World is just 10 minutes away, and an express shuttle is available to take guests to the Magic Kingdom and Epcot Center.

FOR KIDS: All through the year on weekends, during the summer, and at holiday time, the resort's professionally staffed childcare center is open from 9:00 A.M. to 11:00 P.M. The center is equipped with games, toys, stuffed animals, books, movies, art supplies, a marionette stage with puppets for the kids to play with, and most appealing of all, an outdoor playground with sand toys, swings, and climbing equipment. The center is available to kids from 3 to 15 years, and parents may drop their kids off and pick them up whenever they'd like. Cost is $25 per day.

During the summer, beginning in May and at holiday times, a more structured program is put into place. Every weekday from 9:30 A.M. to 1:00 P.M. kids 3–6 get together to do "mousercises," make ice cream, put on puppet shows, play games, go on treasure hunts, and take nature walks. Kids from 7 to 11 get their own Youth Adventure Camps, which includes scavenger hunts, kickball, arts and crafts, golf clinics, boat races, and fitness exercises. They can go at it from 8:00 A.M. to 7:00 P.M. The older kids—up to 17—get to do many of the same activities their parents do but with kids of their own age group. They participate in tennis clinics, aerobics classes, weight-training clinics, and beach and water volleyball tournaments, also from 8:00 A.M. to 7:00 P.M. Two other meeting places for teens are the game room, right in the Grotto area, and the nonalcoholic bar called "On the Rocks" (it's made to look like something out of the Flintstones), which is conveniently located right between the pool and the game room.

Baby-sitting may be arranged for $4 per hour, with a minimum of two hours and 50 cents per hour more for each additional child. The resort will also supply cribs with bumpers, car seats, and strollers to rent.

ACCOMMODATIONS: This is an enormous place—750 rooms, 72 suites. A typical room has two double beds, a ceiling fan, a balcony, and measures 13 by 18 feet.

RATES: Rooms in winter range from $150 to $330 per night, in summer, $130 to $255 and in fall, $155 to $275. One-bedroom suites rent for $305 to $1,200, two-bedrooms from $475 to $1,400.

A three-night Gold/Disney package costs $495 to $600 per person. Kids 18 and under may stay with their parents at no extra charge. A second room for the kids is half-price depending on availability at the time of booking.

Stouffer PineIsle Resort
5000 Holiday Road
Buford, Georgia 30518
Telephone: 404-945-8921; 800-HOTELS1
General Manager: Jerry Phelps

IN THEIR OWN WORDS: "We're nestled in a pine forested island on 38,000 acre Lake Lanier, offering a full array of water sports."

DESCRIPTION: The folks at PineIsle consider golf their number one attraction. Their 18-hole golf course is home of the Nestle World Championship and overlooks the lake and the Blue Ridge Mountains. But there's more than just golf. The enormous lake offers a variety of water sports—swimming, skiing, sailing, and boating, fishing and relaxing on PineIsle's own sandy beach. Right nearby the kids will especially love the waterslides and wave pool at Wild Waves Beach and Water Park. Back on land, there's tennis, horseback riding, and a fitness center for guests. Friends of ours, a family from Nashville, visit here regularly with an 8-year-old and a teenage bicycling freak. They adore it.

FOR KIDS: PineIsle offers two supervised kids' programs—one called First Mates, which is for kids 3–6 and operates from 9:30 A.M. to 12:30 P.M., and the other, Kids Krew for ages 7–12, which operates from 9:30 A.M. to 2:30 P.M. The groups meet daily from Memorial Day through Labor Day and on weekends the rest of the year. The programs are free and are held rain or shine. Kids may join at any time of the day. A picnic lunch can be arranged for $3. Some of the activities planned for the First Mates include magic shows, feeding ducks, nature hunts, pony rides, and water balloon games; Kids Krew participants do seashell crafts, have a magic workshop, learn knot tying, and puppetry. Teens are welcome to join any of the Kids Krew activities, but if they prefer they can choose from some of the events that are regularly scheduled during the day—activities such as poolside bingo, design-a-T-shirt, aerobics, ice cream socials, limbo contests, and, in season, lake cruises. The pool and game room are open 24 hours, which should make most teenagers very happy. Baby-sitting is available for $4.50 per hour for one child, an extra $1 per hour for each additional child; the minimum is four hours. Horseback riding, golf and tennis lessons are all available for kids.

ACCOMMODATIONS: The 250 rooms have balconies with views of either the pine forests or the lake. Thirty rooms have their own whirlpool spa on an enclosed patio, and four of the five two-bedroom suites are penthouses with a sundeck, wet bar, and wood-burning fireplace.

RATES: A standard room for two costs $100; kids 18 and under are free; a deluxe room is $130, and suites range from $275 to $490. For the modified American plan, add $36 per person per day and $20 for kids 12 and under.

Wild Dunes Resort
5757 Palm Boulevard
Isle of Palms, South Carolina 29451
Mailing Address: P.O. Box 1410, Charleston, South Carolina 25402
Telephone: 803-886-6000 or 800-845-8880
President: Michael F. Tinkey

IN THEIR OWN WORDS: "Wild Dunes provides fun for the entire family with activities for everyone. The wide spectrum of programs offered allows parents and children to play together during their vacation and to enjoy some time apart."

DESCRIPTION: Just 15 miles north of the historic district of Charleston, Wild Dunes offers 2½ miles of beach. Since the original property was never cleared and leveled for plantation farming like so much of the land in the area, it still features rolling sand dunes and a variety of subtropical trees—palmettos, pines, magnolias, cedars, myrtles, and live oaks—some as old as 300 years. Both golf and tennis are superb at Wild Dunes. For golfers, there are two challenging courses: the 18-hole Wild Dunes Golf Links, designed by Tom Fazio, the reason that the resort won a gold medal from *Golf* magazine as one of the top 12 golf resorts in America, and the Wild Dunes Harbor Course, located alongside the yacht harbor, where "preserved sand dunes and the forces of nature rarely allow the course to play the same way twice." The resort's racquet club offers 19 Har-tru courts, eight lighted for evening play, and one hard-surface practice court. It has been rated one of the top 50 tennis facilities in the U.S. by both *Tennis* magazine and *Tennis Week*. If that's not enough for the sports-minded, resort guests may also swim in the surf or in one of two pools, go boating, fishing, jogging, windsurfing, or bicycling.

FOR KIDS: If your kids are as interested in tennis or golf as you are, you can enroll them in either the daily clinics for junior golfers or, for future tennis players, either the junior introductory program (for kids 6–16) or the junior mini-camp. The mini-camp is offered to kids 8–16 and cost $8 per session or $27 for four one-hour sessions. The resort also offers a general children's program during the summer and at school vacation times. The program is divided into two age groups. The four-to-seven-year-olds join the Dune Bugs' Club, with different activities each day, including arts and crafts, games, and parent-child swims. Half-day sessions are available from 9:00 A.M. to 12:30 P.M. or 1:00 P.M. to 4:30 P.M. The cost is $15 per child per day or $70 for a full week (the second child in the family gets a reduced rate of $12 and $55, respectively). Older kids, from 8 to 12 years, have a full-day program from 9:00 A.M. to 4:30 P.M. specially designed for this "high energy age level" to include beach games, pool activities, arts and crafts, lunch, and an afternoon "mystery adventure," which might include miniature golf, tours of nearby forts and battleships, fishing, or crabbing. The cost for the full day program is $30 for the first child, $25 for each additional or $140 and $115 for a full week. During the summer, the resort schedules activities that will get the parents and kids together (aerobics, bingo, an island scavenger hunt, "wacky water sports"). In the evenings kids' pizza parties, movies, and a special teen beach party are all possibilities. If baby-sitting is required, the concierge can provide parents with a list of recommended baby-sitters—the arrangements are left to the parents.

ACCOMMODATIONS: One- to four-bedroom villas and cottages are available. All have washers and dryers, fully equipped kitchens, and linens. Daily rates include daily housekeeping services, weekly rates include departure housekeeping only.

RATES: Wild Dunes offers special family vacation packages: the Mini Week Family Plan of three days and three nights costs $580 for a two-bedroom oceanside villa during the summer, $445 in winter; a seven-day, seven-night package cost $1,110 and $805 respectively. The three-day package includes a $50 gift certificate toward resort activities; for seven days, the certificate is worth $100.

Sundial Beach and Tennis Resort
1451 Middle Gulf Drive
Sanibel Island, Florida 33957
Telephone: 813-472-4151 or 800-237-4184
General Manager: Michael Peceri

IN THEIR OWN WORDS: "There's something mystical about this tiny paradise. When you cross over the three-mile bridge from mainland, Sanibel Island begins to cast its magical spell on you. It's a remote and relaxing place. Yet full of natural splendor and activity."

DESCRIPTION: There are 13 tennis courts in all, seven laykold, six Har-tru. The pro shop will matchmake for you, give you private lessons or a clinic, and offer social tournaments. Golf is five minutes away at Dunes Country Club, or you can try sailing, biking, and swimming in five outdoor pools. Throughout the year there are a range of family-type activities scheduled by a full-time recreation director—face painting, tennis clinics, movies, bingo, mom and tot swims, scavenger hunts, and so on.

FOR KIDS: During the summer there's a camp for kids that runs every day of the week from 10:00 A.M. to 2:00 P.M. For Tiny Tots—kids who are potty-trained, 3–6—there are arts and crafts, water play, creative dramatics, games, songs, riddles and stories, nature awareness, beach walks, and more. For kids 7 years and older there are water games, sports, crafts, cookouts, beach parties, water Olympics, and shell crafts. The cost is $10 and includes lunch.

During peak season, November through April, although there's no formal kids' program, the Rec Department coordinates activities daily for kids, teens, and families.

Baby-sitting is available for the youngest, for $5 per hour.

ACCOMMODATIONS: Possibilities include 400 suites—efficiencies, one- and two-bedroom units with full kitchens. Most accommodations have private, screened balconies overlooking the gulf or courtyards. Cribs are available for $5 per night.

RATES: Kids under 14 stay free in the same room as their parents. A two-bedroom suite costs $155 to $320, depending on the season. An "Island Vacation Package" that includes unlimited tennis and the children's program costs $111 to $208 per person for a four-day, three-night stay for four in a two-bedroom suite (this package is not available at holiday time).

Innisbrook Resort
P.O. Drawer 1088
Tarpon Springs, Florida 34286
Telephone: 813-942-2000 or 800-237-0157
General Manager: Cary Brent

IN THEIR OWN WORDS: "Innisbrook is wooded acres rich with gleaming lakes, rolling hills, emerald fairways. Innisbrook is hibiscus, azaleas, citrus groves, and Spanish moss on pine trees. Innisbrook is a natural habitat alive with peacocks, mallards, largemouth bass, and stately turtles. It even has a wildlife preserve."

DESCRIPTION: Besides the natural beauty of the spot, Innisbrook offers excellent golf and tennis, a recreation center, a basketball court, bike rentals, a game room, a playground and miniature golf course ($1 for unlimited play), a par course fitness trail, a fitness center with a full line of Universal and Future Exercise equipment, aerobics, fishing, and five heated swimming pools. There are three golf courses—the 27-hole Copperhead has been ranked number one in the state of Florida, the Island course is the first constructed at Innisbrook, and the Sandpiper is the shortest of the three. The Innisbrook Golf Institute, directed by Jay Overton, is well known. The Institute offers a full three-night teaching package as well as daily clinics; private instruction is available, too, in what the staff calls "golf's most beautiful classroom."

The Tennis and Racquetball Center includes 18 courts (eleven clay, seven hard), seven lighted for play at night; whirlpool baths; a complete fitness center and aerobics workout room; a video training room; a pro shop; and a cocktail lounge. Innisbrook is home of the Australian Tennis Institute, founded and directed by former Australia Davis Cup player Terry Addison. The Institute features stroke improvement, movement drills, strategy for singles and doubles play, slow motion video critique, and more. Students are grouped by playing level, never more than three or four students per instructor.

FOR KIDS: "Zoo Crew" is the name of the activities program Innisbrook operates for kids 4 to 11. Kids are divided into two groups— 4-to-6-year-olds and 7-to-11-year-olds. Zoo Crew runs all summer long and during school vacations. Hours are 9:00 A.M. to 4:00 P.M. For 4-to-6-year-olds, a shorter 9:00 A.M. to noon stay is possible. Counselors are students of education who come from all over the United States to supervise the kids on excursions, at golf and tennis clinics, with arts and crafts, games, pool play, and a variety of theme days, such as "Kids Can Cook" or "Under the Big Top." Kids can be registered by the day or week. The cost is $15 per day, $11 per half-day, $3.50 extra for lunch, $70 for the week.

When Zoo Crew is not in session, a supervised activities program is offered that includes activities from 9:00 A.M. to noon and from 1:00 to 4:00 P.M. (with supervised playground time until 5:00 P.M. for anyone who wants the extra hour).

Lots of activities appropriate for teenagers are scheduled throughout the week at the resort, for instance, Junior Golf Clinics, bike tours, water games, basketball tourneys, and aerobics. Every Friday night there's a "Teen Happy Hour" followed by a "Teen Bash" for kids 12 to 17.

Baby-sitting is available for $3 per hour, day and evening.

And one more thing: Innisbrook offers week-long Junior Golf Institutes in July and August for kids 13 to 17 years of age. Kids staying with their parents can sign up and spend their days at the Institute.

ACCOMMODATIONS: Innisbrook's accommodations are all condos, which the resort prefers to call "lodges." They're two-story buildings with one to three bedrooms. Cribs are available at no extra charge.

RATES: A holiday plan—for Easter, Thanksgiving, and Christmas vacations—costs $60 to $79 per person double occupancy and includes one hour of tennis daily, daily golf and tennis clinics, and unlimited use of the fitness center. There's a three-night minimum, and kids 18 and under in the same room with parents are free.

Sea Palms Golf and Tennis Resort
5445 Frederica Road
St. Simons Island, Georgia 31522
Telephone: 912-638-3351 or 1-800-841-6268
General Manager: John Dow

IN THEIR OWN WORDS: "Since Sea Palms is both a country club and a resort, it caters to a variety of people and offers diverse activities. A beautiful resort, combined with the historical island itself, makes Sea Palms a perfect vacation choice."

DESCRIPTION: This is a resort/residential community set in the heart of St. Simon's Island, one of Georgia's 12 Golden Isles. Sea Palms has 27 holes of championship golf—courses that wind their way through old oaks and sparkling lagoons. The 18-hole Tall Pines course is the site of the annual Georgia PGA Challenge Matches. Mike Cook, the expert we quoted earlier, teaches golf at Sea Palms, and group and private lessons are available. For tennis enthusiasts, there's a three-year-old Health and Racquet Club with 12 composition courts, three of which are lighted for night play. Other possibilities for fun include swimming in a pool that's heated and covered in winter, an exercise room, saunas, a whirlpool, and a fitness course. Guests also like to take island tours, sail, horseback ride, and fish. During the summer there are weekly aerobics, weight, and exercise classes.

FOR KIDS: Keith Massengill is in charge of recreation services at Sea Palms, and he's organized an extensive program for kids. The "Children's Program" for kids 4 to 6 offers a choice of a morning or afternoon session. The hours are Monday through Saturday 9:00 A.M. to 12:30 P.M. or 1:00 to 4:30 P.M. from Memorial Day to Labor Day and during holiday periods. Kids swim, make shell crafts, sing, hear stories, and make ice cream. The cost is $8 per kid. The "Youth Program" for kids 7 to 12 is a full-day program. Lunch is included, and kids play games, go on scavenger hunts, have their own Olympics, and so on. Day trips to Glynn County, Jacksonville, or Savannah are scheduled every Wednesday. The cost is $16 per kid. For teens (13 to 17) Sea Palms offers afternoon and evening activities—windsurfing, cable waterskiing, miniature golf, and so on. In the evening there are movies, tournaments, and teen dinners. Every Saturday a teen trip is scheduled.

Every day at 2:00 P.M. there's an all-family program activity—bingo or water basketball, and at 3:00 P.M. there's a pick-up game of volleyball. At night there are movies and other activities for the whole family to participate in together.

Baby-sitting can be arranged through the front office. All sitters are screened by the personnel department. During high season, give them a week's notice to find a baby-sitter and expect to pay $4 per hour.

ACCOMMODATIONS: The choices include hotel rooms and one-, two-, and three-bedroom villas and suites. Cribs are available for $5 per night.

RATES: A "Warm-up" package includes accommodations with parlor and fully equipped kitchen, free tennis, free golf and tennis clinics, full privileges at the Health and Racquet Club, and a free discount coupon book. The cost is $750 per week for a two-bedroom suite in the deluxe category from November 1 to January 31. Kids under 14 are free.

Mauna Kea Beach Hotel
P.O. Box 218
Kohala Coast, Hawaii 96743
Telephone: 808-882-7222 or 800-228-3000
General Manager: Adi Kohler

IN THEIR OWN WORDS: "Mauna Kea was recently voted 'America's Number 1 Favorite Resort' in a national independent poll of over 15,000 CEOs and presidents of top U.S. corporations. This accolade is only the latest in a long lei of awards that stretches back to the opening by Laurence Rockefeller 24 years ago. . . . You'll find a commitment to excellence in every detail. It begins with a spectacular location, a perfect climate, and Hawaii's finest white sand crescent beach."

DESCRIPTION: The hotel takes its name and inspiration from the nearby snow-topped Mauna Kea, literally "White Mountain" in Hawaiian. The president of the United States and the emperor and empress of Japan have stayed here; art objects from all over the world adorn the grounds. Buildings are terraced to make the most of the panoramic views and, at the same time, to assure privacy for guests. Interior walkways and courtyards bloom with carefully landscaped gardens. The ambience, natural beauty, and warm welcome for families has brought California friends of ours back to the Mauna Kea every year since their now 10-year-old son visited as a babe in arms.

Mauna Kea may very well be golf heaven. Rated among "America's 100 greatest" and "Hawaii's finest" golf courses by *Golf Digest,* the course was designed by Robert Trent Jones, Sr., and built on a 5,000-year-old lava flow that spills into the Pacific. The course, the centerpiece of the resort, rolls over 230 acres of lava hills. The golf pro is John "JD" Ebeksberger. Jack Nicklaus, after competing in a tournament there, was quoted as saying, "It was more fun to play than any course I know." Not a bad review.

And for tennis lovers, too, Mauna Kea offers great possibilities. Rated one of the "50 great Tennis Resorts in America" by *Tennis* magazine and recipient of five-star honors from *World Tennis* magazine, Mauna Kea's tennis park includes 13 plexipave courts. As you'd expect, it has a pro shop, racquet rental, ball machines, and high-tech video-assisted private instruction. Tennis clinics and round-robin doubles tournaments are held every day. The director of tennis is Jay Paulson, who has served as practice partner for Bjorn Borg, Arthur Ashe, and Ken Rosewall.

Want more than tennis and golf? Mauna Kea offers a beach; a freshwater, palm-shaded pool; and snorkeling, surfing, sailing, windsurfing, scuba diving, horseback riding (kids must be at least 8 years to ride), deep-sea fishing, helicopter sightseeing (a bit pricy at $225 per person for an hour "volcanoes flight"). The resort offers three walking tours in the course of a week—a tour of the hotel and gardens, tours of the hotel's Pacific Rim collection given by a professor of art history, and a back-of-the-house tour. Interspersed throughout the week at the resort are Hawaiian crafts classes, movies (contemporary and vintage, complete with hot buttered popcorn), aquatics, volleyball, and dancercise. At night the resort has cocktail music on the Terrace or in the Batik Bar and dancing every night in the Batik Terrace and in the Pavilion. Once a week the resort hosts a luau, traditional food followed by a show of ancient chants and dances of the island of Hawaii.

FOR KIDS: Mid-June through Labor Day, again at Christmas and Easter vacation time there's a supervised program for kids 5 to 12. Trained counselors are available 9:15 A.M. to 4:00 P.M. and again from 6:30 to 8:30 P.M. Some of the activities kids can expect are sand castle contests, Hawaiian crafts and games, nature walks, scavenger hunts, piñata parties, and hot dog roasts.

For kids too young for the organized program baby-sitters are available for $4 per hour day or night.

ACCOMMODATIONS: Families may choose guest rooms that feature spacious lanais (patios) facing the ocean, the beach, or the mountain. Beachfront accommodations feature bedroom/sitting rooms and give families direct access to the beach. The resort is proud of its interiors—rugs and cotton bedspreads loomed in India especially for the hotel and original art on the walls. Some families may prefer to rent one of the villas at Mauna Kea: full vacation homes with two bedrooms within walking distance of the hotel complete with individual pools, lanais, skylighted kitchens, and marble bathtubs overlooking private gardens. Another possibility are the Fairway Homes, three or four bedrooms completely furnished and including a private pool.

RATES: Modified American plan rate, including breakfast and dinner, for a beachfront room is $336 to $481 for double occupancy; the difference in price depends on what your view is—a mountain view is the less expensive, an ocean view is more. Kids 18 and under stay for free, but meals are $58 for kids over 9, $25 for 3–8, and free for under 2s.

Birch Bay Golf Resort and Country Inn
1771 Birch Drive West
Brainerd, Minnesota 56401
Telephone 218-963-4488
Owners: Butch and Kathy Brown, Tom and Peggy Kientzle

IN THEIR OWN WORDS: "Birch Bay has been our year-round home since 1971 and we'd love to share it with you. Because we have only five housekeeping units on the lake (seven are in the country inn) families will small children feel safe; they find it easy to watch their kids because the beach and the playground are all close to the cabins."

DESCRIPTION: You can golf right out your back door on a nine-hole par 36 course. "We have the finest bent grass greens in the area and watered fairways and greens." All guests at Birch Bay are entitled to one free beginner golf lesson and, once they get hooked, can sign up for a golf clinic. Tennis players have a court they can use for free and, there's a sandy beach, snorkeling in the clear waters of Agate Lake, hiking trails, canoeing, and, not far away, a horseback riding stable. One great feature for parents who want to golf but who have kids too young to join them is the free baby-sitting program for golfers—one afternoon a week you'll be assigned a baby-sitter at no extra cost.

FOR KIDS: Birch Bay offers a children's program during the summer (the resort is open from May 1 to October 1) for kids aged 3 to 12, three days a week from 10:00 A.M. to noon. The first hour is spent on a nature hike, the second playing supervised games. At other times, baby-sitting is available for only $2 per hour.

ACCOMMODATIONS: Probably best for families are the house-keeping cottages that overlook the lake. All have carpeting, complete kitchens and bathrooms, and come complete with bedding, pots, pans, and dishes. There's an extra charge for towels and maid service. Another possibility is to stay in a room in the inn and take advantage of a special family plan that offers a second room for half price. Although Birch Bay does not have its own dining room, a restaurant is within walking distance, and there are ten other restaurants to choose from within a five-mile radius.

RATES: The folks at Birch Bay offer a number of package plans. A sampling includes the "Deluxe Weekend" package, three nights and four days in a cabin with use of all facilities for $340 to $410 for two (depending on which cabin you choose) with an extra $30 for each additional person 12 and over. Nongolfing children 11 and under are free. A similar midweek plan costs less. For two rooms in the inn shared by one family (one room with a double bed and one with two twin beds), the special rate is $54 for both rooms.

Ruttger's Bay Lake Lodge
Route 2, P.O. Box 400
Deerwood, Minnesota 56444
Telephone: 218-678-2885 or 800-328-0312
General Manager: Fred Bobich

IN THEIR OWN WORDS: "Our resort is in its 91st year and it's been owned and operated by the same family since it began. We are the oldest family resort in Minnesota. We have always paid special attention to families with children, and our food, served in a log dining room that overlooks the lake, is known throughout the area."

DESCRIPTION: What began as a rustic fishing camp has grown into a full-sized resort. Ruttger's Bay is open all year round but is probably best known for its golf in summer (cross-country skiing on the golf course is fun in winter, too). It offers two nine-hole courses and six tennis courts. When you tire of those two sports, you can try swimming (there's an indoor and an outdoor pool), boating, fishing, sailing, a spa, sauna, hiking, and canoeing. Ruttger's Bay likes to host family reunions—they'll do everything from providing "excellent accommodations to handling arrangements for a family portrait."

FOR KIDS: From Memorial Day to Labor Day, Ruttger's offers a program they call Kids' Camp. It's meant for kids from 4 to 12 and runs 9:00 A.M. to noon. The program is free to guests and includes crafts, treasure hunts, games, fishing, and pizza parties. Baby-sitting is available.

ACCOMMODATIONS: Guests have several choices: lodge rooms, lakefront cottages, villas (next to the indoor pool), golf course condominiums, and Bay Lake Townhomes.

RATES: You may choose from a European plan or an American plan. Since there are a variety of package plans available, we'll give you just a sample: Five nights or more in summer cost from $69 to $82 per person per night, which includes lodging, breakfast and dinner, children's program, maid service, and unlimited use of the tennis court, golf course, and other facilities; for kids up to age 2, $7.50 per night; 2–3 years, $20; 4–19, $40. If you prefer to stay in one of the Bay Lake Town homes, located one mile east of the resort, you can have a full kitchen and a fireplace in a two-level, two-bedroom home for $155 per night. The town homes have their own outdoor and indoor pools, volleyball and tennis courts, sauna and whirlpool.

Grand View Lodge and Tennis Club
May–October: 134 South Nokomis
Nisswa, Minnesota 56468
Telephone: 218-963-2234 or 800-345-9625
October–May: 3950 West 49½ Street
Edina, Minnesota 55424
Telephone: 612-925-3109
General Manager: Mark Ronnei

IN THEIR OWN WORDS: "We are a National Historic Site located on Big Gull Lake and all of our business is families. . . . The phone starts ringing when the last snow melts."

DESCRIPTION: A long way from the Florida-style tennis and golf resort in miles and style as well, Grand View is open from early May to early October and is the quintessential northern lake spa, right down to the deer heads mounted on the wall of the pine-paneled lobby. The resort is a cluster of 50 cabins with a cedar log lodge as a centerpiece, built along the north shore of Big Gull Lake. Golfers enjoy the nine-hole Grand View course carved through stands of white birch and pine trees, and tennis players can take advantage of seven courts. The tennis pro offers a range of tennis activities—instructional clinics, tournaments, and social mixers. Kids 8 to 18 get free group lessons. Use of the courts and golf course is free to guests of the lodge. Besides tennis and golf, a big attraction is the lake itself—motorboating, waterskiing, canoeing, swimming, and surf sailing are all possible, and the resort's marina can equip you for whatever water sport you choose. For those who prefer, there's a semienclosed, heated pool. Adult get-togethers include dances, bingo, backgammon lessons, bridge, and local sightseeing. The atmosphere is casual.

FOR KIDS: Four counselors supervise a children's program for kids 3 to 12 from June to September. The kids are divided into two groups, 3-to-5-year-olds in one, 6-to-12-year-olds in the other. The day starts at 8:45 or 9:30—the choice is yours—and includes nature hikes, beach days, Olympics, arts and crafts, movies, gardening, and lots of other carefully planned activities. Excursions to places of interest nearby are scheduled, too, throughout the week. The hours of the program are until noon for the younger kids and then again 5:30 to 8:00 for dinner and more fun. The older kids meet until noon, then again from 1:30 to 3:30 P.M. and 5:30 to 8:00 P.M. (If you'd like, your kids can have lunch with the counselors; just be sure to arrange it by 9:30 in the morning.)

Baby-sitters are available for $2.50 per hour with three-hour advance notice.

ACCOMMODATIONS: Most guests stay in family cottages with one to six bedrooms. All have decks, views of the lake, fireplaces, and refrigerators, and some have kitchenettes.

RATES: The rates are structured according to the modified American plan, which includes accommodations; breakfast and dinner; golf; tennis; the children's program; use of fishing boats, canoes, and kayaks; maid service; and a variety of daily social activities. A stay in a family cottage that sleeps two to five would be $65 to $95 per adult per night with special rates for kids as follows: 6 to 12, two-thirds the adult rate; 3 to 5, one-half the rate; and under 3, no charge. Nonmeal plans are available early and late in the season. A few housekeeping cabins nearby are available for $450 to $850 per week.

Kiawah Island Resort
P.O. Box 2941201
Charleston, South Carolina 29412
Telephone: 803-768-2121 or 800-845-2471
General Manager: Randy Kolls

IN THEIR OWN WORDS: "The island's 10-mile stretch of wide, sandy beach along the Atlantic Ocean is one of the finest on the East Coast. Kiawah is a quiet place, designed with the family in mind. . . . Kiawah offers all the services and opportunities of most major resorts, but is part of a setting which is unlike any place else. The beach, the forests, the wildlife and the ambience of Kiawah are what people remember and tell their friends about."

DESCRIPTION: Just 21 miles from Charleston, the island is divided into two sections, east and west, and each has its own golf course and tennis courts. The island has both residential and resort areas, and the two are kept quite separate. The West Beach Tennis Center features 12 composition and two lighted hard courts, ball machines, and a practice backboard. The staff there can pair you with a suitable partner and offers clinic and private lessons. The

East Beach Center has nine clay courts, three hard courts, and audio-visual instruction facilities, a pro shop, and automated practice court. Two of the courts are designed for tournament play. (It was Kiawah's tennis pro, Roy Barth, whom we interviewed at the beginning of this chapter.)

The golf course on West Beach is the Marsh Point Golf Course, designed by Gary Player, with water on 13 holes, salt marsh on another three. The Turtle Point Golf Course on the East Beach was designed by Jack Nicklaus and features three oceanside holes that offer golfers who can take their eyes off the ball a stunning view of the ocean. A third course, Osprey Point, was designed by Tom Fazio. It runs through the island's tropical forests and includes water on 15 holes.

Night Heron Park, a 21-acre park near the ocean, has playing fields, a bike rental shop with a video game room, a recreation building, and a 25-meter swimming pool. Guests at Kiawah also like to beachcomb, walk, and try out the 1.1-mile fitness course. When we visited, our favorite activity of all was the jeep safari led by a guide who told us all about island history and the fascinating ecology of the area.

FOR KIDS: From June to August and during Christmas and Easter breaks, guests may take advantage of supervised activities for kids 4 to 12 such as face painting, ice cream making, treasure hunts, puppetry, and games. For kids 4 to 6 the 9:30 to noon session cost $10 per day without lunch; for 7-to-12-year-olds the charge is $25 for a 9:30 A.M. to 4:00 P.M. day with lunch included. If you want a baby-sitter the resort staff will supply you with a list of names. Tennis and golf lessons are available to youngsters.

ACCOMMODATIONS: You have a choice of rooms in an inn or a one-, two-, or three-bedroom villa all to yourself. The inn has 150 rooms, all with balconies. Villas may be beachside, parkside, or linkside; all have fully equipped kitchens, decks and screened porches.

RATES: Double-bedded rooms in the inn are $125 per night; family packages of three days, two nights in a two-bedroom villa cost $458 for a family of four; eight days, seven nights $997. Cribs are available at no extra charge.

Hyatt Regency Hilton Head
Oceanfront at Palmetto Dunes
P.O. Box 6167
Hilton Head Island, South Carolina 29938
Telephone: 803-785-1234 or 800-223-1234
General Manager: Nee Inabinett

IN THEIR OWN WORDS: "This is a luxury oceanfront resort hotel that offers a relaxed, friendly atmosphere. Families are encouraged to visit. There's something about our wonderful ocean and outstanding recreational opportunities that make for a fun time for all."

DESCRIPTION: The hotel fronts on a three-mile stretch of private beach, and every conceivable kind of aquatic sport is possible—waterskiing, windsurfing, sailing, shell collecting, and sunbathing, plus indoor and outdoor swimming pools and a large wading pool for the little ones. The resort features three 18-hole golf courses—the George Fazio Course and the Robert Trent Jones Course, overlooking the ocean, are among the nation's top-ranked courses. Tennis is what the public relations people call "only a serve away" at the Rod Laver Tennis Center with 25 courts, six lighted for night play.

The wide beach is one of the nicest on the island. There's a great kid's playground a few minutes from the hotel just down the beach. Across from the main hotel entrance is a bicycle shop with rentals for all shapes and sizes. Hilton Head has special bike paths, making this mode of transportation particularly appealing.

FOR KIDS: "Pelican Kids" is a camp program for kids 3–15 that runs from Memorial Day to Labor Day and at vacation times and on weekends, from 10:00 A.M. to 4:00 P.M. and 6:00 to 10:00 P.M. Pelican Kids give prop plays, play "pillo polo," get swimming lessons, and do arts and crafts. The day, with lunch included, costs $25. One-to-one baby-sitting is also available with 24-hour advance notice for $5 per hour. For teens, there are teen aerobics and every week a Teen Night with fun, games, and music by the pool or on the beach. The counselors are an unusually cheerful group of young men and women who truly enjoy being with the kids, and the kids know it.

ACCOMMODATIONS: There are 505 rooms altogether, all with two double beds or one king-size bed, a desk, sofa, television, and balcony. Cribs are available at no extra charge.

RATES: The "Family Vacation" package, which includes a gift for the kids, daily breakfast, and dinner buffet, admission to Hyattspa, and a day of family recreation, costs $488 for two nights, $706 for three, and $1,403 for seven for a family of four in high season; $348, $496 and $1,018 respectively in low season (slightly more for an ocean view). Second rooms for a family are available at a reduced rate; see page 50.

The Westin Resort
135 South Port Royal Drive
Hilton Head Island, South Carolina 29928
Telephone: 803-681-4000 or 800-228-3000
General Manager: J. Pat Burton

IN THEIR OWN WORDS: "Golf, tennis, and croquet are immediately within reach, with some of the finest facilities in the world."

DESCRIPTION: The Guest Relations staff is available from 8:00 in the morning to 7:00 at night to help arrange for tennis at the Port Royal Racquet Club (16 courts, eight clay, six laykold, two grass, and six lighted for night games); golf at the Port Royal Golf Club, 36 holes of PGA-rated championship golf; horseback riding; massage; croquet, charter fishing cruises; or use of the health club with exercise equipment, saunas, steam room, and indoor pool.

Physically, the resort is breathtaking. It's large but still offers many smaller nooks and crannies for lots of privacy indoors and out.

FOR KIDS: From April to October, the resort offers "Kids' Corner"—a seven-day-a-week program for kids 4 to 12 from 10:00 A.M. to 4:00 P.M. run out of an Indian tepee behind the pool area. Activities include pool games, beach games, scavenger hunts, arts and crafts, and in the evening, a pizza party, movie, and quiet games. When it rains, there are indoor-type plans—charades, crafts, movies, and so forth.

From 6:00 to 10:00 there's an evening program that includes beach walks, volleyball games, movies, popcorn popping, and more. The program is free. Teens 13 and up participate in supervised activities such as waterskiing, sailing, miniature golf, and trips to Harbour Town. For teens, the charge is $5 to $10; meals are not included for either program. Baby-sitting is available for $5 per hour.

ACCOMMODATIONS: Suites and connecting suites are nice and roomy for families; regular rooms are available as well.

RATES: A Family Fun package in high season (March to November) of three nights with connecting rooms—one for the parents, the other for up to three kids—costs $512 and $247.50. If your stay is in midweek, you can have a fourth night free.

Marriott's Hilton Head Resort

130 Shipyard Drive
Hilton Head Island, South Carolina 29928
Telephone: 803-842-2400 or 800-334-1881
General Manager: Angus Cotton

IN THEIR OWN WORDS: "Here you can have a full vacation experience without ever leaving the hotel's 800 private acres."

DESCRIPTION: For your pleasure there are a health spa, indoor and outdoor pools, bikes to rent, 27 holes of golf, and 24 tennis courts, all within walking distance of your room.

FOR KIDS: "Kids World" is a structured program supervised by trained counselors that operates from 12:30 to 4:30 every day of the week during the summer and school breaks. (There have to be at least six kids signed up to have the program.) It costs $12 per child, and lunch is available at an extra charge. Kids 6 to 11 play lawn games and pool games, go to the beach, have arts and crafts, and take bike hikes. A nice feature of the program is a trip with Captain Zodiac, where kids seek out wild dolphins and beachcomb for sand dollars and shells. Baby-sitting can be arranged for $5 per hour through the Hospitality Desk.

ACCOMMODATIONS: Rooms are in a multistoried complex; some suites are available. Cribs are available at no extra charge.

RATES: A family rate for up to four people in a room costs $399 for four nights, five days.

Wilson Lodge at Oglebay

Route 88
Wheeling, West Virginia 26003
Telephone: 304-242-3000 or 800-624-6988
General Manager: G. Randolph Worls

IN THEIR OWN WORDS: "Oglebay is a family-oriented destination resort park set in the hills of Northern West Virginia. We have a 204-room lodge with a cozy atmosphere where youngsters are always made to feel comfortable."

DESCRIPTION: It all started as a farm, the elegant summer estate of Colonel Earl Oglebay, an industrialist who willed the property to the citizens of Wheeling "for recreational and educational purposes." Oglebay continues to be a nature sanctuary featuring the excellent 65-acre Good Children's Zoo, the Mansion Museum, (the colonel's summer home), a nature center, a garden center, and green house. Throughout the year the park is the site of a number of festivals, including, from mid-November to the beginning of February, the holiday-inspired Festival of Lights. And there's more: two golf courses, indoor and outdoor tennis courts, outdoor and indoor pools, fishing and boating on Schenk Lake, and in winter, downhill and cross-country skiing. In summer, there's entertainment in a 2,500-seat amphitheater, and all year round kids can enjoy two playgrounds and an observatory and planetarium.

FOR KIDS: Guests at the Oglebay may enroll kids age 4 to 15 for a day or a week at a choice of day camps. Three of the camps are based at the zoo: Beast and Little Tykes is especially for kids 4 to 6 and is meant to introduce the little ones to nature and animals. Participants handle some of the gentler zoo animals, do crafts, and share stories and games and songs. Zoo Discovery Camp is for kids 7 to 11, who are given the chance to observe the unique characteristics of a number of animals; they get to feed some of them as well. For "graduates" of the Discovery Camp, there's an Advanced Zoo Camp, where campers study animal anatomy, camouflage, ecology, and animal adaptations and get to spend a morning working as a zookeeper. If animals aren't your kids' thing, there's also a sports camp for 11-to-14-year-olds and a regular day camp for kids from 4 to 14. Hours are from 9:00 A.M. to 3:00 P.M. from June through the middle of August. Oglebay operates the only "Caddy Camp" in the country. Youngsters participate without parents. Ask for details well in advance—it's very popular. Instruction for kids is available in tennis, boating, and riding. Baby-sitting is available for $3 per hour.

ACCOMMODATIONS: The choice is yours: a room in the lodge, one of 24 chalets, or one of the 35 cabins that are rented by the week only during the summer. Cabins have fireplaces, two to four bedrooms, one or two baths, and large living rooms.

RATES: Kids under 18 are free. Oglebay offers a number of packages for holidays. Their summer package, available on weekdays only, costs $59 per person per night based on double occupancy in the lodge with an extra $5 for children. Cabins large enough for eight to 14 people are $500 to $685 per week. Cribs may be rented for $5 per night.

10

Skiing

Skiing is another of our favorite topics. Skiing creates a wonderful family vacation just as long as you pick the right spot and make sure that there are facilities for every member of your family. Ski resorts have really been the leaders in providing family vacation facilities. In this chapter we first present some general information on planning a ski trip with some invaluable advice from experts— Billy Kidd, Christy Mueller Northrop, and Cal Coniff. Then we go on to list some mountains where we think you can have some fun. The information about each ski resort centers around their children's programs. We want you to take a look at what there is and then, when an area appeals to you, to contact the address listed for all the details. *Travel with Your Children* (TWYCH) publishes a guide called *Skiing with Children* every year. It's a compilation of almost 100 ski areas in the United States and Canada with detailed information on each. The entire guide can be purchased for $25 plus $4 shipping.

There's a special discounted price to subscribers to their newsletter, *Family Travel Times*. The guide goes into great detail on individual ski nurseries. It tells you if you need reservations so your kids won't get closed out, how much it's going to cost you (be prepared to pay from $18 to $45 or more per day), who will be responsible for your child at lunchtime (do you really want to stop skiing at 11:00 A.M. because there's a long lift line and you may not be back in time to pick up the kids for lunch?), and more. In short, it answers all those nitty-gritty questions so you can plan the best stay for your family on and off the slopes.

Choosing A Ski Destination

Start by evaluating the individual needs of your children, beginning with the youngest. Carefully determine whether each child will fit into the program geared to his or her age group. Then make certain that the ski terrain meets your own needs and that the resort has all the features beside skiing that you may want from a vacation: restaurants, interesting night life, swimming, tennis, and aerobics. Many ski resorts recognize how expensive it can be to get a family onto skis, so they've come up with special family packages. Shop around for savings, such as Steamboat's "kids ski free program" (free lodging, lifts, and rentals for kids), Okemo's free midweek nursery, and Smuggler's Notch's "Family Fest" weeks. Try to find a resort that has lifts and trails designed for all ages and levels. A variety of trails off one lift means a family can go up the mountain together and then ski down the trail that suits each one best. Remember that virtually all discounts are blacked out over the Christmas–New Year's period.

Choosing Accommodations

Budget will have a lot to do with choice of accommodation. Remember what we've said before, though: a short, great vacation is better than a long, unsuccessful one, so if you have to sacrifice time for comfort, do it. Stay as close to the lifts, childcare, or ski school as you can afford. One quarter-mile may not seem like a long way, but at the end of the day when you're carrying ski equipment and an exhausted child, the distance will seem endless. Slopeside accommodations are particularly nice because not everyone has to come and go together. If a slopeside accommodation seems too expensive, compromise. Stay in a one-bedroom condo instead of a two-bedroom. Ask about daily maid service. Sometimes there's an extra charge for it, but we feel it's well worth it.

If you don't have your own transportation—and often it's not necessary that you do—check out the area's local transportation system and/or whether your accommodation facility has a courtesy van to and from the mountain.

Evaluating Nursery Programs

Some of the questions you should ask about any nursery are the following:

- What age range do they accommodate?
- What are the daily activities?
- Do the kids go outside? Outdoor fun is one of the joys of a ski vacation even for the little kids.
- What is the ratio of care givers to children? Children under 4 years need one adult to four children, infants need a higher ratio of adults.
- What do you have to provide? Always take a change of clothes and warm clothes. Label everything. Don't forget goggles and sun screen. (A good source of well-made, warm winter gear for kids is "Good Gear for Little People," a mail order company located in Washington, Maine 04574. One of their best items is their Bean Bag, a combination snowsuit/sleeping bag that zips on and off in seconds. It comes in two sizes, one for kids up to 15 pounds and one from 15 to 35 pounds.)
- Are hot lunches served? If your kid is a picky eater, can you pack a brown bag lunch?
- How important is "lunch included" to you? Think carefully about this one. Skiing down the mountain at noon may sound uncomplicated right now, but once you're on the slopes, it may not be.
- Are you allowed to visit and take your child out to play in the course of the day?
- Are reservations accepted? Are they necessary? When do you have to be there to ensure a place for your child? Can you think of anything worse than arriving at the mountain only to find your child locked out of nursery or ski school? Not all youngsters can cope with a full day of skiing. A combination of skiing and nursery playtime is a welcome option.
- How does the nursery program combine with the ski school?

Evaluating Ski Schools

Ideally, your child should be in a group with others the same age. Because children get cold and tired, there should be a welcoming indoor space available. Although some kids do very well with formal structured ski instruction, most prefer an emphasis on fun and games. A combined nursery/ski school option is particularly nice for younger kids. Some questions to ask:

- How much time is spent out-of-doors?
- Is lunch served or supervised?
- Can kids ski with parents any time during the day without having to pay extra for a lift ticket?
- For the more experienced, is there a racing program? Or supervised skiing without structured instruction?
- Are the instructors experienced in teaching children?
- Are the areas for kids' instruction private enough so that kids won't feel inhibited by having people looking on?
- Are the facilities for kids—bathrooms and indoor play areas—close enough to the slopes for kids to get to them quickly?
- Are there any special programs? Teen programs for recreational skiers are a relatively new phenomenon, but they're happening at more and more resorts. Some of the spots that offer special teen programs are Snowmass, Vail and Beaver Creek, Copper Mountain, Bolton Valley, and Steamboat (more details in the listings later on). Many other places offer special après-ski programs or facilities for teenagers.

A WORD ABOUT SKIWEE: Although not the only game in town, SKIwee is a ski program we heartily endorse. Having skied at both SKIwee and non-SKIwee resorts, we know that SKIwee is not mandatory to ensure a good ski school experience. But we can say that you most likely will not have a bad one where SKIwee is featured. The SKIwee program is sponsored by *SKI* magazine and several equipment suppliers. It's an all-day program that provides individual attention. Instructors are specially trained and must attend an annual clinic. SKIwee is game-oriented and based on the Montessori philosophy that play is learning. It begins with teaching kids how to put on their ski boots and continues on up to advanced levels of turns and freestyle techniques. The two basic keys to its success are the progress card and the use of a separate terrain garden. The progress card creates a universality of terms—a youngster going from one SKIwee area to another during the season simply picks up wherever he or she left off. Teaching is done through the use of familiar games, soccer, relay races, red rover, and so on. For instance, at SKIwee you don't hear *edging, wedges,* and *weighting*. Four-year-olds don't understand being told to push off and skate, but when trying to win a relay race, they find themselves skating automatically. A race through an obstacle course with a ball between their knees forces children to use their edges and have fun, too. And because kids seem to have such a hard time getting uphill on snow and cannot easily or happily herringbone or sidestep, many SKIwee areas use a carpet on the snow so that climbing becomes easy and fun. The SKIwee program is currently offered at approximately 65 ski areas in the United States. For a complete list, write to SKIwee, in care of *SKI* magazine, 3333 Iris Avenue, Boulder, Colorado 80301.

What the Experts Say

We spoke to three well-known experts on the subject of skiing with kids. All are devoted skiers, and all have had personal experience getting their own kids on the slopes. Here's what they have to say:

Billy Kidd, Director of Skiing, Steamboat Springs, Colorado, and former Olympic champion:

For children under 5 there are three recommendations that I strongly feel will keep your kids on skis:

1. Have your child take a few professional lessons. Kids like to learn with older children and/or adults. And, most importantly, please find a ski resort which caters to children and their individual needs.
2. Buy inexpensive equipment, i.e., plastic ski/snow shoes, often found in toy stores. Have your kids practice wearing these "short skis" on the living room floor to get a feel for balance and movement coordination.
3. Clothing is very important—make sure your children are properly dressed. Parents have a tendency to overdress their kids, who in turn become uncomfortably warm and can't move their arms and legs freely. This results in the child's disliking the sport from the start.

More importantly, kids want to have fun when they learn anything, especially skiing. If your children run into any snags or hangups during the first time out, they'll automatically be turned off. Make it as comfortable as possible in order to get them back on the slopes again. Otherwise, think about the beach for your next vacation.

Here are some tried and true hints: Don't modify old skis to fit your young children. Either rent ahead of time or buy—it is less money than you think. [Note from authors: Investigate buy-back programs where you can trade in one year's equipment for what will fit the next year. Many packages include equipment, so don't buy if this is true.] Choose warm sunny days to introduce your kids to skiing. Minimize your child's time to two to three hours a day on the slopes. Build confidence in your kids. Make sure they're comfortable with any new equipment before starting out on your trip. Get them in the right frame of mind for the ski trip. Familiarize them with the ski area with photos, maps, etc.

Kids naturally love to ski. They enjoy the freedom and independence it offers. Other sports are too team oriented. Skiing offers the first-timer an individual experience not matched by any organized sport. With just a few short lessons, your children will be able to ski down the easier slopes with the rest of the family, one of the key reasons you wanted to go on the ski trip in the first place. Spend time on the slopes with your children and don't try to teach them. Just go out and have fun.

Christi Mueller Northrop, SKIwee National Technical Director, SKI Magazine:

Since families that ski with their children, or are anxious to start skiing with their children, live in different geographical areas across the country, I have answered the question of when and how to start your children skiing according to their accessibility to snow and ski areas.

No matter where you live, it is best not to teach your children to ski yourself, but enroll them in a good children's ski school or special children's ski instruction program, such as SKIwee. Also, never push or force a young child to ski; it is a sport they must want to do and feel comfortable at.

If your family's availability and access to snow is

FREQUENT/EASY: If you live in the snow-belt with ample snow and easy, frequent access to skiing both at an area and in your backyard, children can start skiing as early as 30 months, depending upon the children's coordination.

The best way to start a child with good access to the slopes is to first let them play with their equipment indoors, then out in the backyard for short intervals. Once they are comfortable with the equipment, enroll them in a good children's ski program, since they will learn the most in a game-like atmosphere from their peers. Continue with the lessons, but let the child play on skis at home and at the ski area.

LIMITED/MODERATE: If you live an hour or two drive from the slopes and skiing, it is best starting children skiing at 4 years old at the earliest. If equipment is available, let the child play with it and try it out indoors. Enroll the child in a good program at an area, and try to have the child attend as frequently as possible. Again, the emphasis should be on fun, and the child should not be pressured to learn.

INFREQUENT/DIFFICULT: If you live several hours from skiing or a plane trip away, with the opportunity for only one or two trips a season, children with a very limited chance to ski each season are better waiting until they are five to start the sport.

When a long trip is involved to reach the area, there is a tendency to push the child to like skiing and learn fast. With children who see snow infrequently, it usually takes longer to adjust and learn to ski. If learning to ski is presented in a fun, relaxed way, the child will adapt more quickly. Since skiing is a relatively social sport, it is best that the child is enrolled in a fun program (such as SKIwee) to take advantage of the group, and the games. Also, with a group, a young child not used to snow is less apt to be scared.

No matter where you live remember, children will learn when they are having fun. Too much pressure, either from a ski school or the parents, takes the joy away.

Cal Coniff, President, National Ski Areas Association:

Four or five years of age is a good time for children to take up skiing, and discover that winter is a great time for playing outdoors and having fun. Children take to skiing like ducks take to water, and learning to ski is a happy, rewarding experience for children and parents alike.

Good inexpensive "starter sets" of equipment can be purchased at any ski shop. Most ski areas also rent children's equipment. Fancy ski clothes are not necessary but it is most important that children are dressed in outerwear that will keep them warm and dry. Good mittens and a warm hat are a must.

For the first few times on skis, just let your child walk around on a flat surface to get familiar with the strange "boards" attached to the feet. When you feel the child is at ease walking around, the next step is letting the child slide down the slightest incline that has a flat outrun free of obstacles. The parents should stay with the child at this stage to cheer the child on and, yes, help pick him up from the inevitable falls. This can be done on a little hill in your backyard or near your home. Remember, what may look like a molehill to the parent is Mt. Everest to the child.

For learning the technical maneuvers of skiing, such as turning and stopping, I strongly recommend that you enroll your child in ski school at a nearby ski area. Most have excellent learn-to-ski programs just for children, and many have full-day, learn-to-ski nursery programs where the children are well supervised and cared for. This will allow Mom and Dad a chance to go off and enjoy their day on the mountain.

At the end of the day when you head back to home, your child's pink rosy cheeks and big smile readily tell you it's been a great day full of new adventures and fun. And you won't have to worry about your child not going to bed early!

CROSS-COUNTRY SKIING

Cross-country skiing is another great activity for families. It's nice and low-key and generally less expensive than downhill skiing. Experts recommend starting kids on cross-country skis at age 7 or 8—this kind of skiing requires strength, endurance, and balance that you can't expect from a younger child. The major consideration for families who want to cross-country ski with their kids is the kids' equipment. Gardner Lane, manager of the touring center at Bolton Valley, Vermont, says that "young children need well-fitting equipment. Families who cross-country ski know this and bring their own. The need for rental equipment has not been great enough to warrant a large supply of skis necessary to fit all sizes and abilities of children." It is unfortunate but true that many touring centers have a limited amount of equipment for young children. So you'll either have to take your own or check in advance as to the availability of your particular kid's size. Where should you go to cross-country ski? Practically all downhill ski areas have cross-country skiing nearby. The ones listed here do. But, all you really need is a place to stay where you're made to feel welcome, snow on the ground, proper equipment and clothing, and baby-sitting available for kids who don't want to go along or for cold, windy days. Many of the resorts listed in Chapter 8 offer cross-country skiing in season; check with some of the dude ranches, too, in Chapter 11. Some, like C Lazy U, have a full winter program that includes cross-country. Check also the Appendix for the listing for the Woodstock Inn in Vermont, one of the nation's cross-country pioneers, where kid-sized rental equipment and lessons are available.

For specific information on 161 cross-country ski touring centers in the East, we suggest *Guide to Cross-Country Skiing in New England* by Lyn and Tony Chamberlain, published by Globe Pequot Press ($9.95).

SKI RESORTS

We've listed the mountains that offer comprehensive services to families and covered the topics we think most important to you. These are not necessarily the best skiing spots from the point of view of a ski expert, but we think they're all great for families. Write to the ones that interest you for the reams of information most have on hand and compare.

Most of the resorts listed here offer summer programs, too. Some convert into tennis and golf spots, some continue to run the nurseries even when the snow goes, and most cost 20 to 50 percent less than in the winter. We spent a summer weekend at The Village at Smugglers' Notch and loved it and a week at Snowmass/Aspen. So when making your summer vacation plans, don't forget the mountains.

Northstar-at-Tahoe
P.O. Box 129
Truckee, California 95734
Telephone: 916-562-1010 or 800-533-6787

DESCRIPTION: Skiers can get a view of the waters of Lake Tahoe from the top of Mt. Pluto. The sun shines 80 percent of the time in this corner of California, and the village at the base of the mountains includes on-the-slope lodging and a variety of restaurants, all with children's menus; a cross-country ski center; and a recreation center with saunas, outdoor spas, exercise room, and more.

FOR KIDS: All season long—end of November to end of April— kids 2 (as long as they're toilet-trained) to 6 are welcome at Minor's

Camp Child Care for a full or a half day. Because the nursery is limited to 40 kids, reservations are recommended. Call 916-562-1010. The center is set up as a preschool with supervision in art, science, dramatic play books, blocks, cooking, music, and so on. All children play outside and in. The cost is $30 for kids who don't ski; $38 for kids who want to combine play school and 1½ hours' skiing and are between the ages of 3 and 6.

Kids who attend Minor's Camp and have especially good motor skills can take a 2½ hour lesson at the Ski School, have lunch, and then spend the rest of the day at the Minor's Camp. The cost is $48. Special rates are available for the second child in the family.

Star Kids is an all-day (10:00 A.M. to 4:00 P.M.) lesson program for kids 5 to 12 that includes lessons, lifts, and lunch for $45. Sign-up must be by 9:30 A.M. The Minor's Camp has a list of sitters available for $4 per hour during the day, $5 to $6 at night. Check, too, at the Information Desk of the resort.

ACCOMMODATIONS: There are ten different lodging layouts ranging from hotel-type rooms to mountainside homes. All except Village Lodge Rooms have fully equipped kitchens and gas- or wood-burning fireplaces. Included in all lodging packages is use of the shuttle system and the Recreation Center with its saunas, outdoor spas, and exercise/game room. To give you an idea of cost, let's consider a three-night package for a group of three adults and two children (ages 5 to 12) in a two-bedroom condo with one child taking a three-day Learn-to-Ski program and one adult who is not a skier. The total, with tax included, would be just under $650. Cribs are available at no charge. For an additional charge you can get an interchangeable five- or six-day lift pass that's valid at Squaw Valley, Alpine Meadows, Heavenly Valley, and Kirkwood, too.

RATES: An all-day pass for an adult is $29; for kids 5 to 12 it's $14; and there is no charge for 4-year-olds and under skiing with an adult. Three-day passes cost $78 for adults, $35 for kids. Cross-country trail passes are $9 for adults, $4 for kids for a full day.

Copper Mountain Resort
P.O. Box 3001
Copper Mountain, Colorado 80443
Telephone: 303-968-2882 or 800-458-8386

DESCRIPTION: Copper Mountain is only 75 miles west of Denver, and the ski season is long—mid-November to late April. Of 76 trails, 25 percent are for beginners, 40 percent for intermediates, and 35 percent for advanced. When you're not skiing there's a Racquet and Athletic Club with indoor pool, tennis, racquetball, Nautilus, aerobics classes, and hot tubs. Guests of the Copper Mountain Lodging Services have free access to the club. Ice-skating, horse-drawn sleigh rides, dinner in the woods, and shopping in any of 35 shops in Copper Mountain Village are other possibilities. A good deal offered by the folks at Copper Mountain is the Copper Card; it costs $15 and entitles you to $6 off the adult lift ticket price (with the card lift tickets cost $24). It's good for a free day of skiing at the mountain in April and discounts on rentals, ski school classes, childcare programs, and specials at the Village's shops and restaurants.

FOR KIDS: Belly Button Babies welcomes kids 2 months to 2 years. The cost is $35 for a full day, 8:30 A.M. to 5:00 P.M., with lunch included or $27 for a half, 8:30 to 12:30 or 12:30 to 5:00. A three-day rate is $92. Reservations are required; call 303-968-2882, extension 6344, or 800-458-8386.

Combined with Belly Button Babies, the Belly Button Bakery facility is for kids 2 years and up. It got its name because the kids actually do bake there with help from the staff. Other indoor activities include blocks, music, water play, and dress-up. Kids 3 years and over can ski outdoors with instructors, while those under 3 play in the snow and go sledding. Kids who want to ski have to be registered by 9:30 A.M. for the morning lesson and 12:30 P.M., for the afternoon lesson. Reservations are necessary; call 303-968-2882, extension 6345 or the 800 number above.

In the Junior Ranch, beginners aged 4 to 6 get their own ski lift close to the indoor facilities. More experienced skiers have easy access to the entire mountain.

In the Senior Ranch, whether your 7-to-12-year-old is a beginner or a veteran skier, he or she can stay with the coaches all day, eat lunch with classmates, and ski as much as he or she wants. A full day, 10:00 to 3:15, costs $44 (with lunch and lift ticket); a half-day, 12:45 to 3:15 P.M. costs $30. Three consecutive days and lifts are $114. Special lift plus lessons plus rental packages are also available for kids. Reservations aren't required, but registration for the full day must be made by 9:30 A.M. of the day of the lesson. (Although lessons begin at 10:00, kids can be dropped off any time between 8:30 and 10:00.)

The Belly Button Bakery offers evening baby-sitting in guests' accommodations. Reservations must be made 24 hours in advance. Rates are $5 per hour, 50 cents more for each additional child. Call 303-968-2882, extension 6345, to make arrangements.

Copper Choppers is a program for kids 8 all the way up to 18 who may be "never-ever skiers, progressing intermediates, or hot shot expert skiers." The program runs nine weeks beginning in January; reservations are required.

A relatively new addition to Copper Mountain is the Kid's Arena, an area designed for fun and child-skill development. It's a terrain garden with rolls, bumps, and a variety of snow contours, a fun house, and areas set aside for nonskiing entertainment.

ACCOMMODATIONS: Your choice includes hotel rooms, and one-, two-, and three-bedroom condos and town houses. Everything is within walking distance of the slopes; a free shuttle system is available when you'd rather not walk. Call the 800 number for information. Throughout the winter there are a variety of lodging packages that include kids stay free and ski free benefits.

There's a Club Med at Copper Mountain with a mini-club that's open to kids 3 to 11 (kids under 3 aren't allowed here). Housed in a seven-story hotel adjacent to the slope, all of the club's rooms have twin beds with full bath. Unlimited lessons are included in the price of a stay. Adults pay $800 to $1250 per week, depending on the date, with the highest rate, as you'd imagine, for the week between Christmas and New Year's. Kids from 3 to 11 pay $100 to $580 per week. Kids 6 and under stay in the same room as their parents; older ones have their own room. Weeks run from Sunday to Sunday, and the price of the stay includes just about everything—accommodations, meals, ski instruction (two hours each morning and afternoon), unlimited downhill and cross-country skiing, aerobics, language labs, ice-skating, nighttime dancing and entertainment and, new this year, snowboarding. Kids eat with their friends or their parents and may join mini-club activities at any time from 9:00 A.M. to 9:00 P.M. Lessons and the mini-club are offered daily with the exception of Saturday afternoons and all day Sunday. Transfers from Denver and equipment rentals can be arranged through the club; call 800-CLUB MED for details.

RATES: Some of the special packages at the mountain start at $59.50 per adult per night, kids 12 and under free. Lift tickets are included, and kids under 12 ski free.

Keystone Resort
Box 38
Keystone, Colorado 80435
Telephone: 303-468-2316 or 800-222-0188

DESCRIPTION: Skiing at Keystone (about 70 miles from Denver) can stretch from mid-October all the way into June. Night skiing at Keystone is big—it's the nation's largest night skiing operation with 13 beginner and intermediate runs lit up to 10:00 P.M. Adjacent to Keystone is North Peak, which is for advanced and strong intermediate skiers, and just six miles away, via a free shuttle bus, is Arapahoe Basin, the highest lift-served area on the continent. Lift tickets are interchangeable for all three mountains. Keystone Village has 11 swimming pools, a skating rink, a cross-country center, gift shops, a grocery, and indoor tennis with lessons and clinics available.

"We are known as a family resort and actively cultivate that image. From delivering a "ducky" toiletry basket to crib users in the Keystone Lodge to our new slopeside Children's Center to our New Year's Eve bash . . . we try to make it easy for all members of the family to enjoy themselves." In summer, horseback riding, gondola rides, pedal boating, bicycling, hiking, historical tours, nature walks, and golf are all possible.

FOR KIDS: Keystone Children's Center operates year-round, unlike most ski-oriented resorts. The center is open from 8:00 A.M. to 5:00 P.M. When parents are night skiing, the kids can stay at the nursery, too. Applicable ages are 2 months and up; the nursery at Arapahoe takes kids from 18 months. Kids have free play, story hour, naptime, lunch, arts and crafts. For kids 3 and over, snow play is also offered. The cost is $27 for a half-day, $35 for full. Lunch is included, and reservations are required. A special snow play program for kids 3 and over that includes sledding and building snowmen costs $35 per day, $25 half-day (8:00 A.M. to 1:00 P.M. or noon to 5:00 P.M.).

Mini-Minors Camp combines skiing and nursery with all-day supervision, indoors and out; lunch; and lift ticket, rental equipment, and sledding for kids 3 to 5. It costs $42 per day, $37 half-day. In Minor's Camp kids 5 to 12 can combine lessons, lift, and lunch for $42 half-day, $52 full day with equipment, $3 less without equipment, and for multiday packages. Night skiing lessons are available for $20, with equipment and lift tickets included. If you want to get serious about skiing with your kids, there's a Mahre Training Center at Keystone for four five-day sessions each season. One of the Mahre twins will attend at least one of your sessions. Call 800-255-3715 for details.

Our kids loved ski school here. They skied the entire mountain. One son's class was even taken to A-Basin to ski above the tree line. It's a busy place, especially during holiday weeks. To avoid long ski school lines, check in right at the children's center. The facilities are connected and you can register at either place.

Teens have their very own program at Keystone, three days a week during ski season. It includes ski school, snowboarding lessons, and teen nights with a special outdoor activity such as a moonlit cross-country ski trip combined with dinner. Ice-skating is another favorite for nonskiing hours.

Evening baby-sitting can be arranged in your accommodations. Call 303-468-4182 or 800-255-3715. Cost is $5 per hour for the first child, 50 cents more per hour for each additional child. Requests for evening baby-sitting must be made by 1:00 P.M. that day.

ACCOMMODATIONS: One choice is Keystone Lodge, with a spectacular view of the Rocky Mountains from every window. Condos are available with studios to four-bedroom units possible, all with kitchenettes. Some private homes and many condos are also available for rent. Special packages that are available include free transfers to and from Denver, lift tickets, and no charge for children 12 and under. A resort shuttle bus takes you to and from lodging and the ski area and other recreational facilities. Buses run very frequently day and evening. At the lodge, the per-person rate for a seven-night ski package is $581; in the condos, a deluxe two-bedroom unit is $463 per person in low season, $318 in regular season. For spring skiing, you can take advantage of two-day packages that represent a 22 percent discount over winter rates. In summer, kids under 18 stay for free; in winter it's under 12.

RATES: Lifts are $26 per day on multiple-day tickets for adults, $12 per day for juniors 12 years and under.

Snowmass Resort
P.O. Box 5566
Snowmass Village, Colorado 81615
Telephone: 303-923-2000 or 800-332-3245

DESCRIPTION: Snowmass is 12 miles from Aspen and has lots to offer families. Besides skiing, 90 runs at all levels with a capacity of almost 19,000 skiers per hour, it has a great deal of other activities to lure you: sleigh rides in the moonlight, naturalist-guided snowshoe walks, cross-country skiing (25 miles of trails linking Snowmass and Aspen), swimming and hot tubbing, a genuine dog sled ride, a hot air balloon ride (kids have to be at least 9 years old), and at night, the Snowmass Repertory Theatre and the Top o' the Rockies concert series. Another plus is the fact that 95 percent of the accommodations are slopeside. The resort is owned by Aspen Skiing Company, which also owns Aspen and Buttermilk Mountains, so lift tickets are usable at all three. A free shuttle but connects all of them. Most of the restaurants in Snowmass Village have special children's menus, and another plus is the free Snowmass shuttle that runs all day from 7:15 A.M. to 11:25 P.M.

Snowmass Snowbunnies has a play school for 1½-to 3-year-olds and a ski program for 3-to 5-year-olds. Games are played inside and out. There's a separate nap room for the younger kids, lunch and snacks for both age groups; and for the 3-to-5-year-olds, ski lessons, use of the bunny hill chair lifts, an "Ankle Biters Race" every Friday, and a daily report card. Evening baby-sitting is available through Snowbunnies; call 303-923-4620. The cost of Snowbunnies is $55 per day, $250 for five days.

Another childcare possibility that combines indoor and outdoor play is located on the slope side of the Snowmass Mall, adjacent to Funny Hill. Called Big Burn Bears for 3½-to-6-year-olds and Cubs for 18 months to 3½ years, it costs $235 for five days; evening rates are $7 per hour, with dinner $3 extra. Hours are 8:30 A.M. to 4:30 P.M. seven days a week; evening childcare 5:30 to 11:00 P.M. Call 800-525-6200 for details. This new facility is a cheerful, well-designed environment run by Gracie Oliphant (younger children) and Michelle Tsu (skiers). It's hard not to feel comfortable here. There's so much to welcome kids—an Indian tepee, indoor nature center, a cozy reading room, and piles of books and toys to entice little ones.

At Happy Trails Day Care, another possibility, you'll find day and evening care for infants up to kids age 12. Meals, snacks, arts, crafts, music, and outdoor play are included. Call 303-923-5513. Little Red School House is for kids 2½ to 5 and is open from 8:45 to 5:30 P.M. Call 303-923-3756.

The Ski School at Snowmass gives classes for kids 5 to 12. Kids meet at the Youth Ski School on the slopes at 9:30 A.M. A noontime lunch break is supervised by instructors, and classes end at 3:00. Special events throughout the week include NASTAR, Ski School races, and a Children's Ski School Picnic. Group classes are $55 with lifts for a full day, with multiday packages available (lift tickets are extra). The Ski School runs a program for 13-to-19-year-olds, who are grouped by age and ability. Instructors supervise a variety of activities, including ski racing, sled parties, picnics, and videotaping sessions. Instructors also plan after-ski activities such as movies, sleigh-ride barbecues, and ice-skating parties. The program costs the same as the children's lessons. Snowmass Resort Association keeps a list of sitters at the Snowmass Information Booth on the Mall.

ACCOMMODATIONS: As we mentioned before, 95 percent of the accommodations at Snowmass are ski-in/ski-out, which is great for families. You have lodges and condominiums, studios to four-bedroom units. Most accommodations have kitchens, and many offer kids-free-in-parents' room deals. For information call 303-923-2010.

One spot we especially like is the Mountain Chalet, with full complimentary breakfast, friendly staff, rooms with queen-size bed, pull-out sofa, refrigerator, and kids-only pizza and movie nights during ski season ($9 per child). Walk out the door and you're on the slopes with direct access to two lifts. Ski home to the front door. Their van offers free pick up and delivery to Aspen Airport, 15 minutes away. Some rooms have fireplaces and balconies; a laundromat makes life easier, too. In holiday season, a room with fireplace is $165 double occupancy. Call 800-843-1579 for details.

Another good choice for accommodation in Snowmass is the Crestwood, situated right on the slopes, with a heated swimming pool, a sauna, two therapy pools, and a little sunroom facing the slopes. During ski season a two-bedroom condo costs $290 per night (higher at Christmastime); in summer, the same condo costs $143. Call 800-356-5949 for information.

RATES: A six-day adult ticket costs $186; special rates apply when combined with accommodations packages. For kids, it's $103. Check to see if a Kids Ski Free package is in effect.

NOTE: The entire Snowmass/Aspen area is wonderful in summer, too. We spent a week in Snowmass Village in July (we stayed at the Crestwood in Snowmass and loved our spacious, comfortable condo) and had a terrific time. The best part about the trip was that in this area you can hike to a beautiful mountain lake at the base of snow-capped mountains or go whitewater rafting on the Colorado River during the day, then at night go to a concert at the Aspen Music Festival or to a reading by a well-known author participating in the Aspen Writers Conference. We did it all, and it was great.

Steamboat
2305 Mt. Werner Circle
Steamboat Springs, Colorado 80487
Telephone: 303-879-6111 or 800-332-3204

DESCRIPTION: "Steamboat is so big; we have this corner of Colorado all to ourselves." A great advantage of skiing at Steamboat is that a major airport with direct flights from major U.S. cities is about 30 minutes away. From Denver, Steamboat is about 40 minutes by air. The average snowfall at Steamboat is a total of 27 feet, typically starting in November and lasting through April. Best of all, Steamboat has a "Kids Ski Free" plan: Kids under 12 ski free when their parents buy a five-day or longer lift ticket and stay at a participating property (not valid at Christmastime). And if the parents rent equipment, the kids get theirs free (one child per parent, for the rental deal). Take proof of age for the older kids! The director of skiing at Steamboat is Billy Kidd, the expert we quoted at the beginning of this chapter.

One of our friends just spent a week in Steamboat. Here's what she told us: "Steamboat is a wonderful family ski area. The terrain is varied, with plenty to challenge everyone from the beginner to the advanced skier. Younger kids and learners had a great time in the ski school; older kids or those who are good skiers had no problem meeting other kids. Although our condo was not right on the slopes ($100 per day vs. $300 per day), the shuttle bus system gave everyone the flexibility they needed to come and go as they pleased.

"The 'don't miss' activities in Steamboat include the western barbecue held five times a week at the top of the gondola with a western band for dancing and heaps of ribs, chicken, cornbread, a salad bar and a sundae bar. Also well worth the time are one of the several sleigh rides through the woods to a tent or cabin for a steak dinner and entertainment. Our kids loved the hot springs in town— regular-sized swimming pool plus soaking tubs, but most of all, they liked the three-story-tall warm-water slide to the steaming (at least in winter) pool below. You can also go to the more natural hot springs deep in the woods, but we didn't have time."

We also spent a glorious week at Steamboat. We stayed right on the slopes, which was wonderfully convenient. From our ski school kids we learned about Wally World, a bumps-and-jumps-through-the-woods trail that is unmarked and just for kids. Après ski we had a drink at a bar in the Gondola Plaza while the kids played video games, watched ski movies, and had snacks at SKIDS, Steamboat's

Kids Club. Great snow, great skiing, and lots of sunshine all made for a terrific week.

FOR KIDS: From the end of November to the beginning of April, the nursery operates from 8:00 A.M. to 5:00 P.M. It's open to kids 6 months to 6 years old. A full day for the first child is $30, for the second, $18; a half-day is $22 and the second, $15. Lunch is available for kids 2 and over for $4; you must provide food for the younger children. Kiddie Corral offers group lessons for kids 3 to 5. Half- and full-day lessons are offered. The full day includes lunch and a lift ticket. A half-day lesson costs $30 (including lift ticket), a full day $40. Three-day packages cost $107, five days, $125. Kids 6 to 15 may take group lessons at the Ski School. A two-hour lesson costs $21, a set of three is $57. Three all-day lessons, which include lunches, cost $102.

"Ski Week" is a package of five all-day lessons, five lunches, NASTAR racing, and a pin for $172. The ski school has staff for handicapped skiers, and there are Billy Kidd Racing Camps for three to six days at a time and daily NASTAR racing clinics.

Most lodges have access to baby-sitters. A list of baby-sitters is also available from the Chamber of Commerce, 303-879-0740. Expect to pay $3 to 5 per hour and make arrangements in advance; early mornings are the most difficult time to get coverage.

ACCOMMODATIONS: There are hotels, motels, lodges, condominiums, houses, and guest ranches all within three miles of the mountain. There are lots of slopeside possibilities, too. Most have indoor pools, game rooms, hot tubs, and other amenities. All price ranges are covered, but for a sample let's consider a slopeside condo for a group of four at Bear Claw Condos, with a kitchen, laundry facilities, and a fireplace. The rate for a night is $250 to $330. For information on lodging, call 800-525-2628.

RATES: Remember that kids ski free as long as they're 12 years or under. The only time this deal is not in effect is during the Christmas–New Year's holiday. An adult daily lift ticket ranges from $27 to $32, depending on season. Multiday packages are a few dollars less. Seniors (65 and over) ski for $14, so invite the grandparents to come along.

Another convenient lodging option is at the Sheraton Steamboat Resort. Located at the base of the slopes, the rear entrance, which you can ski directly to, lets you out at the gondola area, and the front at the restaurant/shopping plaza Ski Time Square. This large hotel has a choice of lodge rooms, hotel rooms, and condos. In addition, a Kid's Club, which operates full time during the summer months for ages 4 to 12, is open in ski season Thursday, Friday, and Saturday evenings and some holidays from 6:00 to 10:30 P.M. The hotel boasts two outdoor heated swimming pools, spas, and two video game rooms. Lodge rooms range from $49 to $129, hotel rooms from $59 to $199 and two-bedroom apartments from $139 to $429. All prices are per night, with children 17 and under free in the same room with parents. A variety of package plans are also offered. For information and reservations call 303-879-2220 or 800-848-8877 in Colorado, 800-325-3535 outside Colorado.

Vail Resort Association
241 East Meadow Drive
Vail, Colorado 81657
Telephone: 303-476-1000 or 800-525-3875

Beaver Creek
P.O. Box 915
Avon, Colorado 81620
Telephone: 303-949-5750 or 800-525-2257

NOTE: We're listing Vail and Beaver Creek together because, although they're separate ski destinations ten miles from each other, they offer the same kind of facilities for kids because they are owned by one corporation, Vail Associates, Inc. Lift tickets are interchangeable between the two mountains.

DESCRIPTION: Vail Village nestles right at the foot of Vail Mountain and therefore offers all the extra attractions of a town. Vail Mountain is now the largest ski resort in North America. The new expansion of China Bowl has added 1,881 new acres of lift-accessed intermediate and advanced bowl skiing. Vail's network of six express lifts services acres of gentle learn-to-ski terrain, seemingly endless cruising runs, and some of the most challenging bump skiing on the continent. Vail offers 120 named trails and has a lift capacity of 35,020 skiers per hour.

Beaver Creek is a ski mountain ten miles from Vail. A daily shuttle service ($1 each way) connects it to Vail. Beaver Creek has 49 named trails with a lift capacity of 15,209 skiers per hour. Cross-country skiing is also available on 12 miles of double-set track at the top of the mountain. Vail and Beaver Creek receive an average annual snowfall of 300 to 350 inches, with sunshine for more than 70 percent of the skiing days. For nonskiers, both areas offer snowshoeing, hot air ballooning, iceskating, wildlife and snowcat tours, sleigh rides, and lots of shopping.

FOR KIDS: Vail has recently opened its new $1.2 million expansion of the Golden Peak Children's Center. The center is a one-stop service for families, with a nursery, children's cafeteria, children's rental shop, and Vail/Beaver Creek Ski School for children. Children's Mountain Adventures, a program that allows kids to combine skiing and learning about Colorado's past, is available, as is a "Night Out" program that gives the kids a night off from their parents at a supervised evening of fun; call 303-476-5601 for information.

Vail and Beaver Creek have a Disney connection, too. Goofy and other characters are often seen skiing with the kids at their special mountain hideouts such as Gitchigumee Gulch.

Both mountains feature the Small World Play School, open (from the end of November to mid-April at Vail and year-round except May at Beaver Creek) from 8:00 A.M. to 4:30 P.M. Kids 2 months to 6 years are welcome and reservations are strongly recommended. Call 303-479-2044. A day at the nursery costs approximately $40.

The Children's Skiing Center, operating from 8:00 A.M. to 4:30 P.M., is open to kids 3½ to 12. The cost is $45 per day or $53 with a lesson and a lift ticket. (Lift tickets are interchangeable between Vail and Beaver Creek.)

Mogul Mice is for beginners 3½ to 6. It's a package of 1½hour lessons, lunch, and equipment rental for $53 for a full day. The SuperStar Program is for kids 3½ to 6 who can stop on snow. All-day class lessons, lunch, and lift ticket cost $53 per day. Teenagers can take five hours of lessons for $36 per day; lifts are extra.

At Vail a privately operated facility called ABC School provides day-care to visitors and residents alike. The ages are 2 to 5, and the program includes art, music, stories, outdoor play, rest, and snack time. The cost is $30 per day from 8:00 A.M. to 5:00 P.M. Call the director, Ann Hansborough, 303-476-1420, for reservations at least one day in advance. In Vail and Beaver Creek, many lodges have baby-sitter lists, and in Vail the Youth Center, 303-479-2292, has a list of available sitters, who charge between $5 and $6 per hour.

ACCOMMODATIONS: In Vail, Beaver Creek, and Avon most hotels, lodges, and condos cater to families and may give children's discounts. Call 800-525-3875 for lodging information. In Beaver Creek, the number to call is 800-525-2257. A sample is the Charter at Beaver Creek, a one-, two-, or three-bedroom condo facility at the base of the mountain that has ski season specials such as a two-bedroom suite for $490 per night. Children under 12 are free, and cribs are available for no extra charge. A new 300-room Hyatt opened slopeside at Beaver Creek in December 1989 with all the features of Camp Hyatt mentioned on page 50. A double room with kids 18 and under free in the same room is $225–255.

RATES: At both mountains, a regular adult lift ticket is $35 for a full day; $20 for kids 12 and under. Multiday rates offer additional savings.

Sun Valley Resort
Sun Valley, Idaho 83353
Telephone: 208-622-4111 or 800-635-8261

DESCRIPTION: Fifty-one years ago, a young railroad executive named Averell Harriman established the Sun Valley Lodge. Sun Valley's history is glamorous—Hemingway, Cooper, Crosby, Gable, Garland, Kennedy, Eastwood, and Ford have all signed the register. One of the photos in the promotional brochure shows Louis Armstrong on the slopes with a group of ski instructors. No doubt, you and your family will be in good company at Sun Valley. Sun Valley has two mountains, Dollar for beginners, and Baldy for intermediate and advanced skiers. Free shuttle service takes you from the Lodge, the Inn, or the Village Condos to and from both. There are over 70 runs on the two mountains. The first chair lift ever used in skiing was at Sun Valley; now there are 16 double, triple and quad.

FOR KIDS: The good news is that Sun Valley has a "Kids Stay and Ski Free" plan that's in effect at nonholiday times. Kids 17 and under, accompanied by a parent, get free accommodations and lift tickets for the duration of their stay. Nice deal.

At Sun Valley Playschool, kids 3 months to 6 years play indoors and out. A full day costs $45 with lunch included. Baby-sitting can be arranged through the Playschool for day or evening at a rate of $4 per hour during the day and $7 at night. Kids 5 to 12 can take beginner and intermediate lessons on Dollar or Baldy Mountain. The cost is $42 for one day, $108 for three days, and $145 for five days. Private instruction for kids 3 and 4 years old is available for $35 per hour, and a special introduction to skiing for the same age group is available for $12.

Downhill skiing isn't the only game in town. Sun Valley was the first ski area to establish a children's cross-country track, and the

Nordic Children's Program is enormously popular here. Group lessons are available for $15 per hour and trail fees for kids 6 to 12 are $4; free for anyone under 6. A special rental package including equipment and trail fee is $5 for kids.

ACCOMMODATIONS: Sun Valley Village is within walking distance of the Lodge, the Inn, and condominiums. Sample rates at the Lodge for a standard room are $55 per person double occupancy, $69 per person for a family suite (remember the kids stay and ski free deal). A condo costs approximately $45 per person per night.

RATES: Lift tickets are $35 per day for adults, $20 for kids.

Waterville Valley
Waterville Valley, New Hampshire 03125
Telephone: 603-236-8311 or 800-GO-VALLEY

DESCRIPTION: This very family-oriented ski resort is located in the White Mountains of New Hampshire, just 130 miles from Boston and about 325 miles from New York, and is surrounded by 768,000 acres of national forest. Developed by ex-Olympian Tom Corcoran, the 4,000-foot mountain has a vertical drop of 2,020 feet with an average annual snowfall of more than 12 feet (supplemented, of course, by snowmaking). There are a total of 53 trails, ten of which are expert, 37 intermediate, and six beginner. The Waterville Valley Sports Center (complimentary entry is included in most lodging packages), has a large indoor pool, tennis, racquetball and squash courts, a jogging track, and a restaurant. In addition to activities scheduled by the mountain and the ski school, the town recreation department offers family and children's activities on a regular basis. Among them are an indoor ice-skating arena and sleigh rides. The cross-country ski center has over 100 kilometers of trails, 70 of which are groomed and tracked. There are special kids' lessons offered, and small-size skis are available for rent.

FOR KIDS: The nursery here, lodged in a large, recently built enclave in the basement of the ski school building, is cheerful and well equipped. Children from 6 weeks to five years old are accepted. It is open from 8:30 A.M. to 4:00 P.M. on weekdays and from 8:00 A.M. on weekends. Reservations are recommended, especially during busy holiday periods and weekends. There is the possibility of full-day, half-day, and even hourly stays. There are separate infant and toddler rooms, and a wide variety of play and learning activities are featured. The nursery opens up onto a children's terrain garden making outdoor play, weather permitting, very easy. There's a nice ratio of caregivers here too, 1:3 for infants and 1:5 for older kids. A full day in the nursery costs $33 for children under 2 and $26 for those over 2. Prices are higher on weekends and holidays, and multiple day discounts are offered. The nursery is free midweek on some five-day midweek lodging packages.

Children 3 years and older can enroll in ski school. A Petite SKIwee program is for kids 3–5, Regular SKIwee is for kids 6–8 and Grande SKIwee is for ages 9–12. It is a full day program from 8:30 A.M. to 4:00 P.M., although a half-day is possible. The rate, which includes lessons, lifts, and lunch, is $40 per day for Petite, $50 per day for older children. Multiple-day SKIwee tickets are offered at lower daily rates, and single days are higher on weekends and holidays. More advanced skiers might choose to enroll in the Mountain Challenger Ski Week for 6-to-12-year-old experts who wish to refine their skills. There is a choice here of one or two lessons per day over a five-day week. The cost is $60 with one lesson per day and $95 with two lessons. Reservations are recommended.

Kids 12 and under ski free when one parent purchases a three or more day nonholiday midweek lift ticket except over Christmas, February, and Easter vacation weeks. Kids five and under always ski free.

Baby-sitting is available, but difficult over holiday periods, and costs about $3 to $5 per hour.

ACCOMMODATIONS: The accommodations are serviced by a free shuttle bus system which connects all the facilities (mountain, condos, lodges, Sports Center, etc.). We spent a wonderful week at the Black Bear Lodge, a 107-room all-suite hotel with an indoor/outdoor pool, sauna, laundry room, game room, and free access to the Sports Center. Our one-bedroom suite was quite spacious, and there were lots of other families there with kids for ours to play with. A sample rate at Black Bear, for a family of four with two children under 12 (who are free) starts at about $598 per family for five nights lodging, five days' skiing, muffins and coffee, one ski lesson, access to the Sports Center, a reciprocal ticket to all the Ski the Whites participating resorts, free skiing for kids under 12, and free nursery for younger children (at Waterville Valley only), both midweek. For information and reservations, contact the Lodging Service at the number given above.

RATES: A variety of lift and lesson packages are available. Lift tickets only start at $54 per adult for two days midweek, $65 on weekends, five days at $115. Group lessons, 1½ hours each, are $18 apiece.

Taos Ski Valley
Taos Ski Valley, New Mexico 87571
Telephone: 505-776-2291 or 800-992-SNOW

DESCRIPTION: Only 18 miles from the town of Taos, this resort offers an appealing combination of sun and snow. There are 71 slopes, and the easiest and steepest are accessible from the top of all lifts. Taos's Ski Schools Learn-to-Ski-Better Week is popular with all levels of skiers. The Village includes shops, restaurants, and a pro shop and a shuttle bus to the town of Taos. Ski-related evening programs are offered throughout the valley; up-to-date schedules are available at the Ski School office; après-ski in the village includes dancing, movies, talent shows, and jazz festivals.

FOR KIDS: The Peek-a-Boo Child Care program for kids 6 weeks to 3 years operates in the "Hide 'n' Seek" building, about 100 yards from the center of the village year-round. It is open from 9:00 A.M. to 4:00 P.M., the same hours that the lifts operate. Kids 18 months and over play in the snow. Reservations are required; call 505-758-9076. The charge is $30 per day; you pack your own lunch for your child. In the town of Taos there's a day-care center that will take drop-ins with advance registration. It's called Trudy's Discovery House, 505-758-1659, and is open from 7:45 A.M. to 5:45 P.M. during the week, 9:00 to 5:00 on Saturdays. Kids must be at least 6 months old, and prices range from $8.50 to $14.50 per day. Rumor has it that several mountain employees use this service, though it might be a hassle for you if you're staying right at the ski area.

In the KinderKafig program kids 3 to 6 learn to ski all over the mountain. The 5- and 6-year-olds have two hours of lessons in the morning, lunch, and two hours of supervised skiing with an instructor. The 3- and 4-year-olds' program includes an hour of skiing in the morning and afternoon, play in the snow, and indoor activities such as crafts, games, puppets, and storytelling. The cost is $32 for a full day; $20 for a half. A lift ticket is included, and a six-day package is $168.

In the Junior Elite program kids 7 to 12 get morning and afternoon lessons and a lift ticket for $43 per day. Thursday at 2:00 is race time. The Elite program is for kids 13 to 18. Lessons are fast-paced and geared toward fun. Afternoons are free for skiing with new friends or for ski clinics on racing or other areas of special interest. Taos plans their ski programs to be as flexible as possible—groups can form their own race-oriented classes or challenge classes for kids who can ski and want thrills but aren't interested in racing. The lodges keep lists of baby-sitters who will sit either in their own home or at the resort.

ACCOMMODATIONS: On the slopes there are lodges, all with saunas, jacuzzis, or hot tubs and live entertainment and condos all with kitchens. (At this ski area, we recommend a lodge for a much more picturesque vacation.) If you plan to cook, you can get groceries at Twining's Provisions. Ski packages are also available at accommodations in the town of Taos.

RATES: If you stay on the slopes, the most popular package is the week-long Saturday to Saturday package. For lodges this includes the room, two or three meals per day, six days of lift tickets, and six mornings of ski school classes, and for the condos includes all of the above except the meals. A typical and popular lodge is the St. Bernard, which charges $970 per adult for a ski week with $540 for kids 7 to 12 and $500 for ages 3 to 6 in the same room as the adults. For accommodations information call 800-992-SNOW. Lift tickets are $29 for an adult one-day ticket, $27 per day for a multiday ticket; a child (12 and younger) pays $16 per day; $14 for a multiday ticket. Equipment rental is $12 for the first day for adults, $10 every additional day; for kids it's $7 and $6.

Ski Windham
Route 23W
Windham, New York 12496
Telephone: 518-734-4300 or 800-883-5056

DESCRIPTION: Ski Windham has 33 trails and seven lifts, with a skier capacity of 9,800 per hour. Snowmaking covers 97 percent of the mountain, and there are two lodges, the Wheelhouse and the Lodge at Ski Windham.

FOR KIDS: Kids from 6 months to 7 years may stay for a half- or full day of supervised activities in the new Children's Learning Center. Reservations and prepayment are required (518-734-4300). The full-day session, from 8:30 A.M. to 4:00 P.M., is $40, a half-day from 8:30 A.M. to 12:00 noon or 1:00 to 4:00 P.M. is $24. Kids play inside and out. Smokey Bear Ski School is a learn-to-ski program for kids 4 to 7. A single session is $33, $41 with equipment rentals; a full-day session, which includes two lessons, lunch, a lift ticket, and nursery supervision, is $55, or $63 with rentals. Reservations are highly recommended. Smokey Bear Ski School also has half-day sessions from 8:30 A.M. to noon or 1:00 P.M. to 4:00 P.M. for $33 or $41 with equipment.

Beginner group lessons for first-time skiers are given at 10:00 A.M. and 2:15 P.M. Additional lessons for first-time skiers only are given at 12:15 P.M. on weekends and holidays.

ACCOMMODATIONS: Ski Windham Lodging and Skier Information Service will help you find a place to stay. Call 800-729-SKIW or 518-734-9850.

RATES: Kids 6 and under ski free with a ticketed adult. Daily weekday rates in peak season are $23 for adults and $20 for juniors. Weekend/holiday rates are $32 and $26. Special weekday packages allow kids 12 and under to ski for free with a full-price ticketed adult. Some area lodges offer kids under 12 free accommodations.

Shawnee Mountain
Shawnee on Delaware, Pennsylvania 18356
Telephone: 717-421-7231 or 800-SHAWNEE

DESCRIPTION: A ski resort in the Poconos, this is a gentle hill compared to some of the other areas we've described here, but it is reputed to have one of the best SKIwee programs anywhere in the country. The mountain has 23 slopes and trails with snowmaking on all. Skiing doesn't stop when the sun goes down: Night lights cover 95 percent of the slopes and trails with practically shadow-free illumination.

FOR KIDS: Little Wigwam Babysitting, located at the base of the mountain, entertains kids 1 year and up from 9:00 A.M. to noon and 1:00 to 4:00 P.M. Rates are $3 per hour or $20 for a full day. A lunch option is available, too. Children's Nest nursery is located at the Shawnee Village reception center, a few miles from the mountain, and one mile from the Inn and condos. Kids 1 to 8 are welcome from 8:30 to 5:00 on weekdays and 8:30 to 6:00 on weekends. Rates are the same as the Wigwam.

SKIwee and PreSKIwee offer kids to 12 a full-day program that includes lunch and costs $45; equipment rental is extra. All partici-pants receive the individualized progress card and a SKIwee pin. Boys and girls aged 12 to 16 can join a holiday race camp during the Christmas holiday season. The package includes training on and off the snow, evening clinics, movies, and awards. Two nights' lodging, six meals, constant supervision, and swimming at Shawnee Inn are included for $175 with lift tickets, $130 without. A day-camp option is available for $100 and $70 for teens staying with their parents. The Reception Center at the Village will help you find a baby-sitter.

ACCOMMODATIONS: The Shawnee Village/Shawnee Inn is located on the banks of the Delaware River about 2½ miles from the mountain. The new North Slope town homes are directly across from the mountain. Free transportation throughout the resort complex to the mountain is included with ski packages. If you stay in a condo, a car is recommended. The activities staff provides a full schedule of daily activities, everything from crafts to aquacise classes in the pool to movies at night. Guests can use the facilities of the Shawnee Racquet Club, five miles away. Ice-skating is available. You can choose from rooms at the Inn or two-bedroom villas. Sample rates, per night, are $70 per person double occupancy during midweek at the Inn and $390 to $750, depending on season in the villas and town homes (which sleep up to six). Guests of the Inn, villas and town homes get two free lift tickets during the week and a one-third discount on weekends and holidays. Call 717-421-1500 or 800-SHAWNEE.

RATES: Lift tickets are $28 for day and night (8:00 A.M. to 10:00 P.M.) during the week. Children under 7 ski free when accompanied by a paying adult.

Bolton Valley Resort
Bolton, Vermont 05477
Telephone: 802-434-2131 or 800-451-3220

DESCRIPTION: "The Lodge at Bolton Valley and Trailside Condominiums are within steps of ski lifts, tennis courts, pools, and restaurants. Children can't get lost, cars are not needed, and programs provide a good mix of family time, children's time, and adult time together." Located in central Vermont, 19 miles east of Burlington, this destination resort is located on 6,000 wooded acres. There are 40 interconnected trails with summit views of Lake Champlain and the Green Mountains. There's a cross-country touring center, too, with 100 kilometers of trails. The Sports Center includes two tennis courts, an exercise room, a whirlpool, a sauna, and an indoor pool. Night skiing is possible from 6:00 to 11:00, Monday through Saturday.

FOR KIDS: HoneyBear Nursery, open from 8:30 A.M. to 4:30 P.M. in winter, 9:00 to 4:00 in summer, has a crafts area, a kitchen, a block area, and a separate room for infants and children. Infants through age 6 are welcome, with reservations necessary for children under 2. The cost for preschoolers is half-day with lunch $15, full day $27, five days for $118; infants half-day $18, full $30, and five days for $125. On Wednesday and Saturday nights the nursery is open from 6:30 to 9:00 and the fee is $10 for those hours. (Rates slightly lower in summer.)

The Ski School programs for 4- or 5-year-olds enrolled in the nursery offers one or two SKIwee lessons. Instructors pick them up from the nursery and return them: half-day ($18) and full day ($48) sessions are available. Bolton Cubs SKIwee program is for kids 5 to 7. Operating 9:45 A.M. to 2:00 P.M. every day, it costs $48 with lunch and a lift ticket included; five days costs $180. The Bears program operates for kids 8 to 12 from 9:30 A.M. to 3:00 P.M. and costs $48 per day, $180 for five days with lunch, instruction, and skiing included. The Teen Scene, available for school vacation times only, provides afternoon ski lessons exclusively for teenagers for $10 per day, five days for $40. The Pied Piper of Bolton is a dinner and evening activities program for kids 6 to 11 available three nights a week. It costs $14 with dinner; $9 without. Baby-sitting can be arranged with the front desk for $3 per hour, day or evening. The nursery is also open evenings when the Pied Piper program is in effect, but you will need to feed your child dinner.

Bolton is a favorite of ours. It's easy for kids to maneuver on their own, there's a particularly warm welcome throughout, and their kids' programs are top-notch. Kids program director Julie Frailey creates programs that reflect her understanding of kids and parents (she and her ski school director husband have two kids of their own). She will make certain that your child is in just the right program for him or her.

ACCOMMODATIONS: Right at the mountain there's the Lodge at Bolton Valley, a slopeside hotel (some rooms have kitchens and fireplaces), and Trailside Condos: one-, two-, three-, and four-bedroom units with kitchens and fireplaces and some separate chalets. Down the slopes is Black Bear Lodge, a 20-room country inn. At the Bolton Valley Lodge and Trailside Condos, kids under 6 stay free in the same room as parents. Cribs are available at no extra charge.

RATES: Kids under 6 ski free. Various packages are available, for instance, an "All Frills Vacation," which includes lifts, slopeside lodging, breakfasts and dinners, daily ski lessons, use of the Sports Center, aerobics classes, night skiing, and cross-country skiing, for $485 per adult for five days; "Kidski All Frills Vacation" includes lodging in the same room as parents, enrollment in Bolton Bears or Cubs full-day program, ski lifts, night skiing, sleigh ride, breakfasts and dinners, and use of the Sports Club for $267 for five days. Lodging and skiing only for five days is $299.

Mount Snow Resort Center
89 Mountain Road
Mount Snow, Vermont 05356
Telephone: 802-464-3333 or 800-451-4211

DESCRIPTION: Mount Snow has 77 trails and 17 lifts, and skiing is usually possible from early November to May. The facilities include three base lodges, all with cafeterias; a summit lodge; three rental shops; and a vacation center, which is the focus of the kids' activities. (In summer, Mount Snow hosts a golf school for anyone 12 or over and their popular mountain bike school for the same age group.)

FOR KIDS: The Pumkin Patch (that's how they spell it) is where kids 6 weeks to 12 years go for a variety of programs. The nursery is for infants up to age 8 and operates daily. Kids play indoors and out, and those under 2 have their own room where they can nap and play. Outdoor facilities include slides, monkey bars, rope ladders, and swings.

Ages 3 to 5 years can participate in Peewee SKIwee, which includes two one-hour lessons a day. Kids 6 to 12 participate in the SKIwee program—five hours of supervised skiing and instruction each day with lunch included for all-day programs. Mount Snow was one of the original SKIwee resorts. All skiing lessons begin at the Children's Learning Center, a protected area with its own rope tow and terrain garden. Five weeks a year are designated "Teddy Bear Ski Weeks," which include five days of free skiing for kids 12 and under, rides on a snow-grooming machine, a magic show, teddy bear parade, and more. Vacation Services at 802-464-8501 has details.

ACCOMMODATIONS: Mount Snow Vacation Services, 802-464-8501, represents 56 properties in the area. An example of a facility at the base of the mountain is Snow Lake Lodge, with two pools, a fitness center, and a lounge, which offers ski packages such as a five-day ski week in regular season for $214–$269 for two adults in a room; kids 4 to 12 are free.

A typical condo rate is $115 per day midweek for a two-bedroom facility within walking distance of the lifts.

RATES: Kids under 6 ski free; 6- to 12-year-olds pay $19 per day.

Okemo Mountain
RFD 1B
Ludlow, Vermont 05149
Telephone: 802-228-4041 general information, 802-228-5222 for
snow reports, 802-228-5571 for lodging service

DESCRIPTION: Located in central Vermont, Okemo has 70 trails, including a 4½-mile-long beginner trail from the summit. The village of Ludlow has specialty shops, restaurants, antique stores, and a variety of lodging possibilities.

FOR KIDS: Okemo Mountain lures families with

- free skiing for kids 6 and under
- free beginner lift regardless of age
- free lodging for kids 12 and under at Okemo Mountain Lodge, Kettle Brook, and Winterplace, slopeside condos
- free day-care with lunch included during midweek at nonholiday times
- Saturday evening childcare from 6:00 to 10:00

From mid-November to late April, the nursery operates from 8:30 A.M. to 4:30 P.M. every day and on Saturday evenings from 6:00 to 10:00 as well. Kids 1 to 6 years play indoors and out, hear stories, play games, and do puzzles and arts and crafts. The nursery is free midweek, otherwise $30 for a full session, $15 for a half-session. Lunch is included. An Introduction to Skiing option for kids 3 and 4 is available for $10 extra. The SKIwee program, described in the introduction, offers half-day and full-day sessions. Two-hour snow instruction is included morning and afternoon for kids 4 to 8. At the Children's Ski School ages 6 and up may take lessons 9:45 to 11:45 A.M. and 1:45 to 3:45 P.M.

Young Mountain Explorers, for kids 8 to 12, is meant for kids of average or better skiing ability and offers four hours of supervised skiing and instruction daily. Baby-sitting arrangements can be made with Joyce Washburn in the main office of the resort; rates are about $2 per hour. There's a junior racing team program for ages 8 to 18, divided into age groups. A NASTAR recreational racing program for all ages and abilities is held every day except Monday.

ACCOMMODATIONS: Slopeside accommodations are available at Kettle Brook and Winterplace Condominiums—one- to three-bedroom units—and at Okemo Mountain Lodge with 72 one-bedroom units that can sleep four. Nearby are country inns and lodges, and motels as well. One of our favorites is the Combes Family Inn, a comfortable farmhouse filled with games and pets, a barn with goats, and acres for cross-country skiing and sledding. Call 802-228-8799 or write to Box 275, RFD 1, Ludlow, Vermont 05149. For information about other accommodations, call 802-228-5571.

The cost of your vacation will depend on where you stay. The Okemo Mountain Lodge has five-day midweek packages of $520 for a family with two adults. Children under 12 are free.

RATES: Full-day lift tickets at the mountain are $35 on weekends and holidays; $32 for 12 and under; half-day $25 and $15. A five-day package is $135 and $80, respectively. Ski school is $18 for a class lesson, $35 for a private lesson; the day-care center is free midweek and $30 for a full day on weekends and holidays.

The Village at Smuggler's Notch
Smuggler's Notch, Vermont 05464
Telephone: 802-644-8851
General Manager: Robert Mulcahy

DESCRIPTION: "We're a secluded self-contained village tucked away in the mountains. . . . Everything is within walking distance and there's a sense of freedom and casualness among guests. . . . Everything we do is with the family vacation experience in mind. . . . Our programs and activities are set up to give parents worry-free time to relax . . . while giving their children a chance to make new friends, be challenged and have a lot of fun." One of the nice things about Smuggler's philosophy about children's programming is that parents can always join in on an activity and kids can come and go whenever they'd like.

All amenities at Smuggler's are within a short walking distance of each other—the hot tub, the pool, the restaurants, a pub, all accommodations, and the lifts are all right there. There are three interconnected mountains to choose from: Madonna, Sterling, and Morse, each with a variety of terrain just right for the novice or the expert. Cross-country skiing is available on 23 miles of trails winding through wilderness with a Sugarhouse at the end of the trail. We have lots of friends who've had great family ski vacations at Smuggler's and return winter after winter.

FOR KIDS: Kids 3 months to 6 years may stay at Alice's Wonderland, the new day-care center from 9:00 to 4:00 daily with lunch available. The center is licensed by the state of Vermont, and advance reservations are necessary. The cost is included in ski packages; lunch is $5 extra. Kids 3 to 6 may spend the whole day at Discovery Ski Camp. The day includes two 1¾-hour ski lessons with breaks for snacks, lunch with friends, and games, ice-skating, sleigh rides, movies, arts and crafts, and Cookie Monster races. The full day costs $38, and a special five-day rate of $109 is available. Little Smuggler's Ski School provides daily lessons for 3-to-6-year-olds; groups are small. Each lesson is 1¾ hours long with a hot chocolate break. Five lessons are $70; free with some packages.

Adventure Ski Camp is for kids 7 to 12 and gives them an all-day program that includes two 1¾-hour lessons at 9:30 A.M. and again at 1:00 P.M., lunch with friends, volleyball, soccer, ice-skating, challenging racing, and racing technique instruction. The full day costs $38 with lunch, $109 for five days with special packages.

Young Adults Ski School is the place for people 13 on into the early twenties who want to ski a lot, talk a little, and do some racing. A teen center, with a deejay and dancing, serves nonalcoholic beverages après-ski. Baby-sitting is easy to arrange for $5 per hour. Parents' Night Out gives parents a chance to be together while the kids eat with staff and enjoy some after-dinner entertainment. The cost is $15 but is included in some packages.

ACCOMMODATIONS: These range from efficiency apartments to luxury homes. All are slopeside. A typical condo has a fireplace, fully equipped kitchen, queen-size bed, fold-out sofa in the living room, and patio or balcony. Cribs are available for $12 per stay.

RATES: Smuggler's offers many inviting packages. Our favorite is the Family Fest, which runs nine weeks of the season (including Christmas) and provides accommodations, a five-day ski pass, ski school classes, use of the Aqua Center with a pool and hot tub, hosted parties and free rental equipment for kids 12 and under, free teens' racing clinic, free Discovery and Adventure Ski Camp, and free Parents' Night Out, for one evening. Prices start at $1,060 for a family of four in a studio, $1,235 for a one-bedroom suite.

Jackson Hole Ski Resort
P.O. Box 290
Teton Village, Wyoming 83025
Telephone: 307-733-2292 or 800-443-6931

DESCRIPTION: When you're not skiing on the 3,000 acres of varying terrain, you can take a snow coach tour into Yellowstone National park or a sleigh ride through the nearby Elk Refuge.

FOR KIDS: Kinderschule operates for kids 3 months on up. (There are a few spaces for younger kids with advanced reservations required.) Hours are 8:30 A.M. to 4:30 P.M. from early December to early April. Reservations are required; rates are $20 for a half day, $35 for a full day, with lunch and snacks included. Write to Kinderschule, P.O. Box 290, Teton Village, Wyoming 83025. Kids 3–5 may take two one-hour lessons each day at the ski school. Kids 6–14 are offered the SKIwee: a full day is $25; a half, $15. Lunch can be arranged for kids from noon to 2:00 P.M. for an additional $12, if parents want to stay on the slopes. Lodges and property management offices have lists of baby-sitters. Expect to pay up to $4 per hour.

ACCOMMODATIONS: For details, call 800-443-6931. At the ski area there are condos and lodges, and not far are two full resorts, Americana Snow King and Jackson Hole Racquet Club. One particularly nice-sounding lodge in Teton Village at the base of the mountain is the Alpenhof, a small (40-room) hotel that is the closest to the ski lifts. It has lots of Alpine atmosphere, a restaurant, jacuzzi, game room, and baby-sitting service. A seven-night package, which includes lodging, five days of lift tickets, and one half-day ski lesson on Sunday morning, costs $386 for two in the low season, $1,233 in high season. The phone number is 307-733-3242.

RATES: A one-day adult ticket is $32, for kids 14 and under, $16; a five-day ticket is $140 for an adult and $70 for 14 and under.

11

Farms and Dude Ranches

Dude ranch and farm vacations are two great choices for family fun. Whether you choose a working farm where your kids can help milk the cows and feed the chickens, an elaborate resort where dude ranching is the theme or something in between, this type of vacation can be terrific.

Here we list five farm-type vacation spots and 40 ranches. We've emphasized the facilities for kids, something no other book does. But for the most complete listing of farm and ranch possibilities in the United States, we recommend Pat Dickerman's book *Farm, Ranch and Country Vacations*. The latest—the 40th anniversary edition—includes lots of recommendations from b and b farms to ranches you visit for a week or more. Pat's book is available for $13 postpaid from Farm and Ranch Vacations, 36 East 57th Street, New York, New York 10022, or by calling 212-355-6334 for credit card orders. Pat's listing includes many hosts who provide children's programs and baby-sitters.

Another source of information on guest ranches is the Dude Rancher Association's annual magazine/directory of members. For copies, send $1 to the Association at P.O. Box 471, LaPorte, Colorado 80535, 303-493-7623.

The farms we list here all invite you and your kids to participate in the life of the farm. If possible, choose a farm where the kids of the family are close to the age of your own kids, in other words, instant friends.

The ranches we list fall into three basic types: working cattle ranches that have been established for a long while and now take a few guests, guest ranches where riding in the main activity, and resorts with a dude ranch theme that offer lots of other activities besides riding.

We've taken a few ranch vacations ourselves, and they've been some of the best times we've ever had. In fact, as we write this, we're packing up for a trip to Colorado. We can't wait to get out to the wide open spaces. Besides all the fresh air, exercise, relaxation, and no-frills fun, a dude ranch vacation gives our city kids the kind of freedom they don't get at home. There are no streets to cross or traffic to worry about. A dude ranch is a learning experience, too, since the kids get a feeling for what life was like in the Old West. Most ranches feature—besides the obvious horseback riding—trout fishing, backpacking and hiking, and river-rafting day trips. Many offer full- or part-time childcare, while some simply post a list of daily activities for kids. All offer loads of activities that are perfect for the whole family to do together, like hayrides, chuck wagon dinners, square dancing, and campfire sing-alongs.

As veterans of a number of ranch vacations, we have a few thoughts about choosing the right ranch for your family. A ranch vacation is a substantial investment, and it can be absolutely wonderful. However, if you choose the wrong ranch, it can be a major disappointment. In the following pages we give you lots of choices. Read through them, select the places that appeal to you, and then call them and ask every single question you have. No question is silly. We've found that ranches take their personalities from the owners, so we suggest talking directly to the owner. Get a feeling for what he or she is like. Are they genuinely warm and friendly? Are they flexible? What kind of staff do they have? Although we like to ride, we aren't crazy about horses, so we need a place where other options are available. For us, a ranch near some other interesting tourist attractions is ideal so that we can spend some of our time riding and the rest out doing other things. If you're like us, be sure to have a car so that you don't feel too confined at the ranch. We met a couple who were going stir-crazy because they didn't have a car and were totally dependent on expensive taxi transportation whenever they wanted to go anywhere. Ask about hiking possibilities near the ranch, whether you can arrange whitewater rafting or any other kind of adventure away from the ranch. On the other hand, if you and your family are mad for horses, choose a ranch that's serious about riding and offers you lots of it included in the price of the stay.

And don't worry about having cowboy boots; we found that sneakers were just fine for us and the kids. And bring two pairs of jeans at least—you won't believe how dirty you get on the ranch, and laundry facilities are not often available.

Rates at most ranches will include all meals (lots of hearty food served family-style), accommodations (from rustic to luxurious), and all activities. Some, however, have a separate fee for riding and activities. Most of the ranches we list here require a minimum stay— usually a week—during the summer. Many are open year-round and offer wonderful cross-country skiing possibilities in winter.

Riding is the mainstay of most ranch holidays, although you could certainly enjoy a ranch stay even without riding. Ask ahead to be sure of the type of riding available and whether, if you have an experienced rider in the family, he or she will be given room to lope. Find out whether your kids will be able to ride on the trails or if they'll have to stay within the bounds of the corral, and whether riding lessons are available. With the rise of the cost of liability insurance recently, many ranches have had to establish a minimum age as high as 8 for trail rides.

Again, our listings are in alphabetical order, by state.

FARMS

Glacier Bay Country Inn
Box 5
Gustavus, Alaska 99826
Telephone: 907-697-2288
Owners: Al and Annie Unrein

IN THEIR OWN WORDS: "Deep in the woods, down a narrow, winding road, you'll find the inn. Its log beam ceilings, dormer windows, large porches, cozy wood stove and private baths provide a comfortable, relaxed atmosphere. . . . Al and I and our children, Havila, seven, and Casey, four, treat you as a welcome friend who has come to share our home. Ask Havila for a guided tour to the 'bear tree'—she'll point out all the local flora and fauna along the way."

DESCRIPTION: Hiking and cross-country skiing are nearby, at Glacier Bay National Park. Just three miles away is a beach, and the fishing area is well known for king salmon in May; Coho salmon in mid-July, August, and September; and halibut all summer long. Guests at the inn are welcome to participate in farm activities, hike through the dense rain forest, listen for ravens, or watch for the Northern Lights.

ACCOMMODATIONS: All rooms at the inn have beamed ceilings, gorgeous views, and private baths. Each room has a theme; for instance, the Seaside room has brass porthole mirrors, a fisherman's net draped on the wall, and seagull wallpaper.

RATES: Rates are per person and include three meals and transportation to and from the airport in Gustavus: $84–$89 per day for adults, $49 per day for kids 3 to 11, and no charge for under 3.

There are two cribs available at no extra charge. Baby-sitting can be arranged with a day or two notice for $3 per hour.

Emandal—A Farm on a River
16500 Hearst Road
Willits, California 95490
Telephone: 707-459-5439
Owners: Tamara and Clive Adams

IN THEIR OWN WORDS: "Believing that families truly need time to be together in an unstructured, unpressured environment, we provide no planned activities. . . . Whatever you do, it's your time to do as your wish."

DESCRIPTION: In 1908 Em and Al Byrnes (ergo, the name of the farm) opened up their home to friends in the Bay area who wanted to vacation on the Eel River, which borders the ranch, to get away from the pace of the city, which even in 1908 was fairly hectic. More than 80 years later the farm is still a retreat for city-weary people who like to swim or tube in the river, hike on the 1,000 acres of hilly land, and participate in the life of the farm—doing anything from egg-gathering to berry-picking. In July the farm operates as a camp for kids 7–16, but in May, August, and parts of September the Adams family opens it up to other families who may come for a weekend or for a week or two at a time. This is the kind of vacation that is perfect for families who like to camp but don't want to tote all the equipment and prefer to have someone else do the cooking for them.

FOR KIDS: There's no organized program here but what could be better for kids than a working farm with a river nearby?

ACCOMMODATIONS: In all there are 19 redwood cabins that sit on the oak- and fir-clad hills, all built by Al Byrnes himself between 1915 and 1925. Each has beds (linens and blankets are provided), cold spring water, and electricity. Bathrooms and showers are nearby. Three meals a day are served family-style—vegetables, meat, and eggs all come from the farm.

RATES: Seven days at the farm with all meals included costs $426 per adult; for kids 12–17, $277; for 6-year-olds, $182; 5-year-olds, $160; 4-year-olds, $132, 3-year-olds, $98; 2-year-olds, $71; and under 2, no charge. Weekends, Friday to Sunday, cost $134 per adult for a regular weekend; $201 holiday weekends.

Rockhouse Mountain Farm
Eaton Center, New Hampshire 03832
Telephone: 603-447-2880
Owners: The Edge Family

IN THEIR OWN WORDS: "Rockhouse is a family business. We have second and third generations coming back year after year to our back-to-the-land atmosphere. Our place is small so there's lot of chance for personal contact."

DESCRIPTION: The farm is located on the side of Rockhouse Mountain, a little village in the White Mountains. It operates from mid-June through October and has 400 acres in all with streams, fields, and wildflowers, horses, cows, pigs, geese, and ducks. In the 200-year-old barn you'll find horses ready to be saddled up for a ride along a country trail. Kids like to help milk the cows. At a lake just a half-mile from the farm, guests can swim, canoe, and sail (no extra charge for the boats).

ACCOMMODATIONS: Guests stay in the farm's inn, in rooms with or without private bath.

RATES: The daily rate per person double occupancy with a private bath is $52. For kids the rates are under 1 year, free; 1–5, $22; 6–11, $28; and 12 and over $32. All rates include breakfast and dinner.

Berkson Farms
Route 108
Enosburg Falls, Vermont 05450
Telephone: 802-933-2522
Owner: Sid Berkson

IN THEIR OWN WORDS: "Make your life simple. Come spend time with us and feel yourself in touch with the best things in life—fresh air, Vermont pasture and mountain greenery, farm animals and farm life, along with country home cooking."

DESCRIPTION: This is a dairy farm, and guests are welcome to help milk the 200 head of "country-honored" dairy cows, to collect eggs from the hen house, plant the garden, or help bring in the hay. During spring, maple sugar season, guests can even carry buckets of sap and help boil it down to maple syrup. The farm is located on 600 acres; the farmhouse is over 100 years old, and guests are welcome all year round.

FOR KIDS: There are a children's pool, a playground area with swings and a seesaw, a room full of games for indoor play, and bicycling, running trails, and swimming nearby.

ACCOMMODATIONS: The farmhouse has eight bedrooms, each with its own Vermont view. There's room for 12 to 14 guests altogether. Two cribs and two high chairs are available.

RATES: A six-night, seven-day stay at the Berksons' costs $300 for adults, $150 for kids under 12, 2 and under are free. Dinners are extra.

Rodgers Dairy Farm Vacation
R.F.D. 3, Box 57
West Glover, Vermont 05875
Telephone: 802-525-6677
Owners: Nancy and James Rodgers

IN THEIR OWN WORDS: "We have a quiet, peaceful atmosphere for families to vacation with their children. We have five guest rooms in our home. Our guests live with us; we eat together as a family."

DESCRIPTION: The Rodgers' farm, operated since the early 1800s by Jim's family, is a working dairy farm with lots of open space. It has a swing set, sandbox, ponies to ride, and lots of cats, kittens, cows, and calves. Kids play in the hay barn, learn how to milk a cow, or go to the lake four miles away.

ACCOMMODATIONS: Five guest rooms have twin or double beds, and there's a crib available. The rooms are large, with homemade quilts on the bed. There's an enclosed porch for relaxing, and the large kitchen-dining area is where Nancy serves the meals.

RATES: Rates are per person so a family of four make take either two or three rooms; the choice is theirs. The rate per person is $200 per week, $125 for children under 12; daily it's $40 and $25. All rates include three meals.

RANCHES

Price Canyon Ranch
P.O. Box 1065
Douglas, Arizona 85607
Telephone: 602-558-2383
Owners: Scotty and Alice Anderson

IN THEIR OWN WORDS: "We are a working cattle ranch (that's primarily how we make our living) who take only a few paying guests at a time. We are in an isolated area of the mountains of Southeast Arizona and the nearest town is Douglas, 42 miles away, 150 miles from the nearest airport."

DESCRIPTION: Just as Scotty described above, this is very much an authentic working ranch. Don't expect fancy but do expect "the real thing." In summer, besides accommodating families, the Andersons operate a riding camp for boys and girls where campers learn to ride and care for a horse, do branding and roundups. There's a small outdoor pool, a modest-sized fish pond with a boat, and lots of horses.

FOR KIDS: There's no special program for kids—they're expected to ride and join in on the life of the ranch. This is probably not the right choice for very young children.

ACCOMMODATIONS: The family bunkhouse is a two-room unit with a bath. It sleeps six comfortably.

RATES: Adults are charged $135 per day double occupancy. Kids' rates range from $10 to $35, depending on age. The minimum stay is two days. Rates include lodging, meals, and a horse. The Andersons also operate a trailer park, where they charge $8 per day for a complete hookup with two people, $1 for each additional person, $4 per day for tents.

Rancho de los Caballeros
P.O. Box 1148
Wickenburg, Arizona 85358
Telephone: 602-684-5484
Manager: Dallas C. Gant, Jr.

IN THEIR OWN WORDS: "Rancho de los Caballeros is an elegant, working ranch/guest resort set amid 20,000 acres of rolling hillsides and flowering Arizona desert."

DESCRIPTION: There are lots of things to do—swimming in an outdoor pool, tennis, trap and skeet shooting, golf, horseback riding and at night square dances, movies, cards, and billiards. The ranch is open from October to May.

FOR KIDS: From mid-November to mid-May, children 5 to 12 have an organized program run by counselors. The program begins at 8:00 A.M., when the counselor meets the kids for breakfast; the morning is spent riding and on nature walks. Afternoons are spent with parents until 6:00 P.M., when the counselor meets them again for dinner and after-dinner games until 9:00 P.M. Counselors are with the kids for all meals. The little kids can ring ride in the corral and play in the playground at any time during the day. Baby-sitting is available for $3 per hour. Instructions in horseback riding are available for $18 per ride, tennis and golf at $24 per hour.

ACCOMMODATIONS: Suites have one or two bedrooms, and some have kitchenettes. Cribs are available for $5 per night.

RATES: The basic per person adult rate in high season (February to May) is $96 to $114 per night for double occupancy. Connecting living rooms are extra. Ask for children's rates. Rates include meals, accommodations, and use of some, but not all, ranch facilities.

Scott Valley Resort and Guest Ranch
Route 2, Box 270
Mountain Home, Arkansas 72653
Telephone: 501-425-5136
Owners: Tom and Kathleen Cooper

IN THEIR OWN WORDS: "Here we really work at getting parent and child together. Games—either active or board games—are great. . . . We try to set up an atmosphere where parent and child can relate to each other. . . . Our guests become our friends and we place a high value on friendship. . . . Arkansas is one of the best kept secrets and hidden treasures in this country."

DESCRIPTION: In the midst of the Ozarks, the ranch is set among 214 acres of meadows, streams, and woodlands. There are six different trail rides offered each day (37 horses to choose from), a heated pool with a lifeguard on duty during the summer, tennis, volleyball, softball, badminton, nature and fitness trails. At night, expect cookouts, games, and hayrides. There's all kinds of adventure on the White and Norfork rivers (a box lunch, boat and canoes are available as part of the package). Guided fishing trips can also be arranged for world-class trout fishing on the White River.

FOR KIDS: The Coopers are adamant—they don't believe in children's programs that separate kids and parents—"Granted our parents love the idea that the kids can and do go on supervised trail rides and they don't have to go every time, but that's not the intent and purpose of the vacation. Yes, they love to be able to have someone watch their toddler for a few hours while they canoe, go shopping or just lie in the sun, but that isn't the main point of the trip!" The Coopers go on: "Parents and children don't need more time apart; they need more time together learning how to interact. We do help with that." So the emphasis is clearly on togetherness, with lots of activities of interest to both parents and their kids. For the occasional adult trip, baby-sitters are available for $3.50 per hour with a five-hour minimum. All meals are family-style.

ACCOMMODATIONS: The facilities are motel-like: 16 of the 28 units have two bedrooms and sleep up to six people. Each has a private bathroom and daily maid service, and all are on the ground floor.

RATES: Weekly rates are $450 for an adult, $330 for kids 7 to 12; $210, 3 to 6, and free for kids under 3. Any family or group of four or more who occupy the same unit are entitled to a 10 percent discount. Rates include all activities at the ranch, meals, and lodging. A one-day fishing trip with a guide on the Norfork or White River is approximately $90.

Alisal Guest Ranch
1054 Alisal Road
Solvang, California 93463
Telephone: 805-688-6411
Manager: Jack Austin

IN THEIR OWN WORDS: "The Alisal provides a lovely setting for family togetherness with facilities and activities available for individual pursuits as well."

DESCRIPTION: The ranch takes its name from the Spanish word for "sycamore grove" and has been in operation since the turn of the century, starting out as a prosperous cattle ranch. In 1943 the current owner bought 10,000 acres of the ranch to winter cattle but decided, three years later, to open the place to guests. There's room for 200 people now, and many guests return year after year. According to one guest, "After 12 years of coming to The Alisal, I told my kids I was taking them to Europe next summer. Two of them still aren't talking to me." Riding is important at Alisal but so are tennis and golf: There's a par 72 course designed by Billy Bell and a resident PGA professional on staff year-round, and seven tennis courts with a resident pro and staff offering private and group lessons and clinics. On the ranch's own 100-acre lake, guests may sail, fish, row, windsurf, and swim. If freshwater swimming is not for you, there's an outdoor heated pool. At night, guests get together for country dancing, storytelling, talent shows, and other activities that are fine for any age.

FOR KIDS: For children 4 and older, there are counselors available to direct arts and crafts projects throughout the day and into the early evening. There may be fingerpainting, clay modeling, sand painting, or storytelling. Kids are free to come and go as they wish and are encouraged to go on their own to the pool, playground, or game room if they are old enough. Every afternoon there are two outdoor activities planned with the kids in mind—it might be a hike, a scavenger hunt, or a series of races. For the very little ones, babysitting can be arranged for $5 per hour.

ACCOMMODATIONS: You may choose from a large studio room with twin beds and a fireplace; a two-room suite with a bedroom equipped with king or twin beds, a sitting room with pull-out beds and a fireplace; or a private bungalow with a large front porch, three bedrooms, two baths, and a living room with a fireplace.

RATES: The daily rates for the studio room are $195 double occupancy; the two-room suite, $245; and for the bungalow, $390 for four people. Kids under 2 may stay for free, and from 2 to 12, the rate is $60 per day. Rates include lodging, breakfast, and dinner, but riding, tennis, and golf are additional in the high season—June, July, and August.

Coffee Creek Guest Ranch
HCR 2, Box 4940
Trinity Center, California 96091
Telephone: 916-266-3343
Managers: Mark and Ruth Hartman

IN THEIR OWN WORDS: "The whole atmosphere is like a camp for families."

DESCRIPTION: Set in a canyon surrounded by wilderness, high peaks with lots of conifers, and Coffee Creek flowing right through it, the ranch hosts a maximum of 50 guests per week, keeping the staff-to-guest ratio at one to three. Horseback riding, swimming in the heated pool or a dip in Coffee Creek, gold panning, horseshoes, volleyball, hiking, hayrides, and square dancing are all offered. We get calls from people looking for another ranch like Coffee Creek: "After all," said one parent, "we don't want to spend *every* vacation there."

FOR KIDS: From Sunday through Thursday, from 8:00 A.M. to 5:00 P.M. there's a supervised program for kids 3 to 12 called Kiddie Korral. Mornings involve a nature hike and crafts, and the afternoon is passed in riding and swimming. Horseback riding lessons are available at $10 per lesson.

ACCOMMODATIONS: Cabins have one or two bedrooms. Some have fireplaces; all have full baths and wall-to-wall carpeting.

RATES: During the summer, the adult weekly rate for a two-bedroom cabin plus three meals and ranch activities is $415, for 13 to 17 it $395, and for kids 3 to 12 it's $295. Kids 3 and under are charged $150, which includes baby-sitting during rides from Saturday through Thursday.

Wilderness Trails Ranch
23486 County Road 501
Bayfield, Colorado 81122
Telephone: 303-247-0722
Owners: Gene and Jan Roberts

IN THEIR OWN WORDS: "Parents rave about our wonderful children's and teen programs because the kids love it, and the parents don't have to worry about entertaining their children. The kids are never bored and are always ready for bed with no hassles! Many tears are shed at the end of a week's stay because they've had such a marvelous time."

DESCRIPTION: Located in the heart of the San Juan National Forest of southwestern Colorado, this is Colorado's last frontier. Riding, hiking, fishing at the ranch's private stocked pond or at Vallecito Lake (two miles from the ranch), swimming in a 72-foot pool, waterskiing, windsurfing, relaxing in the spa, rafting down the Animas River, and playing volleyball are all favorites. Evenings may include a magic show, a square dance, or an old-fashioned hayride.

FOR KIDS: Children ages 6 to 12 participate in the riding program, with lessons all week long. They also have crafts, hikes, picnics, games, a hayride and a Frontier Day, which includes archery and Indian lore. The younger children ages 2 to 5 have pony rides each morning and afternoon and spend the rest of the time with their counselors in the tree house, on the swings, hiking, picnicking, or just playing outdoors. Although there's no specific programming for children under 2, staff members are usually available to baby-sit, during the afternoon or evening. Kids 6 to 12 usually eat lunch and dinner one hour before the teens and adults, but families may eat together if they prefer. Teenagers have their own counselors and go off on all-day rides and hikes with them. They picnic together, play volleyball, and have hot tub parties.

ACCOMMODATIONS: Families stay in log cabins with two, three, four, and five bedrooms, nestled among the pines, spruce, and aspens. Cribs are free.

RATES: The Sunday-to-Sunday package for adults is $695, for kids 12 to 17, $600; for kids 6 to 11, $540; for kids 4 to 5, $450; and 2 to 3, $380. Children under 2 are free. Rates include accommodations, all meals, daily maid service, children's program, horses, waterskiing, hayrides, and other ranch activities. The river raft trip is extra.

Sky Corral Ranch
8233 Old Flowers Road
Bellvue, Colorado 80512
Telephone: 303-484-1362
Manager: Greg Cecil

IN THEIR OWN WORDS: "Many of our guests tell us that they came for a vacation and ended up spending time with friends. We are small enough (25 guests at a time) so that a family can get a lot of attention, and when they leave, they leave as friends."

DESCRIPTION: This family-operated ranch sits at the end of the road at an elevation of 7,800 feet in "a valley full of fresh air." The ranch is bordered on three sides by the Roosevelt National Forest, just 24 miles northwest of Fort Collins. The owners keep their own string of mountain-bred, trailwise horses and offer lots of trails to ride. A breakfast ride to the high meadow is a special weekly feature, as is an optional overnight pack trip. There's also fishing for trout, swimming in the heated pool, re-energizing in the hot tub or sauna, as well as tennis, horseshoes, and volleyball. Each week there's the chance to take a raft trip. At night a variety of family-type activities is offered, including a melodrama put on by the staff and square dancing.

FOR KIDS: Baby-sitting is always available at no extra charge as long as 12 hours' notice is given. Kids from 3 to 12 may participate in an organized program that includes play in the sandbox and games for the younger ones and for those 6 and over, nature crafts, artwork, riding instruction, hiking, and barnyard visits. Kids' activities are scheduled every day from 9:00 to 11:00 A.M. and again from 1:00 to 4:00 P.M.

ACCOMMODATIONS: You can choose from one-, two-, or three-bedroom cabins or a room in the Ranch House. Cabins are especially cozy and comfortable and two have their own fireplaces.

RATES: A six-day stay costs $620 for adults, $500 for kids 6–12, $400 for kids 3–5, and free for under 3s. During June and September there's a 10 percent discount. Rates are all-inclusive—lodging, meals, airport pickup, rafting, riding, coffee delivered fresh to the cabin every morning, and all ranch activities.

Home Ranch
P.O. Box 822
Clark, Colorado 80428
Telephone: 303-879-1780 or 800-223-7094
Manager: L. Kendrick Jones

IN THEIR OWN WORDS: "Our ranch offers a gracious combination of western warmth, creature comforts and lively outdoor activities. It is a peaceful, chuck-it-all, wilderness retreat."

DESCRIPTION: When a friend visited, she was immediately impressed by the beauty of the ranch—here is wilderness living complete with antiques, fabulous art, wonderful amenities, and gourmet food. The ranch is open in both winter and summer—she saw it in winter when the guests come to cross-country ski on 40 kilometers of tracked trials that run through the Elk River Valley, all around the ranch, down by the river, and across the valley. Only 18 miles north of Steamboat Springs, the ranch may also be used as a base for downhill skiers but, it is a half-hour ride from Steamboat. Winter rates include cross-country ski equipment and lessons, sleigh rides out to feed the horses, and as much ice-skating as you'd like.

In summer, of course, the emphasis turns to riding—everything from kids' rides to all-day sightseeing trips to roping and barrel-racing for the more experienced. Other possibilities include fly-fishing in the ranch's own trout-stocked pond or the Elk River, hiking with llamas along trails that open onto stunning mountain views, cookouts, and the use of the swimming pool heated to 90 degrees year-round and sauna.

Our own visit here in summer confirmed what our friend had to say. This is a gorgeous place—truly a luxury dude ranch. The attention to detail is impressive—the manager explained to us that only 100 percent cotton 200-thread-count sheets are considered good enough for Home Ranch guests. The ranch is Ken's dream come true—he built it himself over the last 11 years. It is one of the few American properties to have earned the prestigious French designation as a "Relais et Châteaux." When we visited, the people at the Home Ranch were thinking of making 3 years the minimum age for guests. Check to see what they've decided. They don't want their children's program to have to provide baby-sitting-type care; they prefer that it's a more active program for kids who are old enough to get involved in the activities.

FOR KIDS: Baby-sitting may be arranged at no extra charge for kids 3 and under, and for the older kids, counselors are available to lead crafts, supervise swimming, play games, and teach them all about horses. Kids over 6 take part in the regular activities of the ranch, usually spending most of their time either horseback riding or swimming. Lessons in riding, cross-country skiing, fly-fishing, and roping are all available at no extra cost.

ACCOMMODATIONS: Rooms are in separate cabins and in a handful of rooms in the main lodge. The largest accommodation is the two-bedroom, two-bath cabin; also available are studios, one-bedrooms, and a one-bedroom with a loft and a living room. All cabins have covered porches and, luxury-of-luxuries, their own private jacuzzi tucked in under the porch. The rooms are beautifully furnished; the art work is truly remarkable—everything from Vietnamese tapestries to antique crazy quilts to Native American carpets and weavings. Each room has a coffeemaker and mini-refrigerator, and all are supplied with coffee, tea, milk, home-baked cookies, crackers and cheese. The Home Ranch combines the very best of the rustic—unfinished pine, rough-hewn logs—with modern amenities—hair dryers, good reading lights, and a nice, thick terry cloth robe in every closet. The food is spectacular—this is one ranch that has a chef, not a cook.

RATES: In winter, the one-bedroom with loft and living room costs $2,235 for two adults for seven nights; kids 2 and under are free, 3-to-5-year-olds are $45 per night. Children over 5 are charged $90 per night (the regular third- or fourth-person rate). In summer, the same arrangement costs $2,400. All rates include three sumptuous meals per day and entitle guests to one raid on the kitchen in the middle of the night as well as airport transfers, once-a-week laundry service, evening entertainment, a trip to the rodeo in Steamboat, all-day hiking trips into the wilderness, and all riding and lessons. Hot air ballooning, river rafting, mountain bike tours, and massages are all easily arranged for an additional fee.

Vista Verde Guest and Ski Touring Ranch
Seed House Road
Clark, Colorado 80428
Mailing address: Box 465
Steamboat Springs, Colorado 80477
Telephone: 303-879-3858 or 800-526-RIDE
Owners: The Brophy Family

IN THEIR OWN WORDS: "We have a traditional western guest ranch offering good food and comfortable lodging and a year-round mountain recreational experience. Our ranch is fairly small so we are able to give guests a personalized vacation. In the summer, the emphasis is on family activities."

DESCRIPTION: Our family spent a few days not long ago at Vista Verde and had a great time. Most impressive of all was the staff—all extremely spirited young people whose love of ranch life was contagious. My youngest, not generally a joiner, was crazy about the children's counselor and happily went off with her on nature hikes, a trip to town on an antique fire engine, and to a nearby former mining town for gold panning. The Brophys love animals and keep goats, sheep, chickens, and assorted cats and dogs—the kids got to feed the farm animals every day and gather eggs in the morning. Great fun for a city kid. The ranch is beautifully situated, and the trail rides

take guests to places with extraordinary vistas. The food was great—
Jacques, the chef, was terrific about custom-designing menus for our
vegetarian family.

Vista Verde is just 25 miles north of Steamboat Springs, high in
the Rocky Mountains of northwestern Colorado. It's surrounded by
the Routt National Forest and the Mount Zirkel Wilderness Area
and bordered by the Elk River. The Brophys are eager to share the
beauty of their ranch and to give guests a chance to experience as
much of their part of the world as possible in a week's stay. One day
is set aside for an all-day ride up the South Fork of the Elk River,
and once during the week there's an overnight pack trip that gives
guests the chance to "sleep under the stars on top of the world." Any
guests who want to get involved with the real work of the farm are
more than welcome to ride herd on 200 head of cattle, check fences,
do haying or irrigating. Hiking is another favorite activity at Vista
Verde—once during the week the Brophys schedule a day hike to
the 11,000-foot levels for a look at the incredible wildflower display.
On another hike, everyone brings gold pans and a gem and mineral
book, hoping to get lucky. One of Colorado's finest fly-fishermen
holds a weekly clinic at the ranch, and it's easy enough to go out to
any of the mountain streams or lakes in the area to test what you've
learned. Guests are treated, too, to a full day of river rafting on the
upper Colorado River. The ranch is open in winter as well, when the
favorite activity is cross-country skiing along a 20-kilometer network of well-marked trails. If that's not quite enough, there's an
additional 40 kilometers of marked trails in the adjacent Routt
National Forest. We stopped by the ranch in winter and to us, it felt a
little like a visit to grandma's—that is, if grandma owned a ranch!

FOR KIDS: "The entire staff joins in helping kids learn how to
participate in and enjoy western life. Our unique group of small farm
animals become instant friends, and children help to care for everything from grown ducks to tiny lambs, peacocks to pygmy goats."
Kids gather eggs and feed the animals each morning. Starting at
9:00 A.M., kids from 3 to 12 may participate in the ranch's children's
program. For the under 3 set, there's petting the animals, treasure
hunts, games, rides in the ranch fire engine, and hayrides. The 3-
to-5-year-olds do some of the same activities as the little ones, plus
they get a chance to learn about horseback riding on Strawberry and
Tony, two miniature horses that are only three feet tall. At Fort
Smiles, built up high in the trees, there are cots for overnights, toys
for little ones, and swings and a slide for a quick descent. Older
children, from 6 to teenage, do more advanced riding and learn a lot

about fishing. All of the kids get a chance to swim, hike, and have picnics.

ACCOMMODATIONS: Guests stay in one of the mountain log homes that are tucked into the aspen hillside and overlook hay-meadows and the mountains. Wood is the theme inside and outside the rustic cabins, and all are carpeted, have full kitchens and baths, living rooms with fireplaces, and from one to three bedrooms.

RATES: From May 28 to September 17, a one-week stay at the ranch costs $1,050 per adult, $850 for kids 6–12, and $750 for kids under 6. Just about everything is included in the rate except for the hot-air balloon ride, fly-fishing school, and a two-day wilderness pack trip. In winter, rates are $60 per day for the first two guests, $30 for each additional guest for lodging; for meals, add $25 per day per person.

Colorado Trails Ranch
P.O. Box 848
Durango, Colorado 81302
Telephone: 800-323-DUDE
Owners: Dick and Ginny Elder

IN THEIR OWN WORDS: " A vacation at Colorado Trails Ranch is darn good therapy for anyone whether you are a family, a couple or traveling alone. . . . Remember, our job is seeing to it that you forget yours."

DESCRIPTION: Dick and Ginny are serious about horses, horse-back riding, and dude ranching. We had lunch with Dick one after-noon, and he told us all about his theory of dude ranching. He and his wife are the only certified riding instructors who teach at a dude ranch and Dick explained that anyone who comes to stay at Colorado Trails learns a tremendous amount about riding and horses. "We tell guests how they're going to ride these horses and it may be different from what they're used to. We're interested in equitation—not long, arduous trail rides." Dick loves to collect antiques. Some of the highlights of his collection are displayed throughout the ranch. He is extremely proud of his staff—he spends the winter hiring for the three months the ranch is open—and insists that all applicants provide him with a videotape of their riding. As we said, he really is serious about horses.

Riding in groups of six, lessons for beginners and the more advanced, tennis on two courts (you can use their rackets), whirlpool spa, swimming in a heated pool, fishing in a stocked river or on a lake 12 miles from the ranch, hiking, climbing, and photography are all possible during the day. River rafting on the Animas River can be arranged with a local outfitter, and an excursion to Mesa Verde National Park with a ranch guide is easy to plan if you want to leave the ranch for a while.

FOR KIDS: The children are divided into three age groups—5 to 9, 9 to 13, and 13 to 18 years. The program runs from June to August, and each age group has its own counselor. The kids do lots of riding; they swim and learn archery, riflery, and waterskiing. The program is flexible. The kids get a chance to suggest activities. Kids may eat with their parents or their new friends.

ACCOMMODATIONS: There are three basic styles of cabins—Alpine cabins have one or two rooms each with bath; country cabins have two-room suites with queen-size bed and full bath; and mountain cabins are a bit more deluxe.

RATES: Rates vary according to the cabin chosen, but a sample would be two adults, two children in two rooms of the Alpine cabin for $2,775 per week. The rates include lodging, meals, horses, tennis, waterskiing, and all other ranch facilities. The only "extras" are the Mesa Verde trip ($20) and an optional overnight ride ($20 with their sleeping bag, $15 with your own), and river rafting, $15 for kids up to 18, $18 for adults.

Aspen Lodge Ranch Resort and Conference Center
6120 Highway 7, Longs Peak Route
Estes Park, Colorado 80517
Telephone: 303-586-8133
Manager: Boyd LaMarsh

IN THEIR OWN WORDS: "Our true western hospitality makes you feel comfortable. Located in the magnificent Tahosa Valley, the views are the most breathtaking anywhere."

DESCRIPTION: Just 65 miles from the Denver airport, the lodge is located high up in the Colorado Rockies. Riding and hiking are the main summer activities at the lodge; in winter guests like to cross-country ski and take rides through mountain forests on horse-drawn sleighs. Tennis and racquetball are available at the ranch—there are two courts for each—and the heated outdoor pool is fun in any season.

FOR KIDS: Kids 5 and under can have baby-sitters for $2 per hour during the day, $3 per hour at night. For kids 6 and older, there's a children's program that operates during the summer and during Christmas vacation. The program includes hiking, swimming and horseback riding lessons, games, an overnight campout, and excursions to a nearby amusement park or Rocky Mountain National Park. (The program is included in the price of a stay at the lodge, but excursions cost $3 to $5 extra.) Kids may eat with counselors at lunch and dinnertime or, if they prefer, with their parents.

ACCOMMODATIONS: Guests stay in lodge rooms or in private cabins with either one or two bedrooms and separate living rooms.

RATES: In summer, the rate for a family of four with two children between the ages of 2 and 12 would be $80 per adult and $40 per child per night. Kids under 2 are free. Summer rates include all meals, but horseback riding is extra at $10 per hour. Winter rates are for lodging only and range from $60 to $80 per room per night.

Longs Peak Inn and Guest Ranch
6925 Highway 7, Longs Peak Route
Estes Park, Colorado 80517
Telephone: 303-586-2110 or 800-262-2034
Owners: Virginia and Bob Akins

IN THEIR OWN WORDS: "The pace is slow so you have the chance to spend time with your family, friends and by yourself. Also, you experience the friendly atmosphere and hospitality extended because of our small size and family management. Everyone gets a vacation; we do the cooking and the cleaning. You don't have to load up the car each day and travel; just step out the door and you're there."

DESCRIPTION: Longs Peak is the highest mountain in Rocky Mountain National Park and, nestled right at its base, is the Akins' ranch. The horses are reliable and trailwise, and riding instruction is available to all guests. You can choose from short trail rides to all-day rides along a variety of mountain trails; specialty rides include a breakfast cookout, steak fry, and an overnight campout. You can also try hiking, trout fishing, sightseeing in Rocky Mountain National Park, bird watching, or just strolling among the wildflowers and aspens. At night you may get to square dance, play bingo, join a sing-along and there's always the option to do absolutely nothing but relax. The ranch is not very large—never be more than 80 guests at a time—so you'll be able to make new friends easily.

FOR KIDS: Kids from 4 to 16 may join supervised activities

during the summer (the ranch operates from June to September) from 9:00 A.M. until 4:00 P.M. every day except Sunday. Every four to six kids have their own counselor. For the youngest kids, the program involves games, fishing, short walks, picnics, and rides around the corral. The older kids swim, fish and ride; each week there's an overnight campout for the kids 6 and over. For teens, there's no structured program but a counselor is available to suggest and direct activities. Counselors and teens get together to plan a schedule that may include any of the regular activities of the ranch, a trip to town to see a movie, or a special hike or ride.

ACCOMMODATIONS: You stay in bedroom or family units in the lodge or in nearby guest buildings. Family units have two bedrooms and two baths and are large enough to accommodate up to seven people.

RATES: Rates are based on a stay of one week. An adult (over 13) pays $485 for a week in a family unit; for a child 9–12 it's $380, and for a child 4–8, $345. Since there's no programming for kids 3 and younger, the Akins offer a special "nanny" rate—one half the family unit rate for a relative or friend who comes along to baby-sit. Rates include all meals and children's program, but riding is extra. For guests staying a full week there's a weekly riding fee of $115 for adults and $100 for kids 6 to 12. (Kids under 6 are not allowed on the trails.) If you don't plan to do a lot of riding, you can rent a horse by the day—$38—or half day—$27.

Rawah Guest Ranch
P.O. Box K
Fort Collins, Colorado 80522
Telephone: 303-484-5585
Owners: Carol and Eric Jones

IN THEIR OWN WORDS: "This is a family atmosphere guest ranch. . . . Whether riding the mountains, the meadows or the arena, you can bet you'll enjoy it!"

DESCRIPTION: *Rawah* is the Ute Indian word for wilderness; the name is apt, since the ranch sits at the edge of the 76,000-acre Rawah Wilderness Area and is practically surrounded by the Roosevelt National Forest in some of Colorado's wildest and most beautiful country. The Joneses think of their ranch as more rustic than resort—they cater to "folks who want to step back in time a bit and be away from the hectic pace of today's crowded civilization." Riding and fishing are the two major activities at Rawah. Guests are matched with the right saddle and horse when they arrive and keep the same horse until the end of their stay. Instruction is available at no extra charge. The main buildings of the ranch are close to the Big Laramie River, one of the best dry-fly streams in the west, and, for the hardy, the high country lakes offer great fishing as well. Pack trips of three to five days and raft trips on the Cache la Poudre River can easily be arranged for guests.

FOR KIDS: There's no formal children's program, but babysitting is available for kids under 6 every afternoon at no extra charge. There's a sandbox and swings for the little ones and for the 3-to-5-year-olds, an occasional ride on a horse led by a baby-sitter. Kids 6 and over get their own horse and saddle and can go off on supervised trail rides. Kids like to fish in the pond or river, play on the trampolines or join a game of ping-pong.

ACCOMMODATIONS: You may choose from a room in the lodge or a cabin with room for the whole family. Meals are served in the big dining room with a stone fireplace, and since there are only 30 guests at a time, you should get to know everyone pretty well by the time you leave.

RATES: A one week stay, double occupancy, is $595 per person, which includes horses, meals, maid service, and lodging. Kids 3–10 cost $365 per week (under 3 stay in parent's room at no extra cost) and the special rate for nonriders is $520 per week.

C Lazy U Ranch
P.O. Box 378
Granby, Colorado 80446
Telephone: 303-887-3344
Owners: George and Virginia Mullin

IN THEIR OWN WORDS: "We are the highest rated guest ranch in the country with the Mobil 5 Star and AAA 5 diamond ratings."

DESCRIPTION: This is ranching complete with wall-to-wall carpeting, high in the Colorado Rockies. It's a summer, fall, and winter resort. In summer it offers fishing, skeet shooting, horseback riding, a sauna, whirlpool, racquetball, tennis, hiking, and hayrides; in winter, there are cross-country skiing, sleigh rides, ice-skating, snowshoeing, and holiday celebrations. Colorado River rafting trips, golf at a nearby course, boating, and windsurfing can also be arranged.

FOR KIDS: From mid-June to Labor Day and again during winter vacation time through New Year's, there's a full-day children's program for kids 3 to 17. Supervised by counselors, kids learn to ride and fish and appreciate western life. Teenagers 13 to 17 have their own program, which emphasizes riding (morning and afternoon rides), sports, hayrides, cookouts, and games. Everyone has breakfast together, and after breakfast counselors meet with the kids for a full day of activities. Lunches and dinners are eaten with the counselors; after dinner the kids join their parents for the evening entertainment—square dances, swing dances, or staff shows.

ACCOMMODATIONS: You have a choice of one- to three-room units, all with private bath, some with fireplaces. At the center of life at the ranch is the Main Lodge, which includes the dining room, bar, card room, and lounge.

RATES: In summer, weekly rates are $900 to $1,000 for two; children under 6 pay $200 less but do not take trail rides. Winter rates range from $100 to $190 per day per person for two, kids 6 to 12 receive a 10 percent discount, and those 3 to 5 are half-price. From December 19 to January 4 there's a three-night minimum. There is a 10 percent discount all winter long for a stay of seven nights or more.

Drowsy Water Guest Ranch
P.O. Box 147
Granby, Colorado 80446
Telephone: 303-725-3456
Owners: Ken and Randy Sue Fosha

IN THEIR OWN WORDS: "A visit here in our secluded mountain home at Drowsy Water Ranch is a blend of our clean, rustic cabin and lodge accommodations, superb, homemade country-style food and our entertaining and friendly staff."

DESCRIPTION: The ranch borders thousands of acres of backcountry and the Arapahoe National Forest. Trail rides led by wranglers are available every weekday, and for nonriding times there are swimming, horseshoes, jeep trips, pack trips, and trout fishing. Nighttime activities are just what you'd expect at a ranch: square dancing, song fests, campfires, movies, rodeos and hayrides.

FOR KIDS: The littlest ones, under 5, spend time with counselors, riding horses, playing games, hiking, fishing, swimming and doing crafts. Kids over 5 participate in the riding program: They get a horse of their own for the week, and after riding they swim, hike, learn to use a lasso, take archery lessons, and explore nature. Kids can be involved in supervised programming from 9:15 in the morning until 8:00 at night. The children's program runs from June 8 to September 14. Children may eat with or without their parents.

ACCOMMODATIONS: Cabins with one to five rooms are available to families. All are rustic but comfortable, sheltered by stands of aspen and pine and situated along the creek and ranch ponds.

RATES: For one week, a mother, father, or first two family members are $615 per person; all other family members are $560. Kids 5 or under are $325 and any nonriders among you can deduct $105. Rates include all meals, a horse for the week, the children's program and all ranch activities except an overnight pack trip, a river float trip, and golf.

Latigo Ranch
P.O. Box 237
Kremmling, Colorado 80459
Telephone: 303-724-3596
Owners: Jim Yost and Randy George

IN THEIR OWN WORDS: "We're a ranch oriented towards helping families enjoy one another in a secluded mountain setting. Horseback riding is the focus but not the exclusive family activity. . . . In the peak of wildflower season here we have over 95 species blooming at once!"

DESCRIPTION: Nestled in the Colorado's Rocky Mountains, this homey ranch is open in both summer and winter. In summer, the week's activities include riding, of course, and cookouts, an overnight pack trip, nature walks, lectures and at night, square dancing and swing dancing to a live band. The folks at the ranch can also arrange a three-day llama trekking trip for you into the Service Creek Wilderness of Routt National Forest. For one week in July, they sponsor a Wildflower Photography Workshop with experts who teach how to identify the flowers and take the best possible photographs of them.

FOR KIDS: For the youngest, kids 2 and under, you'll need to notify the ranch well in advance so that they can help you find a baby-sitter from the local area. Kids from 3 to 6 are supervised while the adults are out riding. During that time they'll learn about mountain animals, plants, and rocks, hear stories about Indians and horses, work on crafts in the tepee, go on nature walks with their counselor, be led around on Rooster, the ranch's tiny pony, feed Winkle the rabbit, or learn new songs and games. For kids 6–13, the favorite activity is riding. "We emphasize instruction and we structure fun riding activities with sufficient challenge to ensure that these young riders are improving their skills while having a good time." Kids may spend as much or as little time as they'd like with the counselors and may eat meals with their family or at a separate table with other kids and counselors. At times, the kids will get together for their own hot dog roast, but in the evening families are always together for activities that are planned to appeal to all ages.

ACCOMMODATIONS: Modern log cabins have one to three bedrooms, sitting rooms, fireplaces or woodburning stoves, and all are heated.

RATES: In summer, adults pay $777 per person per week; kids 6–13, $577; 3–5, $377; and 2 and under are free in the room with their parents.

Bar Lazy J Guest Ranch
477 County Road 3
Parshall, Colorado 80468
Telephone: 303-725-3437
Owners: Larry and Barbara Harmon

IN THEIR OWN WORDS: "Our ranch is relaxed and unstructured except for meal time and riding time. We want the entire family to have freedom and choice. This is every guest's vacation—from 2 to 80. We feel we have an outstanding children's program."

DESCRIPTION: Bar Lazy J is settled in a peaceful valley of the Colorado River. There's room for 38 guests at a time. Horse rides leave the ranch twice a day every day. Instruction is available. The Colorado River flows through the ranch for "doorstep fishing," and right by the ranch is a 40-foot pool with a children's pool attached. Not too far away you can arrange a river rafting trip, or you can play tennis just five miles away at Hot Sulphur Springs. Every Saturday there's a rodeo, and for golfers there's an 18-hole course about one-half hour from the ranch.

FOR KIDS: The children's program here is for kids 2 and over and operates from mid-June to Labor Day. Local baby-sitters are available to take care of kids under 2. Just let the staff know you'd like one. The program is deliberately flexible and meant to suit the interests of each kid involved. After a family breakfast, a counselor checks with each child to see how much time he or she wants to spend with the counselor that day. The kids can have lunch and dinner in their own dining room if they'd like, and counselors are available from 8:30 A.M. to 7:30 P.M., for example, until after the nightly hayride. With their own counselors, kids ride, swim, fish, and hike, and if they're interested crafts and square dancing are scheduled. Each year there are some new lambs and calves that need to be fed. Usually the kids and their counselors are in charge.

ACCOMMODATIONS: Guest cottages accommodate from two to eight people. They're situated along the Colorado River and all have a screened-in porch. Cribs are available at no extra charge.

RATES: Adults (that's anyone 9 or over) pay $595 for a week; children 5 to 8, $450; 2 to 4, $350; and under 2, $100. Rates include accommodations, meals, maid service, the counselor program, and all recreational facilities.

Lost Valley Ranch
Route 2
Sedalia, Colorado 80135
Telephone: 303-647-2311
Owner: Robert Foster

IN THEIR OWN WORDS: "Lost Valley is an authentic year-round working horse/cattle ranch situated in a beautiful valley on 40,000 acres of the Colorado Pike National Forest. . . . Our aim is to give the entire family a memorable vacation. . . . 90 percent of our clientele are either returning guests or referred by a former guest. To understand you must come and experience the atmosphere that is created by the beauty of the mountains, the service attitude of our staff and the friendships formed with other families."

DESCRIPTION: Lost Valley is a working ranch, homesteaded in 1883. The owners, who say that most of today's young people have learned what they know about ranching from the TV show "Dallas," invite you to come and see the real thing in Louis L'Amour country. Riding is the main event with miles of scenic trails available; guests can help with the roundup or branding or plan an overnight pack trip into the hills. There are a heated pool, tennis courts and trap shooting, volleyball, and horseshoes. Trout fishing is great, and the chef will custom-cook a catch. Nighttime activities are typically ranchlike: barbecues, square dancing, and hootenannies.

FOR KIDS: During the summer Lost Valley offers a program for

6-to-12-year-olds and for teenagers. Three-to-five-year-olds have a program available all year long; the littlest ones may have a baby-sitter for $2.50 per hour. Teenagers ride along with three college student staff members and are encouraged to do "their own thing" while the kids 6 to 12 have a more structured program, which includes riding, swimming, hikes, and picnics. Children may eat with or without their parents; some nights there are special meals just for kids. On Saturdays there are special family rides. Children 3 to 5 have group baby-sitting while adults are off on morning and after-noon rides. Parents can take their 3-to-5-years-olds on a horseback ride, but counselors won't.

ACCOMMODATIONS: Cabins have from one to three bedrooms. All have a living room, fireplace, and one or two baths. Cribs are available at no extra charge.

RATES: The basic adult rate is approximately $850; children 3 to 5, $500; 6 to 12, $675; and teens, $850; kids under 2 are free. Rates include meals, lodging, entertainment, all facilities, horseback riding, fishing, tennis, swimming, the children's program—everything except trap shooting. Nonsummer rates are lower.

North Fork Guest Ranch
Box B
Shawnee, Colorado 80475
Telephone: 303-838-9873
Owners: Dean and Karen May

IN THEIR OWN WORDS: "We believe in family vacations and offer a lifetime of memories. . . . The ranch is our home and we take great pride in our own sense of hospitality, . . . one of the unexpected joys of a vacation at North Fork is getting to know our exceptional staff. You can count on their help, whether it's helping map your trip, cleaning a fish, or getting film for your camera."

DESCRIPTION: An hour from Denver, the ranch has the North Fork of the Platte River (Eisenhower's favorite trout fishing river) right out its back door and a few miles to the west, the snow-capped peaks of the Continental Divide. Riding instruction is available for all guests, and most of the rides will take you into the high country wilderness adjacent to the ranch. The week's activities include a whitewater raft trip and a picnic lunch (kids 8 and over may go along), an overnight trip with all gear provided by the ranch, trap shooting, and a rodeo.

FOR KIDS: Kids 6 and over are invited to join the regular trail rides and participate in all ranch activities with their parents. For the younger ones there are counselors who will play games with them, take them swimming (there's a heated pool), on hikes, and fishing in the pond, where a catch is guaranteed. (All you have to do is ask and the staff will be happy to cook the very same fish for your family for dinner.) Counselors are available from 9:00 A.M. to 5:00 P.M.

ACCOMMODATIONS: The Homestead Cabin is just right for a family of four, with its two rooms and connecting bath. Larger cabins with three rooms are also available. Some cabins have fireplaces, all have daily maid service.

RATES: From June 17 to August 26, the high season, the weekly package costs $750 for adults, $600 for kids 6–12, $500 for kids 1–6 and free for kids under 1 year. The rate is $100 less from May 1 to June 17 and during September. Transportation from the Denver airport costs $80 for a family of four.

Busterback Ranch
Star Route
Ketchum, Idaho 83340
Telephone: 208-774-2217
Managing Director: Jim Root

IN THEIR OWN WORDS: "The atmosphere at Busterback is extremely relaxed and we want people to feel as though they are in their own home and we are their good friends."

DESCRIPTION: In summer, this is a guest ranch. In winter, it's a cross-country ski resort. Cradled in a valley below the peaks of the Sawtooth Range, the ranch is the kind of place that is "tailored for those that yearn to get away from it all but aren't sure how well the wilderness will fit." Besides the riding, guests can try fishing or kayaking in the Salmon River, which flows right through the ranch, or go canoeing on a nearby lake. There are only eight rooms, so you will get a lot of attention from the staff.

FOR KIDS: As you would expect, at a ranch with only eight guest rooms, there is no formal children's program, but kids are welcome. Riding, games, mountain biking, and swimming are all possibilities. For kids 3 and under there's baby-sitting available at $4 an hour for a minimum of four hours.

ACCOMMODATIONS: There are five rooms in the main lodge and three log cabins, equipped with rough-hewn pine beds. Wherever you stay, you're guaranteed a magnificent view.

RATES: The rate of $135 per person per day includes lodging, meals, use of mountain bikes, canoes, and windsurfers. Horseback riding is, however, additional at $25 for two hours. Children's rates are lower.

Flathead Lake Lodge
Box 248
Big Fork, Montana 59911
Telephone: 406-837-4391
Owner: Doug Averill

IN THEIR OWN WORDS: "Our clientele is entirely families—we have between 30 and 40 children each week."

DESCRIPTION: The Averills established the ranch in 1945 on the shores of the largest natural lake west of the Great Lakes, in the Rocky Mountains, just south of Glacier National Park. Horseback riding is the star attraction—trail rides along the mountain terrain, evening rodeos, breakfast rides, and cookouts over open fires. Guests can also sail, whitewater raft, fish, waterski, canoe, or swim in either the lake or a heated pool.

FOR KIDS: From mid-June to mid-September, the ranch has a children's program that operates from 7:00 A.M. all the way until 10:00 P.M. Kids 3 years and up can participate. The ranch offers horseback riding, of course, arts and crafts, swimming and boating, campfires at night, waterskiing for the older kids, tennis, inner tubing on the river. Lessons in sailing, waterskiing, horseback riding, tennis, and fishing are all available. Each week there's a guest rodeo and a special overnight campout in teepees. The kids' activities involve one wrangler (counselor) to every three children—good odds.

ACCOMMODATIONS: For families, there are rustic two- to three-bedroom cottages with room for four to seven people. There are "plenty" of cribs at no extra cost. Meals are eaten at the lodges, and outdoor barbecues of buffalo, roast pig, and fresh salmon are held on a patio overlooking the lake.

RATES: A seven-day package that runs from Sunday to Sunday costs $989 for an adult, $797 for teens, $671 for kids 4 to 12, and $96 for kids under 4. Included are meals, horseback riding, water sports, use of boats, waterskiing, tennis, volleyball, and lots of other ranch activities.

Lone Mountain Ranch
P.O. Box 69
Big Sky, Montana 59716
Telephone: 406-995-4644
Manager: Bob Schaap

IN THEIR OWN WORDS: "Viv, our daughter Laura, our partner Mike and I make the Lone Mountain Ranch our year-round home. We are convinced that it's just about the prettiest spot on earth and that we're mighty lucky to live in such a place. We also feel very fortunate to be able to share our home in the Montana mountains and our own way of life with our guests."

DESCRIPTION: According to Schaap, "The ranch and its surroundings are among the few remaining places to see elk, moose and bighorn sheep in their natural habitat, to walk through fields of wild alpine flowers, ride the mountain trails and watch a Montana sunset over the mountains." Guests set their own pace—do as much or as little as they please. Some of the choices include rides twice a day or, for the adventurous, all-day rides. At least once a week the ranch trailers horses to a remote trailhead for backcountry riding. And, for guests who really want to feel like they belong, there'll be opportunities to join the wranglers mending fences or blazing new trails. Since Yellowstone is nearby, weekly van trips are scheduled. Trout fishing is excellent and can be reached by horse, float, or pack trip. Several times each week the ranch naturalist leads a hike, and overnight pack trips can be arranged (a minimum of three nights is recommended). In winter, the ranch becomes home to cross-country skiers, with a ski shop, ski rentals, instruction at all levels, guided day trips into Yellowstone, and overnight trips to the ranch's backcountry cabin.

FOR KIDS: Kids 6–12 are able to participate in a number of special programs designed for them, such as overnight campouts, cookouts, kids' rides, rodeos, nature walks, and outdoor games. Hours vary from day to day—most take place during the afternoon or evenings. There are also a few organized activities for kids 2–5 and a few afternoons a week reserved for group baby-sitting. The staff recommends bringing along someone to take care of kids younger than 6 if you want to do a lot of activities that won't include them. Sometimes local baby-sitters can be found, but there's no guarantee.

ACCOMMODATIONS: You'll be staying in a cabin, all with electric heat and modern baths. Most are made of native log and all have a front porch. All meals are provided, and if you plan to be away from the ranch at lunchtime, the kitchen will pack you a bag lunch.

RATES: In a large family cabin shared by four the per person weekly rate is $725 for adults, $615 for kids 6–12, and $460 for kids 2–6. Children under 2 are free if they share a room with adults. Most guests stay for a week or two, but shorter stays are possible. Included in the rates is lodging, meals, rides, riding instruction, guided walks, outdoor barbecues, children's activities, evening programs, and the use of all recreational facilities at the ranch. The price of the Yellowstone van trip is $35 for adults and $20 for kids under 12; whitewater rafting is available for about $28 for a two-hour trip on the Gallatin River.

Mountain Sky Guest Ranch
P.O. Box 1128
Bozeman, Montana 59715
Telephone: 406-587-1244 or 800-548-3392
Manager: Alan Brutger

IN THEIR OWN WORDS: "We're the perfect setting for a Western vacation—Swiss-like peaks of the Absarokee-Beartooth Mountain Range, the Yellowstone River flowing through wide-open Paradise Valley, the Gallatin National Forest in our backyard and famous Yellowstone National Park only 30 minutes away."

DESCRIPTION: There are hundreds of miles of horseback riding trails surrounding the ranch. Everyone gets his own horse for the duration of his stay, and lessons for beginners are available. Big Creek, which flows through the ranch, is excellent for trout fishing, and there are also tennis, a heated swimming pool, hiking trails, a volleyball court, a hot tub, and a sauna. Kids have their own playground, game room, and private trout pond.

FOR KIDS: From June 1 to October 15, kids of all ages may participate in a full day of activities planned just for them. Breakfast and lunch are eaten with the family. Kids may eat in a supervised setting at dinnertime with other kids, allowing their parents to dine alone. Kids go on horseback rides with their counselor, do arts and crafts, and play in the playground. After lunch with their parents they go on another ride, swim, and fish. From 4:30 to 5:30 they get together with their parents, and from 5:30 to 8:00 they join their counselors for dinner and an after-dinner treat such as a cookout, a movie, or square dancing. Teens have a similar schedule but with kids their own age and at a different pace and level. The littlest ones, under 3, may have a baby-sitter; it's best to discuss individual needs for this age group with the staff.

ACCOMMODATIONS: A typical cabin at Mountain Sky has two rooms—a back bedroom and a front room with a hide-a-bed. Three- and four-bedroom cabins are also available.

RATES: The weekly package includes lodging, meals, a horse, and all ranch activities. In summers it's $980–$1,120 per adult, double occupancy; $840–980 kids 7 to 12; and $520–735 for those 6 and under.

Sixty Three Ranch
Box 979
Livingston, Montana 59047
Telephone: 406-222-0570
General Manager: Sandra Cahill

IN THEIR OWN WORDS: "We are in one of the world's most beautiful locations and we offer an ideal family vacation where families can spend a lot or very little time together. The parents don't have to worry about their children; the kids have a great time just experiencing regular ranch life. . . . Lasting friendships between families are formed here."

DESCRIPTION: This is a working ranch in Mission Creek Canyon, where guests join in on roundups and other ranch work. Horseback riding lessons are available, and riding is the main event. Trout fishing in the ranch's own stream and excursions to nearby Yellowstone Park are popular with guests.

FOR KIDS: There's no formal kids' program, but baby-sitting can be arranged for $2 per hour.

ACCOMMODATIONS: There are two-, three-, and four-room cabins, some with two baths, tucked in among the aspen and pine.

RATES: A three-room cabin large enough for five costs $525–545 per person per week, including accommodations, meals, use of a saddle horse, riding instruction, and access to all ranch facilities. Pack trips are $150 per day extra. Subtract $25 for kids 3–11 and 50 percent for kids 3 and under who don't need a horse. Free for infants except for a small charge for crib rental.

Rocking Horse Ranch
Highland, New York 12528
Telephone: 914-691-2927 or 800-437-2624
Owner: Billy Turk and his family

IN THEIR OWN WORDS: "Excellent for families . . . endless activity with supervision and instruction. Parents are pampered, too. . . . You arrive as a guest and become a friend."

DESCRIPTION: The long list includes horseback riding, waterskiing, fishing, swimming in an outdoor and an indoor pool, miniature golf, archery, tennis courts, saunas, ice-skating, sleigh rides, volleyball, a fitness gym, and on and on. Insructions in tennis, swimming, waterskiing, and horseback riding are all offered at no extra charge. At night, there's entertainment in the Round-Up Room Nightclub. Throughout the year there are special theme weekends—a "Who Dunnit" weekend, a "Festivale de Columbus," and so on.

We spent a few days at Rocking Horse and had lots of fun. Just be sure you're not expecting a "back to nature" experience or that you want peace and quiet. The ranch is a lively place with nonstop events from early morning until late at night.

FOR KIDS: A day camp for kids operates all summer and at holiday time. Kids from 4 to 14 are welcome to participate from 9:00 A.M. to 4:30 P.M., and in the course of the stay they can learn to ski, waterski, and horseback ride. Children can eat lunch and dinner with their parents or with their counselors. The choice is theirs.

ACCOMMODATIONS: Facilities are motellike, and many rooms are large enough for a family of six. The four of us had plenty of room to maneuver in ours. Cribs are available at no extra charge.

RATES: Rates vary with season but as a sample: A weekend (three days, two nights) in summer costs $101 per adult, $51 for the first child, and $48 for the second. Rates include an enormous breakfast and dinner, riding, and all of the other ranch activities.

Pinegrove Resort Ranch
Lower Cherrytown Road
Kerhonkson, New York 12446
Telephone: 914-626-7345
Owners: Dick and Deborah Tarantino

IN THEIR OWN WORDS: "Pinegrove is a small, family-owned resort specializing in warm hospitality and individual attention. People who came to Pinegrove as children with their families are now bringing their spouses and children to Pinegrove. We do a 90 percent repeat business and our guests return as friends. They have favorite horses, favorite waiters, meet and become friends with other guests and end up booking with them for next year."

DESCRIPTION: Pinegrove breeds its own purebred and half-bred registered Arabian saddle horses. Tours, 1½ hours long, are given twice a week, including Saturdays, and kids love them! Horses are trained in Western and English and carry guests over acres of picturesque mountain trails. Other activities include tennis, an indoor/outdoor pool, a rifle range, archery, mini-golf, bocce, sauna, volleyball, a game room, a stocked lake for fishing, skiing in winter, boating, and hiking.

Please note that this ranch is not for everyone. We have been going for years, and love it. The atmosphere is very caring, but the accommodations are very basic. They're in the process of renovating and fluffing up the rooms; to date 55 rooms have been done over. Be sure to ask for one of these redone rooms; we've had complaints about the cleanliness of the older, more rustic rooms. Like the rooms, some of the facilities could also use a facelift, and that, too, is in the plans. For example, they have an indoor miniature golf course next to the swimming pool. Unfortunately, it is never completely set up, and it's hard to find the right-sized clubs, so it is almost never used! The best time to visit is weekends and holidays and during July and August. At other times, midweek business might include school groups and a less-than-usual roster of activity and entertainment.

FOR KIDS: Families spend a lot of time together here. Children as young as four, if capable, will be taken out on the hourly rides. Ask about the daily instruction hour if your children have never been on a horse before. Children need not be accompanied by parents on the ride, though with the little ones it is recommended. In addition to myriad activities for everyone, including cocktail and coketail parties and bingo, a separate room has been set up for Grandma's Day Care. Welcoming children from about 3 to 9 or 10 (children must be toilet trained), two people supervise the kids in arts and crafts, swimming, pony rides, hayrides, and other ranch-oriented activities. The air-conditioned space has mats for children to rest on, and cookies and juice are served all day. The center is free to all guests and is open from 10:00 A.M. to 1:00 P.M. and again from 2:00 to 5:00 P.M. It is open daily in the summer and holiday weeks and weekends when there are children in-house.

In the evening a free night patrol is offered. For those who would prefer private baby-sitting, the cost is $3.50 an hour. Arrangements should be made as early as possible with the front desk.

ACCOMMODATIONS: Some rooms are located in a two-level, motellike building. They have two double beds, private bath, and carpeting and are heated and air-conditioned. Others are in villas— with one, two, or three bedrooms, kitchen, and sitting rooms. Some have fireplaces. Cribs are free.

RATES: An eight-day, seven-night package is $999 for a family of three sharing a room. Each additional child is $35 per night. For five nights the package costs $799 and for four nights, $699. Weekend rates are $179 for each adult with 50 percent off for children. Rates cover all meals, including a Sunday barbecue, riding, and all ranch activities and entertainment.

Ridin-Hy Ranch Resort
Sherman Lake
Warrensburg, New York 12885
Telephone: 518-494-2742
Owners: Andy and Susan Beadnell

IN THEIR OWN WORDS: "Here families can vacation in a remote spot where children have lots of room to play safely. Our social program includes activities especially for the children and others for the whole family."

DESCRIPTION: Ridin-Hy is located in the Lake George area, in Adirondack State Park, right on the shores of a mountain lake in a heavily wooded valley. There are 800 acres in all, open to guests in both winter and summer. In summer, guests ride on trails in the park and use the lake for swimming, rowboating, speed boating, and waterskiing. When the snows come, there's a beginner-intermediate slope right at the ranch, snowmobiling, cross-country skiing, ice-skating, sleigh rides, sledding, and horseback riding. Each evening, there's a programmed activity—one night it might be a mini-rodeo, another a hot dog roast, a hayride and sing-along, bingo or poolside steak fry. Not far from the ranch guests can spend time at Great Escape, an amusement park, at the Saratoga Race Track, Fort William Henry, or at Lake Placid.

FOR KIDS: Kids from 2 to 17 have activities planned for them. Depending on their age, the choices include pony rides, rainy day videos, boat rides, crafts, hikes, softball, waterskiing, swimming lessons, junior rodeo, and more. Lessons in horseback riding and swimming are free; learning to waterski costs $6 per hour. Baby-sitting can be arranged for a minimum of four hours at $3 per hour.

ACCOMMODATIONS: In all there are 65 rooms, two to eight rooms in each one-story building. Rooms are large, with two twins and one double bed and a full bath; suites with two bedrooms, a living room, and 1½ baths are also available.

RATES: A two-night weekend rate in summer includes meals, riding, and all ranch activities for $170 per adult; 10–17, $116; 7–9, $110; 4–6, $60; and under 4, free.

Rock Springs Guest Ranch
64201 Tyler Road
Bend, Oregon 97701
Telephone: 503-382-1957
Owner: Donna Gill

IN THEIR OWN WORDS: "Special feelings at the ranch emanate from how easy it is to relax and have a good time. This is attributed to the setting, seclusion, quality of staff, and our extensive youth program in the summer."

DESCRIPTION: Rock Springs is about ten miles from Bend, adjoining the Deschutes National Forest. Days can be filled with horseback riding, swimming, tennis, or volleyball. If you're feeling lazy, just stroll through the woods, lie in the sun, or sit by the fire and read.

FOR KIDS: Rock Springs has a children's program that operates seven days a week from the end of June to after Labor Day. It operates from 9:00 A.M. to 1:00 P.M. and again from 5:00 P.M. to 9:00 P.M. and is available to kids 5 to 12. At the beginning of each day, the kids meet in the playroom to plan their day with their own counselors and wranglers. Horseback riding is most popular, but anyone who'd rather not ride can swim, try arts and crafts, or go on a nature hike. At night, there are hayrides, talent shows, dinner hikes, and lawn games. For teens, there are adventure trips and hayrides. Individual baby-sitting can be arranged for kids too young for the organized program, but to encourage parents to bring their own sitters, the ranch offers free accommodations and meals for the sitter in the family cabin (often on a roll away bed).

ACCOMMODATIONS: Cabins are carpeted, sleep two to seven people, and generally include kitchens and fireplaces.

RATES: A week-long package including lodging, daily maid service, three meals, the horseback riding program (guided trail rides, luncheon ride, a weekly skills clinic and corral rides), fishing, tennis and volleyball, outdoor spa, game room, and children's program costs $2,585 a family of four during the summer.

Flying L Ranch
HR-1, Box 32
Bandera, Texas 78003
Telephone: 512-796-3001
General Managers: Klayton and Monica Seeland

IN THEIR OWN WORDS: "Whoever says you can't have it all has never seen the Flying L Ranch. . . . Located in the beautiful Texas Hill Country, we are truly the ultimate for family vacations."

DESCRIPTION: Here in the wide open spaces—542 acres of Hill Country—you'll find a combination resort and ranch. Besides the horseback riding—one-hour trail rides are included in the price of a stay—there's tennis on two courts, golf on a 18-hole par 72 course, riding lessons, an outdoor pool, bicycles to rent, horseshoes, shuffleboard, and when you're finished playing, a hot tub big enough for six. During the summer, there's entertainment every night—barbecues, sing-alongs, hayrides, and creekside buffets. "We'll give you toe tappin', knee-slappin' music from some hot pickers and grinners. Whether it's cloggers, square dancers, crooning duets, or a country dance band, y'all can count on a lively time." It's fun, too, to take a trip into the town of Bandera while you're staying at the ranch. Bandera, founded in 1853, is known as the "Cowboy Capital of the World" and has its very own monument on the courthouse lawn to honor the town's seven world-champion cowboys.

FOR KIDS: During the summer, spring break, Easter and Thanksgiving weekend, the Flying L offers a children's program for kids 3–12. Counselors are available from 9:00 A.M. to 9:00 P.M. to take the kids fishing (every kid who catches a fish gets a souvenir photo with his or her catch), swimming, and exploring. Storytelling, pony rides, crafts, peewee Olympics, and trips to see the nearby dinosaur tracks are all part of the program. For kids under 3, babysitting may be arranged for $2.50 per hour.

ACCOMMODATIONS: You can choose among golf-view condos that come with a king-size bed, refrigerator, microwave, hot plate, balcony, and separate living area with a queen-size sofa sleeper; an "original" or remodeled villa, some with fireplaces; a two-room ranch-view condo with a covered patio, or a three-room ranch-view condo complete with a kitchen, washer and dryer, whirlpool bath, fireplace, and covered patio with a barbecue pit.

RATES: Summer package rates, from May 26 to September 4, for a full week (arrive Sunday afternoon and leave the following Sunday) is $429 per adult in the most expensive facility, the three-room ranch-view condo. The rate in the original villa suite is almost $100 less. For kids 6–17, the rate is $249, and from 1–5, $59; kids under one are free. Rates include Texas-sized breakfasts and dinners, golf green fees, horseback riding (lessons are $15 per hour extra), children's program, nightly entertainment, and, if you're flying your own plane in, don't worry—they won't charge you for the use of their paved and lighted airstrip.

Mayan Dude Ranch
P.O. Box 577
Bandera, Texas 78003
Telephone: 512-796-3312
Owners: Don and Judy Hicks

IN THEIR OWN WORDS: "My parents, Don and Judy, have owned the Mayan Ranch for 35 years and have been very successful running it with their 13 children. We are very family-oriented and feel we can nicely accommodate not only children's needs and wants but teenagers' and parents', too. Throughout the summer months, we have something planned every hour of the day for everyone."

DESCRIPTION: The ranch is situated in Texas hill country, and every day you can expect a morning and afternoon ride into the hills. There are a swimming pool and tennis courts, and golf is about two miles away at a neighboring guest ranch for nonriding hours. When there's been enough rain, you can float down the Medina River in an inner tube. When the sun goes down, there are barbecues, steak fries, mariachi bands, square dancing, and more.

FOR KIDS: All summer long, on Thanksgiving weekend and from December 21 to January 1, the staff at Mayan organize a children's program for kids 2 and over. The kids may eat with their families or, if they prefer, with their groups and supervising staff. Some of the activities planned for the kids are swimming parties, hayrides, horseback rides, coloring contests, and watermelon hunts.

ACCOMMODATIONS: There are two choices: "Western native

rock cottages" with one, two, three, or four bedrooms or motel-type accommodations with two adjoining rooms, with a king-size bed in one and two double beds in the other.

RATES: The rate per day is $75 for adults, kids 13 to 17, $50; 2 to 12, $40; kids under 2 are free. Weekly rates are also available.

Paradise Guest Ranch
P.O. Box 790
Buffalo, Wyoming 82834
Telephone: 307-684-7876 or 5252
Owners: Jim and Leah Anderson

IN THEIR OWN WORDS: "Our guests . . . say it is the best family vacation they have ever had. Many of our activities are geared so that the families can participate together—such as our talent night— or separately—such as our kids' overnight, when the kids go while the parents stay at the ranch for a gourmet dinner and an evening to themselves. . . . They feel like they are part of our family when they visit."

DESCRIPTION: This is a fabulous place. The atmosphere is warm and genuine, primarily because it reflects the personalities of Jim and Leah. The staff seems to love what they're doing and are anxious to share their enthusiasm with guests. Our families had a wonderful time there—riding, fishing, making new friends and learning about the history and ecology of the area.

The ranch is beautifully situated in a secluded valley in the Big Horn National Forest, along the edge of a forest of lodgepole pine and aspen and surrounded by over a million acres of national forest lands. Horses and horseback riding are the focus of a stay at Paradise. The staff matches horses and guests, and a horse becomes yours for the length of your stay. You can arrange anything from an hour-long ride to an all-day ride with a lunch packed on a mule and cooked along the trail. Lessons are available, and many guests like to take their horses to nearby mountain lakes to go fishing. A wrangler is always available to go with you. There's fishing galore (they even supply you with bait), as well as a whirlpool spa, volleyball, badminton, and, of course, horseshoes; and for rainy days, there's an indoor game room. The people at Paradise will also arrange a four-day guided trip into a base camp at Frying Pan Lake. Some guests like to combine the pack trip with a stay at the ranch. Ask for details.

FOR KIDS: The children's activities are unstructured and cater to individual needs; counselors are warm and caring. For the youngest, baby-sitting can be arranged, or they may want to play in the Kiddies' Corral, which includes swings, a sandbox, playhouse, and crafts. For the 3- to 5-year-olds there are crafts and games and rides on kids' ponies. They're supervised in the pool and spend time in the Kiddies' Corral. As soon as the kids are old enough—usually 6 years and up (but they are flexible)—their time is centered around horses and trail rides. One night a week is "Kid's Night Out," a camping overnight much enjoyed by all. Teens do lots of riding and fishing and socializing with the crew, some of whom are teenagers themselves. A special counselor with a degree in early childhood education coordinates activities for kids under 6, and several weeks are set aside each year to cater to families with young children. At night families get together for a variety of activities: a sing-along around a bonfire, a slide show about the area and the ranch, a barbecue on a hill overlooking the ranch; talent night featuring guests and the crew, too; a chuck wagon dinner in Bald Eagle Park; and a steak fry and a square dance. Every Saturday there's a rodeo for kids and adults, and that same night awards are given to all children who participate.

ACCOMMODATIONS: Guests stay in deluxe log cabins, all recently renovated, built into the hillside overlooking the valley. All cabins have full baths, a separate living room, a fireplace (all ready for lighting), and spacious porches. Some even have washers and dryers. Three cribs are available, and all cabins have kitchens. Cabins range in size from one to three bedrooms. Housekeeping services are provided.

RATES: Rates include lodging, three meals, and all regular weekly activities. They're based on a Sunday-to-Sunday stay and cost from $700 to $800 for adults, $600 to $650 for children 6 to 12; $400 for 3–5, and under 2, free. Baby-sitting and activities for this age group are provided while the older kids and adults are riding. The four-day pack trip costs $100 per person for four or more people and includes tack, horse, sleeping bags, cots, food, and the services of a cook.

Castle Rock Ranch and Adventure Center
412 Country Road 6N5
Cody, Wyoming 82414
Telephone: 307-587-2076 or 800-356-9965
Owner: Nelson Wieters

IN THEIR OWN WORDS: "Castle Rock is an unusual 'guest-ranch' in that it provides a wide range of adventure activities for families, all with the theme of environmental awareness and challenge-achievement. The program is especially designed so that all family members are on common ground—they all approach a variety of new experiences on an equal basis."

DESCRIPTION: Activities include llama treks, horseback trips, whitewater rafting, backpacking, fishing, rodeos, ranch chores, arts and crafts with artists-in-residence, photography safaris, exploration of Yellowstone National Park, square dancing, and mule-team trips. Families, assisted by staff, choose and plan their own program. We've heard rave reviews from friends who've visited. They even do guests' laundry!

FOR KIDS: Kids from 3 to 16 may participate in a children's program that runs from 9:00 A.M. to 8:00 P.M., seven days a week. Included in the program are arts and crafts, storytelling, games, fun at the animal petting farm, bicycling, and more. Excursions to Yellowstone, the Buffalo Bill Museum and to the rodeo are part of the program. Kids under 3 may stay with a baby-sitter—the charge is $2 per hour—while the parents and older siblings are busy.

ACCOMMODATIONS: Families stay in log housekeeping cabins. Cribs are available at no extra charge.

RATES: Rates vary with the accommodations you choose. The most expensive, "Rustler's Roost" (which has a living room with a fireplace, kitchen/dining area, master bedroom, private bath, and an enclosed sleeping porch) costs $750 per person double occupancy, half that for kids 6–11, and $80 for kids 3–5. Two and under are free. These are weekly rates; stays of less than one week can be arranged for $100 to $150 daily per adult.

Rimrock Dude Ranch
2728 North Fork Route
Cody, Wyoming 82414
Telephone: 307-587-3970
Owners: Glenn and Alice Fales

IN THEIR OWN WORDS: "There are no 'musts!' Rimrock is a place where everyone does what he pleases. . . . We offer a wonderful family vacation."

DESCRIPTION: Horses are assigned to suit the guests' experience. Anyone who has never ridden before is taught Western-style riding. Offered are fishing in the north fork of the Shoshone River, swimming in the river or at De Maris Hot Springs, and hiking. At night there are square dancing, games, parties, and rodeos. Rimrock also offers wilderness pack trips of varying lengths during the summer. One friend of ours signed up for one and loved it.

FOR KIDS: There's no formal children's program, but a good friend spent a week at Rimrock with her 4-year-old and said he was treated with exceptional warmth and caring. The wranglers made sure to find a horse that would be just right for him and included him on some gentle trail rides. She told us about a breakfast ride that began at 6:00 one morning and led to a beautiful clearing where hot coffee and blueberry pancakes were waiting.

ACCOMMODATIONS: Guests stay in cabins with private baths. Some have stone fireplaces, and all are heated. Cribs are available at no extra cost.

RATES: Rates for a one-week stay are $72 per day per person for four people, including meals and all ranch activities.

Box R Guest Ranch
Box 100
Cora, Wyoming 82925
Telephone: 307-367-2291
Owners: The Loziers

IN THEIR OWN WORDS: "We run a working guest ranch with a family atmosphere. We've been in operation for three generations."

DESCRIPTION: This is an old-time cattle ranch which started out as the homestead of the Lozier family in 1900. Now, guest accommodations have been added, but the Loziers are proud of the fact that they've never lost the atmosphere of a real working ranch. The ranch is the only deeded land to border the Bridger Wilderness Area on the west slope of the Wind River Mountains, the state's highest and largest mountain range. Each summer 250 cattle and 50 horses and mules graze the 1,590 acres of ranchland and nearby foothills. There are only 20 guests at a time at the ranch, and the Loziers offer a choice of seven ranch and wilderness vacations, tailored to the desires and abilities of the guests. For example, the "Ranch River Wrangler" version includes riding instruction, lots of trail rides, guided fishing trips, a float trip on the Upper Green River, and a three-day pack trip into the mountains. Guests are encouraged to participate as much as they'd like in the working life of the ranch.

FOR KIDS: There's no formal children's program at the ranch but kids as young as 3 may ride along with their parents.

ACCOMMODATIONS: Guests stay in rustic cabins in rooms equipped with a queen-size and a twin bed.

RATES: The price varies with the package you choose. The one we describe above, the week-long Ranch River Wrangler, costs $595 per person for double occupancy. Kids 3 and under pay half price. Rates include all meals, cowboy guides, unlimited riding, and all unguided activities.

Bitterroot Ranch
Dubois, Wyoming 82513
Telephone: 307-455-2778 or 800-545-0019
Owners: Bayard and Mel Fox

IN THEIR OWN WORDS: "We have a 9-year-old boy ourselves and there are two girls aged 9 and 12 who live here. Visiting children are drawn into the life at the ranch."

DESCRIPTION: This is a working ranch where riding is the main focus.

FOR KIDS: There's no organized children's program, but there are ponies for the children to ride, and the older ones go off on supervised rides. There are a number of other resident animals—lambs, angora rabbits, ducks, and geese, and a stocked trout pond where kids can learn to fish. A baby-sitter is available every afternoon, so that parents can go off on a ride by themselves.

ACCOMMODATIONS: Log cabins have one, two, or three bedrooms and are heated.

RATES: Adults pay $825 per week, Sunday to Sunday, which includes accommodations, riding, and all meals; kids 4 to 16 pay 25 percent less; and those 3 years and under pay $20.

Lazy L and B Ranch
Dubois, Wyoming 82513
Telephone: 307-455-2839
Owners: Leota and Bernard Didier

IN THEIR OWN WORDS: "There's nothing finer than a good dude ranch that likes families together. All ages will enjoy the Lazy L and B."

DESCRIPTION: The ranch began just before the turn of the century as an old homestead where sheep and cattle grazed. The

Didiers have owned the land since the 1950s, located on the high plains of northwest Wyoming, adjoining the Wind River Indian Reservation. Surrounded by mountains on three sides, the ranch is only an hour away from Togwotee Pass, the gateway to Yellowstone, Jackson Hole, and the Grand Tetons. The setting is magnificent for a variety of trail rides—up valleys, under cottonwood trees, across plains toward an abandoned homestead, to neighboring ranches, across alkaline flats into the forests of the Shoshone Wilderness and to the Wind River Indian Reservation. Riding is why most people come to the L and B, but besides riding there's trout fishing, volleyball, horseshoes, and swimming in an outdoor pool. Every week there's a square dance at the ranch (with instructions for city slickers) and a hayride to a haunted house out on the prairie for kids and adults. Not too far away, in the town of Dubois, guests like to play golf and tennis, and go to local cowboy bars and square dances. The ranch has its own lapidary shop where guests are welcome.

FOR KIDS: In summer, there's babysitting for kids under 3 during the morning ride time and during the adult dinner hour; for kids 3 to 5 there's a program that includes swimming and being led around the corral on a horse. When kids get to be 6, they can go on morning and afternoon rides, play in the game room, swim, and do crafts. Teens like to hang out with the wranglers and learn all about horses; they ride, go on overnight pack trips, and, if interested, may work in the craft shop or study Indian lore. Children may have dinner with or without their parents; the children's dinner is supervised by staff.

ACCOMMODATIONS: Modern log cabins—there are 16 in all with showers and baths—are arranged around a central yard positioned just right for a splendid view of the mountains.

RATES: One week—from a Sunday to a Saturday—costs $545 for adults, $445 for kids under 12. People who stay for two weeks get a two-day pack trip in the Washakie Wilderness at no extra charge. All rates include as much riding as you'd like, meals, lodging, and even transportation to town when the mood strikes.

Trails End Ranch
Box 20311
Jackson, Wyoming 83001
Telephone: 307-733-1616
Owners: Liz and Matt David

IN THEIR OWN WORDS: "Where the road ends, your vacation begins. . . . We are unique in our small size—we accommodate only

10–20 guests at a time. With this small size we enjoy tremendous flexibility, diversity and personal attention for you."

DESCRIPTION: Twenty miles west of Jackson and seven miles north of the Snake River, the ranch's 150 acres spread across the stream valley of Fall Creek and are completely surrounded by the Teton National Forest. Besides the traditional ranch activities, Trails End offers trap shooting, archery, swimming in the pond, darts, and horseshoe pitching. Hiking along streamside trails is fun, and day trips are possible to Grand Teton and Yellowstone National Parks, the Snake River and Hoback River canyons. Fishing for cutthroat trout is popular with guests, and for real fishing enthusiasts, the ranch will arrange pack trips into the Wind River Range, where more than 1,300 lakes and streams beckon.

FOR KIDS: There's no formal kids' program—"our whole ranch is a playground!"—but there are lots of things for kids to do, like rafting and swimming, outdoor painting, kids-only adventure rides, and fishing.

ACCOMMODATIONS: You'll stay in modern log cabins with private bedrooms, bath, and separate living room. From the cabin porch you'll be able to look out over Fall Creek and the Snake River Mountains.

RATES: From June 16 to August 31, the weekly rate for an adult is $735, kids 4–12, $665, and 3 and under, $100. Other dates, the rates are slightly less.

Gros Ventre River Ranch
Box 151
Moose, Wyoming 83102
Telephone: 307-733-4138
Manager: Brad Robicheaux

IN THEIR OWN WORDS: "We have a ranch that makes guests stop and look around. There is a natural beauty here that brings peace of mind and contentment.".

DESCRIPTION: Located on the eastern boundary of Grand Teton National Park, along the banks of the Gros Ventre River, the ranch is completely surrounded by national park and national forest land. The main lodge, cabins, and corrals sit in the middle of the meadows, by forests of pine and aspen. In summer, trail riding is the thing; in winter there's cross-country skiing and snowmobiling. Gros Ventre is a working ranch where real cowboys tend cattle in the hills surrounding the ranch. The ranch breeds its own horses, and branding is a typical summer chore—guests may actually work alongside the cowboys if they'd like. In summer, besides trail rides, there's hiking in the mountains around the ranch or on any of the trails in Grand Teton National Park and the chance to take a guided float trip. You can spend a day touring Yellowstone, swim in the ranch's own swimming hole, or canoe on nearby Slide Lake. In winter, some folks like to use the ranch as a base for a downhill skiing vacation at nearby Jackson Hole ski area.

FOR KIDS: According to Robicheaux, Gros Ventre is best for kids 6 and over so that they can go along on the trail rides. For younger kids, baby-sitting is usually available during mornings and on weekends, but, as Robicheaux puts it, "I've never seen a child bored here. There are lots of things to do. We have high camp, low camp and other places where they like to play on their own. We don't feel supervision is necessary as we are located 18 miles from the nearest town, ¼ mile from the nearest public road and three miles from our nearest neighbors. Kids are safe anywhere here. Their freedom to roam is our baby-sitter."

ACCOMMODATIONS: Log cabins have either twin, double or king-size beds. Some have living rooms with open wood-burning stoves. For those chilly Wyoming nights, all guests get an electric blanket and all rooms have electric heat.

RATES: In summer, a two-bedroom, two-bath lodge with a living room shared by four people costs $980 per person per week. Kids up to 2 years are free, and 2-to-6-year-olds are charged $50 per night; a two-bedroom, two-bath cabin without a living room costs $805 per person per week. Winter rates are about $100 less per week.

Heart Six Dude Ranch
P.O. Box 70
Moran, Wyoming 83013
Telephone: 307-543-2477
Owners: The Garnick Family

IN THEIR OWN WORDS: "We are definitely family oriented. In fact, our own family of five young children live and play on the ranch. Our staff is especially trained to work with kids of all ages."

DESCRIPTION: According to the Garnicks, the old ranch hasn't changed much since 1900. They tell us, "Sure, the old stage to Yellowstone is gone now, and there's a lot more modern con-

veniences, but it's still run by honest, friendly Wyoming people."
The ranch is small—only 35 to 40 guests at a time—but there's lots
to do. Besides riding, there's fishing, swimming in an outdoor pool,
canoeing, nature hikes, badminton, basketball, and the chance to
take a float trip along the Snake River operated by the folks at the
ranch. Float fishing trips are fun—$150 for two people with lunch,
snacks, and a professional guide for a full day. Guests often like to go
into the town of Jackson—for Old West Days, rodeos, or just to hang
out. The ranch is also a good base for tours of Yellowstone. Each
week—from Sunday to Saturday—a number of activities are scheduled—hayrides, square dancing, trips into town for theater and
rodeos, campfire sings, and moonlight rides.

FOR KIDS: During the time that adults and kids are out on their
morning and afternoon rides, the children who don't want to ride or
aren't yet old enough can participate in an organized program. Kids
11 and under may go fishing, go on nature walks, do crafts, and play
games. Baby-sitting can be arranged for $2 per hour.

ACCOMMODATIONS: There are 14 log cabins of varied sizes with
names like Buffalo, Antelope, Wolf, and Grizzly. Some have kitchenettes, some have fireplaces.

RATES: Weekly rates vary with the cabin you choose and include all meals, riding, and other ranch activities. For example, the
rate for Buffalo North, a three-room suite with four double beds,
bath, fireplace and a hide-a-bed costs $725 per person when there
are four people staying. Infants up to 1 year are $100, kids 1–5 are
half price, and 6 and up pay the full rate.

Crossed Sabres Dude Ranch
Wapiti, Wyoming 82450
Telephone: 307-587-3750
Owners: Fred and Alvie Norris

IN THEIR OWN WORDS: "The mountains here and the tall, tall
pines combine to make up what is considered to be some of the most
beautiful country in all of the world."

DESCRIPTION: The ranch is located just nine miles east of Yellowstone in the Shoshone National Forest. A week at Crossed Sabres
includes lots of riding: scenic rides, picnic rides, short rides, long
rides, and even an overnight pack trip. In between the riding, the
ranch offers fishing, usually a day trip to Yellowstone, a day in

historic Cody with a visit to a rodeo, a raft trip on the Shoshone River, cookouts, square dancing, and more.

FOR KIDS: There's no special kids' program; they go along with the grown-ups.

ACCOMMODATIONS: The two-room cabins are rustic but modern, and all are heated.

RATES: Weekly rates for adults are $525 to $625; kids 8 to 17, $475, 3 to 7, $425; and 2 and under free. Rates include accommodations, meals, your own horse and tack, cowboy guides, an overnight pack trip, a rodeo trip and visit to Cody and Yellowstone, and transfer to and from the Cody Airport.

12

CAMPING AND CABINS; ACCOMMODATION IN NATIONAL PARKS

Camping can range from rustic—sleeping bags under lean-tos along the Appalachian Trail—to luxury—queen-size beds in a sleek recreational vehicle (RV) parked at a spot complete with electricity and hot and cold running water. The kind of camping you choose will depend on you and your family, but whatever style you choose, don't embark on a two-week-long camping vacation until you've tried it for a weekend and are sure that you like it. Your first trip should be close to home and civilization.

In this chapter we include information on tent camping, RV camping, as well as a listing of rustic-type "resorts" where families stay in cabins and spend their days enjoying the outdoors. In the West, many of these types of places are called ranches, so check Chapter 11.

Other possibilities for camping families are the outfitters described in Chapter 6.

Our own families have had wonderful camping vacations, usually tenting and often in state or national parks. Naturalist-led walks into the woods or along the coast at low tide have taught our kids a lot about nature; storytelling around the campfire at night is something they talk about all the time. There's nothing quite as nice as life without telephones, televisions, and clocks. Camping gets its rhythm from nature: The beauty of the surroundings takes over, and the stress of everyday life loses its hold on everyone in the family.

Camping is also one of the most economical vacations you can take. Campsites cost only a few dollars per night, and food costs can be kept to a minimum.

FINDING A CAMPGROUND

The United States has over 20,000 campgrounds, 8,000 publicly owned and the rest privately owned. Some national parks are so popular that they need to be booked months ahead and can be reserved through Ticketron outlets. For a list of the 104 areas maintained by the National Park Service and information on their facilities, send $3.50 to the Superintendent of Documents, U.S. Government Printing Office, Washington, D.C. 20402, and ask for *National Park Camping Guide*. For $1.50 more you can also order *National Parks: Lesser Known Areas*. If the idea of camping on Indian lands interests you, write to the U.S. Department of the Interior, Bureau of Indian Affairs (BIA), Washington, D.C. 20242, and ask for its map of Indian areas. On the back of the map are listed the addresses of areas and agency offices of BIA where you can write for specific information on existing sites.

Some of our national forests also have camping facilities. For a list of national forests write to the Forest Service, U.S. Department of Agriculture, Office of Information, P.O. Box 2147, Washington, D.C. 20013, and ask for order number FS-65. The Bureau of Land Management oversees 399 million acres of recreation sites; for information on camping on these sites write to them care of their Public Affairs Office, 1800 C Street, N.W., Washington, D.C. 20240.

And for listings of privately owned campgrounds you can write for the state directories compiled by the National Campground Owners Association, 11307 Sunset Hills Road, Suite B-7, Reston, Virginia 22090; tell them the state or states you want and enclose $1 for each state listing. Kampgrounds of America, the largest campground chain, will send you a directory of its 650 properties—send $3 to KOA, P.O. Box 30162, Billings, Montana 59114.

Free campground information is usually available from local

and state government tourist offices; see the appendix in the back of the book for addresses. Many of the state and national parks have cabins where families can enjoy a bit more comfort than in a tent. Two books that list these cabins are *The Complete Guide to Cabins and Lodges in America's State and National Parks* by George Zimmerman, published by Little, Brown and Company ($12.95), and *State and National Parks; Lodges and Cabins* by John Thaxton, published by Burt Franklin and Company as part of the Compleat Traveler series ($8.95). In this edition, we've added our own section on cabins in the national parks; see page 440.

RV CAMPING

The RV industry's public relations voice, the Recreation Vehicle Industry Association, will be more than happy to send you a bulging packet of information on the benefits of RV travel. You'll get information on rentals, purchase, campgrounds, state and regional RV associations, and more. According to the folks at RVIA, "compared to other means of transportation and lodging, traveling and camping in an RV cost half to three-quarters less." Their address is P.O. Box 2669, Reston, Virginia 22090. Two specific sources of information on renting RVs are Cruise America, American Land Cruisers, 7740 N.W. 34th Street, Miami, Florida 33122, 800-327-7778, and U-Haul International, Inc., 2727 North Central Avenue, Phoenix, Arizona 85004, 800-528-0463.

PREPARING A CAMPSITE

Once you have chosen a campsite, the first thing to do is to set specific boundaries for your kids. We like the idea of taking balls of yarn, a different color for each kid, and using it to mark off the "safe" area for each child. Arrange a play area for your youngest while you set up camp and have everyone participate in the setting-up process. There's plenty for even the youngest to do: spreading the ground cloth, hammering in the tent posts, or filling a pot with water. Older children may enjoy having their own tent. Parents: think of how nice a little privacy will be.

A camping trip gives you the perfect opportunity to work as a team and to teach your kids real respect and love for nature. Two excellent books to help you do the latter are *Starting Small in the Wilderness* by Marilyn Doan and *The Nature Observer's Handbook* by John W. Brainerd. *Starting Small* is a how-to book for parents who are introducing kids to wilderness adventure and a source book for safe, responsible, and enjoyable activities for the youngest campers; the age range is infancy to 12. Information on the right gear for adults as well as kids is also included. It costs $6.95 and is published by Sierra Club Books. *The Nature Observer's Handbook* ($9.95) presents ways to observe, experience, and record the "intricate beauty of nature." Brainerd includes excellent advice on "nature touring" with children; he suggests starting with a tour of your backyard on your hands and knees. The book is published by Globe Pequot Press.

Anyone contemplating family camping should have a copy of Margaret Malsam's *Camping Circus: An Entertaining and Informative Guide to Family Camping* (Beaumont Books, 333 West 55th Avenue, Denver, Colorado, $6.95). When her two oldest kids were only toddlers, Margaret and her husband, George, built a simple chuckwagon unit, put it in back of their pickup, and started a family camping tradition that was to last for over ten years and eventually included two more children and larger trailers. The book is Margaret's delightful account of those years during which her family traveled through every one of the states and much of Canada. Her book successfully combines practical tips with an interesting account of the family's on-the-road adventures: from hoedowns in the Ozarks to the sights of the big cities. Perhaps what makes this book particularly good is that Margaret tells about the bad times (the infamous Bug Day is one example) along with the good, but the overall feeling is that a family who camps together shares something very, very special. Helpful appendices included packing tips, state tourism and parks offices, and Margaret's own time-tested award-winning recipes.

STAYING IN NATIONAL PARKS

Among the most spectacular destinations for families, or for that matter, anyone traveling in the U.S., are the national parks. From our earliest school days we can all remember the photographs of Old Faithful, the breathtaking views of the Grand Canyon, the majesty of the trees in the Sequoia National Forest. Perhaps it's time to take these sights out of the realm of second-hand memory and experience them for yourself. Knowing that many of our readers are turned off by the idea of camping with kids, we want to assure you that there are many alternatives for staying in our national parks. In fact, the accommodations that you'll find in our national parks are as varied as the parks themselves: In one, you may choose to stay in a primitive cabin, in another you may overnight in a first-class hotel listed in the National Register of Historic Places.

As you can imagine, the national parks and the accommodations within their borders are enormously popular, so it is imperative that you make reservations as far ahead as possible. Some parks require reservations as much as one year in advance. What follows is an annotated listing of accommodations (alphabetically by state) in some of the most popular parks in the U.S.

Denali National Park—Alaska

McKinley Chalet Resort
825 West Eighth Avenue, No. 240
Anchorage, Alaska 99501
Telephone: 907-276-7234
Manager: Carson Fleharty

IN THEIR OWN WORDS: " . . .[a] family type atmosphere with beautiful scenery, away from the distractions of city life. . . wholesome outdoor activities, fresh air, spectacular wildlife viewing in the park."

DESCRIPTION: The resort has an indoor pool, a children's game room, and an indoor play area that's open from 10:00 A.M. to 10:00 P.M. High chairs and booster seats are available in the dining room, and although there's no children's program now, the director of sales and marketing tells us that one is being planned.

Some of the highlights of a stay at the resort are the Tundra Wildlife Tour—eight hours under the guidance of a driver/naturalist—which includes a look at grizzly bears, caribou, Dall sheep, moose, wolves, and fox; river rafting (for kids 5 and over); free National Park Service programs, and "flightseeing"—a bush pilot's view of the towering, snow-covered peaks of the Alaska Range.

ACCOMMODATIONS: The resort is located on the east boundary of the park, overlooking the Nenana River. In all, there are 216 two-room suites in chalet-style cedar lodges. Each suite has twin beds in the bedroom and a hide-a-bed in the living room.

RATES: Kids under five are free; cribs are $3 per night. The resort is open from May 20 to September 17; for four people the overnight room rate is $137.

North Face Lodge/Camp Denali

Summer: P.O. Box 67
Denali National Park, Alaska 99755
Winter: P.O. Box 216
Cornish, New Hampshire 03755
Telephone: Summer: 907-683-2290; winter: 603-675-2248
Owners: Wallace and Jerryne Cole

NORTH FACE LODGE

IN THEIR OWN WORDS: "Located in the heart of Denali National Park, the Lodge offers families an opportunity to explore this wilderness area by hiking, fishing, canoeing and cycling. Families can become more in tune with nature by exploring tundra ponds, observing wildlife (grizzly bears, mountain sheep, moose and caribou) and birds. The staff is knowledgeable and enthusiastic about sharing their knowledge of the Park with guests."

ACCOMMODATIONS: Described as a country inn by its owners, the lodge accommodates 35 guests at a time. Rooms are twin-bedded and two cribs are available. There is one family suite, which consists of one double-bedded and one twin-bedded room.

RATES: Children under 4 are free when sharing with parents; children 4–12 pay 75 percent of the adult rate, and a reduction of 10 percent is in effect when three or more members of the same family share a room. All rates cover lodging, meals, equipment, and all activities, including nature walks, canoeing, biking, fishing, nature photography, and evening programs. Two nights and three days cost $410 per adult; three nights and four days, $615.

CAMP DENALI

IN THEIR OWN WORDS: "This is a rustic, informal wilderness lodge for those who are seeking an in-depth wilderness experience. It is our hope that guests will feel a true sense of the Denali Wilderness during their visit and gain an appreciation for this region and its wildlife and fragile eco-system."

ACCOMMODATIONS: One-room cabins are equipped with wood-burning stoves, propane lights, and hot plates; there's running spring water outside the cabin and a private outhouse in addition to centrally located bathroom and shower facilities.

RATES: This facility has the same pricing policy as North Face Lodge. Three nights and four days is $600 for an adult; five nights and six days is $1,000 for an adult. Transportation to the camp from Anchorage (a five-hour trip) is included, as are meals, lodging, and all activities, including hiking, canoeing, fishing, gold panning, nature photography, and the use of a darkroom.

Grand Canyon National Park—Arizona

Grand Canyon National Park Lodges
P.O. Box 699
Grand Canyon, Arizona 86023
Telephone: 602-638-2401
Manager: William Bohannon

DESCRIPTION: One of the seven wonders of the world—need we say more? Visitors may sign up for mule trips, bus trips, and a one-day smooth-water raft trip on the Colorado River.

ACCOMMODATIONS: You have six choices, all clustered at the South Rim: El Tovar is a grand hotel designated as a National Historic Landmark; Bright Angel Lodge and Cabins is rustic but comfortable; Thunderbird and Kachina are modern two-story lodges; Maswik is in the Canyon Village and offers rustic cabins as well as modern accommodations; and East and West Yavapai Lodge is just minutes from the canyon rim.

RATES: Kids under 13 are free in a room with their parents; cribs are available at no extra charge, and baby-sitting may be arranged through the concierge at El Tovar. Rates vary from one property to the next, ranging from $38 for a cabin at Maswik Lodge or a standard room at Bright Angel Lodge to $140–$220 in a suite at the El Tovar Hotel (less expensive rooms are also available at El Tovar).

Sequoia/Kings Canyon National Parks—California

Giant Forest Lodge
P.O. Box 789
Three Rivers, California 93271
Telephone: 209-561-3314
Manager: Glen Becker

DESCRIPTION: Question: What is the oldest living thing on earth? Answer: The General Sherman tree—one of the sequoias you can see in the park. But there's more than just trees here; there's horseback riding, trout fishing, 900 miles of marked hiking trails, and, as soon as the first snow falls, snowshoeing and cross-country skiing all the way until April.

ACCOMMODATIONS: The lodge offers a variety of accommodation possibilities: motel rooms, deluxe cabins, standard cabins, family cabins (two rooms, bed space for six, with a private tub or shower), and two types of what the lodge calls "rustic cabins" (without any private toilet or shower). A cafeteria is located nearby and the lodge dining room is open from late May through mid-October.

RATES: Cribs are $5.50 per night; children under 12 stay free with their parents. Rates range from $70 for the deluxe motel accommodation in the high season (May through October) to $28 for the rustic sleeping cabin without bath.

Yosemite National Park—California

Yosemite Park and Curry Company
5410 East Home Avenue
Fresno, California 93727
Telephone: 209-252-4848

IN THEIR OWN WORDS: "Unlike many contemporary visitor attractions, Yosemite is a work of nature, formed by glaciers many thousands of years ago. Ice—not man—was the sculptor."

DESCRIPTION: The people at the Yosemite Park and Curry Company have put together a listing of seven pages of activities just for kids within the park. As they explain it: "In a child's world, everything is big. In Yosemite everything is even bigger. . . . Because the sheer scale of Yosemite is so bewildering, activities for children have been designed to bring Yosemite National Park down to kid-sized proportions." Some of the possibilities include the rental of walk-and-lead ponies, available by the hour; burro picnics—half-day adventures for kids 7–12 to a site along the Merced River complete with stories and games; two programs for kids 8–9 and 10–12 which involve joining a park ranger in search of adventures and secret places in Yosemite Valley; family discovery walks; guided saddle rides for kids 7 and older; bike rentals; daily art classes; and in winter, skiing at Badger Pass, ice-skating at Curry Village, and ranger-led snowshoe walks and tours.

ACCOMMODATIONS: There are six choices: Curry Village,

Yosemite Lodge, The Ahwahnee Hotel, the Wawona Hotel, and White Wolf Lodge and Tuolumne Meadows Lodge

At Yosemite Lodge you'll find deluxe hotel rooms and cabins with or without baths located close to Yosemite Falls; at Curry Village the choice includes rooms, cabins, or tent cabins. Both facilities have swimming pools. The Ahwahnee Hotel is a magnificent hotel built in 1927 and listed on the National Register of Historic Places. While the preceding three facilities are open year-round, the following are seasonal: The Wawona Hotel is a Victorian-era gem with swimming, tennis, golf, and horseback riding right on the grounds operating from spring through Thanksgiving; the White Wolf Lodges and Tuolumne Meadows Lodge (with a choice of cabins or tent cabins) are open only during July and August and are located high up in the mountains.

RATES: As you'd expect, the costs from facility to facility vary enormously. Just to give you an idea of what to expect, a double room at the Ahwahnee Hotel costs $159.50 per night in high season; a cabin with private bath at Curry Village is $35.50, and a canvas tent cabin at White Wolf Lodge is $27.25. Children 12 and under are charged between $2 and $5, and cribs, when available, are free.

Everglades National Park—Florida

Flamingo Lodge
Box 428
Flamingo, Florida 33030
Telephone: 305-253-2241
Manager: Gary Sabbag

IN THEIR OWN WORDS: "We are located forty miles inside the National Park. The pristine beauty and natural environment are our biggest attractions."

DESCRIPTION: Located right on Florida Bay, the lodge offers canoeing, fishing, hiking, and horseback riding. Houseboats are also available for rent, and tours guided by naturalists are scheduled regularly.

ACCOMMODATIONS: You have a choice of staying in the lodge or in one of the 16 housekeeping cottages. The cottages have a kitchenette, living room, and bedroom; the lodge rooms have two double beds, air-conditioning, and a private bath.

RATES: Kids 12 and under stay free when they share a room with parents; cribs are available at no charge. In high season, from November 1 to April 30, when all facilities are in operation, room rates are $69, cottages are $80 per night. A two-room suite in the lodge costs $105.

Mammoth Cave National Park—Kentucky

Mammoth Cave Hotel, Hotel Cottages, Sunset Point Motor Lodge, Woodland Cottages

National Park Concessions, Inc.
Mammoth Cave, Kentucky 42259-0027
Telephone: 502-758-2225
General Manager: G. B. Hanson

IN THEIR OWN WORDS: "There are two worlds to explore in Mammoth Cave National Park—the extraordinary world of the underground and the more familiar surface world of oak-hickory forests, meandering rivers and woodland wildlife. . . . From the beginning, underground explorers doubted that they would ever find the end of Mammoth Cave. Today the cave still seems to be a wilderness without boundaries."

DESCRIPTION: Above ground, you can hike, take scenic drives, or sign up for a boat trip on the Green River. But it's the underground activities that are the most popular: There are a number of cave tours offered, ranging from a quarter-mile, 1¼-hour tour to a five-mile, six-hour offering. Tours are available every day of the year except Christmas.

ACCOMMODATIONS: The choices are: the Mammoth Cave Hotel, a brick motor hotel right by the entrance to the park; Sunset Point Motor Lodge, at the edge of the forest overlooking Sunset Point Bluffs; Hotel Cottages adjacent to the hotel; and the more secluded Woodland Cottages, tucked away in the forest. The cottages are open only from spring to fall; the hotel and motel are open year-round.

RATES: Children 16 and under may stay free in a room with their parents. The rate for two people in a double- or twin-bedded room at the hotel is $46; a family room at the Sunset Point Motor Lodge is $48; the hotel cottages are $33 for two, and at the Woodland Cottages a family unit is $30. Cribs are available for an additional $5 per night.

Isle Royal National Park—Michigan

Rock Harbor Lodge
P.O. Box 405
Houghton, Michigan 49931-0405
Telephone: May to September: 906-338-4993; October to April:
502-773-2191
General Manager: Rondell G. Sanders

DESCRIPTION: This park, on an island in northwestern Lake Superior, is 45 miles long and nine miles wide. There are no roads or cars on the island, which is reached by boat from Grand Portage, on Minnesota's north shore. Most of what goes on at this park is water-related: fishing and boating are popular as well as hiking, nature study, and photography.

ACCOMMODATIONS: Visitors have a choice of accommodation at the lodge, open from mid-June to September, or staying in one of the housekeeping cottages—one room with an electric stove, refrigerator, utensils, china, one double bed and two bunk beds. Groceries are available at the Marina store or meals can be taken at the lodge.

RATES: A room for two in the lodge, including three meals, is $62 per person, $26 for children under 12; double occupancy in the cottage is $34 per person, $9 each additional person. Cribs are available at no extra charge.

Blue Ridge Parkway—North Carolina

Bluffs Lodge
Route 1, Box 266
Laurel Springs, North Carolina 28644
Telephone: 919-372-4499
General Manager: Colon Sparkman

DESCRIPTION: The Blue Ridge Parkway extends 469 miles along the crests of the southern Appalachians and links two national parks—Shenandoah and Great Smoky Mountains. The parkway is designed for what the Department of the Interior calls "motor recreation." Along the road there are several spots where visitors can abandon their cars and take a walk through the woods.

ACCOMMODATIONS: Bluffs Lodge features views of meadows

and mountains and is located just about halfway along the parkway. There are 24 rooms at the lodge, available to guests from May 1 to October 31.

RATES: The rate for two people is $50; each additional person is $5. Cribs are available for $5 per night.

Big Bend National Park—Texas

Chisos Mountains Lodge
National Park Concessions, Inc.
Big Bend National Park, Texas 79834-9999
Telephone: 915-477-2291
General Manager: Ronnie Houchin

IN THEIR OWN WORDS: "From the lush vegetation in the Rio Grande flood plain to the high country of the Chisos mountains rising from the sea of the surrounding Chihuahuan Desert, the stark contrasts make this one of the most diverse national park areas."

DESCRIPTION: Horseback riding—short trail rides, all-day trips, and overnight pack trips are all available, and hiking is a popular pastime in the park.

ACCOMMODATIONS: Guests may choose from a motel-type room, a room in the lodge itself, and stone cottages accommodating up to six people. All facilities are open year-round.

RATES: A room for four in the motel is $61; a room for three in the lodge, $56, and accommodation in one of the stone cottages in a room with three double beds is $61 for four people. Cribs are available for $6 per night.

Shenandoah National Park—Virginia

Big Meadows Lodge, Skyland Lodge
c/o ARA Virginia Sky-Line Co., Inc.
P.O. Box 727
Luray, Virginia 22835
Telephone: 703-743-5108
Operating season: Skyland, late March–mid-December; Big
    Meadows, mid-May–October

IN THEIR OWN WORDS: "Some of nature's more spectacular displays are yours to discover in beautiful Shenandoah National

Park: from deer, black bear, and bobcat to more than 200 species of birds, all in the virgin hemlock forests dotted with over seventeen kinds of wild orchids."

DESCRIPTION: Not far from either lodge you can horseback ride, hike, picnic, participate in walks led by naturalists, visit the ruins of mountaineers' cabins, go for a wagon ride, fish for native trout, or have the kids try out the playground.

Skyland is located at the highest point of elevation on the Skyline drive so the views are spectacular. Big Meadows is on a high plateau looking out over the Shenandoah Valley; it gets its name from the large grassy area where deer and other wildlife are often seen.

ACCOMMODATIONS: At Skyland, you may choose a motel-style room, a cabin that will accommodate from two to seven people or a suite with a fireplace and room for two to eight people. At Big Meadows the choices are similar, with rooms in the main lodge as one more option.

RATES: To give you an idea of what you can expect to spend, a cabin during the summer costs $32 to $62 per night double occupancy at Skyland; $53 to $55 at Big Meadow. Cribs are free, and there's no charge for kids 16 and under.

Olympic National Park—Washington

Lake Crescent Lodge
HC 62, Box 11
Port Angeles, Washington 98362-9798
Telephone 206-928-3211
General Manager: Walter Sive

Sol Duc Hot Springs Resort
P.O. Box 2169
Port Angeles, Washington 98362-0283
Telephone: 206-327-3583
General Managers: Steve Olsen, Connie Langley, and Rick Langley

IN THEIR OWN WORDS: "Olympic National Park is a magnificent, unspoiled wilderness of glacier-clad peaks, alpine meadows, cascading streams, unspoiled coastline and virgin forests. . . . This park is one of the few to have gained international recognition as A United

Nations World Heritage Site. . . . This spectacular natural scenery is filled with quiet lakes, abundant wildlife, unique plants and delicate wildflowers."

DESCRIPTION: Activities include boating on Lake Crescent, fishing for trout and salmon, hiking, and horseback riding.

ACCOMMODATIONS: Lake Crescent Lodge offers lodge rooms, cottages, and motel rooms, all available from April 30 to October 30. Sol Duc, located in a valley of 150-foot evergreen trees, right beside the Sol Duc River, offers cabins for overnight stays and, as an extra lure, three hot springs pools and one freshwater swimming pool. There are two kinds of cabins: One with two double beds, full bath, stove, and refrigerator but no dishes, pots, or pans and one with full bath, two double beds, two queen-size beds or one double bed plus a double hide-a-bed but no cooking facilities.

RATES: At Lake Crescent Lodge, accommodations range from $38 for two people in a room in the lodge to $88 for three people in a cottage; additional people are $8 each. Cribs are $8 per night. At Sol Duc, cabins with cooking facilities are $58 for two plus $6.50 for each additional person (kids 3 and under are free) and for cabins without cooking facilities, $54 for two. Cribs are available at no extra charge.

Grand Teton National Park—Wyoming

Jackson Lake Lodge
P.O. Box 240
Moran, Wyoming 83103
Telephone: 307-543-2811

IN THEIR OWN WORDS: "Relaxation has never been so exciting. . . . It's all here . . . wildlife viewing, horseback riding, floating, hiking, cruising, fishing, canoeing—to provide unforgettable summer memories."

DESCRIPTION: The resort offers swimming in a large heated pool, horseback riding, and float trips. In the park you can fish, golf, swim, play tennis, or just enjoy the beauty of it all. This is where "The Virginian" was written and where the classic cowboy movie "Shane" was filmed. It is still a favorite of photographers and artists who try to capture its beauty.

ACCOMMODATIONS: This full-service resort, open from June 7 to September 17, is right in the heart of the park. The main lodge sits on a bluff overlooking Willow Flats and offering a wonderful view across the water to the skyline of the Grand Tetons. There are 42 guest rooms in the main lodge and 343 rooms, most with two double beds, in two adjacent wings. The same company that operates the lodge, also operates 30 log cabins at Jenny Lake Lodge and 209 log cabin rooms (some are remodeled settlers' cabins) at Colter Bay Village, also in the park.

RATES: The rate for four people in a room with a view at the lodge resort is $88–$99; kids under 12 are free. Rollaways are $7.50 per night, cribs are free. At Jenny Lake Lodge the rates are $405 per day for four people in a cabin, breakfast and dinner included; and at Colter Bay Village they are $62–82 for two rooms with connecting bath with room for up to four people.

CABIN VACATIONS

The following places offer cabins and a range of outdoor possibilities, a bit more luxurious than tent camping, perhaps, but still very much in the camping mood.

YMCA of the Rockies
Estes Park Center
Estes Park, Colorado 80511-2800
Telephone: 313-586-3341

Snow Mountain Ranch
P.O. Box 169
Winter Park, Colorado 80482
Telephone: 303-887-2152
Operating season: Year-round

IN THEIR OWN WORDS: "These family/conference vacation centers are aimed at creating a welcome environment for families and large groups. Most of our acreage is forested, giving it a secluded feeling."

DESCRIPTION: The YMCA operates these two centers; Estes Park has been operating for more than 80 years, the Snow Mountain Ranch is newer, established in the 1960s.

FOR KIDS: Unlike the other listings in this chapter, Estes Park has a full program for kids. During the winter it operates seven days a week, in summer, it's midweek only. Kids from 3 to high school age can participate in activities from 8:30 A.M. to 4:00 P.M. The cost is $10 per day. Activities include arts and crafts, sing-alongs, swimming, pony rides for the little kids, and horseback riding for the older ones ($10 extra), miniature golf, and a once-a-week overnight. "With our extensive acreage, there's no reason for excursions."

ACCOMMODATIONS: Housekeeping cabins and lodge rooms are available at both sites. At Estes Park, cabins have from two to four bedrooms; at Snow Mountain some have five bedrooms. A two-bedroom cabin with room for five costs $66 per night; $439 for a full week at Estes Park; a similar size cabin at Snow Mountain is $78 for a night, $515 for a week. Most cabins have fireplaces. Both centers have restaurants that serve breakfast, lunch, and dinner; cabins have kitchen facilities if you'd rather do your own cooking.

RATES: The costs of accommodations are given above. All guests must belong either to the YMCA in their own hometown or join the YMCA of the Rockies for the duration of their stay—$5 per family. However, since this is a very, very popular spot you may want to consider joining at a higher category (from $50 to $200) so that you can be one of the first to have a chance at reservations. Write for details.

Hill's Resort
HCR 5, Box 162A
Priest Lake, Idaho 83856
Telephone: 208-443-2551
General Manager: Craig Hill
Operating season: Year-round

IN THEIR OWN WORDS: "Families come to Hill's and Priest Lake to be together as a family and enjoy each other. Hill's Resort is truly a family-run resort for families."

ACTIVITIES: Hill's was established in 1946 by George Hill, starting with a small restaurant, a store, and ten cabins. Forty years later there are 48 cabins, a more ambitious lakeside restaurant and an oyster bar as well as tennis, boating, golfing, fishing, waterskiing and in winter, cross-country skiing and snowmobiling. Priest Lake is 26 miles long with seven islands, all surrounded by the Selkirk Mountain Range.

ACCOMMODATIONS: All cabins feature fully equipped kitchens, fireplaces, electric heat, linens, and towels, and units are large enough to sleep from six to 12 people. The Hills describe them as real "homes away from home."

RATES: In summer, a housekeeping unit that sleeps six and has two bedrooms costs $690 per week. A "Get-Away Weekend" package that includes two nights' lodging, dinner one night and breakfast both mornings costs $155 per couple.

Kawanhee Inn Lakeside Resort
Webb Lake
Route 142
Weld, Maine 04285
Telephone: 207-585-2234 in summer; 207-778-4306 in winter
Manager: Martha Strunk
Operating season: Summer

IN THEIR OWN WORDS: "We have a lodge-type atmosphere here. Our huge living room—the Moose Room, with its fieldstone fireplace, puzzles and a library—is perfect for rainy days. There are no required activities—just an outdoor environment that families love. Our white sandy beach with water that drops off slowly is safe even for toddlers. We have the best family hiking trails in the state."

DESCRIPTION: There's a main lodge situated on a high knoll overlooking the lake and mountains. The lodge has 14 rooms, but for families the housekeeping cabins are best. Guests like to swim, play tennis, sail on the lake, bicycle, and hike. From time to time, watercolor workshops are offered. All-day climbing trips to Mt. Blue, Tumbledown, and Bald Mountains are popular with hikers of all skill levels. The dining room features half-price meals for kids.

ACCOMMODATIONS: The cabins face the lake and mountains, and none is far from the shore. They vary in size and can accommodate from two to seven people. Each has a living room with a large stone fireplace, a complete bath, and a screened porch. Extra cots and cribs are available.

RATES: Cabins are rented by the week. Rates are $400 for a family of four.

Appalachian Mountain Club
5 Joy Street
Boston, Massachusetts 02108
Telephone: 617-523-0636
Owner: Private, nonprofit organization
Operating season: Summer

DESCRIPTION: The Appalachian Mountain Club (AMC) operates a number of camping areas that are available to members and nonmembers alike. The four camps that are recommended for families with young children are the Cardigan Lodge, Echo Lake, and Cold River camps in New Hampshire and the Echo Lake Camp in Maine. Accommodations range from lodges to platform tents to cabins. Family-style meals are served in main dining rooms. Let's take Cold River Camp as an example. It is located on a 90-acre site in a secluded valley on the Maine/New Hampshire border. From the site, the hiking possibilities are unlimited—woodland walks, easy climbs, or more challenging full-day hikes are possible. The camp rents canoes, and the area is great for biking. For kids, there are a sandbox, slide, and swings and play equipment in the recreation hall.

ACCOMMODATIONS: Family cabins are located in the pine grove, surrounding the meadow and overlooking the ravine. The main lodge has a massive stone fireplace and a central dining room.

RATES: At Cold River, adults pay $190 per week (with an additional $20 for nonmembers); children 8 to 15 pay $167 and under 7, $111.

Timber Bay Lodge
Box 248
Babbitt, Minnesota 55706
Telephone: 218-827-3682
Owner: John Rykken
Operating season: mid-May–October 1

DESCRIPTION: One friend who lives in San Antonio raves about this spot; she and her family have gone all the way from Texas to Minnesota for the past two summers and plan to keep on going back for more. Guests at Timber Bay have two choices: staying in a cabin on 26-mile-long Birch Lake or actually going out on the lake and staying on one of the houseboats that are available for rent. The emphasis at Timber Bay is on nature and all of the natural beauty that surrounds this peaceful piece of the world. For kids, the owners have organized a children's program supervised by a college student and open to ages 5 to 12 from 9 to 11:30 A.M. every day, Monday–Friday. Kids can expect to take nature hikes, go on picnics, do arts and crafts, and go on scavenger hunts. During the afternoon, the same counselor supervises the swimming area at the lake, where kids and adults can sail, waterski, canoe, fish, or swim. A naturalist is on staff and is available throughout the week to take kids and parents on hikes in the woods; onto the lake to find eagle nests; or out at night for a lesson in star gazing. Teenagers especially seem to like the group volleyball game that's held once a week, and everyone loves the once-a-week barbecue and bonfire. Teens may also make new friends at a game room open from 10:00 P.M. on.

ACCOMMODATIONS: The housekeeping cabins on the lake are all log-sided with wood-paneled interiors, and guests may choose from one, two, or three bedrooms. All cabins are carpeted, have Franklin stoves with wood provided, decks, and fully equipped kitchens. (There's no central dining room, so all meals must be prepared in the cabin.) Houseboats come in four sizes—the smallest accommodates up to four people, the largest sleeps 10.

RATES: Cabins range from $465 to $695 per week; houseboats from $425 for a three-night weekend in the smallest to $1,150 for a full week in the largest.

Ludlow's Island Lodge
Box 1146 GV
Cook, Minnesota 55723
Telephone: 218-666-5407 or 800-537-5308
Managers: Mark and Sally Ludlow
Operating season: Summer

IN THEIR OWN WORDS: "We think our resort is extremely family-oriented. (We have four children ourselves—13, 11, 8, 6.) Everything here is set up for parents and children to use as they need or want to. . . . Most of our guests take several vacations—Ludlow's is their choice for their family vacation."

ACTIVITIES: There's no lack of things to do at Ludlow's. Much of the activities center on Lake Vermilion and its 1,200 miles of shoreline. There are swimming, boating, tennis, racquetball, golf a ten-minute ride away, waterskiing, sauna, and hiking trails. During the summer, Ludlow's has activities scheduled for kids 2½ years and older, at least three to five days a week. There's no extra charge for the program, which is designed to fit the group of kids staying each week. Some of the activities you can expect are pontoon rides in search of beaver dams or bald eagles, nature hikes, breakfast cookouts, treasure hunts, and horseback riding. Kids can sign up for lessons in tennis, waterskiing, racquetball, and fishing. A fishing contest and a special fishing trip for kids coincide with the weekly adult fishing clinics. Baby-sitting is available for $3 per hour with four hours' notice.

ACCOMMODATIONS: All cottages have fireplaces and decks, are fully carpeted, and have kitchens. There are dishwashers, microwaves, blenders, and automatic coffee pots. All are situated in birches and pines and within 50 feet of the water's edge. Cribs are available at no extra charge. There's no main dining hall; everyone does his own cooking. There's a small grocery store that's open 24 hours.

RATES: Weekly rates based on two people in a cabin ($50 for each additional person) range from $625 to $1,140. Maid service is $60 per week for two, $15 for each additional person. Children under 12 stay free before June 15 and after Labor Day.

Gunflint Lodge
Box 100 GT
Grand Marais, Minnesota
Telephone: 218-388-2294 or 800-328-3325
Owners: Bruce and Susan Kerfoot
Operating season: Summer

IN THEIR OWN WORDS: "The single thing that makes families enjoy a vacation at Gunflint is that children are truly welcome here. We avoid having a lot of rules. We cater to kids at meals—if a child wants a cheese sandwich for dinner, we make it for him or her even though it's not strictly 'on the menu.' Games and puzzles can be left unfinished overnight in the Lodge."

ACTIVITIES: During the summer, staff naturalists lead a variety of activities based on the forest, lakes, plant life, animals, and wilderness that surround the lodge. Twenty or more activities are offered each week, from nature hikes to berry picking (early August is raspberry and blueberry season), from an evening moose search to a breakfast cookout and paddle. Gunflint has a resident fishing pro, and for kids 6 to 15 staying one week or more, there's a free half-day guided fishing trip led by the pro or one of the guides. Baby-sitting, at a cost of $1.50 per hour, can be arranged with two hours' advance notice.

ACCOMMODATIONS: Lakeside cottages have from one to four bedrooms, a living room with a fireplace, a full bathroom, carpeting, and electric heat; some have kitchens. Cribs are available at no extra cost.

RATES: A seven-night package that includes room, all meals, a motorboat, two canoes, gas, and the family naturalist activity program costs approximately $625 for the first two adults and $260 for each child 4 to 15. Children under 3 are $5 per night. Other packages are available for two to six nights.

Brookside Resorts
HC 05, Box 240
Park Rapids, Minnesota 56470
Telephone: 218-732-4093
Manager: Dave Keller
Operating season: Summer

IN THEIR OWN WORDS: "We are a very family-oriented summer resort. We concentrate on activities and care for children 2 to 18. . . . We offer families a chance to enjoy each other and give each family member the opportunity to pursue their personal recreational interest."

ACTIVITIES: Brookside, located in the north woods of Minnesota, boasts lots and lots of recreational facilities—a golf course, tennis courts, an indoor-outdoor swimming pool (one end in the lodge, the other outside, surrounded by a deck), fishing, boating, and waterskiing on Two Inlets Lake. On rainy days it offers ping-pong, movies, a pool table, and a sauna in the lodge. From Memorial Day to Labor Day, there's a seven-day-a-week Kids' Program that begins at 9:00 A.M. and ends at 9:00 P.M. and is available to anyone 2 or over. For kids 2 to 7, there's a Kindernook program that runs from 9:30 to 11:30 A.M. Monday to Friday. The program combines free play, storytelling, nature walks, and crafts. The Kindernook area is a large, fenced-in playground with a playhouse, swings, toys, and a walk-in bunny cage. For kids under 2, baby-sitting is available for $2 per hour with advance notice.

ACCOMMODATIONS: All of the 28 cabins have kitchens and knotty pine interior. There are two- and four-bedroom cabins, and a boat is supplied with each cabin. Some are carpeted; others have room-size braided rugs. Appliances are modern, and all the basics for cooking and eating are supplied. Guests take their own sheets and towels or rent them from Brookside.

RATES: Rates vary with the season and the size of cabin. A sample: A two-bedroom cottage for four people costs $635 for the week of August 12 to 19. Before June 29 and after August 19, kids under 17 stay free; children under 3 are always free.

Chico Hot Springs Lodge
Pray, Montana 59065
Telephone: 406-333-4933
Owners: The Art Family
Operating season: Year-round

IN THEIR OWN WORDS: "At Chico Hot Springs, it's the people who make the place. This dedicated and hard-working staff take pleasure in helping the history and excitement come to life. . . . It's not a fancy place but its quality is unique."

DESCRIPTION: Pray, population 15, is just 22 miles south of Livingston and a 30-mile drive from the gate of Yellowstone. Chico's well known for its natural hot springs; in the past 100 years many have sworn by the restorative powers of this soothing warm water. The pools are open all day, until midnight. The average temperature of the larger pool is 94 degrees, the smaller is ten degrees warmer. Guests at Chico can ride horses (trips from one hour to overnight can be arranged), go fishing (there's a private trout lake about 20 minutes from the lodge), take float trips, or in winter, go cross-country skiing.

ACCOMMODATIONS: You can stay in a room in the lodge or an adjacent motel, but for families, the log houses, cabins, or chalets are a lot more fun.

Two log houses, one large enough for six, the other for up to 20, sit above the lodge on a hill. The largest one—with five bedrooms—has a spectacular view of Emigrant Peak and the west side of Paradise Valley. The large living room has a rock fireplace; there's a complete kitchen, two bathrooms, a laundry, and a large deck with picnic tables. For somewhat more modest accommodations, three cabins are available with two rooms each with a double bed and a separate bathroom (toilet, sink, and shower); a fourth cabin has one room plus a bathroom. Two chalets—one that will sleep six to eight, the other large enough for up to ten, have beautiful views of Paradise Valley, complete kitchens with pots, pans, and utensils, a bathroom with a tub and shower, laundry facilities, and a sauna.

RATES: Rooms in the lodge, with private bath, cost $49 double occupancy (no extra charge for kids 6 and under); the smaller log house is $105 per night, $630 per week, and the larger is $275 per night, $1,650 per week. The two-room cabin costs $55 per night; the one-room cabin, $50, while the smaller chalet costs $110 per night or $660 for a full week, and the larger, $140 per night, $840 for a week. Kids 6 and under are no extra charge when they stay in a room with parents.

Holland Lake Lodge
SR Box 2083
Condon, Montana 59826
Telephone: 406-754-2282 or 800-648-8859
Owners: The Uhls
Operating season: Year-round

IN THEIR OWN WORDS: "Holland Lake Lodge is that special place for your family if the outdoors appeals to you. We feel our atmosphere offers the family a relaxed place to come without costing a year's salary. Our lounge has a toy box and children's books. . . . Many families book one to twenty years in advance."

ACTIVITIES: The lodge is located in the heart of Montana's scenic Rocky Mountains at the gateway to the Bob Marshall Wilderness. In summer, guests horseback ride, canoe, fish, swim, and hike; in winter, they cross-country ski, ice fish, skate, and snowmobile. All meals are served in the Lake Room of the lodge, and there are special meals for children. Baby-sitting is available at $2 per hour by prior arrangement.

ACCOMMODATIONS: There are rooms in the lodge, but for families the cabins are best. The cabins are rustic but comfortable; all but one has a kitchen, and they can accommodate from four to eight people. Cribs cost $5 per night to rent.

RATES: The cabins rent for $44 to $70.50 per night. Meals are extra and moderately priced. Canoes and rowboats are available for rent for $3.50 per hour, and a guided four-hour horseback ride costs $35.

Loch Lyme Lodge

Route 10, RFD 278
Lyme, New Hampshire 03768
Telephone: 603-795-2141
Operating season: Year-round; cabins in summer only
Owners: Judith and Paul Barker

IN THEIR OWN WORDS: "My husband and I have two young sons who have certainly taught us a lot about vacationing with children during the past years. We have found this very helpful in working with our own summer guests. We do not offer, and do not intend to offer, the following: televisions, telephones in cabins, video game room, soda machines, or organized social programs. . . . What we *do* have is 125 acres of New Hampshire fields and woodlands bordering Post Pond, a spring-fed lake."

DESCRIPTION: During the summer Loch Lyme operates as a summer resort, with housekeeping cabins; in the fall and winter it becomes a small bed and breakfast operation using just the main lodge. Located near Dartmouth College, the lodge features a waterfront with a safe, sandy beach for toddlers. Boats and canoes are available, and fishing on the lake is reported to be good. There are two clay tennis courts and hiking trails. Baby-sitting can be arranged with six hours' notice for $2 per hour during the day and $2.50 at night. Usually the baby-sitters are the teenage girls who work and live at the lodge during the summer. Children's portions are available in the dining room, and most of the vegetables are grown in the garden by Mrs. Barker's father.

ACCOMMODATIONS: Cabins are spread out through the woods and along the lakeshore so that there's a feeling of privacy. A typical cabin has a living room with a fireplace, a bath, a kitchen or kitchenette, one to four bedrooms, and a porch. Most cabins have daybeds in the living rooms for additional lodging. Cribs are available for $5 per stay.

RATES: The weekly rental for cabins ranges from $310 to $460. Daily rates on a bed and breakfast or modified American plan (MAP) (breakfast and dinner) are also available. The MAP is $39 to $47 per day for cabins for adults, $16 to $22 for kids 5–15. Children under 4 are free.

Wayfarer Resort
46725 Goodpasture Road
Vida, Oregon 97488
Telephone: 503-896-3613
Owner: Terry Patton
Operating season: Year-round

IN THEIR OWN WORDS: "We provide a cozy home base for people who love to fish, hike, boat, raft, swim, play volleyball and tennis or simply commune with nature."

DESCRIPTION: The cabins at the Wayfarer perch on the banks of the emerald green McKenzie River, one of the country's premier trout streams. Fishing is what brings most people to the resort; this would be a lovely spot for a family reunion.

ACCOMMODATIONS: In all there are 13 cabins with one to four bedrooms. All have kitchen facilities; there's no central dining room.

RATES: The cost of your stay will vary with the type of cabin you choose. One of the more expensive possibilities is "The Old Homestead," four bedrooms, 2½ baths, with two queen-bedded rooms and two twin-bedded rooms for $672 per week for four people, $6 for each additional person. A one-bedded cottage large enough to sleep six, with a hide-a-bed, is $540. Daily maid service is extra.

13

CRUISES

Before we set out on our first cruise with the kids we were less than enthusiastic about the idea. We were afraid we'd be bored, that all we'd do was eat ourselves into oblivion, that we'd go stir-crazy sharing a tiny cabin with our kids, and that the kids would be restless. None of these came to pass. We had a great time, and we've become real fans of cruising with kids. Our cruise was on the *Fairwind* (now part of Princess Cruises), which has a Youth Center open from 9:00 A.M. to midnight, a pool just for kids, a kids' program that operates even when the ship is in port, and other services just right for families.

Our route took us to some scuba diving meccas, and my husband and I wanted to dive at as many ports as possible. We were able to arrange several dives; we spent the morning together as a family and had lunch with the kids, and then dropped them back at the ship before heading off on our dive. On many ships we couldn't have done that because sometimes the children's program doesn't operate when the ship's in port.

More and more cruise ships are tuning in to the needs of families. Fortunately, single parents traveling with their kids are getting attention, too. Combination sea/land packages, free airfare, and other enticements are making cruising with your family more and more affordable. The typical cruise price includes accommodations, meals, snacks, and entertainment, so even if the price quoted seems high at first, consider what's included. More and more ships are offering kids' and teens' programs. Not only does that mean that you'll have a chance for free time yourself but also that other kids are more likely to be along on the ride. New friends are a very, very important part of a successful vacation for your kids. Not every cruise ship is right for families. Here are some guidelines to help you decide which ones are.

- Accommodations: Look for a cabin to accommodate all of you in a category you can afford. Family cabins can accommodate three to four people or have room for a crib. Adjoining rooms are nice but, of course, more costly. Your youngest may not take kindly to a shower, so ask whether you can have a cabin with a tub. And if you need a crib, be sure to ask for it at booking time; this also applies to booster seats, special menus, early seating, or any other requests you have. Even when the cruise line indicates that these options are always available, be sure to reserve what you need.
- Shore excursions: Wherever you dock there will be planned excursions. We think it's better to explore on your own. It's less expensive, and you can control the pace. Consider joining up with another family for a shore adventure. Some ships have shore excursions just for kids. Ask about them.
- Baby-sitting: Most, but not all, ships have some kind of arrangement for baby-sitting. Even if there's no formal baby-sitting arrangement, you can usually make a private agreement with a crew member or find a willing teenager on board.
- Refrigerators: These are always a plus with kids. If there aren't any, take along an insulated bag and ask the steward for ice. If the ship has 24-hour room service, this won't be necessary.
- Pricing: A child with 2 adults usually pays third- or fourth-person rates, less than the rate of the first two people in the cabin. Although more cruise lines are taking single parents' needs into consideration, the second person in the cabin, even when a child, will be charged an adult rate. Also, look for special "kids cruise free" deals.
- Early dining: When there are two seatings, sometimes kids can eat at the early one and parents can eat at the second. Ask at booking time. Full meals may not be available from room service, but substantial snacks are often available.

Coping with the High Cost of Cruising

Cruise specialists all believe cruising offers good value. An "average" cruise in the Caribbean should run about $145 to $280 per day per person, with children less. The price includes food—lots of it—and nonstop entertainment. Plan for extras such as shore excursions and tipping, which is almost uniformly expected. Budget $8 to $10 per person per day for tips, and $35 to $55 per person in port charges. We recommend that families think about doing shore excursions on their own; arranging a car and driver for a day may cost less than the organized trip. Here are a few money-saving tips:

- Share a stateroom: as we said above, it's really not bad at all. Most of the families we've spoken to, ours included, found that being all together in one room didn't detract from the vacation one bit.
- Book well in advance. Many lines offer early booking discounts. Or ask whether there are any standby, last-minute rates if you can mobilize your family quickly.
- Be flexible on dates. High season may only be three or four particular sailings.
- Book a lower deck on an inside cabin. You'll probably spend very little time in your cabin. In all of the cruises we've taken, only once did we actually look out our windows. Most often they were too high or we couldn't see anything anyway.
- Book with a cruise specialist. Many of these cruise-only agencies offer group rates to individuals or have special arrangements with individual cruise lines for specific sailings.

Every year, TWYCH (Travel with Your Children) publishes a special guide called *Cruising with Children,* which lists almost 100 ships and all their child-related services. Copies are $20 (plus tax for New York residents) and $14 for subscribers to *Family Travel Times* (see page 8). Write to 80 Eighth Avenue, New York, New York 10011, or call 212-206-0688 to order.

A cruise-only specialist you should know about is South Florida Cruises, which offers savings as high as $1,500 per cabin on various ships worldwide. They know a lot about facilities for kids. You can contact them at 5352 Northwest 35th Avenue, Fort Lauderdale, Florida 33309, 800-327-SHIP. For a list of other cruise-only agencies, write to the National Association of Cruise Only Agencies (send a self-addressed, stamped envelope to P.O. Box 7209, Freeport, New York 11520).

And now for some specific cruise possibilities for you and your family, listed alphabetically, by cruise line.

Admiral Cruises
1220 Biscayne Boulevard
Miami, Florida 33132
Telephone: 305-373-7501 or 800-226-8064 from Florida

THE SHIPS: SS *Azure Seas*, SS *Emerald Seas*, MV *Stardancer*

IN THEIR OWN WORDS: "Admiral Cruises' shipboard lifestyle is fun, relaxed and comfortable. A friendly crew provides myriad activities which can be enjoyed by every member of the family. Most cabins easily accommodate a family of four, menu selections are varied, and the choices of ports range from historic to tropical to scenic to action-packed. Admiral offers families value and variety for their vacation dollar."

FOR KIDS: Organized programs for children ages 4–16 are offered during the summer (Memorial Day through Labor Day) and holidays (Christmas, Easter, and Passover). At other times, some children's activities but not a full-time program are offered. On shorter cruises activities are planned both on shore (it could be sandcastle building, treasure hunts, and the like) and on board (pool and deck games, contests, movies, parties, and more). A piñata party on the last night of the cruise makes a nice finale for the kids. Other activities may include get-acquainted gatherings, a teen disco, arts and crafts, fun and fitness programs, trivia contests, limbo lessons, and bingo. On the *Azure Seas,* "kids-only" tours to the San Diego Zoo or Sea World are possible. Baby-sitting is not available on any of the ships.

KID'S PRICING: Children sharing with two parents pay third- and fourth-passenger rates; a child with one adult pays full fare.

DESCRIPTION: *Azure Seas'* port of embarkation is Los Angeles; ports of call are Ensenada (Mexico), San Diego, and Santa Catalina Island. The ship has 98 three-bed cabins with upper pullman berths; 44 four-bed cabins with two upper pullman berths; 12 suites with a queen-size bed and a double-size sofa bed. There are no adjoining cabins. Three- and four-night cruises depart on Mondays and Fridays weekly.

Emerald Seas leaves from Miami and calls at the Bahamas:

Nassau, Freeport, and Little Stirrup Cay. It has 88 three-bed cabins, 89 four-bed cabins, no adjoining cabins. It heads out on three- and four-night cruises year-round. Pre- and post-cruise packages to Disney World are available.

Stardancer's ports of embarkation are Vancouver, British Columbia, and Los Angeles; Alaskan ports of call are Juneau, Skagway, Haines, Ketchikan, in Mexico it's Puerto Vallarta, Mazatlán, and Cabo San Lucas. The ship has 111 three-bed cabins, 239 cabins with upper berths, two deluxe suites with sitting area, and 46 connecting cabins. From June to September, there are seven-night cruises from Vancouver to Alaska; from October to May, seven-night cruises depart from Los Angeles to the Mexican Riviera. *Stardancer* also offers pre- and post-cruise tours to Alaska. The ship's pool has a sliding roof and a shallow area just right for kids.

American Hawaii Cruises
550 Kearny Street
San Francisco, California 94108
Telephone: 415-392-9400 or 800-227-3666

THE SHIPS: SS *Constitution*, SS *Independence*

IN THEIR OWN WORDS: "The emphasis on the *Independence* and the *Constitution* is on bringing the destination on board with Hawaiian food, island shows, and a relaxed 'aloha' feeling in everything—from the guests' attire to the warmth of the all-American crew."

FOR KIDS: Full-time children's recreation directors are assigned to each ship depending on the number of children aboard. If there are at least 12 children under the age of 12 on board during the summer months and major holidays, a comprehensive recreational program goes into gear. The program varies daily and is posted in the youth center. Activities are planned according to age—2-to-6-year-olds, 7-to-12s, and 13-to-16s are grouped together for backgammon, ping-pong, shuffleboard, movies, pool games, pizza parties, teen disco nights, and more. The youth center on the *Independence* has a portable disco with a dance floor and soda fountain. Activities are scheduled from 9:00 A.M. to 5:00 P.M. and 7:00 to 10:00 P.M. and operate whenever the ship is in port. There is no baby-sitting provided officially, although it is sometimes possible to arrange it with off-duty crew members.

KID'S PRICING: A summer (June 10–September 2) "Free Kids"

program allows up to two kids, 16 and under, to sail free when sharing a category F or higher cabin with two full-fare adults. At other times (except on Christmas and New Year's cruises) children 16 and under pay $295 each when sharing with two full-fare adults.

DESCRIPTION: Both ships cruise from Honolulu to the Hawaiian Islands. On the *Constitution,* there are 41 three-bed cabins and 84 four-bed cabins with 120 upper berths and seven sofa beds. The *Independence* offers families 64 three-bed cabins and 76 four-bed cabins with 119 upper berths and 21 sofa beds. On both ships rollaway cots for children too young to sleep in an upper berth must be requested at booking time. Two two-room suites on each have a sitting room with sofa beds; there are no adjoining cabins. Seven-day round-trip cruises depart every Saturday. It is possible, too, to take a partial cruise and combine it with a resort stay on one of the islands.

Bermuda Star Line
1086 Teaneck Road
Teaneck, New Jersey 07666
Telephone: 201-837-0400 or 800-237-5361

THE SHIPS: SS *Bermuda Star,* SS *Veracruz,* SS *Queen of Bermuda*

IN THEIR OWN WORDS: "We offer value for money, children's counselors, children's programs, a casual atmosphere, larger cabins, a wide variety of dining choices and friendly service."

FOR KIDS: Children's activities are offered on the *Queen of Bermuda* and the *Bermuda Star* during July and August cruises; at other times it's left to the discretion of the cruise director. Activities are scheduled throughout the day, and the ratio of supervisors to children depends on the size of the group on board. When the ship is in port, no program is scheduled. The Junior Cruisers program, for ages 3 to 10, includes coketail parties, pool games, bingo, hoola-hoop contests, and face painting. A program for ages 11 to 15 offers movies, shuffleboard tournaments, and an "End of the Cruise Blues" party; older teens are welcome to participate if they wish. No programs are scheduled for the *Veracruz.* Baby-sitting is not always available; it depends on staff availability but can usually be arranged once on board through the room steward.

KID'S PRICING: From April to October, children with two full-fare passengers in the same cabin sail free on the *Bermuda Star* between New York or Philadelphia and Montreal. August to September, children 10 and under pay $40 on five-night and weekend cruises out of Tampa on the *Veracruz*. In July and other times there are special children's prices, but children with one adult always pay full fare.

DESCRIPTION: The *Bermuda Star*'s ports of embarkation are New York, Philadelphia, Montreal, New Orleans, Acapulco, and San Diego; ports of call are Newport, Rhode Island, Nova Scotia, Montreal, Quebec, Key West, Playa del Carmen, Cozumel, Puerto Vallarta, Mazatlán, San José, Montego Bay, Ocho Rios, the Panama Canal, and Cartagena. Family accommodations are 53 quads, four triples, and four suites with adjoining rooms.

The *Veracruz*'s port of embarkation is Tampa; ports of call are Playa del Carmen and Cozumel in Mexico; Key West, Nassau, and Bimini. Family accommodations include 61 three-bed cabins, 25 four-bed cabins with upper pullman berths, two suites that accommodate a third person on a sofa bed, and five adjoining cabins. The ship's itinerary includes five-night cruises to Mexico or two-night cruises to "nowhere" in the Gulf of Mexico.

The *Queen of Bermuda* travels from New York, New Orleans, and Key West to St. Georges and Hamilton, Bermuda; the Mexican Yucatán and Playa del Carmen and Cozumel. Family accommodations include 42 four-bed cabins; 17 have two upper berths, and 18 have three lower beds and an upper berth. Four cabins have upper and lower berths plus a sofa bed, one cabin has a king-size bed plus a sofa bed. Three bed cabins are available in the top category only and there are 138 adjoining cabins.

From May to October, seven-night cruises depart Saturdays to Bermuda; from November to May, six- to eight-day cruises from New Orleans to the Yucatán leave on Fridays and Saturdays.

Costa Cruises
World Trade Center
80 Southwest Eighth Street
Miami, Florida 33130-3097
Telephone: 305-358-7325 or 800-447-6877

THE SHIPS: MS *Carla Costa,* SS *Costa Riviera,* MTS *Daphne,* MTS *Danae,* TS *Eugenio Costa*

IN THEIR OWN WORDS: "Not only do the children stay busy having a good time, we slip some educational programs in on them, too: geography, history and travel. There are a lot of things they can learn while they are having fun."

FOR KIDS: A cruise staff member arranges children's activities for kids who are potty trained up through teens. "Because infants and toddlers require very special care and personal attention, regrettably they cannot be cared for under the program." Activities are scheduled throughout the day and may include scavenger hunts, pool games, video game competitions, disco dance contests, arts and crafts, shuffleboard, ping-pong, board games, and lots of contests. Each night, a schedule of the following day's activities is distributed. Teen activities are listed on the adult schedule and on the *Costa Riviera,* there's a special teen club open every day and night. Children eat with their parents and some evening activities are offered. The program operates primarily during the summer and during major school holidays. At other times, youth activities depend on just how many kids are on board. Baby-sitting, at sea or in port, is available; the price is negotiated between parents and crew members.

KID'S PRICING: On the *Carla Costa,* kids under 12 with two adults pay $275; on the *Costa Riviera,* $295. On the *Daphne,* the cost ranges from $595 to $995 depending on destination, on the *Danae* from $770 to $920, on the *Enrico Costa* $270 to $310, and on the *Eugenio Costa,* $380 to $450. These last three rates do not include airfare.

DESCRIPTION: The *Carla Costa*'s port of imbarkation is San Juan; ports of call are Curaçao, Caracas, Grenada, Martinique, and St. Thomas. Family accommodations consist of 76 three-bed cabins and 62 four-bed cabins with upper berths; ten two-room deluxe suites that sleep four, with a double sofa bed; four deluxe cabins with a sofa bed; and two adjoining cabins. Seven-day cruises depart every Saturday year-round.

The *Costa Riviera* starts out from Fort Lauderdale and goes on to St. Thomas, St. Croix, Nassau, or Ocho Rios, Grand Cayman, and Cozumel. For families, there are 130 three-bed cabins with upper berths, 21 with sofa beds, 36 four-bed cabins with upper berths, 11 with sofa beds. Seven-day cruises depart every Saturday all through the year.

The *Daphne* sails between San Juan, Los Angeles, and Vancouver and the Carribean, Trans Canal, and Alaska. Family accommodations include 53 three-bed cabins (25 with sofa beds and 28 with upper berths); 19 four-bed cabins with upper berths, and 27 suites with sitting areas (12 have sofa beds). From October to April the ship is scheduled for seven-day Caribbean cruises and 16-day Trans Panama Canal cruises; from May to September the ship heads out on seven-day Alaskan cruises.

The *Danae, Enrico Costa,* and *Eugenio Costa* all sail from Europe or South America to the Mediterranean or to South American waters.

Cunard Line Ltd.
555 Fifth Avenue
New York, New York 10017
Telephone: 212-661-777 or 800-221-4770

THE SHIPS: *Queen Elizabeth 2, Cunard Princess, Cunard Countess, Sea Goddess I,* and *II, Sagafjord,* and *Vistafjord*

NOTE: Since the children's programming differs from one Cunard ship to another, we list each ship individually. The *Sea Goddess I* and *II, Sagafjord,* and *Vistafjord* have no children's programs. Note, too, that if you travel on the *QE 2* you needn't leave Rover behind—pets can cruise along with you at a nominal fee. Kennel maids supervise the pets in temperature-controlled kennels.

QUEEN ELIZABETH 2

FOR KIDS: Three separate programs are offered on every cruise. For infants up to 2 years, a nursery is available from 9:00 A.M. to 5:00 A.M.; diapers and formula are provided. Cribs and basinettes are both available. A Children's Play Center is for kids 2 to 12 and operates from 8:00 in the morning until 6:00 P.M. A daily newsletter, "Junior Globetrotters Programme," lists such activities such as fingerpainting, contests, storytelling, tea parties, arts and crafts, a children's radio show, and gymnastics. The Slant Floor Cinema has daily showings of Disney films and cartoons. The center is furnished with colorful, child-sized playthings and books. The Teen Scene room is open 24 hours a day; from Memorial Day to Labor Day and at school vacation times, a special teen counselor organizes ping-pong tournaments, disco parties, deck hikes, and other fun for this age group. Baby-sitting is not difficult to arrange; expect to pay $5 per hour.

KID'S PRICING: Kids under 2 years who sleep in a crib pays $20 per day when in a room with two adults; an infant with one adult also pays $20 per day, and adults must pay the applicable single passenger fare. Children 2 and over with two adults pay 50 percent of the minimum rate. A child with one adult must pay full fare.

DESCRIPTION: The *QE2* travels from New York, Baltimore, Boston, Fort Lauderdale, Honolulu, Los Angeles, Charleston, and ports in England, Ireland, and France to Bermuda, Hawaii, Acapulco, Curacao, St. Thomas, Norway, Halifax, Bar Harbor, Newport, a number of cities in Spain, the Caribbean, and in Puerto Vallarta. All first-class cabins accommodate cribs, and many accommodate three or four people. There are over 200 adjoining cabins.

MV CUNARD *PRINCESS* AND MV CUNARD *COUNTESS*

KID'S PROGRAMS: At Christmas and during the summer, the ship has two counselors who organize activities from 9:00 A.M. to noon and 2:30 to 5:30 P.M. for children from 2 to 12 years. The ship is in port every day and most children accompany parents on shore excursions. Activities include arts and crafts, deck hikes, scavenger hunts, storytelling, and more. When the ship is in port a limited schedule of activities is planned. Baby-sitting can be arranged at approximately $5 per hour.

KID'S PRICING: Under 2, the charge is $10 per day when sharing with two adults or with one adult paying the single occupancy rate. Kids over two years, sharing with two adults, pay the third- and fourth-person rate. A child with one adult pays full fare.

DESCRIPTION: The *Princess*'s ports of embarkation are New York, Fort Lauderdale, Malaga, Malta, and Venice; respective ports of call are Bermuda, the eastern and western Mediterranean, and the Canary Islands. There are 134 three-bed cabins with upper berths, 10 staterooms with three lower beds, and 24 adjoining rooms. The *Countess* goes from San Juan to points in the Caribbean; accommodations are the same as those of the *Princess*.

Delta Queen Steamboat Company
30 Robin Street Wharf
New Orleans, Louisiana 70130
Telephone: 504-586-0631 or 800-543-1949

THE SHIPS: *Mississippi Queen.* (The *Delta Queen,* their other ship, is not listed here since it has no three- or four-bedded cabins suitable for families.)

FOR KIDS: A children's counselor will definitely be aboard those cruises where the special "kids cruise free" deal applies (see below). Activities are planned to familiarize kids with the many historical sights en route—the *Queen* passes through Mark Twain country. At other times, when the reservations staff sees that there will be more than eight to ten children on board, they'll alert the on-board staff that a children's activity program is needed. So ask, when you book, what the status of the children's program will be. Baby-sitting is available and can be arranged through the Purser's Office but is not available when the boat is in port and is more difficult to arrange during the day than in the evening. The cost is a pricy $8–$10 per hour.

KID'S PRICING: A summer special for children under 16 traveling with two adults in category C or higher allows one child to travel free sharing a stateroom. On some August, September, and November sailings, two additional children (for a total of up to three) will be accommodated in a separate cabin as space allows. At other times there are a limited number of separate cabins for one or two children at 25 percent off the published rate.

DESCRIPTION: The *Mississippi Queen* sails from New Orleans, Memphis, St. Louis, St. Paul, Cincinnati, and Pittsburgh to a host of interesting river communities along the Mississippi and Ohio Rivers. The ship has 56 three-bed cabins (39 of these are upper berths, 12 are lower, and five are sofa beds), four four-bed cabins, and four adjoining cabins.

Holland America Lines
300 Elliot Avenue West
Seattle, Washington 98119
Telephone: 206-281-3535

THE SHIPS: MS *Nieuw Amsterdam*, SS *Rotterdam*, MS *Noordam*, MS *Westerdam*

IN THEIR OWN WORDS: "The Indonesian and Filipino staff is always eager to accommodate special requests and they love children."

FOR KIDS: Children's programs are organized when bookings "indicate a need"—always at Christmastime and usually at Easter and during the summer. At other times, the daily program usually includes some special children's activities, but programs differ from ship to ship, depending on the whims of each cruise director. Generally, there is one activity during the day specifically geared to school-age kids, and children may be interested in other offerings such as pizza and coketail parties and kite flying that are open to all ages throughout the cruise. Baby-sitting is generally available; it costs $5 for the first hour and $2.50 for each additional hour.

KID'S PRICING: Kids under 3 years (under 2 on Alaska cruises) are free when sharing with two adults; airfare is not included. Children aged 3 to 12 sharing with two adults pay third and fourth-passenger rates. A child with one adult pays full fare except on Alaska cruises, when children 12 and under pay half the regular rate.

DESCRIPTION: The *Nieuw Amsterdam* sails from Tampa and Vancouver, British Columbia, to the Caribbean, Trans Canal, and Alaska. Family accommodations include 20 deluxe staterooms with king-size bed and sofa bed, 72 four-bed cabins with two lower beds and two upper pullman berth, and 24 adjoining cabins.

The *Noordam*'s ports of embarkation are Fort Lauderdale and Vancouver, British Columbia; ports of call include the Caribbean, Alaska, and the Panama Canal. Accommodations are the same as the *Nieuw Amsterdam*.

The *Rotterdam* sails from Fort Lauderdale, Vancouver, B.C. and Acapulco to the Caribbean, Alaska, the Panama Canal, and Mexico. Family accommodations include 180 three-bed cabins and 73 four-bed cabins with upper pullman berths. This includes four three-bed and 18 four-bed suites with separate sitting areas and couch. In addition, there are 42 adjoining rooms and 70 rooms with common hallways.

The *Westerdam* travels between Fort Lauderdale and Vancouver, B.C. and Caribbean ports and Alaska. It offers lots of accommodation possibilities for families: 112 outside standard twin cabins with one single bed and sitting area with sofa bed, 186 inside standard twin cabins with two twin beds, 64 standard double cabins with double bed and sitting area with sofa bed, 154 deluxe twin cabins with two twin beds, sitting area and sofa bed, 13 cabins with queen-size bed plus sitting area with sofa bed and five two-room deluxe suites with two single beds and a sofa bed.

Premier Cruise Lines
1200 Challenger Road
Cape Canaveral, Florida 32920
Telephone: 407-783-5061

THE SHIPS: SS *Atlantic,* SS *Majestic,* and SS *Oceanic*

NOTE: Premier is the official cruise line of Walt Disney World. Some Disney characters are on board all sailings and join several events, to the delight of all ages. Naturally, they help entertain the kids as well. The price of a four-night cruise, includes a free pre- or post-cruise three-day Walt Disney World package with admission to the Magic Kingdom and EPCOT Center, tour of the Spaceport, USA, three nights in an Orlando-area hotel (some on-site at extra cost) and a rental car with unlimited mileage.

FOR KIDS: Up to ten Youth Counselors are on board every cruise year-round. Daily events are scheduled from 9:00 A.M. to noon and 2:00 P.M. to 5:00 P.M. for ages 2–7, 8–12, and 13–17. The focus of the activities is Pluto's Playhouse, the Children's Playroom, and the Teen Center. Children's newsletters, one for each age group, list the daily activities. You can expect to find arts and crafts, storytelling, disco classes, hopscotch, pool games, and more. Activities during the day when the ship calls at an out island include limbo contests, sand-castle building, scavenger hunts, and sack races. Activities often center on the Disney characters on board with special magic shows and lots of creative, thoughtfully designed events. The director of all of the kids' programs for Premier believes that lots of passengers sail with them just because of the kid's program and that the cruise line had better meet the passengers' highest expectations if it is to succeed. We were especially impressed with the teen coordinator, who handled this difficult age group with tact and great understanding; the kids adored her.

When the children's program ends at 10:00 P.M. baby-sitting is available in the playroom until 1:00 A.M. for children 2 years and older. The cost is approximately $3 per hour for one child, $5 per hour for two or more in the same family. Cabin baby-sitting is available on a limited basis by special request to the Youth Director.

KID'S PRICING: Children under 2 are free. In all other cases there are substantial discounts for third, fourth, and fifth passengers in the cabin. Special prices too, for single parents traveling with children up to 18 years old.

DESCRIPTION: All ships leave from Port Canaveral; the *Oceanic* and the *Atlantic* sail to Nassau and Salt Cay (Bahamas out island); the *Majestic* sails to the Abacos Bahama out islands—Treasure Cay, Green Turtle Cay, Great Guana Cay, and Man-O-War Cay. (The ship will dock midway between the islands and a tender runs to each, all day and evening.)

On the *Oceanic* you'll find 177 three-bed cabins with two lower beds and one upper pullman; 163 four-bed cabins with two lower beds and two upper pullmans; 71 five-bed cabins, and 40 adjoining cabins in addition to eight "veranda apartments" and 42 suites. Some rooms have double- or queen-size beds. The cabins we saw, including several suites, were among the largest we'd ever seen on the high seas.

On the *Atlantic* you can choose from 246 three-bed cabins, nine of which have upper berths; six four-bed suites with sofa beds; and 141 four-bed cabins with upper berths.

The *Majestic* has 137 three-bed cabins which are doubles with upper berths, 66 four-bed cabins, six suites, and several cabins large enough to accommodate five passengers.

Princess Cruises

10100 Santa Monica Boulevard
Suite 1800
Los Angeles, California 90067
Telephone: 213-553-1666, 800-421-0522 or 800-421-0880

NOTE: After merging with Sitmar, Princess now operates a total of eight ships: *Island Princess, Pacific Princess, Royal Princess, Sea Princess,* and the former Sitmar ships, *Fair Princess, Sky Princess, Dawn Princess,* and *Star Princess.* Because the programs on the former Sitmar ships are the most comprehensive, these are the only ones we list here.

THE SHIPS: *Fair Princess, Dawn Princess, Sky Princess, Star Princess*

IN THEIR OWN WORDS: "We feel that the service, warmth and friendliness of our Italian crew members make the difference. They make you feel at home and do their utmost to make your vacation a special experience.

FOR KIDS: Every cruise has a minimum of four counselors. The ratio of counselors to children is approximately one to 20 (this ratio includes teenagers). From June to August, the program expands to include a teen coordinator, performing arts director, and at least eight counselors who organize an enriched program designed to "stimulate social skills, self-improvement and natural curiosity." Youth counselors are on duty from 9:00 A.M. to midnight, seven days a week. Hours of the center are lengthened when the ship is in port. A daily newsletter just for kids tells passengers what to expect each day.

Infants from 6 months and toddlers are welcome in the Youth Center, where there are cribs and cots for naps. Formula should be requested two weeks before sailing, and parents are asked to feed and diaper children, although staff is willing to pinch-hit when necessary. The staff is very child oriented, and although diaper changing may not be in their job description, while we were on board we never saw any child left in dirty diapers.

The Youth Center is well stocked with games, books, supplies, and lots of great prizes. Activities include magic shows, arts and crafts, ice cream pizza parties, talent shows, swimming, and more. The children's pool is located right outside the center.

Activities are available during lunch and dinner hours, although meals are not provided for children unless parents make a special request. Parents are asked to check in with the youth activities coordinator throughout the day and are always welcome at the center. Our kids gravitated to it, and as a result, we spent lots of our time on deck just outside the center.

The Teen Center for ages 13–17 is equipped with a dance floor, juke box, and video games. A teen coordinator schedules activities such as aerobics, drama classes, acting lessons, ship tours, Italian lessons, and midnight films. The Sitmar staff is so tuned in to this age group's needs that teenagers really love to hang out at the Teen Center.

In all, there are three swimming pools, one for adults, one for children, and one for both. The gymnasium is reserved for kids during certain hours, when it's supervised by a youth counselor.

Baby-sitting is neither necessary or available, since the Youth Center is staffed and open from 9:00 A.M. until midnight. None of the families we met found the absence of baby-sitting a problem.

KID'S PRICING: Infants to 12-year-olds pay approximately half of the regular third- and fourth-person rate when they're with two adults; a child with only one adult pays full fare.

DESCRIPTION: *Fair Princess* sails between Los Angeles and Vancouver and the Mexican Riviera and Alaska. Most cabins, except suites and mini-suites, have two lower beds and two upper pullman beds. Suites and mini-suites sleep only two people. There are no connecting rooms, but many sets of cabins share a small common hallway.

Dawn Princess, the sister ship of the *Fair Princess,* sails from Fort Lauderdale, Lisbon, Venice, London, Copenhagen, and Los Angeles to the Caribbean, Mexico, and Europe.

The *Sky Princess*'s ports of embarkation are Fort Lauderdale,

San Juan, Acapulco, New York, Montreal, Rio de Janeiro, and Manaus; ports of call are the Caribbean, Mexico, South America, Trans Canal, Canada, and New England. Cabins are spacious, and most have two lower beds and two upper pullman beds.

And finally, the *Star Princess* sails from Fort Lauderdale and San Francisco to the Caribbean and Alaska. One hundred fifty cabins have upper berths; twin beds are convertible to double beds.

The other Princess ships, the *Island Princess, Pacific Princess, Royal Princess,* and *Sea Princess* all offer programs only when there are 25 or more children on board from the age of 2 years through teens, usually during summer and holiday cruises. Baby-sitting is not available. Children under 12 months are not permitted to travel. Children under 12, sharing with two adults, are charged one-half the minimum rate for the occupied accommodations. With one adult, the first child pays full fare, a second child receives a 50 percent discount.

Royal Caribbean Cruise Line
903 South America Way
Miami, Florida 33132
Telephone: 305-379-2601

THE SHIPS: MS *Nordic Prince,* MS *Song of America,* MS *Sun Viking,* MS *Song of Norway,* and *Sovereign of the Seas*

FOR KIDS: On the *Sovereign of the Seas,* the children's programs operate year-round and, on all other ships, on Christmas, New Year's, Easter (the week before and during) and from mid-June through Labor Day. There are three programs in all—for ages 5–8, 9–13, and 14–17, supervised by program counselors who are usually teachers with either guidance of phys ed experience. The *Sovereign* has one room just for kids. The other ships don't, but special times are scheduled for children to use the pool and other public areas when adults aren't using them. Activities are scheduled from 9:00 A.M. to noon, 2:00 to 6:00 P.M., and 8:30 to 10:00 P.M. and include tours of the ship, ice cream and pizza parties, swimming, masquerade parties, sports tournaments, and special shore excursions. Programs are sometimes available in the afternoon while the ship is in port for kids who stay behind.

A newsletter listing all kids' activities is distributed each evening for the following day, and free, supervised shore excursions are part of the program at certain ports.

We were very impressed with the kids' programs on the *Sun Viking*. The counselors seemed to always be available; they were on deck at 9 in the morning for any child who had not yet had breakfast and also took the kids to the on-deck barbecue lunches. The program is quite flexible and may continue past noon during some activities. In fact, some evenings the kids' parties in the Compass Lounge went on until 11:00. On the day of the free kids-only shore excursions, extra ship staff join the group to help watch the kids. The kids loved having an excursion just for them, and though it didn't last a full day, it gave the parents a nice break, too. Baby-sitting is usually available in the evening, although not always during the day. The charge is about $8 per hour, and a minimum of three hours is required. While the ship is in port, sitters are available as well.

KID'S PRICING: Children sharing a cabin with two adults pay third- and fourth-passenger rates. Air/sea fares begins at $495 for the seven-day Bermuda and eight-day Caribbean cruises; there's a $250 discount on Miami and $200 discount on New York cruises if no air transportation is needed.

DESCRIPTION: The *Nordic Prince*'s ports of embarkation are Miami and New York; ports of call are Bermuda, San Juan, St. Thomas, Antigua, Barbados, Martinique, St. Maarten, and Nassau. Family accommodations include 30 three-bed cabins and 48 four-bed cabins with upper pullman berths, 15 large deluxe suites with two beds, and 44 adjoining cabins.

The *Song of America* sails from Miami to Haiti, Jamaica, Grand Cayman, Playa del Carmen, and Cozumel. Family accommodations consist of 74 three-bedded and 43 four-bedded cabins with upper pullman berths, and one large deluxe suite with a third bed.

The ports of embarkation for the *Song of Norway* are San Juan and New York, ports of call are St. Maarten, Antigua, Martinique, Barbados, and St. Thomas. Twenty-five three-bed cabins and 48 four-bed cabins have upper pullman berths, 13 deluxe suites have two beds only, and there are 38 adjoining cabins.

The *Sun Viking* leaves from Miami and sails to Barbados, St. Lucia, St. Barts, St. Thomas, and Guadeloupe. Family accommodations include 26 three-bed cabins and 48 four-bed cabins with upper pullman berths, nine deluxe suites with two beds, and 40 adjoining cabins.

And finally, the *Sovereign of the Seas* starts out in Miami and calls at Labadee (Haiti), San Juan, and St. Thomas. For families, the choices include 178 three-bed cabins, 88 four-bed cabins with upper pullman berths, four deluxe suites with two beds, and 50 adjoining cabins.

World Explorer Cruises
555 Montgomery Street
San Francisco, California 94111
Telephone: 415-391-9262 or 800-854-3835

THE SHIP: SS *Universe*

NOTE: When we first asked World Explorer about children's activities a few years ago, they said nothing special was offered. Our question prompted them to check on how many kids sailed with them, and they discovered that there were many more than they had originally thought. Wanting to provide a memorable experience for all of their passengers, they added special programs for kids.

IN THEIR OWN WORDS: "Probably the most important thing is the adventure of Alaska. Kids really enjoy it when they pull into port; it's sort of like the olden days . . . cowboys and Indians, . . . they love it. The attractiveness of the destination is Number 1, it appeals to kids of all ages, and secondly, the unique shore excursions are special. We have everything from gold-panning to whitewater rafting for the kids; it's hands-on stuff for kids to do, sort of like a Disneyland on the water."

FOR KIDS: A youth program director is on all cruises from June to September when there are enough kids 7 and over on board. The program includes board games, exercise classes, sports tournaments, movies, and more. Evening activities are also scheduled, and if there are at least five or six kids under 7 years old, the youth director will arrange special activities for them, too—activities such as games, skits, and ice cream and cake parties. Baby-sitters can be arranged without much problem for $2–3 per hour and are available for the times that the ship is in port.

KID'S PRICING: Children under 2 are free; children over 2 sharing with two adults are $595 (the third- and fourth-person rate); a child with just one adult pays full fare.

DESCRIPTION: The *Universe* sails from Vancouver to Alaska. For families, there are 110 four-bed cabins. (From September to May the ship serves as a floating campus for the University of Pittsburgh.)

None of the Above/More Places That Welcome Families

In the course of writing this book, we discovered many hotels/ resorts that welcome families but don't fit neatly under any of our chapters. Some have kids' programs, but they're not as comprehensive as the ones we list in the heart of the book. Even so, we want you to know about them so that if you're traveling in their direction you can consider them. We've listed them here by state:

Arizona

Loews Ventana Canyon Resort
7000 North Resort Drive
Tucson, Arizona 85715
Telephone: 602-299-2020 or 800-234-5117

This is a beautiful resort situated high on a plateau above the city of Tucson, in the middle of a saguaro cactus garden in the Catalina Mountains. Golf, bicycling, tennis, jogging, and swimming are all possible, plus guests have full use of the fitness center with a staff of professional trainers. Holidays are special times at Ventana Canyon for families—at Christmas and Easter there are day-care camp programs for kids 3–11; at Christmas the staff schedules ballet and chorus performances, at Easter there are egg hunts and visits from the Easter Bunny and Big Bird. Evening activities for kids from 7:00 and 11:00 are also available at holiday times; the children's activities are free to guests. Baby-sitting may be arranged for $5 per hour. In high season, mid-January to mid-May, rates are $215 to $245 double occupancy with suites for $390 to $1,200 per night. Rooms are spacious, and all have private patios. Special golf, tennis, spa, and holiday packages are available. Kids 18 and under stay free in their parent's room.

California

Lost Whale Bed and Breakfast Inn
3452 Patrick's Point Drive
Trinidad, California 95570
Telephone: 707-677-3425
General Manager: Susanne Lakin

Unlike most California b and b's, this one, located on California's north coast, welcomes kids enthusiastically: "We have four spectacular acres on a bluff leading down to a private beach of tidepools and sea lions. We have a play yard, farm animals, bikes, toys, sleeping lofts for children, hearty breakfasts, and our children, Megan, 6, and Amara, 2, are eager to play with little guests." Kids may eat with their parents in the dining room, or, if they'd prefer, they can sit with Amara and Megan. "We fix whatever parents request." The great room is filled with books, puzzles, and games that will entertain kids when they have to stay inside; on nice days they can have the run of the enclosed grounds. Baby-sitting at night can be arranged for $2 per hour. Rates, which include breakfast and afternoon tea, are $75–90 nightly double occupany, $5 for kids 2–16. Cribs, bassinets, and high chairs are all available with advance notice.

Colorado

Tucker's Mountain Meadows Bed and Breakfast
37951 Highway 184
Mancos, Colorado 81328
Telephone: 303-533-7664
Owners: Keith and Sandy Tucker
Operating season: Year-round

When we called Sandy Tucker to find out how to get to her b and b, we were a little taken aback when she described it as being "just off the highway." Not to worry. The Tuckers' place is situated in a gorgeous spot off the road that winds from Mancos to Dolores, and everything about the place is as close to perfection as we have yet found. As our youngest daughter observed when we sat down to breakfast on our first morning at the Tuckers', "This is a wonderful place to wake up!" It is, in fact, a wonderful place for just about anything—Sandy and Keith are probably the warmest hosts we have ever encountered. The Tuckers' beautiful b and b has four bedrooms on the second floor, two on the first, and a fully equipped immaculate kitchen that guests are sometimes able to use. (The Tuckers restrict use of the kitchen when there are lots of guests, but while we were there our family was the only one in residence so we had full run of the kitchen. We packed our picnic lunches there and made ourselves a spaghetti dinner one night.) Sandy, who believes that people on vacation shouldn't have to spend time in a supermarket, picked up all of our groceries on the day we arrived—we just gave her a list, and a few hours later, everything we needed was ours. The cookie jar at Tucker's is always full (the four of us must have demolished at least three dozen chocolate chip cookies in three days); there's coffee, hot chocolate, and tea available whenever the mood strikes. And the breakfasts are extraordinary; absolutely everything is homemade, including blueberry muffins, an apple crisp, French toast, a vegetable omelet, and scones.

The kids had a wonderful time with the Tuckers' newly acquired resident llama, their seven horses, three cats, and assorted dogs. Anyone who is planning a trip to this part of Colorado (spectacularly beautiful as is the whole of the west of the state) and particularly to Mesa Verde National Park (the gate's only six miles away) should most definitely plan to stay with the Tuckers. And, rates are reasonable: $40–65 per room per night, and remember that includes an enormous breakfast.

Beaver Village Condominiums
50 Village Drive
P.O. Box 3154
Winter Park, Colorado 80482
Telephone: 303-726-8813 or 800-525-3304
General Manager: Kristy Meyer

These one-, two-, and three-bedroom condos are adjacent to Arapahoe National Forest and 1½ miles from the Winter Park/Mary

Jane Ski Areas. Guests can shuttle free to downhill skiing or go cross-country skiing right outside their condo door. To warm up there are jacuzzis, an indoor pool, and a steam room. Tennis, sailing, golf, hiking, and horseback riding are all possible when the snow melts. Cribs are available for $5 per stay, and baby-sitting can be arranged for $1.50 per hour. A two-bedroom condo large enough for six costs $99 to $231, depending on the seas; a one-bedroom for four costs $110 during the regular season.

Florida

Sun Viking Lodge
2411 South Atlantic Avenue
Daytona, Florida 32018
Telephone: 904-252-6252
General Managers: Frank and Mindy Forehand

The lodge specializes in families. The 60-foot-long waterslide is a hit with everyone, and for cooler weather, there's an indoor pool. The kiddie pool is best for little ones, and for everyone there are two game rooms and a sauna, hot tub, shuffleboard, and basketball. Family packages for two-room suites with room for up to six people and kitchens are $70 to $140 per night, depending on season. Smaller rooms starting at $35 per night are also available. Cribs are available at no extra charge. Baby-sitting for $4 per hour can be arranged at the front desk.

Fortune Place
1426 Astro Lake Drive North
Kissimmee, Florida 32743
Telephone: 305-847-9661 or 800-624-7496
General Manager: Jim Schroeder

These are condos with two, three, or four bedrooms; full kitchens; an outdoor pool; a children's game room; and a children's playground. It's near Walt Disney World, Sea World, and so on. Cribs are available. Rates range from $99 to $199 per night for a two-bedroom condo, depending on season.

Lake Buena Vista (Walt Disney World Village)

The following hotels are all operated by the Disney people, all are Official Walt Disney World Resorts: Disney's Caribbean Beach Resort, Disney's Polynesian Resort, the Disney Inn, Disney's Village Resort, Disney's Grand Floridian Beach Resort, Disney's Fort Wilderness Resort (for camping, complete with trailers and campsites), and Disney's Contemporary Resort.

Information on any or all of the above is available from P.O. Box 10,000, Lake Buena Vista, Florida 32830-1000, or by calling 407-W-DISNEY.

Each of these properties is kid oriented, as you'd expect. Their activities are guaranteed to please kids: at the Polynesian Resort kids can have breakfast with their favorite Disney characters, hula at "Mickey's Tropical Review," or go to their own dinner theater while parents have a night out. At the Grand Floridian and the Contemporary, the Mouseketeer Club keeps kids 3 to 9 happy from 4:30 P.M. to midnight ($4 per hour for the first child, 50 cents per hour for each sibling).

Buena Vista Palace
Walt Disney World Village
P.O. Box 22206
Lake Buena Vista, Florida 32830-2206
Telephone: 407-827-2727 or 800-327-2990
General Manager: Robert L. Stolz

This 27-story hotel overlooks Walt Disney World and offers kids aged 3 to 9 free breakfast with the Disney characters as part of the summer package. Special activities are planned, too, throughout the summer for kids 3 to 17. Baby-sitting is available for $5 per hour during the day or in the evening. There are three pools, a recreation island with a Jacuzzi and sauna, tennis courts, golf, and a playground for the kids. Rates in peak season—during Christmas vacation time—are $135 to $235, depending on the room; no charge for kids under 18 in the same room with parents. Family packages that include accommodation, tickets to Walt Disney World, dinner shows, car rentals, and meals are available year-round.

Hilton at Walt Disney World Village
1751 Hotel Plaza Boulevard
Lake Buena Vista, Florida 32830
Telephone: 407-827-4000 or 800-782-4414
General Manager: Samir A. Shafel

This Hilton property operates a Youth Hotel, which provides a place where kids can do arts and crafts, watch a large screen television in the video room, or even nap in a pint-sized dormitory. Kids 4 to 12 may be dropped off any day of the week from 4:00 P.M. to midnight. The ratio of counselors to kids is usually one to 12. All guests at the Hilton are guaranteed admission to Disney theme parks, even during peak attendance periods, and also receive discounted greens fees at three golf courses operated by the Disney people. A Stay 'n' Play ticket package, which includes accommodations, transportation, and admission to the Disney parks, breakfast each morning, and unlimited use of the health club and tennis courts, costs $209.50 per adult double occupancy for four days, three nights during peak season. Kids stay free in the same room with parents.

Fontainebleau Hilton
4441 Collins Avenue
Miami Beach, Florida 33140
Telephone: 305-528-2000 or 800-HILTONS
General Manager: Andre Schaefer

This elaborate hotel has recently had $70 million worth of "refinements" as the management calls them. You'll find seven tennis courts, a swimming pool as big as an island lagoon, and a 1,200-foot beach. For kids 5 to 13 there are activities during the summer and at school break time originating at the Kids' Korner—arts and crafts, sand-castle building, T-shirt painting, and exercises. A double room costs $165 to $235 per night; a parlor plus one bedroom is $360 to $535. Packages such as a seven-day, six-night version cost $925 for a double room plus parking, continental breakfasts, and cocktails. Kids stay free in their parents' room. There's no extra charge for supervised kid's activities.

Sonesta Village Hotel
10000 Turkey Lake Road
Orlando, Florida 32819
Telephone: 407-352-8051 or 800-343-7170
General Manager: Bob Moceri

The Sonesta Kids Club, with its own frequent guest program for kids 4 to 12, provides supervised activities each day from noon to 5:00 P.M. and a variety of evening events, until 7:30, 8:00, or 10:00, depending on the activity. Sonesta Kids have penny dives, balloon tosses, build sand castles, and so on, treasure hunts and picnics. The club also offers a "Tuck-in Service"—Sunny the Seal, the club mascot will come to your villa, give your kids a bedtime snack and wish them sweet dreams. The hotel has a children's pool and three play areas with monkey bars, teeter-totters, and swings.

Accommodations at Sonesta Village are in one- and two-bedroom villas. A special four-night package, "Family Villa Vacation," includes accommodations, a rental car for four days, a three-day passport to Walt Disney World, Magic Kingdom, and EPCOT Center, and a surprise package for kids and costs just under $400 for a one-bedroom, $537 for a two-bedroom villa from the beginning of January to mid-February.

Georgia

Little Saint Simons Island
P.O. Box 1078
St. Simons, Georgia 31522
Telephone: 912-638-7472
General Manager: Ben Gibbens

This is an exquisite, privately owned barrier island with six miles of unbelievably pristine beaches. Our family spent three days here during the summer and will never forget the natural, unspoiled beauty and the kindness and warmth of the naturalists who taught us so much. We spent our days fishing, swimming, boating, horseback riding, exploring the beach for sea turtle nests, and collecting shells. One night, after dinner, we got into a jeep and went out to see an alligator nest. There are only 12 rooms in all, and only 24 guests per night are allowed. The food is excellent; the bird watching is spectacular. This is a place for people who honestly love being in the middle of nature without distractions. The staff sensibly discourages kids under 5. Rates vary from $275 to $375 double occupancy per night with all meals, transportation to and from the island, horseback riding, use of all equipment, private picnics, hors d'oeuvres and wine before dinner, and the full-time attention of the naturalists. Children's rates are available on request.

Hawaii

New Otani Kaimana Beach Hotel
2863 Kaldaua Avenue
Honolulu, Hawaii 96815
Telephone: 808-923-1555
General Manager: Stephen Boyle

A friend en route to Asia spent a few nights here and wrote to tell us about how pleased she and her son were with their accommodations. Their lanai (balcony) faced Waikiki in the distance and the beach of Sans Souci in the foreground. The hotel is right at Diamond Head, close to a lovely park and the Honolulu Zoo. Junior suites with one bedroom and a kitchen are a good value at $112. The hotel's open-air restaurant is a wonderful place to eat—you can order bagels as well as papaya muffins, fruit frappes, and more. Expect to meet lots of kids on the beach—guests and locals together.

Massachusetts

Tara Hyannis Hotel
West End Circle
Hyannis, Massachusetts 02601
Telephone: 508-775-7775 or 800-THE-TARA
General Manager: Kevin M. Howard

The resort is located at the hub of the Cape and offers swimming in outdoor and indoor pools, tennis and golf, and a well-equipped health club. Throughout the week during the summer and at school vacation times, staff schedules activities for kids 5 to 12—things such as a cartoon pajama party early in the morning, a kids-only supper party, splash parties, and movies. In summer, a mid-week package from Sunday to Thursday would cost $133 for two per night, which includes breakfast; kids 16 and under stay for free in a room with parents, and rooms are big enough for four. A weekend package costs $335. Baby-sitting is available for $5 per hour.

New Hampshire

Whitney's Village Inn
Box W
Route 16B
Jackson, New Hampshire 03846
Telephone: 603-383-6886
General Manager and Owner: T. M. Tannehill

When the Tannehills acquired the inn in 1983, they were determined to establish the inn as a family inn run by a family. To do this they offer special rates for kids, a children's menu, a kids' dinner table, a family activities room, nightly movies, and a teen room. In winter there's skiing—downhill at Black Mountain and cross-country in the backyard; ski lessons, ice-skating (they'll provide the skates), and sledding; in summer they offer swimming in a mountain pond, hiking, tennis, volleyball, badminton, croquet, fishing, and all the family-type attractions of the Mount Washington Valley. There are eight family cottages, with living room, bedroom, and bath, with room for six. Cribs are available. The rate for adults is $72 per person double occupancy with breakfast and dinner included in a family suite; for a three-night package the rate drops to $65. Kids 12 and under in a room with parents are $25 per night.

Pennsylvania

Hotel Hershey
P.O. Box BB
Hotel Road
Hershey, Pennsylvania 17033
Telephone: 717-533-2171 or 800-HERSHEY
General Manager: Patrick Kerwin

This majestic hotel, made to look like one of the grand villas of the Mediterranean, is set on 58 acres of lush, rolling green countryside. At the hotel itself there are lots of activities for kids and their families during the summer and at holiday time. Hershey is a wonderful place for a family vacation, with Hersheypark, the zoo, the Museum of American Life and Chocolate World (our daughter is still raving about the tour there that explains how chocolate is made). The Hotel Hershey's appealing mixture of elegance and warmth makes a great base for a trip to this town, where chocolate rules. The hotel has an indoor and an outdoor pool, a whirlpool and sauna, four outdoor tennis courts, a nine-hole golf course plus guest privileges at other gold courses, horseback riding, cycling (bikes are available), jogging trails, a game room, and in winer, tobagganing and cross-country skiing. Daily rates from April to November are $105 per person double occupancy with breakfast and dinner included; $21 for kids under 9 and free for kids 4 and under. Packages are available throughout the year. One most appealing to families is the Hersheypark Classic package, which includes room, breakfast, admission to the park and Zooamerica and free admission to Hershey Gardens. It costs $95 per person per night double occupancy, $186 for two nights.

Hershey Lodge
West Chocolate Avenue and University Drive
Hershey, Pennsylvania 17033
Telephone: 717-533-3311 or 800-533-3131
General Manager: John H. Bogrette

This is where our family stayed when we visited Hershey, and we were delighted. We loved the rooms—spacious and pretty—and especially the pool, the hot tub, and the sauna, which were just great after a busy day of sightseeing in Chocolateville. The staff is all extremely wlecoming to kids, and although there's no supervised children's program, there are lots of family-oriented activities scheduled whenever it's school vacation time. Another surprise feature at the lodge is that it has its very own first-run movie theater. We stayed at the lodge for a few days between Christmas and New Year's and the place was jumping with families who all seemed as happy as we were with their choice. Rates in summer, their peak season, are $114 per night for a room with two adults, with kids 17 and under free. Packages are available, too.

Vermont

Mountain Top Inn
Mountain Top Road
Chittenden, Vermont 05737
Telephone: 802-483-2311 or 800-445-2100
General Manager: William P. Wolfe

In winter, explore the peaks and valleys of this Green Mountain resort on cross-country skis; in summer, stroll through its green fields or swim in the clear water of its lake. This place likes to think of itself as something between an inn and a resort—all the facilities of a resort, like a pool, horseback riding, cross-country skiing, and all the personal attention and warmth of an inn. At Mountain Top there are three types of accommodations: guest rooms, all with lovely views, cottages, and chalets. Nicest of all for families are the roomy chalets with two bedrooms or more, a kitchen or kitchenette, full bath or baths, living room, dining area, fireplace or wood stove. Rates for a chalet in summer, based on double occupancy with breakfast and dinner included, are $316 for one night, $982 for seven. Kids 7–16 would pay 50 percent, 2–6, 35 percent, and under 2, free. In winter, at peak time during Christmas vacation, the same chalets are $358 for one night, $836 for seven.

Woodstock Inn and Resort
14 The Green
Woodstock, Vermont 05091
Telephone: 802-457-1100 or 800-448-7900
General Manager: S. Lee Bowden

In winter, guests at the Woodstock Inn go cross-country skiing, on sleigh rides, ice-skating, dogsledding, or downhill skiing nearby; in the warm weather they offer golf, tennis, biking, swimming, horseback riding, fishing, and hiking. The Woodstock Recreation Center is close by and has supervised playground activity Monday through Friday from 9:00 A.M. to noon. There are 110 rooms in all.

A Ski Vermont Free package, which includes room, lift tickets to Suicide Six, trail fees at the Touring Center, equipment rentals, and use of the Sports Center, costs $85 to $130 per night midweek, $240 for a one-bedroom suite. Baby-sitting is available for $5 per hour.

Virginia

Holiday Inn on the Ocean
3900 Atlantic Avenue
Virginia Beach, Virginia 23451
Telephone: 804-428-1711 or 800-942-3224
General Manager: Steven J. Luchik

Located right at the end of the Virginia Beach boardwalk, this hotel in the heart of an enormously popular resort town offers an indoor and outdoor pool and is within a 15-minute drive of six public golf courses, 146 tennis courts, four fishing piers, and an oceanfront sports fishing marina. During the summer, the staff plans activities for kids around the hotel and excursions to a nearby state park, a dairy farm, a zoo, or the Marine Science Museum. Tuesday and Friday nights in July and August are set aside as family nights, with activities designed to appeal to all ages. Summer packages for an efficiency apartment on the ocean cost $425 for three nights with arrival from Sunday through Wednesday, kids 19 and under stay for free with parents. Baby-sitting is available for $5 per hour during the day and in the evening.

Publishers

Any family planning to travel (and we hope that's every family) should have a copy of a catalog published by the folks at Carousel Press that specializes in family-oriented books. For a copy, send $1 (applied to your order) to Family Travel Guides, P.O. Box 6061, Albany, California 94706, 415-527-5849.

Here we list the publishers of books listed in *Great Vacations with Your Kids*. Many of the books we list are produced by small presses with limited distribution and may not be readily available in your local bookstore. You can always order books by mail; just be sure to add about $2 to cover postage and handling. Better still, call the publisher and ask exactly how much to send.

Addison-Wesley
1 Jacob Way
Reading, Massachusetts 01867
800-447-2226

Adventure Guides
36 East 57th Street
New York, New York 10022
212-355-6334

Anais Press
P.O. Box 9635
Denver, Colorado 80209

Bantam/Doubleday Day
  Publishing Group Inc.
666 Fifth Avenue
New York, New York 10019
800-323-9872

Carousel Press
P.O. Box 6061
Albany, California 94706
415-527-5849

Chronicle Publishers
275 Fifth Street
San Francisco, California 94103
800-722-6657

Congdon and Weed
298 Fifth Avenue
New York, New York 10001
800-221-7945

Doubleday Book and Music Clubs
245 Park Avenue
New York, New York 10167
212-984-7561

Fielding/William Morrow
105 Madison Avenue
New York, New York 10016
212-889-3050

Globe Pequot Press/East Woods
Old Chester Road
Chester, Connecticut 06412
800-243-0495

Harvard Common Press
535 Albany Street
Boston, Massachusetts 02118
617-423-5803

Harcourt Brace Jovanovich
465 South Lincoln Drive
Troy, Missouri 63379
800-543-1918

Hearst Professional Magazines
105 Madison Avenue
New York, New York 10016
212-481-0355

Houghton Mifflin
1 Beacon Street
Boston, Massachusetts 02108
800-225-3362

John Muir Publications
P.O. Box 603
Santa Fe, New Mexico 87504
505-982-4078

Prentice-Hall
Gulf and Western Plaza
New York, New York 10023
800-223-2336

Readers Digest
260 Madison Avenue
New York, New York 10016
212-850-7007

Sierra Club Books
730 Polk Street
San Francisco, California 94109

Simon & Schuster
1230 Avenue of the Americas
New York, New York 10020
800-223-2348

Times Books/Random House
201 East 50th Street
New York, New York 10022
800-638-6460

Williamson Publishing Co.
Church Hill Road,
P.O. Box 185
Charlotte, VT 05445
800-234-8791

Yankee Publishing
Depot Square
Peterborough, New Hampshire
    03458
800-423-2271

Williamson Publishing Co.
Church Hill Road
P.O. Box 185
Charlotte, VT 05445
800-234-8791

United States Tourist Offices

Listed here are addresses and telephone numbers for the tourist offices of all the United States. When you write or call one of these offices, be sure to request a map of the state and a calendar of events. If you will be visiting a particular city or region, or if you have any special interests, be sure to specify this as well.

Alabama Bureau of Tourism and
  Travel
532 South Perry Street
Montgomery, Alabama 36104
205-261-4169; 800-252-2262 (out-
  of-state); 800-392-8096 (in-state)

Alaska Division of Tourism
P.O. Box E
Juneau, Alaska 99811
907-465-2010

Arizona Office of Tourism
1100 West Washington Street
Phoenix, Arizona 85077
602-255-3618

Arkansas Department of Parks and
  Tourism
1 Capitol Mall
Little Rock, Arkansas 72201
501-371-7777; 800-643-8383 (out-
  of-state); 800-482-8999 (in-state)

California Office of Tourism
1121 L Street, Suite 600
Sacramento, California 95814
916-322-1396, 322-1397;
  800-862-2543

Colorado Department of Tourism
1625 Broadway, Suite 1700
Denver, Colorado 80202
303-592-5410; 800-255-5550

Connecticut Department of
  Economic Development/
  Vacations
210 Washington Street
Hartford, Connecticut 06106
203-566-3948; 800-243-1685 (out-
  of-state); 800-842-7492 (in-state)

Delaware Tourism Office
99 Kings Highway
P.O. Box 140
Dover, Delaware 19903
302-736-4271; 800-441-8846 (out-
  of-state); 800-282-8667 (in-state)

Florida Division of Tourism
Fletcher Building
101 East Gaines Street
Mailing address:
126 Van Buren Street
Tallahassee, Florida 32399-2000

Georgia Tourist Division
Box 1776
Atlanta, Georgia 30301
404-656-3590; 800-847-4842

Hawaii Visitors Bureau
Waikiki Business Plaza, Suite 801
2270 Kalakaua Avenue
Honolulu, Hawaii 96815
808-923-1811
or New York Office
441 Lexington Avenue, Room
  1407
New York, New York 10017
212-986-9203

Idaho Department of Commerce
Capitol Building, Room 108
Boise, Idaho 83720
208-334-2470; 800-635-7820

Illinois Office of Tourism
310 South Michigan Avenue, Suite
  108
Chicago, Illinois 60604
312-793-2094; 800-545-7300 (out-
  of-state); 800-359-9299 (in-state)

Indiana Tourism Development
  Division
1 North Capitol, Suite 700
Indianapolis, Indiana 46225-2288
317-232-8860; 800-W-WANDER

Iowa Tourism Office
200 East Grand Avenue
Des Moines, Iowa 50309-2882
515-281-3679; 800-345-4692

Kansas Department of Economic
  Development
Travel and Tourism Division
400 West Eighth Street, Suite 500
Topeka, Kansas 66603
913-296-2009; 800-252-6727 (in-
  state)

Kentucky Department of Travel
  Development
Capitol Plaza Tower, 22nd Floor
Frankfort, Kentucky 40602
502-564-4930; 800-225-8747 (out-
  of-state)

Louisiana Office of Tourism
P.O. Box 94291
Baton Rouge, Louisiana
  70804-9291
504-342-8119; 800-334-8626 (out-
  of-state)

Maine Publicity Bureau
P.O. Box 23000
97 Winthrop Street
Hallowell, Maine 04347
207-289-2423; 800-533-9595

Maryland Office of Tourist
  Development
217 East Redwood Avenue
Baltimore, Maryland 21202
301-974-3517; 800-331-1750

Massachusetts Division of Tourism
Department of Commerce and
  Development
100 Cambridge Street, 13th Floor
Boston, Massachusetts 02202
617-727-3201; 800-533-6277 (out-
  of-state)

Michigan Travel Bureau
Department of Commerce
P.O. Box 30226
Lansing, Michigan 48909
517-373-1195; 800-543-2-YES

Minnesota Tourist Information
  Center
375 Jackson Street
Farm Credit Service Building
St. Paul, Minnesota 55101
612-296-5029; 800-328-1461 (out-
  of-state); 800-652-9747 (in-state)

Mississippi Division of Tourism
P.O. Box 22825
Jackson, Mississippi 39205
601-359-3414; 800-647-2290

Missouri Division of Tourism
P.O. Box 1055
Jefferson City, Missouri 65101
314-751-4133

Montana Promotion Division
1424 Ninth Avenue
Helena, Montana 59620
406-444-2654; 800-541-1447

Nebraska Division of Travel and
    Tourism
P.O. Box 94666
Lincoln, Nebraska 68509
Tel: 402-471-3796; 800-228-4307
    (out-of-state); 800-742-7595 (in-
    state)

Nevada Commission on Tourism
Capitol Complex
600 East Williams Street, Suite
    207
Carson City, Nevada 89710
702-885-4322; 800-237-0774

New Hampshire Office of Vacation
    Travel
P.O. Box 856
Concord, New Hampshire 03301
603-271-2343, 271-2666;
    800-258-3608 (in the Northeast
    outside of New Hampshire)

New Jersey Division of Travel and
    Tourism
C.N. 826
Trenton, New Jersey 08625
609-292-2470

New Mexico Travel Division
Joseph Montoya Building
1100 St. Francis Drive
Santa Fe, New Mexico 87503
505-827-0291; 800-545-2040 (out-
    of-state)

New York State Division of
    Tourism
1 Commerce Plaza
Albany, New York 12245
518-474-4116; 800-225-5697 (in
    the Northeast except Maine)

North Carolina Travel and
    Tourism Division
430 North Salisbury Street
Raleigh, North Carolina 27611
919-733-4171; 800-VISIT-NC
    (out-of-state)

North Dakota Tourism Promotion
Liberty Memorial Building
State Capitol Grounds
Bismarck, North Dakota 58505
701-224-2525; 800-437-2077 (out-
    of-state); 800-472-2100 (in-state)

Ohio Office of Tourism
P.O. Box 1001
Columbus, Ohio 43266-0101
614-466-8444; 800-BUCKEYE
    (out-of-state)

Oklahoma Division of Tourism
500 Will Rogers Building
Oklahoma City, Oklahoma 73105
405-521-2409; 800-652-6552 (in
    neighboring states);
    800-522-8565 (in-state)

Oregon Economic Development
    Tourism Division
539 Cottage Street, N.E.
Salem, Oregon 97310
503-378-3451; 800-547-7842 (out-
    of-state); 800-233-3306 (in-state)

Pennsylvania Bureau of Travel
    Development
Department of Commerce
439 Forum Building
Harrisburg, Pennsylvania 17120
717-787-5453; 800-847-4872

Rhode Island Department of
  Economic Development
Tourism and Promotion Division
7 Jackson Walkway
Providence, Rhode Island 02903
401-277-2601; 800-556-2484
  (East Coast from Maine to
  Virginia; also West Virginia and
  Ohio)

South Carolina Division of
  Tourism
1205 Pendleton Street
Columbia, South Carolina 29201
803-734-0122

South Dakota Division of Tourism
Capital Lake Plaza
711 Wells Avenue
Pierre, South Dakota 57501
605-773-3301; 800-952-2217 (out-
  of-state); 800-843-1930 (in-state)

Tennessee Tourist Development
P.O. Box 23170
Nashville, Tennessee 37202
615-741-7994

Texas Tourist Development
P.O. Box 12008
Capitol Station
Austin, Texas 78711
512-426-9191; 800-888-8839

Utah Travel Council
Council Hall
Capitol Hill
Salt Lake City, Utah 84114
801-538-1030

Vermont Travel Division
134 State Street
Montpelier, Vermont 05602
802-828-3236

Virginia Division of Tourism
202 North Ninth Street
Suite 500
Richmond, Virginia 23239
804-786-4484; 800-847-4882

Washington Development of Trade
  and Economic Development
Tourism Division
101 General Administration
  Building
Olympia, Washington 98504
206-586-2088; 800-544-1800 (out-
  of-state)

Washington, D.C., Convention and
  Visitors' Association
1212 New York Avenue, N.W.
Washington, D.C. 20005
202-789-7000

Travel West Virginia
West Virginia Department of
  Commerce
State Capitol
Charleston, West Virginia 25305
304-348-2286; 800-CALL-WVA

Wisconsin Division of Tourism
P.O. Box 7970
123 West Washington
Madison, Wisconsin 53707
608-266-2161; 800-372-2737
  (within Wisconsin and
  neighboring states);
  800-432-8747 (out-of-state)

Wyoming Travel Commission
I-25 and College Drive
Cheyenne, Wyoming 82002
307-777-7777; 800-225-5996 (out-
  of-state)

INDEX

CONNECTICUT

DISTRICT OF COLUMBIA (WASHINGTON, D.C.)

FLORIDA

GEORGIA

TELL US ABOUT YOUR OWN GREAT VACATION.

We want to hear about the places you've discovered so that we can include them in our next edition. Please take a minute to complete the following form and return it to: *Great Vacations With Your Kids*, c/o **TWYCH**, 80 Eighth Avenue, New York, New York 10011

Your Name: _____

Your Address: _____

Your Telephone: _____

Name of Property/Tour Operator: _____

Address: _____

Telephone: _____

Contact Person: _____

Describe your "find." We'll contact them directly for details.

Many, many thanks.

TELL US ABOUT YOUR OWN GREAT VACATION.

We want to hear about the places you've discovered so that we can include them in our next edition. Please take a minute to complete the following form and return it to: *Great Vacations With Your Kids*, c/o **TWYCH**, 80 Eighth Avenue, New York, New York 10011

Your Name: _____

Your Address: _____

Your Telephone: _____

Name of Property/Tour Operator: _____

Address: _____

Telephone: _____

Contact Person: _____

Describe your "find." We'll contact them directly for details.

Many, many thanks.

FAMILY TRAVEL TIMES®

If you enjoyed reading

Great Vacations with Your Kids,

you'll love reading **Family Travel Times®**

– the only newsletter dedicated to helping parents

• plan fun and successful family vacations.

Come, travel with us across North America and around the globe.   Don't let folks tell you that you can't take an exotic or romantic vacation with your kids. Find out where and how in **Family Travel Times®**. Having read this book you know that the vacation possibilities are endless and, that with proper planning, you can go anywhere you want on vacation, bring the kids along, and *all* come home having had a great holiday.

After all, isn't this what family vacations were meant to be?

Precious time

with our children

enjoying,

learning,

growing,

and being together.

**Great Family Vacations
begin with**

FAMILY TRAVEL TIMES®

hotels with children's programs . . .

travel toys . . . city vacations . . . skiing . . .

sport vacations. . . cruising with kids. . .

where to stay . . . things to do. . .

FTT helps make these times

together even more special

Annual Subscription: $35

Sample Issue: $1

- - - - - - - - - -

☐ Yes, sign me up today:

Name: _____

Address: _____

_____

Telephone: _____

Ages of Children: _____

Family Travel Times® is published by
TWYCH, Travel With Your Children
80 Eighth Ave., New York, N. Y. 10011
(212) 206-0688